RELIGIOUS DYNAMICS IN A MICROCONTINENT

ARCHAEOLOGY OF THE MEDITERRANEAN WORLD

VOLUME 1

GENERAL EDITORS

Lin Foxhall, *University of Liverpool*
Peter van Dommelen, *Brown University*

EDITORIAL BOARD

Laurel Bestock, *Brown University*
Andrea De Giorgi, *Florida State University*
Francesca Dell'Acqua, *Università degli Studi di Salerno*
Lieve Donnellan, *University of Melbourne*
Claudia Glatz, *University of Glasgow*
Paul S. Johnson, *University of Nottingham*
†Joan Sanmartí Grego, *Universitat de Barcelona*
Luca Zavagno, *Bilkent Üniversitesi*

# Religious Dynamics in a Microcontinent

*Cult Places, Identities, and Cultural Change in Hispania*

Edited by

ALEJANDRO G. SINNER and
VICTOR REVILLA CALVO

BREPOLS

British Library Cataloguing in Publication Data
A catalogue record for this book is available from the British Library.

© 2022, Brepols Publishers n.v., Turnhout, Belgium.

All rights reserved. No part of this publication may be reproduced,
stored in a retrieval system, or transmitted, in any form or by
any means, electronic, mechanical, photocopying, recording,
or otherwise without the prior permission of the publisher.

ISBN: 978-2-503-59545-0
e-ISBN: 978-2-503-60094-9
DOI: 10.1484/M.AMW-EB.5.130175

Printed in the EU on acid-free paper.

D/2022/0095/160

# Table of Contents

List of Illustrations     7

Abbreviations     11

**Alejandro G. Sinner** and **Víctor Revilla Calvo**
1. Introduction     13

## Part I
### Rituals in Context

**Ignasi Grau Mira**
2. Ritual Practices and Sacred Landscapes: Identity and Territorial Organization in Late Iron Age and Early Roman Eastern Iberia     27

**Thomas G. Schattner**
3. The Sacred Landscape of Western Hispania in the Roman Period     37

**Marc Mayer Olivé**
4. Rock Sanctuaries and Roman Epigraphy     53

**Alejandro G. Sinner** and **Victor Revilla Calvo**
5. Religious Practices and Rural Cult Sites in Hispania Citerior: Some Reflections     65

**Jonathan Edmondson**
6. Roman Colonies and Local Cults: The Example of Augusta Emerita (Mérida) in Lusitania     79

**María Pérez Ruiz**
7. Private Beliefs, Domestic Religion, and Identity in Hispania     101

**Part II**
Strategies, Mechanisms, and Practice

**Greg Woolf**
**8.** Religion and Identity on a Microcontinent — 117

**Marta Campo Díaz**
**9.** Coinage and the Religious Beliefs of the Peoples of Hispania: Tradition and Foreign Influences — 125

**Ana Mayorgas**
**10.** Rome's Memory and Ritual in Hispania — 139

**Víctor Revilla Calvo**
**11.** Roman Past and Local Identities: The Case of Saguntum — 151

**Francisco Marco Simón**
**12.** The Imperial Cult and Consensus Rituals in Hispania: First Century BCE–First Century CE — 167

**Matthew M. McCarty and Kimberly Edher**
**13.** Localizing 'Oriental Cults' in Roman Iberia: Relationality, Power, and Place — 177

Bibliography — 193

Index of Sources — 231

Index of Names — 239

# List of Illustrations

**2. Ritual Practices and Sacred Landscapes — *Ignasi Grau Mira***

Figure 2.1. Map of eastern Iberia with the sanctuaries studied in the text.    29

Figure 2.2. Example of votive figurines representing worshippers:
A: Terracotta figurines from the sanctuary of La Serreta.
B: Limestone sculptures representing men in Roman dress (*togati*).    31

Figure 2.3. Plans of the main buildings in the sanctuaries of eastern Iberia:
1. La Serreta. 2. El Cerro de Los Santos. 3. La Encarnación. 4. La Luz de Verdolay.    33

**3. The Sacred Landscape of Western Hispania in the Roman Period — *Thomas G. Schattner***

Figure 3.1. The sanctuaries in the Hispanic West discussed.    38

Figure 3.2. São Miguel da Mota. Sanctuary of Endovellicus, hypothetical reconstruction.    42

Figure 3.3. São Miguel da Mota, Sanctuary of Endovellicus, range of sculpture genres.    42

Figure 3.4. Cabeço das Fráguas, Polytheistic Sanctuary, rock inscription in Latin letters but in the Lusitanian language.    47

Figure 3.5. Monte do Facho, Sanctuary of Berobreus, hypothetical reconstruction.    48

Figure 3.6. Mapping of the Roman sites around São Miguel da Motta/Alandroal, Portugal.    50

Table 3.1. Typology of sanctuaries and votive deposits in Western Hispania.    39

Table 3.2. Sanctuary of Endovellicus, sculpture genres.    43

**4. Rock Sanctuaries and Roman Epigraphy — *Marc Mayer Olivé***

Figure 4.1. The Cueva de Román in Clunia.    55

Figure 4.2. a) The Cueva de La Griega in Pedraza; b) The Cueva del Puente.    56

Figure 4.3. a) Inscription A of the Cueva del Puente; b) The sanctuary of Diana in Segobriga.    57

Figure 4.4. a) General view of the sanctuary of Calescoves in Minorca;
b) Some inscriptions in the sanctuary of Calescoves.    58

Figure 4.5. Sketches of the graffiti at Oceja, Cerdanya.    60

Figure 4.6. a) General view of the Cueva Negra of Fortuna;
b) Ensemble of digitalized sketches of the rock-face *tituli* of Fortuna.    61

## 5. Religious Practices and Rural Cult Sites in Hispania Citerior
— *Alejandro G. Sinner and Victor Revilla Calvo*

| | | |
|---|---|---|
| Figure 5.1. | Location of the cities and cult spaces mentioned in the text: 1. Can Modolell. 2. Pla de Prats. 3. El Cogull. 4 Cales Coves. 5. Muntanya Frontera. 6. Santa Bárbara. 7. La Serreta. 8. Cueva Negra. 9. Peñalba de Villastar. 10. La Griega. 11. Panóias. 12. Santa Lucía del Trampal. | 69 |

## 6. Roman Colonies and Local Cults — *Jonathan Edmondson*

| | | |
|---|---|---|
| Figure 6.1. | Map showing the boundaries of the territory of Augusta Emerita. | 80 |
| Figure 6.2. | Reconstruction of the colony's original forum, with imperial cult temple, plus the forum annex with another temple (calle Baños), with another temple (calle Viñeros) just outside the forum proper. | 81 |
| Figure 6.3. | Small votive altars to a) Divus Sigerius Stillifer; b) Dea Sancta Turib(rigensis); c) Dea Sancta Proserpina; d) Dea Sancta, all from Emerita. | 83 |
| Figure 6.4. | Location of the shrine of Endovellicus at São Miguel da Mota in relation to Augusta Emerita and Ebora, showing major and secondary roads, *mansiones*, and the marble quarries near Estremoz and Vila Viçosa. | 87 |
| Figure 6.5. | Votive altar set up to Deo Indovellico by Blandus, slave of Caelia Rufina, São Miguel da Mota. Funerary altar of C. Rubrius Flaccus, Tuccitan(us), Emerita. | 90 |
| Table 6.1. | Votive inscriptions from the urban centre of Emerita. | 93 |
| Table 6.2. | Votive inscriptions from the territory of Emerita. | 96 |
| Table 6.3. | Dedicators of vows to Endovellicus and subjects of vows *pro salute* made at the sanctuary at São Miguel da Mota (Terena, Alandroal, distr. Évora). | 98 |

## 7. Private Believing, Domestic Religion, and Identity in Hispania — *María Pérez Ruiz*

| | | |
|---|---|---|
| Figure 7.1. | a) Layout of the painting that decorated the altar on its four faces; b) Remains of the altar in the peristyle of House 2B in Emporiae. | 105 |
| Figure 7.2. | a) House of Fortune, Carthago Nova (Cartagena, Murcia); b) Villa of El Rihuete (Mazarrón, Murcia); c) House of the Blind Caves, Clunia (Peñalba de Castro, Burgos). | 108 |
| Figure 7.3. | Cult images found in the *lararium* of the villa of Vilauba (Camós, Girona). | 110 |

## 9. Coinage and the Religious Beliefs of the Peoples of Hispania — *Marta Campo Díaz*

Figure 9.1.  1. Rhode drachm. 2. Emporion drachm. 3. Orose drachm. 4. Arse drachm. 5. Ebusus unit. 6. Gadir hemidrachm. 7. Sex unit. 8. Abdera unit. 9. Lascuta unit. 10. Malaca unit. 11. Malaca half unit. 12. Asido half unit. 127

Figure 9.2.  1. Castulo unit. 2. Castulo unit. 3. Carmo unit. 4. Obulco unit. 5. Obulco semis. 6. Kese unit. 7. Kese half unit. 8. Iltirta unit. 9. Untikesken unit. 10. Valentia as. 130

Figure 9.3.  1. Carteia semis. 2. Augustus, semis, Ilici. 3. Tiberius, dupondius, Romula. 4. Tiberius, sestertius, Tarraco. 5. Tiberius, dupondius, Caesaraugusta. 6. Augustus, as, Carthago Nova. 7. Tiberius, as, Emerita. 8. Caligula, as, Caesaraugusta. 9. Lepida/Celsa as. 10. Tiberius, as, Graccuris. 134

## 11. Roman Past and Local Identities — *Víctor Revilla Calvo*

Figure 11.1.  Location of Saguntum and the Roman cities located in the south of the conventus Tarraconensis and the northern territories of the conventus Carthaginensis. 153

Figure 11.2.  The inscription *CIL* II²/14, 327 dedicated to P. Cornelius Scipio as *restitutor* of Saguntum. 161

## 13. Localizing 'Oriental Cults' in Roman Iberia — *Matthew M. McCarty and Kimberly Edher*

Figure 13.1.  Sites discussed with material related to the cults of Isis, Serapis, and Mithras. 1. Caldas de Reyes/Aquae Calidae. 2. Lugo/Lucus Augusti. 3. San Juan de la Isla. 4. Empúries/Emporion. 5. Els Munts. 6. Tarragona/Tarraco. 7. Benifaió. 8. Cartagena/Carthago Nova. 9. Cabra/Igabrum. 10. Belo/Baelo Claudia. 11. Santiponce/Italica. 12. Mérida/Augusta Emerita. 13. Beja/Pax Iulia. 14. Setúbal/Caetobriga. 15. Panóias. 178

Figure 13.2.  The sanctuary at Panóias, with locations of the inscriptions recorded and associated features cut in the rock. 180

Figure 13.3.  Sculpture probably displayed in a Mithraeum at Augusta Emerita. 183

Figure 13.4.  Inscribed sculpture from the Mithraic sculptural assemblage at Augusta Emerita. 185

Figure 13.5.  Location of the sanctuary to Egyptian gods at Baelo Claudia. 187

Figure 13.6.  Plan of the Els Munts Mithraeum, set into an elite villa. 189

# Abbreviations

*AE*    *L'Année Épigraphique* (Paris, 1888–)

*AEA*    *Archivo Español de Arqueología*

*AJA*    *American Journal of Archaeology*

*ANRW*    *Aufstieg und Niedergang der römischen Welt* (Berlin: De Gruyter, 1972–)

*BDH Mon.*    *Hesperia: Banco de datos de lenguas paleohispánicas* (Madrid, 2005–)

*CIBal*    C. Veny, *Corpus de las inscripciones baleáricas hasta la dominación árabe* (Madrid: Consejo Superior de Investigaciones Científicas, 1963)

*CIIAE*    J. L. Ramírez Sádaba (ed.), *Catálogo de las inscripciones imperiales de Augusta Emerita*, Cuadernos emeritenses, 21 (Mérida: Museo Nacional de Arte Romano, 2003)

*CIL*    *Corpus Inscriptionum Latinarum* (Berlin, 1863–)

*CILA*    *Corpus de inscripciones latinas de Andalucía*, 4 vols (Seville: Junta de Andalucía, 1991–2002)

*CILAE*    *Corpus inscriptionum latinarum Augustae Emeritae. Centro CIL II: Mérida* <https://cil2digital.web.uah.es/> [accessed 28 July 2022]

*CILCC*    J. Esteban Ortega (ed.), *Corpus de inscripciones latinas de Cáceres*, 5 vols (Cáceres: Universidad de Extremadura, 2007–2019)

*CIMRM*    M. J. Vermaseren (ed.), *Corpus Inscriptionum et Monumentorum Religionis Mithriacae* (The Hague: Martinus Nijhoff Publishers, 1956–1960)

*CIVAE*    J. L. Ramírez Sádaba (ed.), *Catálogo de inscripciones votivas de 'Augusta Emerita'*, Cuadernos emeritenses, 45 (Mérida: Museo Nacional de Arte Romano, 2019 [2021])

*CMBad*    J. R. Mélida, *Catálogo Monumental de España: Provincia de Badajoz* (Madrid: Ministerio de Instrucción Pública y Bellas Artes, 1925)

*CNH*    L. Villaronga, *Corpus Nummum Hispaniae ante Augusti Aetatem* (Madrid: José A. Herrero, 1994)

*EAOR*    *Epigrafia anfiteatrale dell'Occidente romano* (Rome: Quasar, 1988–)

*EE*    *Ephemeris Epigraphica* (Berlin, 1872–1903)

*ERAE*    L. García Iglesias, 'Epigrafía romana de Augusta Emerita' (unpublished doctoral thesis, Universidad Complutense de Madrid, 1973)

*ERAsturias*    D. Santos, *Epigrafía romana de Asturias* (Oviedo: Instituto de Estudios Asturianos, 1985)

*ERBC*    A. M. Canto (ed.), *Epigrafía romana de la Béturia céltica* (Madrid: Universidad Autónoma de Madrid, 1997)

*ERPLe*    M. A. Rabanal and S. Mª García, *Epigrafía romana de la provincia de León: revisión y actualización* (León: Universidad de León, 2001)

*ERRB*    A. Redentor, *Epigrafia romana da região de Bragança*, Trabalhos de Arqueologia, 24 (Lisbon: Instituto Português de Arqueologia, 2002)

*FE*    *Ficheiro Epigráfico* (Coimbra: Universidade de Coimbra, 1982–)

*GeA*    C. Schmidt Heidenreich (ed.), *Le glaive et l'autel: Camps et piété militaires sous le Haut-Empire romain* (Rennes: Presses universitaires de Rennes, 2013)

*HAE*    *Hispania Antiqua Epigraphica* (Madrid, 1950–1969)

*HEp* Hispania Epigraphica (Madrid, 1989–)

*IGLNovae* Inscriptions grecques et latines de Novae (Mésie inférieure) (Bordeaux, 1997)

*IGUR* L. Moretti, *Inscriptiones graecae urbis Romae* (Rome: Istituto italiano per la storia antica, 1968)

*ILAlg* Inscriptions latines d'Algérie (Paris, 1922–)

*ILER* J. Vives (ed.), *Inscripciones latinas de España romana* (Barcelona: Universidad de Barcelona, Consejo Superior de Investigaciones Científicas, 1971)

*ILN* Inscriptiones latines de Narbonnaise (Paris, 1985–)

*ILNovae* V. Bozilova, J. Kolendo, and L. Mrozewicz (eds), *Inscriptions latines de Novae* (Poznan 1992)

*ILS/D* H. Dessau (ed.), *Inscriptiones Latinae Selectae* (Berlin, 1892–1916)

*IMAPB* J. Salas Martín, J. Esteban Ortega, J. A. Redondo Rodríguez, and J. L. Sánchez Abal (eds), *Inscripciones romanas y cristianas del Museo Arqueológico Provincial de Badajoz* (Badajoz: Junta de Extremadura, 1997)

*Inscr. Aq.* J. B. Brusin (ed.), *Inscriptiones Aquileiae*, 3 vols (Udine, 1991–1993)

*IRC* G. Fabre, M. Mayer, and I. Rodà, *Inscriptions Romaines de Catalogne*, 5 vols (Paris: De Boccard, 1984–2007)

*IRCP* J. d'Encarnação (ed.), *Inscrições romanas do Conventus Pacensis* (Coimbra: Instituto de Arqueologia da Faculdade de Letras, 1984)

*IRG* F. Bouza and A. D'Ors, *Inscripciones romanas de Galicia, I Santiago de Compostela* (Santiago de Compostela: Consejo Superior de Investigaciones Científicas, Instituto Padre Sarmiento de Estudios Gallegos, 1949)

*IRPCádiz* J. González Fernández, *Inscripciones romanas de la provincia de Cádiz* (Cádiz: Diputación Provincial de Cádiz, 1982)

*IRPL/IRPLu* F. Arias, P. Le Roux, and A. Tranoy, *Inscriptions romaines de la province de Lugo* (Paris: De Boccard, 1979)

*IRPToledo* J. M. Abascal Palazón and G. Alföldy, *Inscripciones romanas de la provincia de Toledo (siglos I–III)*, Bibliotheca Archaeologica Hispana, 42 (Madrid: Real Academia de la Historia, 2015)

*JRA* Journal of Roman Archaeology

*JRS* The Journal of Roman Studies

*LIMC* Lexicon Iconographicum Mythologiae Classicae (Zurich–Munich–Dusseldorf, 1981–1999)

*MLH III* J. Untermann, *Monumenta Linguarum hispanicarum: Die iberischen Inschriften aus Spanien* (Wiesbaden: Reichert, 1990)

*OPEL* B. Lőrincz (ed.), *Onomasticon Provinciarum Europae Latinarum* (Budapest, 1994–2005)

*PITTM* Publicaciones del Instituto Tello Téllez de Meneses, Palencia

*PLINovae* L. Mrozewicz, *Paleography of Latin Inscriptions from Novae (Lower Moesia)* (Poznań, 2010)

*RGDA* Res gestae Divi Augusti

*RIB* Roman Inscriptions of Britain

*RICIS* L. Bricault, *Recueil des Inscriptions concernant les cultes isiaques*, 3 vols (Paris: De Boccard, 2005)

*RPC* A. Burnett, M. Amandry, and P. P. Ripollès, *Roman Provincial Coinage: From the Death of Caesar to Vitellius (44 BC to AD 69)*, I (London: British Museum Press, 1992)

*RS* M. H. Crawford (ed.), *Roman Statutes*, Bulletin of the Institute of Classical Studies, Supplement, 64 (London, 1996)

*TIR* A. Balil Illana, G. Pereira Menaut, and J. Sánchez-Palencia (eds), *Unión Académica Internacional Tabula Imperii Romani. Hoja K-29: Porto: Conimbriga, Bracara, Lucus, Asturica* (Madrid: Instituto Geográfico Nacional, 1991)

*ZPE* Zeitschrift für Papyrologie und Epigraphik

# 1. Introduction

> Along with the happy lot of their country, the qualities of both gentleness and civility have come to the Turdetanians; and to the Celtic peoples, too, on account of their being neighbours to the Turdetanians, as Polybius has said, or else on account of their kinship but less so the Celtic peoples, because for the most part they live in mere villages. The Turdetanians, however, and particularly those that live about the Baetis, have completely changed over to the Roman mode of life, not even remembering their own language any more. And most of them have become Latins, and they have received Romans as colonists, so that they are not far from being all Romans. And the present jointly-settled cities, Pax Augusta in the Celtic country, Augusta Emerita in the country of the Turdulians, Caesar-Augusta near Celtiberia, and some other settlements, manifest the change to the aforesaid civil modes of life. Moreover, all those Iberians who belong to this class are called 'Togati'. And among these are the Celtiberians, who were once regarded the most brutish of all. So much for the Turditanians. (Str. III.2.15)[1]

This well-known paragraph by Strabo about the cultural transformation of the populations of Turdetania includes some of the fundamental elements that the Graeco-Roman intellectual tradition used to reflect on cultural otherness. In the first place, the cultural diversity of the Iberian Peninsula and of the elements that characterized it: from language to customs, passing through forms of social life; secondly, the identification of a process of change rather than exchange (from the standpoint of this intellectual tradition) that seemed very fast and of some of the factors that drove it. Among these factors the author placed particular emphasis on the presence of immigrants and the direct action of the Roman power. This cultural diversity, the interactions that were generated by different and constantly changing relationships of power, and the identities constituted were a clear part of the same intellectual reflection on the 'other' and on the various forms of contact between societies and their potential consequences. Strabo understood them as a 'top-down' civilizing process associated with Roman expansion. The description of the different populations of Iberia that Book III of the *Geography* contains continually insists on this point. This was, however, a frequent reflection at the time that Strabo was composing his work.[2]

This analysis of intercultural contact implicitly included in its formulation the question of the identity of local populations, which the author conceptualized as a consequence of their conscious and total integration within Roman culture (conversion into *togati*) encompassing the adoption of new habits and a new language. From Strabo's standpoint, these changes inexorably led to the complete disappearance of local cultures ('The Turdetanians [ … ] have completely changed over to the Roman mode of life, not even remembering their own language any more'). The nature of the deities and rituals of indigenous societies (especially in the north-west and in Lusitania) frequently appears in this analysis, and Strabo highlights the differences in religious practice.[3] These differences, interpreted as part of a specific way of life, enabled the Greek geographer to establish the identity of the other, particularly when he sought to highlight the distance from the Graeco-Roman way of life. With obvious differences in approach, the elements that make up this reflection are still present in modern research discussing the Roman conquest and the cultural transformation of the Iberian Peninsula.

---

1   Jones 1923, 59.
2   Prontera 1999; seminal works: Cruz Andreotti 1999; 2007; 2011; 2015. For Strabo in general: Prontera 1984; Dueck 2017.

3   Str. III.4.16 highlights the particularity of the beliefs and rituals: 'Some say the Callaicans have no god, but the Celtiberians and their neighbours on the north offer sacrifice to a nameless god'; for the supposed atheism of some pre-Roman groups as a differentiating element: Bermejo 1994.

**Alejandro G. Sinner**, Associate Professor of Roman Art and Archaeology (University of Victoria)

**Víctor Revilla Calvo**, Professor of Ancient History (University of Barcelona)

The peoples inhabiting Iberia prior to the Roman arrival were characterized by considerable cultural, ethnic, and social diversity. Such diversity is amply recorded in ancient Greek and Roman historical and geographical sources (with Strabo's analysis being the most complete extant work), as well as by a rich epigraphic corpus of pre-Roman inscriptions. In total, over three thousand inscriptions are preserved in what is certainly the largest body of epigraphic expression in the western Mediterranean world outside the Italian Peninsula. No fewer than four writing systems — in addition to Phoenician, Greek, and Latin — were used between the fifth century BCE and the first century CE to write the vernacular languages of the Iberian Peninsula: Tartessian, Iberian, Celtiberian, and Lusitanian.[4] In addition to this rich cultural and linguistic substratum, two important colonial agents affecting different areas (Greeks in the north-east and Phoenicians in the south and south-east) and with a very diverse impact, higher in the coastal areas and less noticeable inland, influenced the formation and evolution of these extremely heterogeneous socio-economic and cultural realities.[5]

Finally, the gradual conquest of Iberia resulted in one of the longest and most complex colonial processes known in the Roman world. This undertaking took place over two centuries, between the second century BCE and the first century CE and included the arrival of newcomers from Italy and elsewhere in the Mediterranean;[6] it also involved different rhythms of integration and interaction, making use of a wide range of control mechanisms over the existing political entities. The impact of the *restauratio Augustea* in the Iberian Peninsula, which culminated in and completed the conquest of the north-western territories, was equally important. The social, economic, and cultural consequences of these processes of change can be reconstructed thanks to a substantial corpus of inscriptions that includes some of the most significant texts in the Roman world for the republican and early imperial periods.

## Why Hispania?

It is the above distinctive, rich, varied, and dynamic history that makes a volume devoted to cults, rituals, identities, and cultural change and exchange in the Iberian Peninsula during the transition from the late Republic to the early Empire necessary. Political and socio-economic interactions led to cultural change and the formation of a whole spectrum of local and regional identities as a response to the new situation created by the integration of the provincial communities in the global context of the Empire.[7] The analysis and interpretation of the dynamics of interaction and cultural exchange generated in this geographical space — a true microcontinent — over more than half a millennium has undergone a profound renewal in recent decades. This renovation has affected the methodology employed in the field, with the incorporation of laboratory techniques and epistemological approaches.[8] Religious manifestations, thanks to their capacity to define value systems and individual and collective behaviours, played a key part in the construction and negotiation of identities at different levels. Identities could in many cases coexist, contributing to generating responses to the new social, cultural, and economic situation. This lengthy and complex process led to the formation of a multicultural and diverse Roman Empire, therefore making such developments fundamental to our understanding of the ancient Mediterranean.

Recent archaeological work has led to the documentation and analysis of a number of cult sites in the Iberian Peninsula. Among them and without being exhaustive, we can highlight the sanctuaries at Panóias, Santa Lucía del Trampal, Peñalba de Villastar, La Griega, La Serreta d'Alcoi, Muntanya

---

4 For a synthesis including the latest research on Palaeohispanic languages see Sinner and Velaza 2018; 2019 with bibliography.

5 On Phoenician/Punic colonization and settlement in the Iberian Peninsula: Aubet 2001; López Castro 1995. An overview of the Phoenicians' impact in Roman Hispania in Machuca 2019; a more general overview of their impact in the broader Mediterranean in Lopez-Ruiz and Doak 2019. For the Greek impact in Hispania see Cabrera and Sánchez Fernández 2000; Aquilué and Cabrera 2012.

6 The nature and extent of this migration have long been debated. Two diametrically opposed positions predominate. The first one contends that a substantial inflow of Italics settled in Hispania after the Second Punic War: Wilson 1966, 9–12; Marín Díaz 1986; 1988, 47–109; González Román 2010, 13–32, including many soldiers settled after service (Brunt 1971; Gabba 1973). The second tends to minimize the entity of migratory flows to the Iberian Peninsula: Haley 1991; Le Roux 1995, 85–95; Cadiou 2008, 627–61; Sinner forthcoming.

7 Due to its size, it is not possible to provide here an exhaustive list of works. Studies discussing these processes in north-eastern Spain and the Ebro Valley include, for instance: Keay 1990; Abad Casal and others 2006; Beltrán 2003; Sinner 2015; for central Spain: Noreña 2019; for southern Spain and the River Baetis: Fear 1996; Keay 1998. For patterns in Romanization in the Iberian Peninsula as a whole and the debate generated around the validity of the concept: Blázquez Martínez and Alvar 1996; Keay 1988; 2003; Curchin 1991; Coarelli and others 1992; Beltrán 1999; 2017; Johnston 2017.

8 Dietler and López-Ruiz 2009. Ferrer Albelda 2012, 668 questions the essentialist perspective that underlies maintaining a strict distinction between Phoenician-Punic populations and other peninsular communities of non-Semitic, Indo-European, or Iberian roots, in the second–first centuries BCE.

Frontera, Cueva Negra, and Cales Coves.⁹ None of these archaeological sites have been completely excavated. In most cases, the documentary evidence is limited to a corpus of greater or lesser size of inscriptions and materials with a votive or decorative function, rarely contextualized, which only allow us to address certain aspects of the ritual (which can rarely be related to a calendar), or of the circumstances surrounding a votive act and the social condition of the individuals who took part in them. However, the available data have made it possible to produce some very important works of synthesis, of both a thematic and regional nature. This has coincided with new methodological and theoretical approaches in the way religion is studied, as an area particularly sensitive to cultural change. A variety of studies have underlined the role of rituals and beliefs in the creation of mechanisms of integration and social communication, as well as in the definition of individual and community identities.¹⁰ In this context, sanctuaries and other cult spaces are key elements in the analysis of the forms and rhythms of religious and cultural change experienced by the indigenous societies, initially during the Roman conquest and later as part of their integration into the newly established provincial system.¹¹ However, a number of these spaces of worship, those located in rural areas, raise considerable problems of interpretation and will be discussed in detail in several contributions in this volume. The difficulty in their study lies, to a large extent, in the scarcity of literary, epigraphic, and archaeological evidence related to the nature and chronology of cults, rituals, and the protagonists' social and legal status or identities.

This shortage of data is the result, on the one hand, of a research tradition in Spain that was only poorly developed until a few decades ago; on the other hand, it is caused by the characteristics of a large proportion of the religious manifestations among the rural population, which in many cases involved very modest initiatives and were located in humble architectural contexts that cannot always be distinguished from domestic or production spaces.¹²

These circumstances complicate the identification and documentation of initiatives and rituals in the archaeological record as well as the explanation of their possible function; particularly in an area such as religion, where relations between public and private (and the very limits of these spheres) are complex, dynamic, and in constant evolution. Not to mention the difficulty involved in placing the interests and strategies associated with personal initiatives in a broader context (professional, socio-legal, political, cultural). The lack of information on the topography and architecture of these spaces of worship has been especially marked, although some early studies revealed the diversity of possible situations, partly associated with the reconstruction of a natural scenario, and already raised the issue of to what extent these sites indicated continuity from a pre-existing tradition and how often they were visited.

Furthermore, the main problem was of an epistemological nature: the hegemony of a historiographic paradigm that defined the rural world as a social and cultural environment resistant to change, organized according to a traditional value system that seemed to follow its own rhythm and modus operandi; in other words, a backward world that was seen to stand in contrast to the dynamism represented by a pattern of urban life much more open to change.¹³ According to this paradigm, rural religious manifestations, due to their modest nature in terms of material evidence and the (apparent) predominance of a world of pre-Roman beliefs, cults, and rituals, could be presented as a compendium of cultural marginality and political resistance. It is evident that this perspective contributed to reinforcing the image of the so-called Romanization process of the Iberian Peninsula directed from a top-down perspective and understood as a (necessary) phase of historical progress. This perspective has, however, been questioned in recent years.¹⁴

The changes in perspective from which epigraphic documentation has been analysed in recent decades are a good example of some of the theoretical and methodological problems that arise. Traditionally, the presence of Latin inscriptions, accompanied by

---

9 Panóias: Alföldy 1997; Rodríguez Colmenero 1999; El Trampal: Abascal 1995; Peñalba de Villastar: Beltrán and others 2005; Marco and Alfayé 2008; Alfayé 2010; La Griega: Abásolo and Mayer 1997; Abásolo 1998; Santos and others 2005; Alfayé 2014; La Serreta d'Alcoi: Grau and others 2017; Muntanya Frontera: Corell 1996; Cueva Negra: Stylow and Mayer 1996; González Blanco 2003; González Blanco and Matilla 2003; Cales Coves: Orfila and others 2015.

10 Important theoretical and methodological observations in: Diez de Velasco 1992; 1999; 2017; Marco 1996a; 1996b; 2009; 2012; 2013a; 2013b; 2017a; 2017b; Alfayé 2009, 2010; Alfayé and Marco 2008, 2014; Tortosa 2014. Analysis has focused particularly on the field of religious forms of communication and their instruments, as well as on the processes of memory and identity creation: Alfayé and Marco 2008; 2014; for the centres of worship see Alfayé 2009; 2010.

11 For example, Mateos and others 2009; Mangas and Novillo 2014; Grau and others 2017; Grau and Amorós 2017; Tortosa and Ramallo 2017.

12 Sinner and Revilla in this volume.
13 Revilla 2002.
14 See below n. 19.

a text that conformed to a greater or lesser extent to Roman religious practices, had been interpreted as a clear indicator of cultural change in an initial or advanced phase. Recent studies show how the epigraphic habit could be implemented in very different ways, which might have involved the use of different supports and engraving techniques, of particular combinations of text and image, or the modification of Latin formulae and terms as part of a process in which Roman practices were adapted to the needs of indigenous individuals and groups. This implies that the communication techniques of Roman culture underwent complex processes of re-elaboration; these would ultimately come to reflect diverse personal or collective identification strategies as well as social and cultural patterns of interaction generated at different levels: local, regional, and provincial.[15] At the same time, these strategies must be understood in a broad cultural field, on a Mediterranean scale.[16]

## Objectives and Theoretical Framework

The main goal of this volume is to gain a deeper understanding of forms of historical analysis of religious phenomena (cult, rituals, spaces, and strategies) in Roman Hispania and to evaluate their explanatory potential in order to comprehend the processes of cultural and social change as well as the responses that individuals and groups made to the processes associated with the conquest and the subsequent colonial process. The book also aims to provide detailed technical insight into the existing rich datasets that have received scant, if any, scholarly attention to date, especially in English-language publications. The fulfilment of these two goals, together with the discussion of a large number of case studies that cover most — if not all — the Iberian Peninsula, gives rise to a volume in which strong argumentative chapters coexist with others examining the state of the arts of a particular territory and/or area of study.

Religious phenomena are valued as a privileged field of study, since they allow for transversal analysis, from the political to the social and economic spheres, combining the public and private domains (a duality that, on the other hand, appears to be too rigid), and the individual and collective levels (recognizing diverse and heterogeneous forms of grouping and association), from a multidisciplinary perspective.[17]

This volume avoids the consideration of religion as a simple historical epiphenomenon reduced to the cultural sphere that directly reflected political and socio-economic dynamics. Instead, other key questions such as which place the religious sphere might have occupied in the definition of forms of cultural and social identity in Hispania will be explored. Similar perspectives and approaches have been applied with excellent results when processes of change and of territorial and socio-political reorganization have been studied in Italy, for example.[18]

Moving from the broader to a more detailed list of objectives, this volume also envisages the analysis of specific situations at a local and regional level, including their main characteristics and evolution over the course of time. Identifying diverse forms of religious interaction at different levels and scales will also be a key component of the book. Public, private, individual, collective, and institutional forms of religiosity, identity, and memory will be discussed, always in the context of the Roman conquest and its subsequent process of stabilization. The book also aims to explore the role of memory in identity construction and the creation of both individual and collective responses to the processes of socio-economic, political, and cultural change that were wrought in the western Mediterranean between the third to first centuries BCE and the first century CE. In particular, an attempt is made to analyse the potential relationships between memory, past, and religious manifestation. These relationships are evaluated from two perspectives: on the one hand, by analysing the introduction and development of certain rituals and priesthoods, as well as the creation of specific religious landscapes; on the other, by means of identifying myths and episodes that formed an integral part of narratives associated with the remembrance or reactivation of the past. In this respect, some communities in Hispania constitute potentially significant case studies.

The contents of this book are inspired by a double theoretical perspective. Firstly, the contributions of postcolonial theory, which has profoundly renewed the way in which the processes of cultural change triggered by the expansion of Rome in the West and its interactions with a diverse array of indigenous groups are considered. Secondly, and

---

15 The importance of writing, in its various forms (forms, types of support, context), is highlighted in various contributions to this work. Cf. Cooley 2002; Häussler 2008a–b.

16 Especially relevant are the studies of Beltrán emphasizing the role that Rome had in the diffusion of the epigraphic habit: 1995; 1999; 2011; 2012; 2013; 2017; Beltrán and Díaz Ariño 2018. A different perspective in Prag 2013.

17 Religion understood as a form of communication and agency: Urciuoli and Rüpke 2018, 125–26; for agency applied to religion see Rüpke 2015; 2016.

18 Stek 2009.

more specifically, by questioning the excessively schematic and dualistic approaches to certain factors (a perfectly defined homogenous Roman culture versus the indigenous milieu) and mechanisms (a top-down approach). Scholars have recently been particularly interested in applying new perspectives when analysing the formation of identity forms.[19] This change in standpoint also allows the image of a traditional Roman Republic that adopted diametrically opposed attitudes in the West and the Greek East to be questioned.[20]

At the same time, the contributions brought together in this book are intended to define the epistemological importance and limitations of concepts such as Romanization and globalization when studying cultural processes in the ancient Mediterranean.[21] The distinctive features of the Roman Empire are, in this sense, an excellent case study, since it allows us to address both cultural identity formation processes (different thanks to their protagonists, mechanisms, and strategies) and the context in which these same processes were generated and acquired meaning.[22] With the above in mind, it is important to highlight that the editors did not want to exclude other approaches and interpretive frameworks from the volume. Showing the existence of diverse perspectives and models is always necessary in a study that aims to stimulate dialogue and discussion among scholars while presenting and pushing forward the state of knowledge.

The Iberian Peninsula offers a particularly suitable field of study due to the diversity of its cultural and geographical conditions, as well as the complexity and duration of its conquest — over two centuries. At the same time, these factors allow us to analyse the dynamics of the late republican state and society and the changing political, socio-economic, and cultural conditions in which this expansion occurred. The contributions gathered in this book seek to analyse the role of religious manifestations in the construction of forms of individual and collective identities alongside public and private ones in this context of cultural change.

Religious manifestations played a fundamental role in the construction of cultural and identity mechanisms that allowed individuals and communities to place themselves in a changing global context, the last two centuries of the Republic, and the early imperial era, a period in which new conditions and power relations were generated within the Roman state and society. As a result, there appeared a new institutional framework, deployed at various levels, from cities and their associative fabric to imperial administration and law, but also a new social and economic context in which provincial populations would negotiate their respective position and relations with the emperor.[23]

The volume, furthermore, tries to avoid the perspective of a history of the peninsula differentiated in two stages separated by the Cantabrian Wars: a first phase, represented by the two centuries of the Republic, in which cultural change is considered to have been the result of a necessary adaptation to the violence of the conquest; followed by a second phase of stability in which the Roman social model, based on a more or less widespread urbanization process, would only experience minor readjustments. Reconstructing the expansion and evolution of specific cults, in particular the approach that interprets the geography of a cult as a direct indicator of cultural change, is also avoided in this book. All the contributions included give priority to the study of material manifestations of a different nature related to ritual practices. Architecture, texts and their supports, topography, spatial organization are all elements that can, in turn, exercise their own agency.[24]

The editors' wish is that every reader is able to benefit from and engage with the contributions in this volume. To accomplish that, most of the chapters are pitched at a general scholarly audience but are also accessible to advanced undergraduate and graduate students. In terms of academic disciplines, the contents straddle the fields of classical studies, ancient history, philology, numismatics, religion, and archaeology. It is the editors' intention that both students and academics in these areas should find these essays interesting and useful, since a rich body of archaeological, epigraphic, and numismatic evidence that remains largely unknown among English-speaking scholars is presented and discussed in its pages.

---

19  Mattingly 1997; 2011; Webster 1997; 2001; Webster and Cooper 1997; Woolf 1994; 1995; 1997a; 1998; 2009a; Roymans 1997; Terrenato 1998; 2008; Keay and Terrenato 2001; Revell 2009; 2015; Noreña 2019. The value of religious manifestations as an indicator of cultural change and their role in the so-called Romanization paradigm has created a substantial body of literature; see among others: Cancik and Rüpke 1997; 2009; Bendlin 1997; Webster 1997; Derks 1998; Van Andringa 2002; Woolf 1995; 2009; Rives 2010; Häussler 2012. For central and southern Italy see: Stek 2009; 2015; 2016; Terrenato 2013; Stek and Burgers 2015.
20  Marco 2017b, 776.
21  Hingley 2005; cf. Hingley 2011, 108–12, with a methodological reflection on the concept; Webster 1996; 1997; Mattingly 2002; 2011; Hitchner 2008; Stek 2014; 2016; Pitts and Versluys 2015; Witcher 2000; 2017; Terrenato 1998; 2008.
22  Van Dommelen and Terrenato 2007.
23  Marco 2017b and in this volume; an analysis of religious manifestations in Roman Hispania from the perspective of globalization: Díez de Velasco 2012.
24  Urciuoli and Rüpke 2018.

## Structure and Content

Bearing the aforementioned goals and historical and theoretical frameworks in mind, the editors have decided to structure the volume in two parts, each of which aims to systematically examine several interconnected questions.

Part I, *Rituals in Context: Spaces, Scenarios, and Landscapes*, is composed of six chapters (Chapters 2–7) and puts forward a detailed analysis of the spaces and scenarios of interaction from different perspectives, including the temporal dimension, together with calendars and rhythms of celebrations. Special attention is paid to both the private (domestic) (Chapter 7), in which personal beliefs can be expressed more freely, and the public spheres (cultic spaces and religious landscapes), always from an interdisciplinary perspective that includes the study of material culture, without neglecting the epigraphic and architectural evidence. The study of religious landscapes and sanctuaries, which played a key role in the spatial organization of a territory and acted as central points of collective identity, is one of the focal points of this section. A core feature of Part I (Chapters 2 to 4) is to explore how socio-cultural strategies and ritual practices linked to sanctuaries and other kinds of cult spaces served to promote a sense of community before and after the Roman conquest.

The spatial organization of rock sanctuaries, a specific category of places of worship, is also a key component of Part I. In general, rock sanctuaries were places characterized by a location associated with particular natural conditions, the absence of constructions inspired by Hellenic architectural models, and by a variety of epigraphic practices that used rock surfaces and were adapted to the topography of the terrain. The unique features of a location (based on factors such as its accessibility, topography, the presence of woods or water in the form of springs or streams, etc.) are further significant factors that enable us to appreciate the way in which it was transformed into a sacred place and how visits to the site took place. On the one hand, the combination of these factors enabled the space for movement and ritual to be organized; on the other, new meanings that were associated with cultic practice could be generated. The existence of texts in Palaeohispanic languages and the subsequent adoption of Latin in relation to various cults shows the variety of ways in which these places adapted to the dynamics of cultural interaction followed by both individuals and groups, including civic communities, between the third century BCE and the first century CE.[25]

The introduction of writing is one of the effects of contact with the Phoenician-Punic and Greek colonizers, and it was to spread rapidly in the fourth–third centuries BCE. The extension and expansion of the 'epigraphic habit' in all areas of social life in the Iberian Peninsula, however, is a characteristic phenomenon of the last two centuries of the Republic and the first century of the Empire.[26] Part I shows how the selection of these media reflects different factors and strategies, which must be understood in a context of agency and negotiation carried out by both individuals and groups of diverse nature and in different places. It is important to assess the modalities adopted through the use of writing (from content to support, via the writing technique), in various situations, to create forms of self-representation.

In Chapter 2, I. Grau assesses the relationship between the formation of territorially based political entities and the constitution of political identities in the eastern regions of the Iberian Peninsula in the second and first centuries BCE. This process, related to the Roman intervention in the region, led to the development of places of worship and rituals that involved the reinvention and negotiation of previous cultural traditions and the creation of a new shared memory. This gave rise to a set of practices that served as a strategy to legitimize the newly formed political structures. In particular, certain sanctuaries acquired a political and ideological function as centres of population organization and symbolic aggregation. The author highlights the coincidences with similar processes that occurred in other regions of the Mediterranean, especially those that were only moderately urbanized. This is a description that accurately defines the situation in the south-east of the Iberian Peninsula prior to the Augustan urbanization programme.

T. Schattner (Chapter 3) analyses the situation in the western and south-western lands of the peninsula in pre-Roman times as well as after the Roman conquest. In the course of this chapter, the author draws comparisons with some case studies in eastern Iberia (Muntanya Frontera, Cerro de los Santos) also discussed in other chapters of the vol-

---

25 On Palaeohispanic languages see Sinner and Velaza 2018; 2019 with references.
26 It is significant that the oldest Latin text produced in the peninsula, a graffito that appeared in a tower on the fortification of Tarraco, and which dates back to the late third century BCE, is a dedication to Minerva: *M(anios) Vibio(s) Men(e)rva* (*CIL* I² 3449l = II₂/14, 841). The text could be related to a specific cultic practice, as pointed out by Alföldy 1981; 2002.

ume. The vast territory under study was characterized by cultural diversity and its only indirect link to the Punic and Greek colonial exchange circuits, and later by slow integration into the Roman political orbit, which culminated in the second half of the first century BCE. The starting point of the chapter is a dynamic concept of sacred landscape (space as a cultural and social construct). In relation to this idea, Schattner analyses the relationship between population and sacred places through a historical perspective, putting forward a typology based on the study of the architectural characteristics of, offerings found at, and internal organization of the different sites. This approach allows diverse theoretical and methodological approaches applied to the study of the archaeological and epigraphic evidence to be evaluated simultaneously. In particular, Chapter 5 questions the validity of a dualist perspective of the material culture.

The Latin epigraphy of rock sanctuaries is studied from the perspective of agency by M. Mayer in Chapter 4. This contribution highlights the diversity of individual and collective activity, both private and public, as far as visits to some cult centres were concerned. A series of case studies are analysed in connection with the introduction and organization of certain cults, or the rituals that took place, but other possibilities, such as a specific pilgrimage or a visit without any religious intention are also considered. The chapter discusses a wide range of sanctuaries, some without visible architectural features (large rock surfaces, underground sanctuaries), and others in which an architectural programme and the use of the topography of the terrain were combined. In particular, it focuses on the eastern area of the peninsula (Cueva Negra, Cales Coves), but examples in the centre and west (Clunia) are also analysed. A particularly interesting example is the sanctuary of Panóias, in Portugal (also discussed in Chapters 5 and 13). The chapter also addresses a fundamental issue: the dissemination of the practice of writing in the religious sphere and its relationship with processes of cultural change.

Chapter 5 (Sinner and Revilla) evaluates the conceptual and methodological problems posed by the analysis of manifestations of worship and sanctuaries in the rural world of Hispania. In the first place, the difficulties are due to the characteristics of the archaeological and epigraphic evidence available. To a certain extent, these difficulties arise from the ways in which ritual practices were materialized and the diverse forms of frequentation that took place at particular cult places. However, the fundamental problem is that this is a field of study traditionally conditioned by a reductionist perspective that defines the social and cultural processes of the rural world as essentially conservative and ahistorical; at the same time, this perspective separates the territory from the city.[27] Revilla and Sinner's analysis focuses on places of worship; but it does not seek to establish a typology of sites based on their architectural characteristics. These were spaces of intersection for very diverse cultural, social, and political realities, which lay between the public and the private spheres as well as between the city and its territory, or between the local sphere and other frameworks of political and cultural integration.[28] In short, Chapter 5 focuses on the nature of sanctuaries as spaces for interaction and communication in which hierarchies, forms of representation, and socio-political interactions were expressed.

The colony of Augusta Emerita (Chapter 6) allows J. Edmondson to analyse the impact that the foundation of a privileged civic community, which was established in imitation of Rome, had in the organization of the cults and sanctuaries of a territory. This impact can be seen in two ways. In the first place, through the establishment of official cults, in particular those dedicated to the members of the Domus Augusta. Secondly, through the contributions of individuals of all conditions and status, as well as institutions. The initiatives of the two categories of worshippers explain the particular configuration of the cults and rituals of the colony between the first and third centuries CE. These initiatives were unevenly distributed, both in the city and in the surrounding territory. In this context the presence of two local deities, Ataecina and Endovellicus, is especially revealing. The former seems to have been officially integrated in the pantheon of the colony, while the latter was worshipped at a sanctuary lying on the edge of the city's territory.[29] By means of studying both the official and local cults, as well as rituals and sacred places, which were suitably adapted to be used by new settlers and indigenous peoples, it may be possible to define the identity of the new community.

The first part of the volume closes with Chapter 7. Here M. Pérez Ruiz shifts the focus from the public into the private sphere and studies the variety of practices and rites performed in the domestic space between the third century BCE and the first century CE. Material evidence (*arulae* and altars, deposits), situations (rituals and foundational offerings), and spaces (in particular *lararia*) found in settlements

---

27 Cf. Urciuoli and Rüpke 2018.
28 This perspective has recently been employed for the study of Italy: Stek 2009; for Hispania: Alfayé 2009; 2010.
29 See Sinner and Revilla in this volume.

with different characteristics are analysed: from small, nucleated settlements to *domus* and *villae*. In these domestic spaces, a highly diversified set of practices stemming from a wide range of cultural traditions can be identified. In the first instance, some practices that emerged in the Iberian Iron Age related to the self-representation of certain social groups are analysed; these appear to have led to the specialized use of certain domestic spaces. Later, the author discusses how Italic rites were introduced in the course of the second century BCE together with a specific place of worship, the *lararium*. This process parallels the expansion of urbanization in certain regions in the late second century and the early first century BCE.[30] Pérez Ruiz's chapter highlights the particular importance of agency, in the domestic context, to understand the processes in which practices and rituals were combined, modified, and adapted.

Part II, *Strategies, Mechanisms, and Practice: Collective Identities and Private Agency*, aims to define some of the means and procedures used to construct an identity; in some cases, a collective memory with a clear political component was drawn upon. Some of the chapters specifically enable the collective intervention of political elites to be evaluated. In others, the creation or reconstruction process of a cult (with the corresponding definition of its sacred places and the material organization of the cult and its rituals) reflects personal initiatives undertaken by people of a particular rank or condition because of their responsibilities, social position, and mobility. Such cases enable the impact of interaction and movement that came about as a result of the unification of the Mediterranean to be examined.[31] The case studies included make it possible for a wide range of strategies and situations, which were manifested in an equally wide variety of forms, to be reconstructed.

In Chapter 8, G. Woolf questions the validity of using concepts such as 'Mediterranean' to analyse the cultural processes generated in this geographical area in the first millennium BCE. He points out the impact of marked regional diversity, which, at one and the same time, has both facilitated and complicated contacts between societies. In particular, the author emphasizes how the application of generically defined frameworks of reference, as in this case, leads to the importance of factors (communications, trade, unification, politics) that would have generated processes of integration being unconsciously highlighted, while the difficulties arising from the diversity of cultural traditions and geography are underestimated. His analysis can be applied both to the field of religion and to wider cultural and political trends.

In the case of the Iberian Peninsula, Woolf highlights the importance of being cautious when trying to analyse the mechanisms of (political and cultural) identity formation since many factors act in favour of the marked fragmentation of the Iberian Peninsula. Such divisions were the consequence of a combination of historical, cultural, and ecological factors, and they were particularly clear from the first half of the first millennium BCE onwards. The particular geography of Hispania, a microcontinent extending from the Atlantic Ocean to the Mediterranean Sea, has conditioned its social, cultural, and religious landscapes, making it the perfect case study to consider the heuristic validity of traditional frames of reference such as Mediterranean and Atlantic Bronze Age religions as well as the utility of describing large-scale patterning in terms of religious action. The author also demonstrates how the dynamics of religious interaction occurred more often within certain regions of the peninsula rather than between these regions, giving rise to different patterns of expansion for cults and rituals. This regional differentiation reveals the limits to the application of imperial power, which was capable of creating administrative, religious, and cultural integration mechanisms in the peninsula in the face of the combination of historical and geographical factors.

The analysis of the strategies and initiatives related to identity construction starts with a discussion of a controversial but fundamental type of evidence: coinage. In recent decades, the effectiveness of monetary objects as a vehicle for the dissemination of messages has been debated in depth, but in a limited sense, due to its function as a vector for propaganda messages (currency seems to be particularly well adapted to this type of analysis since it is an area generally controlled by a political power) that power imposes on society. In contrast, the role of currency as a transmitter of complex political and cultural messages that involve active negotiation within a civic community has recently been empha-

---

30  Together with the concession of exceptional juridical statutes (unusual in the second century), the appearance of new forms of urban planning must have had a far-reaching impact on the organization of indigenous communities. This development created new spaces of social and political interaction and identity that subsequently contributed to reinforcing these new communities. In the context of religion, this idea has been developed by Urciuoli and Rüpke 2018, 118–21 ('Religious change is always investigated in the ongoing interaction between space and different agents'). Urban development in Hispania: Houten 2021.

31  On mobility in Rome: De Ligt and Tacoma 2016; Tacoma 2016; Woolf 2016.

sized. In these dynamics of negotiation, the elites of each community acted as intermediaries before the Roman power, playing a fundamental role that does not exclude the participation of other social groups.[32]

Chapter 9 (M. Campo) studies the appearance of religious elements (cults, rituals, myths) on coinage minted in the peninsula and their possible meaning. The author analyses the constituent features of the civic issues of Hispania between the sixth century BCE and the first century CE, in addition to evaluating their different uses and the potential that they offer to define cultural interaction and identity construction processes.[33] The starting point is the official nature of coinage and the intervention of elites in the choice of the motifs included in designs, which is a reflection of their control over the political organization of their communities. The creation of images demonstrates that an iconographic language derived from the Hellenic world was adapted. This discussion highlights the lack of information on the internal life and religious manifestations of Hispanic cities and the difficulties involved in identifying a distinctive religious iconography for local deities, which arose from the adoption of classical iconographic designs. These difficulties further complicate any analysis of the reasons that lie behind the choice of an image for a deity (whose specific characteristics remain unknown) and what strategies may have been adopted. The different motifs (deities, rituals) displayed on coins and the usage of coinage for non-economic purposes are also studied.

Chapters 10, 11, and 12 consider the specific problems involved in the relationship between religious manifestations, identity, and cultural change. They analyse several situations in which the definition of a collective identity acquires a political value. They also consider forms of agency in the implantation of cults and rituals. In this context, the construction of a memory of the past, defined and maintained through a combination of rites, rituals, and priesthoods, is a basic mechanism for defining the identity of some civic communities in Hispania and their elites. At the same time, the construction of this memory, which led to a local community becoming an integral part of Roman history, enabled the position and role of provincial elites to be defined within the political, social, and cultural framework that the Empire offered.

Chapter 10 (A. Mayorgas) considers a number of aspects related to the structure and transmission of cultural memory in Rome. The core of her study is the diffusion of certain narratives (including some individuals and episodes dating back to the earliest periods in Roman history) in the Hispanic provinces. In the introduction to her study, the author highlights two particularly important factors: the existence of a cultural memory, which was completed in the Augustan period, starting with the figure of Aeneas and his successors, and the difficulties involved in transferring and adapting this memory to a provincial context. Subsequently, Mayorgas analyses the iconographic, epigraphic, and numismatic evidence derived from very different urban contexts: in the three provincial capitals, where this evidence formed an integral part of the setting of the forum, and in cities with a very different history and juridical status, ranging from urban centres founded or politically active in the context of the Second Punic War (Italica, Saguntum) to small imperial-period *municipia*. The diversity of situations found in the Iberian Peninsula is unparalleled in other Roman provinces. In particular, the significance of the presence of priesthoods linked with the earliest Roman rituals (such as the *salii*) and the remembrance of certain incidents in the past (the she-wolf and the twins; the prodigy of the sow and the thirty piglets) in public and private contexts is analysed. Their presence coincides with the expansion of the imperial cult. Nevertheless, the author is of the opinion that they were isolated local initiatives, which did not reflect a strategy on the part of the Roman state, and which apparently did not give rise to regular rituals, with the possible exception of the practices associated with the *dies natalis* of Rome at the sanctuary of Cales Coves (Menorca), which, however, seem to have been more closely linked with the rural meaning of the *Parilia*. Above all, the remembrance of the mythical past of Rome should be interpreted as part of different strategies of self-promotion used by some Hispanic elites to define their position within the imperial framework. Ultimately, Mayorgas's study enables us to consider the complex relationships between myth, past, memory, and cultural change, and the instruments used to elaborate a cultural and political identity.[34] The creation of this identity and the ways in which it was circulated and adapted among different groups of people in the provinces, groups whose activity was shaped by different civic frameworks, is but one of the components of the system of interactions that regulated the imperial administration.

---

32 Chaves 2008b; 2012b; 2017; Chaves and Marín 1992.

33 For Hispania: Chaves 2012a; Beltrán 2002; Royo Martínez 2016; Mora 2019.

34 The relationship between history, memory, and religion is discussed in Otto and others 2015.

Following the approach of Chapter 10 (Mayorgas), Chapter 11 (V. Revilla) is devoted to the identity construction process of one city in Hispania, namely Saguntum. This analysis takes recent reflections on memory in Rome that have been drawn up from different perspectives as its starting point.[35] In addition, works on identity construction in Hispania inspired by Bickermann's fundamental study are taken into account.[36] The basis for this identity is a memory of the past that combined the recollection and active remembrance of certain episodes in the Second Punic War with mythical features of widely varying origin. In order to activate this memory, use was made of cults and priesthoods (the *Salii*) that enabled a connection to be established between the past of Saguntum and that of Rome. However, it is impossible to ascertain whether the existence of this priesthood implied ritual activity and a calendar that reproduced the practices undertaken in Latium and Rome itself (cf. Chapter 10). The presence of cults such as that of Liber Pater in the Saguntum area, in sanctuaries maintained through the public intervention of the city, implying the presence of its magistrates, should be understood in this same light. Rather than interpreting an ancient local cult of an agricultural nature, the cult to Liber Pater seems to reflect a new meaning being attributed to a cult place by means of a link with the earliest Roman religious tradition. The construction of civic identity seems to have been carried out under the strict control of the local elites. These sectors of society deliberately created an account of the past dominated by themselves, in which values such as class and their own initiatives became the central feature of the community's past. By means of this strategy, they took control of the historical memory of the community, while at the same time re-elaborating it. This undertaking that recalled the past was not an initiative driven by learning or nostalgia, but rather one aimed at legitimizing control over the community. At the same, it enabled the city's own identity to be promoted before other elite groups in the province and also allowed the city to stake a place in the new political and cultural framework promoted by the imperial power. To achieve this, a historical special relationship with republican tradition was emphasized.

Chapter 12 (F. Marco) analyses the different practices and rituals connected with the imperial cult between the late first century BCE and the first century CE. It covers the specific cases of the provincial capitals and the situation found in very different regions: Baetica and the north-western part of the peninsula. The author questions certain traditional hypotheses, such as the idea of a single cult exclusively promoted by the imperial power in the East and the West. In contrast, he proposes the hypothesis of a range of practices, which were not to be united until the Flavian period. This diversity was the result of the combination of very early initiatives undertaken by the representatives of imperial power in the peninsula and the interventions of urban elites of very different communities, whose aspirations and needs varied considerably. The common element in all these practices was the exaltation of consensus, which was expressed in loyalty to the emperor. This exaltation led to the development of ceremonial practices that involved the provincial elites. Through their participation, these elites reinforced their social position and demonstrated their adherence to and place within the imperial order. The author also emphasizes the importance of other elements that contributed to projecting the imperial figure above the life of any community and to unifying the interventions of provincial populations: on the one hand, intangible mechanisms, such as the calendar, oaths or the remembrance of the foundational myths of Rome (cf. Chapter 11: Revilla); on the other hand, tangible means, such as imperial portraits (either large scale or on coin issues) and monumental architecture.[37]

Some of the questions discussed in Chapters 4 and 5 (the role of certain individuals in establishing a cult and promoting a sanctuary) are taken up again in Chapter 13 (M. McCarty and K. Edher). In it, the authors question the dominant metanarratives that explain the diffusion of the so-called oriental cults in the Iberian Peninsula on the basis of the cultural origins of the individuals that promoted them. This principle leads to the assumption that fixed ethnic identities existed, and that variations in them would supposedly serve to indicate the greater or lesser degree of Romanization of a territory or region. In contrast to this idea, the authors put forward a perspective that emphasizes agency as the fundamental factor in the establishment of certain cults and their precise definition. As opposed to an ethnic origin, the factor that explains the creation of specific religious manifestations in a region was the private initiative of certain individuals.[38]

---

35 Mayorgas 2007; 2010; Dardenay 2010; 2012; Sandberg and Smith 2018 includes several studies on the construction of the historical account on the basis of memory and tradition; aristocracy: Hölkeskamp 2017.
36 Bickerman 1952; Johnston 2017.
37 On monumental architecture and religion: Häussler 1999.
38 In accordance with a postcolonial perspective: Mattingly 2011; Revell 2015.

Such undertakings reflected the need to construct a social power and to define a position of authority in a precise context. This need was embodied in the adoption of cults and rituals and the promotion of certain places of worship. The result was a localized religion that developed in specific spaces of social and territorial interaction.

## Final Remarks

The studies brought together in this volume demonstrate that religious manifestations represent a privileged space for analysing relationships between processes of cultural change and the negotiation strategies adopted by individuals, social groups, and political communities. This relationship between dynamics of change and negotiation was particularly intense and complex in the context of Roman Mediterranean expansion as from the third–second centuries BCE. At that point in time, the political and socio-economic balance was drastically altered, and processes of interaction involving individuals and communities, and which supposed the development of forms of identity and formulation of frameworks of reference to provide meaning to the swift and violent changes of the period, were created. Aspirations and expectations related to personal security, promotion and status, wealth, etc. coalesced in the construction of these identities within a rapidly expanding political and cultural framework that incorporated very diverse forces.

The Iberian Peninsula offers an unrivalled setting for analysis, both because of its history and diversity and for its size and location: a microcontinent placed between the Mediterranean, a geographical space supposedly favourable to unification and communication, and the Atlantic world and continental Europe. The subjects analysed in this volume (cult sites and sacred landscapes, the diffusion of specific cults, rituals, the development of traditions) demonstrate the wide range of strategies, initiatives, and means used in the religious sphere by both individuals and communities in Hispania. This diversity reflects the (to a greater or lesser extent clear) perception of the position that it occupied in changing circumstances, the consequence of far-reaching processes that were difficult to understand and to which some form of meaning had to be attributed. However, the religious phenomenon cannot be analysed unequivocally as an automatic response to the 'anxieties' generated by great historical processes. The aspirations and expectations of individuals, linked with the formation of a collective and personal identity, and a limited perception of the social environment, are fundamental for an understanding of religious dynamics at a local and regional level and their specific forms of expression: the expansion of certain cults and their specific forms; the creation of rituals and calendars; the selection of sacred spaces and their particular organization. In other words, it is not a question of interpreting the dynamics of religious practice as simple reactions to historical change, but rather to understand them within a series of initiatives and strategies formulated in everyday life, with a greater or lesser degree of awareness, together with resources to construct new frames of reference that might endow an individual or a collective's position with meaning within a constantly evolving overall context. Obviously, in order to try to reconstruct individual and collective aspirations and strategies, factors such as status, whether an individual belonged to one or more collectives (of different types), gender, socio-economic position, and age need to be taken into account; however, neither should the possible normative value that models of reference elaborated in the centre of the Empire (or elsewhere and redesigned there) be forgotten, since many people originally from Hispania who emigrated to the capital would have been able to discover, assimilate, and spread them, at the same time as they modified them and endowed them with a new meaning.

As some of the contributions demonstrate, memory of the past could play an important role in the creation of individual or collective identity. Some chapters show how a combination of certain events in the history of a community with myth and ritual might help to create a collective memory. In this case the examples analysed also reveal the wide variety of initiatives, above all dominated by the urban elites in Hispania, although not all of them were developed in the same way. The selection of certain (very specific) incidents in Roman history or aspects that were linked to the new imperial power and their combination with some points of reference taken from Greek culture, including clearly mythical elements, or features derived from local history (which in itself was also an artificial creation of the past) gave rise to a wide range of highly original accounts.

In some cases, these constructs could have remained in the realms of pure erudition (this might have been the case of the description of Tarraco that Florus offers in the early first century CE), but in others there seems to have been a conscious desire to commemorate and perhaps even reactivate certain fundamental moments of the Roman past. One explicit aim behind remembering local historical events and combining them with the past of Rome might have been to emphasize a community's prestige. Nevertheless, in certain contexts, their role seems to go beyond that: the regular commemoration of these episodes in a public context, linked with local institutions (which would thus see their activity legitimized), might convert the past into a key feature in defining a collective identity. This identity would place the community, and more specifically one of its constituent parts (the elites) in the wider context of the structure of the Empire.

In this respect, Hispania thus reveals itself to be a microcontinent that acted as a crossroads for different cultural traditions and situations which, as a consequence of their mobilization, adaptation, and combination with external elements, helped its inhabitants to construct frameworks of reference and interaction on different levels: local, regional, and provincial. Some questions still remain to be analysed in greater depth: To what extent were the identity and memory of a community perceived and accepted beyond the local elites and did they serve to generate effective mechanisms for internal consensus? What was the true significance of the narratives based on memory and identity in creating identification with the Empire in comparison with mechanisms such as the imperial cult or service in the administration? And above all else, how were these narratives to develop over the course of the imperial period? Considering all these questions obliges one to analyse the communities of Hispania from all possible standpoints.

### Acknowledgements

The editors would like to express their gratitude to those who have made this book possible: of course, the authors of the different chapters, who kindly agreed to adapt to the norms and deadlines, as well as for kindly engaging in a constant dialogue and exchange of ideas with the editors; to the reviewers for their detailed and thoughtful comments on earlier versions of the volume, which have helped to improve the final text; to the institutions, museums, and collections that have allowed the reproduction of a number of illustrations; Philip Banks and Tim Barnwell, who have ensured the linguistic correctness of the texts; Brepols, in particular Rosie Bonté (Publishing Manager), and the editors of the *Archaeology of the Mediterranean World* series, Peter Van Dommelen and Lin Foxhall, who have been of extraordinary assistance in helping us to improve the manuscript and produce an attractive design; this project would have never been possible without the financial support of the University of Victoria (Book Subvention Fund) and especially of the Social Science and Research Council of Canada, the University of Barcelona, and Generalitat de Catalunya, which have funded the projects *Beyond Contacts: Tracing Identities and Cultural Change in the Roman West* (A. G. Sinner) and *Dinàmiques socioeconòmiques del món rural romà: formes d'hàbitat i cultura material al litoral central català* (V. Revilla). Lastly, but no less important, we must mention our families and beloved ones, especially Anna, Cassia, Rafael, and Antonella. The preparation of this volume required over two years of long working hours with their ups and downs. Their support has been fundamental for ensuring that the book reached completion.

# PART I

## Rituals in Context

*Spaces, Scenarios, and Landscapes*

IGNASI GRAU MIRA

# 2. Ritual Practices and Sacred Landscapes

*Identity and Territorial Organization in Late Iron Age and Early Roman Eastern Iberia*

## Introduction: Landscapes and Sanctuaries

Archaeological research on landscape and territorial organization in eastern Iberia has proposed that there were clear processes of urbanization and that centralized polities were created in the Iron Age. These dynamics were the result of local social processes together with the complex colonial encounters that occurred on the Mediterranean seaboard during the centuries prior to the Roman conquest in the third century BCE.

These territorial developments evolved in two main phases. During the Early and Middle Iberian periods (seventh–fourth centuries BCE) the region was structured around a series of small territories dominated by fortified urban centres. These oppida, to use the ancient term adopted by scholars, controlled dependent farming settlements of varying sizes that existed in each valley, ranging from what may have been single-family farmsteads to hamlets or larger villages. Conflicts and social tensions between oppida and territories were frequent during this period as archaeological destruction layers prove.[1]

The second stage witnessed a shift towards the union of different territories to create larger political units. During the third century BCE some of the existing oppida increased in size, functioned as political and religious centres, and were raised to the category of capital towns of the various regions. However, in terms of territorial organization, the other oppida continued to serve as local centres for each of the valleys although subordinate to the main towns. The surrounding rural sites increased in number in order to sustain these early Iberian city-states.[2] This would have meant eliminating the local community structures established by each oppidum and defining a new societal structure during the third century BCE. This process has been studied in depth in the Valencia region, which covers the northern part of the area under study,[3] but similar dynamics are found in other areas of south-eastern Iberia.[4]

The Roman conquest of the Iberian Peninsula, in the late third century BCE, led to major changes in this territorial organization. The Roman conquerors used part of the existing network of Iberian centres, but dismantled others. Far from bringing it to a halt, Rome fostered the process of establishing communities and territories and encouraged the use of native traditions, which were reinvented in the new social context.

An important component of this territorial process of aggregating communities was the use of social strategies to reinforce the newly created political identities. In other words, the construction of new political entities required symbols that provided authenticity based on shared collective traditions and values.[5] This was an active process of ethnic identity creation,[6] materialized in cult places and ritual practices[7] that evoked shared memories and used them to justify the new political framework and its landscape.[8]

The creation of sacred landscapes through ritual practices as part of the consolidation of identities rests, in my opinion, on two elements that are particularly relevant. The first is the use of the collective memory,[9] established at significant places in the symbolic landscape. The second is the establishment of shared practices anchored in traditions and the past.

---

1 Bonet and others 2015, 261.
2 Bonet and others 2015, 263.
3 Bonet and others 2015.
4 López Mondéjar 2019; Ramos Martínez 2018.
5 Anderson 1991; Hobsbawm 1983.
6 Jones 1997.
7 Demarrais and others 1996.
8 Yoffee 2007.
9 See Mayorgas and Revilla in this volume.

**Ignasi Grau Mira**, Professor of Archaeology (Universitat d'Alacant)

In relation to the first point, the construction of religious buildings at places previously considered as sacred spaces is indicative of a profound resignification of the Iberian religious landscape and a reorientation of ritual practices. In this sense, the force of permanence and immutability is used to shape a new socio-political reality and a new structure of the territory, in accordance with the new Roman interests.[10]

With regard to the second aspect, shared practices, *sensu* Bourdieu, contributed to building the idea of community anchored in the territory. Participating in the ceremonies of the sanctuaries, always in accordance with the rites socially acceptable to the community, contributes, according to the *habitus* principle, to the progressive construction of the collective.[11]

In this respect, the ritual integrative mechanisms that lead to the convergence of diverse groups and communities sharing collective religious experiences, expressed through community practices, are especially significant.[12] The practices shared by the group, such as the action of depositing the same type of votive offerings, in the same sacred space, and at a certain moment, would become a means to consolidate the collective *habitus* of the participants, generating an idea of belonging to a community, as well as an identification with the territory.[13]

In sum, sanctuaries provided reference points for the local communities, centres of settlement systems, and symbolic nodes in the late Iberian and early Roman period prior to the configuration of Roman cities in the late first century BCE.[14] In this sense, the role of the Iberian sanctuaries as spaces of social aggregation and interaction was similar to that of other cult places in the Mediterranean world.[15] During this first moment of Roman expansion in eastern Iberia, the collective identity and power of local groups and individuals was expressed through the development of sanctuaries, rather than through public buildings in towns, as in other parts of the Roman dominions.[16] In the following pages, these ideological and ritual practices carried out in the local sanctuaries as political strategies will be discussed.

## Cult Places, Sacred Landscapes, and Identity in Eastern Iberia

Iberian communities sought to redefine themselves in a climate of change and competition brought about by the new historical circumstances of Roman expansion. In this context, sanctuaries became the focus of affirmation for the new communities, which largely tried to present their traditional identity through ritual practices. This was a complex, plural process of place-making for local Iberian groups in which different aspects would give rise to diverse responses. In this respect, the cult places would be better understood as spaces for negotiation and exchange between the different agents involved, the local Iberian communities and the Roman or Italic populations, as has been proposed for other colonial contexts.[17]

According to these proposals, cult places became spaces of aggregation that played a key role in the new context of Roman expansion, possibly favoured by the new ruler to shape landscapes, but without the risks involved in encouraging political centres that could have acted against the interests of Rome. It is possible that the newly established Roman power would not have welcomed the potential emergence of powerful political entities centralized in urban centres. Roman rulers used local oppida and their territorial structures, but limited the concentration of power, promoting political fragmentation and balance between local factions. In fact, in the whole region of eastern Iberia only the colony of Valentia was founded during the first stage of Roman establishment, in the second century BCE. Similarly, the important port of Carthago Nova was an active urban centre reinforced directly by Roman rulers,[18] but most of the settlement pattern remained under the control of the Iberian oppida that continued to be occupied under Roman rule.

In that respect, sanctuaries contributed to the creation of collective identities, without encouraging political centralization and the urbanization processes that the Romans developed and formalized from the time of Augustus onwards.[19] During this first stage of Roman expansion, the aggregation needed to structure landscapes was better accommodated in sanctuaries than in towns.

The traditional sanctuaries were redefined with the incorporation or reinforcement of certain elements. Important in the Iberian case was the adop-

---

10 Gruel and others 2008; García-Cardiel 2015a, 91.
11 Duplouy 2019; see also Sinner and Revilla in this volume.
12 Sallnow 1981, 163–82.
13 García Cardiel 2015b, 92.
14 Abad Casal and others 2006.
15 Alcock and Osborne 1994; Häussler and Chiai 2019; Stek 2009; 2015; Cifani and Stoddard 2012; Williamson 2012.
16 Patterson 1992, 149–57.
17 Malkin 2002.
18 Ramallo 2006; Noguera and Madrid 2014.
19 Abad Casal and others 2006.

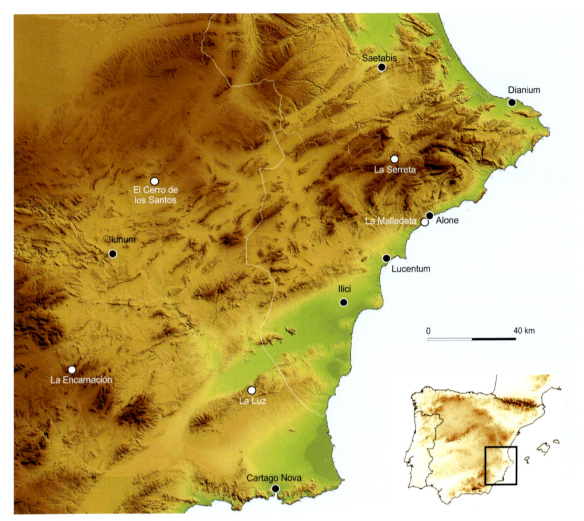

Figure 2.1. Map of eastern Iberia with the sanctuaries studied in the text. Black circles denote Roman cities.

tion of new constructions and votive practices. It might be argued that the constant rebuilding of the sanctuaries, usually with Roman and/or Italic components, which marked the reaffirmation of the ties with the place by different generations of worshippers, was particularly significant.

## Ritual Activities and Identity in the Sanctuaries of Iberia

Different strategies and ritual practices were employed in cult places in order to create identity, attach meanings, and connect people to places. The most prominent strategies recognized in Iberian sanctuaries were the action of building and rebuilding monumental structures and the use of specific votive offerings for each sanctuary. As regards the building of monumental structures, this process was first described by S. Ramallo and his colleagues some years ago for a small group of sanctuaries in the south-eastern region.[20] Analysis of this monumentalization of cult places within a wider geographical and temporal framework has revealed a series of different dynamics in the republican and early imperial periods.[21]

In short, it is possible to state that, prior to the Roman conquest, most cult places in Iberia were natural sites, possibly with ephemeral constructions that have left hardly any trace. During the Roman expansion in the second and first centuries BCE major building work was undertaken at most of the sanctuaries in the region. Differences in the forms and chronologies of these building processes are a consequence of local initiatives framed within similar strategies. The most evident initial monumentalization of these sanctuaries in the second and first centuries BCE[22] was followed by repeated episodes of rebuilding until the first and second centuries CE,

---

20 Ramallo 1993; Ramallo and others 1998.
21 Ramallo and Brotons 2014, 38; Grau and others 2017.
22 Ramallo 1993.

indicating the significance of these building activities in the long term.[23]

Secondly, the most important archaeological evidence of the ritual activity at the Iberian sanctuaries is the hundreds, or sometimes thousands, of votive offerings that make up the sacred deposits at each cult site. A detailed analysis and interpretation of votive offerings is beyond the scope of this paper, and so a single aspect that appears to be particularly important as a strategy for strengthening community identity is focused on here. A specific type of object was chosen to be deposited as an offering for each territorial sanctuary. The objects were not normally of a single, exclusive type, but there is a clear selection of votive objects that were different at each cult place. In this way, the sense of belonging to a territory was expressed through the deposit of a specific offering in each place.[24] Specialist workshops associated with each sanctuary would also have promoted the commoditization of the offerings. However, there can be no doubt that they contributed to the development of a sense of shared practice among those making the offerings and the experience of belonging to a community of practitioners.

## Sanctuaries of Eastern Iberia

In the next section, the archaeological evidence related to these ritual strategies in the region under study, eastern Iberia (Fig. 2.1), will be described. The main characteristics of construction activities and the nature of votive objects will be summarized in order to evaluate the role of sanctuaries in shaping the landscape and creating identities. Recently analysed places of worship that can be used to define the aforementioned processes have been selected.

### La Malladeta (La Vila Joiosa, Alicante)

The sanctuary of La Malladeta is located in the littoral area of the present-day province of Alicante, the central coastal area of ancient Contestania (Fig. 2.1).[25] This cult place is located on a coastal promontory close to the Iberian settlement of Alon, the later Roman city of Allone, under the modern-day urban nucleus of La Vila Joiosa.[26] The location on the top of the hill makes it a geographical landmark visible from any point of the surrounding coastal plain. In addition, it is located next to a key land communication corridor that connected the neighbouring regions.

This sanctuary has been the subject of study by a joint Spanish-French project, which has enabled the site to be known in detail and provided valuable information for the understanding of the transformation processes at Iberian cult sites around the time of Roman expansion.[27] An initial Iberian phase can be identified and dated between 375 and 100 BCE. There are no building remains, but it has been recognized by the presence of terracotta figurines and Attic and Italic Black Gloss pottery in different sectors. In this phase it may have been an open-air cult place similar to those recorded in other Iberian regions.

The second Iberian phase can be dated between 100 and 25 BCE, and it is made up by a series of small departments, ranging in size from 7 to 14 m² and arranged in a row, some of which can be grouped into units composed of two or three rooms. These rooms are not interpreted as domestic units, given the absence of domestic elements such as hearths, and the scarcity of cooking wares and habitat refuse. On the other hand, the presence of other artifacts such as votive terracotta figurines has led researchers to interpret the complex as a place for religious activities, possibly rooms to provide shelter and service to visitors to the cult site. These constructions are distributed on the southern and western slopes of the promontory. Movement would have been articulated by the presence of narrow roads in the form of streets that follow the slope.

The area of ritual activity is recorded in Sector 5, located at the top of the hill. What is known as space 3 is part of a badly preserved building with an ash layer overlying the natural bedrock, which contained votive terracotta fragments. These remains have been related to religious practices that must have included rituals in which fire played a part.[28]

In the last quarter of the first century BCE substantial reforms were to take place in the sanctuary, with the destruction and abandonment of the structures located on the slopes. These changes marked the beginning of the last phase, dated between 25 BCE and 75 CE, which was limited to the hilltop. The end of the cult site coincided with the acquisition of the status of Roman *municipium* in the time of Vespasian. Ritual activities may have been transferred to temples in the new Roman town.

---

23 Grau and others 2017.
24 Grau 2016.
25 Rouillard and others 2014.
26 Espinosa 2006.
27 Rouillard and others 2014, 49–85.
28 Rouillard and others 2014, 85.

## La Serreta (Alcoi-Cocentaina-Penàguila, Alicante)

The Iberian sanctuary of La Serreta (Fig. 2.1) is located on a narrow plateau at the top of the hill adjacent to an Iberian settlement inhabited from the early Iberian period until the Roman conquest in the third century BCE.[29] This cult site was excavated in 1920–1922 and for this reason we lack detailed evidence of the archaeological context of the building and finds. However, recent analyses of the available records have proposed three main phases in the activity of this long-standing cult place.

The first phase in the existence of La Serreta can be dated to the third century BCE and is closely related to the nearby Iberian settlement, which was the main urban centre in the region and the capital of the Iberian territory that stretched along the Alcoi Valley. Hundreds of terracotta figurines representing worshippers belonging to this phase were found. Different types of pieces were recovered: incense burners in the shape of female heads, compositions of groups of figurines, figurines representing male heads and, most abundant, female figurines that have been linked to fertility at the sanctuary (Fig. 2.2a).[30]

The second phase of the Iberian sanctuary can be dated to the second and first centuries BCE, after the Roman conquest, which resulted in the destruction of the nearby Iberian settlement. In this period the cult site attended the religious needs of the entire region as a centre of pilgrimage for the neighbouring Iberian oppida and villages. Most of the offerings associated with this period are female-shaped incense burners of regional origin, the so-called Guardamar-type.[31] During this phase, the cult place may have remained an open-air site, according to the currently available evidence.

The third phase of the sanctuary is marked by the building of different structures and changes in the votive offerings deposited. Excavations found the remains of buildings in two areas on the hilltop of La Serreta. At the highest point of the mountain some worked ashlars and tiles were found, although they were not placed in any specific order, possibly because of the complete destruction of the building. On the basis of the details identified, the building could be defined as a rectangular construction measuring 8 by 10 m.[32] This was located within the earlier Iberian sanctuary; various votive deposits were collected, such as Roman terra sigillata vessels, coins, and lamps. These materials point to the

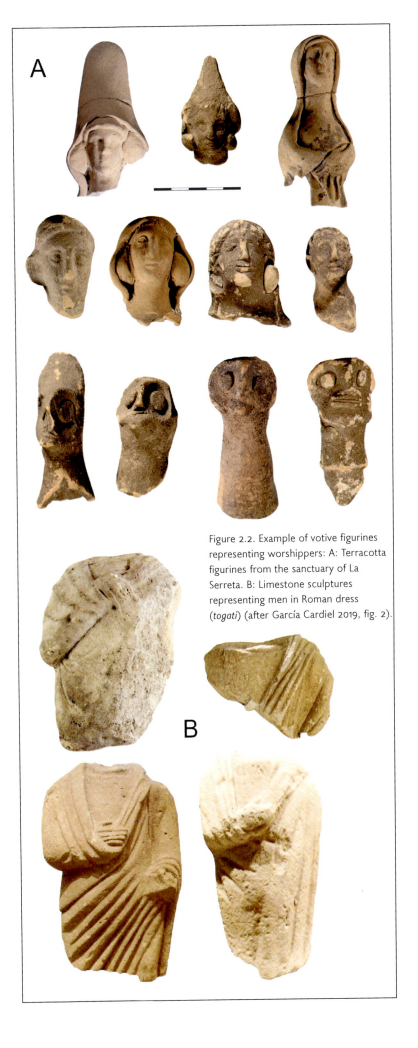

Figure 2.2. Example of votive figurines representing worshippers: A: Terracotta figurines from the sanctuary of La Serreta. B: Limestone sculptures representing men in Roman dress (*togati*) (after García Cardiel 2019, fig. 2).

---

29 Grau and others 2017.
30 Grau and others 2017, 87–118.
31 Grau and others 2017, 80–84.
32 Visedo 1922a, 8; 1922b, 4.

continuity of the Iberian cult site in Roman times, from the first to the fifth centuries CE.[33]

The second area of interest is located a hundred metres to the north-west of the hilltop, where we find an interesting rectangular building composed by different aligned rooms (Fig. 2.3.1). Some years ago, E. Llobregat identified this building as a sanctuary with a Semitic design of the *ulam-kekal-debir* type[34] or a Roman building with an internal distribution comprising an atrium (A-3), *cella* (A-2), and *opisthodomos* (A-1), the floor of which, according to this scholar, was higher than those of the other two rooms. This researcher also pointed out the existence of a large quantity of tegulae and imbrices recorded in a survey carried out in 1988, which undoubtedly indicated that the remains were of Roman date.[35]

Recently, this building has been studied in detail in order to reinterpret the result of the earlier excavations. It is a quadrangular building attached to a series of platforms that regulate the northern slope. This terrace is constructed with local dry-stone and is completed with another platform located at a lower level, with very similar characteristics, which would have provided reinforcement.

The best-preserved wall, built with well-finished ashlars, which defines the northern side wall of a building, stands on this terrace. The other perimeter walls are only partially preserved. However, with the restitution of the surviving sections we can point to the existence of a building measuring 17.95 m long by 6.05 m wide. The internal structure is marked by the presence of three transversal walls, which define three rooms and possibly an entrance on the eastern side, oriented from the south-west to the north-east. It is difficult to identify the latter due to the absence of the closing wall at the eastern end, so it could also be an extension of the longitudinal walls in the form of a portico. This building was covered by tiles, as demonstrated by the presence of abundant tegulae. This type of structure required solid foundations, together with the terraces mentioned, to withstand the pressure of a very heavy roof.

The measurements used in La Serreta follow a pattern close to the 50-cm module used in Hellenistic and Roman republican architecture in the western provinces.[36] We find this pattern in various buildings dating from the late republican era in eastern Hispania, as in the so-called *sacellum* of Osca, dated to the third quarter of the first century BCE, and other buildings in the Ebro Valley, at La Vispesa and Gabarda.[37] This pattern is also recorded in the urban transformations of the late second century BCE in the Neapolis of Emporion.[38] Examples in the region closer to La Serreta are the forum of Valentia[39] or the rural cult place of El Canari, dated to the early first century CE.[40]

It was mentioned above that it is difficult to establish a precise chronology for this building, since it has not been completely excavated, and the materials recorded are not informative from the chronological point of view. This construction may be related to the major rebuilding of sacred spaces that took place in the region during the time of Augustus, a moment when a clear change in the votive objects deposited in the sanctuary is recorded.

## El Cerro de los Santos (Montealegre del Castillo, Albacete)

El Cerro de los Santos is another key place in the monumentalization model of Iberian cult sites during the period of Roman establishment in the region.[41] This sanctuary was located at an important crossroads of some of the main routes in south-eastern Iberia. After an initial phase of the cult site, which can be identified as a possible open-air sanctuary dating to the fourth and especially the third centuries BCE, a series of substantial transformations took place with the building of a temple on the northern edge of the hill.[42]

The main limitation when analysing the temple of El Cerro de los Santos is the scarcity of surviving remains. Recent excavations have found features cut in the underlying rock that help to reconstruct the plan and interpret the drawings and descriptions made by the first excavators, Lasalde and Saviron, in the last third of the nineteenth century.[43] It was a rectangular building measuring 15.60 m in length and 6.90 m in width, with a front staircase that provided access from the northern slope (Fig. 2.3.2). Well-squared blocks of 0.45 m in width were used in this building; they were joined by means of lead clamps and seated directly on the natural bedrock, which had been worked in preparation. Its internal structure is divided into a *cella* of 12.02 m in length by 6 m in width, and the *pronaos*, which occupies the rest of the space. Access to the *cella* would have been

---

33 Visedo 1922a; 1922b.
34 Llobregat and others 1992, 69.
35 Llobregat and others 1992, 69.
36 Jodin 1975.
37 Asensio 2003, 96–97.
38 Sanmartí and others 1990.
39 Escrivá and Ribera 1993, 580.
40 Pascual and Jardón 2014, 132–33.
41 See also Schattner in this volume.
42 García Cardiel 2015a, 88.
43 Ramallo and Brotons 2014, 40.

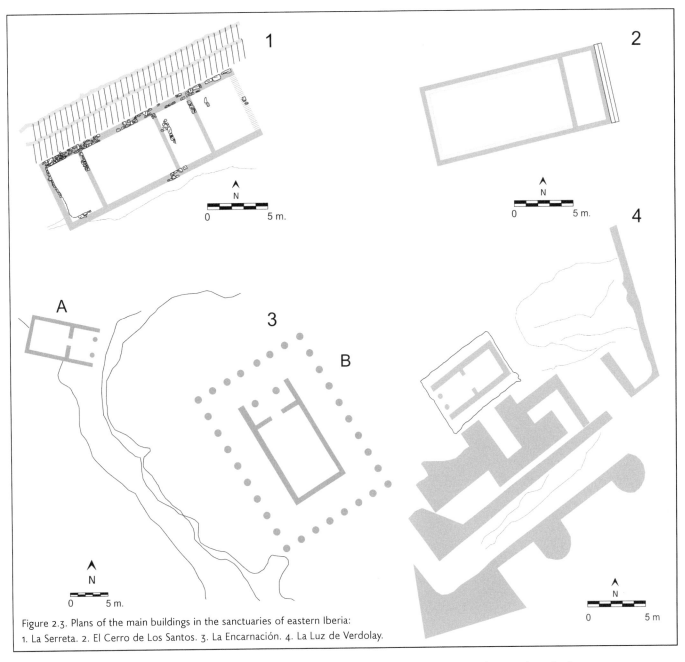

Figure 2.3. Plans of the main buildings in the sanctuaries of eastern Iberia:
1. La Serreta. 2. El Cerro de Los Santos. 3. La Encarnación. 4. La Luz de Verdolay.

through a door 2.60 m wide, preceded by a facade with two columns located between the *antae*, resting on Attic bases without a plinth. As regards the paving of the building, fragments of *opus signinum* and black and white tesserae have been recorded, which could be related to different construction phases in the lifespan of the temple. Finally, some fragments of a column that could be considered as a local interpretation of Ionic-Italic capitals and a roof probably made of tiles have been identified.[44]

In summary, during the late Iberian or republican period an *antae* temple in the Ionic order was built on El Cerro de los Santos; this may have had a tetrastyle facade with half-columns attached to the *antae*, similar to the first phase of temple B at La Encarnación. The chronology of this temple cannot be established beyond doubt, although most specialists currently accept that it can be dated to the second century BCE.[45] However, some elements such as the capitals and the presence of black-and-white mosaics would suggest a rebuilding phase in the Augustan period.[46] The abandonment of the cult site must have taken place in the early impe-

---

44 Ramallo and Brotons 2014.

45 Nicolini 1973, 65; Noguera 1994, 200–03; Jaeggi 1996, 427.
46 Ramallo and Brotons 2014, 40.

rial period, possibly towards the middle of the first century CE.[47]

The offerings deposited in the sanctuary of El Cerro de Los Santos were different goods that included everything ranging from items of clothing, vessels, or natural products to specific objects that were clearly made precisely to be deposited as votive offerings. In this case the most frequent and important are the stone sculptures that represent the worshippers themselves, the power groups in Iberian society. Some of these sculptures are undoubtedly datable to this period of Roman occupation, to judge by their stylistic features and the clothes that they wear, clearly of Roman character. Such is the case of the representation of a man wearing the Roman *palla* and the veiled heads of Italic influence. These sculptures have been dated by several authors to the second and first centuries BCE.[48] These images are an excellent example of the adoption of Italic dress by the Iberian ruling classes.

### El Cerro de la Ermita de La Encarnación (Caravaca, Murcia)

El Cerro de la Ermita de La Encarnación has revealed some of the most interesting evidence related to ritual practices during the period of Roman expansion in Hispania. The origins of this sanctuary are indicated by the deposition of various votive objects dating from the fourth and third centuries BCE in a space not clearly defined by constructions, possibly an open-air cult site or one with some structures of organic material.[49] After this first ritual occupation, the space was transformed from the second century BCE onwards by several periods of construction that stretched over two centuries.

Construction of the building known as Temple A can be dated to the first half of the second century BCE (Fig. 2.3.3). It is a small building oriented north-east to south-west and measuring 9.48 by 5.10 m (32 by 17 Roman feet of 0.295 m). It is composed of a *cella* measuring 6 m (20 feet) and a *pronaos* of 3.48 m (12 feet), all these measurements being largely deduced from the cuttings and foundation pits cut into the bedrock. There is merely one surviving row of large rectangular blocks with a length of between 1.16 and 1.22 m and a width of between 0.50 and 0.60 m. The *cella* and the *pronaos* intercommunicate with each other by means of a door with a threshold of 1.70 m in width.

At the turn of the second to the first century BCE, Temple B was built; this was of much larger dimensions than the previous one and was a far more prominent building, at least in its final phase.[50] The first phase can be defined as an Italic-plan temple, with two columns between the *antae* although it can also be interpreted as a tetrastyle temple. Other characteristic elements of this temple are the *opus signinum* pavement, the absence of a podium, the presence of terracotta architectural pieces, and the roof made of large tiles, the most obvious parallels for which are recorded in the Etrusco-Italic temples of the republican period such as Pyrgi, Lavinium, Ardea, Città Castellana, or Cosa.[51]

At a later date, a profound transformation of the building was to be carried out, providing it with a much more monumental aspect. A second paved platform that surrounded the previous temple on three of its sides, with dimensions of 27.25 m in length and 17.25 m in width was constructed, while an octastyle facade was also erected. The external walls were formed by eight columns on the facade and ten on the side, of Ionic order. The *cella* was 6.10 m wide by 10.90 m long and was built with perfectly squared ashlars whose length ranges between 0.94 and 1.18 m, with a width of 0.45 m and a thickness of 0.60 m, which determines the width of the wall. The *cella* is preceded by a *pronaos* measuring 7.35 m. The parallels for this architectural model of octastyle temples with ten columns on the long sides are found in central Italy from the late republican period onwards.[52] The dating of this reform cannot be pinpointed precisely, although it surely corresponds to the Augustan period, when intense temple-rebuilding activity is recorded in the region.

After these rebuilding activities, the presence of a ritual deposit containing mainly fragmentary Iberian stone sculptures that were buried centuries after they had been carved and used should be noted. The pit was located in the *pronaos* of Temple B and was obliterated following ritual rules that involved its being closed by means of a stone slab and a mortar seal noticeably different from the rest of the pavement.[53] One of the last pieces of evidence for the use of the sanctuary of La Encarnación dates from the second century CE. There an inscription mentions Lucius Aemilius Rectus who undertook some restoration of the temple.[54] At the sanctuary of La Encarnación offerings of almost one hundred pieces

---

47 García Cardiel 2015a, 88–89.
48 García y Bellido 1943, 84–86; Ruiz Bremón 1986, 71–73; Noguera 1994, 210.
49 Ramallo and Brotons 1997, 261; 2014.
50 Ramallo and Brotons 1997, 52–65; Ramallo and others 1998.
51 Ramallo and Brotons 1997, 50–52; Ramallo and others 1998.
52 Ramallo and Brotons 1997, 52–65; Ramallo and others 1998.
53 Ramallo and Brotons 2014, 33–37.
54 Ramallo 1991, 63.

of gold and silver characterize this place of worship. Other votive offerings recorded with them include fibulas, terracotta figurines, vessels, and the above-mentioned Iberian stone sculptures.[55]

### The Sanctuary of La Luz in Verdolay (Santo Angel, Murcia)

The sanctuary of La Luz in Verdolay is another good example of the early monumentalization process of Iberian cult sites in the south-east.[56] The first phase of La Luz began in the late fifth–early fourth century BCE and lasted until the late third century BCE. The remains of activity in this period include various ritual objects, as well as evidence that was interpreted as tumuli, offering tables and pits with votive offerings.[57]

The main transformations took place on the hill that is known as Salent during the late third or early second centuries BCE (Fig. 2.3.4). On this hilltop, a structure of *opus caementicium* with a small temple of rectangular plan, about 6.79 m in length and 4.81 m in width, was built.[58] An internal pavement of *opus signinum* was laid directly on the underlying bedrock. According to the proposal put forward by P. Lillo, this must have been an *antae* temple with two large, plastered brick columns on the front; access to the temple would have been gained by means of a staircase located in the western part. It would have included a *cella* of little more than 2 m in length and a *pronaos*; its roof must have been covered with tiles, including terracotta tiles with Italic-inspired motifs.[59] This temple was very similar to what is known as Temple A at La Encarnación.

The building of this temple of Italic inspiration was not the only construction work carried out on the hill at this time; in addition, it was accompanied by other structures that contributed to the monumentalization of the sacred complex. Close to the temple there was a basin more than one metre in depth, partially excavated in the natural rock with the rest constructed in limestone masonry, which has been interpreted as a *favissa*.[60]

The sloping terrace containing the temple and the *favissa* was delimited by a wall with a thickness of 0.74 m and 15.55 m in length. The lower slope was enclosed by a terrace, with dimensions of 17.38 by 3 m, with a masonry wall of 0.30 m in width and in which there were several bastions. Finally, it was found that the natural rock must have been cut at certain points of the hill, probably to construct the access ramps that would have led to the upper plateau where the temple was located.[61]

This sanctuary had a short lifespan, being destroyed during the second half of the second century BCE.[62] This short existence of less than a century clearly contrasts with the long lives of the other cult places in the south-east. At the sanctuary of La Luz the predominant offering was of bronze human figurines. Nearly seventy bronze figurines were found, accompanied by other pieces such as small votive falcata-style swords, rings, and a large assemblage of pottery, possibly linked to ritual meals.[63]

### Discussion

The traditional view of Roman expansion attributed the process to the ideal superiority of its cultural patterns. These features included its political and legal organization, the establishment of a market economy based on commercial agriculture, an invincible military capacity, and the superiority of Roman arts and engineering.[64] From this perspective, the material culture was the touchstone for assessing the degree of integration of the different communities and regions. This interpretation, however, is derived from an idealist view based on cultural history. Moving away from this perspective, in this chapter the Roman expansion is understood as a historical process in which different cultural and material realities, including those of the ideological sphere related to cult places, were integrated flexibly. This study understands the role of material culture as an active means of social transformation and not only as the gradual vector that allows the evaluation of historical change. In this respect, there can be no doubt that 'material culture was actively used to construct, define, redefine and maintain social identities and relationships',[65] like those that were expressed in the changing times arising from the annexation of local territories to the Roman world.

Overcoming a dualist view that contrasts the terms native and Roman as opposing situations, our approach revolves around a much more intricate reality. The various aspects of Iberian and Roman culture are interrelated to configure a historical process of their own that is different from those of neigh-

---

55 Brotons and Ramallo 2010.
56 Ramallo and Brotons 1997.
57 Lillo 1991–1992; Comino 2015, 587–90.
58 Tortosa and Comino 2013, 125.
59 Comino 2015, 492–505.
60 Lillo 1995–1996, 96–98.
61 Tortosa and Comino 2013, 128.
62 Tortosa and Comino 2013, 128.
63 Tortosa and Comino 2013.
64 Hingley 2005.
65 Metzler and others 1995, 2.

bouring regions. The intention of this interpretative exercise is to understand a historical trajectory beyond referring to neutral native survival, which does not explain historical dynamics. The integration of local traditions occurred within the framework of a new Roman socio-political dominion, which brought about its resignification. The aim is to evaluate the variability of the different local responses to the implementation of Roman power. It is also important to investigate how the different groups reacted to this expansion, beyond a supposed immobility for reasons of cultural rejection or geographical determinism.

In the case of the study in question, the adoption of ritual patterns and practices typical of Roman-Italic culture was selective and combined with other elements of local tradition. However, that did not mean that they represented a failed process of integration according to the canons, an explanation that would be based on the comparison of the evidence with a supposed ideal model of Romanization that is rarely observed in the actual archaeological record. Rather, we propose that the Roman establishment was based on a modality in which Iberian cultural features were intermixed with Roman-Italic patterns. Consequently, local initiatives actively contributed to the historical process.

Within this framework, the groups of the different Iberian regions shared a place of reference and a series of symbolic practices. The cult sites were reinforced with new symbolic and material elements but were also immersed in their traditional cultural values and religious beliefs nested in the identity of the group. This is the approach that should be followed in the interpretation of the meaning of sanctuaries: those places where the different communities could build a religious environment in which they could recognize their place in the world. Thus, although the hegemonic cultural currents laid out the basic lines of the Roman religious maps, the local groups also had the opportunity to build a religious landscape suited to their needs and their perceptions of space and place.

## Final Remarks

As occurred in other areas of the Mediterranean, the territories in the Iberian Peninsula that encountered Rome had to reinforce their regional identities through the aggregation of the different local communities.[66] The Iberian cult sites are undoubtedly linked to the landscape transformation resulting from these contacts. Although their origins lay in the pre-Roman era, the intensity in the frequentation of sanctuaries, even with their recurrent building and monumentalization, must be linked to the development of collective identities. People were anchored in cult spaces in this context of redefinition and change. This process is especially important in the development of new rural communities that constituted the components of society in non-urban areas, in processes similar to the ones that have been studied in some Italic regions.[67]

The parallels recorded in situations around the Mediterranean with those observed in Iberia are more than evident and should be the subject of comparative analysis. This examination must go beyond the architectural similarities indicated in the monumentalization of the Iberian sanctuaries[68] to ascertain the role of the organization of broadly similar social and territorial situations. In this interpretative framework it can be proposed that the similarities and analogies could be due to the use of similar political mechanisms of indirect Roman intervention. These strategies of domination took the local rulers who guaranteed Roman territorial control during the first period of expansion as an instrument of action. Therefore, territorial aggregations and local identities enabled there to be a reordering of the political space that favoured integration into the Roman realm.

These socio-political and territorial functions can be proved by the fact that when Roman cities were founded and religious functions were transferred to the new urban temples, the traditional sanctuaries were abandoned, as many examples demonstrate.[69] However, some of the traditional cult sites remained active in those areas lacking Roman towns, such as El Cerro de Los Santos, which is closely related to the *via Augusta*, or La Serreta in the Alcoi Valley, which articulated a rural district.[70]

---

66 López-Mondéjar 2016; Tortosa and Ramallo 2017; Rueda 2011.
67 Stek 2015, 404.
68 Ramallo 1993.
69 Tortosa and Ramallo 2017.
70 Thanks are due to the editors for the kind invitation to participate in this monograph and the reviewers for their valuable comments. Funding for this research was provided by the Spanish Ministry of Science — Research Project MICINN PID2019-107264GB-I00 'Paisajes romanos en el sur de la Provincia Tarraconense. Análisis arqueológico de la estructura territorial y modelo socioeconómico' and the Generalitat Valenciana (Valencian Regional Government) under Grant PROMETEO/2019/035, LIMOS. LItoral y MOntañaS en transición: arqueología del cambio social en las comarcas meridionales valencianas.

THOMAS G. SCHATTNER

# 3. The Sacred Landscape of Western Hispania in the Roman Period

Although the Iberian Peninsula appears to be a self-contained area, separated from the rest of Europe by the Pyrenees, in reality it is not. The sheer size of the country, measuring nearly 1000 km in every direction, combined with the natural features of its mountains, plains, and rivers, means that, climatologically speaking, a wide range of climatic zones are represented, from the very damp north to the semi-arid and sometimes even arid south.

This extremely diverse landscape was reflected in the ethnographic composition of the population when Gnaeus Cornelius Scipio and his troops landed on the north-east coast near Emporion in 218 BCE. Scipio and the Roman army encountered a mosaic of Indo-European tribes in the west, north-west, and centre of the peninsula, non-Indo-European Iberians on the east coast and in the south, and Punic and Greek populations in the Mediterranean coastal regions in the south and the north respectively. It was only after two hundred years that Rome managed to unite this European subcontinent under one hand for the first time in its history, through a persistent policy of perfidy, brutality, and the skilful exploitation of the internal differences of the natives (*divide et impera*). For the first time, Augustus succeeded in subjecting the extremely different landscapes of Hispania to a new order, which was characterized by the fact that it was created by applying the same principles throughout the peninsula.

However, the diversity of peoples and tribes described above can be divided linguistically and culturally into two major areas: an Indo-European area in the west, where languages apparently belonging to the Proto-Celtic family were spoken and which occupied the greater part of the country, and a smaller area in the east, which was characterized by the presence of non-Indo-European languages (Iberian).

The recognition of these connections is of utmost importance for our research question; for the situation in one area is fundamentally different from that in the other, and this is even reflected in the length of time research has taken place. While the history of research into the respective cults and religious practices in the West goes back more than a century, in the East it is still a young subject, and it has only been increasingly recognized and addressed for a generation. While in the West male deities are predominant, in the East female deities are more likely to be found. While in the West the names of far more than three hundred deities are known and listed as a result of the evidence of inscriptions on altars, only a few names are known from the Iberian area, such as Betatun, Salaeco, Sertundo, Neton, Bokon, and Pales. While in the Indo-European area votive figurines are almost completely missing, and the picture is mainly determined by sacred altars, the sanctuaries of the Iberian area are characterized by extremely diverse votives,[1] similar to the manner known in Greek sanctuaries. This proximity to models found in the East (Phoenician, Punic, Greek) should not, however, hide the fact that a defined cult topography with the components of the *temenos*, altar, temple, and cult image recorded in the Greek world does not emerge. This applies all the more to the Indo-European area, in which (votive) altars are sufficiently present as stray finds without any context, but the archaeological or epigraphic evidence for *temene* is only present in isolated cases.

This being the situation, the aim of this contribution is to typologically structure and order the ancient sanctuaries of pre-Roman and Roman western Hispania, which are mostly rural or located in smaller settlements (Fig. 3.1).[2] In view of the consequences for our understanding of Roman Spain, at the end (see Interpretation below) a conclusion

---

1 See Sinner and Revilla in this volume.
2 I thank my friend and colleague M. Blech (Bad Krozingen) for his advice.

**Thomas Schattner**, Scientific Director of the Madrid office of the German Archaeological Institute

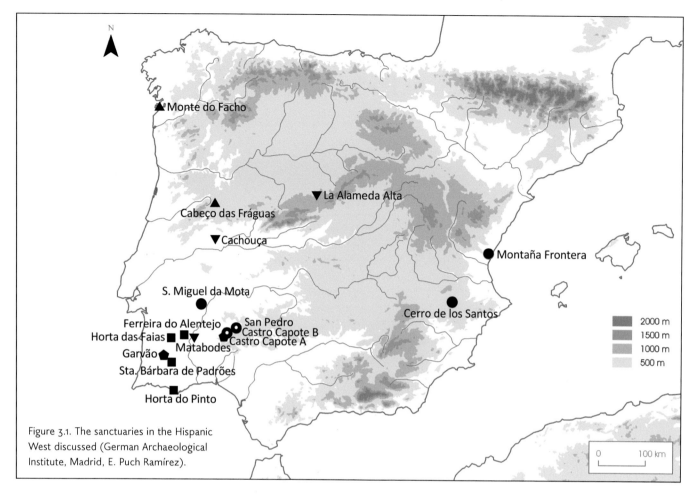

Figure 3.1. The sanctuaries in the Hispanic West discussed (German Archaeological Institute, Madrid, E. Puch Ramírez).

attempted by means of the concept of a 'sacred landscape'. Nevertheless, sanctuaries in other regions like Muntanya Frontera or Cerro de los Santos are taken into account if they contribute to illuminating and clarifying the typological panorama. In this respect it is a summary limited by the length restrictions for this chapter. It allows individual and exceptional cases[3] or even hoards, which usually lack a well-defined context, to be disregarded.[4] Similarly excluded are the typical Roman city sanctuaries with their temples at the centre. However, the attempt seems justified after more than a hundred years of research on the subject, which began in earnest with José de Leite Vasconcellos's *Religiões da Lusitânia* and was continued by a number of important scholars.[5] José María Blázquez Martínez, Julio Mangas Manjarrés, and Francisco Marco will be mentioned here as key figures. While research was initially determined by a philological approach, over the course of time and especially in recent decades, this has expanded into a combination of philology and archaeology, particularly field archaeology. This expansion has led to a juxtaposition of the two approaches, through which the strengths and weaknesses of each are revealed. Archaeology, especially field archaeology, as an artefact science, is of particular importance since the material found is objective and thus requires immediate identification. The extensive excavations undertaken since the 1980s have led to the discovery of a sufficiently large number of sanctuary sites, so that an attempt at typological classification, such as the one presented here, can be ventured. The list can only be provisional and requires continuous updating and completion. An increase in types can be expected from the publication of the Zaragoza thesis by M. J. Correia Santos,[6] and from the ongoing research by S. Alfayé Villa[7] on the grotto sanctuaries, and of course from the ongoing field research,

---

3 For example, the sanctuary of Fonte do Ídolo in Bracara Augusta is not included, as it is located within a necropolis and therefore has its own problems, see in summary Garrido and others 2008 and most recently Schattner 2019a.
4 For example Raddatz 1969.
5 Vasconcellos 1905; 1913.

6 Correia Santos 2015.
7 In her thesis this author has dealt extensively with the sanctuaries and holy places as well as the cult customs of the Celtic area of the Iberian Peninsula; see Alfayé 2009.

Table 3.1. Typology of sanctuaries and votive deposits in Western Hispania.

| Type | Typological references: local, regional, supraregional | Sanctuary | Votive deposit | Dating | Cult, deity (B) Name proven (E) Name deduced |
|---|---|---|---|---|---|
| Walled sanctuaries | supraregional | Cachouça, Idanha-a-Nova | | 8th/7th c. BCE | |
| | | La Alameda Alta, Ávila | | | |
| | | Matabodes, Beja | | 2nd BC/1st c. CE | |
| Tableware | supraregional central Italy | | Garvão | 3rd c. BCE | light, eye healing |
| | | El Castrejón, Castro Capote A | El Castrejón, Castro Capote A | Mid-2nd c. BCE | Ritual extinction |
| Statues | supraregional Greece/ Asia Minor | São Miguel da Motta, Alandroal | | 1st to 4th c. CE | Endovellicus (B) |
| | | Cerro de los Santos, Albacete | | 4th c. BCE to 1st c. CE | Fertility goddess, Pales? (B) |
| | | Muntanya Frontera, Sagunto | | 4th c. BCE– 2nd c. CE | At first the Italic cult of the Vinalia and Liberalia (E), afterwards Liber Pater (B) |
| Tableware, lamps, terracottas | local/ supraregional | | San Pedro, Valencia del Ventoso | Mid-1st until 2nd c. CE | Ataecina-Bandue (E) |
| | | | El Castrejón, Castro Capote B | Mid-1st c. CE | |
| Lamps | supraregional Sicily, Gallia, Greece | | Horta das Faias (Peroguarda, Ferreira do Alentejo | 1st–3rd c. CE | Egyptian gods? Isis, Serapis (E) |
| | | | Santa Bárbara de Padrões, Castro Verde | Mid-1st c.– 3rd c. CE | Egyptian gods? Isis, Serapis (E) |
| | | | Ferreira do Alentejo | | |
| Stone circles with stone pillars | Regional | Cabeço das Fráguas, Guarda | | 8th/7th c. BCE until 1st c. CE | Polytheistic sanctuary, Trebaruna, Reve, Laebo, etc. (B) |
| | | Monte do Facho, O Hío | | 3rd/4th c. CE | Berobreus, resp. Berus breus (B) |

which is increasingly turning its interest to the sanctuaries, as the investigation in the Sun and Moon Sanctuary at Praia das Maçãs, Sintra, Portugal, for example, now shows.[8] An extension to the entire Iberian Peninsula would also be desirable, but this would go beyond the scope of this chapter. The concentration on western Hispania is the result of the research that has been conducted on sanctuaries for several years at the Madrid Department of the German Archaeological Institute.[9]

Turning to the features that differentiate the sites that have been studied, various principles can be used to classify the elements that identify the different categories within the typology presented here. In the first section of this chapter, the internal archaeological appearance of the sanctuaries will be examined, particularly by means of analysing the inventory of portable votive offerings, their type, genus, position, or deposit (section A). Subsequently, the interpretation will assess the results (section B). With regard to the above-mentioned criteria, it is remarkable that none of the votive gifts recorded can be considered as typically Roman. On the one hand, the stone pillars or altars from Fráguas and Monte do Facho belong to the Atlantic world, particularly in the way in which they are organized in stone circles. In contrast, the dedication of statues, altars, terracottas, lamps, and special tableware — among which Roman terra sigillata does not play a prominent role — reflects pre-Roman Mediterranean customs, not specifically Roman ones.[10] As is generally known, it is not until the imperial period that a change can be observed

---

8 Ribeiro 2007; de Hoz 2014; Encarnação 2015; Ribeiro 2016; in the newly founded digital magazine *Portugal Romano* several articles are dedicated to this sanctuary: <https://issuu.com/portugalromano/docs/revista>; also the homepage <http://museuarqueologicodeodrinhas.cm-sintra.pt/escavacoes/1/alto-da-vigia.html> [accessed 3 June 2022].

9 Most recent summary in Schattner 2017; see also Schattner 2015.

10 In general, it is not always easy to describe archaeological artefacts as being Roman, see Gutsfeld and others 2019.

in the sanctuary inventories in the Mediterranean region, and thus in dedicatory practices towards forms that can be described as Roman, when the traditional, Greek-dedicated offerings gave way to large quantities of household ceramics and lamps, which henceforth determined the image of Roman sanctuaries under the Empire. This process is known as the 'votive change in Roman times'.[11] The inherent development described seems to have largely passed Hispania by, and can be observed there in the west of the peninsula alone, and even there only sporadically by means of the emergence of lamps as votive objects. The overall picture of the sanctuaries and votive deposits in question is described below (see Table 3.1). The descriptions of the respective sanctuaries are kept short as they are well known. The names given to the sanctuary types are derived from their distinctive features.

## Typological Order according to the Internal Archaeological Appearance

### Walled Sanctuaries

#### Cachouça (Idanha-a-Nova, Portugal)

The site of Cachouça was only discovered recently. It is characterized by a depressed, circular or elliptical, sunken area (39 × 26 m), surrounded on all sides by a wall of quarried stones and earth.[12] Two vessels were found in excavation trenches cut through the rampart. One is interpreted as a foundation deposit.[13] The other had been deliberately destroyed in situ.[14] Together with other peculiarities, a convincing explanation can be found in the identification of the site as a Final Bronze Age or Early Iron Age sanctuary (eighth/seventh century BCE).

#### La Alameda Alta (Ávila, Spain)

The only information for this site consists of a short reference based on an oral communication. It is characterized by the fact that more than twenty of the animal sculptures (the so-called 'verracos') known from the northern Meseta have been found there.[15]

#### Matabodes (Beja, Portugal)

The site was recently discovered during geophysical prospection in the vicinity of Beja. Surface finds such as Dressel 1 amphorae point to a second/first-century BCE date. The length of the sides (approximately 110 m) in combination with the square shape has led to its identification as a 'Viereckschanze'.[16]

### Description of the Type

The term 'walled sanctuary' is proposed here as a designation. Of all the types of sanctuaries presented here, this one is by far the least frequently attested. The site at Alameda Alta is only known from hearsay; Matabodes only geophysically; Cachouça is identified with reservations. In the publication of Matabodes the term 'Viereckschanze' is used. However, since such sites are generally unknown in Hispania, the new term 'walled sanctuary', which is unencumbered, is to be preferred. With regard to the meaning of the 'Viereckschanzen', the older interpretation as an exclusively sacred area has now given way to a more nuanced evaluation, according to which they are fortified courtyards or small settlements in which a sacred function was also exercised or which accepts that sanctuaries could also be enclosed in this manner.[17] Furthermore, the site at Cachouça (eighth/seventh century BCE) can only be added with reservations due to its considerable chronological distance from the other sites listed, especially Matabodes, which belongs to the second/first century BCE.

### Tableware

#### Garvão (Ourique, Portugal)

In the well-known third-century BCE pit at Garvão (Ourique, Portugal), the finds consist of many thousands of clay vessels of all sizes as votive offerings.[18] Famous is the human skull, which was found covered in a box-like structure in the middle of the *favissa* (depression or pit) between two slate slabs.[19]

---

11 Bookidis 2003, 255–57; Bradbury 1995, 334–36; Rothaus 2000, 129 ('thousands of votive lamps [...] seem to indicate that this was one of the most popular forms of late-antique pagan activity').
12 Vilaça 2007, 72 fig. 28; 2008, 48 fig. 14.
13 Vilaça 2007, 73 fig. 29.
14 Vilaça 2007, 73 fig. 30.
15 López Monteagudo 1982, 13; da Silva and Lopes 2007, 7; see also Salinas de Frías 1995, 283.
16 da Silva and Lopes 2007.
17 Kuckenburg 2004, 137; von Nicolai 2011.
18 The detailed publication of the finds in: de Mello Beirão and others 1985. Subsequently, some members of the group of authors presented their own accounts: Gomes and Silva 1994. The latest contribution about the site by Gomes 2012 does not introduce any new ideas.
19 The *favissa* has so far only been published in preliminary reports. This may be the reason why no photographs of this important find have yet been submitted. For the anthropological investigation, see Fernandes 1986; Antunes and Cunha 1986.

That the pit and its finds indicate a sanctuary is beyond doubt. In view of the small lamp-like plates and the precious metal plates with depictions of eyes, the excavators assumed that eye healing took place, that the cult must have had something to do with light, both in its material form and in a figurative manner, and that life after death, which would be made possible by divine light alone, could be indicated.

### Castro Capote A (Higuera la Real, Spain)

In the interior of the *castro*, a room with a floor space of approximately 4 m² was found in an alley, which apparently represents the north–south axis. It has an opening on its west side.[20] In its centre there is a massive rectangular block made of quarried stones, which is interpreted as an altar. Burnt red earth, charcoal particles, burnt black areas on the stone table, and masses of burnt bone prove the effect of intense fire. The number of finds of pottery was substantial (5170 significant pieces). In a similar way to Garvão, the vessels were stacked one inside the other, according to size, with the small ones inside the large ones. The date of the sealing of the area towards the middle of the second century BCE is close to or coincides with the date of a general destruction of the settlement in the first half of the second century BCE.[21] In brief, there must have been a collective feast.

### Description of the Type

This type of sanctuary is characterized by the appearance of substantial amounts of tableware.[22] The dating of the two examples ranges from the third century BCE and the mid-second century BCE, and the sites thus lie chronologically close together.

The examples present different characteristics. While the cult place itself remains unknown at Garvão — the *favissa* is a secondary feature — at Castro Capote the cult must have taken place around the altar.[23] In this respect the cult place only became a deposit (primary deposit) through sealing and therefore combines two functions.[24] The situation thus illustrates the distinction between sanctuary and votive deposit. In combination with the sealing on the one hand and the organized deposition of large quantities of tableware on the other, the noteworthy peculiarities of this type become apparent. Such sites have been recorded throughout the Mediterranean, but in Hispania they are limited to a few examples,[25] from Baetica and Bastetania.[26] However, they are also found in Italy. In this respect, it could be a rite that was adopted and interpreted differently from place to place.

In the Italic examples, all the characteristics mentioned beforehand, from the surrounding wall to the deposits formed by enclosing and stacking the bowls and plates in large vessels, can be found. Furthermore, depositions outside the area covered by the enclosure wall can also be found in central Italic sanctuaries such as Satricum, Borgo Le Ferriere.[27] The similarity is so close that a direct relationship is immediately obvious.[28] The parallels go so far that perhaps even the presence of central Italian emigrants in southern Lusitania can be assumed. What is not explained by this, however, is the human skull amid the finds of the Garvão deposit, which remains a hapax.

### Statues

### São Miguel da Motta (Portugal)

The sanctuary of the deity *Endovellicus* in the Portuguese region of Alentejo, near the present-day village of Alandroal on the hill of São Miguel da Motta, is one of the oldest subjects studied in Portuguese classical archaeology. Scientific research goes back to the sixteenth to eighteenth centuries[29] and was continued by José Leite de Vasconcellos at the end of the nineteenth century.[30] Vasconcellos's finds were overwhelming in number and, together

---

20 Berrocal 1994.
21 Berrocal 1994, 268.
22 The typological relationship between the two sanctuaries has always been recognized, Berrocal-Rangel 2004, 111; see also Berrocal Rangel and others 2009, 196–204. A find from Vaiamonte, Portugal, which C. Fabião 1996, 51 reconstructed from pieces coming from older excavations, which are stored in the Museu Nacional d'Arqueologia in Lisbon may perhaps be included in this type.
23 The question of primary or secondary deposit is also hotly debated in the parallel example in Satricum, Borgo Le Ferriere given below. While J. Bouma 1996, 67 assumed it was a primary deposit, M. Gnade 2002, 33, 46 considers the context to be a secondary depot, not even sacral, but the substructure of a road passing nearby: Gnade 2002, 39.
24 Berrocal 1994, 268.
25 Cancho Roano: Almagro-Gorbea and others 1990, 278; see also Etruscan palaces: Torelli 1985, 21–32.
26 Baetica: for example Alhonoz (Herrera, Sevilla), see Belén Deamos 2011–2012; Bastetania: for example Adroher 2005, 2012.
27 Bouma 1996.
28 However, the number of finds in the different layers at Satricum differs; see for example Gnade 2002, 39 table 1 the architectural terracottas, which are completely absent from the examples from the Iberian Peninsula.
29 First mention of the inscriptions by Teodósio de Bragança, A. Guerra, in: Calado 1993, 61.
30 A short overview of research in Guerra and others 2003, 418.

Figure 3.2. São Miguel da Mota. Sanctuary of Endovellicus, hypothetical reconstruction (drawing A. Ramos) (German Archaeological Institute, Madrid, archive, A. Ramos; D-DAI-MAD-Z-25-302-2014-ARAM)

Figure 3.3. São Miguel da Mota, Sanctuary of Endovellicus, range of sculpture genres (German Archaeological Institute, Madrid, E. Puch Ramírez).

Table 3.2. Sanctuary of Endovellicus, sculpture genres.

| Type | SRBH | Quantity | Format | Genre | Dating |
|---|---|---|---|---|---|
| Male heads | S | 8 | life-size and below life-size | Ideal sculpture | Hadrianic/Antonine period/later 2nd c. CE |
| Female heads | S | 9 | below life-size | Portraiture | third/early fourth quarter of 2nd c. CE |
| *Togati* | S | 8 | life-size and below life-size | Portraiture | Claudian-Neronian, mid-1st c. CE |
| Caryatid | S | 1 | below life-size | Ideal sculpture | earlier 2nd c. CE |
| Soldiers | S | 3 | below life-size | Portraiture | later 2nd c. CE |
| Female gift-bearers | S | 3 | below life-size | Portraiture | 2nd c. CE |
| Nude male | S | 6 | below life-size | Ideal sculpture | mid-2nd cent. CE |
| Nude male | R | 2 | below life-size | Ideal sculpture | earlier 2nd cent. CE |
| Children | R | 4 | below life-size | Portraiture | 2nd c. CE |
| Half-body male | BH | 6 | below life-size |  | 2nd c. CE |
| Animals | S | 2 | below life-size |  | 2nd c. CE |

with other pieces, formed the core of the collections of the Museu Etnológico Português, founded by him in 1893, which later became the present Museu Nacional d'Arqueología. These finds are currently being examined with the overall aim of studying the rural indigenous Roman sanctuaries in the west of the Iberian Peninsula.[31] The archaeological evidence from the sanctuary is comprised of statues, their pedestals, and altars. In 2002, further statues, which are by far the best-preserved sculptures, were recovered from the features underlying the chapel.[32] The state of preservation was all the more surprising, as the new research in the excavated areas found evidence of very extensive destruction. This is so widespread that even after the conclusion of field research, the lack of corresponding archaeological evidence has not yet enabled the detailed appearance and the external shape of the ancient sanctuary to be defined. Any reconstructions must therefore remain hypothetical (Fig. 3.2). The new finds consist of a supporting figure (caryatid), a robed female figure, an offering bearer, a togatus, a naked male torso, and a wild boar (Fig. 3.3). The spectrum is representative of all the other sculptures, ranging from ideal sculpture (naked torso), to portrait sculpture (togatus, robed female figure), and animal sculpture (wild boar). The assemblage dates from the first/second century CE. Particularly surprising is the occurrence of architectural sculpture (the caryatid); such finds have been recorded in urban (Rome, Mérida) and suburban contexts (Hadrian's Villa, Villa of Herodes Atticus),[33] but they would not be expected in São Miguel da Motta, which is some distance from the nearest Roman city. The presence of the caryatid probably leads to the conclusion that a building may be supposed to have existed, one that had columns made of architectural supporting figures. The overall evaluation of the finds indicates that the sanctuary dates from the imperial period (first to fourth centuries CE). The well-preserved and unambiguously identifiable pieces are statues (S) and reliefs (R) as well as busts (B) and herms (H). They reveal a picture of great typological unity insofar as the votive offerings are almost exclusively statues.

The overview in Table 3.2 presents a more detailed picture of the genres. It is difficult to find parallels for such a wide-ranging assemblage in the Hispano-Roman context, only the sculptures from the sanctuary on the Cerro de los Santos (province of Albacete) being comparable.

Both sanctuaries are exceptions in several respects. What they have in common is the extraordinarily large number of finds, with about a hundred from São Miguel da Motta and some four hundred statues from the Cerro de los Santos.[34] However, the dating is only comparable to a limited extent, as the latter sanctuary dates from the Ibero-Roman period and is therefore older. There, votive practices started in the fourth century BCE and came to an end in the course of the early first century CE.[35] In this respect,

---

31 Guerra and others 2005, 184–234; current overview in Schattner 2017a.
32 Portuguese-language report Guerra and others 2003; German-language report Guerra and others 2005; Spanish-language report: Schattner and others 2005.
33 The list of find-spots of the other known Roman caryatids in Schattner and others 2008, 697–729.
34 Ruano 1987 catalogue contains 404 pieces; Ruiz Bremón 1989; Noguera 1994, 191; Truszkowski 2006, 11.
35 Generally accepted dating by Noguera 1994, 211–13; older dating still at Ruiz Bremón 1989, 177–82; earlier beginning of the votive activity however now in Truszkowski 2006, 29–82.

one sanctuary follows the other in time. The fact that the two sites belong to different periods can be seen as an explanation for the different votive practices that are reflected in the types of statues dedicated. But this interpretation must also be differentiated. In the Iberian period of the fourth–second centuries BCE, it was mainly sculptures of standing orantes, seated people, and animals that were dedicated on the Cerro de los Santos,[36] but in the Roman period in the mid- and later second century BCE onwards, four groups predominate:[37] mainly *togati*, apparently associated veiled male heads (*capite velato*), male portraits, and a bust.[38] The observation is interesting, since between the earlier, Iberian, and the later, Roman, phase, a shift, even a break, in votive behaviour can be observed. The spectrum of statuary types dedicated is more restricted. Of the older types, only the standing male statue in the form of the *togati* survives in Roman republican times. Such changes in composition in votive complexes signify shifts in preferences. They reflect the views, perspectives, experiences, and responding actions of the individual worshipper, but do not necessarily affect the deities, who on the one hand remain constant in their divine destiny and practical competence, but on the other hand develop further alongside their worshippers to the extent that they remain receptive to their changed wishes, needs, and fears. A fertility goddess is thought to have been the cult image at the Cerro de los Santos, but her name remains unknown.[39] Whatever the case, it is true to say that, in view of the change in votive offering described in the assessment and perception of the sanctuary's clientele from the late second century BCE onwards, the area of influence did not remain the same, but changed.

### Comparison between São Miguel da Motta and Cerro de los Santos

Nevertheless, even in the imperial-period sanctuary of the deus Endovellicus not all types are present from the initial phases, as the table shows (Table 3.2). Interestingly, the oldest statues are again the *togati*, which apparently belong to the foundation and installation phase of the sanctuary in the Julio-Claudian period.[40] Against the background of the finds from the Cerro de los Santos described above, it could be concluded from this observation that *togati*, especially in this period of the first half of the first century CE, apparently represented common and popular votive offerings in local, rural Roman sanctuaries. There are no finds for the following period. Only at the end of the first century CE did the tradition of dedicating statues continue in the form of reliefs with nude male representations. In the subsequent period, that is in the second century CE, most statue types were dedicated: the caryatid, reliefs and sculptures of the male nude, statues to which the male heads belong, as well as female gift-bearers, robed female figures, male busts, children and animal sculptures. The series closes with statues for the corresponding female heads and soldiers. In summary, the cautious conclusion is that, in the sanctuary of the deus Endovellicus, certain types of statues were apparently dedicated only in certain specific periods. What could the reason be? Several conclusions are possible. If the point of departure for reflection is the deity, one could assume that this deity, as an oracle god[41] was particularly succinct, appropriate, or plausible at certain times for certain areas of life or for specific concerns. The accuracy of the prediction may have immediately led to follow-up enquiries. But then the accuracy of the prediction might have shifted to another area, which immediately had a similar effect. Be that as it may, the deity only answered when his audience asked him. He was a kind of sounding board for their wishes and fears. If one takes the sanctuary's clientele as a starting point for reflection, the changes in votive offerings, perhaps measurable in generations and therefore appearing relatively quickly, can be understood as reflecting a high degree of individualization that was present in the sanctuary. This leads to the conclusion that the practice of the cult was a highly private form of worship, which, however, as explained, was always time related. In principle, the individual believer would have determined the form of his or her consecration himself or herself. This was not predetermined by a tradition that had been practised for a long time but could be freely chosen — as long as it was a statue. Seen in this light, the uniform appearance of the sanctuaries at São Miguel da Motta and Cerro de los Santos would have been determined by the desire for representation. In the act of consecrating the statue, worshippers them-

---

36 Ruiz Bremón 1989, 88–91; as Mielke 2012, 22 however points out, this is not characteristic of Iberian sculpture, as animal sculpture is usually far more prevalent. For the gender determination of anthropomorphic sculpture see Ruiz Bremón 1989, 85–87.
37 Noguera 1994, 193.
38 Catalogue of statues, Noguera 1994, 95–143.
39 Ruiz Bremón 1989, 184; Stylow 1995, 29 has suggested Pales.
40 Schattner and others 2013, 74.
41 Vasconcellos 1905, 124–46; 1913, 195; Lambrino 1951, 112–29; LIMC III 1: 725 s. v. Endovellicus (Le Glay); most recently Schattner and others 2013, 83.

selves stepped before the deity and put themselves in the spotlight. Jörg Rüpke has recently contrasted individualization with polis religion and described the heuristic possibilities of the concept.[42]

### Muntanya Frontera (Sagunto, Spain)

Although known since the nineteenth century, scientific research in this sanctuary has only begun recently.[43] As far as can be seen, the site was in use from the fourth century BCE to the second century CE. Among the finds preserved in this context we are particularly interested in the bronze votive statuettes and the small pedestals with inscriptions.[44] The pedestals are cube-shaped with dimensions between 9–14 and 10–18 cm and have pin holes on their upper surface for attaching the bronze statuettes. They are inscribed with Iberian characters, although in one case there is also a bilingual one with a Latin inscription.[45] In addition, further statue bases were found, which were intended for (larger) statuettes,[46] none of which have been found. These pedestals are somewhat larger, reaching in one case even up to 70 cm in height. They bear Latin inscriptions in which specific persons are named, such as citizens or freedmen, who make votive offerings to Liber Pater as the cult lord. The existence of bases for statues and statuettes as pedestals is a Roman feature and thus an indicator of Romanization.[47] Of the total of nine bronze votive statues, three are naked, while the others are dressed in a pallium or toga, very similar to the statues from the Cerro de los Santos discussed above.[48] Among the naked people there is a representation of Hercules. With regard to the others, research shows that they are votive offerings of worshippers, that is real people,[49] whose individuality, however, is not reflected in the representation.

### Description of the Type

This is the usual type of sanctuary, as it is commonly found in the eastern Mediterranean area, especially in Greece and Asia Minor, particularly in the Archaic period. Of particular importance is the relationship between the individualization of the statues, which can be observed there, and which, as is well known, is clearly illustrated in the sanctuary of Apollo at Didyma with the Chares of Teichiussa. Chares is testified in the inscription itself, but the figure does not display any individual features.[50] Individualization takes place solely through the accompanying text, not through the image. Exactly this same case is also present in the three Hispanic sanctuaries mentioned. In the Endovellicus sanctuary in São Miguel da Motta, the anonymity of the heads stands in contrast to the numerous statue pedestals with the dedicatory inscriptions of the named worshippers. Although in no case can a statue be successfully assigned to its pedestal, the statement is nevertheless clear from the large number of cases. The situation is quite similar to that of the statues from the Cerro de los Santos. The numerous *palliati/togati* do not exhibit any individual traits. However, in one case, a statue bears the Latin inscription Lucius Licinius.[51] The sanctuary at Muntanya Frontera is characterized by the small, cubic Iberian inscriptions and the larger Latin-inscribed statue bases. The Latin inscriptions give concrete names of citizens and freedmen. Only larger statues could have stood on them, none of which have survived. The dozen or so bronze statuettes that have been found also show the type of a standing male figure dressed in a pallium.[52] Against the background of the descriptions that identified the bearers of the pallium or toga as the ones in which the worshippers in this period of the first century BCE and first century CE were represented in the sanctuaries, they can only indicate specific persons, not divine figures, especially since the posture, clothing, and general representation suggests an attitude of prayer.[53] However, as they do not exhibit any individual traits, individuality can only be expected from the inscription, which is written in Iberian. There are names mentioned. Since our knowledge of the Iberian deity names is very limited, the criterion for distinguishing anthroponyms from theonyms is lacking.[54]

---

42 Rüpke 2013b.
43 History of research in Nicolau 1998a.
44 Most recently Aranegui and others 2018.
45 Summarizing Simón 2012.
46 Simón 2012, 240 with n. 14.
47 Simón 2012, 244 with n. 48. The concept of Romanization continues to be used in this contribution, in the way that it has recently been revalidated, see Gutsfeld and others 2019.
48 Aranegui and others 2018, 467.
49 Aranegui and others 2018, 471.
50 Tuchelt 1970, 78–80 Taf. 43, 2; 4, 1. 2.
51 Noguera 1994, 118–21 no. 26-MO fig. 53, two other statues also bear (Iberian) inscriptions.
52 Museo de Arqueología de Sagunto 2009, 30 fig. at the bottom of the page; Civera 2014–2015, 167; Aranegui and others 2018, 466–69 nos 4–9 fig. 10.
53 Civera 2014–2015, who, referring to García-Bellido 2002–2003, adopts a representation of a god, that of the Liber Pater, who is attested in numerous inscriptions in the Sanctuary at Muntanya Frontera.
54 Simón 2012, 241.

## Tableware, Lamps, Terracottas

### San Pedro (Valencia del Ventoso, Spain)

The range of finds in this sanctuary is defined by ceramics, lamps, and terracottas.[55] Their number is manageable, especially since the finds do not originate from an excavation but represent uncontextualized finds insofar as they were observed and collected at the foot of a hill slope. The terracottas depict Minerva, Fortuna, Mercury, and Venus.[56] The lamps mainly come from regional workshops in Augusta Emerita and Baeturia.[57] Among the ceramics, terra sigillata, thin-walled vessels, and grey ware are particularly noteworthy; open vessels, mainly bowls, constitute the majority.[58]

### Castro Capote B (Higuera la Real, Spain)

This is a votive deposit measuring 2 × 1.60 m found at the entrance to the site of El Castrejón de Capote, which, at the moment of its burial, had been abandoned for 150 years.[59] The panorama of finds is dominated by lamps and terracottas (about thirty pieces) with representations of Venus, Mercury, and Minerva as well as a golden laurel leaf. The finds belong to the second half of the first century CE. Oil traces prove violent destruction by fire, probably sacrificial in nature. Finally, the depot was covered by an accumulation of loose stones. The site suggests the presence of a population living nearby, who must have managed the associated sanctuary.

### Description of the Type

The two deposits are apparently not only located in close proximity. The finds, especially the terracottas, also exhibit close connections.[60] In view of the distribution map, this seems to be a type that occurs locally in the west of Hispania. The relatively small number of finds could indicate a small sanctuary nearby. However, examples of similarly large *favissae* with comparable categories of finds in the inventory, such as in San Miguel de Liria–Edeta (Valencia),[61] demonstrate that the type may have been common in the Iberian Peninsula.

## Lamps

### Horta das Faias (Peroguarda, Ferreira do Alentejo, Portugal)

This is a deposit of Roman lamps, very similar to the finds at Santa Bárbara de Padrões, described below.[62] Discovered by chance in 1954 while planting a tree, the lamps were found in a deposit of approx. 3 × 1.50 m surface area, at a depth of 70–110 cm.[63] The stratigraphy is described. While the lamps from layer 1 were mostly broken, so that intentional fragmentation can be envisaged,[64] those from layer 2 were preserved complete. Furthermore, during the excavation of the site, as at Santa Bárbara de Padrões, accumulations of lamps were frequent. With regard to the figurative representations on the lamps, as at Sta. Bárbara, Helios, Isis, and Serapis are represented. The conclusion that both sites obtained the lamps from the same distribution network is obvious.[65]

### Santa Bárbara de Padrões (Castro Verde, Portugal)

This sanctuary is located nearby. The *favissa* consists of a 15 m-long and approx. 2 m-wide north–south oriented ditch, which was laid out at an acute angle or rather parallel to the edge of a rock outcrop (slate) and contained many thousands of lamps, which appeared directly under the turf.[66] At this site the lamps also differ as regards their state of preservation from layer to layer, six layers having been preserved. In layer 4 (third century CE) most of the lamps were broken. But in layer 5 (mid-first until end of second century CE) the lamps were undamaged. They were found in heaps, which are irregular in shape or circular with diameters of 80–100 cm. A total of thirteen such piles were observed. The excavators explain these heaps as a consequence of the lamps having been brought from the sanctuary in baskets and deposited here.[67] As for the depositional practice, it is important to note that the votive behaviour changed over time.

As regards their form, they are mostly volute lamps, many of them with relief decoration. Thematically they include depictions of amphitheatres and

---

55 Berrocal and others 2009.
56 Blech 2009.
57 Morillo Cerdán and Rodríguez Martín 2009, 233.
58 Berrocal and others 2009, 285 fig. 19; 292 fig. 26.
59 Berrocal and Ruiz-Triviño 2003, 23, 31–50; overview plan of the two deposits Capote A and Capote B in Berrocal 1994, 42 fig. 7, 1.
60 Blech 2009, 222 (head of Minerva).
61 Aranegui 1997.

62 Garcia Pereira and Maia 1997, 21.
63 Viana 1954, 3 (note of the discovery); Viana 1957, 124–37.
64 Garcia Pereira and Maia 1997, 21.
65 Calado 2012, 50.
66 The find was excavated in 1994. In addition to the first preliminary and selective excavation publication Garcia Pereira and Maia 1997, a Lisbon master's thesis on the subject is now available; Calado 2012.
67 Garcia Pereira and Maia 1997, 21.

circuses. In view of the traces of use, such as burnt nozzles, etc., all the lamps had obviously been used.[68] In this respect, the deposition in the trench is indeed secondary, so that its identification by the excavators as a *favissa* seems understandable. However, theoretically it could also be expected that the burning lamp would be deposited in the pit. The corresponding sanctuary is presumed to be in the area of the village church, which means at a distance of more than 100 m from the *favissa*.[69]

### Horta do Pinto (Faro, Portugal)

Finally, the sanctuary at Horta do Pinto also belongs to this series known from the Faro region and is apparently very similar to a *favissa* in its external form and dating.[70]

### Ferreira do Alentejo (Portugal)

There is apparently another lamp deposit from Ferreira do Alentejo, which remains unpublished.[71]

### Description of the Type

Deposits of lamps are a common phenomenon in Greece, Israel, and Sicily, and the custom spread throughout the Mediterranean area as far as Gaul.[72] Against this background the presence of the type in Hispania is not surprising. However, two points must be borne in mind: firstly, with the exception of a few Greek, western Phoenician, and Punic examples, lamps remained almost unknown in Hispania in comparison with other regions until the time of the late Republic, and secondly, the limited geographical distribution of these sanctuaries in southern Lusitania is striking, since all the examples can be found along the route (150 km) from Ferreira do Alentejo to Faro. They are always secondary deposits, and nothing is known about the sanctuaries that they were associated with.

Figure 3.4. Monte do Facho, Sanctuary of Berobreus, hypothetical reconstruction (drawing A. Ramos) (German Archaeological Institute, Madrid, archive, A. Ramos; D-DAI-MAD-Z-25-302-2014-ARAM).

## Stone Circles with Stone Pillars

### Monte do Facho (O Hío, Pontevedra, Spain)

The sanctuary, at the top of Monte do Facho, 140 m high and dominating the entrance to the Ría de Vigo, has been known since the 1960s, when the first altars were found. By the time the new excavation began in 2003, around forty altars had been discovered, most of which were inscribed. The reading of the name of the gods caused great difficulties although they now seem to be accepted as deus lar Berobreus or Berus Breus.[73] The inscriptions on the altars are relatively uniform, a special feature being the regularly missing name of the dedicatee. The new excavation was not only able to uncover a large number of other altars, but some of them were even found in situ. In total, there will ultimately be perhaps a hundred altars, of which about two-thirds will be inscribed. The altars were not arbitrarily scattered around the area. Some of them were located within single-line stone arrangements of round or even angular shape, here called enclosures, of which there are a considerable number, whereas others were located outside them. The space between the enclosures was free, unregulated terrain that could be walked on at will. It seems obvious to associate the enclosures with social groups, which in modern terms can perhaps be described by the terms family, clan, or association. The altars themselves are usu-

---

68 Garcia Pereira and Maia 1997, 23; Calado 2012, 127.
69 Garcia Pereira and Maia 1997, 19; Jorge Calado 2012 concludes in his master's thesis, albeit with a tortuous argumentation, that it could be a Nilotic sanctuary with the Alexandrian deities Isis and Serapis as ritual owners.
70 Franco and Gamito 1997, 346 fig. 3.
71 Short note in Garcia Pereira and Maia 1997, 21 n. 6.
72 Sicily in general: Hermanns 2004, 101–15; Garcia Pereira and Maia 1997, 22; Selinunte, Demeter Malophoros: Hermanns 2004, 101; Greece and Israel: Rothaus 2000, 130–34; Gaul, Châstelard de Lardiers: Deonna 1927, 237; Bérard 1997, 239–50; Lachau, Le Luminaire: Lancel 1973, 534.

73 Schattner and others 2005, 172; 2014; Koch 2019.

## Cabeço das Fráguas (Guarda, Portugal)

This sanctuary, located at an altitude of 1000 m on the mountain of Cabeço das Fráguas, is attested by a rock-face inscription in large Latin letters, but in the Lusitanian language (Fig. 3.5).[74] Lusitanian, or Western Hispanic, belongs to the older Celtic languages,[75] which, like many of the other pre-Roman languages of the peninsula, fell victim to the conquest of Latin. In it, a whole series of deity names are mentioned, which are given animals for sacrifice. At the end, the names of the two superior deities *Trebaruna* and *Reve* are mentioned. Interestingly, the ensemble of sheep, pig, and bull is described as sacrificial animals, the essential components of the ancient Roman sacrifice of Suovetaurilia: a lamb for *Trebopala*, a pig for *Laebo*, a 'commaia' (goat?) for *Iccona Loiminna*, a lamb of 'usseam' quality for *Trebaruna*, and a bull of 'ifadem' quality for *Reve*.[76] To find an inscription of such content here in the seclusion of the western foothills of the Central Iberian Mountain System seems completely astonishing, but it is not singular, since especially in the area between the Rivers Tagus and Douro there are a number of inscriptions of comparable content, which at first were interpreted as votive inscriptions, but are now seen as belonging to the small group of sacrificial inscriptions.[77] The designation as a sanctuary is primarily based on the inscription. It is located within a walled settlement (*castro*), from which it is separated by a wall. Two entrances lead into it. There are also conspicuously laid out patterns of stone, which are deliberately placed in rows. Even if only a few of these stone settings have been preserved in their entirety, both angular and rounded ground plans clearly appear. In the immediate vicinity there are either soil discolorations that have been interpreted as post holes or stone concentrations that obviously served to wedge the stones. In fact, a stone pillar of over a man's height was found in a fallen position in front of one of these stone concentrations.

Figure 3.5. Cabeço das Fráguas, Polytheistic Sanctuary, rock inscription in Latin letters but in the Lusitanian language, A) photograph, B) facsimile drawing (DAI Madrid).

ally characterized by their upright, pole-like form, which may seem somewhat unorthodox against the background of the well-known Roman altar forms. All in all, the sanctuary must have offered the sight of a dense forest of steles, since the area that it covers is small (Fig. 3.4). The sanctuary was established towards the middle of the third century CE, as is very clear from coin (Claudius II Gothicus) and pottery finds, and continued to be used until the end of the fourth or perhaps until the beginning of the fifth century CE (coin of Constantius II).

---

74 The study of this sanctuary is part of the aforementioned research project on the Romanization of indigenous sanctuaries in the west of the Iberian Peninsula; see most recently on Fráguas with bibliography Schattner 2013, 400–03.
75 This point is not undisputed; see the divergent interpretations of Tovar 1985; Untermann 1983; Gorrochategui 1987.
76 The various readings most recently in Correia Santos 2007, 180.
77 Most recently Correia Santos 2007, 179; Schattner 2012, 403; Ribeiro 2013.

### Description of the Type

The two examples are far apart in time and might therefore lead to the initial assumption that no comparison is possible. If they are nevertheless grouped together here, there are several reasons for this. Firstly, phenomenologically, it arises from the fact that both structurally use stone circles in which stones as tall as a man or as tall as votive altars are placed. It is further recommended by the observation that both are sanctuaries with a unique character, each of which is without parallel not only in its own period but also in all other periods. The aforementioned temporal distance in conjunction with the common features leads to the assumption that there was a development, the intermediate stages of which currently remain unknown. There seems to be a gap in research.

### Interpretation

As has been seen in the preceding pages, according to the current state of research, six types of sanctuaries or votive deposits can be identified. In the overview in Table 3.1 the sites are differentiated according to whether they are sanctuaries or votive deposits. At first sight, there appears to be one noticeable typological conclusion, namely that sanctuaries appear only in the form of Walled sanctuaries, statues, and stone circles, while votive offerings appear only as collections of dedicated objects such as tableware, lamps, and terracottas; however, reservations should be expressed about such an interpretation until the function of the votive offerings has been clarified.[78] These may in fact either be evidence of a one-off deposition in the form of a sacred act, which is archaeologically manifested through the deposit alone (a primary deposit), or they may be indicative of a customary *favissa* in the sense given by Aulus Gellius (*Noctes Atticae* II.10), serving as a pit for depositing the remains of a clean-up operation within a sanctuary, in order to ritually bury cult material that is no longer usable (a secondary deposit). Only Castro Capote A appears in both columns, since as a sanctuary it was turned into a votive deposit by filling it in and deliberately covering it up when the settlement was abandoned in the mid-second century BCE.

The substantial proportion of types that are represented in different areas of the peninsula is perhaps surprising. In this context, the walled sanctuary type and those of the tableware type (Garvão) are the earliest. The former appear supraregionally in western Hispania, while the latter recall comparable finds in Italy, particularly in central Italy and Sicily. There is currently no basis for linking the former with the central European quadrilateral enclosures (Viereckschanzen). This would, however, be to name the two regions which historically have always been in closest contact with Hispania, and from which it received its cultural influences directly. However, the lamp deposits also belong to this Mediterranean context, pointing towards Italy, particularly to Sicily, Greece, and as far as the Levant (modern-day Israel). Again, perhaps somewhat surprisingly, and in remarkable numbers, there are the statue sanctuaries, which, in view of the lack of pictorial individualization of the worshippers, appear in a form that was common in the archaic Greek realm. In comparison to all these sanctuaries and deposits, the number of site types that are only regionally and locally distributed is again perhaps surprisingly small. It should, however, be pointed out at this juncture that the sanctuaries mentioned at the beginning and not listed in this preliminary consideration, such as the list compiled by M. J. Correia Santos, will expand the picture, especially in terms of their number. Among the complexes listed in Table 3.1, only the category described as stone circles conveys the impression of being a separate western Hispanic creation, especially when set in the context of its wide chronological range from the eighth/seventh century BCE to the fourth/fifth century CE, since the tableware-lamp-terracotta deposits, together with the lamps and the terracottas themselves, contain objects with Greek-Punic-Roman connotations. The very different chronological range of the type, the duration of their life, and the intensity of their use, that is to say how frequently the sanctuaries and accordingly the votive deposits were used, leads to the question of their relationship to their respective landscape environments and the related settlements in the course of the general historical development, which, however, can only be briefly touched upon at this point.

These are precisely the conditions that the concept of sacred landscape describes. It constitutes its strength, since it overcomes a limitation to the purely geographical dimension, which is reflected, for example, in the traditional concept of geographical space as a container, in which people and things have their fixed, unchanging place.[79] Through its origins in the academic disciplines of human geography

---

78 Lamps are common in Punic and Roman shrines in Sardinia, and mostly associated with Astarte/Demeter; they're also common and long-standing in (W) Sicily.

79 On the term Hard 2003, 16.

Figure 3.6. Mapping of the Roman sites around São Miguel da Motta/Alandroal, Portugal based on Calado and Roque 2013 (German Archaeological Institute, Madrid, E. Puch Ramírez).

and the sociology of space,[80] it allows a dynamic understanding of the construction of space. The term sacred landscape refers to a densely branching system of connections, which is defined by two axes: on the one hand by the location of its components — people, places, and social goods such as sanctuaries in a certain area — and on the other hand by the connection of these elements with each other.[81] Strictly speaking, these are two processes, each of which presents its own problems. It is of the utmost importance that, on this basis, in a further step, a definition of the term 'region' becomes possible. Here, region is understood as a dynamic area in which indications and common features are concentrated in such a way that a large number of common reference points become visible. These can be used to determine and name the regions; the sacred landscape in question can be an area within a region. In a final step, this definition can be compared with those cultures which have come down to us in the names of the peoples that Roman historiography has transmitted. These had an awareness of belong-

---

80 Bourdieu 1998, 15–21; Löw 2001, 130–52, 263–74; Miggelbrink 2002, 43.
81 Löw 2001, 130–52, 263–74.

ing to these areas/regions. As a result, a spatial differentiation of socio-cultural norms in the sense of a historical-cultural regional construct of the peoples can be achieved in the overall view.[82] The concept of sacred landscape also has the advantage of being divisible. The division into smaller spatial or content-related units creates insight into a system, which in turn is a prerequisite for the understanding and interpretation of places and their place within the overall construct.[83]

The study of sanctuaries and places of worship in a specific area such as western Hispania belongs exactly at this interface. Its sacred landscapes are made up of the different cult sites, the sanctuaries, and their corresponding rituals. Their description in conjunction with the inclusion of historical and cultural factors such as the operators of the sanctuary, its purpose, and tasks, as well as the public, the worshippers of the deity, thus creates a new picture that may be surprising. As a result, the sacred landscapes of western Hispania are thoroughly dynamic regions in which, in addition to traditional types of sanctuaries, an astonishing number of types can be found that are closely related to originally non-Hispanic ones. It would therefore seem impossible to deny such a connection. The period of the second/first century BCE and the first century CE apparently represents a temporal and content-related hiatus, whether identified by sanctuary types coming to an end or new ones beginning, or represented by a new orientation in terms of content becoming apparent in the use of the sanctuaries and votive deposits. Historically, it is the period of pacification of the peninsula after the military turning point of the siege of Numantia (154 BCE to 133 BCE), then the period of Caesar, Augustus, and the Flavians, in which Hispania, in the course of processing the effects of the military impact,[84] experienced nascent urbanization, changes in the economic and taxation system, and land distribution, in short, far-reaching Romanization and diffusion of Roman culture.[85] Therefore, when the repertoire of statue consecrations in the sanctuaries of that period changes, as in the case of the Cerro de los Santos from the second century BCE or later, in the first century CE, when, furthermore, in Muntanya Frontera in the second century CE, no more votive offerings are dedicated and the operation of the sanctuary is apparently suspended,[86] this cannot be explained by a lack of population, deserted areas, or the absence of the elite, since the old families — as can be seen everywhere — remained in a leading position.[87] On the contrary, the relevance of these cults for everyday life weakened, which was reflected in the decline in the number of visitors and gifts. The desire to visit these sanctuaries and to offer gifts to their native deities seems to have been receding. The settlements, which were everywhere changing their external appearance in accordance with the Roman pattern, obviously offered an attractive alternative to the followers and worshippers of the deities with the sanctuaries and temples located there. Obviously, a selection process was taking place, which led to the end of the aforementioned sanctuaries of the Cerro de los Santos and Muntanya Frontera. If at the same time, further west in São Miguel da Motta, a sanctuary of exactly this type and layout was founded, which, in view of the large number of statues (about one hundred), was accepted and frequented by the worshippers of deus Endovellicus, the reason cannot be the type of sanctuary, its rites, and cult practices. Nor can it be due to the lack of settlement, as is shown by the mapping of Roman sites in the region, which shows a dense presence of Roman remains (Fig. 3.6).[88] Rather, the reason can be explained on the basis of the selection process described, especially since in the new cities the access of worshippers was made easier by the addition of the corresponding Latin epithets through the inclusion and classification of the native gods in the Roman pantheon.[89]

---

82 Miggelbrink 2002, 121–23.
83 Miggelbrink 2002, 127–29.
84 For the archaeological implementation of this term see now Gutsfeld and others 2019.
85 For example Muñoz Tomás 1995, 124; Sánchez González and Seguí 2005, 38.

---

86 On the contrary, prospection in neighbouring Hellín-Tobarra reveals an increase in settlement points; cf. Jordán Montés 1992, 208 map 7 (distribution of the twenty-five Iberian sites); 213 map 8 (distribution of the 28 Roman sites).
87 For example in Munigua: Gimeno 2003; in Volubilis: Jarrett 1971, 533.
88 The criterion for inclusion in the map was the corresponding classification in the archaeological map Calado and Roque 2013 as a Roman settlement or as a surface find.
89 In the combination of the names of gods and epithets all imaginable variants between Roman and indigenous are possible, see for example the lists in Barberarena Núñez and Ramírez Sádaba 2010: native epithets for Roman deities (ibid., table 1); Roman epithets for native deities (ibid., table 4); native deities who are presented with a Roman Deo (ibid., table 5) or Deo sancto (ibid., table 6); see also Richert 2005, 18–48 (Catalogue of the Names of Gods).

# 4. Rock Sanctuaries and Roman Epigraphy

A wide variety of monuments can be understood under the heading of 'Rock Sanctuaries'; these range from individual peaks and crags to elaborate architectural transformations of rock walls; it is equally apparent that they are known throughout the Roman Empire. The examples in Hispania are relatively modest and do not involve elaborate architectural forms, since they take advantage of rock walls whose surfaces, with very few exceptions, do not seem to have been subjected to substantial preparation or modification. As far as subterranean inscriptions are concerned, they are usually restricted to the walls in existence, although on some occasions the mud present within the cave is also used for sculptural purposes. The techniques by which texts were written on the surfaces varied depending on the support to which they were applied; in the cases that will be studied they ranged from dry-point incision on a rock face to the use of engraving tools specifically for epigraphic purposes; a further well-documented possibility is the tracing of the text on wet clay surfaces of the same type as those recorded on *tegularia*. Finally, reference should be made to paint directly applied to the rock face itself with *atramentum* or red lead by means of a quill or a brush, evidence for both of which is available. There was thus a wide array of writing techniques that clearly reflect the possibilities for setting down the written word available in the Roman world.

## Identity Texts with Some Religious Features

Few texts are likely to have as much potential to identify aspects of the religious beliefs of an individual or a group as those recorded in caves and rock shelters; to a certain extent, these inscriptions are unconventional as regards their support and spontaneous as concerns their contents; the latter tend to be somewhat different from those recorded in conventional epigraphic texts, which are subject to the tyranny of pre-existing concepts, both in their form and their formulaic language; nevertheless, the relative nature of such a statement should not be lost from sight when dealing with the ancient world, which in no way should be interpreted as meaning that the weight of Roman influence was any less present. By this, I do not mean that such inscriptions were improvised in their production or innovative as regards their form or linguistic contents; instead, in the case of these inscriptions, the norms did not represent an oppressive weight on the intentions of whoever might have been writing or commissioning them, even though it was impossible to be totally free of previous traditions and, as a consequence, such influences can be detected in almost all cases.[1] Be that as it may, it should be pointed out that it is an approach that requires further examination and which, as will be seen, offers results that are worth considering. It is evident that the religious features tend to be clearly conventional, as are, more specifically, the ones that identify the individuals concerned, because of the cultured form that they involve; in spite of everything, the inscriptions in caves and rock shelters are still Roman epigraphic texts. For this reason, it is sometimes very difficult to identify their characteristics and, above all, their underlying background. On this occasion, our attention will focus on certain examples from the peninsula that seem to provide significant information, bearing in mind the limitations that have already been mentioned and the large number of examples of different categories that are available for study.

The establishment of this new specialization within the field of epigraphy was due to the work of Professor L. Gasperini: cave and rock-face epigraphy was gradually consolidated on the foundations of his fundamental works and, in particular, it gained impetus in 1989, when he convened a major conference on the subject.[2] Limiting ourselves to the context of the peninsula, some years ago, almost thirty

---

1 See Sinner and Revilla in this volume.
2 Gasperini 1992a.

**Marc Mayer Olivé**, Professor of Latin Philology (University of Barcelona / Institut d'Estudis Catalans)

to be precise, in response to the invitation of Lidio Gasperini and Antonio Rodríguez Colmenero, a number of colleagues and I tried to assess the state of cave and rock-face epigraphy in the Hispaniae and Italy.³ In this work, Javier de Hoz provided an initial overview of Palaeohispanic cave and rock-face epigraphy.⁴ For my part, I tried to do the same with this category of inscriptions in Hispania Citerior,⁵ bringing together references to twenty-four sites and mentioning a number of other related inscriptions. In turn, A. Rodríguez Colmenero established a corpus of cave and rock-face inscriptions of Roman date, with fifty-seven entries, from the north-west quarter of the Iberian Peninsula, among which were included the interesting complex of el Cabeço das Fraguas in Pousafoles do Bispo, Sabugal, Guarda, and also Panóias, which would subsequently be studied by A. Rodríguez Colmenero and G. Alföldy, a site that ought to be reconsidered and an effort made to reinterpret it, even though there have been several worthy attempts at doing so recently.⁶ José d'Encarnação, for his part, took responsibility for providing an overview of cave and rock-face epigraphy in Portugal,⁷ and João L. Inês Vaz considered the interesting inscriptions in the surroundings of Viseu.⁸ In the present context, there is clearly no need to examine the excellent balance for Italy offered by L. Gasperini and his team. It should also be mentioned that a further meeting held five years later, in 1997, published in Viseu in 2001, provided an update on the subject by contributing many new finds from Portugal, some from Tarraconensis and a coherent group of studies on Italian inscriptions,⁹ which should always be considered as models for how to approach epigraphic studies.

## The Limits to this Discussion of the Question

In a study such as the one here proposed, in view of the breadth of the subject matter and the large number of studies available on the examples to be examined, our analysis will be limited to a selection of the published literature. Above all, this has been selected and included particularly for those cases in which the study of the site under consideration was not initially undertaken at least in part by the author of this chapter, as in this case direct observation may also help to avoid overloading the bibliography with variants or different readings.

Restricting the analysis to a short list of several examples that also seem to be of particularly noteworthy interest will enable us to see the range of intentions of this type of inscriptions, as well as the specifically religious features of some of them; in this way the analysis will not become immersed in an attempt to achieve an exhaustive consideration of the evidence. It should be easy to extrapolate the observations that might be put forward in this study to other sites of smaller size and even to isolated examples, which need not necessarily be in the Iberian Peninsula.

## The Possible Purpose of Cave and Rock-Face Inscriptions: An Attempt at Definition

The aim of these pages will be to present an overview of the possible purpose of these inscriptions by using a few examples from among the hundreds known and generally by restricting the consideration to the largest ensembles, although reference will occasionally be made to other examples that may be significant for our purpose, that is to identify their precise objective. The Palaeohispanic texts will not form part of this discussion,¹⁰ even though some reference will be made to them since they are prime examples of language contact, a relationship that must have survived until well into the period of acculturation imposed by Rome, when this process had become thoroughly consolidated;¹¹ this relationship can also illustrate the weight that such contacts, mutual influences, and survivals had in a context that might generically be called religious.

As regards the purpose of the examples to be studied, although the vast majority should be considered as votive in nature, an aspect that might be called, somewhat anachronistically, 'sporting' should not be ruled out; this arises from the possibility of

---

3  Rodríguez Colmenero and Gasperini 1995. Previously, Rodríguez Colmenero 1993 had published a corpus containing fifty-seven examples of cave and rock-face epigraphy from the region.
4  de Hoz 1995, with a distribution map on p. 23.
5  Mayer 1995a; 2020.
6  Rodríguez Colmenero 1995. For Panóias, cf. Alföldy 1997; Rodríguez Colmenero 1999; Correia Santos and others 2014; and, most recently, Gasparini 2020; see also McCarthy in this volume.
7  d'Encarnação 1995.
8  Inês Vaz 1995.
9  'Saxa scripta' 2001.

10 A synthesis is given in Sinner and Ferrer 2022 with bibliography.
11 Adams 2005, 279–83, for a brief but effective summary of the phenomenon of language contact in Hispania. On p. 280, Adams rightly recalls a passage in Tacitus, *Ann.* IV.45.2, for the survival of what he calls *sermo patrius* in 25 CE in the case of the Celtiberian from Tiermes whom he refers to. On this question, see also Beltrán 2011, especially pp. 19–21 for the Tiermes episode. In general terms, Estarán 2016, 249–429 is extremely useful for Hispania.

interpreting some cave examples as being related to male initiation rites. S. Alfayé[12] made use, *cum grano salis*, of J. A. Abásolo's expression about visits to the Cueva de La Griega for purposes that would today be described as tourism-related,[13] which excludes the idea of pilgrimage that this scholar advocates for those cases in which a clearly religious aim is indicated. As I have pointed out on other occasions, sheer curiosity or simple interest of a type that might be described as day trips, challenges, or trials of a sporting or even personal nature are elements that should not be ruled out in some cases and might have coexisted, and they surely did, with the religious worship and devotions taking place at some of the sites studied.

Despite the great effort exerted to prove otherwise, it is far from clear whether these Roman inscriptions represented continuity, either in the form of possible dedications or in what might be called ritual activity, from other texts that might be described as native; there can be no doubt that the possibility of continuity is evidenced in the location of these places of worship, but it is far less apparent either in the formulae used or in the dedications to the deity, even in those cases in which the said deity is not strictly Roman. This can be seen in the Latin inscriptions, since superimposition of elements that can be considered intrusive also occurs with cults that are not strictly Roman; we might even be able to refer to a re-Celticization as a consequence of Roman rule itself caused by the displacement of inhabitants that it involved.

The supports found in cave, rock-face, and subterranean or hypogean sites are of many types, ranging from simple crags and peaks to the use of rock walls and shelters or caves, which leads to an interesting subterranean variant of this type of epigraphy, which to a certain extent is similar to graffiti on walls in some cases; however, it should be noted that the text was sometimes written on soft clay, and the climatic conditions inside the cave have preserved it in this state down to the present day, as will be seen in the case of the Cueva de La Griega and the Cueva de Román in Clunia. Three case studies will be examined in this section to illustrate the different reasons why these caves were visited.

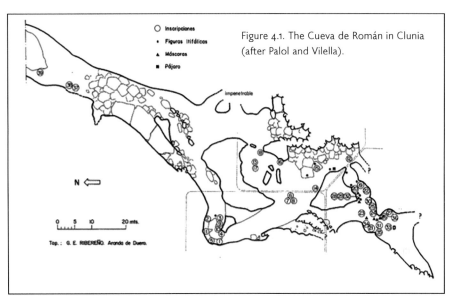

Figure 4.1. The Cueva de Román in Clunia (after Palol and Vilella).

### The Cueva de Román in Clunia

The fact that the almost forty inscriptions in this flooded cave are only accessible with great difficulty (Fig. 4.1) means that we still largely rely on the initial publication of the texts.[14] It is apparent that criticism of the initial interpretation simply as a sanctuary to Priapus led to this idea soon being rejected, with the possibility of it being dedicated to Liber Pater subsequently replacing it. The thoughtful contribution made by L. Gasperini, who associated what seems to be a spring or underground stream with a health-giving application of the same for some form of mud therapy, is undoubtedly on the right path towards achieving a suitable interpretation. However, it is not possible to define which deity may have been invoked when the cure was being undertaken; it may also have had a very specific feature revealed by the depictions of phalluses, which were what led to the mistaken initial interpretation of the complex. The presence of magistrates, to whom reference will be made below, although not exceptional, was to a certain extent a way of officially endorsing the curative properties of the mud and the waters, provided a possible link to the city's water supply can be ruled out as an option, although not all scholars have done so.[15]

The evidence for visits to this cave is ambiguous even though it is considered to have been a subterranean sanctuary.[16] Nevertheless, L. Gasperini's

---

12 Alfayé 2010.

13 Abásolo 1998, 32, where reference is made to *turistas hispanorromanos* (Hispano-Roman tourists), an expression that reflects the possible purpose of some visits to the Cueva de la Griega very clearly.

14 Palol and Vilella 1986; 1987; 129–32, S-1–S-39; Gasperini 1992b; 1998, 283–96; also Crespo and Alonso 2000a.

15 Cuesta 2011.

16 Alfayé 2009; 2016, especially 362–78 for the specific treatment at the sanctuary; reference is made to clay dolls or busts on p. 369; this scholar clearly rejects the interpretation as a sanctuary to Priapus (370), and accepts the proposal made by L. Gasperini

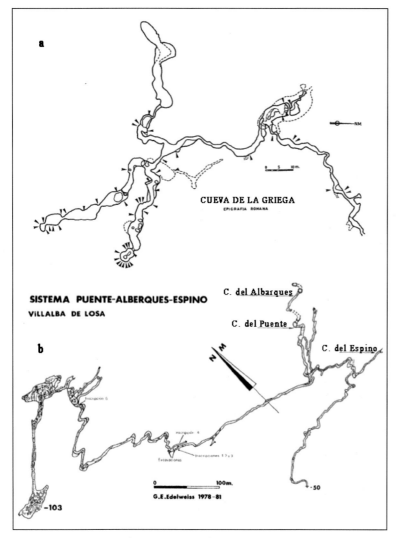

Figure 4.2. a) The Cueva de La Griega in Pedraza (after S. Corchón and others); b) The Cueva del Puente (after Grupo Edelweiss).

observations[17] for S-19, *oblitus | argila*, and S-20, which records a *lutor*, should not be forgotten, as they leave no doubt as regards the function, perhaps the main purpose, of the site: mud therapy. In antiquity gratitude for this cure was expressed by means of ex-votos to a healing deity whose identity cannot yet be specified.

P. de Palol and J. Vilella proposed that there were topographical indicators of the vertical accesses to this cave on the surface in the city, an idea that has also been taken up by S. Alfayé.[18] This is an important detail that should be investigated in greater depth, seeking other parallel cases that should be reconsidered. The context clearly seems to be totally Roman without any hint of an earlier presence on the site.

## The Cueva de la Griega in Pedraza

Perhaps the most significant assemblage in order to appreciate the survival of cave and rock inscriptions and their partially innovatory nature is the collection of 107 inscriptions, some on soft clay, in the Cueva de La Griega in Pedraza, Segovia (Fig. 4.2a).[19] Although this site does not offer examples of the sculpture found in the Cueva de Román, a number of anthropomorphic clay figures seem to have been found on some of the ledges, even if the date of these representations was not clear, and for this reason this material was not collected.

As regards the inscriptions, it should be noted that they reveal evidence that records people simply being present at or frequenting the site[20] as well as definitely votive inscriptions, among which the presence of such a clearly Celtic god as Nemeton in the Romanized Hispanic form of Nemedus stands out.[21]

Names in isolation indicate human presence in the cavern, for instance inscriptions nos 1, 2, 4, 9, 10, 23, and 60 to give just a few of the many examples; others include a verbal specification: *Arcontius | hic intravit*, inscription no. 6, and *Eustatius hic fu|it*, in no. 7. The presence of at least one soldier in inscription no. 30, a *decurio* of an *ala Asturum*, who bore a fully Roman name, should be noted.

There are also more complicated inscriptions: for instance, no. 15, in which the formula *V(otum)·A(nimo)·S(olvit)* follows the name; in addition, no. 37 *vota hic II* and no. 48 *II vovimus hoc*. As far as deities are concerned, *Nemedus* is present with the epithet *Augustus* in inscription no. 32, and as *Nemedo V[- - -]* in no. 54. A *deo Moclevo* is recorded in inscription no. 40 and a *Deva* in no. 83.

If this is a place of worship, as it seems to be, the two dates in inscriptions nos 70, 71, and 84 could be important;[22] the motivation that is made apparent in inscription no. 75, *pro | itu*, would also be significant.

---

by considering that its specialist role was a curative mud-therapy treatment, a subject covered in Alfayé 2010, 190–91 and 206–13.

17 Gasperini 1992a, 286 and 286–87 for the inscriptions mentioned.
18 Alfayé 2016, 365.

19 Mayer and Abásolo 1997; partially included in *AE* 1997, 883–907, and almost entirely in *HEp.* 1997, 659–763. Santos and others 2005 reproduces this first edition, as is pointed out by the editors with the corresponding updated bibliography, particularly as regards the references to Crespo and Alonso 2000b, 64–93; nos N113–N217. More recently Alfayé 2010, 197–99 proposes some possible new readings.
20 Reference is here made to the inscriptions with the numbering to be found in Mayer and Abásolo 1997.
21 Cf. for these last examples, in addition to the works mentioned in the previous note, Solana and Hernández 2000, 155, 202, 220, 226–27, and 277 for Nemedus and his sanctuary; cf. Marco 1993.
22 It would be worth revising our reading of inscription no. 21 since it could contain the name of a consul in the year 160 CE, Tiberius Oclatius Severus, which would indicate a clear second-century date for some of these texts.

## The Cueva del Puente in Villalba de Losa

A different pattern is presented in the Cueva del Puente in Junta de Villalba de Losa, in the province of Burgos, which displays a series of cave inscriptions distributed in three panels, recording a Roman presence and the gradual penetration of a group of people towards the back of the cave (Fig. 4.2b). The date is clear for at least two of them: 21 October 235 CE. The inscriptions do not seem to have a votive purpose, contrary to what was proposed from the original reading of the V in the first inscription, which was understood as *votum* and not as *quinquies*; the latter seems far more probable in view of the context and the form of expression found in these inscriptions. It should also be remembered that inscription no. 56 in the Cueva de La Griega explicitly states: *Rubenus | ter ven(it)*. For this reason, I am inclined to believe that these inscriptions may have celebrated the fact that the individuals involved were brave enough to enter the cave. Only very recently have we succeeded in putting forward a complete reading of the inscriptions, and for this reason it may be useful to reproduce their text:[23]

*Placidus venit V (quinquies)*

*qui antea hic fuit et supra | scripsit timuit ultra ire | dex (vacat) trum parietem lege hic et cum ad extremum fueris lege sic pariete dextra | et scies qui id parietis si quis vestri fecerit | id que sagacius.*

*Ultra accede mil<l>e passus | quattuor quam fueru(nt) | et dirado hic fuit Nicolavus cum hominibus n(umero) X (decem) | Severo et Quintiano co(n)s(ulibus) XI Kal(endas) nov(embres)*

Figure 4.3. a) Inscription A of the Cueva del Puente (overlay by Grupo Edelweiss; photograph by J. A. Abásolo); b) The sanctuary of Diana in Segobriga.

*Hoc viri fortes venerunt | duce Nicolavo Severo | et Quintiano co(n)s(ulibus) XI Kal(endas) nov(embres) | homines n(umero) VIIII (novem)*

As regards the dating of texts B and C, and as a consequence of A2 and A3, there can be no doubt, on account of the consulate of Cn. Claudius Severus and L. Ti. Claudius Aurelius Quintianus: the year was 235 (17), and specifically the eleventh day before the calends of November; I am of the opinion that it would not be the sixth (27 October), as I had proposed in an earlier reading, but instead 21 October. If the extant calendars are examined, for the moment no celebration or noteworthy event that seems to coincide with this date can be found and neither for the previous interpretation of 27 October. It would clearly be very difficult to consider the cave in question to have been a sanctuary in the light of the texts preserved.

---

23 Mayer 2019a; previously Abásolo 1998, 31–32 for the proposal that it was a subterranean sanctuary. Abásolo and Mayer 1999, 283, with an incomplete reading; the tracings of the inscriptions on pp. 260–62. In the same monograph, especially Ortega 1999, 258–63 for the cave in question and its inscriptions. More recently, Ortega 2004; Rioseras and others 2011, 67–68; and Abásolo and Rios 2009, 454 have returned to the question of this cave. Alfayé 2010, 214–15 on previous readings to the latest version may also be useful.

Figure 4.4. a) General view of the sanctuary of Calescoves in Minorca; b) Some inscriptions in the sanctuary of Calescoves (photographs G. Baratta).

the most frequent myths that she frequently appears in are related to hunting: that of Actaeon and that of Hippolytus. It should be emphasized that four of the dedicators of the five inscriptions are women; moreover, three of them were presumably freedwomen, as only one is stated to be a slave, while the fifth individual is male, also of freed status, who significantly makes a dedication to Diana Frugifera. The majority of the *cognomina* recorded are Greek, which would seem to indicate not only a Roman cult, but also an imported one. A female cult to Artemis/Diana is likely to have been combined with her condition as a deity who propitiated fruits and hunting in wooded areas; hence the rudimentary rock sanctuary in a rugged landscape. Nobody would have failed to recognize that this was reminiscent of Diana Nemorensis, an association that it would have been very difficult to resist in this case; although we know that there are few examples outside Italy, and that these seem to have arrived through members of the army, the social context and location could be indicative in a city that experienced profound Italic influence. In the case of the two definite freedwomen, the freedman, and the female slave, it should be noted that the circumstances indicate the name of the *patronus* or *dominus*, which would lead one to think that the vow had been delegated by these figures.

### The Sanctuary of Diana in Segobriga

The only site where the rock face is worked is the so-called *lucus Dianae* in Segobriga (Fig. 4.3b).[24] G. Alföldy's reading of the five inscriptions is totally satisfactory.[25] As Juvenal (XIII.80) well expresses, the goddess is *venatrix puella*, and

## The Intervention of Local Magistrates: A Way of Making a Cult Process Official?

In this section, attention will be paid to the presence of magistrates that is recorded in some cases; this can be detected easily through their condition being mentioned in the cave or rock-face *tituli*.[26] A useful study by S. Alfayé emphasizes such involvement in the case of the Cueva de Román in Clunia.[27]

---

24 Almagro Basch 1976; 1984, 37–39; Alföldy 1985. Almagro-Gorbea 1995b.
25 See now the recent edition in *CIL* II²/13, 207–11, with a substantial number of illustrations.

26 Initiatives undertaken by local magistrates are recorded in other sanctuaries in Hispania: Sinner and Revilla in this volume.
27 Alfayé 2016, 362–78 for this subterranean sanctuary with an analysis of the magistrates' presence on p. 368 and 377; Alfayé 2010, 200–01.

The presence of *IIIIviri* and of an *aedilis*, Bergius Seranus, may indicate that the ritual practices in the sanctuary had been made official, although the magistrates might only have been users that had decided to indicate their social condition before the deity or protective and health-giving force. The expression *IIII viri venerunt* can be understood in many ways.[28] The fact that certain common formulae, such as a person's presence being recorded by the verb *venire*, which is also used by some individuals in other cave and rock contexts, are found should be pointed out as well. However, it should be highlighted that in one case at Clunia a far more complex and meaningful form is recorded: *Bergius Seranus aedilis dicit | quisquis hic venerit*.[29] The case of the sanctuary of Cales Coves may be able to shed some light on this possible process of officialization or perhaps even on the implantation of Roman features on earlier phases.

### The Sanctuary of Cales Coves (Minorca)

The group of inscriptions is located on the wall to the left of the entrance to a cave or cavern in the small cove of Cales Coves (Figs 4.4a and 4.4b), where a sanctuary is likely to have been situated since there are abundant traces of one. This site may well have had native precedents in addition to, in view of the funerary context and perhaps the sacred nature surrounding it in the cove itself, Punic ones.[30] Furthermore, the relative abundance of rock and subterranean inscriptions on the island should be borne in mind.[31] At present, the results of our research enable us to identify twenty-nine inscriptions distributed in relatively well-preserved and fragmentary panels, including the clear remains of the existence of other, now almost completely lost examples. Their features have been described and the possible criteria for their order or sequence dealt with in previous studies;[32] for this reason, I will limit myself to mentioning some evidence that is reflected by the frequent, almost identical repetition of the same formulaic pattern, a clear indication of a scheduled periodical intervention, probably of an annual nature, in accordance with a pre-established procedure or ritual.

R. Zucca pointed out that the formula began with the consular date, continued with the date within the year, which he rightly supposed was always the eleventh day before the calends of May (21 April), and continued with the phrase HOC VENIMVS AEDI, which introduced a series of names in the genitive and ablative;[33] he discussed at some length the use of *hoc* for *hunc* and put forward the possibility of considering *aedi* as an abbreviation of *aeditui* or alternatively of *aediles*; the latter was preferred by J. Juan.[34] In the future, a more detailed comparative study will enable us to consider these aspects in greater depth once the new edition of the collection of inscriptions that I prepared has been published; this is referred to with the letter E when the inscriptions are mentioned.

As far as can be ascertained, the possible sanctuary outside the cave was used, in accordance with the available epigraphic evidence, in a time frame that stretched between 125 CE (E 3 = *CIBal* 143) and 230 CE (E 2 = *CIBal* 144). In addition, another four inscriptions are tentatively dated to 140 CE (C 4 = *CIBal* 141); 150 CE (E 1 = *CIBal* 143); 179 CE (C 3 = *CIBal* 140) and 214 CE (F 2 = *CIBal* 149) respectively.

The cult to Rome is apparent because of the date; further archaeological fieldwork might be able to provide more evidence for the ritual, which may have followed the traditional *Palilia* or *Parilia* festival, which coincided with the traditional date for the birth of Rome. The doubt that remains is what criteria could have led to the choice of this type of sanctuary to celebrate what seems to be, because of the date, the *Natalis Vrbis*, re-established during the reign of Hadrian. In addition, its location is particularly unclear; one argument that has been put forward is the possibility of native cult precedents, which may have had some connection, although a very distant one, with the original pastoral condition of these ceremonies in Rome and their archaic role in marking the beginning of the year, which the short-lived emperor Pertinax seems to have wanted to restore anew.

### The Inscriptions in Oceja (Cerdanya)

The recent publication of a collection of twenty-nine rock-face inscriptions in Oceja, near Llívia in Cerdanya (Fig. 4.5), has provided an important new dataset for the aspect of the subject studied in this section.[35] Among other texts incised on the rock

---

28 Alfayé 2016, 367 and fig. 8, 191; fig. 8, 196; 2010, 206–13.
29 Inscription S-2 in the edition by Palol and Villella 1987.
30 For the context cf. Orfila and others 2010, 395–433. A reference in Alfayé 2010, 200–01.
31 On the subterranean inscriptions from the island of Minorca, see now Obrador and others 2020.
32 See most recently, Mayer 2015, with the previous bibliography; Orfila and others 2013, 109–17. The inscriptions had been published previously with different readings in Veny 1965 (= *CIBal*.), nos 135–56; *HEp.* 2010, 65–76; *AE* 2015, 698–702.

33 Zucca 1998, 201–02 and especially p. 216, notes 46–50.
34 Juan Castelló 2005.
35 Ferrer i Jané and others 2018. A general panorama in Velaza 2018–2019, with references to the previous literature.

Figure 4.5. Sketches of the graffiti at Oceja, Cerdanya (after Ferrer i Jané and others).

face is a list of four individuals with native names, but with an indication of a patronymic that finishes with the formula *IIII viratum | scriptum est*. As the editors point out, these figures could have been the *IIII viri* of the neighbouring town of Iulia Lybica; they would demonstrate that an elite indigenous group still exercised control in this Romanized settlement. There is no reason to disagree with this interpretation, but attention should be drawn to the formula used. It is clearly aimed at making the process of occupying the post official or to mark the record of this event by means of a written form, such as the one found in this text. It is therefore apposite to wonder whether the presence of the *titulus* at this point reflects a previous tradition, without any written record, according to which the officers of the community fulfilled a specific ritual even prior to Romanization, which can be understood as an example of imitating Roman forms and behaviour. Naturally, we cannot go any further than simply suspect that this was a way of sacralizing power in a traditional place that survived on at least one occasion in the early stages of the institutional Romanization that was to transform society through the inhabitants themselves.

### Cave and Rock-Face Inscriptions as Proof of Religious and Literary Acculturation. The Example of the Cueva Negra in Fortuna (Murcia)

Cave and rock-face inscriptions can contain very significant elements that reflect scholastic or, if one prefers, literary culture; even in a sanctuary where the survival of a native cult is evident, such as that of Peñalba de Villastar,[36] two lines, 268–69, from the second book of Virgil's *Aeneid*: *tempus erat quo prima quies mortalibus aegris inc[ipit et dono divum gratissima serpit]* were found. According to M. Gómez Moreno, this inscription, which has now disappeared, must have dated from the first century CE, and it can undoubtedly be assigned to the early stages of the Flavian period.[37]

This section will be devoted to a specific examination of the ensemble of rock-face *tituli picti* in the Cueva Negra in Fortuna (Murcia) (Figs 4.6a and 4.6b), which has revealed, and is still capable of revealing, totally literary texts of considerable magnitude, quality, and originality.[38] The progress of

---

36 Beltrán and others 2005; Beltrán 2013, 171–75. For the perplexity that the presence of Virgil gives rise to, see also Marco and Alfayé 2008, 509–10 for these lines.

37 Gómez Moreno 1949, 207 and 399; Mayer 1993, 862 and plate 3; 2019b, 17–21, for this type of Virgilian documents.

38 The first study of the texts in Stylow and Mayer 1987; subsequently, Stylow and Mayer 1996 [1999]; 2003; the most complete edition is to be found in Mayer 1996 [1999]. See also Letzner 1992, 29 n. 38, 120, 175 n. 19 and 275 no. 11; Díez de Velasco 1998, 110–11.

Figure 4.6. a) General view of the Cueva Negra of Fortuna; b) Composite of digitalized sketches of the rock-face *tituli* of Fortuna (after A. González Blanco).

research has been constant, although it has slowed down in recent years.[39]

When we refer to the Cueva Negra in Fortuna (Murcia), the very name of the site, and nowadays of the town, is in itself of immediate interest, undoubtedly being derived from a location called *Fortuna Balnearis*, so called because of the existence of hot-water springs.[40] It should also be borne in mind that the symbolism of the place name, probably of Roman origin, is not limited to this, as it is likely to have included other values of Fortuna, such as a defining abstraction of Rome's destiny as is reflected in the *De fortuna Romanorum*, ΠΕΡΙ ΤΗΣ ΡΩΜΑΙΩΝ ΤΥΧΗΣ, to be found in Plutarch's *Moralia*, in which *virtus* and *fortuna* come together to accompany the Romans' *bona fortuna*; the writer sees this as a gift of nature, *phisis*. He also recalls the Fortuna Fortis, the Fortuna Muliebris, and the fact that fortuna, tyche, accompanied the history of Rome from its beginnings and that it is almost considered as a mother to the city, in fact its guardian spirit and the guarantor of its prosperity.[41]

The painted texts are located above a spring in a cavern at some considerable distance from the Roman baths where water drips from the rock, as one of the verses indicates: *guttae cadunt de vertice* in a *concava rupe* and where *semper stillant nymphae gaudentes in antro*.[42] The description is very apposite; it is precisely in this *titulus pictus* that a reference is made to the *sodales Heliconi* as the individuals who may have visited the Cueva Negra and have written the supposed poem or hymn. It should be remembered that the *Musae Heliconiae* are also related, as Plutarch reveals in his *Amatorius*, ΕΡΩΤΙΚΟΣ, in which the dialogue between Flavianus and Autobulus is located on Mount Helicon next to the altar of the Muses (Plut., *Amatorius* 1); in addition, the festivities in honour of Cybele and the ecstasy of the faithful in the ceremonies of this goddess are mentioned in the same work; he also refers to Attis as a barbarian superstition, which, however, is not without significance in a dialogue in which deities of a traditional nature, especially Eros, played a leading part.[43]

Catullus's poem 61 reminds us of Hymenaeus as a *Heliconii cultor*, which leads us to the possibility of considering, as has already been proposed,[44] these *sodales* as a collective reference to those who cultivated poetry, which in principle would not be impossible; however, the social context of the moment encourages us to think of an organization of collegiate nature, obviously very different from the archaic Roman *collegium poetarum*, but, nevertheless, an organization with both collegiate and cult aims under the apparently festive patronage of the Muses of Mount Helicon. If the context of the Cueva Negra and the clearly erotic contents of some of the poems are borne in mind, it will soon be realized that the syncretism goes far beyond the survival of Punic cults[45] under a Roman or, better, Hellenistic appearance; in fact, we are presented with proof that the contents of the texts recorded in this cave reveal how, from the late first century CE onwards, a fusion of cults that has sometimes been attributed to later times was gradually taking place. In such a context, neither is it a surprise that a *sacerdos* of the Ibizan Aesculapius, a clear reminiscence or *interpretatio* of Melqart, should honour the Phrygian deities, *Phrigia numina*, inscription no. 14 (II/14) [grid squares B-1 / B-2 / B-3], precisely on the day when the *lavacrum* of the image of the Magna Mater was held in Rome, namely the sixth day before the calends of April, in other words 27 March, thus transforming the landscape of Fortuna into a new Mount Ida, as is evoked, to quote but one example, by Catullus's poem 63, since it might be supposed that the surroundings of Fortuna had not yet been dramatically modified and deforested.[46] I will not consider the rituals that some have sought to see in the Cueva Negra, a subject with

---

39 For the development of the project: González Blanco and others 1993. Also Mayer and González Blanco 1995; Mayer 1995b, 84–86 and 92; González Blanco and others 2002; González Blanco 1996 [1999]; again in González Blanco 2003. For the state, future, and conservation of these *tituli* cf. Gasca and others 2003. As the inscriptions have been published, they have regularly been included in HEp from 1990 onwards and in AE 1987, 655; 1992, 1078; 2002, 849; Cugusi and Sblendorio Cugusi 2012, 78–85 include some of the *tituli* under no. 90.

40 For the recovery, excavation, and use of the Roman spa: González Blanco and others 1996 [1999], 177; González Fernández and others 1996 [1999]; Matilla and others 2002; Matilla and others 2003, 79–182. In addition, González Fernández 2003, 373–86 for the connection between Fortuna balnearis and military personnel.

41 Cf. Babbitt's edition in the Loeb Classical Library, 1972, 322–77.

42 Inscription no. 30 [grid squares B-3 / B-4]. The wording of the inscription will be cited according to the edition contained in Mayer 1996 [1999]. P. Cugusi has drawn attention to this passage, pointing out the repetitions of the theme in texts nos 30, 33, and 37, to which no. 34 might also be added as a variation on the same theme; cf. Cugusi 2007, 61–81 (= Cugusi and Sblendorio Cugusi 2016, 1415–38 with addenda, the version cited here); this scholar had previously made this point in Cugusi 2003, 449–66 (= Cugusi and Sblendorio Cugusi 2016, 263–85, with addenda, esp. pp. 278–80). For these poems, see also Gómez Pallarés 1995; Hernández Pérez 2007.

43 See the edition in the Loeb Classical Library and Minar, Sandbach, and Hembold (eds) 1969, 306–441.

44 Cf. on this question Baños 2003, who considers that *sodales Heliconi* is simply an expression equivalent to 'companions of the muses'.

45 Mayer 1990; 1992; Stylow 1992.

46 Ubiña 1996.

many ramifications.[47] The field of literary influences and references is undoubtedly a more secure context.[48] It is also essential to mention inscription no. 1 [grid squares A-1 / A-2], where *locamus xoana* is recorded on the same date as is stated in the above-mentioned inscription.[49]

It should also be remembered that, in my opinion, the chronology of the *tituli* in the Cueva Negra might continue, on palaeographical grounds, down to the early third century CE.

Other texts can be reconstructed relatively easily or have come down to us in their entirety, among which, and merely to provide an example that does not make one despair, the following example will be provided:[50]

NVMPHARVM LATICES
ALIOS RESTINGVITIS IGNIS
ME TAMEN AT FONTES
ACRIOR VRIT [A]MOR

This couplet is repeated on two occasions and reveals the standard of these texts, enabling us to evaluate to what extent the literary culture associated with Carthago Nova, which the sources do not even refer to, should be considered as high.

What seems to be a *carmen responsivum* also reveals the presence of a cult or dedication to a deity in no. 11 (II/7) [grid square B-1]:

VOTA REVS VENERI NYMPHIS
CONVICIA DONA
NIL PECCANT LATICES PAPHI-
EN PLACATO VALEBIS

In this case, it can be seen how Venus and the Nymphs represent the fundamental idea of the purification or healing brought about by the waters.

The waters of the spring and its Nymphs, which are also referred to in poem 31, could have had purifying and health-giving properties for those who visited them; going there must have been a complement, or perhaps the main attraction, for those who frequented the thermal baths and their spring, now well known as a result of the excavations undertaken. The poetic vein present is both of a high standard and quite singular, especially if it is placed alongside the *carmina epigraphica*[51] recorded in the capital of the region, Carthago Nova; in some cases, they also display a high level of originality, and the city was presumably the cultural source from which a substantial proportion of the poems at Fortuna were derived.

Finally, at this juncture it is worth remembering that the poem in the inscriptions numbered 33 (III/6) [grid squares B-7 / B-8], 38 (III/2) [grid squares D-6 / D-7] and 41 (III/4) [grid square D-8] is, in different states of preservation and varying in length, almost a Virgilian cento, since they repeat and contain different passages of the *Aeneid*: I.139, 166–67, 310–11 and III.229–30; the description of the port of Carthago gives way to the lines of Virgil, a description that, according to Servius's commentary on the *Aeneid* I.159 *et seq.*, was a matter of poetic licence, of a *topothesia* since it was referring to the port of Hispaniensis Carthago. This fact would undoubtedly prove the source of the poetic current that is abundantly recorded on the rock face of the Cueva Negra at Fortuna.

## The Deities Present in this Type of Epigraphic Monuments in Hispania

In view of the wide range of deities that can be found in cave and rock-face epigraphy in Hispania, this discussion will be limited to the examples studied or alluded to in the selection that has been made.

There can be no doubt that, especially in the light of the Lusitanian inscriptions on rock, it is partially justified to link some of these rock texts with Celtic deities.[52] Evidence for this statement is also to be found in the *tituli* of the Cueva de La Griega in Pedraza, to which reference has already been made. It should also be emphasized that a Celtic god Lug appears at Peñalba de Villastar,[53] in an extremely varied epigraphic context that has attracted renewed attention in recent years. In the case of the Cueva de Román at Clunia the health-giving deity remains unknown, although we might be able to extrapolate

---

47  Cf. for different proposals on the nature of the cave, among them a Bacchic one: Fernández Ardanaz 2003; Rodríguez Colmenero 2003; Fernández Nieto 2003; Ramírez Sádaba 2003b.

48  For the literary aspects: Molina 2003; Velaza 2003; Espigares 2003; García Jurado and Velázquez Soriano 2003; Fernández López 2003; Cristóbal 2003.

49  This inscription is worth studying anew insofar as it contains another date linked to the *Kalendas octobres*, written using *hoc scripserunt* according to those who made this observation.

50  It is no. 13 [grid squares B-1 / B-2], p. 413; this text is repeated with spelling and phonetic variations in no. 10 [grid square B-1], p. 412 in our edition cited in n. 36. P. Cugusi discussed it in Cugusi 2011, 96–106 (= Cugusi and Sblendorio Cugusi 2016, 1439–55, which will be referred to here; see especially pp. 1446–47).

51  Cf. Hernández Pérez and Gómez Font 2006, with an analysis that is nothing short of exhaustive.

52  Cf. for example Olivares 2002, 27–66 for Lusitania and pp. 100, 114, and 119 for the Cueva de La Griega in Pedraza. Prior to this, in general terms, Marco 1994.

53  Marco 1986; Marco and Alfayé 2008.

its identity if the deities present in Fortuna are considered: the Nymphs and Venus herself.

The Cueva de la Losa need not be taken into account in the discussion of this point, while in the case of the lucus Dianae at Segobriga, the name and the dedication speak for themselves. The *Natalis Romae* seems to have been the ultimate objective of the sanctuary of Cales Coves in Menorca, with the *dea Roma* perhaps having replaced a previous cult, although this is a possibility that cannot be confirmed for the moment.

## A Concluding Proposal

In view of what has been presented, no reservations can be expressed as regards the profound Roman influence or even the specifically Roman nature of the examples studied. Not only did the intervention of Roman acculturation involve phenomena such as the one that is conventionally known as *interpretatio*, but it also introduced new factors, which could be considered to have been imported into the contexts in which it intervened. As the examples included in this study show, we cannot rule out Roman innovation or even the identification of new cult elements that may or may not have had precedents. The elements that were introduced were not always strictly Roman; a superimposed population might bring native cults from elsewhere into a territory, such as, for example, certain Celtic deities perhaps, or even Oriental cults. This superimposition makes it difficult to separate the *substrata* from the *adstrata*. Assimilation easily overcomes any resistance and produces epigraphic horizons in which the very structure of expressions and formulae gradually negates the survival of previous features. There can be no doubt that the rituals and procedures became increasingly Roman, in view of the final results that it has been possible to study. Even though it might be expected to have been less official in character at least because of its appearance, rock and subterranean epigraphy also seems to have been deeply influenced by the colonizers. This, however, should not be decoupled from the habit of writing and the language used to record these texts, bearing in mind that at present we cannot evaluate to what extent the Roman trend towards recording events and worship in writing may have been influential even in the birth of the parallel native habits in the Iberian Peninsula.

This concluding proposal seeks to advocate the observation of the available data from what might be called a Roman point of view, insofar as it seems clear that, as we have been able to see, it was intended to present the contents, whether cult-related or not, in a way that could be totally integrated within Roman patterns of use and was understandable from this perspective, whatever the origins of these contents may have been. Nevertheless, it can sometimes be appreciated how, in spite of this apparent integration, the native elements are indispensable in the contents and intention, however much the form of presentation may have been a decisive influence. As a result of the way in which the inscribed features are displayed, some cases do not even allow us to suppose the existence of a previous layer, which, in some instances, such as that of the Cueva Negra de Fortuna, may not actually have existed or which, because of the limitations of the currently available data, it is extremely difficult to trace back in time; to such an extent is this true that, unless there are clear traces of earlier features, supposing the existence of such antecedents is sometimes conjectural or even extremely foolhardy.

# 5. Religious Practices and Rural Cult Sites in Hispania Citerior

*Some Reflections*

Cult places play a fundamental role in processes of social interaction and in the formation of individual and collective identities in the Roman rural world, both in Italy and in the provinces. This function can be explained as a result of the wide variety of forms of social and political aggregation that rural communities might belong to; these made it necessary to create specific mechanisms that would allow interaction and communication. Sanctuaries, as meeting places that were associated with a temporal dimension and which were frequented in certain conditions, are a key area of study. The function assumed by the sanctuaries involved the materialization, through architecture and material culture, of various forms of interaction between individuals as well as between individuals and divinities. Architecture and material culture are related to the organization, modalities, and rhythms of practices and rituals. However, analysis of this evidence has to face serious problems that are clearly described in a fundamental work by J. North.

> If indeed religion is an integral part of all activities, then in principle, its modalities should reflect patterns of life as well as any other sources of information. However, as will become very clear, although there is no shortage of evidence about religious aspects of country life (references in texts to the country and countrymen, religious sites in remote or rural locations, deities with agricultural duties to perform, rituals carried out in the villages), making use of this information in any spirit other than the antiquarian raises formidable problems of method. At this stage, defining the problems may be as much as can be expected.[1]

It is particularly problematic to analyse the religious manifestations in the Iberian Peninsula in the republican period and the early Empire. Complex cultural processes in which the introduction and adaptation of many kinds of cults and rituals played an important role flourished in this extensive geographical area, which can be defined as a true microcontinent.[2] This chapter aims to analyse the conceptual and methodological difficulties that are raised by the study of rural cult places in Hispania. The challenges involved in such an examination are due to, in the first place, the nature of the available archaeological and epigraphic evidence. The rural worlds of the Iron Age, Punic, and Roman Iberia are poorly researched to begin with, and ritual sites always have received (much) less attention than farms and other settlements. This fact can be explained, in part, as a result of the materialization of ritual practices and forms of frequentation of specific cult places, by nature, private and modest, were materially expressed. Nevertheless, the fundamental problem resides in the long-established approach to the study of the field, which is conditioned by a reductionist perspective that defines the social and cultural processes taking place in the rural world as essentially conservative and ahistorical; at the same time, such an approach separates the rural hinterland from the city. Even though this analysis focuses on cult places, it does not aim to establish a typology of such sites on the basis of their architectural features. In fact, equal importance will be given to the examination of the material culture associated with ritual practices.

We consider that sacred spaces and sanctuaries constitute privileged evidence to analyse religious manifestations in rural areas, as well as to deter-

---

1 North 1995, 141.

2 Woolf in this volume.

**Alejandro G. Sinner**, Associate Professor of Roman Art and Archaeology (University of Victoria)

**Víctor Revilla Calvo**, Professor of Ancient History (University of Barcelona)

mine their (changing) function in diverse contexts and the factors associated with the appearance and evolution of religious practices. These spaces took on various roles and reflected the complex relations existing between city and countryside.[3] In them, one can detect the intersection between different cultural, social, and political situations, between the public and the private realms, the local sphere and other frameworks of organization and integration that coexisted within an Empire that was more than just a political superstructure. They were spaces for interaction and communication in which all kinds of relationships and power structures were generated.

Although architectural remains are less monumental than in other regions of the western Mediterranean, the Iberian Peninsula provides a substantial body of information. The study of these spaces has made it possible to undertake thematic studies and outline categories not based on their adaptation to architectural typologies, but on the functions, situations, and dynamics that converged in these spaces of worship, and whose configuration reveals agency in play and the negotiation of ideas in contexts of cultural change and exchange.[4]

## Studying Rural Cults and their Scenarios in Hispania

Manifestations of worship in rural areas have traditionally occupied a limited amount of space in the extensive literature on religion in Roman Spain.[5] Historiographically, scholarly works on the topic have only mentioned the evidence for the diffusion of certain deities and, occasionally, some particularities of their cult in relation to a specific settlement, territory, or the socio-cultural background of the worshippers.[6] The discussion of the ritual and religious practices of rural areas never takes centre stage. Furthermore, these forms of analysis are integrated in traditional classifications based on conventional categories of Roman religion: the official gods, the imperial cult, the indigenous gods, and the deities of oriental and colonial origin (Punic or Greek).

This limited perspective was particularly applied to those gods with rustic and natural attributes in Italic cults such as Liber Pater, Diana, or Silvanus, as well as to deities that had a close relationship with the places in which they manifested and exerted their beneficial character (e.g. springs, caves, mountains, forests). Apollo and the nymphs, present in numerous thermal springs, are good examples.[7] In this respect, the presence of Liber Pater, Silvanus, or Diana in a rural area was easily explicable as an example of the direct *interpretatio* of indigenous deities.[8] Following this reductionist model, some modern historians established an index indicator of the adoption of Roman culture in a specific area. However, this method underestimated the complex factors and processes (e.g. individuals, political collectives, as well as institutions, social and juridical categories) that determined and promoted this assimilation as a Roman cult and its forms. The result was a rigid model, with only a limited potential to interpret the evidence and unable to explain specific situations that lay outside this rigid framework.

The rural world has also been marginalized in studies discussing the expansion of certain cults in Hispania. Their diffusion was related to the existence of supposedly more advanced and dynamic cultural contexts, the city, as a heterogeneous space, or the Greek East as the focus of innovations, being the most common examples. In this scenario, the rural implantation of a cult served as marker of its capacity for expansion. However, this theoretical approach was based on a hazardous assumption: the interpretation of rural societies as culturally passive realities, whose reaction against innovations could only be explained in terms of resistance or acceptance.

The analysis of the implantation of the so-called Oriental gods in the rural sphere is a good example.[9] Traditionally, the presence of these deities has been connected with the arrival of specific collectives (e.g. merchants, soldiers, and imperial administra-

---

3 Alfayé 2009; 2010, 179–82. For Italy: Stek 2000.
4 Mangas and Novillo 2014; Mateos and others 2009; Tortosa 2014; Tortosa and Ramallo 2017; Alfayé 2009; Marco 1996, 86–87.
5 For A. Sinner, this chapter is part of the research project 'Beyond Contacts: Tracing Identities and Cultural Change in the Roman West', funded by the Social Science and Research Council of Canada thanks to an Insight Grant.
6 Mangas 1982; Vázquez Hoys 1982; 1987; *Religión romana* 1981; *Paganismo y Cristianismo* 1981; Mayer and Gómez Pallarès 1993; a state-of-the-art overview of studies on sanctuaries in Hispania in Mangas and Novillo 2014. In this section, the ritual and religious practices that took place in a domestic context, from foundational offerings to *lararia* (see Pérez Ruíz 2014; this volume) are not considered. We have also excluded specific practices related to agriculture, such as those expressed in the limited epigraphic corpus on *instrumentum*; these do not seem to be merely invocations of fertility but could also surpass the religious sphere assuming social and cultural connotations: Revilla 2002, 220–21.

7 Díez de Velasco 1992; 1998.
8 For the classical paradigm of the *interpretatio romana*, see G. Wissowa 1916–1919, 1–49; together with a revision of the concept of *interpretatio* in Ando 2008, 43–58; Häussler 2012, 147; Rives 2015, 426–27; Parker 2017, especially chapter 2.
9 The bibliography on this topic is quite extensive; see among others: García y Bellido 1967; Alvar 1993a; 1993b; 1993c; 1999; Bendala 1982; 1986, 345–408; Sayas 1982; 1986; de Francisco 1989.

tors) with a high degree of mobility, displacement, and relocation.[10] Their acts and behaviours were envisaged as being linked to the special position that such groups occupied in the imperial social order, as well as in the lives and careers of their members. This rigid characterization made them vectors for the dissemination of new ideas. In this regard, there is a noticeable insistence on highlighting the existence of special conditions created by urban environments or places of exchange (ports). This approach was suggested to justify the presence of Mithraism in areas of the Iberian Peninsula that do not exhibit a high degree of urbanization.[11] The attention received by the initiatives of these groups and individuals led scholars to overemphasize factors such as their marginality and originality when compared with local societies,[12] neglecting the fact that cultic practices were also the result of mundane, diverse, and individual choices that created webs of connections that permeated throughout society, time, and territory.[13]

Rural religion should not be seen through the heuristic prisms just mentioned, but rather by looking closely at practices of worship and their archaeological remains. By doing so, their potential for analysing the creative agency that religious actors had in society increases significantly.

The nature of the available epigraphic and archaeological material also raises issues and explains the construction of some of the aforementioned theoretical approaches. A substantial part of the surviving evidence comes from domestic contexts — or at least not from an official one — thus complicating its analysis. This situation, more closely related to the poor preservation of the archaeological record than to the cults themselves, facilitates an analysis of these cults as exceptional, rather than as integrated in everyday rural social dynamics. We are facing the consequences of the hegemony of an urban-centric paradigm stemming from core–periphery models, which defined rural religious manifestations as a marginal form in the social and cultural life of Roman society. In this archetype, the beliefs, mythical constructs, and rituals that existed in rural societies were perceived as pieces of a fragmented mosaic of the past that could only survive in private circles and/or in the initiatives of small, isolated groups inhabiting the periphery of the urban world. This view was also rooted in the ideas of the Roman elites themselves.[14]

As a result, an archetype that saw a passive and immobile rural world that opposed the dynamism represented by the public life and economic activity of the Roman city, the true indicator and generator of historical progress, was created.[15] These religious manifestations have been analysed from a modern nationalistic perspective, interpreting them as expressions of conscious and articulated political and social resistance against a colonial power and its institutional, social, economic, and cultural policies.[16]

These recurrent pictures perpetuate a simplistic vision in which rural cults are the result of marginal situations constructed on a set of practices that can barely be explained and understood. Why did some practices survive — and even become traditions — while others failed to do so? How did they react in new contexts to external pressures and stimuli? This vision involves the risk of reducing the importance of the dynamics of change in the rural environment, hindering any reflection on the meaning and function of cults in relation to the various forms of collective life and social grouping present in a territory, as well as in terms of their strategies of adaptation. This problem is further complicated when the heterogeneous process of contact and interaction between Rome and the diverse societies of western Europe are analysed.[17] As a result, until recently, a branch of Spanish historiography interpreted the geographical spread of certain deities as a comfortable indicator of a 'Romanization' process, understood as a gradual process imposed from above. In this context, scholars have insisted on using terms such as 'survival' or 'adaptation' through the lens of the *interpretatio*, as if this mechanism produced identical results regardless of the protagonists, places, and historical conditions.[18]

In Hispania, references to indigenous survivals have been decisive in assessing the location and nature of many sanctuaries (located in high places or in a specific natural landscape determined by the

---

10 García y Bellido 1948, 22–23; Alvar 2016; 2018.
11 Adán and Cid 1998, 135–36 and 143.
12 cf. Alvar 1993a–c.
13 See McCarty and Edher in this volume.
14 cf. North 1995, 141–42.

15 From a different perspective some scholars have tried to evaluate the impact of the interaction between the urban space (including diverse social, political, economic, and cultural dynamics) and religious manifestations; cf. Urciuoli and Rüpke 2018, 122.
16 A critique of this perspective in Terrenato 2013, 48.
17 The Romanization and globalization debate in: Hingley 2005; Mattingly 2002; 2011; Webster 1996; 2001; Webster and Cooper 1997; Woolf 1992; 1995; 1997a; Roymans 1997; Witcher 2000; Terrenato 1998; 2008. The analysis of Witcher 2017 on the concept of globalizing the countryside may contribute to a better understanding of the diversity that shaped religious phenomena in the rural world.
18 A critique of the concept of *interpretatio* in Marco 2012; 2013. For *interpretatio* as a multicultural and bidirectional system see Parker 2017, 40–45.

presence of water, rocks, etc.) as well as the characteristics of certain gods.[19] Recently, more complex theoretical approaches that take into account elements of negotiation generated within the framework of a particularly intricate historical situation have been put forward. They resulted from the combination of colonial, Phoenician-Punic and Hellenic characteristics with indigenous cultural processes — which continued to act after the Roman conquest — and with factors triggered by the evolution of an imperial state and society. Such processes, which involved the development of mechanisms of selection, resignification, and reinterpretation, cannot be reduced to the adaptation-resistance binomial.[20] A more useful way of addressing the meaning of indigenous continuities seems to be to discuss their role as part of the processes of identity construction of various groups (social, professional, cultural) that made up Roman imperial society and who faced the diverse situations generated by the dynamics of this society. This position offers greater potential and implies reconceptualizing the analysis of rural cults from different perspectives: on the one hand, in relation to the evolution of religious practice in the public and private civic framework; on the other, in relation to the complex mechanisms of interaction and social and cultural communication employed by individuals and diverse collectives driven by heterogeneous motivations. Whatever the case, it would seem to be fruitless to propose the existence of a homogeneous universe of rural beliefs throughout the Roman world as a whole and to separate it drastically from the urban sphere.

## The Chronology and Space of Religious Practice

In order to identify a rural cult place, one is obliged to make certain preliminary reflections on the nature of the sources available and the methodology involved in their analysis. Only the correct evaluation of this evidence will make it possible to consider a series of basic questions: how to define the spatial context in which interaction between the devotee and the divine power took place, but also with other individuals and groups; how to reconstruct the practices and principles (whether institutionalized or not) associated with the organization of a cult place; and, finally, how to identify the participants that ensured that these places continued to be visited and used.[21]

Literary and epigraphic sources on rural religious manifestations in Hispania are scarce and difficult to locate in chronological and geographical terms.[22] They also have limited value because they are the expression of a diverse set of social and cultural strategies that affected individuals, groups, and communities differently over several centuries. These limitations are particularly clear in epigraphic studies.[23] Hispania has provided a substantial volume of data on individual and collective actions generically linked to religion. Its value, however, is very uneven, both due to the data it contains as well as because the data is concentrated in the Mediterranean coastal territories and the Guadalquivir Valley. It is also chronologically somewhat restricted to the period of time lying between the first and third centuries CE.

The few literary references are, furthermore, conditioned by socio-cultural factors. The vast majority of allusions speak of the patron deities of cities, generally assimilated to the Hellenic pantheon, which were linked to the foundation of the earliest (Punic and Greek) colonial or indigenous communities (Gadir, Emporion, Saguntum). In most cases, the information is restricted to comments of clear aetiological value about the location of sanctuaries and the specific features of the cult, emphasizing complementary aspects. First, their antiquity; second, the local implementation, which depended on the presence of eastern, Hellenic or Italic settlers; third, the association with the foundation of a city, a process that, at the same time, could be integrated into a mythological framework (appealing to Heracles, the Homeric heroes, etc.). These are traditions elaborated a posteriori, in many cases related to processes of urbanization during the Augustan era that generated forms of civic identity and cultural memory. The insistence on archaism and similarities to ancient Mediterranean models are key features of these constructions that provided the community with a self-image that projected itself back to its origin and elaborated the idea of continuity over time.[24] Such foundational cults/myths mask the characteristics that a specific cult could assume, because in these narratives the surrounding territory rarely appears as a political or symbolic space.

---

19 Tarradell 1973; 1979.
20 Díez de Velasco 1992, 143; 1999, 91, 97; Marco 1996a; 1996b; Marco and Alfayé 2008; Alfayé and Marco 2008.
21 Cf. Scheid 1997, 54, 56–57.
22 Vázquez Hoys 1977; 1982; 1995; García 1990; in numismatics, García-Bellido 1991; Ramírez Sádaba 2000.
23 Epigraphy and provincial religion in: Rives 2010; general views: Rives 2001; Scheid 2012.
24 Bickermann 1952; Mayorgas in this volume. For the Iberian Peninsula: Martínez Pinna 2008.

Regarding religious inscriptions, several problems can be pointed out.[25] In the first place, reference should be made to the lack of archaeological context and, consequently, an unclear chronology that complicates our understanding of the use and occupation of a place and its subsequent evolution. Context is essential to place an inscription in its cultural and social environment. Likewise, displacements and the reuse of materials in late Roman or medieval buildings must always be taken into account.[26] Perhaps the best example in Hispania to illustrate this issue is the Visigothic church of Santa Lucía del Trampal (Alcuéscar) (Fig. 5.1), where up to fifteen votive altars dedicated to Ataecina were reused in its walls. This concentration of texts, has made it possible to suggest that a space of worship devoted to this deity with a power of attraction that extended as far as nearby cities, especially Augusta Emerita,[27] was located in its vicinity during the second century.[28] The Mediterranean coast and the interior of Hispania Citerior reveal similar examples, such as the epigraphic corpus of the sanctuary of Santa Bàrbara, in the territory of Saguntum.[29] Therefore, the lack of context and chronology prevent the meaning of a text from being defined and fully contextualized and, more specifically, from being attributed to a specific location. Poor preservation of the material can also prevent us from establishing whether homogeneous categories of forms of expression and types of offerings applicable to specific cults, traditions, territories, and chronological periods existed.[30]

Analysis of sculptural representations and decorative programmes that once might have accompanied the texts also suffer from the problems described above. Consequently, it is difficult to identify differences in the economic capacity and/or the feelings and objectives that drove the promoter of a religious initiative. The diversity of materials and supports (marble, bronze, lead, rock surfaces, clay) used to inscribe texts and elaborate objects is evident when comparing the actions of individuals and those promoted by municipal magistrates and elites. However, the factors that determined the choices are not always clear and aspects such as traditions linked to artisanal practice, the natural resources available, and the material culture of the communities in a specific territory must be added to the equation.

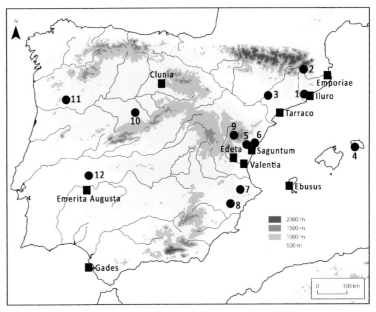

Figure 5.1. Location of the cities and cult spaces mentioned in the text: 1. Can Modolell. 2. Pla de Prats. 3. El Cogull. 4. Cales Coves. 5. Muntanya Frontera. 6. Santa Bárbara. 7. La Serreta. 8. Cueva Negra. 9. Peñalba de Villastar. 10. La Griega. 11. Panóias. 12. Santa Lucía del Trampal (image: R. Álvarez Arza-UB).

At the same time, the survival of epigraphic texts makes it difficult to assess the specific ways in which a local community employed writing and could establish connections between certain categories of objects and inscriptions in specific contexts, from everyday life to economic and cultural activity.[31] In a sanctuary, it is common to find texts that reflect the intention to make certain initiatives clear or to inform about someone's presence.[32] However, the opposite situation can also occur, and some types of offerings do not provide any information about those who deposited them. An interesting case study is the sanctuary of La Serreta de Alcoi (Fig. 5.1), frequented between the protohistoric period and the first–second centuries CE. Analysis of its material culture has revealed an interesting cultural practice that included the deposition of specifically selected objects of low economic value (tableware, lamps, coins), which seems to avoid the use of writing. Such practices have been interpreted as a conscious wish to exclude situations of social and economic competition. It also highlights the absence of iconographic representations, which also seems intentional.[33] This is especially true when compared with the sculptural and deco-

---

25 Marco 2009.
26 Cenerini 1992, 92.
27 Abascal 1995, 87; Edmondson in this volume with bibliography.
28 Edmondson in this volume.
29 Corell 1994; 1996, 123–24.
30 See Revilla 2002, 196–98.

31 Beltrán 2011. An example of epigraphy in rural contexts in Mari and Revilla 2018.
32 For the process of communication in religious contexts, see: Veyne 1983; Beard 1991; Scheid 1992; North 1995, 136.
33 Grau and others 2017, 187–90 and 194–96 for coins.

rative repertoire of the sanctuaries in the territory of Saguntum, linked to a classical iconographic programme both in their forms and through the habitual use of marble.[34] The particularities described above clearly illustrate the diversity of practices observed at a local or regional level, responding to very specific cultural dynamics and social strategies that are difficult to reconstruct without any additional context and archaeological evidence.

The second important issue is the physical structure of epigraphic source material, which scarcely allows one to appreciate the intentions, experiences, and feelings of devotees.[35] Some of its characteristics depend on the support used, which in turn was related to more generic factors (simplicity of the offering, dimensions, personal preferences, and local customs) that define the length of the text and its content. In some cases, dedications are especially simple. This is the case of the bronze *tabulae ansatae* from Can Modolell (Fig. 5.1) that only mention the dedicator or simplify the elements and formulae.[36] A similar case, although in a private context, can be seen in the references to Jupiter and Liber Pater in small labels engraved on press weights from the Trull dels Moros (Sagunto).[37] In certain cases, the support and the technique employed involve significant problems (linked to the site itself) that do not, however, prevent the elaboration of complex texts. Examples of this are engraved (Peñalba de Villastar, La Griega, El Cogull, Cales Coves, Panóias; Fig. 5.1) and painted inscriptions (Cueva Negra) on rock faces and in caves.[38]

The formulae also raise questions. Religious manifestations in the Roman West clearly show how the use of epigraphy responds to a combination of several factors, such as the needs of the protagonists (complex and difficult to define) and the practices and traditions of the socio-cultural environment of the devotee and the place of worship. These variables translate into a variety of formulae that are directly related to the motivations of the protagonists. All these elements adjust well to the practice of a ritual; even their stereotyped nature shows that these are terms with familiar meanings to those who used them, which served to define their relationship with a god through ritual, the obligations of the contracting parties, and their material expression in the form of offerings.[39] In this sense, it should be noted that the use of forms and names in rural Hispanic epigraphy indicates an effort to translate that recognizes the categories of the Roman pantheon and certain equivalences of powers or nature that are publicly accepted by the dedicator, while being useful in the field of their social and religious behaviour. This use involves processes of interpretation and redefinition that must have affected indigenous beliefs. Consequently, the epithets of a deity, the formulae, and the support used to honour it must be understood as an ensemble that should be analysed globally, including its spatial and cultic context, as well as the social and cultural one, avoiding simplifications.

The nature of places of worship and the evolution of the cult practice in them present some specific problems. In the first place, neither the formulae nor the texts of the inscriptions provide details to define the concrete character that a god could assume in relation to a place (especially if it presented a special condition: a thermal spring, a cave, etc.) and some individuals or groups. Solving this problem by referring to the attributes and powers usually accredited to a known deity is always hazardous. An example of this could be *IRC* II, 17, a *pro salute* dedication to Jupiter that has parallels in the region north of the Pyrenees:[40] slave dedications to *Iuppiter Optimus Maximus*, for the benefit (health and protection) of their owners, which invite one to think about a specific health-giving function, different from the one expected from the official Jupiter. In this action, however, a relationship of dependency integrated in the context of the hierarchies and ideology that define the order of a domestic group is also visible. Jupiter himself could be acting as a guarantor.[41]

Inscriptions, on the other hand, can provide evidence that helps to better define and understand the character of a sanctuary, but the quality of the information provided can vary significantly. Only on rare occasions, does it offer all the data necessary to characterize a cult place. Thus, the inscription *IRC* I, 88, from Can Modolell, mentions an object offered *ex stipe* by the *duumviri* of a city, perhaps the nearby city of *Iluro*, but that is not certain. In contrast, in the sanctuary of Muntanya Frontera an inscription

---

34  Vicent 1979; Arasa 1998.
35  Marco 2009; Alfayé 2010, 186–88 and 192; in general: Rives 2010, 426–27.
36  *AE* 1983, 630 = *IRC* I, 89 = *AE* 2003, 1012; *AE* 1987, 729 = *HEp* 2, 1990, 74 = *HEp* 5, 1995, 135 = *IRC* I, 207: Mayer 2012.
37  *CIL* II²/14, 597–14, 598: Beltrán 1980, no. 288, table LXXVII, no. 289, table LXXVIII; Corell 2002, no. 321; Revilla 2002, 220.
38  A synthesis in Alfayé 2010; Sinner and Ferrer i Jané 2022; Mayer in this volume.
39  Cenerini 1992, 98–99; for the meanings of the formulae see Sartori 1993, 425; likewise, the use of Latin or native languages in inscriptions must be understood in a broader context than the contrast between resistance and assimilation; for this issue and the language-identity relationship: Beltrán 2011; Cooley 2002.
40  *CIL* XIII 37 and *CIL* XIII 310.
41  Fabre 1993, 185–87.

(CIL II²/14, 656) displays a more complete and markedly civic formula.[42] The text mentions the main, or exclusive, deity of the place and could be related to a building programme promoted by the magistrates of the nearby city of Saguntum.[43] The information provided by these texts, although useful, is limited: they allow us to glimpse the function and meaning of a place for diverse groups and institutions. We can even take as read some of the ways in which its operation was usually managed, in particular when the intervention of a civic community is recorded. However, this does not presuppose that the legal status of a place can be precisely defined.[44]

Inscriptions also create problems when evaluating the rhythm and intensity of the religious life in a sanctuary, as well as its meaning for the population of a specific territory. In general, inscriptions and their associated objects tend to appear outside their spatial and cultural context and can rarely be accurately dated. Only a few places provide a certain number, clearly insufficient, of texts that may be considered useful because they mention a deity, the dedicant, and include formulae related to the ritual or the action performed: at Can Modolell, among over a dozen texts, only five name gods and one refers to a formula (*ex stipe*); at Muntanya Frontera, of forty texts, eight dedications mention Liber Pater and a total of seven bear the formulae *v.s.l.m.* and *ex voto*; at Santa Bàrbara, with a total of twelve inscriptions, eight include a religious formula (*ex voto, v.s.l.m., v.s.l.a.*) and some possible allusions (not without problems) to Apollo.[45] Cases such as the Cueva de La Griega, in Segobriga, illustrate the problem better: from more than a hundred texts, fewer than a dozen can be safely related to cult acts or mention deities.[46] Another important issue is that inscriptions usually do not contain indications of festivities and/or dates that are useful for the definition and reconstruction of a calendar of worship, its frequency, and specific activities. This prevents us from establishing the temporal 'density' of practices and their materialization, since it is also unusual to be able to relate inscriptions to precise initiatives or to a specific material culture.[47]

Finally, in certain cases the nature of some of the texts that appear in a sanctuary should be taken into consideration. This problem of interpretation arises, for example, with the literary character of the *tituli picti* identified at Cueva Negra.[48] But it also affects a part of the personal names present in many sacred places. As some researchers have argued, some may reflect both a cult activity as well as visits to the place for reasons of a profane nature.[49] The impossibility of securely linking an epigraphic text with a religious practice illustrates the interpretative limits of the epigraphic message, the nature of which cannot always be deduced from the context.

In short, the contents of most of the extant inscriptions do not allow us to consider certain fundamental questions to evaluate the nature of a cult place: the attributes of the deities worshipped; the specific conditions of the cult; or the donors' intentions. In general, the inscriptions only indicate the fulfilment of a vow, making use of the conventional formulae recorded in Roman religious practice; however, these formulae rarely make it possible to reconstruct an individual's feelings and motives, the context in which his or her initiative was undertaken, or the strategies that were used to fulfil the vow. In addition, limiting our interpretation of a cult and its rituals in a rural space to an analysis of the inscriptions poses the danger of homogenizing practices that may have displayed considerable geographical and chronological variations. In contrast, however, restricted use of inscriptions, or particular features of their palaeography, of their formulae, and of the supports used cannot systematically be interpreted as expressions of cultural otherness or as indicating the donor's social condition. The specific context of a cult place and the possibilities of interaction that it offered must have been assessed in a different way by each and every individual or collective, who employed different procedures to highlight their initiatives. This had significant consequences for the selection of the objects offered and the messages showcased in each case.[50]

The archaeology of places of worship constitutes another fundamental source of information. This field is based on the premise that the architecture and the spatial organization of these places (with the simultaneous support of epigraphy)

---

42 [*Lib*]*ero Patri*|[- *F*]*abius Felix*|[*et - F*]*abius Fabianu*[*s*]|[*I*]*Iviri ex d(ecreto) d(ecurionum)*|[*p*]*ecun(ia) publi*[*ca*]|[*f*]*aciend(um) cu*[*ra*]|[*v*]*erun*[*t*].
43 Corell 1996, 126; Revilla 2002.
44 *Leges sacrae* in Italy: Aberson and Wachter 2010.
45 Sinner and Revilla 2017; Corell 1994; 1996; Grau and others 2017, 213 mention nineteen inscriptions related to Liber (as well as eight uninscribed ones and eighteen in the Iberian language).
46 Theonyms: *Nemedus, Deva*; formulae: *v(otum) a(nimo) s(olvit), vovi(t)*: Abásolo and Mayer 1997; Abásolo 1998; Santos and others 2005; Alfayé 2014.

47 Dates related to moments of worship in Cueva Negra, the Cueva de La Griega and Peñalba de Villastar: Alfayé 2010, 197–200.
48 Velaza 2003.
49 Alfayé 2010.
50 Scheid 1997, 56.

can provide data to reconstruct the rituals and, to a lesser extent, the ways in which a place was visited and the rhythms of activity involved. It is more problematic to define the motives of a devotee or a collective (the wealth and prestige of a place, exhibited in its architecture?) for visiting a place. However, the use of archaeological evidence faces two problems. First, the lack of archaeological exploration at most places of worship and, second, the poorly preserved state of many remains as a consequence of erosion and/or intentional destruction.[51] These circumstances lead to our almost total ignorance of architecture, ornamental programmes, and liturgical furniture and offerings, which prevents us from reconstructing the spatial organization of a sanctuary and hinders any attempt to define the specific function of its components or the ritual structure.[52]

Pliny the Younger's references to some Italic sanctuaries demonstrate the different ways in which a sacred space (of the god) and a space open to the activities of the audience that gathered in these places were perceived. This is a distinction that is particularly necessary for the existence of festivities that brought together large numbers of people and allowed them to carry out other activities.[53] The state of the archaeological evidence does not enable the characteristics of the spatial and ritual organization in most Hispanic sanctuaries to be established. However, it is possible that the need to rigorously organize the areas of a centre of worship was not felt equally strongly in all cases. As the sanctuaries mentioned by Pliny clearly show, it is not the same to speak of a complex under the control of a civic authority, or subject to the investments of a senator, as of a small place of worship whose sacred character is not officially recognized, and which is only sporadically frequented by a small group or individuals of modest social status. It was at the important sanctuaries, those which attracted large audiences and included different activities and a well-organized calendar of festivities, that it was necessary to separate spaces and functions.

The nature of archaeological evidence also poses problems of interpretation since a relationship between architectural typologies and specific ritual practices cannot be established. Obviously, there could not be simply one single scenario or a rigid correspondence between a deity and the physical organization of a sanctuary; each situation would have depended on the possibilities and motivations of the protagonists, their social context, and traditions. On the other hand, many places of worship dating from the imperial era show a particular relationship with the topography and the relief features (rocky walls, shelters, caves, summits) that seem to have been specially valued; the case of caves is the most obvious.[54] In many of these sacred places the architecture is minimal or totally absent. This fact cannot be explained simply as a reflection of pre-Roman survivals but must be understood as a result of strategies carried out by the individuals and the communities at these places.[55]

In fact, in many places it can be observed how the topographical components of the landscape, taken separately or globally, are valued and integrated into a broader conception that uses and, at the same time, reinforces the messages created by the architectural language. In this context, certain natural elements or conditions associated with a divine character have a special role: peaks (which imply visibility and isolation), water, cavities, and rocks.[56] The indigenous precedent is not the only possible explanation, nor the main one, to understand the way in which a place was chosen and organized. However, no sanctuary allows for specific motivations to be identified, since, as we have seen, epigraphy does not inform us sufficiently about deities or about individuals or groups interested in the promotion of worship.

In those cases that are better known, a complex coexistence between architecture, image, and inscriptions can be detected. In this context, the topographical appreciation of architectural elements and the use of a language composed of decorative elements and construction techniques do not seem to depart from models known in Italy and elsewhere. At the same time, variations in a number of projects must have been considerable due to the prestige of the place and the possibilities of the promoters. Panóias is a case that demonstrates the problems

---

51 Corell 1996, 126.
52 See Scheid 1997, 52; Glinister 1997, 62 gives less importance to the definition of interpretative categories. For the terminology and its architectural correlations, see Jordan 1879; Fridh 1990; Castillo 2000.
53 Pliny perceived the relationship between the religious calendar and the influx of public: *Ep.* 8.39.2-3 and 9.39.

54 Alfayé 2009; 2010 shows the relationship between the topography of a place and the (possible) conditions of frequenting it and worship.
55 It is interesting to note that some sanctuaries built in the second century BCE in the Murcia-Valencia region reflect Italic construction models that rarely appear in imperial times: Tortosa and Ramallo 2017; this could perhaps be explained by their role in territorial and political organization during the early stages of the Roman conquest.
56 This topic was already discussed by Tarradell 1973; 1979 and there is abundant bibliography; see among others: Alfayé 2009; 2010; Alfayé and Marco 2008; Grau and others 2017.

and possibilities of combining the use of different types of evidence particularly well. There, only the in situ conservation of many inscriptions and their relationship with the topography of the place allow an itinerary linked to an initiatory process and its rituals to be reconstructed with a certain degree of certainty.[57] The definition of places of worship cannot start from the search for correspondences with architectural models.[58] The underlying problem is the impossibility of establishing categories of sacred places, much less a hierarchy, in relation to the functions of a place, the cult entity, rituals, and its radius of influence and prestige.

Ultimately, our limited knowledge of the material organization of a cult site (from its topography and architecture to offerings) means that we are ignorant of fundamental aspects related to public and private religious behaviour. It is also difficult to analyse some of the dynamics of interaction and social communication among the population of a territory. These problems can be seen especially in two areas that are discussed below: the relationship between sanctuaries and elites, who may have acted when exercising magistracies or privately, and the capacity of attraction that some cult sites had, which depended on multiple factors and strategies generated by diverse individuals and groups.

## Civic Communities and Rural Sanctuaries

One way in which urban elites participated in religion was by serving as magistrates, since the office involved strict obligations in relation to the maintenance of civic cults. These responsibilities reflect the intimate relationship between urban life and religion. A detailed description was included in the founding charter of the colony of Urso, which is especially interesting because it shows the official Roman practice in this regard and its implementation in Hispania.[59] This practice also applied to the rural environment, both in Italy and in the provinces, especially in relation to certain categories of sanctuaries.[60] In his description of the sanctuary of the Clitumnus, Pliny the Younger listed all the elements that characterized this practice: a privileged location, an architectural scenography associated with nature, the coexistence of several gods with the main deity of the place, the variety of functions that the latter could assume (and which, like oracular activity, explained its capacity of attraction) and, finally, the control of a city (Hispellum) and the reason for this connection (the intervention of Augustus). The example is interesting, additionally, because it shows that the religious significance of the place exceeded the limits of a territory, contributing its prestige to the political and administrative importance of the city.[61]

In Hispania, inscriptions that indicate the interest of a city in a rural sanctuary are scarce and provide little information on the conditions required for such an initiative to take place. Although evidence is scattered, this circumstance allows us to sense some of the mechanisms mobilized to specify such initiatives and the relationship with the functioning of a sanctuary. However, it is impossible to establish the forms of administration of these places precisely. In these circumstances, the temptation to resort to the norms recorded in Roman laws to explain particular cases is very strong, but this can lead to a false impression of homogeneity.

The available evidence includes specific terms and procedures. The text of *IRC* I, 88 from Can Modolell, which mentions a sum offered *ex stipe*, is recorded on a bench or *mensa* made in an expensive material, *giallo antico* from Chemtou. It is, therefore, a specific offering related to the equipment and decoration of a space in the sanctuary. In another case, the inscription *CIL* II²/14, 656 from Muntanya Frontera is better preserved, allowing us to appreciate a regular scheme of municipal action that explicitly mentions the authority of the local *ordo* (*ex decreto decurionum*), the responsibility of the magistrates (*curaverunt*), and the type of resources allocated (*pecunia publica*). In both places, the initiative seems to be showcasing *duumviri*, although the fragmentation of the Can Modolell text generates problems to appreciate the precise terms of their participation.[62] Equally interesting are the cases of collegiate action recorded in very diverse contexts. At Cales Coves (Balearic Islands), magistrates are mentioned in relation to a precise date that reflects an annual pilgrimage.[63] In the underground sanctuary of Clunia, a *quattuorvir* and an *aedilis* appear. The latter, recorded three

---

57 Alföldy 1997; Rodríguez Colmenero 1999; Correia Santos and others 2014.
58 Sartori 1992, 81, 84, and 90; Marco 1996b, 85.
59 Rüpke 2006.
60 Fincker and Tassaux 1992; Hispania: Marco 1996b.

61 Scheid 1996, 246–47, 251–53, and 255–56.
62 The recent discovery at Can Modolell of a fragmentary inscription that mentions a citizen — currently in the course of publication — already known as *aedilis* in another text from the immediate territory (in *CIL* II 4528 = IRC I, 126), suggests the regular presence of magistrates from a nearby city in the sanctuary, but does not solve the question of the functioning and status of the place.
63 *CIL* II 3718–24 = 5992–6000; Veny 1965, 160–70 nos 135–56, figs 91–96; Orfila and others 2010; 2016. Mayer in this volume.

times, is associated with a text that could be interpreted as a regulation of the operation of the place.[64]

It is difficult to interpret the material differences of the epigraphic support and the preparation of the texts mentioned. A certain proportion of the inscriptions reflect costly investments and formalized official forms. It is interesting to note, however, that in other cases, the presence of magistrates does not reflect a particularly important epigraphic initiative (the texts from Clunia were incised in clay, as were some at La Griega). Whatever the case, the nature of this evidence does not allow us to establish clearly in which situations municipal interest was expressed. Nor can the administrative, social, and cultural contexts in which the intervention of municipal governments occurred be identified, let alone the frequency and modalities of the interventions (with the exception of the annual celebrations at Cales Coves). Can Modolell, for example, reveals occasional actions, despite the value of the object offered. In the case of Muntanya Frontera, building activity has been suggested, which would fit well with the official nature of the inscription and the explicit mention of municipal funding. Other cases, such as Clunia, also suggest an isolated initiative (an inspection? Specific rituals?), although the mention of a possible *lex* would indicate a more regular civic control and management of the place. This place was also located in an urban context, which makes the presence of magistrates normal.[65]

How can the municipal action in these and other Hispanic sanctuaries be explained? Undoubtedly, a generic concern that facilitated private expressions of devotion that resulted in very specific initiatives existed. Along with this, we must assume compliance with the competences of every urban community.[66] However, the specifications of municipal laws accept other possibilities: first, the need to generate situations and define messages that promoted civic identity and, through it, the power of an elite. This relationship between civic identity and religious tradition appears in many cities in diverse forms and is reflected in a range of evidence. One part comprises literature, which collects, in detail, legendary narratives integrated within the Mediterranean colonial tradition.[67] Another privileged area, more directly related to the expression of certain messages because it was controlled by urban governments, can be found in the civic mints of the first century BCE and first century CE.[68] On many occasions, these issues insisted on the cohesion of a community highlighting the antiquity, exclusivity (based on a precise origin), and originality of its institutions, social order, and beliefs. In this context, the spatial location of the specific gods, myths, and rites of a community must have played an important role, since they ensured their appropriation of a territory. An example of the construction of an identity is precisely the case of Saguntum, whose elites developed a complex 'bricolage', which included religious elements and the mythical and real past (colonial, Roman, and native) of the city to define a civic identity in the transition from the Republic to the Empire.[69] This mechanism constructed a religious landscape organized around several cults (Artemis-Diana, Venus, Liber Pater) located in both the city and its surrounding territory.[70]

Be that as it may, in general, the epigraphic evidence does not allow the issue of the status of sanctuaries to be addressed.[71] The inscriptions already mentioned (*IRC* I, 88 and *CIL* II²/14, 656) indicate the symbolic value that a place might acquire for a community, but cannot help us to specify how this was related in legal and material terms to a city and how it was organized internally; nor even in what context the location and material development of the sanctuary took place. The interest of a city's institutions, which must have generated diverse actions, seems to have depended on a complex combination of factors: concern for the preservation of the cult; integration of a place and a cult in the ideological framework forming the civic identity; and the material benefits and the prestige derived from the protection of a sanctuary with its capacity of attraction.

---

64 Palol and Viella 1987; Gasperini 1992b; 1998; Gasparini 2020; cf. Alfayé 2010, 200–02, 206–11; 2016, 362–83.

65 Alfayé 2010, 210; 2016; some laws in republican Italy, such as *CIL* I² 756 = *ILLRP* 508 = *ILS* 4906, show a particular interest in regulating economic aspects: Aberson and Wachter 2010; incidentally, it is interesting to note the thoroughness with which the text *CIL* I² 756 describes the architectural elements of the sanctuary. This can be related to the description given by Pliny the Younger — see below — of a sanctuary located on his estates; the coincidence in the materialization of a precise architectural language seems to reflect strategies of self-representation and social control on the part of elites that express themselves in a similar way in different contexts (public and private).

66 The lack of epigraphic evidence makes it impossible to specify the intensity and regularity of these interventions.

67 Johnston 2017.
68 Ripollès 1998; 2010; 2012b; Chaves 2008b; 2017; Campo in this volume.
69 Beltrán 2011; Revilla in this volume.
70 Corell 1996, although some cult attributions are hypothetical; cf. Grau and others 2017, 213–16.
71 Scheid 1997, 54.

## Elites, Self-Representation, and Social Power

The literature of the early Empire provides examples of the private initiatives undertaken by the Roman elite in the organization of the 'space and time' of religious practices in rural areas. This action is another facet of their economic and social power as a class of landowners that resided, whether permanently or not, in a territory and who were central to a network of social relations. A revealing text for its details is an epistle of Pliny the Younger (*Ep.* 9.39) that describes the state of an ancient sanctuary located on his lands and his intention to restore it.[72] His initiative reflects a double perception in his condition as owner: in the first place, his obligations with respect to the inhabitants of the territory, obligations that assume the acceptance of a material commitment; secondly, awareness of the impact (and prestige) associated with his initiative. In this sense, Pliny's action goes beyond the strict field of religion since it implies possibilities to manipulate some of the interaction/socialization processes of a community.[73]

At the same time, its objectives exceeded the strictly local context. First, because the euergetic action was embedded in a pattern of behaviour generally accepted by the imperial elites (the true recipients of an action carefully described in the epistle). Secondly, the consequence of his action was the dissemination of some forms of ritual, artistic, and architectural settings, adapted to models emanating from imperial society and contributing to a process of homogenization at local scale.

In Hispania, the best example of the impact of a member of the elite's initiatives in a rural context is provided by the sanctuary of Panóias, which involves the implantation of a specific deity and a ritual, the creation of a material scenario and the extensive use of inscriptions as a means of ordering spaces and worship. The initiative was based around an individual of senatorial status who acted as the founder. This figure corresponds to the condition of a 'pilgrim founder', well known in the second–third centuries CE.[74] The leading role of this individual can be noted, in the first place, in the presence of Eastern deities, whose cult is introduced without any apparent precedent (Hypsistos Serapis, the Diis Severis, Isis) together with the local gods of the Lapiteae. Parallel to this, the rituals of the cult were carefully specified. This precision also shows the prominence of the promoter in the creation of a cult practice.[75]

However, the inscriptions are limited to the ritual and its topography. The circumstances, context, or interests of the promoter are not described — it is not in the nature of the epigraphic message. There is no precision such as is shown by Pliny's epistle regarding social, ideological, and artistic pretensions and forms of action; nor do we know the position of the individual in the territory. This prevents us from appreciating the real objectives of the initiative, the social context in which it was immersed and, finally, how local, not only religious, interaction and social communication practices could be managed.

This problem is a general one. Individual interventions such as the one carried out by Pliny must have been common, but their frequency, specific initiatives, and, above all, the intentions that moved their protagonists cannot be determined. Possibly, the vast majority of these actions did not result in the architectural and ornamental transformation undertaken by Pliny and were limited to specific offerings. The scarcity of allusions could also suggest a certain lack of interest among the urban upper classes in rural spaces as appropriate areas for the expression of their prestige and the construction of social power. A partial explanation is the existence of alternative spaces for action that allowed them to act with independence and greater possibilities for impact (in the exhibition of luxury and messages): for example, the funerary constructions located on family estates or on the periphery of cities.[76]

The boundaries between public and private were very fluid and could easily be crossed by a *dominus*, depending on his interests. The various forms of action were specified in the promotion of architectural and ornamental, epigraphic and artistic programmes, of greater or lesser importance depending on the capacity and aims of the promoter. The most significant fact is, however, that these actions might involve a conscious redefinition of a cult and its function, which could modify its influence. The procedures and language used, the forms and rites that transformed the setting hide important changes behind the introduction of what seem to be merely

---

72 Commentary of the passage in Scheid 1996.
73 On this matter see: Plin., *Ep.* 5.14.8, 7.30.3, 9.36.6, and 9.15.1 (lawsuits) and 9.37 and 8.2 (property management); de Ligt 1993.
74 Alföldy 1997, 240; a comparable example of the foundation of a private sanctuary by a high-ranking Roman officer can be seen in C. Iunius Silvanus Melanio, who founded the sanctuary of Zeus Theos Megistos in Segobriga, which is known thanks to other cult inscriptions around the Empire: Abascal and Alföldy 1998.

75 Alföldy 1997; Rodríguez Colmenero 1999; Correia Santos and others 2014; Chaniotis 2005, 163 emphasizes the importance of private initiatives in the introduction of a cult and the problem that elucidating the reasons for doing so may present; cf. McCarty and Edher, in this volume.
76 For Mediterranean Spain: Sanmartí 1984.

minor reforms. Private action must have had profound effects as it could manifest itself in very diverse fields (funerary, sacred, residential, and economic) and with varied means that allowed the landscape and local traditions to be redefined, integrating the memory of an individual or a family group into them.[77]

## Rural Sanctuaries as Spaces of Interaction and Communication

References to legal status in sanctuary inscriptions, in particular situations of dependency, are quite rare. In some places the presence of slaves and freedmen is noted, specifically indicated with the terms *servus* and *libertus*. However, the usual situation is a simple onomastic indication, which does not allow the individual's socio-economic status to be identified. This circumstance can be seen, for example, in the sanctuary of Diana in Segobriga, where only a few people indicate their status with the term *libertus*, while the legal status of other individuals has been deduced from the onomastics.[78] It can also be seen at Muntanya Frontera, where thirteen inscriptions mention individuals, with a total of fifteen names, but only one name is accompanied by the word *libertus*. The absence or inclusion of legal terms does not directly reflect the social and legal composition of the groups that visited the sanctuaries or the population of the territory, as the case of Muntanya Frontera itself demonstrates. The apparent scarcity of *liberti* at this site contrasts with the numerous references in the nearby territory and in Saguntum itself, the vast majority in the rigorously formalized context of funerary inscriptions, clearly indicating socio-familial relationships and testamentary provisions.[79] This disparity shows that visitors to a sanctuary could build a personal image, as devotees, with some freedom. It would be interesting to see to what extent certain practices that respected or modified social conventions could be performed, bearing in mind the context (religious, funerary, domestic) and the interaction between various groups; but the evidence in this regard (the vast majority of the rural population remain anonymous) is very limited.

In other cases, in contrast, the reference to a servile condition can be understood as necessary, given the reason for the dedication (the slave who prays for the health of his or her owner),[80] or as an expression of a particular situation. This is the case of imperial slaves (at Can Modolell), whose indication of dependence (*servi Caesaris*) replaces any other (*natio, origo*) and indicates their special position.[81]

The apparent lack of interest in emphasizing social and legal hierarchies and the modesty of many offerings could lead us to consider that the majority of rural sanctuaries were natural spaces of expression for simple popular religiosity, or clearly marginal to the world of civic values. They would, therefore, have been secondary areas for the interests and intervention of the urban upper classes. This conclusion seems so easy because of our archaeological ignorance of most sites. Behind this approach lies the above-mentioned image that the Roman elites associated with the peasantry. In this context, sanctuaries would have appeared as appropriate spaces for the preferential expression of individual feelings and less committed to municipal life or to the community in general. However, some of the known sanctuaries reveal, precisely, an architectural and ornamental wealth that does not fit at all with the image of modesty applied to rural religion. Neither does this image coincide with the protagonists' heterogeneity, other than the simple local peasantry, even sometimes including people with an important position in society, even if it is ambiguous (members of the *familia Caesaris*), as well as with the manifest interest of civic institutions in the dignity of the sanctuary and the material maintenance of the cult, as the site of Muntanya Frontera demonstrates. In the same respect, the case of Panóais shows the difficulty involved in directly relating individual initiatives and the material expression of a cult and, in particular, to what extent it would be dangerous to deduce the status and social position of a dedicant from the entity of the architectural remains of a place.

In fact, some rural sanctuaries seem to serve as privileged spaces in which individuals in a particular situation (legal status, professional status, etc.) express wishes and act in accordance with their own needs, using formal procedures with some freedom. Among such situations, officials, soldiers, merchants, or simply travellers (freeborn individuals, freedmen, and slaves) must be considered. In this sense, the presence of individuals who served in the house-

---

77 Residential buildings: Leveau 1983; Bodel 1997; Terrenato 2007; economic exhibition: Purcell 1995, 155, 166–67; tombs: Purcell 1987; an example of the importance that these types of projects could have for a senator and the religious form they assumed can be seen in Cicero's actions building a sanctuary to his daughter Tulia: Cic. *Att.*, XII.18 and XII.19.
78 *CIL* II 3093b = *CIL* II 5874b (Diana); *CIL* II 3093d = *CIL* II 5874d (Dianae Frugiferae); cf. the warning of Marco 2017b.
79 Beltrán 1980; Corell 2002.

80 *IRC* II, 17; *CIL* II²/14, 587.
81 *IRC* I, 206; *IRC* I, 89. Mayer 2012 suggested that the place should be related to an imperial *fundus*.

hold of the *princeps* in certain places does not seem to have been fortuitous. These individuals occupied an ambiguous position in Roman society, due to the combination of inferior status and the power associated with their dependence on a special *dominus* or *patronus*. The rural places of worship would have offered a stage for imperial freedmen to exhibit a pattern of behaviour close to the euergetism of the imperial and provincial elites that could not be adequately displayed on the urban scene, monopolized by the elites and where local freedmen had their own environment as *seviri Augustales*.

At the same time, the presence of slaves and freedmen of imperial officials could indicate another of the functions of a sanctuary: its definition as a space that provided opportunities to develop forms of communication and interaction between special categories of the administration and the local population. In this respect, contributing to the promotion of a cult could help to establish contacts that would aid the establishment of communication channels with the population and local elites, favouring the official's own interests. Of course, purely personal needs of a religious or broader scope (prestige?) cannot be excluded. Participation in the religious life of a territory, therefore, would have contributed to providing roots and opportunities for interaction for individuals characterized by their mobility.[82] Sanctuaries, as centres of attraction and an occasion for social gathering, could serve as communication spaces that would facilitate the integration of these individuals. This factor would play a greater role, both in urban and rural places, in relation to 'initiation cults'. Their particular character, with identical practices and hierarchies throughout the Empire, with a special presence in the administration and the army, would have provided a meeting point for officials with those who shared their faith. At the same time, within the recognizable hierarchy of a religious group based in one place, this official, or a soldier, could identify his own position and a way of relating to local society.

However, it is very difficult to define and quantify the attractiveness of sanctuaries and the factors (social, cultural, economic) that determined it, identifying the possible levels of its projection: local, regional, provincial, or even interprovincial.[83] In most sanctuaries, epigraphy does not allow the origin of the individuals who frequented them or contributed to their activity to be established; not to mention the fact that the number of records is very small. In the case of Muntanya Frontera, the *nomina* recorded (Baebius, Cornelius, Valerius) frequently appear in Saguntum and, to a lesser extent, in Edeta and Valentia, but it is impossible to determine the origin of these individuals and, therefore, the radius of influence of the sanctuary cannot be defined; the possible presence of a dedicant from Tarraco has also been indicated. The range of possible situations is considerable. In the case of the Cueva de La Griega, it has been proposed that it should be interpreted as a regional sanctuary, while in that of Cueva Negra the presence of priests of Aesculapius from Ibiza could reflect a simple visit or pilgrimage (the motivations cannot be specified) of individuals from Ebusus.[84] At sites such as Can Modolell, the presence of individuals who, due to their function and their membership of the *domus Caesaris*, stand beyond the local context seems exceptional, but this is also a consequence of the lack of information about other cases. At all events, this site is also an example of the coexistence between foreigners, magistrates, and the local population. The diversity of situations is a good indication of the dynamism and the capacity of adaptation to very different factors that centres of worship had.

## Final Remarks

Religious manifestations in rural areas constitute a complex conglomerate of beliefs, practices, and scenarios. These situations include a multitude of deities, of diverse origin, whose personality and attributes (with regard to their qualities, field of action, and mythical context) and worship underwent changes over several centuries due to variable conditions. It does not seem methodologically useful, therefore, to analyse the implantation of these deities on the basis of archetypes or personalities defined only by a cultural origin (Punic, Hellenic, indigenous, Italic), which must have influenced and conditioned each other to a greater or lesser extent. Nor is it right to radically separate city and territory as if they were scenarios in which antagonistic social and cultural relations and values developed: the city as the core of the official religion; the territory as a reserve of indigenous beliefs, organized according to rhythms of evolution and resistant to external influences.

Analysis of rural cults and their scenarios must start from the verification of the multiple relations that every Roman city maintained with its territory

---

82 Perhaps it is in this context that we should place the actions of C. Iulius Siluanus Melanio.
83 Alfayé 2010, 192 and 202.

84 González Blanco and others 1987; Mayer 1996; Stylow and Mayer 1996.

and population. Religion occupied a special position in this process since it generated mechanisms of social integration and civic identity in which people participated through diverse forms of association. These mechanisms were projected outside the urban space through a topography of religious spaces, the definition of deities, and rituals. This religious geography and the concrete forms it adopted were essential for a community since they contributed to defining its territorial limits, its relations with other cities or with the imperial power, as well as its identity. In the formation of this complex of religious manifestations, very diverse, particular and collective forces intervened; the latter were organized and institutionalized in several ways.[85] In many rural sanctuaries it is possible to observe, in particular, a private performance free of some conventions that appear in urban worship; but the importance of this fact should not be exaggerated, as the repetition of votive expressions or the legal language of some initiatives reveals.

However, the dynamics of the constitution of landscapes and sacred places cannot be reduced to the exclusive action of urban elites acting as magistrates or rural owners. Together with the dynamics of the polis-religion, it is necessary to evaluate individual necessities such as the initiatives of 'itinerant founders'.[86] The presence of an individual or a group in a centre of worship or sacred place (visit, pilgrimage, regular worship) might involve very different motives that sometimes transcended the field of religion. An additional factor of complexity is the different needs that the population of the territory, of very diverse social status, and outsiders, whether settled or passing through, had. In this context it is possible that, on occasions, certain extra-urban settings also served to develop specific forms of communication and social expression, which may have been more or less necessary for the community.

It is evident, in sum, that one cannot approach the study of rural sanctuaries and/or religious landscapes from a catalogue of literary, epigraphic, and archaeological survivals alone. It is essential to adopt an approach that integrates the dynamics of settlement structure and the evolution of the urban communities that controlled and modelled a territory. The location, nature, and frequentation of a sanctuary, understood as a space where identities and social interactions are constructed and negotiated, are directly and indirectly related to these dynamics.

---

85 cf. Urciuoli and Rüpke 2018.

86 On 'individualization' Rüpke 2013b; on agency Rüpke 2015; 2017.

JONATHAN EDMONDSON

# 6. Roman Colonies and Local Cults

## *The Example of Augusta Emerita (Mérida) in Lusitania*

In 25 BCE Augustus took the decision to found a Roman colony on the banks of the River Anas (modern Guadiana) for the veterans discharged from the legions V Alaudae and X Gemina at the end of the first phase of his Asturian and Cantabrian campaigns in the far north of the Iberian Peninsula. This new colony of Augusta Emerita assumed still greater importance after Augustus, arguably in 16 BCE, split the republican province of Hispania Ulterior into two new provinces — Baetica and Lusitania — and selected Emerita as the main administrative centre of Lusitania.[1] After more than a century of intense archaeological and epigraphic research, the urban layout of the new colony and its chronological evolution are now better understood, while the almost two thousand inscriptions known from its urban centre and rural territory, ranging in date from the first century BCE to the seventh century CE, allow some key aspects of its social, political, cultural, and religious history to be reconstructed.[2]

The colony was granted an unusually large territory (cf. Frontin. *De limit.* 9, Thulin; Agenn. Urb., *De controv. agr.* 44, Thulin), and individual colonists were given larger than normal land assignations within the centuriated *pertica* (cf. Hygin. Grom. *De limit. constit.*, 135–36, Thulin).[3] The precise limits of its territory remain controversial for certain stretches, but a workshop on the topic held in Mérida in February 2020 revealed that a growing consensus is emerging (Fig. 6.1).[4] To the north, Emerita's territory was bounded by that of the pre-existing *colonia* of Norba Caesarina (Cáceres), to the north-east by that of the community of Turgalium (Trujillo), to the east by that of the pre-existing *colonia* of Metellinum (Medellín), to the south-east and south by the territories of a series of communities along the northern fringe of Baetica (from east to west, Artigi, Iulipa, the *Municipium Fl(avium) V(- - -)* located at Azuaga (prov. Badajoz), Regina, possibly the so far unlocated *municipium* of Arsa, Contributa Iulia Ugultunia, Segida Restituta Iulia and Seria Fama Iulia), to the south-west and west by the territory of the Augustan *municipium* of Ebora (Évora) in Lusitania, and to the north-west by that of the Flavian *municipium* of Ammaia (São Salvador de Aramenha, Marvão, distr. Portalegre).

In addition, the colony controlled at least three *praefecturae* outside its main *pertica*.[5] One of these included land some 120 km east of Mérida close to the *trifinium* where the provinces of Lusitania, Baetica, and Hispania Tarraconensis converged, since a boundary stone from the reign of Domitian has been found in the area of Valdecaballeros that marked the limit between this *praefectura* of Emerita and an enclave of territory of the Baetican *colonia* of Ucubi, while another, dated to 73 CE, marked the boundary between this same enclave of Ucubi and the territory of the *municipium* of Lacinimurga. Another *praefectura* was located about 20 km south of the *pertica* of Emerita within the territory of the Baetican *municipium* of Contributa Iulia Ugultunia, as indicated by the discovery of two further *termini Augustales* marking the limits of the territory of this *praefectura* of Emerita at Los Altos de Solaparza and at El Cañuelo, 3 km apart in the *término municipal* of Valencia del Ventoso (province of Badajoz).[6]

---

1 For details, see Edmondson 2011; 2016; 2018.
2 For a recent synthesis, see López Díaz and others 2018, chs. 7–11.
3 On the territory and traces of parts of its centuriation, see Ariño and Gurt 1992–1993; Étienne 1995; Gorges and Rodríguez Martín 2011; Olesti 2014, 390–414.
4 It was held in conjunction with two current research projects: 'Names and Identity in Roman Spain: The ADOPIA Project', supported by a Partnership Development Grant from Canada's Social Sciences and Humanities Research Council (PDG 890-2017-0039), and 'Inscripciones latinas de *Augusta Emerita* (ILAE)', supported by the Spanish Government's Ministry of Sciences, Innovation and Universities (PGC 2018-101698-B-I00), directed by Professor A. Alvar Ezquerra, Universidad de Alcalá.
5 Hygin. *De limit. constit.* 135–36, Thulin.
6 *Termini* from Valdecaballeros: CIL II 656 = II²/7, 871 = Cortés Bárcena 2013, 62–66 no. 11: *Imp(eratori) Domiti|ano Caes(ari) Aug(usto) | Divi Aug(usti) Vesp(asiani) f(ilio) | Augustalis te|rminus c(olonorum) c(oloniae) C(laritatis) Iul(iae) | Ucubitanor(um) | inter Aug(ustanos)*

---

Jonathan Edmondson, Distinguished Research Professor of History and Classical Studies (York University)

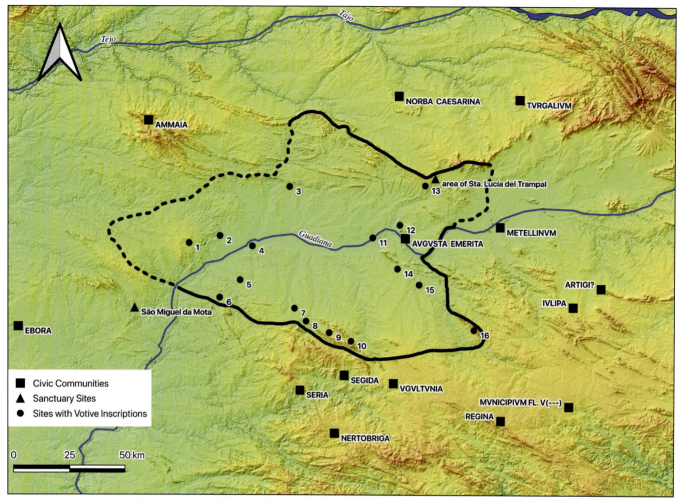

Figure 6.1. Map showing the boundaries of the territory of Augusta Emerita. The solid line indicates where the boundary is secure, the dotted line where it is plausible. 1. Elvas. 2. Herdade da Fonte Branca, Caia e São Pedro, Elvas. 3. Villar del Rey. 4. Badajoz. 5. La Cocosa, Roman villa. 6. Olivenza. 7. Torre de Miguel Sesmero. 8. Nogales. 9. La Morera. 10. Feria. 11. La Garrovilla. 12. Roman reservoir 'Proserpina', Mérida. 13. Valley of the River Zarza. 14. Torremejía. 15. Alange. 16. Hornachos. (Map by H. Forsyth).

*Emeri(tenses)*; *CIL* II²/7, 870 = Cortés Bárcena 2013, 43–48 no. 4, Mojón Gordo, 13 km N of Valdecaballeros: *Imp(erator) Caes(ar) Aug(ustus) | Vespasianus po|ntif(ex) [max(imus)] trib(unicia) p|ot(estate) [IIII i]mp(erator) X p(ater) | p(atriae) co(n)s(ul) IIII design(atus) | V ter(minavit?) inter Laci|nimurg(enses) et Ucu|bitanos c(olonos) c(oloniae) Claritatis Iuliae*. Termini from Valencia del Ventosa: (1) *AE* 1993, 917b = *HEp* 5, 1995, 115 = Cortés Bárcena 2013, 75–78 no. 15: *terminus Augu|stalis finis Em|eritensium*; (2) Paniego and others 2020: *term[inus Augusta|l]is fini[s Emeritens(ium)]*. The reading of an inscription found at Montemolín (Badajoz) to attest the limits of pastureland of Emerita — *[t]ermin|[u]s Aug(ustalis) pra(torum) | [co]loniae Aug(ustae) Emer[itae]* (Fita and the Marqués de Hinojares 1918, 155 = *HAE* 1483 = *AE* 1993, 917a) — must now be rejected in light of J. González's new edition of the text based on autopsy following the stone's rediscovery at the Dehesa de El Santo (Montemolín): González Fernández 1996, 84 no. 1 = *HEp* 5, 1995, 109 = *AE* 1997, 785: - - - - - - | [- - -f]lam[ini? - - - | - - - Caesar]is Aug(usti) prae[fecto - - - | - - - co]l(oni-) Aug(ust-) Emer[it - - -]*.

The fact that Emerita controlled such a vast territory, amounting to about 8500 km²,[7] even if it was not as densely occupied as, for instance, the Guadalquivir Valley to the south in Baetica, means that its colonists would have been forced to confront various indigenous peoples and communities and their cultural and religious practices.[8] Some of these local indigenous people were incorporated into the citizen body of the new colony or took up residence there as *peregrini*.[9] As a result, Emerita provides a very interesting case study for an exploration of how the authorities of a Roman colony, which was also a provincial capital, interacted with local reli-

[7] For this estimate, Cordero 2010, 160; Houten 2021, 242.
[8] For the region prior to the foundation of Emerita, see Heras 2018.
[9] Str. III.2.15 includes Emerita as one of a group of 'synoecized' communities, where native inhabitants were incorporated into Roman towns. Epigraphic confirmation: C. Allius Tangini f. Pap. [- - -?] (*AE* 1993, 892 = *HEp* 5, 1995, 52, Rincón de Gila, territory of Emerita); C. Iulius Mandi f. Sangenus (*HEp* 9, 1999, 95 = *AE* 2006, 597, Emerita). See further Edmondson 2018, 64–65, with fig. 4.

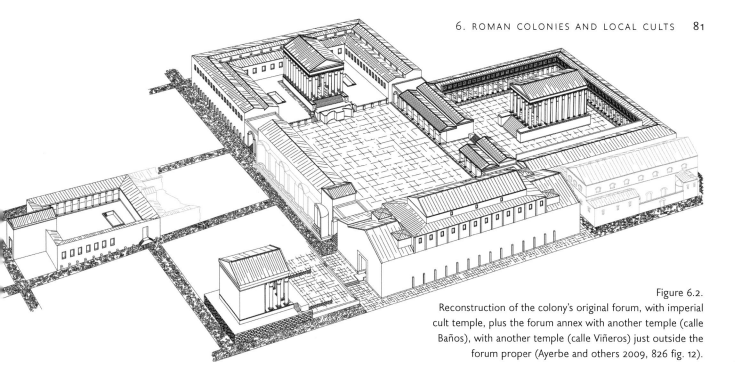

Figure 6.2.
Reconstruction of the colony's original forum, with imperial cult temple, plus the forum annex with another temple (calle Baños), with another temple (calle Viñeros) just outside the forum proper (Ayerbe and others 2009, 826 fig. 12).

gious cults and cult places in, and near, its territory.[10] The chapter will examine some of the multiple reactions that Rome's occupation of this region provoked.

## Cults in the Urban Centre

The foundation of a Roman citizen *colonia* at Emerita inevitably led to the formation of a religious pantheon made up largely of Roman state cults. As in other Roman colonies, the local senate and magistrates had responsibility for determining the annual religious calendar and regulating all civic cults and festivals in both the urban centre and its rural territory.[11] The distinctively metropolitan nature of Emerita's urban centre has frequently been noted, and many elements of its urban architecture were calqued on that of the city of Rome. Not surprisingly, temples formed a significant component of its urban fabric, as a series of archaeological projects of the Museo Nacional de Arte Romano (MNAR), the Consorcio de la Ciudad Monumental de Mérida (CCMM), and the Instituto Arqueológico de Mérida (IAM) of Spain's Consejo Superior de Investigaciones Científicas (CSIC) over the last forty years have done so much to elucidate.[12] Alongside the emblematic imperial cult temple that formed the focal point of the colony's original forum (the so-called 'temple of Diana'), which was modelled on the temple of Divus Iulius in the Roman Forum,[13] the colony came in time to boast the massive temple of the provincial imperial cult in the calle Holguín, whose plan was based on that of the temple of Concord also in the Forum Romanum,[14] the *sacrarium* of the *Lares et imagines* [*domus Augustae*?] inserted into the *ima cavea* of the theatre under Trajan,[15] the temple of Mars known from the inscribed epistyle reused in the sixteenth century in the small shrine ('hornito') of Santa Eulalia and possibly restored in the mid- to later third century thanks to the intervention of a Roman equestrian governor of Lusitania,[16] a possible shrine of Nemesis built into the amphitheatre in the late second or early third century CE, as also occurred at Tarraco,[17] plus a whole series of smaller temples now revealed archaeologically in or near to the original colonial forum (see Fig. 6.2).[18]

Not surprisingly in a provincial capital, of all cults (see Table 6.1, with references) it is the worship of the deified members of the *domus Augusta*, the *divi* and *divae* (nos 20–22), and sacred offerings

---

10 For previous studies, Ramírez Sádaba 1993; Goffaux 2006; Ramírez Sádaba and Jiménez Losa 2011; Ramírez Sádaba 2019. For a new catalogue of votive inscriptions from Emerita and its territory, Ramírez Sádaba 2019 [2021].
11 As laid down in the *lex Coloniae Genetivae Iuliae*: RS 25 = CIL II²/5, 1022, ch. 64; cf. chs. 65–72, 125–27 for other religious matters, with Rüpke 2006a; Strothmann 2020.
12 For an overview of recent work, see Álvarez Martínez and Mateos 2011.

13 Álvarez Martínez and Nogales 2003; Ayerbe and others 2009.
14 Mateos 2006.
15 Trillmich 1989–1990; cf. AE 1990, 515 = HEp 4, 1994, 167 = CIIAE 26, rev. Stylow and Ventura Villanueva 2018, 166–74 no. 4 and figs 22–27, 29 = AE 2018, 832; CIVAE 63.
16 CIL II 468; third-century restoration: Edmondson 2007 (AE 2007, 721 = HEp 16, 2007, 12).
17 Nogales 2000a, 40.
18 Ayerbe and others 2009, 807–31 on the creation and development of the forum area, including temples, from the Augustan period to Late Antiquity.

to the *Genius* of the ruling emperor (no. 31) or the emperor himself (nos 10–15) that have left the greatest weight of evidence not just in terms of dedications, but also through the attestation of *flamines* and *flaminicae* involved in their cults at both the municipal and the provincial levels.[19] Roman state cults also loom large, with dedications to Jupiter (nos 34–36), Juno (no. 33), Liber Pater (no. 39), Mars (nos 40–42), Venus Victrix (no. 59), Fortuna (nos 29–30), and perhaps Neptune (no. 54).[20] The statues of Ceres, Proserpina, and Pluto displayed on the *scaenae frons* of the theatre would also suggest that the cult of each of them was important at the colony.[21] In time, some of these Roman divinities came to have the epithet 'Augustus' associated with them, as dedications to Jupiter Aug(ustus) from the later first century (no. 35), the L(ares) A(ugusti) or, less likely, L(iber) A(ugustus), depending on how this abbreviated theonym is expanded, from the second half of the second century (no. 38), or Deus Mars Aug(ustus) from the mid- to later third century CE (no. 42) illustrate. A small pedestal that supported a votive palm was dedicated to the Genius of the Colony (no. 32) — *Genio C(oloniae) I(uliae) A(ugustae) E(meritae)* — in the late first or first half of the second century, most likely in a shrine of the Genius located somewhere in the urban centre.[22] As we have seen, Nemesis had a small sanctuary in the amphitheatre, from where an early third-century painted dedication to Dea Invicta Caelestis Nemesis survives (no. 52), made by a visitor from Rome, M. Aurelius Fhilo (*sic*). That the small votive pedestal dedicated to 'the Mistress who cures the soul' (no. 53) — *Dominae cur(atrici) anima[e]* — may also relate to Nemesis is strengthened by the verbal parallelism with this exact same title found on a votive plaque from the amphitheatre at Italica, where a shrine of Nemesis was also located.[23] But it might alternatively be connected to the cult of Salus or that of Proserpina-Ataecina, to which we shall return.[24]

In addition, some minor Roman divinities also received cult (Table 6.1): Fontanus (nos 26–27), the Nymphs (nos 55–56), and the water-springs (*Fontes*) (no. 28), as well as a catch-all pantheistic dedication to 'all the gods' (*deis omnibus*) (no. 19). A Mithraeum, which was thriving in the mid-second century, located near the site of the modern Plaza de Toros, has provided a rich haul of votive altars and sculptures of Mithras and figures associated with Mithras (nos 16, 44–51), as well as Mercury, Venus, Chronos, and Aesculapius or Serapis,[25] while isolated dedications also attest to cults of the Magna Mater, styled Mater Deorum (no. 43), and Serapis (no. 58).

Not surprisingly, the large majority of these dedications were set up by individuals who, from their names, appear to be Roman citizens of the colony, including a freedman who set up a votive offering to the Genius of the colony (no. 32). The decurions of the colony were responsible for a dedication to the Genius of the emperor in the later first or early second century (no. 31). Slaves are on record making offerings to Mithras (nos 47, 49), while the Dionisius (*sic*) who made a vow for the well-being of [S]empronius Fronto (no. 61) may also have been a slave. Soldiers serving on the staff of the Roman governor or procurator are also represented: a *frumentarius* of the Legio VII Gemina dedicated an altar to Mithras in 155 (no. 51), while lower-ranking soldiers from the same legion set up an unusual circular slate votive plaque in the late first century for a deity whose name has not survived, if it was ever inscribed, on the damaged monument (no. 62) and a miniature altar to the L(ares) A(ugusti) (or possibly to L(iber) A(ugustus)) (no. 38) in the second half of the second century.

Visitors to Emerita could make offerings during temporary sojourns in the city, such as Quintio, slave of a citizen of Conimbriga in north-western Lusitania, who set up a votive to Mithras (no. 49), or the parents of M. Arrius Reburrus from the *civitas* of the Lancienses Transcudani (Mileu, São Vicente, distr. Guarda) who dedicated a pedestal to Jupiter Augustus in honour of their son (no. 35). More substantially, (Domitia) Vettilla dedicated a shrine to

---

19  Among a huge literature, Étienne 1958; 1990; Edmondson 1997; Fishwick 2002, 53–60, 166–69; 2004, 41–70, 189–94; 2017. For the epigraphic evidence, Ramírez Sádaba 2003a; Delgado 1999 (provincial priests); 2000, 113–26, 132–48 (*flamines* and *flaminicae* of the colony).

20  Díaz y Pérez 1887, 354, where he reports that a dedication to Neptune by 'la república ó municipio Emeritense' (*sic*) was found in 1849 'antes de llegar al puente', but was soon thereafter reused for a building in the Plaza de la Constitución, now the Plaza del Parador. No trace of, nor further reference to, this stone to my knowledge exists.

21  García y Bellido 1949, 89. no. 72 (Pluto), 153–54 no. 164 (Ceres), 154 no. 165 (Proserpina). For alternative interpretations of the statues of Pluto and Proserpina, Ojeda 2018, 201–03 nos 7–8.

22  García Iglesias 1984, 145–48 no. A (*AE* 1984, 485), reading *G(enio) ci(vitatis) A(ugustae) E(meritae)*; but for the revised text *G(enio) C(oloniae) I(uliae) A(ugustae) E(meritae)*, see Étienne and Mayet 1984, 168; Edmondson 2007, 547–48 no. 3, with fig. 6; cf. Trillmich 2016–2017 [2020]. On cults to municipal *Genii* in Hispania, Goffaux 2004.

23  *AE* 1984, 486, rev. Edmondson 2007, 548 no. 4, with fig. 7a–b. cf. ERItalica 11 = CILA II, 15* (HEp 4, 1994, 754); HEp 9, 1999, 511; *AE* 1908, 151; 1955, 151; 1984, 505: … *Domin(a)e cur(atrici) animae* (a modern copy of a genuine ancient text).

24  As argued by García-Bellido 2001, 67 and n. 62.

25  For a full recent catalogue, Alvar 2018, 81–122; for remains of the Mithraeum in the calle Espronceda, ibid., 73–81, with Barrientos 2001.

Mars at Emerita in the mid-second century (no. 41); she was from a senatorial family from Vercellae in Transpadane Italy and wife of L. Roscius Paculus, a senator perhaps of Lusitanian origin.[26] In the second half of the third century Roman provincial governors, now of equestrian rank, made major dedications to Deus Mars Augustus and Deus Jupiter at the provincial capital (nos 42, 34). The former was triggered by rebuilding work to the god's shrine sponsored the governor, while the pedestal to Jupiter was set up in the main forum of the colony.[27]

But arguably the most interesting feature of the known votive dedications from the urban heart of the Roman provincial capital are those made to local divinities.[28] These include dedications to the otherwise unattested Divus Sigerius Stillifer (no. 23 = Fig. 6.3a), the equally obscure Edigenius Domn[i]cus (nos 24–25), and a local divinity called Lacipaea (no. 37), whose name is strongly suggestive of a connection with the *mansio* Lacipaea, located on the road from Emerita to Caesaraugusta in the territory of Emerita (*It. Ant.* 438.4), and whose cult is also attested in the territories of Norba Caesarina and Turgalium, two communities that bordered on Emerita.[29] Two of these local gods received votives from men with fully Roman names: Val(erius) Festianus in the case of Sigerius Stillifer (no. 23 = Fig. 6.3a); in the case of Lacipaea (no. 37), two brothers Valerius Proculus and Valerius Vitulus from the *municipium* of Termes (Montejo de Tiermes, prov. Soria) in central Hispania Citerior. Details about the dedicator have survived on just one of the offerings to Edigenius (no. 24), and this was set up by Trophimus, whose name strongly hints that he was a slave.[30] The recently published dedication to Jupiter Solutorius (no. 36) involves a case of syncretism between the supreme divinity of the Roman pantheon and a local chief divinity. Evidence for the cult of Jupiter Solutorius is concentrated in the territories of Norba Caesarina,

Figure 6.3. Small votive altars to a) Divus Sigerius Stillifer (Table 6.1, no. 23); b) Dea Sancta Turib(rigensis) (Table 6.1, no. 7); c) Dea Sancta Proserpina and (Table 6.1, no. 57) d) Dea Sancta, all from Emerita (Table 6.1, no. 8). Mérida: MNAR (a, b, d); Consorcio de la Ciudad Monumental (c) (photos: J. Edmondson).

Turgalium, and Caurium, with isolated cases in the territories of Ammaia, the Civitas Igaeditanorum, and Caesarobriga. As such, we would seem to have a case where regional religious practices had an impact on cult activity at the Roman colony and provincial capital of Emerita. The fact that the surviving dedication includes an official date of the colony (a[nno] col(oniae) C[---]XX[---] or C[---]XV[---]) suggests that it was a public cultic act.[31]

---

26 For her full name, cf. *CIL* V 6657 = *ILS* 6741a, with Navarro Caballero 2017, cat. no. 239,1. For Paculus, see Caballos 1990, 2.291–92 no. 163. See further Saquete 2016–2017 [2020].

27 For these third-century governors, see Edmondson 2020. For votive dedications by provincial governors in Hispania in general, Le Roux 2006.

28 Rothenhöfer 2009.

29 Territory of Norba: *CILCC* I 2 = *AE* 1994, 877 = *HEp* 6, 1996, 187, Albalá: *G. I(ulius) Pele|cus La|cibaea | v(otum) s(olvit) l(ibens) m(erito)*; *CILCC* I 353 = *HEp* 6, 1996, 249, Torre de Santa María: *L. Cav(---) S(exti) (f.?) | [B]alanus | Lac(ipeae) v(otum) s(olvit)*. Territory of Turgalium: *CILCC* II 485 = *HEp* 6, 1996, 226, Conquista de la Sierra: *T. Iulius | Ammin|us Laci[p]|aiae v(otum) l(ibens) | s(olvit)*. On Lacipaea, see further Olivares 2002, 37, 248–49.

30 For the frequent use of Trophimus and Trophime as slave-names in the city of Rome, see Solin 1996, II, 488–90.

31 *Editio princeps*: *CIVAE* 41, with fig. 37 (photo): *Iovi S[ol]u[t]or[io] | C(aius) [I]ulius [---] | inp[e]n[sa] sua [---]|*

Even more striking is the relatively substantial sample of votive offerings made to the goddess Ataecina, a divinity whose surviving dedications are concentrated in the territory occupied in the period prior to the Roman occupation by the Vettones and who in the Roman period came to be syncretized with the Roman goddess Proserpina.[32] In the urban centre of Emerita she was offered cult under several variant theonyms: *Ataecina Sancta* (no. 1), *Dea Ataecina Turobrigen(sis) Sancta* (no. 6), *Dea Sanc(ta) Turib(rigensis)* (no. 7 = Fig. 6.3b), *Dea Turibrig(ensis)* (no. 2), or just *Dea Sancta* (no. 8 = Fig. 6.3d; no. 9) or in syncretized form as *Ataecina Turibriga Proserpina* (no. 3) or as *Dea Sancta Proserpina* (no. 57 = Fig. 6.3c). Her familiarity within the colony's cultic landscape is suggested by the fact that her name could be abbreviated to just a series of initials as *D(ea) S(ancta) A(taecina) T(uribrigensis)* (no. 4).

As for those attested setting up dedications to the goddess, apart from Artemas, slave of Claudius Martilinus (no. 6) and a dedicant who appears to have had a single name, Musa or Musa[eus] (no. 3, although the text is impossible to decipher in this key section), in each of the other six cases where the dedicant's name can be read, they all have good Roman *tria nomina*: L. Cornel[ius] Herc(u)la[nus] (no. 1), L. Iuventius Iulianus (no. 7 = Fig. 6.3b), L. Caelius Philinus (no. 9), Q. Cor[nelius - - -] (no. 2), [-] Sentius Marsus (no. 8 = Fig. 6.3d), and P. Vitia[- - -] (no. 4, where the name has apparently been corrupted in the manuscript tradition). This would all suggest that this local divinity Ataecina, assimilated to Proserpina, had become fully integrated into the cult life of the colony. The Roman citizens were happy to co-opt her into the civic pantheon and the local senate and magistrates thus had overall supervision of her cult, as they did of all other established cults in the urban centre and rural territory.[33] A significant number of further cases are known from Emerita's territory, to which we shall now turn.

## Cults in the Territory of Emerita

As we have seen, it is not easy to define the limits of Emerita's territory in certain stretches, and in particular the boundaries of the *praefectura regionis Turgaliensis* and the colony's other *praefecturae* are far from clear. As a result, some previous studies of religious activity in the *ager Emeritensis* have included some votives from what now seems to be the territory of the independent municipality of Turgalium rather than from the *praefectura regionis Turgaliensis* that fell under Emerita's jurisdiction.[34] The *IIviri*, aediles, and local *pontifex* attested at *Turgalium* confirm that Turgalium was a civic community in its own right, as does the dedication to the *Genius Turg(alensium)*.[35] As a result, discussion of cults in the *praefecturae* of Emerita is omitted in this study, which concentrates solely on the colony's actual *pertica*.

Scattered evidence exists for cult activity in Emerita's territory, but for the most part it is quite thinly spread (see Fig. 6.1 and Table 6.2, with references). Nevertheless, enough survives to provide some insights into the relationship between cults in the urban centre and those in the countryside. Not surprisingly in the territory of the Roman colony just as in its urban centre, there is a good representation of Roman state cults: Jupiter, either simply as Jupiter (no. T24) or as Jupiter Optimus Maximus (nos T25–27), Juno (no. T22) and Juno Regina (no. T23), Diana (no. T19), Mercury (no. T29; in the form *D(eus) D(ominus) S(anctus) Mercurius*), Silvanus (nos T35–36) and 'Mistress Isis' ('Isis Domina') (no. T21). The dedication to Juno Regina is a special case in that it was made by a senator and his wife from Baetica, Licinius Serenianus and Varinia Flaccina, for the well-being (*pro salute*) of their daughter, Varinia Serena, when they visited the thermal springs at Alange, 20 km south-east of Mérida.[36] In addition, minor cults such as those of Fontanus and Fontana (or perhaps Fontanus and the Fontes) (no. T20) and the Lares Viales (no. T28), who protected travellers, are found. Once again it is difficult to say from these isolated finds whether they were set up at rural sanctuaries that had a formal cult organization or if they were private dedications

---

a[nno] col(oniae) C[---]XX[---] vel C[---]XV[---]. Attestations from the territories of Norba: *CIL* II 728, 5290 = *CILCC* I 383, 342; *CILCC* I 98, 99, 228; Turgalium: *CIL* II 661 = *CILCC* II 842; *CILCC* II 637, 718; Caurium: *CIL* II 5031–32 = *CILCC* IV 1268–69; *CILCC* IV 1278; *AE* 2017, 646; Ammaia: *AE* 1946, 199 = *HEp* 7, 1997, 22; Civitas Igaeditanorum: *AE* 1971, 159; Caesarobriga: *CIL* II 944 = *IRPToledo* 81; *IRPToledo* 19. For discussions of the cult, Peeters 1938, 171, 173–74, 182, 184, 186–87, 190; Salas and others 1983; Esteban 2012–2013 [2015].

32  For discussions, Abascal 1995; 2002; García-Bellido 2001; Olivares 2002, 37, 247–49; Rojas 2016. For Ataecina in Emerita, Méndez Grande 2015.

33  See above, p. 75 and n. 11.

34  This is particularly true in the otherwise valuable study of Goffaux 2006; to a lesser degree in Ramírez Sádaba and Jiménez Losa 2011.

35  *IIvir*, aedile: *CIL* II 5276 = *CILCC* II 728. Pontifex: *CIL* II 657, rev. *CILCC* II 485 (cf. *HEp* 2012, 179); *Genius Turg(alensium)*: *CIL* II 618 = *CILCC* II 726. For the view that the latter refers to the Genius of the *municipium* of Turgalium, see Goffaux 2006, 55–56, *contra* Iglesias Gil 1986, 128–29, 132, arguing that it refers to the Genius of the *praefectura Turgaliensis*.

36  See further Gimeno 1997.

made along the roads, in the case of the Lares Viales, or on rural estates, as was evidently the case with the dedications to Diana (no. T19) and to a deity whose name is lost on a damaged altar (no. T42), which were both discovered at the site of the Roman villa at La Cocosa, 17 km south of Badajoz.

In addition to dedications to these Roman divinities, the cult of Ataecina-Proserpina seems to have flourished just as much in the colony's territory as it did in its urban centre. Evidence survives of the goddess's invocation both in the immediate environs of Emerita and at the fringes of its territory. Hence a *defixio* invoking *Dea Ataecina Turibrig(ensis) Proserpina* (no. T1) to take action against whomsoever was responsible for stealing several items of clothing, including tunics and cloaks, was discovered at the site of the Roman reservoir (now popularly known as the 'Proserpina reservoir') 7.5 km north of Emerita.[37] Similarly, a small votive altar (no. T2) was set up to Proserpina — or more likely, since the top of the altar is broken off, to *Dea Sancta Ataecina Turibriga Proserpina* — in the vicinity of La Garrovilla, some 12 km west of Emerita on the north side of the Guadiana, along the road that led from Emerita to Olisipo. In this case the dedicant gave his name in a simplified form, using just his *cognomen*, but he did not hesitate to record the fact that he was an *Augustalis*, presumably at Emerita; as such, he would in actuality have borne the *tria nomina*. By means of this vow a member of the colony's sub-elite sought to enlist the support of a divinity local in origin, but one that was well accepted into the civic pantheon of the Roman provincial capital.[38]

At the far western edge of Emerita's territory five dedications to Proserpina survive from the area of modern Elvas (distr. Portalegre) in which the deity was invoked as simply *Proserpina*, *Proserpina Sancta*, *Dea Proserpina*, or *Proserpina Servatrix* ('the Preserver') (Table 6.2, nos T30–34). Whether these should be seen as dedications to Proserpina *tout court* or to the divinity syncretized with Ataecina is unclear, but the use of the epithet *sancta* in one of the dedications from Elvas (no. T33) hints at a connection, since, as we have seen, Ataecina was frequently invoked with this epithet.[39] At some point during the second century a votive was offered to *Dea Sancta Burrulobrigensis* (no. T18), a local tutelary deity, it would seem, of a rural *vicus* Burrulobriga, but her invocation as *Dea Sancta* has led to the theory that she too was connected to the syncretized cult of Ataecina-Proserpina.[40] In three of the votives for Proserpina, the person responsible for the dedication bears the *tria nomina* of a Roman citizen: Q. Helvius Silvanus (no. T31), G. Iulius Panthenopaeus (no. T33), and C. Vettius Silvinus (no. T34); in the other two cases, the texts are worn, but the dedicators seem to have had indigenous names: [- - -] Rustri? (f.) (no. T32) and Toncius [- - - - - -] (no. T30).[41]

But the most significant cluster of dedications so far known are the fifteen votive altars to Ataecina (nos T3–17) and several other fragments reused as building material in the Visigothic church at Santa Lucía del Trampal, Alcuéscar (prov. Cáceres) at the northernmost extreme of Emerita's territory, 35 km north of its urban centre, on the southern slopes of the Sierra de Monesterio. This concentration of votives clearly points to an organized sanctuary somewhere in the vicinity. Excavations, directed by Luis Caballero between 1982 and 1990, revealed no traces of a prior Roman-period shrine beneath the church;[42] so it appears that the votives had been brought from elsewhere to be used in its construction, while their typological homogeneity suggests a single place of origin.[43] Where precisely that sanctuary may have been located remains uncertain. Juan Manuel Abascal, in publishing the altars for the first time in 1995, argued that the deity's principal sanctuary, perhaps an open-air *temenos*, was at Turibriga/Turobriga, which he locates in the vicinity of Santa Lucía del Trampal (perhaps near the site of 'Las Torrecillas') and which would explain the frequent appearance of the epithet *Turibrigensis* in the goddess's titulature.[44] María Paz García-Bellido, in an article full of learning and ingenuity, preferred to argue that Turibriga/Turobriga may have been the pre-Roman toponym for the site later occupied by the Roman *municipium* of Augustobriga (Talavera la Vieja, prov. Cáceres) and that Ataecina's cult centre should rather be associated with the sacred grove of Feronia (*lucus Feroniae*) mentioned by Agennius

---

37 *CIL* II 462, with comments.
38 Stylow 1997 (*AE* 1997, 804a): [*Deae Sanctae* | *Ataecinae* | *Turibrigae*] | *Proserpinae* | *Severianus* | *Aug(ustalis)* | *a(nimo) l(ibens) v(otum) s(olvit)*.
39 The only other occurrences in Latin epigraphy of *Proserpina sancta* occur in dedications from Emerita (Table 6.1, no. 57) and from Ilipa Ilia in Baetica (*CIL* II 1044 = *CILA* II.1, 336). On Ataecina's titles of *dea sancta* and *dea domina sancta*, see Abascal 1995, 83–86.
40 Encarnação 1984, 633, commenting on the text (*IRCP* 566).
41 The name Rustrius is otherwise attested only at Vindobona, Pannonia Superior: *CIL* III 4581. Toncius/Tongius is one of the commonest native names found in Lusitania: see Vallejo Ruiz 2005, 418–20.
42 Caballero Zoreda and others 1991; Caballero Zoreda and Sáez Lara 1999.
43 So Abascal 1995, 79–80.
44 Abascal 1995, 97–105; 1996.

Urbicus in his work *De controversiis agrorum* as belonging to the 'Augustini', which she holds was another term for 'Emeritenses' and hence would place the sacred grove in the territory of Emerita.[45] This allowed García-Bellido then to posit a connection between Feronia, an Italic deity, and Ataecina-Proserpina and hence to situate here a syncretized cult of two goddesses who both had connections to the underworld. Even though 'Augustini' was not normally the term used to denote citizens of Augusta Emerita, who were described occasionally as 'Augustani', but much more frequently as 'Emeritenses',[46] Brian Campbell was too hasty to reject this association when he argued that the *lucus Feroniae Augustinorum* more likely refers to a sacred grove of Feronia in Italy in the territory of one of the colonies founded there in the triumviral period or after the Battle of Actium.[47] For another of the *agrimensores*, Frontinus, uses exactly this term with reference to Emerita when he reports that 'multis enim locis adsignationi agrorum inmanitas superfuit, sicut in Lusitania finibus Augustinorum' (in many places a huge quantity of land was left over after the assignation of land [sc., to colonists], for example, in Lusitania in the territory of the *Augustini*), by which he must mean 'in the territory of Augusta Emerita'.[48]

Even if it cannot be located precisely, it seems logical to suppose that Ataecina's sanctuary was situated in the vicinity of Santa Lucía del Trampal; that is, in a very strategic position near to the main Roman road that led north from Emerita to Asturica Augusta (the so-called 'Via de la Plata') and very close to the boundary between the territories of Emerita and Norba Caesarina. It was thus ideally situated to welcome devotees coming from the urban centre of Emerita 35 km to the south (about one day's travel on foot) or from the colony of Norba 40 km to the north. The significant traces of the cult in Emerita's territory, with important extensions to the north and north-east in the territories of Norba and, especially, Turgalium would suggest that this region was a focal point of her cult.[49] If the assumption that her cult existed prior to the arrival of the Roman colonists is correct, then we would have here an example of a local cult being officially adopted into the pantheon of the colony, perhaps even a case of *evocatio*, where a local divinity's power was recognized and harnessed by the Roman authorities for the ongoing benefit of Augusta Emerita.[50]

From the surviving texts found on the granite altars from Santa Lucía del Trampal, once again it is clear that the deity was invoked by a diversity of names, even more variegated than the sample from the urban centre discussed earlier: *D(ea) D(omina) S(ancta) T(uribrigensis) A(taecina), D(ea) D(omina) S(ancta) Turibri(gensis) Adaecina, D(ea) D(omina) S(ancta) Turibri(gensis) Attegina, D(ea) D(omina) Turibri(gensis) Adecina Sancta, Do(mina) D(ea) S(ancta) Turibri(g)e(nsis) Adegina, Domina Turibr(igensis) Attaeg[i]na S(ancta), Domina Turibri(gensis) [A]degina, Domina Turibri(gensis) Addaecin[a]* (Table 6.2, nos T3–10, T12–17), as well as one case where she is simply addressed as *Dom(ina)* (no. T11).[51] But for our purposes, the predominance of completely Roman onomastics among the devotees is once again what is most interesting. The two women whose dedications survive (nos T8, T10) each bore the *duo nomina* of a Roman citizen: Flavia Patricia and Iulia [S]ever(a), while among males, there are five individuals with the full *tria nomina* (nos T5, T6, T11, T13, T14) — L. Norb(anus) Severus, C. C(aecilius?) Severus, C. Val(erius) Telesphorus, L. Pontius Severinus, and [-] Caesius Cresce(n)s — and two with *duo nomina* (nos T7, T39): Annius Severus and Licinius Rusticus. (The omission of the *praenomen* became commoner at Emerita as the second century progressed, which provides a dating criterion for these dedications.) In just one surviving case did an individual with a single name make a dedication, Secun[d]u[s] (no. T17). While this might denote that he was a *peregrinus* or a slave, it might also be the case of a citizen using just his *cognomen* in making a private dedication.

---

45 García-Bellido 2001; Agenn. Urb., *De controv. agr.* 37 Thulin: '… ad lu>cum Feroniae Augustinorum iugera M haec in discrimen si venerunt, omnia supra dicta convenienter habere debent, ut illa si<nt>, quae secundum forma<m> proponuntur' ('If these thousand *iugera* at the sacred grove of Feronia of the Augustini have come into dispute, they ought to have by agreement all the features mentioned above, so that they should be those that are being proposed on the basis of the map (*forma*)', trans. B. Campbell). For further discussion of a possible link between Turobriga and Augustobriga, España-Chamorro 2021, 159–71.

46 For the ethnic *Augustanus*, see Edmondson and Hidalgo 2008, 483–93 nos 1–2 (= *AE* 2006, 615–16), with discussion at 496–98 and fig. 9 (table).

47 Campbell 2000, 342–43 and n. 36.

48 Frontin., *De Controv.* 9 Thulin.

49 For the diffusion of her cult, see Abascal 1995, 80–91, with fig. 55 (map).

50 See García-Bellido 2001, 68. In general on *evocatio* in the Roman Empire, Ando 2008, 128–48.

51 See further Abascal 1995, 64–65, 80–86.

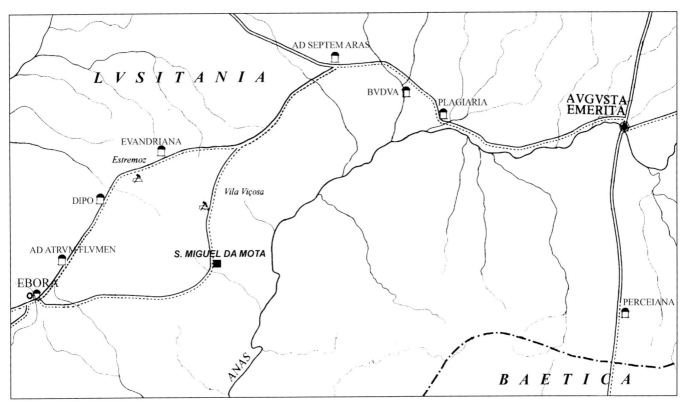

Figure 6.4. Location of the shrine of Endovellicus at São Miguel da Mota in relation to Augusta Emerita and Ebora, showing major and secondary roads, *mansiones*, and the marble quarries near Estremoz and Vila Viçosa (Schattner, Fabião, and Guerra 2013, 75 fig. 3).

## The Cult of Endovellicus at São Miguel da Mota (Terena, Alandroal)

The role that this shrine of Ataecina played in Emerita's cultic network was replicated at the sanctuary of another local divinity, Endovellicus, that flourished during the Roman period just outside the south-western limits of Emeritan territory at São Miguel da Mota (Terena, Androal, distr. Évora). This was linked by a secondary road (see Fig. 6.4) that allowed easy access both to Emerita, 120 km north-east, and the *municipium* of Ebora 'Liberalitas Iulia' (Évora), 70 km south-west, which gained the Latin rights of citizenship under Augustus (Plin., *NH* IV.117) and was one of the few Lusitanian cities ever to boast senators among its citizens.[52] It has recently been suggested that the sanctuary was extraterritorial, laying outside the *ager Emeritensis* and the *ager Eborensis*, and hence controlled by neither community.[53] It is difficult to say in the absence of any clear evidence one way or the other, but it would imply that the two communities had come to an agreement about this when Emerita's territorial boundaries were being established, with the full approval of the Roman provincial governor. What is certain is that the sanctuary lay near to the frontier between these two communities and, as a result, became a natural meeting place for the residents of both Emerita and Ebora.

With its eighty-nine inscribed votive altars, plaques, pedestals, and inscribed statues and statuettes and more than a hundred fragments of uninscribed sculpture, including four portrait-heads of the god, it boasts one of the largest assemblages of votive artefacts known from any local shrine in the Western Roman Empire. The majority of these were disengaged from the ruined early medieval chapel of São Miguel da Mota and uncovered in excavations in the vicinity of the chapel in the 1890s and 1900s by the leading Portuguese archaeologist, philologist, and ethnologist José Leite de Vasconcellos (1858–1941).[54] Excavations conducted since 2002 by a Portuguese-German team from the Universidade de Lisboa and the DAI Madrid under the direction of Carlos Fabião, Amílcar Guerra, and Thomas Schattner have resulted in further important new finds of sculpture in the

---

52 For senators from Ebora, Étienne 1982.
53 Schattner and others 2013, 78–79; see also Sinner and Revilla in this volume.

54 Vasconcellos 1905, 111–46. On Vasconcellos's career and accomplishments, see the articles published to mark the 150th anniversary of his birth in *O Arqueólogo Português*, 4th ser., 26 (2008).

chapel and done much to resolve a number of (though not all) archaeological issues relating to the site.⁵⁵ The god's sanctuary developed in an imposing natural setting with commanding views of the landscape for 30 km all around, as the site of an oracle and possible healing shrine in which incubation may have been practised.⁵⁶ It was in operation from the early-mid-first century CE to the fifth or even sixth century.⁵⁷ Firm traces of sanctuary buildings continue to elude archaeologists, though the marble caryatid discovered in the foundations of the chapel in 2002 evidently once fulfilled an architectural function in a Roman-style building on the site.⁵⁸

Endovellicus has traditionally been treated as a — or rather the — major 'indigenous' divinity of the province of Lusitania.⁵⁹ Studies of his cult in the late nineteenth and early twentieth centuries served to enhance Portuguese nationalism, as is visibly evoked on the title page of Vasconcellos's classic work *Religiões da Lusitânia*, which shows Henry the Navigator and a medallion commemorating the 400th anniversary of 'the discovery of India' by Vasco da Gama. However, the Luso-German excavations since 2002 have now make it clear that there was no identifiably pre-Roman phase of worship of the divinity at São Miguel da Mota. Furthermore, the cultic rites, as far as they can be reconstructed from the surviving votive texts, are completely in line with Graeco-Roman cult practices, which requires us to question just how 'indigenous' a deity Endovellicus was during the Roman period.

Like Ataecina, the god was invoked in a multiplicity of ways: *Endovellicus, Endovelicus, Endovollicus, Endovolicus, Enobolicus, Indovellicus, Deus Endovellicus, Deus E(- - -), Deus Indovellicus, Deus Sanctus Endovellicus, Deus Sanctus Indovellicus, Endovelicus Sanctus*, and *D(eus) D(ominus) Ennov(olicus)*.⁶⁰ As for cultic rites, three of the dedications were set up *ex responsu* (IRCP 484, 513, 530), i.e. following a response of this oracular deity, while three more were prompted explicitly 'by command of the divine power' (IRCP 488: *ex i(ussu) numin(is)*; 522: *ex relegione (sic) iussu numinis*, 487: *iussu ipsius*).

Some of these responses came, it appears, in dreamlike visions, as when Sit<o>nia Q. f. Victorina was inspired to set up a dedication to the god in light of a vision her father had experienced (IRCP 527: *ex visu Q. Sitoni Equestris patris sui*). Endovellicus also seems to have had connections to the underworld. One of the votive offerings was made 'as a result of an order from the underworld' (IRCP 528: *ex imperato averno*), to date an unparalleled expression in Latin epigraphy,⁶¹ while a number of iconographic elements sculpted on the votive dedications such as palm branches (symbolizing victory over death) or pine cones (symbolizing immortality) might also point to an infernal connection.⁶² The fact that a shrine of St Michael the Archangel, responsible for triumphing over the forces of Hell and for escorting Christian souls to heaven, was established on the site of Endovellicus's shrine in the seventh century and the fact that the small river that runs near the sanctuary is today known as the Ribeira de Lucefecit, a toponym etymologically connected to Lucifer/Satan, provide further hints of the infernal significance of this sacred space.

At least eight (about 10 per cent) of the known votives were set up explicitly to guarantee the good health of a family member (*pro salute* ... ) (see Table 6.3, with references) by a process very familiar from the cults of many other Greek and Roman divinities. So, for instance, M. L(icinius?) Nigellio 'set up a dedication to the god Endovellicus to guarantee the good health of L(icinia?) Marciana, his own daughter, fulfilling his vow in an enthusiastic frame of mind' (nos E46–47).⁶³ There are another two (or possibly three) examples of dedications set up in the hope of securing a daughter's good health (nos E43–44 and possibly no. E3), as well as single instances seeking to ensure the well-being of a father (no. E57), a son (no. E65), a slave (no. E13), and possibly a *mamma*, i.e. an affectionate term used to denote a surrogate mother-figure (no. E68).⁶⁴

---

55 Guerra and others 2003; 2005; Guerra 2008; Schattner and others 2013; Fitas 2013; Schattner 2019b, 141–45, with figs 2–3; 2022; this volume.

56 See Renberg 2006, 119, 133–34.

57 Schattner and others 2013, 74–77.

58 Schattner and others 2008; Schattner 2019b, 142–44, with fig. 2.

59 Encarnação 1975, 181–85; Blázquez Martínez 1975, 93–95; Garcia 1991, 310–29 no. 64–148 (in a chapter on 'indigenous divinities'); J. C. Ribeiro 2002b; Rives 2007, 77.

60 See Encarnação 1984, 802–03; J. C. Ribeiro 2002b, 88 (table); d. d.Ennov.: HEp 13, 2003–2004, 981 = AE 2004, 704; Guerra 2008, 164–65 no. 3, with fig. 28.5.

61 However, the phrase *ex imperato* is found in two votive texts from Castellum Elefantum in Numidia (ILAlg. II.3, 10123–24; cf. CIL VIII 6353 = 19335: *ex imperato domini Saturni*).

62 Palms: IRCP 495, 504, 511, 520; pine cone: IRCP 511, with Encarnação 1984, 805.

63 CIL II 5207 = IRCP 516: M. L(icinius?) Nigellio | deo Endovellico | sacrum pr[o] | salute | L(iciniae?). Marcian[(a)e?] | filiae su(a)e | v(otum) a(nimo) l(ibens) s(olvit).

64 CIL II 134 = IRCP 508, if we accept Hübner's suggestion, which he derived from Scaliger via Jan Gruter, that the text on the fragmentary altar was erroneously inscribed in line 6. Rather than *pro salute | Vivenniae | Venustae | Maniliae suae*, the stonecutter should have recorded that it was being set up *pro salute | Vivenniae | Venustae | mammae suae*. A polyonymous name with the *cognomen* Venusta sandwiched between two *gentilicia*, Vivennia and Manilia, is distinctly anomalous and

A number of the votive statues set up at the shrine were classically Roman in appearance, notably the eight statues or reliefs of togate males, dating to the mid-first century CE, and two second-century robed female figures carrying offerings.[65]

The social profile of Endovellicus's devotees also suggests that it was a local cult fully integrated within the ritual world of two of the most Roman communities in the province of Lusitania. The onomastics of those who dedicated votive offerings and those whose well-being was the object of a vow to the deity (Table 6.3) are in very large part Roman — both in the linguistic root of the names used and in their overall onomastic structure.[66] *Tria nomina* or — in the case of women — *duo nomina* are very well represented among those of free status who are attested. The overwhelming majority of names do not include filiation or libertination, and so these individuals are, in epigraphic terms, 'incerti'; i.e. it is unclear whether they were of free birth (*ingenui*) or freedmen/freedwomen (*liberti*). In fact, just eight include filiation (nos E1, E3-9), proving their free-born status, to whom we may safely add the polyonymous Roman equestrian, Sex. Cocceius Craterus Honorinus (no. E2). Of these nine, only one — Q. Sevius Q. f. Pap. Firmanus (no. E5) — has his Roman voting tribe included: the *Papiria*, indicating that he was a citizen of Augusta Emerita, clear proof of the participation of Emeritenses in the rural cult.

The text on the votive column set up by the one securely attested freedman, Hermes [...] P. [l]ib. (no. E10), is so damaged that it is impossible to reconstruct his full name. Other freedmen and freedwomen might well lurk among the 'incerti', but there are no characteristically servile *cognomina* represented that would provide some possible clues. On the other hand, three male slaves are attested as dedicators of vows: Blandus, slave of Caelia Rufina (no. E11; Fig. 6.5a), Hermes, slave of Aurelia Vibia Sabina (no. E12), and Vitalis, son and slave of Messius Sympaeron (no. E14). In addition, a female slave, Vernacla, slave of Treb(ia?) Musa (or Treb(icia) Musa) (no. E13), was the object of a vow for her well-being, initiated by Q. L(icinius?) Catullus (no. E45), although it is difficult to deduce Catullus's motives for seeking Endovellicus's aid to help someone else's slave. One of these slave dedicators is particularly intriguing: Hermes, slave of Aurelia Vibia Sabina (no. E12). Not only does he identify his profession — he was a marble-worker (*marmorarius*), which very likely connects him to the exploitation of the marble quarries of the Vila Viçosa–Estremoz region, just 10-15 km from the sanctuary — but he was possibly also an imperial slave, if we identify his owner, Aurelia Vibia Sabina, as the daughter of Marcus Aurelius, who was born *c.* 170 and lived into the reign of Caracalla. This identification was proposed by Hübner (at *CIL* II 133 and p. xxxviii) but rejected by José d'Encarnação in his more recent edition of the text (*IRCP* 497) on the simple assertion that he did not consider it plausible that a slave linked to the imperial family would be active in this region. But if the Vila Viçosa–Estremoz marble quarries had passed, at least in part, under imperial ownership, which is certainly plausible, and specifically under the ownership of Marcus's daughter, then there would be a perfectly good reason for the imperial slave to be present at the nearby quarries and, as a result, active at the sanctuary of the most powerful local god.[67]

In terms of the individual elements of the names attested, there is a strong preponderance of Roman *gentilicia* and *cognomina*. Not surprisingly, Iulii predominate, but other standard Roman family names are also well represented: Annius, Antonius, Arrius, Calpurnius, Helvius, Iunius, Livius, Petronius, Pompeius, Pomponius, Sempronius, Terentius, Tullius, Valerius, and Vibius. A very similar onomastic profile is found at the two civic communities located in closest proximity to the sanctuary: Ebora and Augusta Emerita.[68] On the other hand, a handful of very rare *gentilicia* also survive: Critonius (nos E3, E26), Magolius (no. E49), Olius (no. E9), Sitonius (nos E6, E56), Turrecius (no. E60), Vesidius (nos E64–65), and Vivennius (no. E68). Of these, Magolius, Sitonius, and Turrecius are unparalleled anywhere in the Roman world (though Sitnia, a syncopated form of Sitonia, is attested once on a ceramic stamp from Bagacum in Gallia Belgica),[69] while the names Olius and Vesidius, which occur occasionally in Italy and in certain provinces, are otherwise

---

difficult to accept. For *mammae* in general in Roman society, see Bradley 1991.

65 *Togati*: J. C. Ribeiro 2002a, 383 no. 35 see Table 6.3 on p. 98, nos E64–65), 386 nos 40–42 (togate statues or reliefs); Guerra and others 2003, 466 no. 4, with figs 43–44. Female figures: Guerra and others 2003, 463–65 nos 2–3, with figs 39–42. See further Schattner, this volume.

66 For an earlier onomastic study of the cult's devotees, see Dias and Coelho 1995–1997.

67 On the quarries, Alarcão and Tavares 1988; Carneiro 2019. For arguments that Marcus Aurelius's daughter did own some of these quarries, see Mayer 2008.

68 For details, consult the ADOPIA digital atlas of personal names from the Iberian Peninsula: <http://adopia.huma-num.fr> [accessed 15 July 2020].

69 *Carte archéologique de la Gaule*. 59.2. *Le Nord, Bavay* (Paris 2011), 360.

Figure 6.5. Votive altar set up to Deo Indovellico by Blandus, slave of Caelia Rufina, São Miguel da Mota (*IRCP* 489, MNA, Lisbon). Funerary altar of C. Rubrius Flaccus, Tuccitan(us), Emerita (*CIL* II 522; MNAR, Mérida) (photos: J. Edmondson).

unattested in the Iberian Peninsula.⁷⁰ Critonius is found in the variant form Cretonius in single examples from Rome (*CIL* VI 35067), Ostia (*CIL* XIV 5032), and Badajoz in the territory of Emerita (*AE* 1971, 147), while a Vivennia Badia is attested in the territory of Ebora (*IRCP* 408, São Pedro, Évora). Of all the communities in Lusitania, Emerita has by far the largest percentage of such rare *gentilicia*, which may well reflect the more variegated onomastic range of the earliest settlers at the colony.⁷¹ These 'fossiles onomastiques' were not in general taken up by local families when they assumed Roman names after gaining Roman citizenship or the Latin rights; they were much more likely to originate with immigrants from Italy who arrived in the province in the late Republic or as settlers in the five triumviral or Augustan colonies.⁷² As such, devotees with these rare *gentilicia* are more likely to have come from Emerita than from any other Lusitanian community.

Conversely, only a handful of 'local' or 'indigenous' elements are detectable in the onomastic record from the sanctuary. The single name Conicodius (no. E15) has been interpreted as an indigenous name, connected etymologically to the Conii, a pre-Roman people from the far west of the Iberian Peninsula.

However, the interpretation of this text is very difficult and the reading of the name far from certain. A small number of *cognomina* do have a local flavour: (a) Arrius Badiolus (no. E22): Badiolus is only otherwise attested in Lusitania at Emerita and Salacia and in the neighbouring province of Baetica at Hispalis;⁷³ (b) [- C]alpurnius Dobetianus (no. E24): Dobetianus is a hapax, but it may be connected etymologically to the distinctively Lusitanian names of Dobiteinus/Doviteinus and Dobiterus, of which twenty or so examples are known almost exclusively from northern Lusitania;⁷⁴ (c) C. Iulius Caturonis [f. - - - ], i.e. whose cognomen is lost because of damage to the stone (no. E42): this man might be a first-generation Roman citizen or first-generation holder of the *ius Latii*, since he gives his filiation not in the Roman manner by reference to his father's *praenomen*, but by his father's single name, Caturo, of which another twenty-six attestations are known from central and northern with another ten from the far north-west of the Iberian Peninsula.⁷⁵ Otherwise, individual scattered examples are known only from Transpadane Gaul, Sardinia, and Mauretania Caesariensis, while two cases occur at military bases in Dalmatia, where both Meduttus Caturonis f. and Veranus Caturonis f. (*AE* 1907, 249; 2000, 1179) served in the *cohors I Bracaraugustanorum*, i.e. an auxiliary unit that took its name and very likely these two conscripts — and perhaps others too — from people from the area of Bracara Augusta (Braga in northern Portugal).⁷⁶

Of all the devotees, Antubellicus Priscus (no. E21) has arguably the most strikingly unusual *gentilicium*. The name Antubellicus, which in form looks like a *cognomen* but here apparently serves as a *gentilicium*, is unparalleled anywhere in the Roman Empire. It may, however, be related to the native name Antubelus, found only in Lusitania in two instances from the modern province of Cáceres.⁷⁷ Nevertheless, the altar that Antubellicus Priscus dedicated (92 cm tall by 50 cm wide by 42 cm deep) was one of the largest and finest to have survived with very carefully executed lettering.⁷⁸ Indeed a number of the votive altars are very similar in form and fabric to votive

---

70 cf. *OPEL* 3.112 (Olius/Ollius); 4.161 (Vesidius).
71 See Edmondson 2006a, 109–20; forthcoming.
72 'Fossiles onomastiques': Navarro Caballero 2000; 2006.

73 Emerita: *HEp* 11, 2001, 58; Salacia: *IRCP* 195; Hispalis: *CIL* II 1223 = *CILA* II.1, 64.
74 cf. Vallejo Ruiz 2005, 304–10.
75 Lusitania: <http://adopia.huma-num.fr/names/565> [accessed 8 July 2022]. North-western Iberia: Vallejo Ruiz 2005, 267–71.
76 According to a search on the Epigraphik-Datenbank Clauss/Slaby (EDCS) <http://www.manfredclauss.de/> [accessed 15 July 2020].
77 Boutius Antubel(i) f. (*CIL* II 756 = *CILCC* I 24, Alcántara); Amoena Antubeli f. (*AE* 2000, 698 = *CILCC* IV 1313, Villamiel).
78 *CIL* II 5202; *IRCP* 487; J. C. Ribeiro 2002a, 392–93 no. 54, with photo.

and funerary altars from Emerita (see Fig. 6.5), and some of the votive and architectural sculpture from the shrine bears an uncanny resemblance to sculpture found at the provincial capital.[79] This suggests that the marble workshops of the provincial capital played some role at the sanctuary site.

This generally Roman onomastic profile and the lack of much of an indigenous imprint are telling, I would argue, in how we should interpret the cult. From what may be deduced from the surviving votives, Endovellicus was not some popular indigenous god worshipped by non-Romans among the local population, anxious to assert something of their pre-Roman identity. Still less can the god be seen as a locus of resistance against Roman rule. Rather, his cult attracted full Roman citizens and even men of the equestrian order. Soldiers too seem to have been active here. One of the surviving votive sculptures depicts a man in military uniform wearing *caligae*,[80] while a reference to a *cohors* in one of the ten small fragments of a metrical dedication (perhaps a hymn) to the god (*CIL* II 6333 = *IRCP* 482, fragment c) led Hübner to argue that it was set up by a soldier. If it is legitimate to identify Hermes (no. E12) as the slave of a daughter of Marcus Aurelius (see above, p. 89 and n. 67), then imperial slaves were involved in the cult as well. In sum, it seems more prudent to conclude that it was the Roman citizen inhabitants of the *colonia* of Emerita and those with the Latin rights of citizenship from the *municipium* at Ebora who were the main participants in the cult of a god whose sanctuary lay near the boundary between the territories of these two communities.

## Conclusions

An examination of cult activity in the urban centre and rural territory of Emerita and its environs shows that the texture of religious activity in this part of Lusitania was complex and multifaceted in the imperial period. Emerita certainly had the cult places and organized civic cults that one would expect in a Roman colony, a type of community that was 'propagated from the Roman state', to borrow Aulus Gellius's formulation, and which had 'all the laws and institutions of the Roman people, not those of their choice'. As a result, 'this condition' was felt to be 'preferable and superior because of the greatness and majesty of the Roman people, of which those colonies are seen to be, as it were, small replicas

and mirror-images'.[81] Aulus Gellius needs to be corrected, however, on one point: Roman colonies did have some choice of their own. We have seen how in a provincial setting there was some latitude for a colony to develop the most appropriate religious pantheon in the particular geographical and cultural environment in which it was founded. To be sure, colonies were expected to cultivate the state gods of the Roman people and to play a lead role in worshipping the *divi* and *divae*, the deified members of the *domus Augusta*, at both the municipal and provincial levels. But the local senate and magistrates of a colony such as Emerita could choose at the same time to incorporate local gods into local cultic activity, as they saw fit. This is clear from a *lex sacra* regulating the cults of the Roman colony of Carthage in Africa Proconsularis (*AE* 1999, 1835–41 = 2007, 1721–37), in the surviving fragments of which the Capitoline triad, Volcanus, Spes, the Cereres, Isis, Bona Dea (possibly), and a local divinity Abbadir are all mentioned.[82] As we have seen, precisely that same phenomenon occurred at Emerita, in its urban and rural cultic activity.

What does seem clear is that the implantation of a Roman colony at Emerita did have an impact on the cults of local deities. They came to incorporate at least some Graeco-Roman ritual practices that made them comprehensible and palatable to the original colonists, who had been born in Italy or other parts of the Mediterranean before serving in the legions and then being discharged and granted land at the new colony.[83] It was in this Roman colonial context that a fully fledged sanctuary of Endovellicus developed in the early first century CE at São Miguel da Mota, a cult place that came to attract devotees from Emerita, a Roman colony, and also from Ebora, a *municipium* with the *ius Latii*, whereby the community's elite gained full Roman citizenship after serving as local magistrates. Emeritenses and Eborenses could participate in these local cults without feeling they were betraying their full or partial Roman status.

Doubtless at the same time these local gods also retained their appeal for those Lusitanians who were not full Roman citizens or Latins, but who remained, in Roman legal terms, *peregrini*. Performing cult acts at such shrines facilitated the preservation of cul-

---

79 For the relationship of the caryatid and togates from the shrine to sculptural workshops at Emerita, Schattner and others 2008.
80 J. C. Ribeiro 2002a, 387 no. 43, with photo.
81 Gell. XVI.13.8–9: 'ex civitate quasi propagatae sunt et iura institutaque omnia populi Romani, non sui arbitrii, habent. Quae tamen condicio, cum sit magis obnoxia et minus libera, potior tamen et praestabilior existimatur propter amplitudinem maiestatemque populi Romani, cuius istae coloniae quasi effigies parvae simulacraque esse quaedam videntur'.
82 See further Ennabli and Scheid 2007–2008; Ando 2020, 353–56.
83 For their origins, Edmondson 2006a, 107–21.

tural memory of some aspects of the pre-Roman past and perhaps even the invention of tradition about that Lusitanian or Vettonian past. The processes in play here may have been somewhat analogous to the appearance of inscribed texts in the language modern philologists call 'Lusitanian', which only occurred after the region was firmly under Roman imperial control.[84] As a result, local cults such as those of Ataecina-Proserpina or Endovellicus offered a cultural setting in which both Romans and non-Romans could assert their distinctive identities, as they congregated for devotional purposes in the *lieux de rencontre* that these sanctuaries provided. During the Roman imperial period, these cults were neither indigenous nor Roman, but rather a subtle amalgam of both, with local gods reinterpreted and re-visioned in a world now firmly controlled by Rome.

As elsewhere, the Roman authorities preferred, for the most part, not to eradicate the local pasts they came to confront, but rather to harness local traditions and especially local divinities to become part of the new political, social, and cultural world that was Roman Lusitania.[85]

---

84   For a recent synthesis, Luján 2019.

85   The author would like to thank Dr José María Álvarez Martínez and Dr Trinidad Nogales Basarrate, successive Directors, and all the staff of the Museo Nacional de Arte Romano, Mérida, and Félix Palma García, Director, and Luis Ángel Hidalgo Martín of the Consorcio de la Ciudad Monumental de Mérida, for all their assistance during my work on the inscriptions of Emerita. He would also like to thank the Social Sciences and Humanities Research Council of Canada/Conseil de recherches en sciences humaines for its ongoing support of his research. This study forms part of the research project 'Inscripciones latinas de Augusta Emerita (ILAE)' (PGC2018-101698-B-I00, P.I.: Prof. A. Alvar Ezquerra). He is also most grateful to Dr José Luis Ramírez Sádaba (Universidad de Cantabria) for making available the text of *CIVAE* prior to its publication.

Table 6.1. Votive inscriptions from the urban centre of Emerita (m = marble; gr = granite).

| | Deity | Dedicator | Type | Date | Reference |
|---|---|---|---|---|---|
| 1 | Ataecina: [Ataec]inae [Sanc]tae | L. Cornel[ius] Herc(u)la[nus] | block (m) | 75–125 | *AE* 2009, 527–28; *HEp* 20, 2011, 19; *CIVAE* 5; *CILAE* 1512 |
| 2 | Ataecina: [Deae] Tur[ibrig(ensi) | Q. Cor[nelius ---] | pedestal (m) | 150–250 | *AE* 2015, 542; *CIVAE* 7; *CILAE* 1540 |
| 3 | Ataecina/Proserpina: Ataecinae [T]urebrigae Proserpinae (JE reads [T]uribrigae) | Musa[---] (Mus[aeus]?) | altar (m) | 50–200 | *AE* 2016, 686; *CIVAE*, Apéndice no. 2; *CILAE* 1567 (now in Oña, BU, but likely from Mérida or region) |
| 4 | Ataecina: D(eae) S(anctae) A(taecinae) T(uribrigensi) | P. Vitia[---] | ? | ? | *CIL* II 461; *CIVAE* 4; *CILAE* 1559 |
| 5 | Ataecina: Deae Atae[ci]n(ae) Tur[ibrig(ensi)] | ? | altar (m) | 75–125 | *AE* 2009, 529; *HEp* 20, 2011, 21; *CIVAE* 3; *CILAE* 1523 |
| 6 | Ataecina: Deae Ataecinae Turobrigen(si) Sanctae | Artemas Claudi [M]artilini ser. | altar (m) | 1–100 | *EE* IX 42; *CMBad* 758; *ILER* 732; *CIVAE* 2; *CILAE* 1552 |
| 7 | Ataecina: Deae Sanc(tae) Turib(rigensi) Fig. 6.3b | L. Iuventius Iulianus | altar (m) | 50–150 | *EE* IX 43; *CMBad* 759; *ILER* 733; *CIVAE* 6; *CILAE* 1509 |
| 8 | Ataecina: Deae Sanctae Fig. 6.3d | [-] Sentius Marsus | altar (m) | 125–200 | *HEp* 2, 1990, 34; 6, 1996, 135; *CIVAE* 9; *CILAE* 1526 |
| 9 | Ataecina: Deae Sanctae | L. Caelius Philinus | altar (m) | 50–150 | *AE* 1976, 269; 1983, 486; *HAE* 2681; *CIVAE* 8; *CILAE* 1547 |
| 10 | Aug(usto) sacr(um) | none | pedestal (m), theatre | 98–117 | *CIL* II 471; *CIIAE* 27; *CIVAE* 64; *CILAE* 1577 |
| 11 | Aug(usto) sacr(um) | none | pedestal (m), theatre | 98–117 | *CIIAE* 28; *AE* 2003, 868; *CIVAE* 65; *CILAE* 1606 |
| 12 | Aug(usto) sacr(um) | none | pedestal (m), theatre | 98–117 | *CIIAE* 29; *AE* 2003, 869; *CIVAE* 66; *CILAE* 1612 |
| 13 | Aug(usto) sacr(um) | none | pedestal (m), theatre | 98–117 | *CIIAE* 30; *AE* 2003, 870; *CIVAE* 67; *CILAE* 1604 |
| 14 | Aug(usto) sacr(um) | none | pedestal (m), theatre | 98–117 | *CIIAE* 31; *AE* 2003, 871; *CIVAE* 68; *CILAE* 1605 |
| 15 | Aug(usto) sacr(um) | none | pedestal (m), theatre | 98–117 | *CIIAE* 32; *AE* 2003, 872; *CIVAE* 69; *CILAE* 1613 |
| 16 | Cautes: Caute | Tib. Cl(audius) Artemidorus, pat[er] | ? | 130–200 | *CIL* II 464; *CIVAE* 82; *CILAE* 1561 |
| 17 | Concordiae Augusti | — | pedestal (m) | 50–60 | *CIL* II 465; *AE* 2005, 760; 2006, 582; *CIIAE* 52, Röring and Trillmich 2010; *CIVAE* 72; *CILAE* 1603 |
| 18 | ? Deae [---] Genio [---]? | M. Aur(elius) [---] | plaque (m) | 250–300 | *AE* 2006, 587; *HEp* 15, 2006, 53; *CIVAE* 94; *CILAE* 1543 |
| 19 | Deis omnibus | Rufus | altar (m) | 50–200 | *CMBad* 769; *ILER* 527; *CIVAE* 28; *CILAE* 1514 |
| 20 | [D]ivo Au[gusto] | ? | pedestal (m) | 14–42 | Gamo and Murciano 2016–2017 [2020] (*AE* 2018, 825); *CILAE* 1674 |
| 21 | Divo A[ugusto] et Diva[e Augustae] | ? | ? (m) | 42–68 | Edmondson 1997, 89–91 no. 1 (*AE* 1997, 777a; *HEp* 7, 1997, 110); *CIIAE* 20; *CIVAE* 61; *CILAE* 1622 |

Table 6.1. Votive inscriptions from the urban centre of Emerita *(cont.)*.

| | **Deity** | **Dedicator** | **Type** | **Date** | **Reference** |
|---|---|---|---|---|---|
| 22 | Divo Augusto et [divae Aug(ustae)] | Albinus Albui f., flamen d[ivi Augusti et] divae Aug(ustae) provinciae Lusitan[iae] | pedestal (m) | 42–54 | *CIL* II 473, rev. Edmondson 1997, 91–103 no. 2 (*AE* 1997, 777b; *HEp* 7, 1997, 111); *CIVAE* 62; *CILAE* 1586 |
| 23 | Divo Sigerio Stillifero Fig. 6.3a | Val. Festianus | altar (m) | 125–200 | *CMBad* 768; *HAE* 409; *AE* 1955, 234; *ILER* 6004; *CIVAE* 27, rev. JE; *CILAE* 1507 |
| 24 | Edigenio Domn[i]co | Trophimus | altar (m) | 100–200 | *ERAE* 30; Gamer 1989, BA 57, fig. 85d; *CIVAE* 25; *CILAE* 1511 |
| 25 | Edigenio? | ?Iul. Ascani[u]s | altar (m) | 100–200 | *EE* IX 72; *CIVAE* 103; *CILAE* 1564 |
| 26 | Fontano | Seranus | altar (gr) | 1–100 | *HEp* 7, 1997, 124; rev. Edmondson 2006a, 57 and n. 115, fig. 1.50; *CIVAE* 30; *CILAE* 1533 |
| 27 | Font(ano) or Font(anae) or Font(ibus) | pro salute Q. C(---) P(---) | altar (m) | 100–200 | *ILER* 541; *ERAE* 6; *CIVAE* 32; *CILAE* 1557 |
| 28 | Fontibus | Iul. Lupu[s] | altar (m) | 125–200 | *CIL* II 466; *CIVAE* 31; *CILAE* 1553 |
| 29 | Fortunae | [---]atius [D]emetrius | altar (m) | ? | *CIL* II 467; *CIVAE* 33; *CILAE* 1556 |
| 30 | Fortunae | none | altar (m) | 100–200 | *CIL* II 5262; *CIVAE* 34; *CILAE* 1565 |
| 31 | G(enio) Augusti | d(ecreto) d(ecurionum) | plaque (m) | 98–117 | *CMBad* 761; *HEp* 18, 2009, 42; *CIIAE* 33; *CIVAE* 70; *CILAE* 1520 |
| 32 | G(enio) c(oloniae) I(uliae) A(ugustae) E(meritae) | C. Antistius C. lib. Iucundus | pedestal (m) | 75–150 | *CMBad* 762; *HAE* 557, rev. *AE* 1984, 485; cf. Étienne and Mayet 1984, 168; Edmondson 2007, 547–48 no. 3, fig. 6; *CIVAE* 35; Trillmich 2016–2017 [2020] (*AE* 2018, 827); *CILAE* 1508. |
| 33 | Iunoni | Claudius Daphnus | altar (m) | 125–200 | *EE* IX 44; *CMBad* 757; *ILER* 367; *CIVAE* 36; *CILAE* 1551 |
| 34 | Deo Iovi | Aemilius Aemilianus, v.p., p(raeses) p(rov.) U(lterioris) L(usitaniae) | altar (m) | 275–282 | *AE* 1992, 957; *HEp* 5, 1995, 81; *CIVAE* 39; *CILAE* 1530 |
| 35 | Iovi Aug(usto) | M. Arrius Laurus + Paccia Flaccilla, in honorem M. Arri Reburri, Lanc(iensis) Transc(udani), filii optimi | pedestal (m) | 75–100 | *CIL* II 5261, rev. Stylow 1987, 116–17 no. A3 (*AE* 1987, 484; *HEp* 2, 1990, 36); *CIVAE* 40; *CILAE* 1555 |
| 36 | Iovi S[ol]u[t]or[io] | C. [I]uli[us ---] | plaque (m) | 150–220 | *CIVAE* 41; *CILAE* 1541 |
| 37 | Lacipaea(e) | Valerii Proculus et Vitulus, Termestini | plaque (m) | 58 | *EE* VIII 23; *ILER* 859; *CIVAE* 26; *CILAE* 1521 |
| 38 | L(aribus) A(ugustis) or L(ibero) A(ugusto) | Q. Nonius Prim(us), miles leg. VII Gemin(a)e F(elicis) | altar (m) | 150–197 | *AE* 2015, 544; *CIVAE* 49; cf. Le Roux 2019; *CILAE* 1532 |
| 39 | L(ibero) P(atri) | none | altar (m) | 50–200 | *CIL* II 5937 (from Emerita, not Carthago Nova); *CIVAE* 50; *CILAE* 1549 |
| 40 | Marti | L. Cocceius Vi[---] | altar (m) | 50–150 | *HEp* 1, 1989, 108; *CIVAE* 52; *CILAE* 1566 |
| 41 | Marti | (Domitia) Vettilla Paculi (uxor) | epistyle (m) | 140–180 | *CIL* II 468; *CIVAE* 51; *CILAE* 1546 |
| 42 | Deo Marti A[ug(usto)] | Iul. Maximinu[s], v.p., proc(urator) Aug(usti) n(ostri), a(gens) v(ice) p(raesidis) p(rov.) [L(usitaniae)] | pedestal (m) | 260–280 | Edmondson 2007; *AE* 2007, 721; *HEp* 15, 2007, 12; *CIVAE* 53; *CILAE* 1516 |
| 43 | M(atri) D(eorum) | Val(eria) Avita | altar (m) | 175–200 | *CIL* II 5260; *CIVAE* 73; *CILAE* 1548 |

Table 6.1. Votive inscriptions from the urban centre of Emerita *(cont.)*.

| | Deity | Dedicator | Type | Date | Reference |
|---|---|---|---|---|---|
| 44 | Mithras (statue of Oceanus) | G. Acc(ius) Hedychrus, p(ater) patrum | statue (m) | c. 155 | AE 1905, 26; CMBad 1089; HAE 667, 1637; CIMRM I, 779; CIVAE 83; CILAE 1501 |
| 45 | Mithras: Deo Invicto | pro salute G. Iuli | altar (m) | 130–200 | CMBad 776; HAE 686, 2693; ILER 284; CIMRM I, 795; CIVAE 78; CILAE 1503 |
| 46 | Mithras: Deo Invicto | C. Camilius Superat(us) | altar (m) | 130–200 | CMBad 767; HAE 2692; ILER 280; CIMRM I, 796; CIVAE 79; CILAE 1506 |
| 47 | Mithras: Invict[o Mithrae?] | Hector Cornelior(um) (ser.), ex visu | altar (m) | 150–175 | HAE 1840; AE 1962, 67; 1984, 487; HEp 1, 1989, 99; CIVAE 81; CILAE 1528 |
| 48 | Mithras: Invicto | C. Curius Avitus, Acci(o) Hedychro pa(tre) | statue (m) | c. 155 | AE 1915, 67; 1919, 87; CMBad 1083; HAE 815, 2691; CIMRM I, 773; CIVAE 80; CILAE 1513 |
| 49 | Mithras: Invicto Deo | Quintio Flavi Baetici Conimbrig(ensis) ser., pro sal(ute) Coutii Lupi | altar (m) | 130–175 | AE 1905, 24; CMBad 765; HAE 668, 2694; CIMRM I, 794; CIVAE 77; CILAE 1562 |
| 50 | Mithras: Invicto Deo Mithrae | G. Accius Hedychrus, pater | statue (m) | c. 155 | AE 1915, 68; 1919, 86; CMBad 1088; CIMRM I, 781; CIVAE 75; CILAE 1502 |
| 51 | Mithras: Invicto Mithrae | M. Val. Secundus, fr(umentarius) leg. VII Gem. | altar (m) | 155 | AE 1905, 25; ILS 9297; CMBad 764; HAE 666; ILER 278; CIMRM I, 793; CIVAE 76; CILAE 1504 |
| 52 | Nemesis: Deae Invictae Caelesti Nemesi | M. Aurelius Fhilo (*sic*) Roma | plaque (stucco) from amphitheatre | 200–235 | AE 1961, 48; HEp 6, 1996, 127, rev. EAOR VII 58, reading *Fhilo* rather than *Felic(i)o*; CIVAE 84; CILAE 1525 |
| 53 | Nemesis: Dominae cur(atrici) anima[e] | name missing | pedestal (m) | 125–200 | AE 1984, 486; Edmondson 2007, 548 no. 4, fig. 7a-b; CIVAE 85; CILAE 1510 |
| 54 | ? Neptune | ? respublica Emeritensium | ? | ? | Díaz y Pérez 1887, 354 |
| 55 | Nymphi[s] | M[- - -]? L[- - -]? | altar (m) | ? | ERAE 8; CIVAE 56; CILAE 1519 |
| 56 | Nymphis | I(ul.) Saturninus | altar (?) | 125–225 | CIL II 469; CIVAE 55; CILAE 1558 |
| 57 | Proserpina: Deae Sanc[tae] Proserpin[ae] Fig. 6.3c | L. Claudiu[s] Donatus | altar (m) | 100–150 | AE 2015, 541; CIVAE 57; CILAE 1538 |
| 58 | [S]arapi[di] | ? | ? | ? | CMBad 763; HAE 669; CIMRM I, 792; CIVAE 86; CILAE 1560 |
| 59 | Veneri Victrici | L. Cordius Symphorus, medicus | altar (m) | 100–150 | CIL II 470; EE VIII 16; CIVAE 60; CILAE 1550 |
| 60 | not given | D. Paccius Agathopus pro salute Marciae Matronae | altar (m) | 100–150 | HEp 1, 1989, 105; CIVAE 90; CILAE 1522 |
| 61 | not given | Dionisius [pr]o sal(ute) [S]emproni Frontonis | altar (m) | 70–100 | AE 2009, 530; CIVAE 92; CILAE 1529 |
| 62 | ? | [- - -, mil. Leg. VI]I G.F. (centuria) Mercato[ris] | circular plaque (slate) | 75–100 | Hidalgo Martín and Chamizo 2012–2013 [2018] (AE 2017, 626); CIVAE 95; CILAE 1545 |
| 63 | ? | M. Antistius Marcellianus | altar (m) | 50–120 | ERAE 33; CIVAE 88; CILAE 1505 |
| 64 | ? | ? | altar (m) | 50–200 | CIVAE 96 |

Table 6.2. Votive inscriptions from the territory of Emerita (m = marble; gr = granite).

|  | Deity | Dedicator | Type | Date | Reference | Find-spot (see Fig. 6.1) |
|---|---|---|---|---|---|---|
| T1 | Ataecina/Proserpina: Deae Ataecinae Turibrig(ensi) Proserpinae | none | *defixio* plaque (m) | 150–225 | CIL II 462; CIVAE 1; CILAE 1517 | Roman reservoir 'Proserpina', 7.5 km N. of Mérida (BA) |
| T2 | Ataecina-Proserpina: [Deae Sanctae Ataecinae Turibrigae] Proserpinae | Severianus Aug(ustalis) | altar (m) | 175–225 | HEp 5, 1995, 76; CIVAE 10; CILAE 2170 | La Garrovilla (BA) |
| T3 | Ataecina: [T]uribri(gensi) A[t/d]ecin[ae ------] | (name missing) | altar (gr) | 175–300 | AE 1995, 747; CILCC I 40; CIVAE 21; CILAE 2009 | Sta. Lucía del Trampal, Alcuéscar (CC) |
| T4 | Ataecina: D(eae) D(ominae) S(anctae) [------] | (name missing) | altar (gr) | 1–200 | AE 1995, 735; CILCC I 39; CIVAE 15; CILAE 2008 | Sta. Lucía del Trampal, Alcuéscar (CC) |
| T5 | Ataecina: D(eae) D(ominae) S(anctae) T(uribrigensi) A(taecinae) | L. Norb(anus) Severus | altar (gr) | 75–200 | AE 1995, 738; CILCC I 33; CIVAE 13; CILAE 2002 | Sta. Lucía del Trampal, Alcuéscar (CC) |
| T6 | Ataecina: D(eae) D(ominae) S(anctae) Turibri(gensi) Adaecinae | C. C(aecilius?) Severus | altar (gr) | 100–200 | AE 1995, 737; CILCC I 44; CIVAE 12; CILAE 2013 | Sta. Lucía del Trampal, Alcuéscar (CC) |
| T7 | Ataecina: D(eae) D(ominae) S(anctae) Turibri(gensi) Atteginae | Annius Severus | altar (gr) | 150–200 | AE 1995, 736; CILCC I 36; CIVAE 11; CILAE 2005 | Sta. Lucía del Trampal, Alcuéscar (CC) |
| T8 | Ataecina: D(eae) D(ominae) Turibri(gensi) Adecin(a)e Sanct(a)e | Flavia Patricia | altar (gr) | 75–125 | AE 1995, 734; CILCC I 42; CIVAE 22; CILAE 2011 | Sta. Lucía del Trampal, Alcuéscar (CC) |
| T9 | Ataecina: D(eae) Dom[i]nae Tur(ibrigensi) ------ | (name missing) | altar (gr) | 75–100 | AE 1995, 740; CILCC I 43; CIVAE 16; CILAE 2012 | Sta. Lucía del Trampal, Alcuéscar (CC) |
| T10 | Ataecina: Do(minae) D(eae) S(anctae) Turibri(g)e(nsi) Adegin(a)e | Iulia [S]ever(a) | altar (gr) | 1–200 | AE 1995, 739; CILCC I 41; CIVAE 14; CILAE 2010 | Sta. Lucía del Trampal, Alcuéscar (CC) |
| T11 | Ataecina: Dom(inae) | C. Val(erius) Telesphorus | altar (gr) | 50–125 | AE 1995, 745; CILCC I 47; CIVAE 42; CILAE 2016 | Sta. Lucía del Trampal, Alcuéscar (CC) |
| T12 | Ataecina: Domina[e ------] | (name missing) | altar (gr) | 75–125 | AE 1995, 744; CILCC I 38; CIVAE 24; CILAE 2007 | Sta. Lucía del Trampal, Alcuéscar (CC) |
| T13 | Ataecina: Domina[e] Turibr(igensi) Attaeg[i]nae S(anctae) | L. Pontius Severinus | altar (gr) | 75–125 | AE 1995, 741; CILCC I 34; CIVAE 17; CILAE 2003 | Sta. Lucía del Trampal, Alcuéscar (CC) |
| T14 | Ataecina: Dominae Turibri(gensi) [A]deginae | [-] Caesius Cresce(n)s | altar (gr) | 75–125 | AE 1995, 742; CILCC I 32; CIVAE 18; CILAE 2001 | Sta. Lucía del Trampal, Alcuéscar (CC) |
| T15 | Ataecina: Dominae Turibri(gensi) Addaecin[ae] | (name missing) | altar (gr) | 75–200 | AE 1995, 743; CILCC I 35; CIVAE 19; CILAE 2004 | Sta. Lucía del Trampal, Alcuéscar (CC) |
| T16 | Ataecina: S(anctae) D(eae) D(ominae) [T]uri[b]ri(gensi) +++[---] | (name missing) | altar (gr) | 100–300 | AE 1995, 748; HEp 6, 1996, 194; CILCC I 45; CIVAE 23; CILAE 2014 | Sta. Lucía del Trampal, Alcuéscar (CC) |
| T17 | Ataecina: Tur(ibrigensi) Ad(d?eginae) | Secun[d]u[s] | altar (gr) | 100–200 | AE 1995, 746; CILCC I 37; CIVAE 20; CILAE 2006 | Sta. Lucía del Trampal, Alcuéscar (CC) |
| T18 | De(a)e Sanct(a)e Burrulobrigensi | Q. I(ulius) Em(eritus?) | altar (m) | 125–200 | IRCP 566 | Elvas (PT) |
| T19 | Dianae | C. A(---) H(---) | altar (gr) | ? | CIL II 980; CIVAE 29; CILAE 2117 | Dehesa la Cocosa, Badajoz (BA) |
| T20 | Fonta[no et] Font[anae]? | ? | altar (m) | ? | EE IX 162: ERBC 98; Ramírez Sádaba 2013, 152 no. 69; CIVAE 110; CILAE 2153 | Feria (dehesa de Los Rapados) (BA) |
| T21 | Isidi Dominae | ex testamento Scandiliae C. f. Campanae | ? | ? | CIL II 981; CIVAE 74; CILAE 2139 | Torre de Miguel Sesmero (BA) |

Table 6.2. Votive inscriptions from the territory of Emerita (m = marble; gr = granite) *(cont.)*.

| | Deity | Dedicator | Type | Date | Reference | Find-spot (see Fig. 6.1) |
|---|---|---|---|---|---|---|
| T22 | Iun[oni] | none | altar (gr) | ? | *EE* IX 161a; *HEp* 2013, 43; *CIVAE* 38; *CILAE* 2147 | La Morera (BA) |
| T23 | Iunoni Reginae | Lic(inius) Serenianus, v(ir) c(larissimus), + Varinia Flaccina, c(larissima) f(emina), pro salute filiae suae Variniae Serenae | altar (m) | 200–250 | *CIL* II 1024, rev. *AE* 1997, 805; *CIVAE* 37; *CILAE* 2047 | Alange (BA) |
| T24 | Iovi | Teusca Petrei f. | altar (gr) | 1–100 | *IMAPB* 56; Ramírez Sádaba 2013, 51–52 no. 1; *CIVAE* 44; *CILAE* 2087 | Villar del Rey (BA) |
| T25 | I(ovi) O(ptimo) M(aximo) | Furnia G. F(urnii) l. Turran(ia) | altar (gr) | ?100–200 | *CIL* II 1015; *HEp* 2013, 18; *CIVAE* 45; *CILAE* 2090 | Badajoz (BA) |
| T26 | I(ovi) O(ptimo) M(aximo) | Q. Va(lerius?) V(- - -) | altar (gr) | 100–200 | *EE* IX 156; *CIVAE* 46; *CILAE* 2143 | Nogales (cortijo de Maricara; Endrines Altos) (BA) |
| T27 | [I]ovi Opt[i]mo Max[imo] | ? | altar (gr) | ? | *EE* IX 160; *CIVAE* 47; *CILAE* 2138 | Torre de Miguel Sesmero (BA) |
| T28 | Laribu[s] Viali[bus] - - - - - - | (name missing) | altar (gr) | 100–300 | *AE* 1995, 749; *CILCC* I 48; *CIVAE* 48; *CILAE* 2017 | Sta. Lucía del Trampal, Alcuéscar (CC) |
| T29 | Mercury: D(eo) D(omino) S(ancto) Mercurio | none | altar (gr) | 175–300 | *HEp* 6, 1996, 208; *CILCC* I 46; *CIVAE* 54; *CILAE* 2015 | valley of River Zarza, 9 km from Alcuéscar (CC) |
| T30 | Proserp(inae) | Toncius [---] | altar (m) | ? | *EE* VIII 10 = *IRCP* 574 | Herdade da Fonte Branca, Caia e São Pedro, Elvas (PT) |
| T31 | Proserpinae | Q. Helvius Silvanus | ? | 1–200 | *CIL* II 143 = *IRCP* 570 | Elvas (PT) |
| T32 | Deae Proserpinae | [---] Rustri? (f.) | altar (gr) | ? | *EE* VIII 9 = *IRCP* 573 | Herdade da Fonte Branca, Caia e São Pedro, Elvas (PT) |
| T33 | Proserpinae Sanctae | G. Iulius Parthenopaeus | ? | 1–200 | *CIL* II 144 = *IRCP* 571 | area of Elvas (PT) |
| T34 | Proserpinae Servatrici | C. Vettius Silvinus pro Eunoide Plautilla, coniuge sibi restituta | ? | 1–200 | *CIL* II 145 = *IRCP* 572 | area of Elvas (PT) |
| T35 | Silvano | L. Iulius Iulianus | plaque (?) | 100–200 | *EE* IX 169; *CIVAE* 59; *CILAE* 2075 | Torremejía (BA) |
| T36 | [S]ilvano | (name missing) | altar (m) | ? | *HEp* 5, 1995, 112; 7, 1997, 155; *CIVAE* 58; *CILAE* 2133 | Olivenza (BA) |
| T37 | missing | [- - -]+avi + f. | altar (gr) | 75–125 | *AE* 1995, 751; *HEp* 6, 1996, 205; *CILCC* I 50; *CIVAE* 98; *CILAE* 2019 | Sta. Lucía del Trampal, Alcuéscar (CC) |
| T38 | missing | (name missing) | altar (gr) | 200–300 | *AE* 1995, 752; *HEp* 6, 1996, 196; *CILCC* I 63; *CIVAE* 99; *CILAE* 2032 | Sta. Lucía del Trampal, Alcuéscar (CC) |
| T39 | not given | Licinius Rusticus | altar (gr) | 150–200 | *AE* 1995, 753; *CILCC* I 49; *CIVAE* 97; *CILAE* 2018 | Sta. Lucía del Trampal, Alcuéscar (CC) |
| T40 | altar with 2 votive dedications | ? | altar (gr) | 1–300 | *HEp* 6, 1996, 204; *CILCC* I 51; *CIVAE* 100; *CILAE* 2020 | Sta. Lucía del Trampal, Alcuéscar (CC) |
| T41 | ? | [Iul]ius Nicero[s]; [Iu]lius Clemens | altar (m) | | *EE* IX 181; *CIVAE* 102; *CILAE* 2055 | Hornachos (BA) |
| T42 | ? | Maroanus | altar (m) | 100–300 | *IMAPB* 10; *HEp* 7, 1997, 33; *CILAE* 2115 | Dehesa la Cocosa, Badajoz (BA) |
| T43 | ? | Secundytius Victori[nus] | altar (m) | 100–300 | *IRCP* 575 | Elvas (PT)? |

Table 6.3. Dedicators of vows to Endovellicus and subjects of vows *pro salute* made at the sanctuary at São Miguel da Mota (Terena, Alandroal, distr. Évora). Subjects of vows *pro salute* are marked *.

| | **A. *INGENUI* (9)** | |
|---|---|---|
| E1 | Ann(ia) Q. f. Mariana | CIL II 6265; IRCP 484 |
| E2 | Sextus Cocceius Craterus Honorinus, *eques Romanus* | CIL II 131; IRCP 492 |
| E3 | *Critonia C. f. [- - -] | CIL II 132; IRCP 494 |
| E4 | Iulia P. f. Maxuma | IRCP 501 |
| E5 | Q. Sevius Q. f. Pap. Firmanus | CIL II 139; IRCP 526 |
| E6 | Sit<o>nia Q. f. Victorina | CIL II 140 = 5201; IRCP 527 |
| E7 | Terentia G. f. | CIL II 141; IRCP 529 |
| E8 | Tullia C.f. Modesta | IRCP 502 |
| E9 | Tusca Olia Tauri f. | CIL II 142; IRCP 519 |
| | **B. *LIBERTI* (1)** | |
| E10 | Hermes [- - -] P. [l]ib. [- - -]? | IRCP 498 |
| | **C. SLAVES (4)** | |
| E11 | Blandus Caeliae Rufinae servus | CIL II 130; IRCP 489 (Fig. 6.5a) |
| E12 | Hermes Aureliae Vibiae Sabinae ser., *marmorarius* | CIL II 133; IRCP 497 |
| E13 | *Vernacla Treb(iae?) Mus(a)e s(erva) | CIL II 6267a; IRCP 515 |
| E14 | Vitalis Messi Sympaerontis f. et servus | IRCP 536 |
| | **D. PERSONS WITH A SINGLE NAME (3)** | |
| E15 | Conicodius?? | CIL II 6330; IRCP 493 |
| E16 | Eutichius | FE 188; AE 1992, 938; HEp 3, 1993, 477 |
| E17 | Sestio | AE 2004, 704; HEp 13, 2003–2004, 981 |
| | **E. *INCERTI* (56)** | |
| E18 | Albia Ianuaria | CIL II 127; IRCP 483 |
| E19 | T. Annius Aper | CIL II 5206; IRCP 485 |
| E20 | Antonia L. [f.?] Manliola | CIL II 128; IRCP 486 |
| E21 | Antubellicus Priscus | CIL II 5202; IRCP 487 |
| E22 | Arrius Badiolus | CIL II 129; IRCP 488 |
| E23 | L. Calpurnius Andronicus | CIL II 6265a; IRCP 490 |
| E24 | [-] [C]alpurnius Dobetianus | IRCP 491 |
| E25 | [-] [Calp?]urni[us] [- - -] | IRCP 543 |
| E26 | Critonia Maxuma | CIL II 132; IRCP 494 |
| E27 | C(- - -) S(- - -) | AE 2004, 703; HEp 13, 2003–2004, 980 |
| E28 | M. Fannius Augurinus | CIL II 6266; IRCP 495 |
| E29 | Helvia Avita | CIL II 6267; IRCP 496 |
| E30 | (H)elvia Ybas | CIL II 136; IRCP 514 |
| E31 | Iulia Anus | IRCP 499 |
| E32 | *Iul(ia) Marcella | CIL II 5204; IRCP 504 |
| E33 | Iulia Maxuma | IRCP 501 |
| E34 | Iulia [Pro]cula | CIL II 5205; IRCP 503 |

| E. INCERTI (cont.) | | |
|---|---|---|
| E35 | G. Iulius Capito | *IRCP* 505 |
| E36 | [Iu?]liu[s Iu?]lianus | *CIL* II 6269b; *IRCP* 507 |
| E37 | L. Iulius Novatus | *CIL* II 134; *IRCP* 508 |
| E38 | L. Iuliu[s ?P]aesicus | *IRCP* 509 |
| E39 | Marcus Iulius Proculus | *CIL* II 135; *IRCP* 510 |
| E40 | Q. Iulius Pultarius | *IRCP* 511 |
| E41 | Caius Iu[lius Se]ptumi[nus?] | *CIL* II 6331; *IRCP* 513 |
| E42 | C. Iulius Catur[o]nis [f. - - -] | *IRCP* 506 |
| E43 | Iu[l. - - -?] (pro Iul. Marcellam (!)) | *CIL* II 5204; *IRCP* 504 |
| E44 | *Iunia (A)eliana | *CIL* II 136; *IRCP* 514 |
| E45 | Q. L(icinius?) Catullus | *CIL* II 6267a; *IRCP* 515 |
| E46 | M. L(icinius?) Nigellio | *CIL* II 5207; *IRCP* 516 |
| E47 | *L(icinia?) Marciana | *CIL* II 5207; *IRCP* 516 |
| E48 | M. Livius Severus | *IRCP* 517 |
| E49 | M. Magolius C[ar?]us | *CIL* II 6267b; *IRCP* 518 |
| E50 | Petronia Albilla | *IRCP* 520 |
| E51 | *Pompeia Prisca | *CIL* II 6265; *IRCP* 484 |
| E52 | M. Pompeius Saturninus | *CIL* II 6268; *IRCP* 521 |
| E53 | Pomponia Marcella | *CIL* II 138; *IRCP* 522 |
| E54 | C. Qu[inctius?] V[- - -] | *IRCP* 548 |
| E55 | P. Sempronius Celer | *CIL* II 6269; *IRCP* 525 |
| E56 | (*)Q. Sitonius Equestris (*ex visu Q. Sitoni Equestris*) | *CIL* II 140 = 5201; *IRCP* 527 |
| E57 | *Quintus Statorius Taurus, father of Tusca Olia | *CIL* II 142; *IRCP* 519 |
| E58 | C. S(ulpicius?) C(- - -) | *IRCP* 523 |
| E59 | S(ulpicia?) Romula | *IRCP* 524 |
| E60 | Turrecia I[- - -] | *AE* 2004, 705; *HEp* 13, 2003–2004, 982 |
| E61 | L. T(- - -) M(- - -) | *IRCP* 528 |
| E62 | T(- - -) M(- - -) | *IRCP* 528 |
| E63 | Valerius CIICA...? | *CIL* II 6269a; *IRCP* 533 |
| E64 | [-] [Ve?]sidiu[s - - -], father of G. Vesidius Fuscus | *CIL* II 5203; *IRCP* 534 |
| E65 | *G. Vesidius Fuscus | *CIL* II 5203; *IRCP* 534 |
| E66 | M. Vibius Avitus | *CIL* II 5208; *IRCP* 535 |
| E67 | M. Vibius Bassus | *CIL* II 5208; *IRCP* 535 |
| E68 | *Vivennia Venusta, *mamma* | *CIL* II 134; *IRCP* 508 |
| E69 | C. V(- - -) M(- - -) | *IRCP* 530 |
| E70 | M. V(- - -) M(- - -) | *CIL* II 137; *IRCP* 531 |
| E71 | T. V(- - -) M(- - -) | *IRCP* 532 |
| E72 | [-][- - -]ius [N]arcissus | *IRCP* 540 |
| E73 | [- - -]s Saturninus | *IRCP* 512 |

María Pérez Ruiz

# 7. Private Beliefs, Domestic Religion, and Identity in Hispania

The analysis of identity and cultural change through religion is a particularly interesting field of study in the domestic realm, in which the individual's own beliefs can be expressed quite freely. Domestic cult — understood as the set of rites developed by the members of the family within the home and devoted to the worship of the deities, spirits, and ancestors in charge of protecting them and providing their subsistence and perpetuation — is customized by each household within some general parameters, much less strictly defined than those of public religion.

In Hispania, the evidence for domestic cults during the Roman period suggests that Italic traditions were introduced at the same time as pre-existing beliefs were profoundly transformed, to the point that many of the latter seem to disappear. However, a more attentive examination of the gods revered, domestic worship spaces and materials, as well as the continuity of certain rites, allows us to recognize evidence of a complex religious hybridism. In this chapter the specific information that domestic religion can offer on the characterization of cultural and religious identity in Hispania will be surveyed.

## Some Observations on Domestic Religion during the Late Iron Age in the Iberian Peninsula

The first evidence for Italic domestic worship in the Iberian Peninsula can be traced back to the end of the second century BCE, in the form of anepigraphic *arulae*, which are first recorded in the northeast of the peninsula.[1] Prior to that date, in spite of the effective Roman presence after the end of the Second Punic War in the territories previously controlled by Carthaginians, the evidence for domestic worship still reflected only indigenous traditions.

Although these traditions were not homogeneous, some common features are observed within each of the two great cultural areas into which the peninsula was divided, Iberian on the one hand and Celtic and Indo-European on the other, with regional — and even local — differences within each one of them. Although gradually increasing, the accumulated evidence about this worship is limited; thus, it is not currently possible to offer a detailed view of the beliefs, rites, or deities venerated in the domestic sphere during the Late Iron Age. Nevertheless, it may be of interest to review briefly the patterns that can be seen in the archaeological record to gain a better understanding of domestic worship in Hispania.[2]

The first aspect to be considered is the existence of spaces with a religious function within dwellings in both cultural areas, although such spaces were also frequently used for other purposes, often of a social nature.[3] In the Iberian area, and also in the Celtic and Indo-European one although to a lesser extent, the combination of religious and social uses in the same space has led to the suggestion that dynastic or 'group identity'[4] rituals took place in them, with the aim of sanctioning the predominant position of one household and of joining together the community

---

1 The earliest are *arulae* from Building B at El Camp de les Lloses (Tona, Barcelona) in Álvarez Arza and others 2000, 278–79 and from a house on Carrer de Lleida (Tarragona) see Montón 1996, 59 no. 71, both dated to the late second or early first centuries BCE.

2 This necessarily synthetic view of domestic worship during the Late Iron Age very briefly summarizes the review of the situation by Pérez Ruiz 2014, I, chap. IV. Although some references for the argument are provided here, more specific case studies, detailed bibliography, and more extensive conclusions can be found in that Ph.D. dissertation.

3 Alfayé 2005, 233; 2009, 162–67; Belarte 2009, 99.

4 We refer here to rituals devoted to underlining the belonging of its members to the same community and strengthening their kinship ties, as a way of reinforcing a social organization of clientelism. This type of rituals is based upon the concept of *gens*, initially understood as an extended family group united by a common ancestor and common divinities which later evolved towards more complex social groups based on a hierarchical organization of dependence.

Maria Pérez Ruiz, Curator at Museo Nacional de Antropología (Madrid)

around it, sometimes through a connection with — real or legendary — ancestors that legitimized this position.[5] This makes it difficult to establish a distinction between the familiar, domestic cult and the communal, identity-based one and, consequently, between the ritual spaces that were strictly domestic and those that were related to the reinforcement of community identity ties.[6]

The rooms where these cults took place do not differ architecturally from the rest of the house but can be distinguished by certain structural elements or fittings, as well as by the material culture, that make them stand out as singular.[7] Hearths used as altars are repeatedly found; together with some objects related to fire rituals, they suggest the sacralization of fire, a practice that is common in many contemporary cultures, including the Roman one.[8]

Other features frequently found throughout the Iberian Peninsula are child burials and deposits of animal bones under house floors.[9] The interpretation of both rituals is not straightforward, nor do they appear to have a single explanation. Child burials are sometimes understood as funerary rites for infants who died before reaching the age at which they were considered part of the community, but they have also been interpreted as foundational, purification or protective rites.[10] Such interpretations, as well as propitiatory and expiatory ones, have also been attributed to animal bone deposits, as well as ritual banqueting.[11] Both types of ritual evidence have also been found combined or associated in the same domestic space, which emphasizes their matching meaning in some contexts and even the substitutive role that animal bones could play in the development of the rites.[12]

There is little information on the deities worshipped. Different types of evidence — painted pottery, incense burners — refer to an Iberian chthonic goddess of fertility, linked to agriculture and the cycle of life and death, identifiable with the Greek Demeter-Kore or Carthaginian Tanit.[13] In the Celtic and Indo-European area, there is epigraphic evidence from the Roman period for the worship of the Matres, deities with similar connotations to those of the Iberian goddess, but also linked to water (see below).[14] Dagda or Dis Pater may also be related to the domestic realm, according to literary evidence, as well as a deity associated with animals, thereby reflecting one of these peoples' main forms of economic activity as cattle breeders.[15]

On the whole, the panorama of domestic cults in the Iberian Peninsula during the Late Iron Age can only be roughly sketched, as the available evidence is neither sufficiently extensive nor eloquent. In addition, a further difficulty in studying them is posed by the heterogeneity shown by the available case studies, possibly related to a certain flexibility in domestic religious practices, which allowed each household or community to customize them accordingly to their interests or needs. In spite of this heterogeneity, the patterns here briefly referred to shed some light when interpreting certain manifestations of domestic worship that can rightfully be considered Hispano-Roman. Some evidence of late date, especially in the Iberian area, also serves as a link to connect the situation in existence with the new one brought about by the Italic presence in the Iberian Peninsula during the republican era.

## The Transformation Process under the Republic

In the period between the arrival of the Romans in the Iberian Peninsula and the turn of the Era, the evidence for domestic worship is scarce, but, in general terms, it reveals the coexistence of cultural traditions of different origin. Some of them are the result of hybridism with Punic or Greek components (already present during the Late Iron Age) recorded in contexts such as Mas Castellar de Pontós (Girona), a rural settlement within the area of influence of the Greek colonies of Emporion and Rhode.

A large dwelling (house no. 1; 225–175 BCE), with a plan that recalls the Greek *pastas* house, stands out on this settlement. Its main room (no. 3) differs from the other ones in its distinctive architecture, its fittings, and its material culture: several hearths, a pit to hold water, an area for the cremation of dogs, offering vessels and an oil lamp, as well as human

---

5 Ruiz 1998, 289.
6 Domínguez Monedero 1997, 394.
7 Alfayé 2007, 316–17; Domínguez Monedero 1997, 393. A review of the structural elements and material culture that typify spaces for domestic cult in the Iberian area in C. Bonet 2010, 178–81. Different authors (Bonet and Mata 1997, 117; G.I.P 2005, 663; Arruda and Celestino 2009, 43–44), based on the guidelines given by C. Renfrew 1985 in his classic work on the 'archaeology of cult', have underlined the validity of these indicators when considering the coincidence of more than one in the same space, which supports its singular use, usually for religious purposes, whether it is exclusive or not.
8 Pérez Ruiz 2014, I, 57; 197–98.
9 Belarte and Valenzuela-Lamas 2013.
10 Alfayé 2007, 317; 2009; Gusi and Muriel 2008, 288–302.
11 Belarte and Valenzuela-Lamas 2013, 178–81.
12 Grau and others 2015, 75–82.
13 Grau and Rueda 2018, 52–53.
14 Beltrán and Díaz Ariño 2007, 37–38.
15 Pérez Ruiz 2014, I, 202–03; Sopeña 1995, 29–42.

bones, were found inside it.¹⁶ But the most outstanding feature is an object of Pentelic marble in the form of an Ionic column, which seems to have been ritually destroyed.¹⁷

This Greek object must have reached Mas Castellar from one of the nearby Greek colonies.¹⁸ In fact, it is very similar to a small column found in the so-called 'Asklepieion' in Emporion, but the quality of the one found at Mas Castellar is higher.¹⁹ Several interpretations of its use have been proposed: from a support for a basin, a table, or a statue to a ritual altar.²⁰ However, the most interesting is the one put forward by J. Ruiz de Arbulo, who considers that its considerable value as a highly regarded imported item must have led to its interpretation as a cult object, possibly as a *baetylus* linked to Semitic traditions.²¹ Other finds in the same room, such as a large number of dog bones or the presence of human bones, also suggest cult rituals of a foreign origin, although whether they were Celtic or Greek is not clear.²²

Analysis of this archaeological evidence has led to this room within the most prominent house in Mas Castellar being interpreted as a space with a religious and social function,²³ which is defined as such thanks to its structural elements and material culture, as was typical of Iberian religion in the domestic realm. Its function must have been to legitimize the prevailing position of the settlement's main family through a group identity cult, as seen above.²⁴ However, some ritual objects, such as the small Ionic column, also point towards those other cultural traditions that have been mentioned, the Greek one because of its origin and the Punic one that seems to have influenced its reinterpretation. Other finds seem to be the remains of rituals of either Celtic or Greek origin, which is coherent with the material record found in some storage pits at the same settlement.²⁵

The so-called 'incense burners'²⁶ in the form of a female head, often found in Iberian settlements along the Mediterranean coast between the fourth and the first centuries BCE, are also of Greek or Carthaginian origin.²⁷ 'Incense burners' are considered ritual objects related to the worship of a goddess of agriculture and fertility, whose identity and cultural origin are still not resolved: Tanit, Demeter-Kore or an Iberian deity syncretized — at least in iconography — with the other two Mediterranean goddesses.²⁸

One of these 'incense burners' is from a house in Ilici (La Alcudia de Elche, Alicante), where the evidence for domestic cults dating to the republican period or around the turn of the Era is very interesting.²⁹ In the domestic space, these objects have been considered representations of the deity that received offerings from the family;³⁰ their presence in a late context like Ilici shows that worship of her continued in the Iberian area for a long time after the Roman arrival. One important question to bear in mind is if another degree of syncretism could be added through the identification of this deity with a similar Roman goddess.³¹

---

16 Pons i Brun 1997, 73–84; Pons i Brun and others 2002, 120–21, 534.
17 Pons i Brun 1997, 81–82. All the column fragments were found to one side of the central hearth of the room. This has led researchers to the conclusion that it must have been intentionally destroyed in the same place where it was usually located inside the room, in order to avoid its desecration or theft when the settlement was abandoned.
18 Pons i Brun and others 1998, 60; Ruiz de Arbulo 2002–2003, 183.
19 Ruiz de Arbulo 2002–2003, 182. While the Mas Castellar column is made of Pentelic marble, the one from Emporion is made of local sandstone.
20 Pons i Brun and others 1998, 60–61.
21 Ruiz de Arbulo 2002–2003, 181. The presence of baetyls in the Iberian Peninsula is well attested in Seco 2010, with some examples clearly related to Punic cult traditions, such as the pillar-style baetyl from the sanctuary of Torreparedones (Cordoba) (ibid., 291–94, 306–08). It is also interesting for the interpretation of the column from Mas Castellar as a baetyl to consider that the Ionic column was added to the traditional types of Carthaginian baetyls in the context of the wider Hellenistic influence that affected this culture from the fourth century BCE onwards (ibid., 238).
22 Colominas 2008, 228–29; Pons i Brun and others 1998, 62.
23 Pons i Brun and others 2002, 120–21.
24 This concept of domestic cult still differs from the Roman one, not restricted to the elite, but understood as a consubstantial part of the concept of 'family' see Pérez Ruiz 2014, I, 35–36. See below, n. 32.

25 Ruiz de Arbulo 2002–2003, 181–82.
26 The name given to these ritual objects is controversial in Pena 2007, 28–29, because many of them do not have traces of burning that justify the term 'incense burners'. J. Ruiz de Arbulo 1994b, 164–65 considers that '*kernoi*' fits their use and symbolism better.
27 M. J. Pena 2007, 18 has proposed a Greek origin and Carthaginian dissemination for these terracotta objects. In this sense, an object made of stone that represents a very schematic female bust has been found precisely in a Punic household context in Carthago Nova (Cartagena, Murcia) (Noguera and Madrid 2013). This artefact, dated to the late third century BCE, is quite similar to the 'Guardamar'-type 'incense burners'.
28 Tortosa 2006, 49–50.; López and Niveau de Villedary 2014, 174–75; Horn and Marin Ceballos 2007 point out that these objects were not spread as part of specific cults, but the deities related to them shared some characteristics that made them very similar, such as protection against death, nursing and maternal attributes, and support for land fertility.
29 See these finds, with bibliography, in Pérez Ruiz 2014, II, 52–53, 64–68. Some of them will be dealt with below.
30 Ruiz de Arbulo 1994b, 159.
31 This type of syncretism has been proposed for another sort of representation of the Iberian goddess in the same city, as will be seen below.

In addition, these 'incense burners' have been related to a process that seems to have developed from the third century BCE onwards throughout the Iberian area, namely the spread of individual religiosity, both in the public and the private sphere. Its most apparent manifestation is the widespread occurrence in sanctuaries of personal votive offerings and the iconographic representation of social groups not present before, usually by means of small bronze figurines.[32] This change was to lead to a more favourable cultural background for the spread of Roman concepts of the domestic cult.[33]

Precisely, before analysing other discoveries from Ilici that refer to the worship of a goddess of fertility and agriculture, it is interesting to focus on another settlement that illustrates how Italic components were gradually introduced in the realm of domestic beliefs during the republican period and coexisted with this already rich compound of religious traditions.

At the republican *vicus* of El Camp de les Lloses (Tona, Barcelona), dated between 125 and 75 BCE, a significant set of domestic religious rites has been recorded. The foundation of the site has been related to the construction of a complex road network promoted by the Romans in the area, in the context of the logistics behind the conquest and control of Hispania.[34] The material culture shows key evidence for Italic traditions in the community that inhabited the *vicus*, coexisting with the maintenance of indigenous ones.[35]

In this context, it is worth focusing on the religious finds on this site. Building B, which has been considered as the dwelling of a prominent inhabitant of the *vicus* — maybe an *apparitor* —[36] is particularly noteworthy. In its probable main room (no. 11), an anepigraphic *arula*, a Campanian B ware dish, Iberian painted ware *kalathoi*, and iron and bronze locks were found. Besides, a wall niche, with a *denarius* of the *Bolskan* mint in it, has been interpreted as the *lararium* where the *arula* would have been located. This is not the only cult evidence: in a second room (no. 13), an infant burial with rich metallic grave goods was recorded; in another one (no. 14) the remains of a domestic ritual with ashes mixed with animal bones, pottery, a millstone, and a half-unit of the Ausesken mint were found; finally, in a last one (no. 12) a votive deposit made up by an Iberian fine-ware vessel containing microfaunal remains, an ankle bone, and a bronze unit also issued by the Ausesken mint stands out.[37]

Thus, in the same building evidence for both Italic and indigenous cult activities and materials coexists. The *arula* is a ritual object of Italic origin, most possibly located inside a *lararium* with a coin, a common offering in this type of worship space.[38] The votive deposit has also been interpreted as a Roman-type foundational rite,[39] while the infant burial[40] and the ash deposit relate to indigenous traditions.

These two indigenous rites are not unique instances at El Camp de les Lloses. The infant burial in Building B is the richest but not the only one on the site, where ten more have been recorded, all of them inside dwellings, under the floors of both domestic and metalworking spaces. Deposits of animal bones have been also found both in domestic and non-residential buildings.[41]

Therefore, El Camp de les Lloses reveals the coexistence — apparently without friction — of both indigenous and Roman domestic beliefs and traditions. In a settlement founded for the purposes of the Roman conquest, both Roman and indigenous individuals seem to have coexisted with their own traditions,[42] eventually enriching the hybridism of domestic worship traditions already existing in Hispania, as the findings in Building B more clearly show. A drastic breakdown or a foreign imposition on the existing domestic beliefs does not appear to have taken place at that moment, it being more

---

32 Rueda-Galán and others 2008, 478; Tortosa 2006, 50.
33 In the formative period of Roman society, family and religion took shape as consubstantial elements of the same reality. As a consequence, the Roman domestic cult was not a prerogative of the elite, but a right and a duty of each family that was inherited generation after generation, see Pérez Ruiz 2014, I, 35–36. Thus, the 'democratization' of domestic religion in the Iberian Peninsula from the third century BCE onwards favoured the better integration of the new religious traditions brought by Romans.
34 Duran and others 2017, 160, 182–85.
35 Duran and others 2017, passim.
36 Duran and others 2017, 165 n. 27.
37 Duran and others 2004, 434–36; 2017, 179, 181.
38 Pérez Ruiz 2011, 292–94. In Hispania, there are two other examples of coin offerings in the *sacraria* of the villas of Vilauba (Camós, Girona; see Castanyer and Tremoleda 1999, 330) and Cornelius (L'Enova, Valencia; see Albiach and Madaria 2006, 121), both from a considerably later date.
39 Duran and others 2004, 435.
40 This child burial is, in fact, very similar to another found in the Iberian settlement of El Molón, see Camporrobles; Duran and others 2017, 181 n. 41.
41 Duran and others 2017, 181–82.
42 The researchers who have studied the site propose, in fact, that these child burials should be considered a funerary tradition maintained by the indigenous women that lived in the *vicus*, many of them as partners of the Roman soldiers, see Duran and others 2015, 304. Although this type of burials has also been recorded in the Italian Peninsula under house floors, by this time they were almost exclusively limited in Roman culture to the ones known as *subgrundaria*, outside the house and under the roof eaves.

feasible to suggest that new objects and rites were added to the existing ones and *vice versa*.

The Roman religious finds from El Camp de les Lloses are also significant due to their early date. The *arula* from Building B is the oldest recorded in Hispania along with one found in a *domus* in Lleida street in Tarragona, both being dated between the late second and the early first centuries BCE. *Arulae* like these must have entered the domestic realm, in fact, by means of contact with Roman-Italic culture, since there is no record of this type of object before the Roman arrival. They are made of local stone, so, unlike the small column from Mas Castellar de Pontós, they were not imported, nor were they made of sumptuous materials.[43]

Both of them come from the *conventus Tarraconensis*, the area of the peninsula with the earliest Italic presence, and from settlements with a noticeable Italic cultural component, which could lead us to conclude that these *arulae* were not only introduced but also used by Romans during this early period, especially considering that, both at El Camp de les Lloses and in Tarraco,[44] they are related to spaces and structures that can be interpreted as *lararia*, that is, domestic shrines of Italic tradition,[45] also the earliest ones recorded in Hispania. However, El Camp de les Lloses shows that the ethnic and cultural reality was more complex, as rites of different origins coexisted in the same household unit, probably as a reflection of the different roots of the members of the family. In this context of social hybridism, the existence of these cultural exchanges must not be dismissed, especially as it concerns such a private sphere as domestic beliefs, which are not easily understood without knowledge of the social roots of the inhabitants of the houses. Regarding the *arulae* analysed, it is significant that other similar ones of the same date and with the same geographical distribution were ritually placed in storage pits in apparently indigenous rituals.[46]

During the first century BCE *lararia* become more common in the archaeological record, usually, but not exclusively, responding to the category of Roman *sacraria*, small cult spaces inside larger rooms.[47]

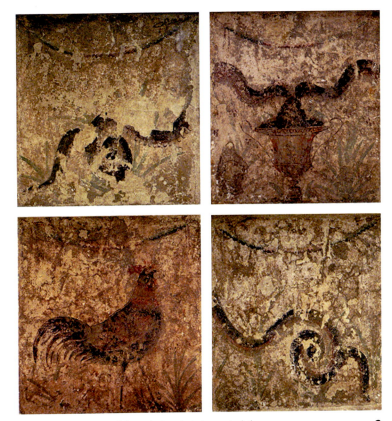

Figure 7.1. a) Layout of the painting that decorated the altar on its four faces; b) Remains of the altar in the peristyle of House 2B in Emporiae (M. Pérez Ruiz).

One of the most interesting case studies during this

---

43 Álvarez Arza and others 2000, 278–79; Montón 1996, 59 no. 71.
44 Cortés 2014, 145.
45 There is nothing similar to *lararia* in Hispania before the arrival of the Romans. As has been mentioned in the previous paragraph, cult spaces within dwellings were usually rooms that only differed from the rest of the house in certain structural elements or their material culture, but they contained nothing that might be considered similar to a shrine.
46 Ros 2005, 152–55.
47 The *sacraria* from the House of the Rosettes in Osca (Huesca; see Uribe and others 2014, 177–81), the House of Fortune in Carthago Nova (Cartagena, Murcia; see Pérez Ruiz 2014, II, 219–21), the villa of El Rihuete (Mazarrón, Murcia; see Pérez Ruiz 2014, II, 229–39), the House of the Black and White Emblem in Celsa (Velilla de Ebro, Zaragoza; see Pérez Ruiz 2014, II, 341–42), and from a *domus* in Acinipo (Ronda, Málaga; see Pérez Ruiz 2014, II, 34), as well as another possible *sacrarium* inside the kitchen of an atrium-style *domus* at Emporiae, in Campo and others 2016a, II, are all dated to the first century BCE, mostly to the closing decades.

period is, however, an altar found in House 2B in Emporiae (L'Escala, Girona), as it belongs to a very clear Italic tradition. It is a large masonry altar (late first century BCE–early first century CE) located in the southern peristyle of the *domus*. On three of its faces, it was painted with two snakes, which approached a gilded *kantharos* crowned with a pine cone, against a plant background in which pink flowers stand out; on the fourth side a rooster is represented, also on a plant background. The scenes are framed by a red and green garland (Fig. 7.1).[48] The confronted snakes are very similar to many Pompeian paintings in *lararia*, both in the representation of the reptiles and through the presence of the pine cone as an offering, in the plant background and the garland.[49] Roosters are also represented in Pompeian *lararia* — some of them on altars — although more rarely.[50]

Therefore, the altar from Emporiae is decorated with Italic domestic cult motifs, and it is a religious structure used for this type of worship,[51] usually located in gardens and peristyles, as in the house in Emporiae, which follows the traditional *domus* structure with *atrium* and peristyle, not very common in Hispania.[52]

The first evidence for domestic deities of Roman tradition, such as the Lares and the Genius, associated with dwellings also dates from this period. Lares are mentioned in an inscription on a stone block (last quarter of the first century BCE) from an altar or an *aedicula* that was probably part of a space for worship inside a villa (Rambla de la Boltada, Cartagena-La Unión, Murcia).[53] The word 'Genius' was written on the base of a small column (second half of the first century BCE–early first century CE) found in a Roman house in Corduba (Córdoba).[54]

Returning now to Ilici, the Ibero-Roman evidence of domestic worship there repeatedly refers to the goddess of agriculture and fertility already mentioned. Pottery related to domestic worship was found in a room with a possible ritual use inside what is known as the Sector 4-C House (228/218–42/38 BCE). The most interesting object is a *kernos*, whose typology refers to Greek and Carthaginian forms,[55] and which is paralleled by other finds in areas of the Iberian Peninsula under Greek influence.[56] However, its painted decoration is Iberian in style, with an outstanding blushing female face on the base of the bowl, where libations prepared in the other vessels of the *kernos* were poured. The face has been interpreted as the representation of the goddess of the land, on which liquid offerings were directly made.[57]

In the House of the Hellenistic Mosaic, in the same room where the votive deposit with the 'incense burner' was found, another offering was discovered,[58] an Iberian *krater* painted with anthropomorphic motifs. On the front, a female winged head arising from the land is accompanied by two birds; on the back, two male faces are separated by two entwined snakes with crest and beard. According to the most widespread interpretation, the female figure must be the great Iberian goddess of fertility and the land, from which she herself emerges, emphasizing her chthonic character,[59] while the two male faces must be the witnesses to the divine epiphany, related to the aristocracy of the place,[60] possibly as heroized ancestors.

However, an alternative interpretation was recently proposed for this object, considered to be a *kantharos* for drinking wine.[61] According to this proposal, the painting on the back would represent Augustus and a *flamen*, separated by two snakes similar to the ones found on the altar from Emporion, which represent a connection between the real world and the underworld. The front depicts the Mediterranean (and Iberian) great goddess, iconographically assimilated as Dea Caelestis. This hypothesis would be supported by the interpretation of the engraving on a carnelian found inside the vessel as Capricorn, the zodiac sign of Augustus.[62]

This new interpretation is significant because the vessel should be considered evidence of domestic worship dedicated to the emperor, undertaken close to the change in the Era and, at the same time, linked to the Iberian great goddess, whether syncretized or not. Thus, it might be stated that the most

---

48 Pérez Ruiz 2014, II, 140–45.
49 Among the clearest parallels are the *lararia* from the House of the Ephebe, see Boyce 1937, 26 no. 40; House of the First Floor, see Fröhlich 1991, 258, L20; House of Pinarius, see Boyce 1937, 58–59 no. 224, or the recently discovered *lararium* in the House of the Enchanted Garden (report in *Il Messaggero*, 5 October 2018 <www.ilmessaggero.it/spettacoli/cultura/pompei_casa_giardino_incantato-4019123.html> [accessed 3 June 2022]).
50 House V, 4, 3 in Boyce 1937, 67 no. 285; House I, 2, 3 in Boyce 1937, 21 no. 4, and Villa of the Mosaic Columns in Boyce 1937, 97 no. 479.
51 Pérez Ruiz 2007–2008, 215.
52 For houses in Emporiae and north-eastern Spain, see Cortés 2014.
53 Pérez Ruiz 2014, II, 235–37.
54 Now lost; Pérez Ruiz 2014, II, 28.
55 Tortosa 2004, 157.
56 Ramos and Ramos 1976, 21; Santos and Sourisseau 2011, 225.
57 Olmos 1988–1989, 94–95.
58 It has been dated by the associated material, among which there are some coins of Augustus (27 BCE–14 CE), see Ronda and Tendero 2015, 264–65.
59 Ramos 1992, 175–78.
60 Olmos 1998, 152–53.
61 Ronda and Tendero 2014, 203–04.
62 Ronda and Tendero 2015, 265–67.

defining manifestation of Roman religion, the imperial cult,[63] must have coexisted in the same iconographic space with one of the most characteristic and recognizable deities of the Iberian pantheon, both realities being coherently present in the domestic rites in which this object must have taken part. However, caution should be exercised regarding this interpretation, since for the moment this would be almost the only recorded evidence for the imperial cult in the Hispano-Roman domestic sphere[64] and contemporary with the first public evidence for the imperial cult in Hispania, where it was introduced at a relatively early date.[65]

## Domestic Worship in Hispania during the Imperial Era: Acculturation or Hybridism?

Around the turn of the Era there is a change in the archaeological record. From that moment onwards the evidence for domestic worship is mainly of Italic or Roman tradition, at least in its form. The presence of this type of evidence gradually prevails, and indigenous traditions are almost exclusively relegated to child burials and votive deposits, although these deposits changed substantially in comparison with Late Iron Age ones. As from the first century CE, the number of recorded examples of domestic cults starts to increase exponentially compared with the previous period.[66]

The archaeological record for this period exhibits a variety of forms of evidence: spaces and built structures for domestic cult inside houses — with or without associated material culture — different types of worship and ritual objects, epigraphy, child burials, and votive deposits.

Spaces and structures for domestic cult in Hispania are mainly of the types known as *lararia*[67] — largely identified on the basis of the evidence from Vesuvian sites — that is, shrines devoted to the worship of the deities of the house and the family, as well as its ancestors. These can be painted *lararia*, niches with or without associated paintings, masonry altars, *aediculae*, *sacraria*, and *sacella*.[68] The most common are *aediculae* and *sacraria* or *sacella*,[69] rather than painted *lararia* or niches, which are the most frequent types in Pompeii and Herculaneum.[70] Regarding the material culture, the most common objects are cult images, *arae* and *arulae*, vessels for liquids, oil lamps, and coins. Epigraphy is mainly found on *arae* and *arulae*, but also on plaques and some architectural elements. The panorama is completed by the two types of evidence of a more local tradition: child burials and votive deposits. As will be seen, they coexist, even in the same house, with Roman-type evidence.[71]

### The Locations of lararia within the House and their Meaning

After this brief review of the archaeological record for the domestic cult in Hispania from the turn of the Era onwards, there are some peculiarities worthy of attention. One of them is the high number of *aediculae* and *sacraria*, which differs from the Vesuvian archaeological record, where simpler *lararia* are the most common types.[72]

The explanation may partly be a consequence of the characteristics of the archaeological record in the two areas. While in the Vesuvian area houses have been almost completely preserved — including walls, where these simpler *lararia* were located — in Hispania the degree of preservation seldom allows wall structures or elements to be recorded. However, it is possible to offer another type of critical appraisal of this state of affairs.

---

63 See Marco in this volume.
64 It is only at a considerably later date that a bust of Septimius Severus found in a suburban *domus* in Augusta Emerita (Mérida, Badajoz) could be related to a domestic cult devoted to the emperor, see Corrales 2016, 227, although there is insufficient information to be confident about this hypothesis. Other evidence of worship of the emperor as part of domestic religiosity can be found in other parts of the Roman world, but none of the examples are dated as early as the one from *Ilici*, see Pérez Ruiz 2015.
65 Ruiz de Arbulo 2009, 169–72; see Marco in this volume.
66 For the mid-first century BCE some fifteen cases of domestic worship have been recorded. Around the turn of the Era the numbers increase to around fifty and at the beginning of the second century they reach their peak with around one hundred instances.
67 Here we will not enter the debate about the appropriateness or not of the use of this term according to its chronology in written sources. We will use it as a customary term used in the academic literature to refer to the shrines for domestic cult of Roman tradition, see Pérez Ruiz 2007–2008, 212–13.
68 Bassani 2008, 23–33; Boyce 1937, 10–18; Pérez Ruiz 2014, I, 79–96.
69 *Sacraria* are small rooms included in the plan of the house, while *sacella* are free-standing, usually located in courtyards and gardens.
70 Pérez Ruiz 2014, I, 226–27.
71 This summary has been extracted from the study made of the domestic cult in Baetica and Tarraconensis during the Roman period, see Pérez Ruiz 2014. The subsequently recorded data from both provinces, and also from Lusitania, do not substantially change this panorama.
72 According to the main *corpora* for Pompeian *lararia*, for which see Boyce 1937; Orr 1972; Fröhlich 1991; Bassani 2008; Giacobello 2008, there are eighty-eight painted *lararia* and 176 niches, while *aediculae* number fifty-nine and *sacraria* thirty-two.

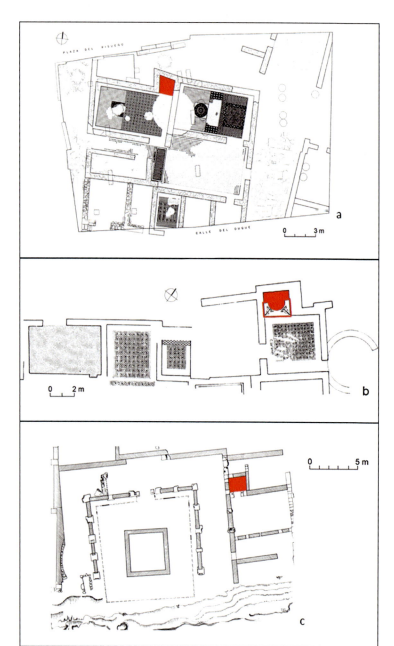

Figure 7.2. a) House of Fortune, Carthago Nova (Cartagena, Murcia). The *lararium* (red) is inside the *tablinum*; b) Villa of El Rihuete (Mazarrón, Murcia). The *lararium* (red) is inside the representational room; c) House of the Blind Caves, Clunia (Peñalba de Castro, Burgos). The *lararium* (red) is adjacent to the banquet hall (a) Fernández Díaz 2008, II, 259 fig. 42; b) Ramallo 1985, 83 fig. 14; c) Palol 1994, pl. 61).

In the Vesuvian cities, there is a relationship between the type of *lararium* and its location in the house. These shrines have been traditionally associated with the *atrium*, but they could be found in almost any part of the dwelling, from the most public and representational rooms to the most private, the kitchen being a common place to locate domestic shrines in Pompeii. It was precisely in these spaces that painted *lararia* were preferentially placed,[73] while niches with and without paintings were common in kitchens, *atria*, and peristyles.[74] *Aediculae* and *sacraria* were almost exclusively found in public and representational areas, such as *atria*, peristyles, and gardens.[75]

The location and monumentality of *lararia* must be related to their function in the domestic realm. It is not by chance that the most monumental types were placed in those spaces of the house by and large freely open to those not forming part of the household and in which the family's social position and respect for tradition were displayed by means of sumptuous decoration, *imagines maiorum*, or trophies obtained by the ancestors. In this context, the *lararium* added to its religious function a social one, linked to the values that the family wished to show towards the exterior — such as the *pietas* of the *paterfamilias* and the respect for the *mos maiorum* — as part of the language of self-representation and self-legitimization expressed in the public parts of the house.[76]

This relationship between the type of *lararium* and its location in the house also exists in the Hispano-Roman evidence. Most shrines — *aediculae*, *sacraria*, and *sacella* — are in the noble areas — open and distribution spaces and rooms and areas for representation — while only a few have been found in *cubicula*, productive and secondary areas and entrances.[77] However, there is a peculiarity in the Hispano-Roman record in comparison with the Vesuvian one: the noticeable presence of *lararia* in rooms and spaces for representational purposes, not common in the Campanian region (Fig. 7.2).[78]

---

73 Forty-nine of the eighty-eight painted *lararia* recorded in Pompeii come from kitchens.
74 Fifty-one, forty-six, and fifty respectively.
75 Fifty-six of the fifty-nine *aediculae* and twenty-seven of the thirty-two *sacraria* have been found in these types of spaces.
76 Pérez Ruiz 2013, 410.
77 Pérez Ruiz 2014, I, 270 fig. 115. New evidence collected during recent years does not substantially change this panorama, as many of the *lararia* are also placed in the main areas of the house. Some examples include the *aedicula* found in the peristyle of the North House of Arucci (Aroche, Huelva; see Corrales and others 2016) or the *sacrarium* in the great peristyle of the villa of Puente de la Olmilla (Albaladejo, Ciudad Real; see García Bueno 2015, 212).
78 Some interesting examples are the *sacraria* from the House of Fortune, in Carthago Nova, and the villa of El Rihuete, both set back in one wall of the *tablinum* or representational room; or the *sacrarium* in the House of the Blind Caves, in *Clunia* (Peñalba de Castro, Burgos), adjacent to the *triclinium* and with a direct access to it; see Pérez Ruiz 2014, II, 219–21, 229–31, 96–99, respectively. More examples in Pérez Ruiz 2013, 409–12. In Pompeii, only around ten *lararia* out of more than four hundred have been found in rooms for representation.

Hispania is not the only territory with differences from the Vesuvian area. Examples can be found in Gallia and south-central Italy, where there are many subterranean spaces for the domestic cult,[79] a feature that is not common in the Vesuvian record.[80] Regarding the peculiarity mentioned for Hispania, there are interesting similarities in other areas of the Roman world. In Ostia, most domestic shrines (second–fourth centuries CE) are placed in peristyles, prestige and representational rooms, and banqueting halls, being mainly monumental niches and pseudo-*aediculae*.[81] In Gallia *lararia* linked with representational areas have also been recorded in the first and the second centuries CE,[82] while in Tunisia, the *sacraria* studied by M. Bassani[83] — contemporary with the ones from Ostia — are mostly placed in peristyles, but sometimes clearly linked to representational spaces apparently with a prominent social value.

As mentioned above, the relationship between *lararia* and domestic representational spaces is justified by both their religious and social function, inserted in the symbolic language of the aristocratic Roman house, in which the social and the religious concepts were inseparable.[84] Some literary sources give us an idea of the significance that cult and the display of religious scenography had during banqueting in order to reinforce the political and economic power of the host before dinner guests.[85]

However, according to the archaeological record, it seems that the social dimension of the domestic cult started to be emphasized by the display of the *lararium* inside — or directly associated with — representational spaces especially from the second century CE onwards, while in Hispania this location is recorded earlier as a common choice.[86] Moreover, this preference for the combination of religious and social activity in the same domestic space recalls what is recorded in singular rooms in some Iberian dwellings, as has been stated above.[87]

Thus, in Hispania the social dimension of the Roman domestic cult must have been influenced and reinforced by the vernacular traditions. Consequently, rooms of an early date for representation and banqueting with associated *lararia* should be considered as a reinterpretation in the Roman period and with Italic forms of the multifunctionality of the outstanding rooms devoted to social and religious ritual in Late Iron Age dwellings, especially in Iberian settlements. Therefore, in *triclinia*, *tablina*, etc., worship in the *lararium* became part of the social ritual as a complement to banqueting and reception. Over time this trend eventually converged with the development of worship in other areas of the Roman world, as evidence from Ostia, Gallia, and Tunisia shows.

## Deities Worshipped

Another subject of interest is the analysis of the deities worshipped in the house from the turn of the Era onwards. As previously mentioned, in Ilici there is evidence for the cult to an Iberian great mother goddess at the end of the republican period. However, as the domestic cult of Italic tradition started to prevail, references to indigenous deities became residual.

In fact, from the iconographic representations and the epigraphic records it can be borne out that most of the deities worshipped were common in the Roman pantheon and domestic cult or had been assimilated into it: Lares, Genii, Penates with different identities[88] — Mercury, Jupiter Optimus Maximus, Hercules, Fortuna, Mars, Bacchus, Minerva, Venus, Tutela, Silvanus, Cybele and Attis or Isis. Even the serpent, common in Pompeian painted *lararia*, is documented. Thus, the question that is posed is whether indigenous deities continued to be present in domestic religion or if they were worshipped by means of syncretism.

---

79  Bassani 2007, 111–14.
80  Bassani 2008, 107–08.
81  Bakker 1994, 32–42, 54–55, 179, 181–82.
82  Bassani 2008, 105; 2011, 110–22.
83  Bassani 2003, 171–75.
84  Gros 2006, 20–21.
85  That is how Sallust explains it regarding Metellus Pius (Sal., *Hist*, Frg. 2.70) and Petronius in his *Trimalchio* (Petr. 60).
86  The *sacrarium* of the House of the Blind Caves, in *Clunia*, has been dated to the Tiberian period. The *sacraria* of the House of Fortune, in Carthago Nova, and the villa of El Rihuete were built in the first century CE. The painted altar in House 2B in Emporiae, with an interesting relationship with the banquet hall, is dated between the first century BCE and the first century CE. In the House of the Lararium, also in Carthago Nova, and in the house of the same name in Bilbilis (Calatayud, Zaragoza), a pseudo-*aedicula* and a *sacrarium*, both linked with spaces for representation, were built at the beginning of the first century CE, see Pérez Ruiz 2014, II, 217–18, 333–36.

87  The main room in House no. 1 of Mas Castellar de Pontós (Girona) has already been mentioned, but other examples are the shrines in House E at Castellet de Bernabé (Liria, Valencia) and in House IIIL at El Oral (San Fulgencio, Alicante). See Pérez Ruiz 2014, I, 139–44, 161–67, with bibliography.
88  The concept of 'Penates', which originally referred to an amalgam of deities without form responsible for the protection of the supplies and the pantry (*penus*) of the family, eventually shifted to apply to any protective deity of the house and the family — 'Penates sunt omnes dii, qui domi coluntur' (Serv., *Aen*. II.514). However, their special relationship with the means for household subsistence does not appear to have been completely lost (Pérez Ruiz 2014, I, 52–54).

Figure 7.3. Cult images found in the *lararium* of the villa of Vilauba (Camós, Girona) (M. Pérez Ruiz).

The most frequently recorded deities in Hispania are Mercury and Jupiter.[89] Mercury was one of the most revered gods in the domestic space, and small bronze sculptures of him are especially numerous in the Western Roman provinces; the difference between Hispania and other regions, such as Gallia and Germania, is that in Hispania there are no signs of interpretation in his iconography.[90] Regarding Jupiter, his presence in *lararia* in other parts of the Roman world is not as common as that of Mercury; in Hispania he is recorded in epigraphy and always with the epithet *Optimus Maximus*, which is peculiar to the Hispanic corpus. But the reason for this particularity is not clear; nor can it definitely be assigned to any type of syncretism; it may only have been the consequence of a particular influence of public religion over private forms.[91]

However, if an overall assessment of the deities recorded is made, it is interesting to note that many of them had a chthonic or agricultural dimension: Lares, Mars, Cybele and Attis, Fortuna, Bacchus, and Silvanus. The Iberian great goddess was also a deity of this type and the agricultural dimension was precisely one of the most outstanding characteristics of Iron Age domestic cults in the Iberian Peninsula, in direct relationship with the cycle of life and death.[92]

Agriculture also played a fundamental role in the definition of the most ancient domestic religion in Rome, but the original attributes of its deities, related to this dimension, had apparently already been forgotten by the early Empire. An interesting example is the *Lar familiaris*, who originally had a chthonic and rural nature, linked to the protection of the country-estate household. This character was lost at a relatively early date due to its transfer from the land to the house, becoming its protector. However, the epithet *agrestis* with which it is alluded to in some inscriptions shows that the memory of its link to agricultural property was not completely lost.[93]

In Hispania only one Lar statuette from a *lararium* has been recorded to date.[94] It was found in the villa of Vilauba (Camós, Girona) along with bronze figurines of Fortuna and Mercury and the remains of a Silvanus (Fig. 7.3),[95] all fallen on the floor — probably from a niche in the wall — of a *sacrarium* destroyed by fire in the third century CE.[96] Lar and Silvanus are complementary deities. Silvanus, the protector of the *silva*, had a domestic dimension that went back to an archaic period when he protected the 'close nature' beyond the domestic property. Thus, the protection of Silvanus started where the Lar's ended and the close relationship between them, domestic property, and nature, can be appreciated in some inscriptions[97] and representations, such as the altar found in Piazza dei Lari at Ostia.[98]

Thus, at Vilauba the worship of two complementary deities, protectors of the country-estate household and the surrounding land, in a context

---

89 Mercury is portrayed in Hispanic houses both in small bronze sculptures and epigraphs on *arulae*, see Pérez Ruiz 2014, I, 369 no. 34, as well as in a herm from a room identified as a kitchen in Ilerda (Lleida), as discussed in Cortés 2014, 159. All of the references to Jupiter are epigraphic, see Pérez Ruiz 2014, I, 369 no. 34.
90 Some bronze sculptures of Mercury found in Hispania have *torques*, as is usual in Gallia (Baratta 2001, 126), but none of them come from *lararia*.
91 Pérez Ruiz 2014, I, 369–71.
92 Grau and Rueda 2018, 61.
93 Pérez Ruiz 2014, I, 39–44.
94 Other statuettes come from domestic contexts but not from *lararia*, and most of them do not have a known context that enables us to relate them clearly to the domestic cult.
95 See the analysis for the identification of this figure in Pérez Ruiz 2014, I, 294–97.
96 Castanyer and Tremoleda 1999, 62–64.
97 *CIL* III 3491; *CIL* VI 646.
98 Calza 1916, 145–48. In the words of G. Dumézil 1974, 306, 'Silvanus can be a sort of Lar, shaggier'.

in which the subsistence of the family relied upon this land, has been recorded. In the third century CE, this *lararium* still fulfilled the same function as the earliest Roman domestic shrines: protecting the country estate and ensuring the family's prosperity. The cult images had been made in the first century CE, which shows that the purpose of the domestic cult remained unaltered by the owners of the villa for more than two centuries.

Finally, Fortuna and Mercury are also complementary and coherent in their context as well. They are also frequently invoked and represented together in Pompeian domestic spaces,[99] and they share some epithets, forming the perfect union between business and luck, more precisely luck in business.[100] Their presence in the Vilauba *lararium* as Penates sought to assist the successful conclusion of the family's economic activity, based on the wealth of the land favoured and protected by the Lar and Silvanus.

The deities worshipped at Vilauba, the meaning of the domestic cult, and the characteristics of its cult images were all Roman, just as the ritual must have been. Nevertheless, examples like Vilauba may show that, in this widespread dissemination of Roman religious beliefs throughout Hispania, the elements chosen and promoted were those that best fitted vernacular traditions with a strong agricultural component. This even favoured the recovery of certain attributions of deities, such as the Lar, which had already fallen into disuse in the original Italic cult.

In fact, the Lar from Vilauba is not the only one found in Hispania whose agricultural dimension seems clear. Near Mérida (Badajoz) an almost one-metre-tall stone Lar, dated to the third century CE, was found next to a sickle and a pruning knife, all the artefacts most likely coming from a villa. The agricultural tools found alongside the Lar lead us to think that, once again, in a late context and far away from the centre of the Empire, the archaic agricultural dimension of this Italic deity was recovered and emphasized, fitting in with the domestic religious tradition in Hispania.[101]

As regards indigenous deities in the domestic sphere, we only have one clear example: the plea to the Matres in two *arulae* from Clunia. Other inscriptions were also devoted to these local deities in public contexts in the same city, where they were related to water and its salutary power.[102] Another possible reference to indigenous deities, assimilated to the Roman theonym Lares, has been found on an *arula* in the *atriolum* of the House of the Fountains, in Conimbriga (Condeixa-a-nova, Coimbra); in this case it is devoted to the Lares Aquites, who have been related to water and also with a health-giving character, perhaps as a replacement for the Roman nymphs.[103]

In other areas of Hispania, there are also epigraphic references to water cults in household contexts, but not all of them can be clearly related to domestic religion. Three *arulae* devoted to the nymphs have been found in villas — the villa of Cabriana (Lantarón, Álava),[104] a possible villa in Casa Santa (Valladolid),[105] and in the villa of Saucedo (Talavera de la Reina, Toledo);[106] another *arula* devoted to Fortuna Balnearis might have come from a rural domestic context, or maybe a Roman bath in Duratón (Segovia).[107] All this evidence could be pointing towards the maintenance during the Roman period of a domestic dimension of water cults already widespread throughout the Iberian Peninsula — especially in the north-west and Lusitania — in the Iron Age; however, doubts about the provenance of the finds and their function invite caution regarding this hypothesis.

Finally, it is worth mentioning the existence of female figurines made of bone, found only in Lusitania, some of them in villas, and of late date. Some of these figurines have recently been considered to have been religious amulets linked to the cult of Magna Mater, especially widespread in this province. This cult has been interpreted as a continuation of a relatively popular indigenous one, devoted to a goddess of fertility and fruitfulness, such as that of Ataegina (Ataecina).[108]

### Child Burials and Votive Deposits

Infant burials and votive deposits constitute one of the most peculiar and abundant categories of evidence for domestic worship in Hispania. The tradition of burying foetuses and newborn children under house floors in Hispania dates back at least to the Bronze Age. As has been discussed above, during the Late

---

99 Also in Hispania, in an *atrium*-style *domus* in Emporiae, dated to the first half of the first century BCE, a figure of Fortune and a *caduceus* of Mercury have been found in a cult space (perhaps a *sacrarium*) inside the kitchen (Campo and others 2016a, 11).
100 Hild 1896, 1273.
101 Pérez Ruiz 2008.
102 Alfayé 2016, 371–72; Beltrán and Díaz Ariño 2007, 35–38.
103 Fernandes 2002, 181; Ribeiro 2002a, 472 no. 145; 2002b, 196; Andreu 2017a, 212 proposes, however, that the relationship of the Lares Aquites with water should be reconsidered.
104 Andreu 2017b, 179 nos 4.2–4.3.
105 Andreu 2017c.
106 Andreu 2017d.
107 Andreu 2017e.
108 Heras and others 2012; Edmondson in this volume.

Iron Age these burials took place both in the Iberian and the Celtic and Indo-European areas. From the second and first centuries BCE, the tradition is also recorded within settlements with noticeably Italic architecture and material culture, such as Ca l'Arnau and Can Mateu (Cabrera de Mar, Barcelona),[109] El Camp de les Lloses,[110] or Celsa (Velilla de Ebro, Zaragoza) — a Roman colony —[111] in a period in which there is no record of such burials in the Italian Peninsula.[112] Child burials continue to be recorded in domestic contexts during the Roman period in Hispania, especially in the north-east.[113]

Almost all these burials are very simple individual inhumations, with infants placed in a lateral or supine position, without grave goods. There is no pattern to their location inside the house, but they are usually next to walls and at some distance from doors.[114] Most of them must have been the result of a specific funerary rite for stillbirths and neonates, but in some cases other interpretations have been proposed — foundational, purification, or propitiatory practices —[115] not always without doubts, as the archaeological record is not sufficiently eloquent. For this reason, each one of them has to be analysed individually in order to understand its meaning, because it could change according to the region, the moment, or the intention.

Other types of ritual finds are also frequently recorded in domestic buildings with child burials, both indigenous (votive deposits) and Roman (*lararia, arulae*, sculptures...); for instance, in Celsa and Bilbilis, where they coexist in some houses with *lararia* and other Roman evidence for cult activity,[116] or at El Camp de les Lloses (Tona, Barcelona), at as early a date as 125–75 BCE (see above). Consequently, this rite must be considered as complementary to others celebrated within the house, all of which were compatible. This situation invites us to reflect on whether the difference between indigenous and Italic-Roman worship is more of a present-day idea than an ancient reality, since these rites could have been part of the same undifferentiated domestic cult, no matter what their origin may have been.

Regarding votive deposits, they are made up by different types of objects that are sometimes mixed with animal and even human bones. In the Late Iron Age period, deposits of animal bones, especially ovicaprids, were relatively widespread throughout the Iberian Peninsula, yet this rite had almost disappeared in the Roman period. Deposits were mostly made up by one or two ceramic vessels with offerings inside. They were mainly concentrated in the north-eastern part of the Iberian Peninsula and are recorded until the third century CE.[117]

The location of these deposits within the house is variable and the function of the room where they were found is not always known. Two (or sometimes more) deposits are frequently found in the same building, and further archaeological evidence of domestic cult is also often found in the same context.[118] The most homogeneous group of votive deposits comes from the area of modern Catalonia. They were usually made up by coarse-ware vessels that were no longer useful for domestic activities (broken, without a handle, etc.). Inside them, there were animal remains — usually birds or eggshells — or liquids (not preserved). The vessels were placed inside pits that were under or next to walls, mainly in villas.[119]

In sum, the tradition of placing votive deposits inside the house is an ancient one in Hispania, but the types of deposits during the Late Iron Age and Roman periods were different.[120] Some of these votive deposits have been interpreted as foundational rites, while others were considered to have been part of propitiatory and purification ones, related to the fertility of the fields, since the presence of remains of hens, roosters, and eggshells referred to the underworld and to an idea of regeneration in the ancient Mediterranean world, a chthonic dimension underlined by the act of burying the votive offerings. That is why these deposits have been related to acts of purification and protection of the family's country

---

109 Martín Menéndez 2004, 382; Sinner 2015, 15–16.
110 Duran and others 2015.
111 Mínguez 1989–1990.
112 See above, n. 41.
113 Lorencio and others 1998.
114 Pérez Ruiz 2014, I, 346–47.
115 As an example, a child burial under a house in the settlement of Can Mateu (Mataró, Barcelona) has been interpreted as a foundation rite, see García i Roselló and others 2000, 35.
116 House of the *Lararium*, in Bilbilis, House of the Black and White Emblem, and House of the Turtle, in Celsa, see Pérez Ruiz 2014, II, 333–38, 341–48, 350.
117 Casas and Ruiz de Arbulo 1997.
118 House of the Antic Portal de la Magdalena, in Ilerda (Lérida); House of the Plinths, in Uxama Argaela (Burgo de Osma, Soria); villa of Vilauba (Camós, Gerona); Pérez Ruiz 2014, II, 152–66, 188–210, 254–59.
119 These characteristics are best fitted by the votive deposits in the urban building of the Antic Portal de la Magdalena (Ilerda, Lleida; see Pérez Almoguera 1998, 200–01) and in the villas of Corbins (Lleida; see Casas and Ruiz de Arbulo 1997, 217–18), Vilauba (Camós, Girona; see Casas and Ruiz de Arbulo 1997, 217), Mas Gusó (Bellcaire d'Empordà, Girona; see Casas and Ruiz de Arbulo 1997, 212–17), Tolegassos; see Casas and Ruiz de Arbulo 1997, 211–17), and Casa Blanca (Tortosa, Tarragona, see Pons Pujol 2003.
120 Belarte and Valenzuela Lamas 2013.

estate, also with a propitiatory meaning linked with the egg as the seed of procreation.[121] The location of some deposits immediately outside the perimeter of some villas and the repetition of these offerings over the course of time reinforce the idea of protecting the family and the property and of favouring the fertility of the fields.[122]

Hence, a sort of hybridism seems to be synthesized in these deposits, whose tradition as propitiatory and/or purification rites existed in Hispania before the arrival of the Romans. However, finds from the first and second centuries CE onwards are different, with offerings related to fertility and a concept of regeneration widespread throughout Mediterranean cultures — including the Roman one — and which differ from Iron Age offerings. As a result, votive deposits as a domestic rite seem to have been long-lived, but with a certain adaptation in their form and meaning to influences that may have been brought by the Romans.[123] However, this new type of deposits and their meaning fitted perfectly in a cult deeply influenced by the importance of fertility and the cycle of life and death, a mainstay of Iron Age domestic religion that was in particular maintained in the logical context of the family's rural estate, as we have also seen in the villa of Vilauba.

## Conclusions

The evolution of domestic worship in Hispania in the course of the Roman period shows a gradual transformation of rites from indigenous traditions towards Roman ones, a shift that seems to reach its peak around the turn of the Era, when indigenous evidence almost disappears from the archaeological record. However, it can be seen that the hybridism that quite clearly appears in some republican contexts, with the coexistence of rites, traditions, and material culture of different origin in the same settlement and even in the same house, continues to exist if we consider not only the form but also the meaning of this worship.

In the assimilation of foreign traditions, Hispano-Romans seem to have preferred the ones that best fitted with relatively deeply rooted beliefs, such as the relationship between religion and social representation inside the house or the agricultural character of domestic religion and domestic gods, related to fertility and the cycle of life and annual regeneration. The maintenance of some specific rites, such as child burials and votive deposits, even with some adaptations, and their coexistence with characteristic Roman elements in the domestic cult, such as *lararia*, demonstrate that hybridism was not a reality restricted to the Republic, but that it shaped domestic worship in Hispania by means of creating a corpus of beliefs and rites that mixed both indigenous and Romano-Italic traditions and elements in a new reality in which their origin did not seem as significant as it is for us.

Hispano-Roman families chose the rites, deities, and beliefs that best fitted with their concerns, longings, and also with their own vernacular traditions from among the ones that they had at hand. Not in vain was the domestic realm a privileged context for freely expressing individuals' own beliefs, and this seems to have been the case to judge from the archaeological record preserved in Hispania.

---

121 Casas and Ruiz de Arbulo 1997, 218–25.
122 Bowes 2006, 82.
123 It must be said, however, that some of the ideas contained in them also had a long tradition in the Iberian Peninsula as part of the Mediterranean *koine*, such as the interpretation of the egg as a symbol of regeneration, see Pérez Ruiz 2014, I, 143–44.

# Part II

# Strategies, Mechanisms, and Practice

*Collective Identities and Private Agency*

# 8. Religion and Identity on a Microcontinent

## Ancient Mediterranean Religions

Ancient Mediterranean religions are a recent invention. The term has been recently used to describe a field that brings together ancient Judaism and early Christianity alongside Greek, Roman, and sometimes a wider group of ancient Near Eastern traditions and even occasionally early Islam.[1] This cross-disciplinary activity has been very successful, helping specialists work out what is genuinely distinctive about their own material, and sometimes suggesting wider trends that are less visible from within particular disciplines. But the extent to which the term 'Mediterranean' serves more than short-term heuristic aims is not always clear. In some cases, the term is clearly a flag of convenience.[2] For classicists and archaeologists 'Mediterranean' has often been a convenient alternative to either 'classical' or 'Graeco-Roman', while for some of those working on ancient Judaism it offers refuge from the equally uncomfortable term 'biblical'.

Some do see the Mediterranean 'as a unifying feature', a space of relatively fast communication, a zone within which certain kinds of connectivity might be activated.[3] Those themes are more evident in relation to some religious phenomena than others. The growth of maritime connections in the first three centuries of the last millennium BCE made possible what have been termed 'orientalising periods' in archaic Greece, Etruria, and Iberia. Mostly this is evident in the spread of various luxuries and with them aspects of style, but these included religious imagery and perhaps already some of the syncretic creativity characteristic of the middle of the millennium. At a later period, Greek iconography was widely adopted, for the portrayal of humans as well as gods, but again with consequences for what is sometimes called a Mediterranean *koiné*. During the second half of the last millennium some deities did begin to have a broadly Mediterranean distribution. Melqart is a case in point, from Tyre to Cádiz and at many points along the way.[4] The distribution of cult to Isis, in her Hellenistic and Roman form, is also largely Mediterranean, especially after her association with the sailing season.[5] The modes by which deities, and especially their images, were disseminated were very varied: some travelled with soldiers and merchants, some came as booty or as the results of inter-state diplomacy, in some cases there were certainly missionaries.[6] Naturally these distributions reflect emergent networks of trade and travel, and the prominence of Mediterranean seafaring among them.

But some other religious phenomena are less obviously Mediterranean. Consider the cult of Jupiter. During the early Empire, dedications to Jupiter outnumber those to any other deity except in North Africa. The chief god of the Roman pantheon was widely syncretized and worshipped in a variety of versions throughout the Empire, especially in areas with strong military presence, such as the Rhineland and the Danube provinces, and in areas

---

1 For instance Knust and Várhelyi 2011; Rüpke 2013a; Spaeth 2013; Orlin 2016; Stephens 2016; SAMR, the Society for Ancient Mediterranean Religions. The term, or some variant of it, has also been used to describe some interdepartmental programmes.
2 Woolf 2004.
3 The quotation is from the foreword to Orlin 2016, citing the inspiration of Horden and Purcell 2000 while acknowledging that they also note the Mediterranean operates as a medium of religious differentiation and a barrier which promotes divisions between cultural systems.

4 Bonnet 1988; Bonnet and Jourdain-Annequin 1992.
5 Bricault 2000; 2004a; 2004b; Bricault and others 2007; Versluys 2004.
6 Collar 2007; Bonnet and Bricault 2016.

**Greg Woolf**, Ronald J Mellor Professor of Ancient History (UCLA)

where Italians settled overseas. Completely different is the cult of Mithras.[7] The version best attested in the Roman world was created either in Anatolia or in central Italy and particularly widely worshipped in the northern provinces, but the theonym can be traced back via Achaemenid religion to Bronze Age Syria and the Indian Vedas, and he continued to be worshipped across Iran and in India. The Jewish diaspora also extended eastwards through Persian territories and south into Arabia as well as westward to Italy. Christianity covered some of the same area and in Late Antiquity also reached beyond the Roman frontier into Ireland, Gothic territory beyond the Danube, and Armenia.

If instead of deities, we look at the distribution of classical-style temples, of statues making use of iconographies we recognize from *LIMC* and similar reference works, of votive traditions of various kinds, of altars with inscriptions in Greek or Latin, we find no clear correlation to Mediterranean regions. There is a slightly better correlation to the limits of Roman Empire. There are few classical-style temples attested beyond the frontiers of the Empire. Garni in Armenia is the best attested archaeologically, and the Peutinger Map records a Temple of Augustus at Muziris in southern India. Statuettes of Roman deities have been found in northern Europe beyond the Roman frontier, but whether or not they were objects of worship is unclear. Tacitus reports the worship of Isis among the Suebi, but it is uncertain whether the identification is his or that of locals. Ritual traditions common in the provinces such as votive altars and religious epigraphy are not known beyond the frontiers of the Empire and not all were uniformly practised within it.

A determined collaborative investigation conducted over a decade into whether or not there was something that could appropriately be termed an imperial religion concluded that, short of the cult of Jupiter, there was not.[8] Ruler worship, once thought a candidate for an imperial religion, now seems better understood as something that emerged within a large number of local ritual traditions, with no central control and few common features beyond use of the images and names of emperors.[9]

Where does this leave Mediterranean religion? While there were a few traditions that had a distribution that was largely Mediterranean, there were others that spilled beyond it. Empire had a greater impact than geography in shaping large-scale religious patterning but did so mostly accidentally. Most deities were worshipped quite locally and religious authority, before Late Antiquity, was never exercised at more than a regional scale. The Mediterranean divided as much as it connected.

## Microcontinents of Difference

The Iberian Peninsula is a good place to attempt a different kind of religious geography, one that takes into account the distinctive features of the various inhabited spaces connected by empire and the sea. Some of these spaces were large islands each with their own character, Cyprus and Crete in the eastern Mediterranean, Sicily, Sardinia, and Corsica in the west. Others were archipelagos and the narrow coastal strips linked to them in regions like the south Aegean and the northern Adriatic. Then there were coasts that opened onto various kinds of continental hinterland, the Sahara, Syria, the Pontic steppe.

Iberia itself may be considered a microcontinent. By this I mean a region connected by various seaways and narrow land route passages but enclosing its own massive hinterland. Iberia may be compared in different ways to Gaul, the Maghreb, and Anatolia. Each has a central massif. Although formed in different geological eras and of different size and shapes, the Atlas, the Meseta, the Massif Central, and the Anatolian plateau all exercise centrifugal pressures that push human populations out from the centre.

The principal way in which this happens is to do with drainage. Relief structures hydrology, relief and hydrology determine the distribution of fertile soils, and all these shape demography and human settlement. In all these regions large river systems drain down from the highlands, and over time have deposited alluvial soils around their lower courses in broad valleys which open onto the coast. The first human populations of Europe often clustered along the coasts in any case because they were generally rich trophic environments, even allowing some hunter-gather populations to become sedentary. Farmers, when they arrived, were most successful on alluvial soils. Differences in altitude were also reflected in temperature differences. Most early domesticated crops were adapted to relatively warm climates, and most early tree crops were intolerant of frost. The cultigens that the first farmers brought from the Near East did better at low altitudes. By late prehistory many populations had learned to exploit neighbouring uplands in a variety of ways, including as summer pasture and

---

7  See McCarty and Edher in this volume.
8  Cancik and Rüpke 1997, 2009; Ando 2003.
9  Price 1984; Small 1996; Cancik and Hitzl 2003; Gordon 2011; see also Marco in this volume.

a source of timber.[10] But the uplands could not support such large populations and so the demographic centres of gravity always remained around the edge of the microcontinents, in broad valleys and on low plateaux.

The Middle Sea offered a potential for connection, at least when navigational skills and technology were developed.[11] The central massifs of microcontinents, by contrast, frustrated communications. The shape of the central massifs made a difference to how connected the lowland centres were to each other. The central massif in France is relatively low and not large in extent, and so there were easy connections across the broad Gallic isthmus that connects Languedoc with the Garonne basin, or from Provence via the Rhône corridor to the river systems of the Loire, the Seine, and the Rhine. The Anatolian plateau, higher and larger in extent, is a more formidable barrier separating the western valleys of the Hermus, the Cayster, and the Maeander from the plains of Bithynia in the north and Pamphylia and Cilicia Pedias in the south. None of these central ranges cut off all communications: even the Alps could be crossed as early as the Bronze Age. But these upland barriers did generate some geographical caging, or perhaps better allowed peripheral populations to be more or less as isolated from each other as they chose.

The effects have been felt in all historical eras and continue today. The long work of nationalism means that we are accustomed to considering the microcontinents as natural unities. But in the past, they were often politically and socially disunited. Despite long processes of political growth since the later Middle Ages and enormous changes in communications technology, the recent history of each region shows the difficulty political centres have had in enforcing their will over their margins.[12] Even today Paris struggles to impose its will on major metropolitan centres such as Bordeaux, Lyon, Marseille, and Strasbourg; Madrid faces rival centres of power in Barcelona, Valencia, and Seville; and Rabat has limited influence over Casablanca, Tangier, Marrakesh. Atatürk placed Ankara in the centre of Anatolian Turkey, but even so control of the eastern regions is difficult, and Istanbul and Izmir remain rival attractors. The connectivity brought by the Middle Sea and the Atlantic has in many cases raised up port cities as rivals to their landlocked capitals.

Every microcontinent has its own distinct cultural history, but they have a family likeness. These are not areas characterized by peer-polity interaction, that widely attested pattern in which a cluster of centres or states share a common and accelerated historical trajectory driven by emulation and competition between local rivals.[13] None of these microcontinents were truly isolated, but when innovations from outside were accepted and adapted, they seem often to have developed in distinctive ways.[14] Technologies, ideas, and styles that took root in one or another of the more densely populated peripheral zones did not necessarily spread to other parts of the microcontinent. It is a feature of microcontinents that peripheral population concentrations are often better connected to distant territories than to other parts of the microcontinent. Geography also imposes a certain cultural fragmentation with political consequences. De Gaulle is said to have asked of France, 'How can you govern a country that has two hundred and forty-six varieties of cheese?'[15] The religious history of microcontinents reveals similar patterns.

## Iberia as a Microcontinent

The core of the Iberian microcontinent is the Hesperian Shield, a mass of granites and other metamorphic rocks raised up by tectonic collisions which also form the core of the main Iberian mountain ranges and of the central plateau of the Meseta.[16] Around it are a series of sedimentary basins formed by later erosion and now shaping the great river systems. The Douro and the Tagus-Guadiana system lie over the Meseta running west. The Guadalquivir in the south and the Ebro in the north-east form two other basins. Only the Ebro flows into the Mediterranean, and it draws most of its water from the Pyrenees. The pronounced difference in rainfall between Atlantic Iberia and Mediterranean Iberia has shaped vegetation and later agriculture and settlement.[17]

Farming arrived in the south in the sixth millennium BCE, and it was a long time before it was established in the north and west. Prehistoric agriculture there developed a distinctive path more dependent on livestock. In Mediterranean Iberia irrigation would be more important. Differences in geology,

---

10 For a model study, Thonemann 2011.
11 Broodbank 2013.
12 For France, Fox 1971; Weber 1976; Braudel 1986. On the Maghreb, Shaw 2004. For a characterization of the Iberian Peninsula, Loidi 2017.
13 Renfrew and Cherry 1986.
14 Shaw 2004 on the Maghreb.
15 'Comment voulez-vous gouverner un pays qui a deux cent quarante-six variétés de fromage?'
16 Loidi 2017.
17 Cunliffe 1995.

pedology, and the availability of timber probably lay behind different traditions of architecture. But ecology does not explain local traditions of sculpture. The *castros* of the north-west, the *stelai* of the south-west, and the coastal *oppida* of the north-east all exemplify the fragmentation of the microcontinent.

From early in the ninth century BCE, if not earlier, some parts of Iberia began to be connected by sea to much more distant societies. Phoenicians visited the Atlantic coasts of southern Iberia and also the Mediterranean regions within the Straits of Gibraltar, connecting them via Sardinia and what is now Tunisia to the Levant and also to North Africa.[18] Greek visitors moved from central Italy to the Rhône mouth and thence to what is now north-east Spain.[19] Burial rites and ethnonyms from the north-east suggest connections between this area and central Europe. By the middle of the fifth century BCE Etruscans and then other Italians established connections with southern France.[20] Sites like Ullastret on the north-east littoral seem to form part of a cultural continuum that stretched to the Rhône. At an uncertain point in the last millennium BCE sailing vessels began to be used on the Atlantic, connecting western coastal societies in Iberia with each other and across the Bay of Biscay with parts of Gaul. Carthaginian and Roman campaigns in the late third century BCE impacted on Mediterranean Iberia from south and north.

Yet these various connections with different places did nothing to diminish the cultural fragmentation of Iberia. This may be exemplified by the variety of scripts that began to be used in different parts of Iberia, and the linguistic diversity they reveal.[21] Linguistically there is a complex mixture of Celtic and other Indo-European languages, and several non-Indo-European ones. Iberian was written in three or four different scripts, Celtiberian in three scripts, Lusitanian and Basque were certainly spoken (and very occasionally written) in particular parts of the microcontinent. Several languages were written in the south-west. There were also regions from which no epigraphy has survived.

Nor did Rome's slow conquest of the region end this fragmentation. The Iberian Peninsula was one of those regions in which Rome first had to develop instruments of government given there was no royal or civic infrastructure to metabolize.[22] It did not do this by conceptualizing Hispania as an object of control, as it had done Sicily, Sardinia, or Asia. There was certainly no plan for systematic conquest in the republican period.[23] The labels Hispania Citerior and Ulterior betray the perspective of armies marching from Italy towards Punic territory. The interior was initially of little interest. Triumphs when they were won in the second and first centuries were announced over particular peoples, not spaces. Short-term military advantage and the desire for metals directed Roman policy beyond the point where Iberia had, like the Balkans and Africa, become a convenient place to stage civil wars.[24] Only with the Augustan reorganization in the last decade BCE is there much sign that the microcontinent was considered as a whole. Revealingly the new provincial structure reflected geography much better than the republican one. Tarraconensis had at its heart the Ebro basin with most of Mediterranean Iberia, Baetica was based on the Guadalquivir drainage system, while Lusitania was framed by the Atlantic-facing river systems of the Douro, the Tagus, and the Guadiana.

## Small Iberian Worlds

In all periods the geographical fragmentation of Iberia has formed a key framework within which communal identities have been created. Around Iberia's rocky core different populations emerged into history at different points.

The content of prehistoric identities is difficult to establish prior to the appearance of indigenous epigraphy. Tellingly this happened at different points around the microcontinent between the seventh and last centuries BCE.[25] From the second century BCE external testimony gives a little help in some regions, but even when we do have ethnonyms like the Vaccaei and the Celtiberians it is not always obvious how long-lasting or unified any particular group was: often the territories of each people are unclear. A huge literature has been created trying to make the best sense of a handful of references to Tartessos in the south. An added difficulty is that communal identity was represented at several levels. The Celtiberians, as portrayed in Greek and Latin texts, are a vast and amorphous group, but occupied a terrain in which dozens of other groups are also attested. Culture-historical approaches to material culture have added confusion, as has a too easy asso-

---

18 Aubet 2001; Sagona 2008; Crawley Quinn and Vella 2014; Crawley Quinn 2017.
19 Dietler 2009.
20 Dietler 1989; 2005; Bats 2013.
21 Sinner and Velaza 2019 and see <http://hesperia.ucm.es/> [accessed 6 April 2020].
22 Richardson 1976; 1986; Edmondson 1992–1993 [1994].
23 Keay 1990.
24 Crawford 2008.
25 For a good discussion based on material from Baetica, Downs 1998; Celestino and López-Ruiz 2016; Cruz Andreotti 2018.

ciation of language and ethnicity. Some of the narratives written around the interactions of groups like the Iberians or the Celts rest on very shaky evidential foundations. The recent controversy over 'Celtic from the West' shows how quite different interpretations can be supported from the same linguistic and archaeological material.[26]

One thing that is clear is that political communities were in most regions relatively small. Settlement archaeology is a good indicator. The small scale of the coastal communities of the north-east — part of that long continuum of related groups stretching from the Ebro to the Rhône — may be judged from the size of even major settlements such as Ullastret and Ensérune. There are none of the vast oppida known from eastern France and central Europe, complexes like Mont Beuvray, Manching, or Stradonice, which enclosed areas of three to five hundred hectares within vast complex earthworks. Things were a little different in the Iberian interior: Numantia is said to have covered more than one hundred hectares, but recent research suggest that the size for both the Celtiberian (6–8 ha) and the Roman town (c. 12 ha) are much smaller.[27] Most Celtiberian centres were under 30 ha in area. The *castros* of Galicia and Asturias were typically small, hillforts that rarely enclosed as much as 10 ha, and they are generally 5–10 ha apart. The proto-urban centres of the south are different in planning, architecture, and engagement with the outside world, but they are also small.

Coinage provides another indicator. More than 160 communities minted coins with Iberian legends.[28] Like writing, coin use followed regional trends, but while the earliest Iberian scripts are in the southwest, coins first appeared in the north-east in the fifth century BCE.[29] Only in the second century, when they were minted by numerous communities in the Ebro Valley, did local coin use take off in the Guadalquivir basin. As in the case of writing, there were many communities that never produced their own coinage.

Finally, there is the fact that under Roman rule community size remained relatively small. By the early imperial period there were around four hundred communities in Iberia as a whole.[30] This compares to fewer than thirty in Britain and around one hundred in the four Gallic provinces. The basis for this is largely classical testimony supplemented by epigraphy, the latter richest in areas of Roman settlement. Pliny the Elder states that Pompey claimed he had defeated more than 870 oppida from the Alps to the borders of Hispania Ulterior, but as he realized claims made on a victory monument are rarely reliable. Strabo picked out a similar claim from the early second century BCE, and his source Posidonius's scepticism.

> Polybius said that M. Metellus exacted a tribute from Celtiberia of 600 talents. He [Posidonius] also made fun of Polybius for stating that Tiberius Gracchus overwhelmed 300 cities, alleging that Polybius was pandering to Gracchus by calling forts cities, as happens in triumphal processions.[31]

Caesar's claims for his conquests in Gaul would also be exaggerated (or at least count some very small settlements as *urbes*). But Pliny's description seems to be using records which in part relate to the Augustan provincial organization of the Hispaniae a century or so before he was writing.[32] Baetica contains 175 communities of which nine are *coloniae*, ten are *municipia* of Roman citizens, twenty-seven have been given Latin rights, six are free, three bound by treaty, and 120 are tributary. Tarraconensis contains 189 autonomous towns, twelve of them colonies, thirteen are *municipia* of Roman citizens, eighteen have Latin rights, one is bound by treaty, and 135 are tributary. He also notes that nearly 293 additional towns are dependent on others. Lusitania includes forty-five peoples including five colonies, one *municipium* of Roman citizens, three with the Latin rights, and thirty-six tributary.

Several points emerge from this list. First, the mean size of communities clearly varied considerably between the three provinces. Lusitania had forty-five communities as opposed to the 189 in Tarraconensis. A check is provided by the number of *conventus* in each province. The function of the *conventus* was to limit the number of places at which justice was given by Roman officials. Lusitania had three, Baetica four, and Tarraconensis seven. Second, Pliny's catalogue also makes it clear that alongside these autonomous communities were many smaller oppida and *populi*, communities attached to others,

---

26 Cunliffe and Koch 2010; Koch and Cunliffe 2013; 2016.
27 Jimeno Martínez 2011.
28 Ripollès 2012b.
29 Ripollès and Sinner 2019.
30 Mackie 1983. Plin., *Nat.* III.3.7–17; IV.4.18–30; IV.35.113–18, listed a number of 399 *civitates* and 114 *populi*. See below.
31 Str. III.4.13 translation Kidd Fragment 271.
32 Plin., *Nat.* III.1.6–III.3.30 and on Lusitania IV.20.110–20. On his partial use of administrative documents for his geography Shaw 1981. The section on the Hispaniae shows an awareness of the pre-Augustan provincial organization but classifies communities by *conventus* as well as *provincia*. It is unclear how far Pliny updated this information. There is little sign in his lists of urban statuses of the impact of Vespasian's grant of the Latin right of 74 CE.

even communities that were in effect clusters of villages. Third, to Roman administrators and to Pliny the relative statuses of different communities were very important. This matters quite a lot when we consider communal identities.

Why was Iberia divided up into so many communities? Roman rule in general sought to impose organization on the provinces, not just to make the giving of justice feasible as in the *conventus* system, but also for the collection of taxation. But there seems to have been a reluctance to expend much energy homogenizing local arrangements. There were a few cases in the East where Romans redrew the political map at this scale, as when the kingdoms of Macedonia in the second century BCE and Pontus in the last century BCE were broken up into new city-states. In most cases pre-existing units were preserved in the administrative geography, perhaps in some cases 'freezing' political communities that were relatively new or fluid, and probably in a few cases determining disputed boundaries. It is very unlikely that the Augustan provincial reorganization of Iberia *divided* indigenous communities. A smaller number of medium-sized communities might have been preferable from the point of view of government. It is most likely, then, that the majority of epigraphically attested communities had had some sort of pre-conquest existence. Indeed, it is likely that as in other parts of the Roman West the political geography of Roman-period communities closely reflected that of their pre-conquest predecessors.[33] In some areas of the Empire, Romans did create new communities, generally to settle Roman citizens. A small number of new settlements were created in Iberia during republican wars such as Carteia and Gracchuris in the 170s BCE.[34] Most of the new communities were Caesarian or later. This is the case for the twenty-six colonies mentioned by Pliny. But this added only slightly to the total number of communities.

Epigraphic documents confirm the impression that in most populous areas political communities were small. One of the first Latin documents from the region is the *Lex Contrebiensis*, which gives some idea of arrangements in the Ebro Valley in the early 80s BCE.[35] The landscape it conjures up is one of small communities pressed close together and struggling over water rights in one of the most arid parts of Iberia. The copies of Flavian municipal charters so far recovered suggest Baetica too was a region in which small communities were pressed close together and even inconsequential centres had full autonomy. Urbanization was concentrated along the valley of the Guadalquivir with urban centres just tens of kilometres apart.[36] Settlement was much sparser to the north and to the south. Another epigraphic indicator of how closely packed communities could be is the relatively large number of *incolae* attested epigraphically: *incolae* were members of one community resident in a neighbouring one. Records of members of one community buried in another show that mobility tended to be short-distance, movement between adjacent communities and mainly in the same region.[37]

These small social worlds were clustered in the richest farming areas, along the valleys of the Guadalquivir and the Ebro, on the north-eastern Mediterranean coastal plain, around the estuaries of the Douro and the Tagus, and so on. Roman colonization, road-building, and administration, and also the development of mines and fish production, created additional nodes of attraction, but did not diminish regionalism.[38] We should conclude that identities most likely continued to be formed at a very local level. Within each region there tended to be competition between neighbours. Pliny's catalogue took care to differentiate communities by their formal status in relation to Rome. The information probably derived from his source document, but there are signs that local communities in Iberia had internalized the hierarchies of status expressed in these distinctions. For instance, the surviving copy of the colonial statute establishing the Caesarian colony of Urso was set up long after its foundation, quite likely in response to the setting up of monumental versions of the statutes that created Latin *municipia* in the Flavian period. Then there is the story of Hadrian responding to requests of 'promotion' to colonial status from Italica and other cities.[39] Promotion, as he pointed out, brought no practical advantages and might even diminish the autonomy of local communities. Competition for status was apparently more important than preserving autonomy. On rare occasions this could result in violence.[40]

Civic statuses were entangled with personal status, especially for those municipal elites who might win Roman citizenship by holding office in a Latin *municipium*. Does this mean a new identity community emerged in Iberia, marked by shared Roman citizenship? Probably not, given that the Roman citizens

---

33  Almagro-Gorbea 1988; Álvarez and Ruiz Zapatero 2001.
34  Herzig 2006.
35  Richardson 1983.
36  Fear 1996; Keay 1998.
37  Mackie 1983; Haley 1991.
38  Edmondson 1987.
39  Gell. XVI.13.1–9 with Boatwright 2000, 36–56.
40  Syme 1981.

of the Iberian Peninsula in the late first century CE were very diverse. They included recent magistrates of Latin *municipia*; all the citizens of the Roman colonies; the legionaries of Legio VII Gemina, formally still based at León in the north-west but in practice with detachments in various sensitive spots such as the governor's base at Tarragona, or the gold mines at Astorga; traders and entrepreneurs from Italy; aristocratic governors, legates, and procurators on short tours of duty; and the ex-slaves of any or all of these. It is difficult to imagine such a disparate group having a common identity in any meaningful sense. Legal status was intersected by class, gender, descent, origin, wealth, and so on.[41] The diversity of the citizen body was only enhanced when most of the population was enfranchised after Caracalla's Edict of 212 CE. Our first definite sign that 'Roman' formed a significant identity in Iberia comes in the Visigothic Law codes.

Nor is there much sign of the emergence of identities at the level of the province in Iberia. Pliny the Younger refers to the *Baetici* in the context of the prosecution of a governor,[42] but that is shorthand for the provincial assembly of Baetica which was too exclusive to incubate a common identity. Local politics might now be expressed in a different idiom, but they remained local. Iberia was not unusual in this respect, but some other regions had different experiences. Local identities and local mythologies grew in importance on both sides of the Aegean, but the broader identity of Hellenism was tolerated by most emperors and promoted by some.[43] But this was perhaps the exception. A few passages of imperial Latin suggest *Hispanus* had a slightly derogatory sense, at least when seen from the cultural centre.[44]

Unsurprisingly then, when we can gain glimpses of collective identity building in Iberia, it took place at the most local level.[45] A cluster of origin myths are preserved by Greek and Roman writers, mainly within geographical or historical works. Most of these stories seem to have been created in the last decades BCE and resemble contemporary stories from Gaul and North Africa and slightly earlier ones from Italy. They typically asserted connections to mythical figures such as Hercules or Odysseus, or to archaic migrations, and the evidence for them was often based on the supposed etymologies of place names or ethnonyms. Quite a few included input from both locals and metropolitan scholars, who contributed not only the broader mythic frames, but also the techniques of this genealogical science, which was often called *archeologia*.[46] How widely known these mythical genealogies were in Iberian communities is difficult to judge. Occasionally they seem to be alluded to on coinage.[47] But apart from Heracles-Melqart there are few monumental traces of them. Perhaps these stories mattered most to those who created them. Some Roman observers at least did not take these stories seriously. Pliny the Elder, in the midst of trying to sort out the geography of the Hispaniae, notes:

> Marcus Varro records that the whole of Hispania was invaded by Hiberi and Persians and Phoenicians and Celts and Carthaginians. He says it was the game (*lusum*) of Father Liber or the frenzy (λύσσα) of the bacchants that accompanied him that gave the name to Lusitania, and that the prefect of the whole was Pan. But what has been said about Hercules and Pyrene or Saturn I consider to be completely mythical.[48]

## Ritual and Identity

Like all parts of the Roman West, Iberia underwent major transformations between the last decades BCE and the first CE. Urbanism appeared in areas that had no previous experience of it, and the physical appearance and government of existing towns was reshaped. Indigenous languages were rapidly replaced by Latin, at least as far as public writing was concerned. Local coinages were replaced by Roman, as they were everywhere in the West.[49] Latin epigraphy maps the arrival of new institutions at all levels of society. A deluge of imported objects and new technologies reshaped the material environment of everyday life.[50] Pre-Roman traditions and styles were eroded and the various cultural zones of Iberia look more similar than ever before, to each other, and also to those of Aquitania and Narbonensis, of the Mauretanias and Africa Proconsularis, even of Italy.

---

41 For how Roman dimensions of identity intersected with considerations of age, sex, status, and other considerations at the level of the individual, see Revell 2009.

42 Plin., *Ep.* 3.4, 3.9.

43 Spawforth and Walker 1985; 1986; Woolf 1994; Swain 1996; Whitmarsh 2010.

44 Mart. XII Preface; Sen. *Apocol.* III.

45 Woolf 2011 relying on the work gathered in Moret 2006; Cruz Andreotti and others 2006; 2007; Cruz Andreotti 2009. With a different emphasis see also Johnston 2017; Revilla in this volume.

46 On the method, Bickerman 1952; Wiseman 1974; Malkin 1998; Hartog 2001; Erskine 2005.

47 Jiménez Díez 2015.

48 Plin., *Nat.* III.1.8.

49 Crawford 1985; Howgego and others 2005.

50 For a variety of assessments Keay 1990; Edmondson 1992–1993 [1994]; Blázquez Martínez and Alvar 1996; Downs 1998; Beltrán 1999; Keay 2001; Revell 2009.

During the triumviral period and the century that followed members of the provincial propertied classes were drawn together by education and by new roles in the military and in government. Many spent time away from home on military service or in the capital: they returned to Iberia with new perspectives and experiences. In some contexts, many of them probably did now feel Roman in some sense or other. It is difficult at this distance for us to be sure how far they felt part of a new ethnic group and citizen body, and how far simply marked by a new class or a new relationship to power. No texts have survived to help us decide if they formed an extensive, but thin, imagined community. But perhaps their consciousness matters less when we consider the many ways in which they embodied Roman ways of life: how they ate, how they washed, how they dressed, how they had themselves portrayed all make them seem Roman whatever label they gave themselves.

Habits of religious practice took their place alongside other new habits. Religious identities in the modern sense did not exist in antiquity. What names someone called the gods, and the rituals in which he or she participated, reflected and affirmed their membership in a community. Those who belonged to more than one community — temporarily as in military service, or permanently in the case of those who were both Roman citizens and members of some tiny Iberian city — might call the gods by two sets of names and participate in more than one ritual tradition. As far as we know (which is not very far), no sense of conflict or dissonance was felt. Jupiter, Hercules, Ceres, and the other gods slipped easily into Iberian spaces, just as Phoenician and Greek deities had before them.

Religion does, however, provide a field within which these transformations can be observed particularly well. That is because, in both pre-conquest and post-conquest Iberia, a great proportion of texts and images were religious in nature. A central part of Roman (and some local) religious thought was that it was important to create monuments. From the outside we might see this as the amassing of symbolic capital, and the transformation of religious monumentality as a transfer of that capital. But this was not organized wholly from above, or wholly by Roman rulers. Few theonyms survive from the pre-conquest period, but once Latin epigraphy was available literally hundreds of names of gods appear that are unknown in other parts of the Empire. Virtually all had very local distributions, and most of these gods are attested by very small numbers of inscriptions. In effect new technologies of displaying and storing religious knowledge were used to bolster the localism of many local communities. This might be true even when Roman gods seem to appear. Jupiter Optimus Maximus is well attested in the north-west of the peninsula, but as in Syria or the Rhineland he seems to have been fitted into local systems of belief and ritual. Other Roman gods also seem to take up regional characters: it has been suggested that Vulcan, Juno, as well as Hercules in the south represent transformations of Punic deities long worshipped there.

This is not the place for another discussion of the dynamics of syncretism and translation, of whose ends these processes served, and how they were understood in the provinces. But their progress does make clear that beneath the apparent homogenizing effect of the Roman takeover, regional and local traditions kept re-emerging. Perhaps the best example is provided by ruler worship. This is attested in various forms from the reign of Augustus, and perhaps rested in some cases on indigenous traditions too. Most visible to us are the urban manifestations of ruler worship, in the Roman colonies of Mérida and *Tarraco* that were made provincial cult centres and in the elaborate regulations for civic cult in the municipal laws. But it is striking that there was apparently no attempt to create a unitary centre for the Hispaniae like that created at Lyon for the Tres Galliae. In fact, it looks as if a provincial cult of the emperor was created in Baetica only under the Flavians. No doubt the reasons were contingent and political, but this is another illustration of how Iberian societies associated most naturally within each of the basins on the edge of the microcontinent. Interaction within each of these main regions remained more intense than interaction across it. This is also being illustrated by recent result of surveys of material relating to new 'Oriental' gods in Roman Iberia. Mithras worship is most concentrated in the Mediterranean littoral in the north-east with an important cluster of material in Mérida. Isiac material by contrast is most concentrated in Andalusia.

The point does not need to be elaborated. Like all micro- (and macro-) continents, Iberia was marked by the development of distinct societies and cultures around its edges. This is reflected in the identities and religious practices of the prehistoric and Roman periods. Our impulse to find a unified experience reflects a modern view of Iberia that rarely coincides with any ancient one. Empire might draw things together, at least in the short term, but geography insists on its divisions.[51]

---

51 I am very grateful to the editors for their advice and bibliographical help. All errors remain my own.

MARTA CAMPO DÍAZ

# 9. Coinage and the Religious Beliefs of the Peoples of Hispania

*Tradition and Foreign Influences*

## Problems of Interpretation in Religious Images on Coinage

The great importance that religious beliefs had in ancient societies resulted in deities, sacred myths, and local cults occupying a preferential place in coin iconography. In the Iberian Peninsula these images appeared at the end of the sixth century BCE on the first issues of Emporion and continued until the closure of the Roman provincial mints during the reign of Caligula. The oligarchies that ruled the cities were responsible for choosing the designs and legends on their issues and the ones who decided the message they wished to project as regards their identity through coin issues. Coins were official documents and no image of a sacred or socio-political nature was ever chosen at random even though their interpretation now presents many difficulties.

Ancient literary, epigraphic, and archaeological sources contribute little, and in many cases no, information as regards the characteristics of the majority of the cities that minted coinage in the Iberian Peninsula. Even when historical and archaeological evidence is available for the coin-issuing cities, identifying their religious structure is complicated, as has been pointed out for many cities in the south of the peninsula.[1] The same situation arises as regards the religious beliefs of the Iberian and Celtiberian populations, about which many studies have been undertaken on the basis of textual and archaeological sources, although their conclusions barely help to decipher the meaning of the coin iconography of these peoples.[2] Moreover, there is little evidence concerning the formal aspects of the deities that the indigenous population worshipped. The scarcity or lack of their own iconography resulted in many cities adopting foreign classical images to represent local deities and cults on their coins, which greatly complicates their interpretation. A local deity about which insufficient documentary evidence is available for its identification may be hidden behind a sacred design of Hellenistic or Roman origin.

Most coin-issuing cities opted to choose a limited number of images related to their religious practices; for this reason, in many cases their issues fail to provide an overall panorama of the local cults and pantheons. Some mints maintained their designs unchanged throughout their issues, whereas, over the course of time, others introduced new images, which provided more information about the development of their religious beliefs and the progressive assimilation of foreign cults. Another question to be considered is that of certain plant and animal images, which may sometimes have both a religious and an economic meaning. On many occasions they are likely to have combined the two symbolic meanings since the deity on the obverse protected the elements related to the economy depicted on the reverse.

It should also be pointed out that, although an attempt is made here to systematize the coin issues of Hispania in several sections in accordance with ethnic and cultural criteria, there was considerable interaction between them; hence, it is not always clear to which cultural grouping mints should be assigned, as has been emphasized in the case of the south of the peninsula.[3]

---

1 Chaves 2012a, 40–41; Marín Ceballos 2012, 32–33; Mora 2019, 148–49.
2 Gozalbes 2006b, 114.

3 Mora 2019, 148–49.

**Marta Campo Díaz**, Institut de Recerca Històrica, Universitat de Girona

## Greek and Phoenician-Punic Imagery

In the closing years of the sixth century BCE, the small Greek colony of Emporion was the first city in Iberia to issue coinage.[4] In the first instance, the city minted above all fractional silver coinage with a wide variety of images, which do not reveal a well-planned iconological programme; neither can a relationship be established between them and the cults of the city, about which very little information is available.[5] Different designs seem to have been adopted from a broad pan-Hellenic repertoire; these evolved depending on fashion, the engravers' knowledge, or the preferences of the magistrates that chose the types.[6]

At the turn of the fourth and third centuries BCE, Emporion struck drachms with a female head surrounded by three dolphins and a horse crowned by a small Nike, which was subsequently replaced by a Pegasus. At the same time, Rhode established a mint that also struck drachms with the head of a female deity, inspired by the design created by Euainetos, at the turn of the fifth and fourth centuries BCE, for the mint of Syracuse and subsequently copied by several Greek mints (Fig. 9.1.1). In general, this effigy has been identified as Artemis, on the basis of Strabo's texts,[7] which state that Artemis Ephesia was venerated in both colonies, although there is no archaeological or epigraphic proof of this.[8] While the female representation on the Rhode issues lacks any attribute that might help to identify her, in the case of Emporion it is significant that in the final issues the deity's head appears with a bow and a quiver, which seems to indicate that, at least in these last drachms, the figure was Artemis.[9]

The Iberians' contacts with the Mediterranean world enabled them to be aware of a wide variety of imported objects with foreign sacred images, among them those represented on the coins struck by Greek mints; over the course of time, these were to have a clear influence on the religious iconography of the different issues minted in the Iberian Peninsula. From the late sixth century BCE, the finds of Greek issues resulted in the Iberian communities on the Mediterranean coast acquiring a degree of knowledge of the existence of struck coins, and in the second half of the fourth century BCE, the city of Arse became the first Iberian settlement to strike coinage. The city chose designs taken from Hellenistic prototypes, such as Hercules, Apollo, or Athena. A good example are the third-century drachms, which display on the obverse a female head with a Corinthian helmet, inspired by the gold staters of the reigns of Alexander the Great and his successors. On the reverse was engraved a bull with a bearded human face, which has been interpreted as a river deity, perhaps of the river that flows beside the city (Fig. 9.1.4).[10]

In the context of the Second Punic War, the Pegasus head on the Emporion drachms underwent a curious modification, being converted into a small human figure whose arms stretch down to his feet and who wears what might be a *petasos* on his head; this figure has given rise to several interpretations, without a unanimous interpretation having been agreed (Fig. 9.1.2). At the same time, some of the Iberian populations produced large amounts of silver coinage with designs that imitated those of the drachms (Fig. 9.1.3) and fractions issued by Emporion and, to a lesser extent, the obols of Massalia. From this moment onwards, we find the continuation of the phenomenon started in Arse, which was to be repeated throughout the second and first centuries BCE, namely the adoption of foreign types by indigenous societies; however, there is no evidence to appreciate the meaning that these peoples gave to the iconography that was copied.

The first city in the Phoenician-Punic sphere to strike coinage was Ebusus, located on the island of Ibiza. Its issues started in the fourth century BCE and later, towards the end of the century or in the early third century BCE, the city of Gadir on the southwestern coast of the Iberian Peninsula also began to mint coins. During the Second Punic War, some cities in southern Iberia, such as Malaka or Baria, minted small amounts of low value coinage, but it was not until the second and first centuries BCE, when the area had become the Roman province of Hispania Ulterior, that the number of mints of Phoenician-Punic tradition increased substantially. At the same time, other cities in the south struck coins with Latin and Iberian legends, on occasions adopting Phoenician-Punic-influenced designs.

Although the written sources provide evidence about the main deities in the Phoenician-Punic pantheon, there is little information about their iconography, which makes deciphering the meaning of the coin designs very uncertain, above all without the support of other sources on the local popula-

---

4 Ripollès and Chevillon 2013, 8.
5 Pena 2000.
6 Campo 2003, 36.
7 Str. III.4.8 and IV.1.4.
8 Pena 2016, 961.
9 Pena 2012, 22–23 and 24.

10 Ripollès 2012a, 203–05.

Figure 9.1. 1. Rhode drachm. 2. Emporion drachm. 3. Orose drachm. 4. Arse drachm. 5. Ebusus unit. 6. Gadir hemidrachm. 7. Sex unit. 8. Abdera unit. 9. Lascuta unit. 10. Malaca unit. 11. Malaca half unit. 12. Asido half unit (Museu Nacional d'Art de Catalunya/Gabinet Numismàtic de Catalunya). (Scale: 120%, 4:5)

tion's religious beliefs.¹¹ It is also venturous to interpret coin images and symbols on the basis of those depicted on other objects, such as razors or the steles from Carthage and other North African cities, the symbolism of which it has still not proved possible to decipher suitably.¹² In the south of the peninsula, the cities that were heirs to early Phoenician foundations, such as Gadir, Malaca, or Abdera, were the ones that adopted the most classical iconographic models on their coinage.¹³ In contrast, other mints that similarly used Punic or neo-Punic script, but which also received other cultural influences, adopted more distinctive images.¹⁴

Ebusus and Gadir were the first two Phoenician-Punic cities to strike coinage and are also the ones about which we have most historical and archaeological information. As a consequence, the interpretation of the deities that presided over the greater part of their issues presents fewer problems than those of other mints. The continued presence of the image of Bes on the coinage of Ebusus indicates that he was worshipped on the island, at the same time as being the main evidence for this cult, since on Ibiza his image has only been traced on some scarabs, amulets, and in the form of some terracotta figurines (Fig. 9.1.5).¹⁵ The legend 'ybshm was engraved on the reverse of the bronze issues of Ebusus in the first century BCE; this has been interpreted as a place name formed by two elements, the first of which, 'y, should be understood as 'island', while there is less consensus as regards the translation of the second element, bshm, although Bes would seem to be the most probable.

From the start of its many issues, the mint of Gadir chose the figure of Melqart, who was the most important deity of the city, with information about his cult in the renowned Herakleion being provided by the ancient literary sources (Str. III.5.5). There is also evidence for a Kronion or a sanctuary dedicated to Baal Hammon and for another in honour of Astarte-Marine Venus, but these two deities do not appear on its coinage.¹⁶ In order to represent Melqart, the Gadir workshop adopted an iconographic model of Hellenistic inspiration, which can easily be identified due to the characteristic lion-skin headdress and club on his shoulder (Fig. 9.1.6). In turn this design was widely adopted, or imitated with more or fewer details, by other mints of Phoenician-Punic tradition such as Sexs or Lascuta (Fig. 9.1.7 and 9.1.9). Some mints engraved variants that are of difficult interpretation, such as the one introduced by Bailo, which replaced the club by an ear of corn.¹⁷ It would be hazardous to state whether the adoption of this iconography on the part of several cities in the south of the Iberian Peninsula should strictly be considered as evidence for the diffusion of the cult to Heracles-Melqart in the region, or whether the process was also influenced by the wish to adopt an attractive and easily copied image.¹⁸

Malaca was a prolific and easily identifiable mint that, in the second century BCE, depicted a male head wearing a conical cap, similar to the classical artisan *pileus*, and later a cylindrical headdress like the Persian *cidaris* on its obverses (Fig. 9.1.10–11). Beside the effigy, a pair of tongs which, together with the *pileus*, identify it as an artisan deity in accordance with the identity of Hephaestus-Vulcan, the god of metal-working in the Graeco-Roman pantheon, was engraved. As it was a city of Phoenician tradition, it is logical to think that it was Chusor-Ptah, the Phoenician Kusor, an artisan and inventor of metal-working and sailing, among other attributes.¹⁹ Another mint that adopted clearly identifiable types was that of Baria, which used a female head of orientalizing design, which has been identified as Astarte-Isis, whose cult is recorded in the city.²⁰ Some cities occasionally displayed images of more enigmatic meaning, such as the helmeted heads of Sex, Olontigi, and Abdera, or the bearded head wearing a diadem of Iptuci and Asido, which has been identified as a possible Baal Hammon.²¹

The reverse designs usually complemented the obverse ones, in addition to helping to decipher their meaning and to contributing more information about the religious beliefs of the cities that issued them. On its reverses the mint of Malaca displayed symbols that were clearly inspired by astral symbolism, with the depiction of stars, a crescent with a pellet, and a radiate-headed bust, which imitated the classical image of Helios-Sol (Fig. 9.1.10–11). This bust might represent the Phoenician-Punic god Shamash, bearing in mind the inscription *šmš* engraved beneath the tetrastyle temple on some low denomination coins of the first century BCE.²² Taken as a whole, the iconography of these Malaca issues points to the possible

---

11  Mora 2003, 49.
12  Marín Ceballos 2012, 32–33.
13  Mora 2012, 27.
14  García-Bellido 1991, 78–79.
15  Campo 2006, 49–50.
16  Marín Ceballos 2001.
17  CNH 124.5.
18  Mora 2012, 28–29; Marín Ceballos 2012, 33.
19  Chaves and Marín Ceballos 1992, 175–90; Mora 2003, 59; Marín Ceballos 2012, 34 and 36.
20  Alfaro 2003; Mora 2019, 155–56.
21  CNH 125.1–3 and 5; 122–23.2 and 6; García Bellido 1993, 126.
22  CNH 102.18; Mora 2014–2015, 141.

existence of a solar cult in the city, similar to those recorded in other Mediterranean and Atlantic ports. Like Malaca, the mint of Abdera (Fig. 9.1.8) also displayed a monument dedicated to worshipping its deities in the form of a tetrastyle temple with a pediment, although in both cases the classical structure that appears on the coins is unlikely to have been a faithful representation of reality.[23] Another interesting cultic monument is the one that was engraved on some coin reverses from Lascuta, which combined the effigy of Melqart on the obverse with a stepped altar, from which spring plant motifs interpreted as palms or perhaps corn ears (Fig. 9.1.9).[24]

A frequent reverse, and less frequently obverse, representation is that of different types of animals. The tunny fish shown on issues from Gadir stand out from its first issues onwards (Fig. 9.1.6); these were adopted by other mints in Hispania Ulterior such as Sex or Abdera (Fig. 9.1.7–8). They probably allude to the importance of the fish-salting industry on the south coast of the peninsula, which must have been under the protection of the deities on the obverses in these cities. Dolphins and bulls were two types of animals that formed part of the iconographic repertoire of the different Mediterranean coin-issuing peoples and cultures. Mints such as Asido (Fig. 9.1.12) depicted dolphins, which are related to marine deities and are considered symbols of good omen. The bull must usually have had a religious symbolism, which in general was associated with strength, fertility, and sacrifices (Fig. 9.1.5 and 9.1.12). Its precise meaning may depend on the sacred cults and rituals practised by the different issuing cities, in addition to being related to the obverse image.[25] An exceptional case is the depiction on the issues of Bailo of a bull adorned with some form of triangular mitre over its head, which seems to indicate that it was being prepared for sacrifice.[26]

## The Religious Beliefs of the Native Populations

Once the Roman provinces of Hispania Citerior and Ulterior had been established, at the same time as the cities of Phoenician-Punic tradition were opening new coin workshops, many cities with native roots also took similar steps. In Hispania Ulterior, the majority of these new mints struck coinage with Latin inscriptions, as was the case of Carmo, Ilipa, or Ulia; to a lesser extent, they issued coins with legends in the south-eastern Iberian script, as in the case of Castulo and Obulco, although these mints also made use of Latin legends. The information available about the religious beliefs of these native populations is even less than that for the Phoenician-Punic cities, and there is hardly any clear evidence for the deities worshipped and the cults that were practised. Be that as it may, the epigraphic and archaeological evidence shows that, without abandoning their own traditions, the peoples of Turdetania gradually adopted foreign customs; by the first century CE, Roman cults and gods had come to form a significant part of their everyday life.[27]

The native mints of Hispania Ulterior sometimes adopted classical designs in order to represent their deities, such as the case of Carmo, which engraved one of its issues with a Mercury-type head with a *petasos* and his symbol, the caduceus.[28] Cities also created their own designs, among which stand out a range of male and female heads, which must represent deities about which there is no iconographic or written evidence. Some of these helmeted heads may depict the city's protective deities, which at the same time could have several nuances in warrior, fruit-bearing, or astral manifestations, depending on the symbols accompanying them or the reverse types.[29] For example, the helmeted head on some issues of Carmo (Fig. 9.2.3) might be a local deity of warlike nature, although it has also been suggested that it should be identified as Tanit as a warrior goddess.[30] Another exceptional design is the female head on issues from Obulco, which appears with a plaited hairstyle terminating in a low bun and her neck adorned with rows of beads, ornaments that, even though they were used by Greek and Roman goddesses, also recall those of the ladies in Iberian sculptures (Fig. 9.2.4). These female heads have been interpreted as local deities, which, when accompanied by crescent, have a clear astral character. Furthermore, the plant motifs accompanying them on the obverse or reverse also point to their fruit-bearing qualities.[31] This female-head design was copied by other mints such as Ilipa and Ulia, whose issues probably allude to the same deity.[32]

These mints sometimes broke with their traditional coin types and introduced other new ones, usually inspired by foreign patterns. A good example

---

23 Chaves 2012a, 42.
24 CNH 126.1.
25 López Monteagudo 1973.
26 Chaves 2012a, 42.

27 Chaves 2012a, 40 and 43.
28 CNH 383.9–12; Chaves 2012b, 180–82.
29 Chaves and Marín Ceballos 2004, 365.
30 García-Bellido 1991, 64.
31 Arévalo 2002–2003, 251.
32 Chaves 2012b, 179.

Figure 9.2. 1. Castulo unit. 2. Castulo unit. 3. Carmo unit. 4. Obulco unit. 5. Obulco semis. 6. Kese unit. 7. Kese half unit. 8. Iltirta unit. 9. Untikesken unit. 10. Valentia as (Museu Nacional d'Art de Catalunya/Gabinet Numismàtic de Catalunya). (Scale: 120%, 4:5)

of the late introduction of a new design can be found in a first-century BCE issue by the Obulco mint, in which the traditional female head with a low bun was replaced by a male head with a laurel wreath, whose hairstyle includes Apollo's characteristic ringlets (Fig. 9.2.5). Chaves has emphasized the similarity between this iconography related to Apollo and that depicted on denarii of the Roman Calpurnia family, who were connected with Hispania. This replacement of a local deity by another from the classical pantheon has been interpreted as the consequence of the interest of the local elites in Obulco in demonstrating their increasing proximity to Rome or, perhaps, in manifesting their recognition of a family or individual who favoured the city.[33]

The coin reverses of the native mints of Hispania Ulterior reveal a wide variety of designs, some of which reproduce myths with distant origins and fantastic beings. The mint of Ilturir engraved a triskeles (or triskelion) with the Gorgoneion on the reverse of some issues,[34] and the Castulo workshop showed Europa — the daughter of the king of Sidon who was abducted by Zeus — riding on the bull (Fig. 9.2.2). Both images are rather crude, and they were probably the work of local engravers who were unaware of the significance of the original design, which led them to make modifications that are difficult to interpret and which must have reached Hispania Ulterior after having passed through the filter of the Roman world.[35] The sphinx found on the abundant issues of the Castulo mint (Fig. 9.2.1) also has geographically distant origins, to be more precise oriental ones, and its presence in the south of the Iberian Peninsula is difficult to explain; crude copies of it were made by the less productive workshops of Ilturir and Ursone.

A substantial number of native mints in the south of the Iberian Peninsula chose to depict animals and plants as the main design on the reverse of their coins. As in the case of the issues of other cultures, the most commonly represented animal was the bull, which is normally shown in a standing position, walking (Fig. 9.2.5) or charging, with a religious meaning that seems clear, but which it is difficult to define as occurs in the vast majority of the issues struck in Hispania. Certain bull designs that seem to allude to Roman rituals related to the sacrifice of these animals, as has already been mentioned in the case of Bailo, and as seems to be indicated by the postures with which the bull is represented by other mints, deserve special attention. The Ipora workshop showed a bull lying before an altar, in a position that suggests that it was tied down,[36] while that of Orippo used an apparently kneeling bull with its nape inclined forwards.[37] These animals were sacrificed in Rome during the *suovetaurilia* ceremony; for this reason, according to Chaves, by using this iconography the inhabitants of the area wanted to draw closer to the Romans' religious habits.[38]

Some reverse designs appear to allude to the agricultural wealth of Hispania Ulterior through plant designs such as corn ears and grapes, as well as agricultural implements such as the plough and the yoke. On some occasions, these designs might indicate the role of the female deities depicted on the obverse in protecting the fertility and abundance of crops although this need not be the meaning implied. Among the plant imagery, the most frequently depicted were ears of cereals, probably wheat in the majority of cases although it is impossible to be certain in view of the small size of the representations. The ears were engraved as the main image on the reverse or as symbols, sometimes alongside others incorporating astral features. On the reverses from Carmo, the ears demonstrate the symbolic importance of this plant element, enclosing the city's name written in the centre (Fig. 9.2.3). On the reverse of the coins minted at Obulco there was a corn ear and a plough, as well as a yoke on some occasions, probably indicating the quality of the astral and fruit-bearing deity whose head was depicted on their obverse (Fig. 9.2.4).

Under Roman administration, more than ninety Iberian and Celtiberian cities in Hispania Citerior established coin workshops, whose peak production period was between the second half of the second century BCE and the early first century BCE. These mints correspond to two clearly differentiated cultural spheres, but all of them had legends in Iberian script and used a largely uniform range of types.[39] The vast majority of these mints adopted a male head and a horseman as the main designs of the silver and bronze units; these could have been inspired by the bronze issues of Hiero II of Syracuse (274–217 BCE) or perhaps by the Dioscuri (Castor and Pollux) on Roman denarii (Fig. 9.2.6).[40] Kese may have been the first city to engrave these designs, which gradually, and with slight variations, were copied by almost all the mints in Hispania Citerior, reaching as far as Celtiberia and the Vasconic area.

---

33  Chaves 2012b, 184–86.
34  *CNH* 357.1–5.
35  Pena 2012, 21–23 and 25.
36  *CNH* 365.1.
37  *CNH* 394.1 and 3.
38  Chaves 2012a, 42–43.
39  Gozalbes 2012, 46.
40  Gozalbes 2006a, 296–97.

One significant exception was the types adopted by the mint of Untikesken, a city with a long tradition of issuing Greek coinage, which is reflected in its choice of types. A helmeted female head in Graeco-Roman style was depicted on the obverses, while on the reverses of its bronze units there was a Pegasus with a modified head, similar to that of the Greek drachms of the city (Fig. 9.2.9). In turn, the Arse-Saguntum mint only adopted the design of the male head and the horseman for some of its bronze units, preferring to continue to engrave increasingly Romanized classical images, behind which local deities and cults must still have been hidden.

The male head on the obverse might be beardless or bearded and, on occasions, with a diadem or laurel wreath, in addition to wearing a cloak fastened round his neck, sometimes fastened with a fibula, or to the neck being adorned with torcs. Once again, no historical or archaeological sources are available to understand the identity of this head and to determine whether it was interpreted in the same way in all the different regions. Another dilemma is whether there was any symbolic link between this male head and the horseman that appeared riding on the reverse of these issues. Generally speaking, the male head is linked to a warrior or a native war deity, although other interpretations have also been proposed.[41] For instance, it has been considered that it was originally related to Melqart-Heracles or to a *heros ktistes* (a hero that founded a settlement), who, with the passage of time, came to be identified with the portrait of the issuing authority.[42]

Signs in Iberian script and symbols taken from the classical repertoire, which acted as production marks rather than as identifiers of deities or local heroes, were often engraved next to the male head. A good example can be found in the issues of Kese, one of the Iberian mints with the highest outputs, which made use of a wide variety of Iberian signs and symbols, such as a spearhead or a rudder (Fig. 9.2.6–7), as well as others including a palm, a caduceus, a bundle of thunderbolts, a laurel wreath, or a dolphin. It does not seem logical that the city would have sought to give a new meaning to the male head each time that it introduced a new mint mark, in spite of the undeniable symbolic value of many of them.

The choice of the horseman on the reverse is in accordance with the strong equestrian tradition in Iberian and Celtiberian societies for which horsemen and horses symbolized power; such depictions were frequent in other forms, such as on pottery or Celtiberian steles, in Iberian sculpture or as bronze figurines.[43] In the coin iconography, the horsemen often carry a spear or a sword and occasionally a shield, which endows them with a warrior aura. They may also hold a palm and exceptionally a sceptre, a bird, or a crown, each of which would have given a different symbolic value to their identity. The religious aspect of these horsemen is less clearly defined than that attributable to the obverse male head; in general, they are considered to refer to the local elites, although their meaning could involve different nuances depending on the region. Scholars who have studied the question have proposed several interpretations,[44] such as that of a *heros equitans*.[45] In the case of the spear-wielding horsemen of Celtiberia, they might be related to a celestial and solar deity, one of whose names could have been Lugus.[46]

On some silver issues, the mints of Kese, Turiazu, and Ikalesken included a variant of the horseman type in which the latter is accompanied by a second horse, a design that, in terms of its form, seems to be inspired by that of the Roman denarii reverses that bear the Dioscuri on horseback.[47] Very occasionally, other mints engraved iconography also taken from the Graeco-Roman repertoire on fractional bronze coinage, although, as on other occasions, we do not have sufficient evidence to determine whether local deities were hiding behind these classical images;[48] for instance, Saiti used a Cupid on a dolphin,[49] and Kese a head wearing a Mercury-style *petasos*.[50]

On the reverse of the lower value bronze issues, representations of animals occupied a fundamental place, which reflects their importance in Iberian and Celtiberian societies. Generally speaking, common animals were chosen, the most frequently depicted being the horse and the bull; others, such as the dolphin, the eagle, the boar, or the cock, were less frequent. Moreover, they engraved exotic animals, such as the lion, and mythological ones, like the Pegasus. The workshops usually associated each type of animal with a specific value, with the consequence that their designs seem to reflect a double interpretation: a more religious one, related to animals that could intervene in local cults and another, more practical one to differentiate coins of distinct value, in the same way as the gods on the obverse

---

41 Gozalbes 2006b, 118–19 and 2012, 48.
42 Almagro-Gorbea 1995a, 259.
43 Gozalbes 2006a, 302–12.
44 Gozalbes 2006b, 121 and 2012, 49.
45 Almagro-Gorbea 1995a, 246.
46 Abad Lara 2008.
47 *CNH* 160–61.17–19; 264.19; 324.1–2.
48 Gozalbes 2006b, 115–18.
49 *CNH* 315–16.8–10.
50 *CNH* 160.16.

of the issues of Rome served to identify the different bronze denominations.[51] A unique case is the wolf on the reverse of some issues of Iltirta; the wolf was considered to be the Ilergetes's totem animal, and it may reflect a mythological event associated with the foundation or protection of the community (Fig. 9.2.8).[52]

## Classical Designs in the Issues of the Colonies of Carteia, Corduba, and Valentia

Prior to Caesar's death, only three privileged cities in Hispania minted coinage, namely Carteia, Corduba, and Valentia. The juridical status of these cities and the origin and composition of their population promoted the adoption of fully classical images without any connection with those used by the Phoenician-Punic or native mints in their vicinity on their issues. The Latin colony of Carteia was located in Ulterior; it was founded in the year 171 BCE[53] in order to house the offspring of Roman soldiers and native women, although it seems to have maintained a substantial underlying Phoenician-Punic component in its population. From the mid-second century BCE until the reign of Tiberius, the city produced a substantial number of issues with images largely taken from classical prototypes that showed its affinity to Rome and the importance of its maritime economy, which does not prevent them from presenting problems of interpretation.[54] One example is the bearded male head found on some of the first issues, which might represent either Jupiter or Saturn, since they both had beards.[55] Another image that should be emphasized is a towered female head characteristic of the personification of cities and used both by Phoenician and Hellenistic mints and on Roman denarii, and datable to between the late first century BCE and the early first century CE (Fig. 9.3.1).[56] As regards the iconography of a fisherman sitting on a rock and holding a fishing-rod from which a fish hangs, it is a unique design in Mediterranean issues and must recall a typical figure in the everyday life of this port city (Fig. 9.3.1).[57]

Less evidence is available for the origins of Corduba, the future Colonia Patricia, the date of whose 'foundation' by Rome and exactly when colonial status was conferred on it are much debated. On the obverse, its issues display a female head, with the hair in a low bun, adorned with earrings and a necklace, which in terms of form is similar to that of some Roman denarii. It has been proposed that it should be identified as the goddess Venus, above all because on the reverse there is a naked winged figurine holding a cornucopia and a torch, which might represent her son Cupid, although the torch would be somewhat irregular. Each user could have opted to interpret this image either as a local deity or as the Roman goddess Venus.[58]

The third case to discuss is Valentia in the province of Citerior, founded in 138 BCE to settle soldiers probably of Italic origin and which was awarded the juridical status of *colonia* at a later date. Between the late second century BCE and the early first century BCE, it struck three issues with the same iconography, which copied fully Roman types, in line with the origin of a substantial proportion of its inhabitants, who preferred to adopt images known in their area of origin rather than the native ones of neighbouring mints. The obverses depict a helmeted female head, similar to the image of Rome found on republican denarii, and the reverses a cornucopia with a bundle of thunderbolts, surrounded by a laurel wreath, which copies the iconography of the denarii issued under the magistrate *Q. Fabius Maximus* by the mint of Rome (Fig. 9.2.10).[59]

## Roman Religious Designs in Provincial Issues

From the mid-first century BCE onwards, and especially during the reigns of Augustus, Tiberius, and Caligula, some privileged cities in Hispania, above all *coloniae* and *municipia*, issued coinage of completely Roman design, in line with the characteristics of their inhabitants, who had Latin rights or Roman citizenship.[60] In general, prior to the Battle of Actium (31 BCE), the senates of the issuing cities chose deities or allegorical figures inspired by prototypes on Roman coinage for the obverse designs, such as the case of Lepida, which engraved a helmeted male head on some asses, which might be a reference to Mars (Fig. 9.3.9).[61] Subsequently, with the exception of Emporiae and Carteia (Fig. 9.3.1), obverses bore the emperor's portrait and occasionally that of a member of his family, thereby proclaiming

---

51 Gozalbes 2006a, 313.
52 Giral 2006.
53 Liv. XLIII.3.
54 Chaves 2012b, 187.
55 Chaves 2012a, 40.
56 *RPC* 120–23; Chaves 2012a, 44.
57 Chaves 2012b, 188.

58 *CNH* 401–02.1–6; Chaves 2012a, 45.
59 Ripollès 1988.
60 Ripollès 2010, 24–29.
61 *RPC* 264.

Figure 9.3. 1. Carteia semis. 2. Augustus, semis, Ilici. 3. Tiberius, dupondius, Romula. 4. Tiberius, sestertius, Tarraco. 5. Tiberius, dupondius, Caesaraugusta. 6. Augustus, as, Carthago Nova. 7. Tiberius, as, Emerita. 8. Caligula, as, Caesaraugusta. 9. Lepida/Celsa as. 10. Tiberius, as, Graccuris (Museu Nacional d'Art de Catalunya/Gabinet Numismàtic de Catalunya, numbers 3, 6, and 8; Museo Archeologico Nazionale di Firenze, numbers 1–2, 4–5, 7, 9–10). (Scale: 120%, 4:5)

these cities' adhesion to the *princeps* and the imperial house.⁶² The reverses tended to express local interests that in particular referred to the city's identity, as well as its social and religious life.

Among the designs related to religion, the cult of the imperial family occupied a key position in the coin iconography of these cities. On the death of Augustus in August 14 CE, the Senate decreed his apotheosis — *consecratio* — and he was declared a god. This gave rise officially to what is known as the imperial cult, which was to be consolidated under the rule of Tiberius. From his reign, the issues in Hispania offer clear examples of the recognition of the figure of the *Diuus Augustus*, as well as depicting monuments associated with the imperial cult.⁶³ The effigy of the divine Augustus with a radiate crown (Fig. 9.3.4), often surrounded by an inscription that showed his category as a *Diuus*, was present on coins of the reign of Tiberius. Good proof of the cult to the imperial family can be found on the dupondii of Romula, on the obverse of which we find the effigy of the divine Augustus with a star over his forehead, referring to the *sidus Iulium*, and in front the *fulmen* or bundle of thunderbolts that symbolized Jupiter's power. On the reverse there was a portrait of Augustus's wife, Livia, who was still alive, with a crescent, the symbol of Venus-Luna, over her forehead and the *orbis* under her head (Fig. 9.3.3).⁶⁴

The reverses display many images that allude to the religious life of the cities of Hispania with depictions of temples, altars, sculptural groups, priests, religious instruments, legionary standards, bulls, or yoked oxen. Several mints included temples, altars, or statues on their issues; it is difficult to determine whether these were faithful representations of reality, if their existence is confirmed by written or archaeological sources, or even if they really existed.⁶⁵ Tarraco is one of the cities about which we have most evidence, both literary and numismatic, on this type of religious monument. In addition to the effigy of the *Diuus Augustus*, the issues of Tiberius's reign bear other evidence of the cult to Augustus in the city. One such case is an octastyle temple that must have represented, with a great or lesser degree of accuracy, the one that Tiberius gave permission to be constructed in honour of Augustus in Tarraco.⁶⁶ Other examples depict an altar with a palm, which refers to that dedicated to the cult of Augustus in his lifetime (Fig. 9.3.4).⁶⁷ Its existence is known from a mention by Quintilian,⁶⁸ who narrates the prodigy that a small palm had grown in the centre of the altar, to which the *princeps* replied that it was probably because it had been used very little. Other cities also included temples, such as, for example, Ilici, which represented a tetrastyle temple dedicated to Juno, as is indicated by the inscription IVNONI carved on the architrave (Fig. 9.3.2).⁶⁹ Emerita also exhibited a tetrastyle temple dedicated to Augustus, as can be deduced from the legend AETERNITATI AVGVSTAE, which must refer to the temple that existed in the city (Fig. 9.3.5).⁷⁰

Some designs allude to the religious ritual linked to the city's foundation, through which new colonies demonstrated their wish to adopt Roman customs. This ritual was expressed on reverses from Emerita and Caesaraugusta, in which a priest — *capite velato* — can be seen leading a yoke of oxen with which he ploughs the *sulcus primigenius* that defined the surface of the new colony (Fig. 9.3.7).⁷¹ Military standards were also present in the foundation process ritual of Roman colonies, and their meaningful symbolism is reflected in the reverse designs of some mints. The colonists under the orders of the person responsible for the foundation proceeded towards their new city following a standard, which afterwards would become a cult object, as it was considered a foundational symbol.⁷² Among other cases, the importance of these ensigns is made apparent on dupondii of the reign of Tiberius from the mint of Caesaraugusta, which depict a *vexillum* between two circular standards on the reverse. An inscription stated that the colony had been founded by veterans of the Legio IV Macedonia, Legio VI Victrix, and Legio X Gemina. All of this was represented on top of a pedestal, which indicates the significance that these standards had for the city (Fig. 9.3.6).⁷³

The importance that priests had in the performance of religious activities in the cities of Hispania is also made apparent by the designs that show instruments alluding to the main Roman priestly posts and colleges.⁷⁴ On some occasions, symbols of the religious colleges of greatest prestige were represented together with the effigies of members of the imperial family, expressing the sacred functions that

---

62 Beltrán 2002.
63 Beltrán Fortes 2012.
64 *RPC* 73; Beltrán Fortes 2012, 83.
65 Ripollès 2010, 27.
66 Tac., *Ann.* I.78.
67 *RPC* 225.
68 *Inst.* VI.3.77.
69 *RPC* 192.
70 *RPC* 48.
71 *RPC* 371.
72 Domínguez Arranz and Aguilera 2012, 73.
73 *RPC* 346.
74 Domínguez Arranz 2004; Domínguez Arranz and Aguilera 2012.

the latter carried out. For example, to emphasize Augustus's condition as pontifex and augur, the mint of Caesaraugusta depicted a *lituus*, the emblem of the augurs, and a *simpulum*, the symbol of the pontificate, next to the emperor's portrait.[75] In some cases the symbols that represented the priestly colleges were the main design on the reverse, referring to the religious duties of the magistrates responsible for the issue or the significance of the city as a religious centre. The city of Carthago Nova depicted priestly instruments on several issues, such as that of the reign of Augustus with the name of the *duoviri quinquennales*, C. Varius Rufus and Sex. Iullius Pollio (Fig. 9.3.8).[76] This issue bore a *simpulum* (a ritual vessel for libations), an *aspergillum* (an implement with a handle that was dipped in purifying water in religious ceremonies), a *securis* (a ceremonial axe used in sacrifices), and an *apex* (the headdress worn by priests).

The bull was a very frequent image on the reverse of coinage from Tarraconensis, especially on issues from mints in the Ebro Valley, where its iconography seems to have spread by means of the imitation of types. The first mint in this area to depict a bull was the colony of Lepida, which adopted it from the time of its initial issues before the Battle of Actium; in the first instance it was shown in a standing position and shortly afterwards charging or leaping (Fig. 9.3.9).[77] Other cities, such as Graccuris, opted to represent the bull in a position of rest and mitred, that is with a *frontale* or a triangular piece above its horns (Fig. 9.3.10).[78] Some mints made reference to the bull on their semis by simplifying the design and engraving its full-face head alone. It is difficult to interpret these bulls exactly, as in the case of Greek, Phoenician-Punic, or native issues in the Iberian Peninsula, and several proposals have been put forward. In general, a religious symbolism is attributed to the bull, related to its value as an animal to be sacrificed, especially when it is depicted in a position of rest and with the frontal above its head, as this was an ornament that in Roman iconography is typical of bulls that are going to be sacrificed as an offering to a deity.[79] Exceptionally, it might also have a meaning related to a military victory and as the emblem of different legions, as in the case of one of the first issues from Lepida, in which a bust of Victory is combined with a standing bull.[80]

## Using Coinage for Cult Purposes: Offerings and Amulets

The intense religious message of coin imagery, together with the intrinsic value of the coins themselves, resulted in their becoming suitable objects to make offerings to the gods.[81] Some coin assemblages found in cult spaces should be interpreted as votive deposits offered to deities. A clearly significant example is that of three republican-period Roman asses found under a column in the sacred area of the city of Emporion.[82] The coins were deposited in the first half of the second century BCE when silver and bronze issues with images of deities of Greek tradition were being minted in the city; for this reason the choice of Roman asses cannot be considered to have been fortuitous. Those who made the offering may have belonged to the new Roman population living in the city, who selected asses with the image of two faced heads of Janus, one of their main tutelary gods. Furthermore, these asses had a significant role in Roman cult activity because of their considerable religious significance.

Some hoards with coins and other objects are also likely to have been deposits with cult-related aims rather than a concealment of wealth, as has been proposed for the hoard of Salvacañete (Cuenca), hidden around the year 100 BCE. The deposit contained Iberian and Roman denarii — many of them perforated — and silver objects with a noteworthy symbolic value.[83] Small coin assemblages found in domestic contexts could have been modest votive offerings, as has been suggested for a find from the Roman city of Iesso (Guissona, Lleida).[84] This was a small group of coins concealed beneath the floor of a house of the first half of the first century BCE, made up by two bronze coins of Kese, one of Iltirkesken, and one of Sekaisa, which had been placed in a broken jug and covered with a stone. Offers to deities have also been identified in industrial contexts, such as the case of a modest foundational offering at the fish-salting plant in Baelo Claudia (Bolonia, Cádiz), dated around the years 140–130 BCE. Two bronze coins of the local mint of Bailo and another from Carteia were buried beneath an underground water channel.[85]

In addition to serving as offerings to the deities, at sanctuaries coins could be used to buy cult objects or to pay for religious services and sacri-

---

75 *RPC* 322.
76 *RPC* 167a.
77 *RPC* 262–64; Hurtado 2013, 130–31; Gozalbes García 2019.
78 *RPC* 429.
79 Ripollès 2010, 27.
80 *RPC* 261 62; Domínguez Arranz and Aguilera 2012, 77.

81 Alfaro 1993, 266–76; Campo 2012, 58–60.
82 Campo 1993, 195–96.
83 Arévalo and Marcos 2000, 33–34.
84 Pera 2001, 58.
85 Arévalo 2006, 88–91.

fices, as is explained by classical sources.⁸⁶ In this context, hoards or small coin deposits can be interpreted as offerings to the gods, but the function of coins lost by chance cannot be determined. At the sanctuary of La Algaida, next to the former mouth of the River Guadalquivir, offerings such as pottery vessels, semi-precious stones, and objects made of metal or glass paste were deposited from the sixth century to the first century BCE. Furthermore, stray finds of coins have also been made, among which thirty-eight silver and bronze examples of the powerful nearby mint of Gadir stand out, the majority with the image of Melqart, one of the leading deities in this area. Some of these were perforated, probably to be used as pendants as some kind of amulet or talisman, but it is impossible to determine the function of the remaining coins.⁸⁷

The worship of water-residing deities was very widespread in antiquity, and different types of offerings, among them coins, made with the aim of ensuring the fulfilment of a request or facilitating the concession of a petition are often found. In the Iberian Peninsula, above all in the north-west, the Celtic zone and the eastern Iberian area, coin offerings in lakes, rivers, and springs have been located.⁸⁸ The period for which most offerings have been traced ranges from the first century BCE to the second century CE and coincides with the period in which thermal waters were most used. The coins selected tended to be low denomination pieces, and they are usually found together with other material of a votive nature. First- and second-century CE Roman issues usually bear the emperor's head on the obverse and, in many cases, a deity on the reverse. However, no preference for a specific deity among this type of coin offerings can be identified.

The religious content of the majority of the images on coins sometimes led to them being used as amulets or talismans. We normally identify this use of coins because they were perforated so that they could be used as pendants, although the holes might have had other purposes. As in the case of the sanctuary at La Algaida, perforated coins are often discovered at sacred sites, but where their use as amulets or talismans is most evident is on cemetery sites. Coins forming part of necklaces with which the deceased were buried so as to protect them in the afterlife have been located in some tombs. A good example can be seen in a child's inhumation burial in the cemetery of el Puig des Molins (Ibiza) of the first half of the third century BCE, in which two perforated Carthaginian bronze coins were found together with a glass paste bead, forming a necklace of which the string that linked them together was preserved, and some other modest jewels.⁸⁹ The finds in this cemetery show that, while the inhabitants of Ibiza valued coins with the image of Bes, they also appreciated examples with depictions of Carthaginian deities, especially that of the goddess Tanit, as is revealed by the coins from this child burial.

Coins might also play a protective role without any need to perforate them, since they could ward off negative influences simply as a result of carrying them on one's person or of keeping them in certain places. The presence of bronze coins under the masts of thirteen ships that sank between the second century BCE and the fourth century should be interpreted in this way.⁹⁰ Roman coins, generally very badly preserved, have been found under the masts of six of these vessels, among which an example with an image of Fortuna stands out, as the choice of such a coin must have been intentional. In the waters of Hispania, the Cap de Vol wreck off the Cap de Creus, whose sinking should be dated to the turn of the Era, should be noted.⁹¹ An Iberian bronze unit of Bolskan was found under the mast of this vessel, which has led to the proposal that this was a locally built ship operated by indigenous Iberian individuals.⁹²

It seems logical to suggest that perforated coins found in cemeteries were intended to be used as amulets, but it is more difficult to define the purpose behind burying unperforated coins on or next to the corpse. In addition to serving as amulets, they could have been used as money to facilitate the deceased's journey to the hereafter and their life there. In native cemeteries, coin finds are unusual, but from the fourth century BCE, their presence is occasionally recorded in tombs in the Greek cemeteries of Emporion and in Phoenician-Punic ones such as those of Ebusus and Gadir, although their deposition was more frequent in first- and second-century CE Roman cemeteries. By way of example, reference can be made to an inhumation in what is known as the Martí cemetery of Emporion, in which a fractional silver Emporitan coin of the issue with an Athena head and an owl — dated around 395–375 BCE — was found on the body's head, while in the right hand there was a small perfume jar.⁹³ In an inhuma-

---

86  Campo 2012, 58.
87  Arévalo and Marcos 2000, 33; Arévalo 2006, 85–86.
88  Abad Varela 1992.
89  Campo and others 2016b, 64 no. 17.1.1.2.
90  Caslson 2007.
91  Nieto 1982.
92  Sinner and Ferrer i Jané 2020, 381.
93  Almagro 1953, 99; Campo and others 2021, 127–28.

tion burial in a trench, dated after the mid-first century CE, in the cemetery of Gadir/Gades, a fraction of Gadir and an as of Tiberius from Italica were found between the legs at the height of the body's knees, as well as eleven perfume jars and a lamp, the exact position of which remains unknown.[94]

## Conclusions

The great diversity of designs and legends on the coins of the Iberian Peninsula reflect the ethnic and cultural characteristics and the evolution of the different peoples that inhabited it between the sixth century BCE and the early first century CE. While this iconographic wealth may, at first sight, seem to be an important source for the study of the religious beliefs of the peoples of Hispania, its interpretation presents many difficulties. The coin legends tell us about the issuing authority, but rarely do they help to decipher the identity of the deity or the cult depicted. Furthermore, ancient literary sources, as well as epigraphic and archaeological evidence, contribute hardly any information concerning the religious beliefs of the issuing cities and make even less reference to the imagery of their coins. In many cases, all this has led to researchers reaching very different conclusions about the meaning of the same sacred design.

The adoption of foreign images to represent local gods and cults was a habitual practice in coin-issuing cities, started by the Greek colonies of Emporion and Rhode, which usually preferred to reproduce designs of other Hellenistic mints rather than creating their own. However, the deity represented on the drachms issued by these mints could be Artemis since, according to Strabo, this deity was worshipped in both these colonies. Phoenician-Punic cities, without any iconographic tradition of their own, also generally opted to copy images from the Hellenistic repertoire, choosing and adapting the designs to the messages they sought to transmit. Be that as it may, the historical and archaeological information for these cities enables us to propose identifications for the deities depicted on their coins, whom they would have worshipped. Thus, Bes was venerated in Ebusus, Melqart in Gadir, Chusor-Ptah in Malaca, and Astarté-Isis in Baria.

The native mints of Ulterior used a wide range of sacred images, in part borrowed from classical repertoires, revealing their gradual tendency to draw closer to Rome, copying images that alluded to Roman deities such as Mercury and Apollo, in addition to certain designs including bulls that seem to reflect rituals related to the sacrifice of these animals. They also depict fantastic beings and myths of distant origins, such as that of Europa riding a bull. These cities also created some of their own designs, such as male and female heads, which may represent tutelary deities of the city, with different variants such as warrior, fruit-bearing, or astral versions. The diversity of sacred images in Hispania Ulterior contrasts with the great uniformity of types of the Iberian and Celtiberian mints in Hispania Citerior, which contribute little to our knowledge of the religious beliefs of these peoples. Most obverses bear a male head that is usually interpreted as that of a warrior or a native war deity. As for the reverses of silver and bronze coins, it is noticeable that they tend to bear a horseman, which is likely to refer to the power of local elites, although its religious component remains far from clear.

The religious iconography of the issues made by Carteia, Corduba, and Valentia reflect the origin of these colonies, which chose classical designs that, although not without some problems of interpretation, illustrate the importance that Roman gods and cults had for their inhabitants. From the mid-first century BCE and until the reign of Caligula, some privileged cities in Hispania struck coinage with clearly Roman images, many of which refer to their religious life. Among such representations, the cult of the imperial family occupied an important place, depicting monuments related to the imperial cult and recognizing the significance of the *Diuus Augustus*. Several mints included sacred monuments, such as temples, altars, or statues, the images of which lead to discussion as regards the extent to which they were faithful representations or even whether some of them really existed at all. Other designs show religious rituals such as the foundation of the city, or priestly implements that alluded to the main Roman colleges and priestly posts.

Coinage played a significant role in the various religious practices of the inhabitants of the Iberian Peninsula. In temples and sacred spaces, coins could have been used to pay for religious services or to buy offerings. They were also used as offerings to the gods when a temple or any other type of public or private building was founded. The intense religious message in most iconographic representations on coins led to their being suitable objects for use as amulets or talismans. On occasions coins were found in certain rituals associated with death, as payment to facilitate the deceased's journey to the hereafter or to protect him or her in their next life.

---

94 Arévalo and Moreno 2016, 155 no. 34.1.1.4.

# 10. Rome's Memory and Ritual in Hispania

## Introduction

By the time of Augustus, the complex story of the origins of Rome was well established. The local account of the twins, miraculously saved by a she-wolf, had been connected with the presence of the Trojan hero Aeneas in Latium. Romans had, thus, a distant relationship with the Greek world as well as an original foundational tale. This story was celebrated by poets and historians, and commemorated in art. Furthermore, it stressed the noteworthy affiliations of the winner of the last civil war. As an adopted Julian, Augustus could claim to be descended from Aeneas's son, Iulus for the Romans (Ascanius for the Greeks), and therefore from Venus herself. In the preface to his work, Livy claimed that the military glory of the Roman people was so great that the nations of the earth (*gentes humanae*) had to accept the idea that Mars was the father of Romulus as willingly as they submitted to Roman dominion.[1] Nevertheless, the remark, and the whole passage, is imbued with clear scepticism about divine intervention in the origins of Rome. By the early Empire, Livy and some of his readers distrusted the myth of the twins as a poetic legend (*poetica fabula*). But they were most likely an exception. Venus and Mars were officially promoted as remote ancestors of the Julians and the Romans. A powerful and visually attractive discourse of this remote past was elaborated, especially by Augustus in the Ara Pacis and his new Forum.

Augustus's times also witnessed a curb on imperial expansion. He completed the conquest of Hispania, which had started two centuries before. Colonization ensued. Several Roman colonies were founded and about 150,000 Italics were settled in these new cities.[2] They were islands of veterans and peasants in a sea of defeated indigenous groups. For the most part, the age of Augustus was a fresh start for Hispania. It was no longer a war scenario. The urbanization process took off, and the urban elites, especially in south and eastern Iberia, led the economic and social integration of the peninsula within the Empire, a link that was not to be broken until the fifth century CE. Despite the role that the remote past might have had in legitimizing Augustus's one-man rule,[3] Roman memory did not play any particular role in the integration of provincial territories, at least not in the case of Hispania. Returning to Livy's words, provincials perhaps could not but accept Rome's divine origins, but nothing was done for them to be confronted with this past. The message that Augustus encoded in the Ara Pacis and the new Forum was meant for a Roman audience and particularly for the population of the city and its visitors. There was barely any official memory of Rome's origins outside the city. It may have been felt that there was no need to present Rome's and Augustus's credentials to the provincial population of Hispania, because victory in war itself legitimated Roman power and its representative. Be that as it may, it does not follow, however, that Rome's past was not remembered in Hispania in imperial times. It was, both in public as well as in private contexts, but the evidence points to disconnected local initiatives rather than a planned Roman strategy. In the following pages, I will review the evidence for this memory in order to evaluate its historical meaning.

## The Immovable Memory of Rome's Origins

Greek colonization is a good example of how memory can be moved by a people exploring and populating new lands. For Greek settlers dragging Greek heroes to the western Mediterranean minimized the impact of encountering the unknown and converted, to some extent, a foreign territory into a familiar place

---

1 Liv., *Praef.* 7–8.
2 MacMullen 2000, 50–84.
3 Zanker 1990, 193–215; Evans 1992, 43–53.

**Ana Mayorgas**, Professor of Ancient History (Complutense University of Madrid)

to live. They also played a mediating role in communication with the non-Greek world. Odysseus was one of those heroes whose presence reached Italy.⁴ But there were others such as Hercules, who ended up fighting the three-headed monster Gerion in Iberia and the cattle rustler Cacus in Rome, or Aeneas, who was located in Sicily and even considered the founder of Rome by the fifth-century historian Helanicus of Lesbos.⁵ Roman memory did not share this feature of mobility. For Aeneas, Latium was the end of the journey. He died during a battle against the Rutulians and was buried by the River Numicus in Lavinium. In addition, Romulus was the opposite to the wandering type. Born in Alba Longa, he founded a city less than 50 km away from where he had grown up as a shepherd and would spend the rest of his life as a king. No matter how far Romans reached, conquered, or colonized, the memory of Aeneas and Romulus was always exclusively linked to Latium, and no other mythological figure related to their past or symbol of their identity was located anywhere outside Latium.

There is no question that, apart from wandering heroes, there exist other ways of moving memory from one place to another, such as reproducing the means by which that memory is re-enacted and upheld. The founding figure of Christianity lived and died in ancient Palestine. By Late Antiquity a sacred landscape especially associated with his death had been identified and would eventually become a place of pilgrimage.⁶ However, there is no need to travel to remember Christ's sacrifice. Christians do it regularly in mass, and certain festivities such as Easter Week are particularly aimed at re-enacting his life. In short, ritual might contribute to reproducing and moving memory to distant places. In general, pagan Rome does not tally with this model either. First of all, no cult of Aeneas or Romulus is attested whatsoever. Admittedly both figures were assimilated to divinities. After their disappearance from earth, the Trojan hero was thought to have become Pater or Jupiter Indiges, and Romulus experienced the same kind of transformation into Quirinus.⁷ Interestingly, Livy does not give the same credit to both assimilations. In the case of Aeneas he casts doubt, leaving the reader to decide whether the Trojan warrior became divine after his death or not.⁸ In contrast, he asserts that after his death the people of Rome 'all with one accord hailed Romulus as a god and a god's son, the King and Father of the Roman City, and with prayers besought his favour that he would graciously be pleased forever to protect his children'.⁹ That would seem to mark the beginning of a royal cult, but neither Livy nor any other ancient author indicate any actual ritual in their honour at that time or later. Therefore, it is not clear whether any of these assimilations had any real effect in ritual. Most probably they did not since no dedication to Indiges-Aeneas or Quirinus-Romulus has ever been found.¹⁰ Indeed, the very fact of the assimilation to another divinity points in the opposite direction. Why should two demigods, sons of Venus and Mars respectively, be venerated under the disguise of another god? Could they not be honoured for themselves as was Heracles, son of Zeus and Alcmena, or Asclepius, begotten by Coronis and Apollo? They definitely could in the Greek world, but they were not among the Romans. In Greece the heroic status of those born from a human being and a divinity could lead to the creation of a cult, although it did not always happen, and in a few cases eventually to their integration among the gods.¹¹ Originally, in Rome, the notion most probably did not even exist, since the noun *heros-ois* is a loanword from the Greek language. This fact makes the absence of a cult devoted to Aeneas or Romulus more comprehensible. The lack of evidence is especially meaningful for the age of Augustus considering the relevance that the origin myth had for the first member of the Julio-Claudian dynasty, who according to Suetonius was close to having received the epithet of Romulus.¹² In fact, the non-existence of a cult of Aeneas and Romulus might explain the assimilation to other divinities. At a certain moment, prior to the end of the third century BCE, both figures must have been considered of such major relevance for Rome's past that their honouring as other divinities was inferred or

---

4   Malkin 1998, 178–209.
5   Galinsky 1969, 63–102. It is one of the numerous versions of Rome's foundation transmitted by Greek authors. See Bickerman 1952; Cornell 1975.
6   Halbwachs 1971.
7   On Aeneas Horsfall 1987, 17–19. On Romulus Bremmer 1987, 45–47.

---

8   Liv. I.2.6.
9   Liv. I.16.3: 'Deinde a paucis initio facto deum deo natum, regem parentemque urbis Romanae salvere universi Romulum iubent; pacem precibus exposcunt, uti volens propitius suam semper sospitet progeniem'. And he repeats the idea in 1.40.3.
10  For the controversial inscription to a supposed *Lar Aeneias* published M. Guarducci see Cornell 1977 and Mayorgas 2010. See Dury-Moyaers 1981 for the so called *heroon* of Aeneas in Lavinium and the cult of the hero. *Contra* see Mayorgas 2010.
11  Ekroth 2007.
12  Suet., *Aug.* VII.2. Evans 1992, 87–103; Ferriès 2009; Brandt 2015; Castiello 2021. For the associations with Romulus in the Republic see Ver Eecke 2008.

devised.¹³ It was no more than a verbal statement, which elevated their status, at the same time as no effort was actually being made to implement or develop a real cult to them.

If there was no founder cult in Rome to be moved to the provinces, other rituals were associated with the memory of its origins, specifically the *Lupercalia* and *Parilia* festivals.¹⁴ The former is well attested in our sources although some key aspects are still debated, such as the god or goddess for whom the ritual is performed, the symbolism of the *luperci* who run half-naked in a goat skin or the route they followed in their ritual race.¹⁵ The connection with the myth of the twins is, nonetheless, unquestioned. The rite of the *luperci* took place at the Lupercal cave on the Palatine Hill, which the Romans identified as the abode of the she-wolf that suckled the twins near a wild fig tree, *Ficus Ruminalis*. Furthermore, the performance of the *luperci* was interpreted as the re-enactment of Romulus and Remus's activity as herdsmen when they ran after the cattle around those hills still uninhabited. *Parilia* was celebrated on 21 April, the day that the city was supposed to have been founded. It was, therefore, Rome's birthday. The rite was performed in honour of the god or goddess Pales, and it was not attached to any relevant point in the city. In fact, unlike the *Lupercalia*, it was performed in Rome but also in the countryside. Ovid pinpoints the interpretation of the main rite, which consisted of jumping over bonfires made by the peasants. It was celebrated in memory of the destruction and abandonment of the old huts by those who were to populate the city founded by Romulus.¹⁶ Both festivals were originally meant to protect and purify the livestock. They stemmed from one of the basic concerns of any agropastoral society, the survival of its cattle. However, they later acquired a new meaning by relating those rites to the foundational myth of Rome.¹⁷ The association must have been triggered by the idea that Romulus and Remus grew up as herdsmen. Since both festivals were especially linked to the pastoral life, they ended up serving as a means of remembering the pre-civic and pre-urban atmosphere of the origins of Rome. The topography of the Palatine Hill contributed to sustaining this perception. The area had become a rich neighbourhood by the end of the Republic. Luxurious houses occupied much of the space. However, the cave of the Lupercal and an old hut considered the house of Romulus (*casa Romuli*) stood as symbol of the simple life of the primitive times.

The festival of the *Lupercalia* survived until the fifth century CE, and throughout this time it remained largely unaltered. The main change must have taken place by the time of Theodosius, when professional actors and actresses replaced the traditional *luperci*.¹⁸ Thus, in the face of the criticism of the Christian authorities, in particular the pope, it became a completely pagan theatrical performance. *Parilia* represents a different case. Hadrian gave a new impetus to the old pastoral festival, which adopted the title of *Romaia*, and commissioned the construction of a temple of Venus *Felix* and Roma *Aeterna* in the Forum. The cult of the political abstraction that had begun in the Greek world in republican times was finally endowed with its own sacred space in the *Urbs*, being transformed into a goddess for the whole Empire. Next to her, in the eastern *cella* stood the mother of Aeneas, venerated as a divinity of fertility and fortune.¹⁹ The temple exhibited and preserved the memory of the city's origins as the building was decorated with reliefs of Aeneas and the twins.²⁰ But the new religious space was not consecrated to them. From a religious point of view they were still second-rate dependent figures. The temple was dedicated in 121 CE, the same year that the festival was renamed as *Romaia–Natalis Urbis*.²¹ It is hard to know how much the ritual changed due to this reorientation. In the third century CE the grammarian Solinus still refers to the *Parilia*, claiming that no sacrifice was performed in order to keep the day pure without bloodshed.²² Perhaps the old celebration in honour of Pales was still held, but it must have been overshadowed by Venus and Roma and the cultic activity of their priests at the same time that the festival acquired a new denomination.²³

---

13 Weinstock 1971, 175–77; Porte 1981, 223–25; Evans 1992, 103–08. On Brelich's identification of Quirinus and Romulus as the same divinity see Ferri 2017.
14 Mayorgas 2010.
15 The bibliography on the Lupercalia is extensive. A general religious reevaluation has been made by Quaglia 2019. For specific aspects see recently Vuković 2018 on the topography of the festival, Vé 2018 on the meaning of the rite, and Ferriès 2008 on its evolution.
16 Ov., *Fast.* IV.793–806.
17 On the potential of the Roman calendar for resignification, see Beard 1987.
18 McLynn 2008, 169–70.
19 Mellor 1981, 1016–17 and 1021–24; Boatwright 1989, 99–133; Mols 2003.
20 Dulière 1979, 101–10.
21 Ath. VIII.63.
22 Solin. I.18: 'Observatum deinceps ne qua hostia Parilibus caederetur ut iste die sanguine purus est'. Marcos Celestino 2002, 155–56.
23 Mellor 1981, 1023–24.

## Roman Cults of Memory in Hispania

*Lupercalia* and *Parilia* showcase the close link between memory and ritual calendar in Rome. There is no evidence that *Lupercalia* or *Parilia* were officially celebrated anywhere but in the city of Rome. In fact, it seems that, in general, it was the case that the traditional religious festivals of the city of Rome were never exported to conquered territories.[24] Certainly, the ritual of the *luperci* was strongly anchored to Roman topography and especially to the Palatine Hill, so it could have been difficult to reproduce in another landscape. By the Late Republic and Early Empire there is epigraphic evidence of *luperci* outside the *Urbs*. The inscriptions come from Latium (Lanuvium, Praeneste), Italy (Otricoli in Umbria or Clusium and Nepet in Etruria), and even from provinces such as Gallia Narbonensis (Nemausus), Numidia (Cuicul), or Dalmatia (Narona). As far as the offices of the priests involved can be recovered, they can mostly be ascribed to the equestrian order even though some of them also reveal that they had a local career.[25] Therefore, in all likelihood all of these references are related to a sole priesthood, that of the *Urbs*, and the existence of local *luperci*, who would have led the local celebration of the *Lupercalia* festival in Italy or in the provinces, is much less likely. The only evidence for a *lupercus* in Hispania should be interpreted in the same way.[26] It is an honorific inscription on a statue base from the Roman colony of Palma (Balearic Islands). Due to its fragmentary state, the name of the person commemorated is not preserved, and his career cannot be fully recovered. The priesthoods of *flamen Romae et Augusti* and *lupercus* are, nonetheless, clearly recorded and besides he was probably a duumvir three times. Other possible honours are lost.[27]

A cautious approach to the evidence leads us to consider that the above-mentioned honouree from Palma belonged to the equestrian rank and was a *lupercus* in Rome. Notwithstanding, it must be admitted that the existence of local *luperci* is not totally inconceivable.[28] Another case of a traditional Roman priesthood is attested in Hispania, the *salii* of Saguntum. The evidence dating to the early Empire comprises seven honorific inscriptions dedicated to decurions and members of the leading families of the town such as the Baebii, Fabii, or Voconii.[29] In some cities of Latium, *salii* are also recorded in the early Empire, especially in Tibur, and they have similarly been attested in other regions of Italy (Trebula Suffenas in Samnium, Opitergium and Patavium in Venetia-Histria, and Ticinum in Transpadana).[30] This is also the case of another archaic Roman priesthood, the *rex sacrorum*, for which there is evidence in Latium as well as in Mauretania Caesariensis (Caesarea and Altava) and Numidia (Lambaesis).[31] The attestations of both priesthoods from Latium and Italy might be a matter of debate, since it is not entirely clear whether they stem from a local tradition prior to the Roman conquest or are instead the result of later Roman influence. The first possibility seems more likely in the case of the *rex sacrorum*, which would imply that no transfer of this traditional Roman cult to the Latin cities was encouraged or accepted by the Romans.[32] However, the evidence from the *municipia* of the Po Valley or outside Italy leaves little room for doubt. It is highly improbable that in those towns or provincial territories there were, prior to the Roman conquest, particular local priesthoods whose ritual responsibilities were those of the *salii* and *rex sacrorum* at Rome. On the contrary, these communities must have adopted the priestly titles later with imperial consent. In the case of the *salii* of Saguntum, it probably happened in the time of Caesar or Augustus when the town was granted the status of Roman *municipium*.[33]

What ritual activities these priests performed is a matter of total guesswork. It is hard to believe that when the *salii* of Saguntum paraded, they used to jump, sing, and carry a replica of the twelve shields of Mars. There is no evidence in this regard.[34] Probably the safest thing we can say is that beyond the particular ritual responsibilities that might have been associated with the priesthood in each town, it was, above all, a prestigious and exclusive religious title

---

24 Woolf 2009b, 247–50.
25 For instance, *CIL* XI, 406. See Scheid-Granino 1999, 84–85, and 129–34 for the corpus and also U. Bianchi *Dizionario epigrafico* s.v. Luperci 2207–09.
26 García Riaza and Sánchez León 2000, 89–90. *Contra* Zucca 1989, 226–27.
27 *HEp* 9, 237: [---]s+++ ol[---] + (duo)v(ir) ter |³ [flamini] Romae | [et Au]gusti lupercọ | [---in i]nsulis [Baliar(ibus)? |⁶ ---] pria [--- | ---] C + [--- | ---] +++o opt[imo?].
28 See Johnston 2017, 221–22.

29 *CIL* II²/14 349, 351, 352, 359, 364, 365, and 390. They have been also collected in other *corpora*: Beltrán 1980; Corell 2002.
30 Delgado 2005, 122–23.
31 For the evidence of Latium Bianchi 2010, 41–71. For that of North Africa Delgado 1998, 35 and 2005, 122.
32 For the *reges sacrorum* see Bianchi 2010, 81–88. For the Latin *salii* Delgado 2000.
33 On the special local identity of the Saguntines and their relationship with Rome, see the contribution of Víctor Revilla in this volume.
34 J. A. Delgado 2014, 156–60, assumes that the *salii* of Saguntum followed the model of the *salii Albani* created by Augustus, so they would have been in charge of the celebration of *Feriae Latinae* in their town.

imported from Rome where the holders had to belong to the senatorial order (as opposed to the *luperci* who were equestrian). In fact, something similar happened in the case of the better attested pontiffs and augurs in provinces. They seem to have been outranked by magistrates and decurions as a whole, who were given responsibility for tasks that were assigned to the priests in the city of Rome, such as the supervision of cults, their funds, religious spaces and burial places, or determining the religious calendar.[35] Therefore, several conclusions can be drawn from what has been said. The *luperci* epigraphically recorded outside Rome (including the one from Palma in Hispania) are for the moment better explained as members of the equestrian order who held the priesthood in the *Urbs*. Due to the existence of other archaic religious titles in the provinces (*salii* and *rex sacrorum*), it is not impossible that further epigraphic finds might reveal the existence of local *luperci* in provincial territories. But even if a local priesthood of *luperci* is finally attested, it is still uncertain whether it should be concluded that the *Lupercalia* were celebrated anywhere outside the city of Rome, since the Roman priestly titles seem to have lost at least part of their original meaning in the transfer to the provinces.[36] Finally, in all this dispersal of traditional Roman priesthoods, there seems to be more local initiative than encouragement by the central government. The latter was more concerned with assuring political alliances through religion than any memory of Rome. The epigraphic statutes of *Urso* and the Flavian *municipia* in Hispania are proof thereof.

As can be attested in the legal charter of Urso (Osuna, Sevilla), a Roman colony founded by Caesar after the civil war, few specific public cults were established in the settlement by law, and nothing was regulated about private cults.[37] The only public cults explicitly mentioned are those of a clearly political character, the Capitoline triad and Venus. The charter obliged the magistrates to organize games in their honour. The rest of the public cults were supposed to be decided by the town council. And the same was applied to the calendar. The town council headed by the duumvirs was in charge of determining the particular festivals and public sacrifices to be celebrated throughout the year, but no specific festival is stipulated as compulsory. In sum, there was no intention of replicating the religion of the city of Rome in a Roman colony beyond the overall idea of a public cult that was taken for granted and placed under the supervision of the decurions, and the existence of public priests, of whom only two are mentioned, pontiffs and augurs.[38] Therefore, no ritual conveying the Roman memory was meant to be exported to the provinces either. Admittedly, the cult of Venus could be interpreted as a reminder of the link of her son to Rome, and to some extent it might have acted in this way. However, the goddess had a place in Roman religion of her own, so the memory load of the cult must be considered a secondary consequence of her introduction in the charter of Urso and not so much the main reason. In other words, the games in her honour that the magistrates were obliged to organize did not primarily aim to maintain the memory of Aeneas as a Roman forebear.

In general terms, the *Lex Irnitana*, one of the several Flavian charters found in a fragmentary state in Hispania, is in line with the legislation of Urso. They are intended for pre-existing towns in Baetica that were granted the status of Latin *municipia* and allowed to use Roman law. In this case, the previous religious practice was admitted as valid. The only cult mentioned is that of the imperial family, to which certain days had to be devoted; hence they were considered festive and non-working days for the administration of justice. Besides, the magistrates had to swear their oaths of office by Jupiter, Augustus, Claudius, Vespasian, Titus, the genius of Domitian, and the Penates. It is no surprise that, next to Jupiter, the deified emperors appear as the divine representatives of the Empire. As Domitian was still alive, the reference to the genius of the reigning emperor is also understandable. The mention of the *dei Penates* has raised more doubts. Robert Étienne considered that they should be interpreted in the local context as the tutelary divinities of the town, namely Irni.[39] More recently Clifford Ando unquestionably identifies them with the *penates populi Romani*, whose cult was originally located in Lavinium.[40] The author expresses some surprise that a 'notionally alien community' was expected to swear by the Penates, who resided far away in Latium, considering it more appropriate of a Roman colony. He also presents the example of these Penates, which according to Valerius Maximus refused to move from Lavinium to Alba Longa, to underline the idea that not all Roman gods were movable, and there-

---

35  As is attested in the *Lex Ursonensis*. See Rüpke 2006b, 19–20.
36  On the contrary A. C. Johnston 2017, 221–22, who considers it possible.
37  Rüpke 2006a, 38–42.
38  See also Rüpke 2006b. Delgado 1998 on priests in Betica and Mauretaniae provinces.
39  Étienne 1974, 457.
40  Ando 2007, 439–41. Dubourdieu 1989, 263–317.

fore there were some internal constraints against the export of Roman religion.[41]

The argument holds true, although it can be nuanced. It is true that at the beginning of their office Roman magistrates with *imperium* had to sacrifice first to Vesta in Rome and next to the Penates in Lavinium, to where they had to journey. This tradition, however, did not prevent a temple of the Penates from being built on the Velia by the end of the Republic.[42] So finally if the 'original' Penates did not move out of Lavinium, at least some kind of replica was installed in Rome. Whatever the case, the oaths performed by the magistrates of the Flavian *municipia* do not have to be taken as indicative of any cult of the Penates in Hispania for which there is so far no evidence. In the city of Rome, the magistrates travelled to Lavinium for the purpose of making a sacrifice in their honour as a religious and cultural statement of the origins of the city. In the towns of the Baetica the context was quite different. The Penates followed Jupiter and the deified emperors in an oath that had a clear political target, proving not so much how Romanized the *Irnitani* were, but how committed to the Empire and to the imperial house to which they had to present themselves. Ultimately, the memory of the origins of Rome was somehow reproduced every time the local magistrates of the Flavian *municipia* took their office, but admittedly that was a collateral consequence and of limited relevance. It would have been more effective to include Romulus and Aeneas in the oath, but for that to be the case they had to be considered divinities in their own right. And they were not.

Since there is no indication that the Romans encouraged the celebration of rituals in memory of the origins of Rome in Hispania, the evidence of a local initiative to this effect takes on a special light. Sound testimony has been found in Cales Coves in Menorca (Balearic Islands). The cave of Cales Coves, located to the south of the island by the coast and also known as Cova dels Jurats or Cova de l'Església, is a sanctuary in which ritual activity has been recorded from the end of the third century BCE to the beginning of the first century CE.[43] Most of the pottery found is local, of the Talayotic culture, which indicates an indigenous tradition that continued after the Roman conquest of the islands by Quintus Caecilius Metellus in 123 BCE. However, by the second century CE, the ritual activity had largely moved to the entrance of the cave, where oil lamps have been found, as well as two rocky platforms probably to place altars and statues, and a group of at least twenty-nine inscriptions, carved or painted on the entrance wall. Due to the deteriorated state of the rock, the inscriptions have been largely lost and are difficult to identify and read. However, in some of them the structure is clear. They are headed by the name of the consuls followed by the calendar date *XI Kal(endas) Maias*. Below there appears the formula *hoc venimus*,[44] the abbreviation *aedi-* or *aed-*, and one or several personal names. The following is one of the best-preserved examples:[45]

*M(arco) Gavio Sq[u]illa Ga|[l]liano S[exto] Car|³minio Vetere co(n)s(ulibus) · XI | K(alendas) Maias hoc venimus AEDI|NTE Gn(eus) Cor(nelius) Baria X v(ir) S o O CV T o L ATI |⁶ [---?] VM II + [..]LINO (hedera)*

This inscription is dated to 150 CE during the reign of Antoninus Pius. Not all of them are securely dated, but those with a clear chronological reference are framed within a period of around one hundred years, from 125 to 230 CE. What the abbreviations *aed-* / *aedi-* refer to is hard to solve. It has been suggested that they should be read as *aedilis-es* or *aedituus-ui*, 'guardians of the temple', and some of them also contain the abbreviation *Xvir-*, which could imply the additional involvement of certain *decemviri* of difficult identification.[46] The epigraphs and the archaeological remains are proof of an annual celebration at the cave of Cales Coves with the presence of public authorities whose names were recorded in the inscriptions. Those magistrates or priests were likely to have been attached to one of the two Roman settlements known on the island, *Mago* (modern-day Maó), the closer one about 20 km away, or the more distant *Iamo* (present-day Ciutadella), both of which are attested as having the status of *municipia*.[47] Once a year the authorities, presumably accompanied by other worshippers, travelled to the coastal Cales Coves to participate in a ritual. No divinity is recorded in the inscriptions, but the reiteration of the calendar date of 21 April might indicate that they met to celebrate the Roman *Parilia* or more precisely Rome's birthday.

The earliest inscriptions at Cales Coves coincide with the reign of Hadrian. Thus, it is very tempting

---

41  Val. Max 1.8.7.
42  Dubourdieu 1989, 387–451. Coarelli 2012.
43  Orfila and others 2010; 2015, 58–88. See also Mayer in this volume.
44  The expression is present in other rock inscriptions in Hispania.
45  *CIL* II 3718 = *CIL* II 5992; *HEp* 6, 1996, 148; *HEp* 19, 2010, 71. For a global study of the inscriptions see Zucca 1989; Mayer 2015; García Riaza and Sánchez León 2000; Juan Castelló 2005, 754–66.
46  Juan Castelló 2005, 752.
47  García Riaza and Sánchez León 2000, 152.

to link the reactivation of cult activity in the cave with the new impulse given by the emperor to the *dies natalis* of Rome in the *Urbs*.[48] In fact, in this local context one could even speculate whether the *Xviri*, clearly attested in some of the rockface inscriptions, might have played the role of the *XIIviri urbis Romae* documented in the epigraphy of the city of Rome and identified with the new priesthood created by Hadrian to serve at the temple of Venus and Rome.[49] No answer can be given, but whatever the identification of those local civil or religious authorities, it is unlikely that the cult of Rome was not part of the annual celebration on the 21 April at Cales Coves.[50] The chronology of the inscriptions coherently points to the second and third centuries CE and from Hadrian onwards both elements were definitely intertwined in the ritual calendar of the *Urbs*. There is also evidence for the worship of Rome in Hispania, although associated with the imperial cult, from the first century CE.[51] In fact we have already seen an example in the inscription of the *lupercus* from Palma who was *flamen Romae et Augusti* as well. In this interpretation only a final aspect remains undefined. When the old pastoral festival of *Parilia* was superseded by the *Romaia* of Hadrian, the temple of Venus and Rome must have become the ritual focal point, in contrast with the undetermined but rural-like scenery of the celebration in honour of Pales which implied the setting up of bonfires. However, in the second century CE the inhabitants of Menorca chose a cave by the coast to go to every 21 April (*hoc venimus*). Why did they not remain in *Mago* or *Iamo* to celebrate Rome's anniversary? The answer probably lies in the previous religious activity that had taken place in the cave since the late third century BCE, which was somehow associated with the cult in honour of Rome in a manner impossible for us to recover. Notwithstanding, we cannot completely exclude the possibility that, despite the late date of the inscriptions, the celebration at Cales Coves did not follow the model of the *Natalis Urbis* but that of the *Parilia*, i.e. the cult in honour of a pastoral divinity invoked to protect and purify the livestock, because worship of similar nature could have previously been performed in that place, which incidentally offered a natural rural setting for the ritual.

No further examples of the celebration of *Parilia* are recorded in Hispania, and yet Cales Coves is unlikely to have been an exception.[52] Other local initiatives that might have left no epigraphic evidence can be presumed. The possibility must also be considered that the worship of Rome implied the annual celebration of the *Natalis Urbis*. This worship is well attested in Hispania from the end of the first century CE always attached to the imperial cult at the provincial as well as the local level. The connection between the two emerged in the reign of Augustus in the eastern part of the Empire, where the city of Rome had received divine honours since republican times, and there was a long tradition of a ruler cult. To a great extent Greeks had included Rome first and then the emperor in their previous local festivals and religious celebrations, paying no heed to the way Romans commemorated the origin of their city.[53] In the western Empire the worship of Rome accompanied that of the emperor from the very beginning. Therefore, one could conclude that it was never relevant by itself and was probably more centred on extolling the imperial power than remembering the origins of the city. To summarize, in Hispania just one calendar date remained of the re-enactment of the pre-foundational times implied in the celebration of the *Parilia*, either because of the difficulty in adapting the traditional rituals of the *Urbs* to the provincial territory, or because of the lack of political will to implement them.

## Representations and Dedications to the Origins of Rome in Hispania

There is definitely more evidence for representing the remote Roman past in Hispania than for re-enacting it. Moreover, the documentation found so far, dated to the reign of Claudius, has no parallel in other provinces.[54] A couple of coin issues of earlier date depicting the she-wolf can be mentioned. The first one comes from Ilerda (Iberian Iltirta and modern-day Lleida) in Citerior. In this case, the local Iberian tradition of the town is the key to understand-

---

48  Juan Castelló 2005, 751–53.
49  Mellor 1981, 1023–24.
50  Contra Juan Castelló 2005, 753 who considers that the worship of Roma and the celebration of the *dies natalis* must be distinguished.
51  Fayer 1976, 185–236; Marco in this volume.

52  An inscription from the rock sanctuary of Peñalba de Villastar (Teruel) has been tentatively interpreted in this way. See Beltrán and others 2005, 939–41. It is one of the four epigraphs that a large rockface panel includes and reads as follows: [?]*II Kal(endas) Maias* | *Cornuto* | *Cordono* | [*C*?]*aius Atilius* | ++++++. The calendar date is uncertain. If a missing *X* is supposed, the resulting date would be 20 April, not 21. Also, it has to be mentioned that the god worshipped is a local horned divinity, Cornutus Cordonus.
53  Mellor 1981, 966–68.
54  La Rocca 2011, 1004–10.

ing the decision taken around the time of Augustus to strike the image of a female wolf on the coinage. Since the late second century BCE this settlement of the Ilergetes had issued coinage with the image of a male-wolf on the reverse, which should probably be explained as a totemic animal and symbol of the community. Iltirta/Ilerda was granted the status of Roman *municipium* under Caesar or Augustus, and it was at that moment that the male-wolf turned into a she-wolf as a civic legend on the coinage.[55] The inhabitants of Ilerda, however, did not go any further in the identification of their town with Rome. They did not complete the image with the twins. Of course, they must have known about the myth of the origin of Rome. Nonetheless, despite enjoying the legal condition of Roman citizens, they did not mean to evoke that remote past as their own, but only to accommodate their local tradition to that of the conquering power. This fact is more clearly appreciated when compared with the contemporary coinage of the Roman *municipium* of Italica.[56] It was the oldest Roman settlement in Iberia, established by P. Cornelius Scipio Africanus after the Second Punic War.[57] Under Augustus the town issued several monetary series for the first time. The bronze semis (half an as) had the emperor's head on the obverse and the twins under the she-wolf on the reverse. The latter motif resumed a republican coin legend — not used however by the *princeps* himself — that depicted the monument erected by the Ogulnii aediles near the Lupercal in 296 BCE.[58] While the Augustan coinage issued in Spain such as the monetary series of Emerita Augusta commemorated recent events, the inhabitants of Italica preferred to look back to the remote past to appropriate the Roman origin myth at the same time as they paid tribute to Augustus and the *Genius populi Romani*. Their initiative did not stop there. It is quite likely that at least part of the decoration of the Forum of Augustus was adopted in the civic centre of Italica, and a relief belonging to a fountain and dating to the reign of Hadrian, when the city was granted the title of Roman colony, represented the complete mythical scene of the discovery of the twins with the presence of Faustulus and a tree standing for the *Ficus Ruminalis*.[59] The inhabitants of Italica were probably exceptional for their penchant for remembering the miraculous aspects of the origin of Rome as well as for being the only non-provincial capital that adopted the iconographic programme of the new Forum of Augustus, which is especially well documented in Emerita Augusta.

In the 1980s several archaeological campaigns uncovered part of a portico that had been added to the main forum of Emerita Augusta in the reign of Claudius. Fragments of statues wearing a toga or armour were also found and were presumably part of the decoration of the portico niches. The discovery resulted in the re-evaluation of previous findings, namely fragments of three statues now reidentified by Walter Trillmich as part of the group of Aeneas, Ascanius, and Anchises leaving Troy. At the same time, part of an inscribed marble plaque discovered during the archaeological excavation received scholarly attention. Despite its mutilated fragmentary state, a few key words could be easily identified, especially the name *Indiges pater*, which surely led to the whole text being completed as follows: *regnavit annos tris. In luco | Laurenti subito non comparvit | apellatusq(ue) est Indiges pater | et in deorum numerum relatus* ('reigned three years. He suddenly disappeared from Laurentum and was named *Indiges pater*. He is counted among the gods').[60] It was part of the *elogium* of Aeneas from the Forum built by Augustus in Rome.

All these remains indicate that by the time of Claudius the forum of Emerita Augusta was enhanced to accommodate a copy of the iconographic decoration of the Forum of Augustus in Rome. This comprised a large collection of statues of *summi viri* identified by individual eulogistic epigraphic texts (*elogia*) and situated along the two porticoes that flanked the temple of *Mars Ultor*. In them a special point, in the form of two confronted exedrae, was reserved, one for the statue of Romulus accompanied by *summi viri*, the other for Aeneas together with the *Iulii* and the Alban kings. Aeneas was represented carrying his father and holding Ascanius's hand in the most iconic image of the Trojan hero in Roman art as a symbol of *pietas*. Romulus held a trophy standing for military victory.[61] Thanks to the fragment of the marble plaque from Emerita, we know that the inscription accompanying the group of Aeneas recalled his transformation into *Pater Indiges*, and a similar reference can be assumed for that of Romulus indicating his assimilation to *Quirinus*. No other forebear, apart from Julius Caesar, shared this divine status, which was spatially marked by

---

55 Villalonga 1978, 16, 271; Johnston 2017, 214–15.
56 Blázquez 1974, 11–12; Chaves 2008a, 123–24.
57 Canto 1999; Caballos 2010; Padilla Monge 2017.
58 Dulière 1979, 39–47.
59 For the Forum of Italica, see Peña Jurado 2005. For the fountain see León Alonso 1995, 164.

60 Álvarez Martínez 1982; Trillmich 1996. AE 1996, 864a; HEp 7, 1997, 109a: - - - - - - | [ - - - ]R · | [ - - - i]n luco · | [ - - - n]on comparvit. | [ - - - e]st · Indiges · pater · | [ - - - nu]merum · relatus. De la Barrera Antón 1996.
61 Zanker 1990, 201–10; Moatti 2015, 271–83.

the central location they occupied in the exedrae. However, from the point of view of memory, Aeneas and Romulus did not differ from the rest of the historical characters whose statues adorned the porticoes. All of them represented a distant past closed by the new era inaugurated by Augustus. It was a past to behold while strolling around the forum, not to re-enact or venerate in a ritual ceremony. It was also a past summarized in a gallery of glorious military men who had contributed to building the Roman Empire. For that reason, Romulus was depicted as a victor. In this scheme there was not room for the more traditional iconography of the twins suckled by the she-wolf, which above all represented the miraculous saving of the descendants of the Alban dynasty.

This approach to the Roman past was adopted not only by the inhabitants of Emerita Augusta, but also by those of Tarraco, Corduba, and Italica, since evidence has been discovered in these towns showing that the iconography of the porticoes in the *Forum Augustum* was adapted to their civic centres as well.[62] The case is exceptional. There is no sign of any similar transfer of Roman urban design to the provinces in other parts of the Empire. Only these three Hispanic capitals, all of them promoted to the status of Roman colony to the time of Caesar and Augustus, decided to copy the new political space inaugurated by the latter, probably around the reign of Claudius. They imitated the *Urbs* and in doing so they reproduced the main Augustan discourse about the Roman past. Lacking the traditional festivals of *Parilia* and *Lupercalia* that involved the population in re-enacting and witnessing the atmosphere of the origins of Rome, the provincials become familiar with a static image of the Roman past in which Aeneas and Romulus stood at the same level, the former as a symbol of *pietas*, the latter as the initiator of the Empire. As part of the decoration, the written *elogia* recalled the assimilation of both figures to previous divinities. Nevertheless, those verbal statements did not entail any cult of Aeneas or Romulus in the Hispanic capitals, just as it had not existed in republican times. The *elogia* did not reflect any cultic experience but historical knowledge now accessible to the provincial inhabitants in a public space together with the short biographies of the other *summi viri* whose statues decorated the *fora*. Along with Corduba, Emerita, and Tarraco, Italica, the hometown of Trajan and Hadrian, finally decided, in the time of the latter, to rise to the level of the capitals by copying the iconography of the porticoes of the Augustan forum.

For the first time the inhabitants of Hispania visiting those civic centres had the chance to peruse the faces of great Roman men and learn about their deeds. One might presume that those collections of statues must have conditioned the memory of Rome in Hispania. The evidence, however, does not support this idea. Aeneas as a forebear of the *Julii* and remote ancestor of the Romans had as relevant a place in Augustan memory discourse as Romulus. He was depicted in the *Ara Pacis* sacrificing a sow and placed in one of the exedrae of the new forum. In contrast, virtually no image of Aeneas has been discovered in Hispania apart from the above-mentioned statues in the civic centres of capitals. The inhabitants of Hispania did not find any interest in this figure. They preferred to remember Romulus, although not as a military victor but as an infant saved together with his twin brother by a she-wolf. They discarded, thus, the iconography of the *Forum Augustum* and favoured that of the *Ara Pacis*, which ultimately summarized — and complemented with *Faustulus* and *Mars* — the image of the original monument of the Ogulnii situated in the Lupercal.[63]

Two inscriptions have been found reporting the erection of a statue of the twins and the she-wolf in Hispania.[64] Both of them come from the province of Baetica, one from Singilia Barba (Antequera, Málaga) and the other from Epora (Montoro, Córdoba). In the former, the donor Marcus Cornelius Primigenius gives a statue of the she-wolf and the twins (*lupa cum infantibus duos*) in recognition of the allocation of public space by the local senate in which to erect a statue of his son.[65] In the second one, a *sevir Augustalis* named Marcus Valerius Phoebus, who had been invited to a public banquet with the decurions and granted other honours (*ornamenta*) because of his munificence in the town, donated a statue of the she-wolf to which he also dedicated the

---

62 On Tarraco see Koppel 1990; on Italica Peña Jurado 2005; on Corduba Márquez 2004.

63 The possibility that the iconography of the *Ara Pacis* in Rome was reproduced in Hispania cannot be rejected either, as remains of the *Ara Providentiae* in Emerita Augusta seem to indicate. These remains show a clear dependence on the Roman monument although no fragment related to the Aeneas or Romulus scene has so far been discovered: Nogales 2000b.

64 The evidence has been previously studied by Dulière 1979, 219–24; Dardenay 2011, 86–89; Johnston 2017, 211–15.

65 *CIL* II²/5 772; *CIL* II 5063: M(arcus) Cornelius Primigenius Sing(iliensis) | ob beneficium quod ab ordine Sing(ilensi) | locum acceperam | in quo statuam ponerem | M(arci) Corneli Saturnini f(ilii) mei | lupam cum infantibus duobus | d(onum) d(edi). On the use of public space for private monuments, see Melchor Gil 2006, 207.

inscription.⁶⁶ There is no reference to the twins, but some lines of the stele before the word *statuam* are lost. They could have been mentioned in this space, since in other epigraphs of imperial times found in North Africa the she-wolf is always accompanied by them.⁶⁷ These are three epigraphs from Tunisia also indicating the wish of three Roman citizens to erect a statue of the group as a public gift. In one of them from Henchir-El-Meden, the donor Quintus Severus Macer claims to have entered one of the lowest offices of the equestrian rank (*adlectus in quinque decurias*) thanks to the emperor Hadrian, which moved him to perform such an act of munificence in his hometown. In the other two, the donors have been elected as duumvirs, and their expenditure is part of the *summa honoraria*, the disbursement they have to make when entering office. Thus, the common point behind all these statues of the she-wolf and the twins is that they were commissioned and donated by the private initiative of elite members with Roman citizenship in Latin *municipia*.⁶⁸

These monuments have been considered an expression of Romanness and loyalty to Rome, and a means for their donors to climb socially or legitimize their positions.⁶⁹ Certainly, the latter can be said of any public move of the elite, including this case. The key question is why this monument was chosen. To begin with, it is worth noting that, despite their relevance, they are exceptional. Some other examples are surely lost. But based on the epigraphic evidence, it was not a widespread habit, probably because the expressions of loyalty to Rome only needed to be directed to the figure of the reigning emperor and the imperial family, and self-promotion at the local level was better achieved when funding urban infrastructure or public events. The statue of the twins added something else. It was a monument that embellished the town in imitation of the *Urbs*, and it emphasized the divine element in the origins of Rome.

The dedication of the inscription from Epora points in this direction. It was addressed to the *Lupa Romana* by a *sevir Augustalis*. Another inscription from Baetulo (Badalona, Barcelona) in the province of *Tarraconensis* reflects a dedication to the *Lupa Augusta* by the freedman and also *sevir Augustalis* Lucius Visellius Tertius.⁷⁰ There is no mention of a statue this time, although it cannot be ruled out that one already existed in the town. Be that as it may, both dedications highlight the divine element in the childhood of the twins, namely a she-wolf, a wild animal associated with Mars, which instead of attacking the babies saved them. Furthermore, Alexandra Dardenay has rightly pointed out that there is a close link between this iconography of the origins of Rome and the imperial cult.⁷¹ In fact, this iconography is much more significant in imperial times than under the Republic. The association was first made in Rome by Augustus and later transferred to the provinces, at least to Hispania and North Africa.⁷²

There is another instance of the representation of a miraculous scene of the remote Roman past in Hispania. In Obulco (Porcuna, Jaén), a father and a son holding religious positions in the town — the former a *flamen* and the latter a *sacerdos Geni municipi* — funded the casting of a statue of a sow with thirty piglets.⁷³ The group represented a famous event after the arrival of Aeneas and the Trojans in Latium. They were about to sacrifice a sow when the animal, which was pregnant, ran off until it stopped to give birth to thirty piglets. The event was taken as a divine indication that the Trojans would found a city in thirty years, Lavinium in some versions, Alba Longa in others.⁷⁴ According to Varro, there were 'bronze images of them standing in public places', even in his time, presumably in Lavinium but he might have meant in other places as well. Besides, a relief of the same theme dating to the first century BCE was found in Rome.⁷⁵ Those were probably the models for the statue from Obulco.

---

66 *CIL* II²/7 139; *CIL* II 2156: *Lupae Romanae | M(arcus) Valerius Phoebus | VIvir Aug(ustalis) | cui ordo munic(ipii) Epor(ensis) ob merita | cenis publicis inter decur(iones) con|venire permisit aliaque ornamenta decrevit | insertis [3] | [6] | [6] | [3 sta]tuam ponendam*.

67 They come from locations in the province of Africa Proconsularis (modern-day Tunisia). *CIL* VIII 958 (*Vina*, present-day Henchir-El-Meden): *lupa cum insignibus suis*; *CIL* VIII 22699 (*Gigthis*, present-day Bou Grara): *lupa cum Romulo et Remo* and *CIL* VIII 12220 (El-Haouaria): *lupa cum gemellis suis duobus*. See Dulière 1979, 219–24.

68 Dulière 1979, 221.

69 Edmondson 2006b, 275; Dardenay 2011. Andrew Johnston 2017, 213–14 emphasizes local agency.

70 *CIL* II 4603.

71 Dardenay 2007.

72 Dardenay 2017, 213–14, stresses the contrast between these provinces and Gaul.

73 *CIL* II²/7 93; *CIL* II 2126: *C(aius) Cornelius C(ai) f(ilius) | C(ai) n(epos) Gal(eria) Caeso aed(ilis) | flamen IIvir mu|nicipi(i) Pontifici(ensis) | C(aius) Cornel(ius) Caeso | f(ilius) sacerdos | Geni municipi | scrofam cum | porcis trigin|ta impensa ipso|rum d(ederunt) d(edicaverunt) | PONTIFEX | ------*. Some scholars have suggested that the inscription was dedicated to the genius of the *municipium* (Rodríguez and Melchor 2001, 178).

74 Dion. Hal., *Ant. Rom.* 1.56. For other authors the portent signalled the founding of Alba Longa (Fabius Pictor F3 Cornell; Varro, *R.* II.4.18).

75 Varro, *R.* II.4.18: 'Huius suis ac porcorum etiam nunc vestigia apparent, quod et simulacra eorum ahenea etiam nunc in publico

For Andrew Johnston the group was a symbol of 'Latinness' and could also have expressed the idea of Obulco as a new Lavinium representing the expansion of Roman power in Hispania.[76] This is probably reading too much into the evidence. On the one hand, there was nothing 'Latin' in the *ius Latii* in the first century CE, apart from the name. The towns of Latium had all been Roman *municipia* since the first century BCE. It would have taken a historian or antiquarian to understand the evolution of Latin rights from the fifth century BCE to the Flavian age. On the other, if that had been the case, one would expect to find more evidence related to the sow and the piglets by the end of the first century CE due to the expansion of the *ius Latii* in Hispania. But the inscription from Obulco stands alone. Probably the explanation lies elsewhere. In fact, the statue of the sow and piglets, like the one of the she-wolf with the twins, meets the same criteria. Both represent divine intervention in the origins of Rome and had already been encoded in an iconographic language by the Romans themselves under the Republic. Thus, if there were some particular inhabitants of Hispania that wanted to go beyond a demonstration of loyalty to the Empire or of local self-promotion and decided to commemorate Roman origins, they had models to copy to hand. Their particular choices show that they found myth more attractive than history and miraculous events more inspiring than the individual figures of Romulus or Aeneas. For that reason, they did not find inspiration in the civic centres of the provincial capitals that replicated the Forum of Augustus, but in the old monuments of the *Urbs*.

## Concluding Remarks

There is little evidence of Roman memory in Hispania. Part of the explanation might be simply found in the loss of attestation over time. However, there is some indication that no effort or intention was made by the Romans to transfer their memory from the city to provinces. There were religious constraints. No cult of Aeneas or Romulus actually existed. Both were assimilated to divinities such as Pater Indiges and Quirinus but this identification did not entail any ritual activity. Their lives were linked to Latium. Contrary to the Greek heroes they were not located in those new territories conquered and colonized by the Romans. Only Aeneas had some imprint outside of Italy in those places he had previously visited on his way to the western Mediterranean. Furthermore, the festivals associated with the twins and the foundation of the city, *Lupercalia* and *Parilia*, were never exported nor in general terms were the rest of the pageants of the Roman calendar. If Roman religion had not changed over time, one could conclude that it was impossible for the Romans to adjust their traditional memory to the newly conquered land. But we know that this was not the case. From Augustus's times onwards they developed a ruler cult which had virtually no precedent in the Republic. They could have equally instituted a cult of Aeneas or Romulus but they chose not to do so or probably did not feel the need to do so. This should lead us to conclude that the legitimation of their dominion must have laid somewhere else than in the divine ascendency of the founder.

The existence of *salii* at Saguntum and in other localities of northern Italy shows that it was not impossible to transfer a traditional Roman religious title to the provinces whatever its ritual prerogatives and activities might have been. It also indicates that the local initiative must have had some weight in the transfer since there is no indication of any official Roman policy in this regard. In Hispania neither the chart of Urso nor the Flavian legislation contain regulations indicating the adaptation of Roman memory cults to colonies and *municipia*. In fact, they let the decurions decide on the public cults and festivals and only required from them some performances. In Caesar's foundation games had to be organized in honour of the Capitoline triad and Venus. In the Flavian towns the new magistrates had to swear on Jupiter, the emperors, and the Penates to enter office. In both cases the selection of divinities has some relation to the Roman myth of origin and it might have contributed somehow to remembering the remote Trojan connection of the *Urbs*, but it does not seem to be the main objective of both rituals.

Notwithstanding the lack of official initiative, evidence has come down to the present demonstrating that the Hispani, or some of them, were familiar with and remembered the foundational story of Rome. As far as we know this memory was not transmitted by festivals or re-enactments as was the case in the *Urbs*. So far the only exception is Cales Coves in the Balearic Island. There, representatives of the community met every 21 April, Rome's birthday, at a cave by the southern coast of Menorca in a clear appropriation of the symbolic date which must have made sense in connection with the previous ritual activity performed in the place before the conquest. The rest of the evidence points to a contemplation of the Roman past by means of public monuments rather than a ritual celebration. The decoration of

---

posita, et corpus matris ab sacerdotibus, quod in salsura fuerit, demonstratur'. Dardenay 2010, 63–64.

76 Johnston 2017, 211–12.

the forum of Augustus that was copied in the civic centres of Emerita, Corduba, Tarraco, and Italica testifies to the wish of the inhabitants of the more relevant settlements in Hispania to provide themselves with the scenery of Roman power and memory. Thus, they could behold the gallery of great men who had built the Empire in which they lived. Among them Aeneas stood out as the representative of *pietas*, Romulus as the first military victor. The inscriptions linked to their statues recalled the divine status of both. However, with no specific ritual associated, those statements were little more than antiquarian information rather than the reflection of actual religious practice. Impressive as these *fora* must have been, they do not seem to have set the tone for other commemorations. The few recorded instances when the elite of other towns — most of them public officers or priests of the imperial cult — chose to erect monuments representing the origins of Rome, they turned to more traditional iconography from the *Urbs* such as the statue of the she-wolf and the twins or that of the sow with the thirty piglets. This choice indicates an interest in the miraculous and divine rather than in Roman virtues or power. Both images captured the moments when a heavenly act or communication mark Rome's destiny: the foundation of Alba Longa and the survival of the founders. In this sense, they are more than tokens of loyalty to Rome or of Romanness. The honours to the imperial family and the cult of the emperors fulfilled that role nicely. They convey a desire on the part of some provincial population to remember the exceptional origins of Rome, a memory that the Roman authorities themselves did not consider necessary to propagate.

VÍCTOR REVILLA CALVO

# 11. Roman Past and Local Identities

## The Case of Saguntum

The city of Saguntum offers an exceptional example of the construction of an identity narrative among Hispanic civic communities, both for its components and for its dynamic nature. This narrative combined specific historical episodes and mythical references that aimed to provide an account of the origins and nature of the community with a profound political and social value. Its content, which allowed multiple connections to be established with the Greek and central Italic worlds, reveals the diversity of cultural traditions that converged in the Iberian Peninsula in the second half of the first millennium BCE. At the same time, its development reflects diverse interpretations of the past that seem to be related to the political circumstances in which the city was immersed throughout its history. This link with the past, which includes initiatives involving active remembrance, cannot therefore be interpreted as the expression of an antiquarian project that only sought to build a prestigious image.

The aim of this chapter is to define the features and approaches in the construction process of the historical memory of a Roman city in Hispania, and the role of this memory as a fundamental element of a political identity. At the same time, it attempts to evaluate the degree of internal coherence of a memory that was not a static structure. The creation of this identity seems to respond to a twofold need on the part of the local elite between the Republic and Empire: firstly, to construct a specific image of the community's past, led by this same elite, which would help to legitimize its political and social power; secondly, to define its position in the face of imperial power and in relation to other elites in Hispania. Religion seems to play an essential role in the construction of this past in two ways: by remembering some of the circumstances of the founding episode and as a means of establishing a deep connection with Rome. This initiative seems to be integrated within the wider context of the reconstruction of Roman history and cultural values associated with the Augustan *restauratio*, but it includes older elements that seem to merge in different ways at certain historical moments. Of particular note are the elements incorporated into the historiography of the second and first centuries BCE. These are related to Saguntum's stance in the Second Punic War and the civil wars of the first century BCE.

On the other hand, the analysis of the case of Saguntum can contribute to knowledge of the forms of interaction between diverse groups, as part of the internal socio-economic and cultural dynamics of the cities of Hispania between the second century BCE and the second century CE. The possible existence of local histories, in the form of traditions that might be repeatedly re-elaborated owing to their oral nature, seems an important factor in understanding the processes behind the constitution of a community and the resolution of its conflicts. In the elaboration of a local memory, the elites played an active role derived from their control of civic institutions. Their efforts seem to reflect the need to legitimize their position and to define both their own situation and that of their community, using elements that had been in circulation in the Mediterranean region since archaic times: divinities, rituals, mythical cycles, and historical episodes. These elements acquired new meaning under Roman rule; particularly during the early Empire. The appropriation and resignification of ancient themes allowed the position of an urban community to be defined in different scenarios: vis-à-vis other cities, in the regional and provincial setting, and before the imperial power.

## Roman Past, Civic Life, and Local Identities

The internal history of Roman cities is a complex subject. Generally, knowledge of their history does not go beyond political episodes that attracted the attention of classical writers because of their exceptional and/or violent nature. In contrast, the devel-

**Víctor Revilla Calvo**, Professor of Ancient History (University of Barcelona)

opment of cultural and socio-economic structures poses significant problems of analysis, apart from the possibility of defining some institutional aspects and identifying social hierarchies through epigraphy. In particular, it is difficult to reconstruct the forms of representation of the various groups that made up a civic community, forms that were in turn integrated within mechanisms of communication and social interaction. This situation prevents a full understanding of essential aspects of urban life in the Empire and its regional nuances. These nuances were determined by cultural and socio-economic factors, the conditions of incorporation into the Roman domain, and widely varying political traditions. This problem is particularly serious in the case of Hispania, whose cities, many of them republican or imperial foundations, lacked the urban tradition of the Greek East. The few Punic and Greek colonial cities, on the other hand, seem to have replaced their pasts by a new historical memory in the course of the last century of the Republic; both in the case of the former Punic cities (Gadeira/Gadir, Ebusus) and the Greek ones (Emporion).[1] By an apparent paradox, while these ancient colonial cities transformed the memory of their past, others, of indigenous origin, were to create a past linked in part precisely to the Greek colonial tradition.[2]

However, the information available on the local history of Roman cities in Hispania is minimal. Only Tarraco offers some fragmentary references to historical events, characters, and mythical-religious aspects that are combined in a very synthetic foundational narrative, but one that is still effective because of its political value.[3] In other cases, the only information available is of an epigraphic and/or numismatic nature. In the case of the coin issues the best-known examples can be seen in the context of the foundation of some Augustan colonies and recall the moment when the community was constituted; but there are also references to the Roman past, through the evocation of rites and mythical episodes, in some cities without privileged status.[4]

In this context, Saguntum is a remarkable case. The city appears with some frequency in various literary genres, particularly in historiography, between the second century BCE and the second century CE.

This literary dossier includes references on a wide range of subjects: origins and institutions, data on its territory and resources, and key historical episodes. This information is fragmentary and often of later date or anachronistic (in relation to the scenarios or episodes it seeks to explain), but it does allow the question of the construction of the identity of a civic community in Hispania to be addressed. In addition, Saguntum has the advantage of an indigenous origin and early development as a political community, as its coinage shows; in parallel, the confluence of Greek, local, and Roman cultural traditions enables us to assess which elements and mechanisms were used for the creation of this identity. The analysis is particularly complex because of the link between these narratives and the debate on what caused, and who was responsible for, the outbreak of the Second Punic War and the significance that this conflict had within the Greek and Roman historiographic tradition.

Other documentary evidence can be incorporated for this analysis. Firstly, Saguntum and its territory have provided a very large body of inscriptions that include important information on institutions and civic life, including administrative and religious aspects. This corpus has been exhaustively studied.[5] This has made it possible to identify the composition of the local elites and the historical development of the community.[6] Analysis of coins issued by the city between the fourth century BCE and the first century CE has also enabled scholars to study in greater depth both institutional aspects (and the successive legal statuses) and the socio-cultural transformation that is reflected, among other things, in the community's name-change and the use of coin legends in Latin after the late second century BCE.[7]

## Arse-Saguntum

Knowledge of the earliest history of the community is very much dependent on accounts by Greek and republican- and imperial-period Roman authors of its role in the Second Punic War. Archaeological evidence indicates the existence of an indigenous settlement on an elevation overlooking the River Palancia and the coastal plain.[8] This settlement, which must

---

1   On Punic communities: López Castro 1995; Machuca 2019; also Celestino and López-Ruiz 2016. Civic identities in Ferrer Albelda 2012; Chaves 2017.
2   Gómez Espelosín and others 1995; Cruz Andreotti and others 2006; Martínez Pinna 2008; Johnston 2017; in general: Bickerman 1952. See also Mayorgas in this volume.
3   Richardson 2000.
4   Marco 2015.

5   Beltrán 1980; Corell 2002.
6   Alföldy 1977; 1984; Abascal and Cebrián 2004.
7   Ripollès and Llorens 2002; Estarán 2022 analyses the numismatic and epigraphic evidence, which suggest the coexistence of the Iberian and Latin languages during the second and first centuries BCE.
8   The city is located on the coast of the modern region of Valencia. In the imperial period, this area, densely urbanized since the Iron Age, formed the southern sector of the *conventus Tarraconensis*.

have been the place named Arse on the first coins, was protected by a wall datable to the fifth to fourth centuries BCE.[9] The first coin issues, which show Greek influence, belong to this period (second half of the fourth century BCE).[10] The community also seems to have had a commercial enclave located by the sea, the interpretation of which is problematic.[11] The community was involved in the Second Punic War alongside Rome. The outcome was the well-known episode of its destruction, reported by many authors, and its subsequent reconstruction. In the second century the city seems to have expanded, with new sectors of the hill being urbanized. A temple with a tripartite *cella* and various public buildings belongs to this phase. New defensive works can also be identified.[12]

Throughout the second century the city remained an ally of Rome, but it was not until the first century BCE that information about its legal status is available. Cicero's *pro Balbo* (*Balb.* 23), dated 56 BCE, identifies its status as a *civitas foederata*. However, some coins from the period indicate that it was a Latin colony. This change in status has been attributed to an initiative by Pompey, between 55 and 50 BCE.[13] Nevertheless, there are some problems in pinpointing this undertaking, which could have been both earlier (in the event that Cicero was ignorant of the precise condition of the city when he composed his speech) or later.[14] In Caesar's Civil War, Saguntum seems to have taken sides with Pompey. This decision subsequently forced its elites to seek rapprochement with Caesar.[15] At the end of the century, Saguntum became a *municipium* of Roman citizens, as can be deduced from the mention of the *municipes Saguntini* in CIL II²/14, 305, dated

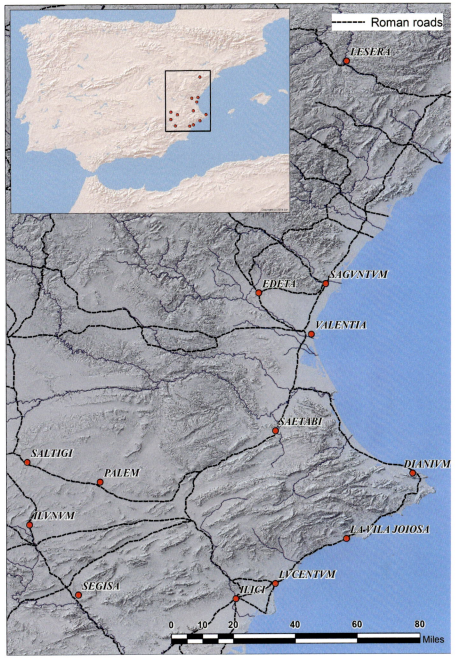

Figure 11.1. Location of Saguntum and the Roman cities located in the south of the conventus Tarraconensis and the northern territories of the conventus Carthaginensis (image: D. J. Martín-Arroyo Sánchez).

4/3 BCE.[16] Pliny the Elder (*Nat.* III.20) also mentions that it was a *municipium*.

The history of the city in imperial times is partly known through epigraphic evidence (the few literary references still focus on the memory of the Second Punic War) and must be understood in a densely urbanized regional context, as it existed

---

9  Aranegui 1992; 1994; 2004a; 2006.
10 Ripollès and Llorens 2002. Beltrán 2011 highlights the relationship between the evolution of Saguntum's coins and its political development between the third and first centuries BCE.
11 Domínguez Monedero 2011–2012.
12 Aranegui 1992; 2006; Hernández Hervás 2004. Republican temple: Aranegui 2005.
13 Ripollès and Velaza 2002.
14 Ripollès 2002b, 340; Llorens 2002, 67. Triumviral chronology: Amela 2009; 2011, 155, 159; but cf. Pena 2022.
15 Nic. Dam., *Vit. Caes.* 11: Perea Yébenes 2017; cf. Abascal 2006.

16 Date of granting around 8/7 BCE: Bonneville 1987, 138–39; collected by Ripollès 2010, 146.

alongside cities of different characteristics and legal status (Fig. 11.1).¹⁷ Among these, the nearby city of Valentia, a republican foundation destroyed in the Sertorian War in 75 BCE, stands out. Valentia was rebuilt in the time of Augustus, although evidence for its urban and architectural development does not become apparent until the end of the Julio-Claudian period and especially in Flavian times.¹⁸

Archaeological activity in recent decades has provided a reliable, albeit incomplete, picture of urban planning in Saguntum.¹⁹ The layout of the city was conditioned by its very irregular topography, which forced settlement to be distributed on terraces. The forum, on the highest part of the old hill, included a temple and civil buildings. Its construction, on top of the second-century BCE temple, dated from the Augustan period. On the same hill there were important civic buildings such as the theatre, dated to the Julio-Claudian period. These urban development projects were the result of initiatives by powerful members of the local elite.²⁰ The organization of the road network also took place at this moment. Between the first and second centuries CE, Saguntum underwent major transformations that particularly affected the area near the river (the forum area seems to have lost importance to such an extent that it was abandoned), which became densely occupied. A mid-second-century circus was located here.²¹ Other monumental constructions of a religious and funerary nature have also been identified, laid out alongside a porticoed road: a temple and a possible honorific arch, built between the Flavian and Trajanic periods.²² Some public buildings were renovated in the third century;²³ but they were abandoned and plundered between the mid-fourth and fifth centuries, parallel to the reorganization of certain sectors of the urban space. At the same time, substantial private buildings and infrastructures were erected.²⁴ All this is indicative of the dynamism of local life into the fourth and fifth centuries.

## The Origins of the Saguntine Community

As has been pointed out Saguntum's past appears with some frequency in the literature of the late Republic and early Empire.²⁵ The memory of its past was built up by combining two arguments: the origin of its first settlers and the alliance with Rome. These arguments seem to have acquired political value, since both allowed the condition of the city as a self-governing community to be highlighted. Through the former, the conditions of the foundation by an organized human group were revealed. From the perspective of the Mediterranean colonial world, this situation implied a conscious political act; at the same time, the origins made it possible to establish a cultural link. For its part, the idea of the alliance made it possible to highlight the functioning of civic institutions (which intervened in the dramatic context of the war against Hannibal) and included an ethical reference, also linked to the episode of the destruction of the city. This event allowed the community to be represented as a political actor, but also its ruling class, the main player in the initiative, to maintain (and show) the alliance with Rome.

The first of the arguments, the origins of the city, appears in many works, with varying detail and with some differences. Livy (XXI.7.2–3) mentions the mixed origin, Greek and Latin, of the foundation, created with colonists from the island of Zacynthus and the city of Ardea (*Rutulorum generis*). Strabo mentions its foundation by the Zacynthians (III.4.6). Subsequently, Pliny the Elder and Appian used various procedures to insist on the Hellenic origin (always in Zacynthus) of the Saguntines. Pliny the Elder establishes a link between the origin of the settlers and the foundation of a temple to Artemis/Diana, supposedly two hundred years before the Trojan War (*Nat.* XVI.216). This reference is significant because of the connection between the Phocaean foundations in the West and the worship of Artemis Ephesia.²⁶ Appian (*Hisp.* 7), in the second century CE, is even more explicit in including the Saguntines among a group of Greek settlements in the Iberian Peninsula that were freely governed by their own laws (which is a way of affirming the Hellenic char-

---

17 Aranegui 2011.
18 Ribera 2008; Ribera and Jiménez Salvador 2012.
19 Aranegui 2002; 2004a; 2004b; 2006; Hernández Hervás 2004; Ferrer Maestro and others 2018.
20 Alföldy 1977; Aranegui 1992; 1994; 2004a; 2004b; 2006; Aranegui and Jiménez Salvador 2013.
21 Hernández Hervás and others 1996; Pascual Buyé 2002; Melchor Montserrat and others 2017; Ferrer Maestro and others 2018.
22 Benedito 2015; Ferrer Maestro and others 2018; 2019.
23 Aranegui 2004b.
24 Aranegui 2004b, 108; Hernández Hervás 2004, 118–21; Ferrer Maestro and others 2018; 2019; similar processes in other cities in Hispania: Ruiz Bueno 2018.

25 In general: Coarelli 2001; Schettino 2006; Wicha 2002–2003; Domínguez Monedero 2011–2012; Johnston 2017.
26 Domínguez Monedero 2009–2011; Bats 2014; Pena 2016 proposes a political interpretation to explain the construction of the 'Ephesian tradition', which she places in the second century; an onomastic connection between Saguntum and Latium is proposed in Pena 2022.

acter of these communities) and were protected by the Romans. Except for Pliny (who only makes an indirect allusion), all the authors deal with the origin of the Saguntines to introduce the preparations for Hannibal's attack that would trigger the war between Rome and Carthage.

Silius Italicus offers an apparently more complete narrative. This author takes up the idea of the mixed origin, with Greek settlers from the island of Zacynthus and Latins from Ardea, of the city and places it in a complex mythical construction full of genealogical and topographical allusions.[27] His account explains, first of all, the origin of the place name, which is derived from the hero Zacynthus, who accompanied Hercules in his labours and who died and was buried in the place that would later house the city. The presence of this character and the link to Hercules' cycle of adventures enabled a tie to be established with the Greek (and Trojan) past. This link is reinforced by the reference to the presence of migrants from the island of Zacynthus. In the same respect, the presence of settlers from Ardea (*rutuli*) establishes another connection with the same past, in this case through the *Aeneid*, in which this community plays a key role in the circumstances generated by Aeneas's arrival in Latium.[28] As a consequence, the poem by Silius Italicus establishes a direct connection between Rome and Saguntum based on ethnic-cultural kinship; but it also generates more complex (ethical and religious) interpretations of that relationship based on the circumstances surrounding the destruction of the city by Hannibal and its parallels with the struggles between the Trojans and the Rutuli.[29]

This reference set, which enhanced the value of various traditions, could be placed in the context of the cultural climate of the mid-first century CE, in which there was a new interest (sponsored by Nero) in the Trojan legend and the link with the origin of the *gens Iulia*; these initiatives had a contemporary effect, as is shown by some of Nero's undertakings concerning Ilium.[30] But these evocations seem to have had a deeper ideological meaning that affected the new Flavian dynasty. In this framework, a narrative that closely linked Rome and Saguntum through the memory of the Italian kinship (Ardea) and the *fides* of an ally became more meaningful.[31] In this scenario Heracles-Hercules also allowed multiple references to be made, because of his condition as a civilizing hero and the personification of *virtus*. In this specific sense, his figure also adopted a political and ethical value since he could be connected with the imperial power. However, the diversity of cultural, religious, and political connotations that are associated with this hero also allowed other appropriations.[32]

This shaping of the foundational story is also related to the name of the city, which is recorded in several ways in the classical sources and on the coins; in this case, moreover, it includes two names: Arse and Saguntum. This duality has been explained as a consequence of the existence of two population centres of different and complementary nature: the main nucleus, Arse, and its maritime enclave in the form of an emporium, which the Romans would later know as Saguntum.[33] This duality and the similarity of the indigenous names with the Greek Zakynthos or with Ardea could serve to elaborate the idea of the Greek (later Graeco-Latin) origin of the local population, incorporated in the literature between the second and first centuries BCE; from there it would pass into the literature of the imperial age.[34]

The few literary references to the establishment and location of certain cults help to strengthen the city's cultural links with the Greek world. To Pliny's aforementioned text about the temple of Artemis, we must add the quote from Polybius about a temple to Aphrodite (III.97.6–8). Pliny places the former inside the city. This location, which followed the practice of Phocaean foundations, helped to reinforce the cultural link with the Greek world that it was intended to highlight in the accounts.[35] In contrast, the temple of Aphrodite would have been located 40 *stadia* away from Saguntum.

---

27 *Pun.* I.271–75; I.291–93; I.378–425.
28 Ardea's *Sacra*: *Pun.* I.665–69; *penates*: II.604–05; furthermore: I.332; I.572; II.541; II.567; IV.62. Greek origin: III.178; *rutuli* and Greeks: I.377–79; I.654–61; II.604–05. Cf. Schettino 2006, 59.
29 Vessey 1974; Pérez Villatela 1990; Barzanò 1992; Coarelli 2001; Wicha 2002–2003, 183–84; Schettino 2006; Martínez Pinna 2008, 256–57; Mayorgas 2017; Johnston 2017, 156–58, 205–08.
30 Tac., *Ann.* XII.58; Suet., *Nero* 7: Schettino 2006, 59–60.

31 Schettino 2006, 59–63; Mayorgas 2017.
32 Augustan propaganda: Wicha 2002–2003, 181. Link between Hannibal and Heracles/Hercules in Liv. XXI.21.9 and especially in Liv. XXI.41.7 and Sil., *Pun.* IV.4–5: Martínez Pinna 2008, 251–52 and 257–58. A local coin with a possible image of Heracles (third century BCE): Llorens 2002, 91–93. Heracles in the Iberian Peninsula: Gómez Espelosín and others 1995, 93–97.
33 Santiago 1990, 129; Domínguez Monedero 2011–2012, 403; but cf. Pena 2022.
34 Coinage: Ripollès and Llorens 2002. Place-name development: Sanmartí and Santiago 1987; Santiago 1990; 1994.
35 Domínguez Monedero 2009–2011.

## *Oppidum fide nobile*: The Use of the Past and the Construction of a Political Identity

The second element that appears in Saguntum's corpus of narratives is its loyalty to Rome and the implications of this. This theme is closely linked to the circumstances of the war against Carthage by various classical authors. Polybius addresses the issue of the relationship between Rome and Saguntum on several occasions to consider the question of ultimate responsibility for the outbreak of war with Carthage. In this context he asserts the existence of some kind of alliance involving Roman protection (Polyb. III.15.5–8; III.17.7; III.30.1).[36] More specifically, Livy refers to the alliance on several occasions (XXI.7.3, *Per.* 21.2); in one of them rather ambiguously, since the destruction of Saguntum is presented as an example of the negative consequences that alliances with Rome could bring to indigenous peoples (XXI.19.6–11).[37] Neither Polybius (in particular) nor Livy clearly defines the terms of this alliance; in fact, neither do the later writers who mention the episode. However, this lack of precision does not affect the building of a narrative that is structured around the idea of this episode being an *exemplum* and embodying a moral value revealed as a consequence of the community's willingness to maintain the obligations imposed by an alliance, adapting its actions to the principles of Roman political culture.[38]

The argument of loyalty appears in another author of the Augustan period, Valerius Maximus (VI.6 ext. 1), in a set of *exempla* of *fides publica*. Most of these are situated in the context of the Second Punic War, which confirms the importance that this conflict had in Roman historical memory. Only two episodes, which the author explicitly relates, have allied communities, namely Saguntum and Petelia, as protagonists; both of them were in confrontation with Hannibal. The historical moment, the opponent, and the collective decision of both communities, which suffered the same end, allowed Valerius Maximus to construct a coherent narrative centring on the importance of *fides* as a key feature in the relationship between Rome and its allies; in reality, as the only important element and, surely, as the only valid option for an ally, regardless of the effectiveness of Roman support.[39] In this sense, the episodes are complementary: respect for *fides* is voluntary in both cases. This respect leads to sacrifice in the face of the impossibility of Roman support, which is recorded in Livy's account in the Saguntum episode, and which is made explicit in that of *Petelia*, authorized by the Senate to negotiate with Hannibal. The absence of this Roman support is a fundamental feature, because it underlines the apparent freedom of their allies to choose even a destructive option. This circumstance made it possible to create an example with a profound moral value and therefore worthy of being remembered in the future. Moreover, the value of this example was sanctioned by the divinity.

It is interesting to note that the Petelia episode had already been picked up by Polybius and Livy.[40] Both authors' texts contain the essential aspects of Valerius Maximus's narrative. In the case of Polybius (VII.1): extreme resistance to the Carthaginians, which resulted in the destruction of the city, driven by the free acceptance of the obligations of the Roman alliance. For his part, Livy (XXIII.20.4–10) mentions the request for help from Rome invoking the terms of an alliance and the Roman recognition of its inability to fulfil its obligations, which led to the Petelians being authorized to act freely; all this came with the parallel recognition of this community's faithfulness. The narrative also includes other aspects that show Petelia's political autonomy: the dispatch of an embassy to Rome and the internal debate in the community, led by the local senate and the elite, about the line to be taken. The subsequent narrative (Liv. XXIII.30.1–5) once again captures the extreme resistance of the community. In short, the cases of Petelia and Saguntum (and it should be remembered that both cities gained this leading role in the same historical context) enabled a political and moral archetype that would serve as a reference model for the actions of Rome's allies and which could be adopted by other provincial elites with the necessary modifications.[41]

The moral function of the narrative surrounding the alliance with Rome was supported by highlighting another aspect: the leading role of a community that was able to act as an autonomous political entity. The political initiative of the city and its elite

---

36  Wicha 2002–2003, 180; Domínguez Monedero 2011–2012, 396–97; cf. Scardigli 1991.
37  Ambiguity: Wicha 2002–2003, 189; Johnston 2017, 206–08 and 226.
38  Domínguez Monedero 2011–2012, 396–97.
39  'Ne a societate nostra desciscerent' (Saguntum); 'deficere nostra amicitia noluerant' (Petelia: Val. Max. VI.6 ext. 2).

40  cf. Frontin. Str. IV.5.18; App. *Hann.* 29 (referring to the harshness of the siege and the destruction of the city, rebuilt by Rome in return); Ath. XII.36.
41  The theme converted into a slogan appears in other works (Mel. II.92; Plin., *Nat.* III.4) and is still collected in late Roman writers (Amm. Marc. XV.10.10). Classical authors' assessment of other episodes of self-immolation by an indigenous community are ambivalent, as shown by Appian's (*Hisp.* 95–98) account of Numantia; cf. Flor., *Epit.* I.34.18.11–17. Wicha 2002–2003, 183–84.

is clearly mentioned by authors like Livy in various ways. Firstly, by showing the action of local institutions and social hierarchies headed by the elite. The use of certain vocabulary by this author (*praetores, senatus, concilium populi*) is significant, since he interprets the Saguntine institutions by means of Roman political categories.[42] Although in a simplified manner, Livy's narrative includes other elements that can be interpreted in the same way; in particular, his allusion to the wealth of the community, which appears in two instances: first, as collective goods, which also responds to the parameters of a civic ideology;[43] second, as a result of its capacity to adequately exploit commercial opportunities and natural resources. This reference is mentioned in a description of the city that includes its demographic potential (a source of wealth in the eyes of any Graeco-Roman writer) and the allusion to the inhabitants' 'high moral values' (*disciplinae sanctitate*). These values are precisely the ones that would lead Saguntum to respect its alliance with Rome, assuming the consequences. Behind all these elements appears the idea of a civilized community, closer to the parameters of a Greek city than a barbarian entity; Appian insists on this idea later when he includes the people of Saguntum among the communities of Greek origin in Iberia that were governed according to their own laws under Roman protection.[44]

Livy's account also refers to the internal debate in the Saguntine community. This discussion, which certainly does not question the principle of the Roman alliance, is another fundamental element in the creation of the city's image, since it implied the existence of civic institutions and a modus operandi regulated by the elites. This debate also has an ethical and political value, as it allows the importance of *fides* as a mechanism for relations between communities to be highlighted.

Such institutions and debates convey the impression of an institutionalized relationship between states (Saguntum and Rome) based on sharing the same value system. But the repercussions of this image of the community go beyond the political, as they allow the relationship between the elites of the two cities to be particularly highlighted. In this context, it is significant that the rescue of the Saguntine captives after the Roman victory is mentioned. This episode showed the social and political reconstruction of the city, while insisting on continuity from the original community and its traditions. Through this connection, the legitimacy of the social order was ultimately revealed. At the same time, the emphasis on loyalty provided a moral reference that also contributed to the prestige of the Saguntine elite and legitimized their position.[45] Loyalty, maintained with all its consequences (since it implied the physical destruction of the community and the extermination of its inhabitants), could thus be exhibited as a model of behaviour applicable to the political and social sphere that could be presented as the exclusive patrimony of the local elite, and which could only be understood and shared by the Roman senatorial elite; therefore, it constituted a means of social and political communication exclusive to two aristocracies that headed their respective communities and could give the illusion of a relationship of equals to Saguntum's aristocracy.

Another aspect to be highlighted in the various accounts is the importance attributed to diplomatic activity. Livy gathers references to the dispatch of embassies to Rome before and during the conflict,[46] but also to acknowledge Roman support for the reconstruction of the city. A significant paragraph (Liv. XXVIII.39) includes the speech of gratitude of a Saguntine embassy formed by ten individuals (the number is also revealing) before the Roman Senate. This discourse is articulated around two issues: on the one hand, the Roman–Saguntine alliance and its consequences; on the other, the reconstruction of the community, which was recovering its condition as a politically autonomous entity. This initiative includes some fundamental features: the restoration of the civic body, thanks to the rescue of the enslaved Saguntines after Hannibal destroyed the city ('Saguntum restituerint ciuesque Saguntinos seruitio exemerint') and the re-establishment of the material bases of the community with the concession of the right to exact tribute from other communities. It is in this context that the activity of the first Cornelii Scipiones and the future Publius Cornelius Scipio Africanus Maior took place. They were recognized as being responsible for this restoration, but in accordance with the Senate's authorization and confirmation. In this same diplomatic context

---

42  Liv. XXI.12.7–8; XXI.14.1.
43  'argentum aurumque omne ex publico priuatoque', Liv. XXI.14.1.
44  *Hisp.* 7.
45  This position was also supported by the granting of Roman citizenship to some inhabitants in the first century BCE: *Balb.* 50–51.
46  Liv. XXI.6 narrates the previous reception of an embassy in Rome and the debate in the Senate, where the Saguntines' status as allies is asserted. Rome also claimed to defend the Saguntine cause before the Senate of Carthage. Liv. XXI.10.13 mentions the proposal of the opponents of Hannibal's policy to send an embassy to Saguntum as an act of reparation. The initiative is linked to the dispatch of other ambassadors to Rome and to Hannibal himself. The narrative, therefore, shows Saguntum to have been fully integrated into a diplomatic circuit.

we can include the allusions to the *hospitium* relationships between the city and certain inhabitants of Hispania, which are described in terms of Roman political language ('Saguntinis amicus atque hospes': Liv. XXI.12.6) and specifying their antiquity ('pro vetusto hospitio': XXI.13.2). Embassies are also mentioned in Appian's later account (*Hisp.* 7, 10, 11), in which the Saguntines engage in active diplomacy.

With regard to these references to diplomatic activity, several meanings can be pointed out. First, they show a frequent relationship between political entities that recognize each other as active participants in an international scenario. In Rome's case, the aim was to integrate a community within the space of its alliances, with the consequences that this implied. This scheme of action is recognized in other instances in the Greek colonial sphere, as the case of Massalia shows. It was a relationship built from the perspective of Roman needs and accompanied by forms of self-representation that defined the position of the participants and a protocol for diplomatic interaction.[47] Some of these elements can be recognized in the case of Saguntum: the use of diplomacy in a context of military emergency and the call to loyalty and mutual obligations imposed by an alliance. The episode in Liv. XVIII.39, with Saguntum's speech of gratitude before the Senate, is very informative. The discourse has a well-defined structure and is accompanied by expressions of respect before the Senate that give an insight into the leading role of this institution (and conveys the vision of Livy himself). The speech is accompanied by acts of homage of high symbolic value (an offering to Jupiter on the Capitoline, and the visiting of Italic cities),[48] which are accepted and reciprocated by the Senate with hospitality and material rewards. Through this exchange of rhetoric and gifts, the existence of a regular diplomatic relationship was made explicit, with its language and practices, established between two theoretically equal cities, but insisting on Saguntum's status as an ally.

Here again, it is an image constructed in the realm of Roman historiography. It could be assumed that it was constructed in an Augustan context, but also incorporating elements that had accumulated over the previous two centuries and which had been continuously recalled in Saguntine elite circles.[49] They were the main players in the diplomatic activity that linked Saguntum to Rome, with its constant appeal to the alliance and the memory of loyalty. Rome's failure to help the Saguntines, unlike other episodes in the history of the Republic, would reinforce the meaning attributed to the episode, since *fides* is an important historiographical theme for the construction of a specific image of Rome and the justification of its foreign policy activity.

In this context, the reference to loyalty can be reinforced by alluding to some kind of kinship between the communities that maintained this relationship, and this approach was used in certain instances.[50] In the case of Saguntum this function could be the reference to the participation of settlers from Ardea in the foundation of the city recorded by Livy.[51] The connection with Rome was not direct, but it was sufficiently prestigious and close (the Latin past and the connection with the Roman foundational legend) to be used. At the same time, the argument of kinship was also a way of establishing a link with the Greek cultural world since political practices typical of this sphere were used. In fact, in the image of the Saguntum–Rome relationship several factors appear that characterize another relationship, the one that existed between Massalia and Rome: *dignitas, vetustas, utilitas*. Through them, the elements of social, cultural, and ethical coincidence that made an alliance and a diplomatic relationship possible were highlighted.[52]

In fact, in the construction of the account of a privileged relationship between Saguntum and Rome, it is impossible to exclude the image of Massalia (and its elites) as a faithful ally of the Republic having been influential. This image, carefully constructed from the third century BCE, in the context of the Punic wars, displays noticeable coincidences with the case of Saguntum: respect for the obligations of the *fides*, military support, and intense diplomatic relations between states led by their elites. Some writers (Cicero, Strabo) report on Massalian allegiance on various occasions and also include religious references that allow for the establishment of multiple cultural and political connections between Massalia and Rome, the origins of which must have lain in the foundational stages of the Phocaean *apoikia*. Among these references, the account of the stopover of the Phocaean settlers in Rome and their friendship with Tarquin the Elder, recorded by Pompeius Trogus, as well as Strabo's description of the details of the rituals and the image of Artemis in Massalia stand out. According to this author, the image of the Diana on

---

47 Torregaray 2018; also Torregaray 2006; Bérenguer 2010; Burton 2011.
48 Highlighted by Johnston 2017, 207 as an opportunity to connect with the traditions of the Italic communities.
49 Johnston 2017, 204–08.
50 For example, in diplomacy: Torregaray 2018.
51 Coarelli 2001; Schettino 2006; Johnston 2017.
52 Torregaray 2018.

the Aventine must have reflected the same model as that in Massalia.⁵³ These reports have a political value, since they are related to the foundation of the *apoikia*, which is also shown as a conscious act that involved the definition of a cultural identity and civic and religious institutions. At the same time, the accounts enabled a relationship between the foundation of Massalia and Rome similar to the case of Saguntum to be established.

The histories of Saguntum and Massalia have other points of contact that could have inspired the later construction of Saguntine narrative. Both cities played a significant, although different, role in the Second Punic War and in the dynamics of Roman expansion in their respective regions in the course of the second century BCE. Moreover, during the civil war between Caesar and Pompey, Massalia was in the same complicated scenario as Saguntum, but the latter succeeded in solving it in its own favour. Such similar historical traditions were added to the attempt (in the case of Saguntum) to claim a Greek origin. By way of hypothesis, it might be proposed that the account of the Saguntine elites was drawn up partly inspired by the image of Massalia, but also in contrast to it, claiming a mixed identity with Greek, Trojan, and Latin origins (something that Massalia could not or did not want to allege) that would justify a particular condition as a Roman ally in the West. Moreover, the exhibition of a *fides* that had led to its destruction was another aspect with which Massalia could not compete.

In short, these origins and the Roman alliance were part of a global image that allowed a political identity to be expressed, one in which very different meanings converged. Such a complex image, which harks back to diverse cultural contexts, must have been formed gradually, incorporating new components and modifying the meaning of others according to new circumstances; in particular, as shown by the case of Massalia, adapting to the evolution of relations between Rome and her western allies in the second and first centuries BCE as a result of the internal dynamics of the Roman state.⁵⁴ In the case of Hispania, special mention should be made of the impact that the reorganization following the Celtiberian and Lusitanian Wars would have, including the foundation of Valentia in 138 BCE, and the subsequent civil wars. These had a serious effect on the region (the destruction of Valentia in 75 BCE). This scenario may have generated reactions on the part of the Saguntine elite aimed at asserting their position in a competitive and dangerous regional and global context.⁵⁵ It was precisely at the end of the second century when the city introduced elements on its coinage (the ship's bow motif, Latin legends, Roman onomastics of its magistrates) that were intended to show the city's link to Rome. This process was followed by the adoption of exclusively Latin coin legends.⁵⁶

Both the initiatives of a part of the Roman aristocracy and those of the elites of some ancient Greek and Iberian cities in the West can be placed in the conflictive context of the period. In both cases, these initiatives were carried out through a self-interested exploration and reconstruction of the past; for the senatorial elite this reconstruction insisted on full control of the senate, as a collective entity, over foreign policy, basing this control on its prestige, on the *mos maiorum* (which the concept of loyalty allowed them to highlight, even through non-Roman examples), and on the privileged relationship with other elites. Particularly interesting, for example, are Cicero's allusions to the ancient case of the Saguntum embassies, which he introduces into the debate on the Senate's action against Mark Antony (Cic., *Phil.* v.27 and vi.6).⁵⁷ In this scenario, the Saguntine elite were able to develop an image that established their leading role and their privileged relationship with the Senate. Furthermore, Saguntum had been involved in the confrontation between Caesar and Pompey and reacted quickly to the changing political circumstances.⁵⁸

Whatever the case, Saguntum's origin and loyalty mutually reinforce each other. The Roman alliance was made possible precisely because they shared a common origin which, in both cities, involved a supposed foundation by human groups of mixed origin. The two themes, moreover, include an ethical-religious component: a divine intervention, which implied a cultural kinship, foreshadowed the future alliance and its consequences, which would be sanctioned by the same goddess *fides*.⁵⁹

---

53 Str. IV.1.4–5. On this subject: Bats 2014. On Trogus Pompeius: Just., *Epit.* XLIII.3 and XLIII.5 (Massalia's aid to Rome after the attack of the Gauls).
54 Johnston 2017, 204–05; Wicha 2002–2003 (Augustan chronology). Coarelli 2001 proposes an earlier composition (mid-fourth century BCE).
55 cf. Alföldy 1984, 214.
56 Ripollès 2002a, 273–302; Ripollès and Llorens 2002, nos 317, 318, 319–30, 331–32, 379–81, 283–386; Beltrán 2011, 31–33.
57 Pina Polo 2018, 201. Overview: Sandberg and Smith 2018.
58 Abascal 2006; 2017; Perea Yébenes 2017.
59 cf. Val. Max. VI.6.ext.1.

## Dynamics of Remembrance: The Augustan Period

In Augustan times, the two components of the Saguntine myth were converted into a coherent narrative of intense political value that would complement and give meaning to new undertakings related to the memory of certain historical episodes. These initiatives must have been projected onto the urban topography and the organization of the community's collective life in a way that is difficult to specify through architecture, ritual, and calendar. Their objective, as expressed in the epigraphic evidence, seems to be remembrance of a (supposed) past that would place the city in the new imperial framework. This aim was sought, in the first instance, through rituals linked to very specific divinities and carried out by religious *collegia* controlled by the local elite.

The most obvious case is the *collegium* of the *Salii*, the only case known outside Italy.[60] A total of seven known inscriptions mention members of this *collegium*, of whom four are named as *magistri*. The corpus can be dated between the time of Augustus and the mid-second century CE, with one group of *Salii* in the Julio-Claudian period and another that dates from the late first and the second centuries. The inscriptions suggest that membership of the *collegium* was the privilege of a limited group of elite families and that there was a close relationship between the local *cursus* and religious functions. This instance has been interpreted as a demonstration of the conservatism of the elite and their monopoly over the institutions of civic life.[61]

The activity of the *collegium* (which is otherwise unknown) allowed multiple connections to be established with the Roman past.[62] On the one hand, because of its antiquity, since tradition linked its foundation to Numa Pompilius, the creator of some of the main Roman religious institutions. At the same time, a different tradition linked the etymology of the word with Salius, a character in the myth of Aeneas, and connected the *collegium* with the cult of Hercules, a hero who appears precisely in some variants of the founding myth of Saguntum. The possible associations with the Roman past also implied a close relationship (a further one) with the Latin world.[63]

The establishment of the *collegium* has been linked to Augustus's religious reconstruction project, with various hypotheses about the level of involvement of the Saguntine elites before the imperial power.[64] However, it seems more appropriate to think of a complex process of interaction and negotiation, carried out in the Augustan and Julio-Claudian periods, which must have taken advantage of a pre-existing basis: the various elements present in the founding myth of Saguntum (which already included numerous references to the account of the origins of Rome and its geography, with a noteworthy Latin and Trojan connection) and the theme of *fides*. This negotiation would have been based on the search for coincidences to build a coherent image of a common past with Rome, and this coherence must have been reinforced by the recreation of rituals and priesthoods.

This process must have involved, in the first place, the Saguntine elites, who had directly contacted the young Caesar after Munda, and who would have had the opportunity to interact later, at the time when Saguntum changed its status from colony to *municipium*. At the same time, the available options, using the religious tradition, fitted into Augustus's policy of recovering (and redefining) elements of the past, carefully selecting those that presented the greatest possibilities of creating new meanings; those most useful to Augustan culture, full of nuances and particularities in the revaluation of the Roman tradition.[65] In this culture, the recovery of ancient rituals centred on the origin of Rome and its historical relationship with the Latins, which had their expression in the *Feriae Latinae*, occupied a prominent position. The celebration of the *sacra* of the *gens Iulia*, which took place in one of the ancient cities of Latium: Bovilae, came to form part of this same context.[66]

Against this background, a new meaning was given to the promotion of worship and specific rituals that allowed a relationship between Rome and provincial elites to be established, based on the recovery of elements of tradition. The creation of new connections between myths, episodes, and places could be a suitable procedure because of the variety of possibilities it offered. The *Salii* and the associated cult enabled these new connections to be established, since they reinforced the meaning of Saguntum's founding stories while at the same time explaining the reasons for the old alliance. The existence of this *collegium* might also have acquired a complementary and deeper meaning. The relationship

---

60 Alföldy 1984, 216–17. A systematic study: Delgado 2014; also Wicha 2002–2003; Johnston 2017, 250–51.
61 Alföldy 1984, 212–18; Delgado 2014, 149 and 151–52.
62 There is no evidence about the rituals and precise calendar associated with the *collegium*, which makes it impossible to determine how it must have been established in Saguntum and its relation to the life of the community: Delgado 2014, 152–60.
63 Plut., *Num.* 13; Fest. P. 329; Verg., *A.* IV.298 and VIII.285. Connections with the Latin world: Delgado 2014.
64 Wicha 2002–2003; cf. Delgado 2014, 157–58.
65 Scheid 2005.
66 Grandazzi 2008.

between priestly offices and the local *cursus*, monopolized by the Saguntine elite, reproduced the connection between the Roman priestly *collegia* and the republican *cursus honorum*. This reaffirmed the profoundly Roman character of the local institutions and their elites, while establishing new cultural connections with Rome's past and its aristocracy, claiming a position close to equality in terms of prestige and behaviour that was anchored in tradition and cult.

It would therefore be a simplification to see this process as the result of merely importing a religious project that would fit into the conservative outlook of an elite. On the contrary, the performance of this elite, from the Augustan period onwards, seems to reflect a remarkable capacity to adapt to a changing global political and cultural context. In fact, the definitive organization of the priesthood of the *Salii* seems to have taken place at a late date, between the Flavian period and the first half of the second century CE, when Saguntum's *cursus honorum* exhibits greater complexity.[67] Nor can one think of an isolated religious enterprise justified by the existence of a previous foundational myth. The establishment of a priesthood only made sense in a global construct, as one of the elements that gave meaning to the claims on which the identity of the Saguntine elite was based.[68]

Another component of the Saguntine past, the alliance with Rome, also appears in the Augustan period through the memory of one of its protagonists: Publius Cornelius Scipio Africanus. An inscription of this moment, without a precise context, commemorates Scipio as the *restitutor* of the city.[69] The inscription mentions Scipio as *imperator* and *consul* and explicitly includes the formula *ex senato consulto* to indicate the circumstances of the figure's actions. These elements recall the episode of the Saguntine embassy before the Senate to give thanks for the reconstruction, according to Livy (XXVIII.39). In their speech the Saguntine people attribute the *restitutio* of the city to the Scipio

Figure 11.2. The inscription *CIL* II²/14, 327 dedicated to P. Cornelius Scipio as *restitutor* of Saguntum (image: R. Álvarez Arza-UB; after Archivo fotográfico Centro *CIL* II-UAH).

brothers previously sent by the Senate, the father and the uncle of Scipio Africanus, but the protagonist of Livy's narrative is the latter. Significantly, the previous paragraph (XXVIII.38) summarizes his actions in Hispania, presented by him in a speech when running for consul. This victorious action and the expulsion of the Carthaginians had ensured the reconstruction of the allied city, and the subsequent historical memory would unify the merits of all the Scipio family in the most important individual in the family.

The direct message of the inscription is clear, as it remembers the episode of the destruction of the city. But the mention of this factor seems to respond to the desire to specifically recall the conditions of the rebirth of the Saguntine community and the recovery of its political status after Hannibal's destruction. This objective acquires full meaning in the broader context of Augustus's reconstruction of the past exemplified in Livy's work. In his account, the embassy–senate relationship is fundamental; hence the precise description of protocol and diplomatic

---

67 Delgado 2014, 151–52. The changes could reflect a moment of institutional consolidation and the formation of new balances within the elite (as a process of local adaptation to the circumstances created by the Flavian reforms in Hispania); this could also be related to the urban development that the city underwent in the second century CE.

68 It cannot be said if the functioning of this priesthood implied the reproduction of the rituals employed in Rome: Delgado 2014, 156–60; Mayorgas in this volume is sceptical and suggests that the significance of the *Salii* existence lies in its prestige as institution.

69 *P(ublio) Scipioni co(n)s(ul)i | imp(eratori) ob restitu|tam Saguntum | ex s(enatus) c(onsulto) bello Pu|nico secundo*: *CIL* II²/14, 327.

language, as well as the circumstances surrounding the stay of the Saguntine legates.[70] All this is summarized in a formula ('ex senato consulto') which condensed the links between two allies.[71] In this context, Scipio's action could be presented as an example of a foundation-reconstruction practice common among republican *imperatores*, but the significance, and the exceptionality, of the figure in republican history helped to reinforce the very importance of Saguntum, which deserved a re-foundation hero on a par with its antiquity and prestige.

The specific mention of Scipio in the inscription allowed for further interpretations, with meaningful political and religious connotations. On the one hand, because of his leading role in the Second Punic War, which made him an essential figure in Roman history, Scipio was often remembered by republican-era writers, who turned him into an archetype of the values and behaviour of an aristocracy that had built the Empire. This memory would be extended to other members of the Cornelii Scipiones, in particular those linked to Hispania, such as Scipio Africanus.[72] At the same time, his figure acquired a religious connotation that is also found in Augustan-period writers such as Livy. He points out the specific link of Scipio Africanus with Jupiter, including his possible divine origin, which, in turn, he related to his military qualities (XXVI.19.1–7; *Per.* XXVI.7).[73] This portrayal, both charismatic and ambiguous, is also found in later authors. Appian, for example, relates Scipio Africanus's initiatives to his military capacity and his claim to act under divine protection (*Hisp.* 19, 23, and 26).[74] Finally, the construction of this image includes a connection with the myth of the origins of Rome. This link can be seen in the episode of the visit to Ilium by the two Scipio brothers, Africanus and Asiaticus, in 190 BCE, during the campaign against Antiochus. The visit, which included the celebration of public rituals, had a clear political and symbolic objective, as it was presented as Rome's return to her origins.[75] The figure of Scipio, therefore, became a genuine crossroad because of its combination of symbolic and religious, historical and contemporary references, which allowed him to be used for the promotion of Saguntum (and of its elites) in the Augustan period.

The literary continuity of this memory demonstrates the conscious wish to preserve and transmit the fundamental episodes of Roman history, in this case the Second Punic War, under the early Empire.[76] This wish must have received its response in certain provincial platforms; and the case of Saguntum was surely one of them. Through the recovery of Scipio's deeds, the local elites remembered their place and that of their city in the history of the Republic. At the same time, they were linked to a central *exemplum* in the memory of the Roman aristocracy.[77] This image seems to hold true in later times, as shown by a late inscription (dated in the second century CE) that seems to repeat the *titulus* of the Augustan period.[78] This specific case raises the interesting problem of the spread and transmission mechanisms of Roman history in the provincial sphere after Augustus.[79]

This recovery of republican history cannot have been incompatible with other initiatives related to the memory of the foundational moment. A coin issue by Saguntum at the turn of the Common Era could be placed in this scenario. The reading of the coin legend poses some problems, but the use of Greek and the content (with a plausible mention of the word 'polis') could be understood as an intentional reference to the city's cultural kinship.[80] These issues (contemporary to the above-mentioned circulation of various literary accounts) show the complexity of the portrayal of Saguntum's past, which integrated different features and which could resort to using other (and prestigious) language (Greek) from that of the local inhabitants. This image included diverse elements that could be activated or deactivated at different times depending on the political and cultural context in which the community evolved. Additionally, the use of Greek on

---

70 See above, pp. 157–58
71 Liv. XXVIII.39.18: 'Suos imperatores recte et ordine ex voluntate senatus fecisse, quod Saguntum restituerint civesque Saguntinos servitio exemerint'; cf. Johnston 2017, 225–26.
72 Polybius contributes to building a narrative about the Scipio family that would be developed by other authors in the next century, in particular Cicero and Livy. Torregaray 1998; 2002; Hölkeskamp 2018.
73 This particular condition appears in Scipio Aemilianus's dream: Cic., *Rep.* VI.11. In addition, Gell. VI.1. Finally, the revaluation of Scipio's memory could include other factors, such as his condition as a *Salius*: Liv. XXXVII.33.7. Wicha 2002–2003, 187.
74 Appian notes that in his time the image of Scipio was still displayed in the processions that departed from the Capitoline Hill, a place to which this character was linked (*Hisp.* 23); this image played a role in the funeral ceremonies of the family members: Hölkeskamp 2018, 440–42.

75 Liv. XXXVII.37.1–3; Just., *Epit.* XXXI.8.1–4. Gabba 1976; Marco 2002, 108.
76 Schettino 2006 suggests the existence of performances associated with the memory of the republican aristocracy's deeds in the first century CE.
77 Hölkeskamp 2018.
78 *CIL* II²/14, 328.
79 Marco 2015.
80 The precise chronology of the issue is debated, but Ripollès proposes to place it in the Augustan period: Ripollès and Llorens 2002, 478 nos 412–15; Velaza 2002, 144; Beltrán 2011, 35; Amela 2012, 176–77.

the currency, a traditional symbol of the autonomy of a city, was a mechanism that reinforced explicitly some elements of the message and introduced new nuances in an already ancient narrative. This initiative was a prerogative of the local elite, who must have evaluated the possible impact of issuing a certain type of coinage.[81]

This set of initiatives must be understood in a political and cultural framework, namely the first decades of the Principate, in which very diverse factors and dynamics converged. First of all, it is possible to point out the connections with some aspects of the *renovatio* and *restauratio* promoted by Augustus. On the one hand, there is a connection with the foundation of Rome through the Trojan myth; on the other hand, the aim was to connect with the value system of the Republic through the link with some of the most important episodes and biographies of Roman history. Some elements of the myth of Saguntum could be linked to the vision of the past promoted by Augustus which was embodied in, among other places, the *Forum Augusti*, with the memory of the protagonists of Rome's foundation as a community; from there an indirect but effective connection could be established with the imperial house itself. But there is also a connection with the republican past through the *summi viri* whose effigies and *elogia* were distributed in the portico of the *Forum Augusti*.[82]

At the same time, the definitive form of the Saguntine myth and the remembrance of some of its components could be integrated into the new regional context created by the juridical promotion of some nearby cities in the Augustan period; in particular, with the reconstruction of Valentia.[83] This initiative must have led to a reorganization of territorial and administrative balances, as well as social and economic ones. Simultaneously, the new scenario implied the creation of efficient forms of political communication with the imperial power. In this context, Saguntum could exhibit an instrument that none of the neighbouring communities had: a prestigious past of autonomy and political alliance with Rome. This instrument seems to be used, in addition to other possibilities, such as rituals and iconography related to the imperial cult.

In fact, the selective insistence on some aspects of Rome's foundational myth and republican history could reflect a strategy on the part of the Saguntine elites that finds very specific parallels in other cities in Hispania: on the one hand, by means of the representations of Aeneas (and the values that his figure incarnated), which appear in capitals like Augusta Emerita and possibly in Corduba;[84] on the other hand, in rituals similarly related to the foundation of Rome, like the worship of *Lupa* (*CIL* II 2156 from Montoro; 4603: Badalona; 5063: Antequera) or the memory of the *scrofa laviniana* (*CIL* II 2126 = *CIL* II²/7, 93: Porcuna).[85] Some of these elements are also reproduced on Augustan-period coins from cities such as Italica.[86]

Many of these parallels are associated with *coloniae*, founded *ex novo* or honorific ones, whose nature placed them entirely within the political and cultural framework of Roman society. An interesting example is Carthago Nova, which could also claim a place in republican history; in this case because of its Punic origin. The city received its colonial status from Pompey, but after Munda its elites sought to draw closer to Caesar, in an episode in which the future Augustus participated (Nic. Dam., *de vita Aug.* x.11).[87] In the Augustan period, the patronage of various members of the imperial family (Agrippa, Tiberius, and possibly the former's sons, Caius and Lucius) and political collaborators (*legati* such as P. Silius Nerva; or King Juba II), who acted as *patroni* and contributed substantial funding, can be witnessed. In addition, several members of the imperial family (Augustus, Agrippa, Tiberius, the sons of Germanicus) also adopted honorific functions in the colony, including the quinquennial duumvirate.[88]

Saguntum was also granted the status of *colonia* in the mid-first century BCE, and this allows us to understand its appearance in the same episode recorded by Nicolaus of Damascus. However, the city later acquired the status of *municipium*. In this context, Saguntum seems to have chosen to develop diverse and complementary strategies to become integrated into the imperial framework. On the one hand, a series of initiatives for establishing ties with the emperor that were undertaken in two ways: an iconographic programme (centred on the forum);[89]

---

81 Cf. in this sense Estarán 2022, 152.
82 Wicha 2002–2003. For the Augustan *Forum*: Zanker 1989.
83 Aranegui 2011; Abascal 2006.

84 Nogales and González Fernández 2007. Linking cities in Hispania to Augustus and members of the imperial house, as *deductores* and *patroni*: Melchor 2017.
85 Marco 2015; Marco in this volume. Johnston 2017, 211–15. Dardenay 2011 analyses the diffusion of the iconography of the Roman foundation myth in Hispania; also, Dardenay 2010; 2012.
86 She-Wolf Breastfeeding Twins and the *Genius Populi Romani*: Chaves 2008a; coinage and local identities: Beltrán 2002; 2011; Chaves 2008b; Ripollès 2010; Royo 2016.
87 Abascal 2002; Perea Yebenes 2017.
88 Melchor 2017, 335–37.
89 Aranegui 2011, 18–20: a sculpture of a young man clad in a toga (Caius or Lucius, Augustus's heirs) and fragments (head and

and a substantial series of tributes that are mainly found in the central years of Augustus's rule and the beginning of that of Tiberius, with references to both emperors and their family, and particular attention being paid to the designated heirs (Caius Caesar; Drusus minor; Germanicus and Drusus Caesar).[90] There are also inscriptions related to his cult and to Augustan divinities.[91] The latter seem to be the result of initiatives by individuals of lesser social status and range across the first and second centuries. This suggests the use of diverse and changing strategies to establish ties with the imperial power. Some were implemented at an early date under the exclusive control of the Saguntine elites and must have been integrated into a complex narrative that insisted on the exceptional nature of the history of Saguntum; other generic ones would have focused on the traditional Roman pantheon. This also includes contacts with leading senatorial families.[92]

At the same time, the Saguntine elite resorted to recovering and recalling episodes from the republican past in order to establish a direct connection with Rome. These initiatives, unlike the previous ones, could not be countered by other cities in the region and could only be paralleled in a few cities in Hispania. At the same time, they could be related to Saguntum's status as a *municipium*. These strategies, while emphasizing the role of the elite, seem complementary to the messages and images that arose around their authority, their control of institutions, and their euergetic undertakings. The combination of present and past thus contributed to reinforcing the prestige of the ruling class. However, it is difficult to say whether this procedure was exclusively the result of the conscious choice of a set of myths that other privileged communities lacked, or an adaptation strategy dictated by the complexity of a dynamic regional/provincial context in which it was necessary to resort to effective forms of communication with the imperial power.[93]

Some of the features that made up the identity of Saguntum seem to have had a specific impact on the surrounding territory. The available evidence is, however, limited. One initial reference can be found in Polybius's words mentioning a temple to Aphrodite outside the city. Different locations have been suggested for this temple, none of which offer conclusive arguments. More recently a connection with the port area has been proposed, as it would have acquired a role as centre of exchange and cultural mediation in the fifth to fourth centuries BCE.[94] The location of several rural sanctuaries, some of which are relatively well known, in its territory is more significant; they were in use from the end of the republican period and, in some cases, were still being visited in the first and second centuries CE. The best known are Muntanya Frontera and Santa Bárbara.[95] These two sites display considerable similarities: their relatively isolated hilltop location; the monumentalization of the site, making use of topography, architecture, and decoration; and a large number of inscriptions and offerings in the form of sculptures. Their location could be explained as reflecting the survival of cults in hilltop sanctuaries, but the systematic use of the epigraphic habit and the iconographic language of Roman statuary is indicative of a new context. The inscriptions found on both sites are of marked votive nature, making use of the habitual formulae. The only divinities recorded are Apollo, at Santa Bárbara, and Liber Pater at Muntanya Frontera. Among the nineteen inscriptions of Muntanya Frontera there is one that mentions a municipal initiative undertaken by the local magistrates and *ordo*, with a clear differentiation of responsibilities and the use of public financial resources.[96]

The divinities present in Saguntum's territory (Polybius's reference to Aphrodite should be added) represent a wide range of powers and attributes, but they can all be related to the Greek and Italic cultural sphere. These connections are particularly complex in the case of Liber Pater, which can be linked with both Greek and italic traditions and allow a specific association with the Latin past. Furthermore, this cult appears in other forms in the territory, with inscrip-

---

body) of a larger than life-sized imperial portrait, made of Paros marble (Tiberius, Caligula?).

90 *CIL* II²/14, 305 (Augustus); *CIL* II²/14, 306 (Caius Caesar); *CIL* II²/14, 307 (Tiberius); *CIL* II²/14, 308 (Germanicus); *CIL* II²/14, 309 (Drusus Caesari Tiberi Augusti filius); *CIL* II²/14, 310 (Drusus Caesari Germanici Caesaris filius).

91 Gods: *CIL* II²/14, 291 (Asclepius Augustus); CIL II²/14, 296 (Lares Augusti); *CIL* II²/14, 297 (Mars Augustus); *CIL* II²/14, 298 (Mercurius Augustus); *CIL* II²/14, 579 (Venus Augusta). Priestly functions: *CIL* II²/14, 731 (*flamen Augusti*; second half of first century CE). At present, there are no known *seviri augustales*.

92 *CIL* II²/14, 329 *CIL* II²/14, 329 (a *patronus* from the time of Tiberius).

93 Italica's coinage has been interpreted in the same way: Chaves 2008a. It is interesting to note that the foundation of this city, in 206 BCE, was commissioned by Scipio Africanus.

94 Domínguez Monedero 2011–2012, 405–06.

95 Nicolau 1998b; Civera 2014–2015; Grau and others 2017, 190–92, 198–99, 213–16; also Revilla 2002; the Iberian inscriptions in the sanctuary of Muntanya Frontera are dating between the second and first centuries BCE (one dated at the beginning of the first century CE): Estarán 2022, 146–47.

96 [*Lib*]*ero Patri*|[*- F*]*abius Felix*|[*et - F*]*abius Fabianu*[*s*]|[*I*]*Iviri ex d*(*ecreto*) *d*(*ecurionum*)|[*p*]*ecun*(*ia*) *publi*[*ca*]|[*f*]*aciend*(*um*) *cu*[*ra*]|[*v*]*erun*[*t*] (*CIL* II²/14,656).

tions that go beyond mere religious invocations.⁹⁷ The cult of Liber Pater in both public and private contexts could be understood as the expression of its link with the natural world and agriculture. For this reason, it would be tempting to interpret the establishment of such a cult in the area as an expression of the continuity of native traditions. However, its spread and the interest of the civic authorities might also be explained by the inclusion of this god in Saguntum's foundational narrative, as part of the system of allusions to the Greek and Latin world. In this case, this would have led to the creation of new places of worship or the redefinition of previous cults and sanctuaries. Such initiatives would have made it possible to construct a local religious geography that would recall some episodes of community's past.

## Elites Looking into the Past? By Way of Conclusion

The identity built by the elites of Saguntum combined very diverse historical and mythical elements. Their formation is an example of a patchwork formed at different times, reworking and relating various themes to create new meanings. This combination was embodied in initiatives (both religious and honorific) related to civic life, as shown by the city's Augustan and later epigraphy. The image offered by the literature or the inscriptions does not reflect simple erudite reconstructions. This operation seems to form part of the wider context of the reconstruction and resignification of Roman history associated with Augustus's *restauratio*, but it started from older elements that were combined in different ways at certain historical moments. Religion occupied a particular space in this process, since the use of cults and rituals allowed for the insistence on essential factors; above all, the city's origins and the link with Rome. In this way the political nature and autonomy of the city were highlighted. This could be reaffirmed, on the one hand, with the specific mention of cults and myths associated with the founding act; on the other hand, through the existence of particular *collegia* closely linked to the local *cursus honorum*. At the same time, the memory of the Roman alliance also had a religious connotation, expressed in terms of an obligation and its consequences, which refers back to the moral and religious language with which political acts were expressed in Rome. The image of the goddess *Fides* that appears in Valerius Maximus's account, in recognition of the actions of the Saguntines, is revealing. This could also be interpreted as an attempt to recover elements of republican political culture and place them in a provincial context, but in that context those elements could receive new meanings that are difficult to identify due to lack of evidence.⁹⁸

The construction of the local identity seems to have been carried out under the strict control of the local elites, although it is not possible to establish the procedures used by them, their specific connections with the Roman aristocracy, or their knowledge of the cultural trends promoted in Rome.⁹⁹ It was the Saguntine elites who opted for the Roman alliance and who guided the community in the resistance against Hannibal, but also in its rebirth and in the subsequent privileged relationship with Rome. The remembrance of past sacrifices justified the identification between the community and its leading group and, especially, the latter's claim to a monopoly of the community's leadership in the early Empire. The construction of an identity seems to include also other mechanisms such as the adaptation of onomastics and the use of the Latin and the Iberian languages in different contexts and specific supports (coinage and inscriptions, as has been proved recently).¹⁰⁰ Saguntum can be defined, in this sense, as a bilingual community, at least during the second and first centuries BCE and until the middle of the first century CE: its inhabitants, led by the elites, used different languages in their self-representation to construct forms of interaction in the local life and in relation to the imperial framework.

The memory of Saguntum's past displays some peculiarities that also force us to question the nature of the local elites. In a seminal study, G. Alföldy defined Saguntum as a society 'closed to the outside world', with a homogeneous elite that monopolized the functioning of institutions and scant possibility of social mobility. This position set it apart from other cities on the coast of Hispania Citerior, such as Tarraco or Barcino. This interpretation implied the idea of its future decline.¹⁰¹ The apparent obsession with the past that stands out in the construction of the local identity would seem to strengthen this hypothesis. However, it would be dangerous to interpret these factors as indicators of immobility

---

97  *CIL* II²/14,597–98. The context of the inscriptions suggests a large number of allusions associated with land ownership as well as the production and consumption of wine, see Revilla 2002, 199.

98  Ando 2000.
99  cf. Johnston 2017, 157–58, 204–09.
100  Estarán 2022. This social bilingualism will finally lead into a linguistic change; also Beltrán 2011.
101  Alföldy 1984, 219; Beltrán 2011.

and isolation.¹⁰² On the contrary, the complexity of the allusions that integrated the local memory, as well as its restatement in Augustan times, prove the capacity of the elite to create an original narrative. This account selected from the past the elements that allowed the creation of an updated discourse that was integrated into the Roman historical narrative and the new political and cultural framework promoted by the imperial power. This narrative was to be maintained, enriched, and more loaded with allusions later, as the work of Silius Italicus shows. It does not seem, therefore, that the Saguntine elites would have oriented their efforts towards the simple remembrance of a static past. On the contrary, the renewal and enrichment of the image of the Saguntine past revealed in the literature of the first century CE suggests a complex process of communication and interaction undertaken in a particular cultural and social setting: the Rome of the Julio-Claudian and Flavian emperors.¹⁰³ In this scenario, in which value systems and behaviours were configured so that the ideology of the republican aristocracy was recovered, members of diverse provincial elites were involved; among these were the aristocracies of Hispania. Within these, moreover, members of important Saguntine families appear.¹⁰⁴ In this competitive process of promotion, the recovery and renovation of some myths could serve to define their own identity against other elites. At the same time, the link of this identity with Roman historical memory (now mediated by the emperor's power) contributed to defining its position in a new social hierarchy on an imperial scale.

In this context, the Saguntine elite seems to have continued to use its past as a central feature of its image and power. This might explain the insistence on remembering the past or the initiatives in the religious field that could be related to a redefinition of the functioning of the *collegium* of the *Salii* (in the late first century or the first half of the second century) or the promotion of certain rituals.¹⁰⁵ This process seems to have been related, at the same time, to the increasingly well-known urban and architectural changes undertaken in the city between the mid-first century and the second century CE.

Could one speak of a specific and conscious project on the part of the Saguntine aristocracy as opposed to the path followed by other elites in Hispania? Raising this question presupposes an excessive internal cohesion, continuity, and cultural awareness being attributed to them. It seems more appropriate to think of the coexistence of strategies, evolving over generations, within both the elite and the same various family groups. A central element of these strategies would be the remembrance of the past; not an erudite or nostalgic initiative, but an approach that would allow some values to be exhibited and some privileges to be legitimized. A broad ideological framework, solidly connected to the Roman past, would enable members of the Saguntine elites to make very different choices. These options could be adjusted to personal and family ambitions (and strategies) to pursue a career or to limit the dangers of it, as well as to avoid the estrangement of local families — and their wealth — from the community. The behaviour of the Saguntine elites, in other words, seems to have been flexible and capable of adapting to diverse circumstances and stimuli.

---

102 A nuanced analysis, with some examples of members of the elite integrated into the imperial aristocracy in Alföldy 1984, 225–28.
103 In this scenario an antiquarian recovery process of the past is carried out, which is also followed by the elites of some cities in Hispania: Marco 2015, 85; Johnston 2017, 227–28.
104 Alföldy 1984, 227.
105 Inscriptions *CIL* II²/14, 292; *CIL* II²/14, 293 are related to the worship of Diana: García y Bellido 1963 and 1966; Bonneville 1987; Alföldy 2000. Dating is problematic and it cannot be determined whether it is evidence of continuous activity throughout the imperial period or an initiative related to the intentional recovery of a connection (Artemis/Diana) with Saguntum's past.

FRANCISCO MARCO SIMÓN

# 12. The Imperial Cult and Consensus Rituals in Hispania

*First Century* BCE–*First Century* CE

## The Diversity of the Imperial Cult

The political centre of any complex society contains a governing elite as well as a series of symbolic elements. It is precisely these elements which mark that society's centre as the centre and imbue it with the aura of not only being important, but also of somehow conditioning how the world is structured.[1] The existence of a shared history, that of the Roman Empire, was one such important symbolic element that Rome sent to its provincial audiences. And it was this shared narrative that gave rise to the restructuring of provincial identities and provided a shared political theology that was centred on the figure of the emperor.[2]

Yet worship of the emperor was not uniform.[3] Generally speaking, the organization of this cult was left in the hands of local elites, who sought to associate themselves with the 'theodicy of good fortune' that the emperor represented;[4] accordingly, the fragmentation of ritual manifestations was the norm, not the exception. In this way, the ubiquity of the imperial cult cannot be taken to imply an existing uniformity or homogeneity, and therefore diverse scholars have found it difficult to see how the imperial cult could have obtained a 'symbolic unity' that was not characterized by multiple contacts between local communities and the centre of the Empire.[5]

In response to theories that maintain the Roman emperor's divinity,[6] there has been a general scholarly tendency to highlight the ambiguity that existed in the emperor's relationship with the divine realm,[7] given that in the Roman Empire there were various autonomous religious practices that were carried out in different contexts (e.g. cities with different legal statuses, families, and other types of associations). All of this makes it rather difficult to posit any single unified religious system with a shared and unitary theology.

Recently, there have been new critiques of the double model,[8] common to much historiographical work dedicated to explaining the imperial cult that theorizes a process of imposition in the West compared to spontaneity in the Greek East. Fishwick[9] encapsulates this understanding of the situation in the West as follows: 'By and large provincial cult in the West appears as an instrument of imperial policy, a device that could be manipulated in whichever direction the purposes of central authority might require'. In contrast to this view,[10] others have emphasized the high level of imperial passivity in a process that is understood as unfolding more spontaneously from below. In short, this double model forces us to reflect[11] on the explanation that is traditionally given for the expansionism of the Roman Republic: on the one hand imperialism in the West (with Carthage and Numantia taken as representative) and hegemony in the East on the other.

The truth of the matter, however, is that it is much more difficult to fit real practices into such neat dichotomies. Fishwick himself[12] contrasts the imposition of provincial cults with the spontaneous development of local cults driven from below, something already recognized by Mellor.[13] The heterogeneity of provincial communities and practices

---

1 Geertz 1983, 124.
2 Ando 2000, 23–24.
3 Nogales and González Fernández 2007; Kantirea 2007; Frija 2019.
4 Gordon 1990.
5 Hopkins 1978; Trimmlich 2007, 14; Woolf 2008, 255.
6 e.g. Clauss 1999.
7 Panciera 2003; Benoist 2018.

8 e.g. Lozano Gómez 2011, 477.
9 Fishwick 2002–2005, 219.
10 Millar 1977, 387; Beard and others 1998, 352–53.
11 Marco 2011.
12 Fishwick 2002–2005, 219 n. 22.
13 Mellor 1981, 1004.

**Francisco Marco Simón**, Professor of Ancient History (University of Zaragoza)

precludes the creation of any one singular framework by means of which historians of imperial cult can account for the existing — and normally rather scarce — types of documentation, such as panegyrics, epigraphy, numismatics, and Christian religious literature.[14] And quite logically, rituals would be carried out in distinct manners depending on the legal status of a community (i.e. whether or not it was a Roman colony).

Generally speaking, such initiatives came from prominent members of the *ordo decurionum*, who had the most at stake in setting up a cult that would become a further source of their own power and advancement.[15] The active participation of governors in the establishment of these cults, however, adds a layer of nuance to the notion of provincials merely taking the initiative on their own. For this reason, ideas of inducement and emulation, instead of imposition or spontaneity, seem to be much more useful for understanding the situation at hand. In short, instead of speaking of *the* imperial cult, we are better served by positing imperial cults.[16]

## The Case of Tarraco and other Early Evidences

The first instance of a cult devoted to the *princeps* in Hispania comes from Tarraco, the capital of Hispania Citerior, which was later renamed Hispania Tarraconensis. Augustus was personally leading the military campaign against the *Cantabri* and *Astures*, but fell ill and had to return to Tarraco, where he stayed for nearly two years. We know from Suetonius[17] that while there Augustus accepted his eighth and ninth consulships (i.e. in 26 and 25 BCE). For a two-year period, then, Tarraco became the centre of the Roman world and the place where Augustus received delegations, like those from India and Scythia, from the other end of the known world.[18] Among the various embassies that came to Hispania, we know of one from Mytilene (Lesbos) that announced that the city had dedicated a temple to Augustus with different divine honours (*isotheoi timai*), all of which was explained in a decree that had been sent to different cities.

According to a brief mention in Quintilian,[19] Tarraco announced that it had dedicated an altar to Augustus from which a palm tree had miraculously sprung; upon hearing this, the emperor wryly responded that apparently the altar must have been used very little for that to happen. Augustus's witticism aside, the symbolic importance of this initiative is as clear as the link of this miraculous tree to Augustus's adoptive father: a palm, sacred to Apollo, had appeared before the Battle of Munda[20] and also at door of Augustus's house in Rome.[21]

The altar in Tarraco was represented on bronze *dupondii* and *semisses* that were struck during the reign of Tiberius and whose obverses imitated a contemporary Roman series depicting *Divus Augustus Pater* with rays emanating from his head. The reverses depict a small palm growing on the *focus* of the altar, the front of which is decorated with bovine skulls joined by garlands and flanking a central panoply of a shield and spear; to the sides of the altar we can read *C(olonia) V(rbs) T(riumphalis) T(arraco)*.[22] The available evidence indicates that the dedication of this altar to Augustus was the fruit of an initiative undertaken by the *ordo decurionum* and that this place was the site of a local cult.[23] In contrast,[24] other scholars have argued that this monumental altar ought to be taken as an early manifestation of the provincial management of the imperial cult.

On the provincial level, the cult of Augustus was associated with the worship of goddess *Roma*, which also took place in the same temple. This demonstrates the adoption of the Hellenistic practice of worshipping kings as *synnáoi theoí*,[25] as happened in Rome for the first time with the placing of Caesar's image in the temple of *Quirinus*. Be that as it may, the *Ara Tarraconensis* is the earliest of a long series of monumental public structures to honour the princeps, which would include the Sestian Altars, the *Ara Trium Galliarum* in Lyon, the *Ara Ubiorum* in Cologne (8–5 BCE), the possible altars from northern Lusitania (*c.* 6 BCE), the altars from Bracara (3–2 BCE) and Asturica Augusta (1 CE: the altar of the *Lougei*), and the altar from Narbonne (11 CE), as well as the altars from Rome: *Fortuna Redux*, *Ara Pacis*, the altars to the *Lares Augusti* and the *Genius* or *Numen* of Augustus.[26]

---

14 Lozano Gómez 2011, 481.
15 Rives 1995, 63.
16 Kantirea 2011, 522; Frija 2019. This variety of the imperial cult in general corresponds to the diversity of the Hispanic cults and identity as stressed by Woolf in this volume.
17 Suet., *Aug.* XXVI.3.
18 Oros. VI.21.9.

19 *Inst.* VI.3.77.
20 Suet., *Caes.* XCIV.11; Cass. Dio XLIII.41; Montero Herrero 2017c.
21 Suet., *Aug.* XCII.1.
22 Ruiz de Arbulo 2009, 170.
23 Fishwick 2014.
24 Ruiz de Arbulo and others 2015, 344.
25 Nock 1972.
26 Montero Herrero 2017b, 138–39.

According to Tacitus,[27] one year after the death of Augustus (i.e. 14 CE), residents of Hispania Tarraconensis asked Tiberius for permission to build a temple to the new *divus*, an initiative that would go on to serve as a model for the rest of the Empire's provinces. On the reverse of coins, we see an octastyle temple in which Augustus sits on a throne, holding a Victory astride a globe in his right hand and a sceptre in his left; below we can read the legend *Deo Augusto*.[28] This legend has surprised some scholars[29] since it shows that Augustus was already venerated as a god (*deus*) between 14 and 19 CE, though officially he only had the title *divus*. That said, although Augustus, who was surely cognizant of the unhappy precedent set by Caesar, avoided direct deification on a state-wide level, there is no evidence that he resisted the idea of being worshipped as such in provincial, municipal, or private cultic contexts.[30] In fact, it is known that *cultores* of Augustus could be found in all Roman houses immediately following the emperor's death,[31] which must also have been the case during the final years of his reign.

In light of the absence of information concerning provincial priests in Hispania Citerior before the Flavian period, it is doubtful whether the temple in Tarraco was a provincial rather than a municipal institution. In the Flavian period, the temple of Augustus, which had previously been separated from the urban core of the city, became the central focus of an extraordinary new complex, which was religious (in the upper portion), theatrical (with a large plaza filled with statues in the middle), and ludic, with the circus that Domitian built on a lower terrace.[32] In carrer del Paradís in Barcelona stand the remains of a temple that dates to the time when the city was founded near the end of the first century BCE and which contained two statues of women, perhaps Livia and Faustina Minor.[33] An altar dedicated to Augustus when the *princeps* was still alive was built in one of the galleries of the southern portico in the forum of Segobriga, which can be dated between 2 BCE and 14 CE.[34] The existence of this altar undoubtedly furnished an important precedent for the processes that led to the spread of the imperial cult throughout the province. Similarly, a group of statues linked to the imperial family was erected in the northern portico at some time in the late Augustan period, while in the Augustan basilica there was yet another group of statues representing the Julio-Claudians in addition to other pre-Flavian monuments discovered in the northern exedra of the forum plaza.[35]

Coins struck during the Flavian period also provide evidence for two temples (one hexastyle and the other tetrastyle) dedicated to the *Pietas Augusta* in Caesaraugusta, where archaeological work has discovered a temple and forum dating to the Augustan period beneath the city's Cathedral of the Saviour, as well as another temple dating to the Tiberian period.[36] Carthago Nova provides further important information about the beginning of cult honours paid to other members of the imperial family during the Augustan period. When Augustus's heirs Gaius and Lucius died prematurely near the end of the first century BCE, various altars were erected for the offering of worship to the new heroes, for whom temples, such as that in Nemausus, were also built.[37] In Carthago Nova both brothers were depicted on *tabulae* that adorned the entrances to the orchestra of the newly built theatre; furthermore, a prominent local citizen, L. Iunius Paetus, built an altar to Gaius (while he was still alive) in a building dating between 5 and 1 BCE.[38]

## The Origins of the Imperial Cult in North-Western Spain

A central element for understanding the beginnings of the imperial cult in Hispania Tarraconensis and the north-western conventus is Lucus Augusti. This appears to have been a sacred forest, which, perhaps building upon a previous local cult, may have been connected to a sanctuary in which cult was paid to the *princeps*.[39] It would therefore constitute an early instance of the imperial cult.[40] In further support of the existence of an ancestral wooded sanctuary, there is an abundance of toponyms such as Nemetobriga.[41] In Semelhe, a settlement located near

---

27 *Ann.* I.78.1.
28 Rodà 2007, 744, fig. 3.
29 García-Bellido and Blázquez 2001, 69 and 363–64.
30 Gradel 2002; Koortbojian 2013.
31 Tac., *Ann.* I.73.
32 González Herrero 2015, 67.
33 Rodà 2004, 421–22.
34 Abascal and others 2007, 695–96.
35 Abascal and others 2007, 698–99.
36 Martín Bueno 2007, 729–30.
37 Gros 1991.
38 Ramallo 1999.
39 Étienne 1974, 384; Tranoy 1981, 197–98.
40 There is another Lucus Augusti in Gaul (*CIL* XIII 5207, 6978, 7011). Today it is known as Luc-en-Diois (Dto.de Drôme) and it was in the area inhabited by the Vocontii.
41 Through antonomasia, *nemeton* is the Celtic term for designating a sacred clearing in the forest as a sanctuary, an idea similar to Latin *nemus* and *lucus* in Marco 2015; 2019. On the sacred landscape of western Hispania in the Roman period see Schattner in this volume.

Braga, an inscription was found that mentions a certain *sacerdos Romae et Augusti ad Lucum Augustum*, who would later become the provincial *flamen* in Hispania Citerior.[42]

The establishment of Lucus Augusti, like that of the remaining capitals of other north-western conventus, took place during Augustus's second journey to Hispania in 15 BCE, although the *princeps* did not personally go to these other settlements (Bracara, Lucus, Ara Augusta), which were located in mountainous regions and therefore would have required that a special legate be sent, perhaps the very same individual in all cases.[43] If this were the case, this person would have been Paulus Fabius Maximus, who is mentioned on a monolith from Lugo, measuring 2.75 m in height and dated between 3 and 1 BCE.[44] This same individual is mentioned on a cylindrical altar erected by the *Bracaraugustani*, which is now housed in the Museu de Guimarâes.[45]

Bracara Augusta, the capital of another conventus, may provide one of the few known cases of a ritual refoundation from the Roman world. From this city, we have an inscription, now part of the Cathedral's facade, dating from between 5 and 2 BCE.[46] Building upon the analyses of Leite de Vasconcelos, Tranoy[47] as well as Montero and Perea,[48] Morais has maintained that the text, which alludes to the consecration of a place struck by lightning with the sacrifice of an adult animal (*bidens*), commemorates the refoundation of Bracara through the ritual burial of the lightning bolt, probably in the settlement's forum.[49] The imperial cult is also attested in other inscriptions that have unfortunately been lost, such as those from Dume (dedicated to the *Genius Caesaris*) and Bracara Augusta (dedicated to the *Genius Augusti*).[50]

A place name that clearly alludes to the presence of the imperial cult in these parts of the north-western Iberian Peninsula is Ara Augusta, mentioned in the *Tabula Lougeiorum* (O Caurel, Lugo) as the capital of the conventus in which the *ciuitas Lougeiorum* lived,

a people with whom Augustus's friend *C. Asinius Gallus* established a truce in 1 CE.[51] Dopico Caínzos[52] thought that this Ara Augusta was the 'provisional capital' of the conventus during the construction of Asturica Augusta, whereas Rodríguez Colmenero[53] considered this place was the capital of one of the four north-western juridical conventus.

We also know of the consecration of several *Arae Sestianae*, which were dedicated to Augustus. In all likelihood, these altars were erected by the imperial legate L. Sestius Quirinalis, who was the governor of Hispania Citerior between 22 and 19 BCE, to commemorate Augustus's visit to Hispania between 16 and 13 BCE as well as the creation of the new provincia Transduriana, alluded to in the *Tabula Paemeiobrigensis*.[54]

When it comes to identifying the location of these altars, the literary record provides two different possibilities.[55] The first option comes from Pomponius Mela,[56] while the second possible hint for the location of the *Arae Sestianae* is found in Pliny[57] and Ptolemy.[58] Though Mela places the altars in the coastal part of the lands inhabited by the *Astures*, it is preferable to follow the lead of Pliny and Ptolemy who locate them on a peninsula of the *Celtici Supertamarici* that can be identified as Finisterre, Monte Louro or the end of San Adrián in Malpica de Bergantiños.[59] The fact that these altars are associated with an individual name is paralleled by the *Arae Flaviae* (found in present-day Rottweil) in the region of the Agri Decumates, which was another centre of the imperial cult. Furthermore, we should maintain the possibility that these altars (of which Pliny and Mela claim that there were three) were conceived of as the cultural expression of the three north-western conventus that were created in the Augustan period: Lucus, Bracara, and Asturica.[60] Be that as it may, the three Sestian altars would have been the earliest ritual spaces that expressed and established their adhesion to the emperor and Rome in this part of pacified Hispania. And in parallel to the accomplishments of Alexander the Great in Asia and India, these three altars would have marked Rome's arrival at the very edge of the inhabita-

---

42 *CIL* II 4255; Rodríguez Colmenero 1996, 296 and 298 n. 156.
43 Rodríguez Colomenero 1996, 287–88.
44 *CIL* II 2581 and *EE* IX, p. 108, with the secure reading *Caesari | Paulus Fabius | Maxumus | legat(us) Caesaris*. Fabius Maximus was married to Martia, a niece of Augustus, and therefore it is hardly surprising that he is mentioned as one of the *princeps*'s *amici* (Tac., *Ann.* I.5; Ovid, *Pont.* XII.3.3, 4.6, etc.). Rodríguez Colmenero 1996, 288.
45 *CIL* II 2411; *EE* VIII, 280 = *ILER* 1028. In both cases, the initiative for the imperial cult was taken by an *amicus principis* such as Fabius Maximus.
46 *CIL* II 2421.
47 Tranoy 1981, 318–19, 328.
48 Montero and Perea 1996.
49 Morais and others 2010, 13.
50 Morais and others 2010, 52–53.

51 *AE* 2004, 758.
52 Dopico 1988, 56 *et seq.*
53 Rodríguez Colmenero 1996, 299 *et seq.*
54 Sanchez Palencia and Mangas 2000; Montero Herrero 2017b.
55 Rodríguez Bordallo and Ríos Graña 1985.
56 Mela III.13.
57 Plin., *Nat.* IV.111.
58 Ptol., *Geog.* II.6.3.
59 *TIR* K 29: 1991.
60 Fishwick 2014, 54.

ble world[61] in line with the notion of the *propagatio Imperii*.[62]

These north-western Hispanic altars are comparable to the *Ara Trium Galliarum* and the altar of the *Ubii*;[63] furthermore, the erection of sacred monuments with similar symbolic content has well-known parallels from the Augustan period, ranging from the monument from La Turbie, which commemorates the victory over the Alpine peoples,[64] to the triple trophy from Lugdunum Convenarum, which commemorates Augustus's victories at Actium in Gallia and Hispania.

The Asturian peninsula mentioned by Mela should probably be identified as Cabo de Peñas and the precise location of the altar as Campa Torres (near Gijón). There, archaeologists uncovered a dedication by Cn. Calpurnius Piso, the governor of Hispania Citerior, to Augustus, which can be dated to 9–10 CE.[65] As is well known, Calpurnius would later suffer a *damnatio memoriae* after having been accused of murdering Germanicus (see below, p. 174). The monumental inscription, which measures 162 by 84 cm and was clearly meant to be displayed prominently, refers, in all likelihood, to the consecration of a structure in Augustus's honour; in fact the inscription would probably have been inserted into the monument, which was most likely a tower. The inscription from Campa Torres is the only monumental inscription that is known from the northern portion of the Iberian Peninsula. A clear parallel for Calpurnius Piso's inscription is found in the inscription from Bavay that commemorates Tiberius's visit to Bavacum in 4 BCE/CE,[66] which is part of a large monument to the imperial cult. In both inscriptions, the lexeme *sacrum* is used to refer to the act of consecration, a feature that is shared by both Augustus and his successor, though not to the worship of any deity.[67]

There are two other toponyms that may very well reflect the existence of possible monuments dating to the Augustan period: Turris Augusti, located on the banks of the River Sar in Galicia,[68] and Portus Victoriae Iuliobrigensium, which is mentioned by Pliny.[69] The latter was probably conspicuous for its monument to Augustus's victory on the Somorrostro hill in Santander.[70]

## Lusitania: Emerita Augusta

Emerita Augusta, which would become the capital of the province of Lusitania, was founded in commemoration of Augustus's victory in the wars against the *Cantabri* and *Astures* in the north.[71] The very name of the new colony obviously contains a clear reference to the conqueror himself (Augusta) as well as to the soldiers who fought in those wars (Emerita).[72] Recent archaeological research allows us to distinguish between two different public spaces that were suitable for representation: the so-called colonial and provincial fora. While the latter is associated with urban development dating to the reign of Tiberius that took place in light of the city being established as the capital of Lusitania and the expansion of the imperial cult at the initiative of the governor L. Fulcininus Trio,[73] the older colonial forum's large plaza betrays clear signs of the settlement's Augustan phase. A temple to the imperial cult, which is known as 'the temple of Diana', though it was possibly dedicated to Rome and Augustus, dominated this square. A second temple was placed in a neighbouring plaza and emulates the temple of *Divus Iulius* in Rome.[74]

The *Ara Providentiae*, possibly from the colonial forum, deploys a cohesive symbolic programme that can be compared to that of the altar from Tarraco. Taking inspiration from Rome's own *Ara Providentiae* in the *Campus Martius* and surrounded by a wall covered in historical reliefs like the altar from Tarraco,[75] this altar from Emerita (again like the altar from Tarraco) is represented on a series of coins com-

---

61 Grüner 2005.
62 Roddaz 2014, 37–41.
63 The *Ara Lugdunensis*, located *ad confluentes Araris et Rhodani*, was erected at Rome's initiative as a consequence of the problems related to the implementation of the census in Gaul, which led Drusus to summon the area's dignitaries to a *concilium* in Lugdunum in order to celebrate a festival in honour of Rome and Augustus in 13 BCE (Liv. *Per.* 139; Cass. Dio LIV.32.1). The altar's iconography contains symbols of Augustan ideology, such as the *corona civica*, the laurel branches and two Victories, see Zanker 1989, 321 fig. 23. In addition, the functions of the *Ara Vbiorum* Tac., *Ann.* I.39.2 found near modern Cologne and founded by the very same Drusus with the intervention of a *sacerdos* (probably between 12 and 9 BCE) suggest that, as was the case in Lugdunum, cult was offered jointly to Rome and Augustus, see Fishwick 2014, 55.
64 Plin., *Nat.* III.20.
65 Fernández Ochoa and others 2005.
66 *CIL* XIII 3570.
67 Fernández Ochoa and others 2005, 144.
68 Mela III.1.11.
69 Plin., *Nat.* IV.14.110.
70 Iglesias Gil 2019, 324.
71 Álvarez Martínez and Nogales 2015; 2019. See also Edmondson in this volume.
72 Cass. Dio LIII.26.1.
73 Saquete 2005.
74 Nogales and Álvarez Martínez 2014, 243–44.
75 Poveda 1999, 403 n. 20.

memorating *Divus Augustus Pater* (the city gate and the tetrastyle temple dedicated to Augustus are also shown). The *Ara Providentiae* has been compared to the extraordinary historical reliefs from Pan Caliente, dated to the reign of Tiberius or Claudius,[76] which depict a *suovetaurilia* sacrifice below a freeze of garlands, bovine skulls, and sacerdotal jars. According to the interpretation of Trimmlich,[77] Agrippa himself is shown leading the ceremony. Between the reliefs, there is a flowering laurel, which is a clear allusion to the two laurels planted in front of Augustus's home by a decree of the Senate in 27 BCE;[78] the iconography of the laurel is quite similar to others depicted on the altar of the *Lares* from the Vatican or the altar from Lugdunum, which is known thanks to the depictions found on coins.[79]

A series of inscriptions dating to *c.* 6 BCE found in the *termini augustales* of the northern cities of Lusitania point to the possible existence of monumental altars, which could have been similar to the Sestian altars and would have been erected by Q. Articuleius Rufus and other legates.[80] In Salacia (present-day Alcácer do Sal) there is an inscribed lintel that a certain Vicanus, the son of Boutius, dedicated as a sacred monument (*sacrum*) to Augustus. It is possible that this belonged to a surprisingly early temple to the imperial cult, since the inscription can be dated to 5 or 4 BCE.[81]

An inscription dating to *c.* 42 CE has been found in Mérida that a certain Albinus, identified as the *flamen Divi Augusti et Divae Augustae provinciae Lusitaniae*, dedicated to Augustus and Livia.[82] Before this date, however, there is already a reference to L. Cornelius Bocchus in Salacia, who held this same priesthood in Lusitania during the reign of Tiberius; this inscription implies that the *consilium provinciae* was already meeting in Emerita Augusta in this period and was presided over by the provincial *flamen*.[83]

The *Ara Pacis* in Rome has a symbolic relationship to the altars from Hispania: a large central rectangular altar placed on a tiered platform and surrounded by a *peribolos* with two doors for entering, a feature that has been analysed as a symbolic reference to Rome's double foundation.[84] The *Forum Augustum*, which was the heart of the new regime, also exercised a pronounced influence over the design of important spaces in the western provinces generally and in Hispania in particular. Decorative elements clearly inspired by the *Forum Augustum*, such as the sculptural group depicting Aeneas and Anchises, have been unearthed in the fora from both Mérida (in the upper portion of the provincial forum, perhaps as part of a possible *Augusteum*)[85] and Córdoba. In this respect, we should also mention the *clipei* of Jupiter-Ammon found in Tarragona and Mérida, which have been dated to the post-Augustan period.[86] There are yet other altars depicted on coins from Italica and Ilici, which share a similar post-Augustan date.[87]

## Hispania Baetica

Although the organized imperial cult, understood as the worship of deceased emperors (*divi*), would not appear in the whole province of Hispania Baetica until the reign of Vespasian, there can be no doubt that when Augustus was still alive he did receive cult worship on a more local level, as the result of both public and private initiatives. So much is clear from sculptures like those found in Italica and Axati (Lora del Río), monuments like the puteal from Trigueros (Huelva), which contained four Zodiac signs, including Capricorn — Augustus's birth sign,[88] inscriptions like that from Urgabo Alba, which confers upon Augustus the title of *pater patriae* as early as 6 BCE (i.e. four years before he would receive the same title from the Roman Senate),[89] or even the inscriptions that mention municipal priests.[90]

The relative fervour of the cities of Baetica, which is also evidenced by coins and the honours rendered to Augustus's heirs Gaius and Lucius, can be explained both by the establishment of new colonies in places previously settled by Caesar as well as their continued enjoyment of Latin rights, which they had first received in the time of Augustus's adoptive father.[91] Coinciding with the foundation of Colonia Augusta Firma Astigi (Écija, Seville) in the Augustan period, a temple was built, whose remains have been unearthed in the town's Plaza de España. At the rear of the temple, there was a monumental pool, similar to those found in the cultic complexes

---

76 Nogales 2000b, 418.
77 Trimmlich 2007.
78 *RGDA* 34.
79 Nogales 2000b, 411.
80 Salinas de Frías and Rodríguez 2007, 587.
81 *CIL* II 5182: *Imp(eratori) Caesari divi f(ilio) Augusto | pontifici max<i = U>mo co(n)s(uli) XII | trib(unicia) potestate XVIIII | Vicanus Bouti f(ilius) | sacrum*; Encarnacão 2017, 769.
82 González Herrero 2015, 3.
83 *CIL* II 2479; González Herrero 2015, 57.
84 Marco 2002; Ruiz de Arbulo 2009, 173 *et seq.*; Delgado 2016.

85 Nogales 2000b; Nogales and González Fernández 2007.
86 Marco 1990.
87 Nogales 2000b, 418.
88 Beltrán Fortes and Stylow 2007.
89 *CIL* II 2017 = II/² 70.
90 González Fernández 2007, 182–83.
91 González Fernández 2007, 178–79.

in Ebora, Emporiae, Munigua and also the so-called 'temple of Diana' in Mérida. Many epigraphic fragments from this pool have gilded letters, which indicates that the local elite understood the Augustan notion of the arrival of an *aurea aetas* (similar letters are also attested in public buildings in Córdoba and Italica). The collection is clearly related to the imperial cult in the Flavian period.

Of all the materials discovered in the temple in Astigi, a certain ritual text stands out, since it contains a formula for a solemn vow (*votorum nuncupatio*) for the *princeps*'s health;[92] this formula is also found in the protocols of the *Fratres Arvales* in Rome.[93] In the case of the text from Astigi, the emperor's name suffered a *damnatio memoriae*; given the inscription's chronology, it could have referred to Galba, Otho, Vitellius or Domitian.[94]

The temple found in calle de la Morería in Córdoba dates to the reign of Tiberius. This site of imperial cult worship in the province was dedicated to *Divus Augustus* and was almost an identical copy of the *Forum Augustum* in Rome; furthermore it bears a strong resemblance to the temple in calle Holguín in Emerita Augusta.[95] In contrast, the complex found at the junction of calle Claudio Marcelo and calle Capitulares, which contained a hexastyle temple on the model of the Maison Carrée in Nîmes, dates to the mid-first century CE.[96] As was the case in Lusitania, the imperial cult in Hispania Baetica began during Tiberius's reign, though no inscriptions that mention a priesthood predate the Flavian period, when we find an inscription mentioning the *flamen Divorum et Augustorum provinciae Baeticae*.[97] This provincial priesthood seems to be a reflection of the *lex de flamonio provinciae Narbonensis*,[98] which was inscribed on a bronze tablet found in the amphitheatre of Narbonne and which ought to be dated to the reign of Domitian.[99]

## Consensus Rituals

As is well known, a central motif of Rome's self-representation is its *pietas*: divine favour recognizes the universal *pietas* of the Romans.[100] For that reason, Roman law laid out the importance of consensus in religious matters, given the way that religion was embedded in social practice. This centrality of consensus is well explained through the metaphor of Rome and her Empire as a single body that could only have one head, that is the emperor.[101] The ritualization of consensus (*Konsensritual*)[102] in the Empire's western provinces was a clear manifestation of the provincials' loyalty towards the emperor. And it was this loyalty, *fides obsequiumque*,[103] that was the necessary precondition for holding and wielding power on the local level.

These ceremonies that displayed consensus and adhesion had three objectives: first, to demonstrate the local elite's loyalty toward the leader of the Empire, which would allow them to maintain the highest possible degree of autonomy; second, to win concessions from the emperor's representatives;[104] third, to partake in a system of *aemulatio* in a bid to surpass the *fides* and *obsequium* of neighbouring communities.

A standardized symbolic system maintained this consensus in the Roman Empire, ranging from a shared calendar in all privileged communities that celebrated the same days and events that were important to the imperial family,[105] to the ubiquity of imperial portraiture on coins and in other media. Given that the emperor enjoyed a special relationship with the gods,[106] his portrait was placed inside all temples across the Empire and would even be taken out as part of processions during local holidays celebrating the emperor's good deeds on behalf of the local community. It was the charismatic power of the imperial institution (and not so much the power of the individual actors in that institution) that guaranteed the proper functioning of the Roman administration.[107]

One physical expression of this consensus is embodied in monumental architecture.[108] The boom in construction (and even epigraphy)[109] that characterized Augustus's rule was particularly intense in the cities of Hispania that did not have their own indigenous traditions of urban architecture. The manifestations of loyalty that were embodied in the

---

92 Tac., *Ann.* XVI.22; Plin., *Ep.* 10.35–36.
93 Scheid 1981.
94 García-Dils de la Vega and others 2007, 103–08.
95 Ventura 2007, 237.
96 Garriguet 2007, 316–17.
97 Panzram 2003.
98 *CIL* XII 6038 = *ILS* 6964.
99 Marco 2004, 418.
100 Plácido 2002.

101 Ando 2000, 292–93.
102 Flaig 1992, 198.
103 *Immobilem fidem obsequiumque* are the words of the emperor Claudius, as reported in the *tabula aenea* in Lyon, to refer to the 100-year loyalty of Gallia Comata, which had been conquered by Caesar (*CIL* XIII 1668, II, 30 *et seq.*). See also Jaczinowska 1989.
104 Bedon 2001, 247.
105 Ando 2000, 407.
106 This special relationship is shown in the numerous reliefs that depict the emperor carrying out sacrifices, thus demonstrating the *pietas* of all Romans; for further discussion, see Gordon 1990.
107 Ando 2000, 410.
108 Trimmlich and Zanker 1990.
109 Alföldy 1991.

urbanism and architecture of these cities were the most concentrated and on display in the forum, a space dominated by the temple of the dynastic cult. The presence of colossal statues of the emperor in the forum represented the eternal vigilance of the *princeps* as the *divinarum humanarumque rerum rector*.[110] Architectural monumentalization constituted the most direct reminder of how the *victoria augusta* had brought peace and created the conditions for the *felicitas temporum*, prosperity, abundance, the development of civic life, as well as the establishment of civic institutions.[111] From this perspective, it has been suggested that the Principate was fundamentally a 'system of acceptance' (*Akzeptanz-System*)[112] that was not exactly built upon the alleged legitimacy of imperial powers so much as on the adhesion that the main social forces (i.e. the army, Senate, and plebs) felt towards the actual *princeps* as an individual.

Beyond a shadow of a doubt, the oldest and most important epigraphic expression of this consensus from Hispania is the 100-pound golden statue that the inhabitants of Hispania Baetica paid for and erected in the *Forum Augustum*, the symbolic heart of the new regime.[113] In all likelihood, the statue represented the province[114] and contained a dedication to Augustus that expressed the community's appreciation for the perpetual pacification that he brought to the province.[115] The inhabitants of Baetica publicly displayed their thanks and loyalty for the *cura perpetua* and *providentia* brought by Augustus, whom they recognized as their patron and protector.

The reference to *consensus universorum civium* appears both in the *Res gestae*[116] as well as in other texts, such as the oration that Augustus delivered at Agrippa's funeral in 12 BCE[117] or the *senatus consultum* about the funerary honours for Germanicus in 19 CE. We know the content of this *senatus consultum* thanks to two fragments of the *Tabula Siarensis* found in Utrera (Seville), which stipulates[118] that the decree should be exhibited in the most conspicuous places in the *municipia* and *coloniae* throughout Italy and the provinces. Therefore, the *Tabula Siarensis* shows how the same factors that motivated the *Vrbs* (i.e. the funerary honours for members of the imperial family) also gave rise to a feeling of *unanimitas* in provincial contexts. The same is revealed in the decree from the *colonia* in Pisa that honoured the memory of Gaius Cesar after the death of his mother in 4 CE: *per consensum omnium ordinum*.[119]

Likewise, in the *senatus consultum de Cn. Pisone patre*, dated to 20 CE, the Senate praises the equestrian order, plebs, and soldiers for their unanimous condemnation of Piso (see above, p. 171) and expression of their *pietas* towards the memory of Germanicus and the imperial family (ll. 151–60). Like the *Tabula Siarensis*, lines 165–72 of this decree mandate that the text be inscribed on bronze and publicly displayed, stipulating that the consuls arrange for copies of the text to be provided to all the provinces.[120]

In addition to the visual representation of political bonds, another important means of expressing loyalty was the taking of an oath to the emperor, a practice attested both in the eastern and western provinces. For our present purposes, there are two especially interesting cases from Hispania: the first is the oath that the Lusitanian city Aritium took to Caligula on 11 May 37 in the conventus of Scallabis (perhaps in Tamazim).[121] The swearing of this oath is attested in an inscription that was discovered near the Tagus and which, unfortunately, has been lost. In this text, the community vows to assist the friends of the *princeps* and to pursue his enemies until they are vanquished; the text even adds that *Jupiter Optimus Maximus* will punish those who do not follow through with their promises.[122]

Something quite similar can be found in an inscription from Baetica that details a loyalty oath (*ius iurandum*) that the *populus* of Conobaria (referred to as 'Colobana' in Pliny)[123] made to Augustus, which can be dated between 12 and 6 BCE.[124] This oath, in which the *proconsul* and *quaestor* of the province took part, was for the health, honour, and victory of the *princeps*, his heirs Gaius and Lucius, and even his grandson Agrippa.[125] The oath, which took place on the occasion of the new *princeps*'s arrival,

---

110 A phrase used in an inscription from Apulum that is dedicated to Jupiter, see *CIL* III 1090; cf. Whittaker 1999, 150.
111 Strothmann 2000.
112 Flaig 1992.
113 Spannagel 1999; Marco 2002.
114 Alföldy 1991, 309–10.
115 *Imp. Caesari | Augusto p. p. | Hispania ulterior | Baetica, quod | beneficio eius et | perpetua cura | provincia pacata | est. Auri p(ondo) C(entum)* (*CIL* VI 4,2 31267 = *ILS* 103).
116 Ramage 1987; Belloni 1987.
117 Cass. Dio LIV.28.3.
118 González Fernández and Arce 1988, 310–11.
119 *CIL* XI 1421 = *ILS* 140.
120 Caballos and others 1996, 127.
121 Alarcão 1988, 57 and 135.
122 *CIL* II 172 = *ILS* 190.
123 Plin., *Nat.* III.3.11.
124 The community was located between Hasta Regia and Nabrissa Veneria, perhaps in the same place as the inscription was discovered, the so-called Las Palmillas estate, located near the estuary of the River Guadalquivir.
125 González Fernández 1988, 113; 2007, 186–87.

was renewed annually on 1 January, beginning with Caligula at the latest.¹²⁶

In addition to oaths and funerary honours, there were other occasions that served to demonstrate the collective's loyalty to the *princeps* in the provinces, such as solemn vows for his health that were taken on 3 January or the celebrations of important anniversaries for the imperial family (e.g. births, adoptions, the donning of the *toga virilis*, or marriages) that local officials would include in each community's public calendar.¹²⁷ Likewise, the arrival (*adventus*) or departure (*profectio*) of the *princeps* constituted events worthy of celebration in various cities with ceremonies in which collective loyalty was put on display.

The importance that religion had as a system of communication¹²⁸ can be appreciated in coinage in particular. As has been recorded for Spanish issues,¹²⁹ the choice of iconography and religious messaging greatly contributed to the cohesion of communities and the Empire, since coins, in many cases, provided a mechanism for redefining local identity.¹³⁰ Additionally, we should not overlook the importance of emphasizing certain events that demonstrated adhesion to the new regime, such as the founding of the city, an emphasis on its urban features (e.g. through the depiction of temples and altars), and devotion to the emperor (evoked through the common inclusion of his likeness on the obverse or well-known symbols like crowns or religious imagery).

Female members of the Julio-Claudian dynasty (most notably Livia) also played an important role in legitimizing the monarchy.¹³¹ After her son Tiberius's reservations and rejection of the proposals of divinization that came from Hispania in line with the requests from Asia (Tacitus tells us that the proposal of the delegations from Hispania Tarraconensis and Baetica were turned down),¹³² on 17 January 42 Livia was declared *diva Augusta*, which ushered in the cult worship of female members of the imperial family during the reign of Claudius. Fragments of marble statues of Livia have been found in Hispania Tarraconensis and Baetica, both alone and in conjunction with statues of other members of the family. The seated statue from *Iponuba* (near Córdoba) that shows Livia holding a cornucopia (a symbol of *Abundantia* or *Fortuna*) is of particular interest. Of all the issues depicting Livia (e.g. those from Tarraco, Caesaraugusta, or Emerita), that from colonia Romula (Triana) is of particular note: the *dupondius* struck during the reign of Tiberius shows a deified Augustus (with rays emanating from his head) and Livia with a crescent moon standing on a sphere and bears the legend *Iulia Augusta Genetrix Orbis*, which is also found on statue bases from Hispania (e.g. one from Anticaria, which was dedicated by a *pontifex*).¹³³ A decree by the decurions of Urgavo (Arjona, Jaén) commemorates the erection of a statue dedicated to Livia as *Iulia Augusta*¹³⁴ and we also know of two *flamines* in Lusitania who were tasked with maintaining the cult of *Diva Augusta*.¹³⁵

In connection with these strategies of adhesion and consensus on the part of provincial populations, we also ought to mention the diffusion of (re)creation myths stressing Roman identity. In addition to the iconographic programmes found in the fora of the capitals of Hispania Lusitania and Baetica or that on the *Ara Providentia* from Emerita, which was modelled on the *Ara Pacis* (see above, p. 172), various statue bases have been found throughout Hispania that are dedicated to the she-wolf,¹³⁶ a theme that was also repeated in mosaics. We can also mention lamps that depict Aeneas's flight from Troy in this regard.¹³⁷ Of particular note is an inscription from Obulco (present-day Porcuna, Jaén), datable to the second half of the first century CE,¹³⁸ in which C. Cornelius Caeso, aedile, *flamen*, and *duovir*, and his son of the same name, who was a priest of the *Genius Municipalis*, dedicate a statue of a female pig with thirty piglets. This undoubtedly constitutes an allusion to the appearance of the *scrofa laviniana* that showed Aeneas the place to found Lavinium upon arriving in Latium.¹³⁹ Of equal interest is the funerary monument from Urgavo for a *duovir* and Roman citizen (M. Horatius Bodonilur) and his wife (Lucretia Sergieton), who, judging from their names, were clearly of indigenous stock. The two ploughing scenes that flank the inscription display the foundational yoke, which is well known from late republican reliefs from Italy and certain coin series from cities such as Caesaraugusta or Emerita.¹⁴⁰

---

126 Le Gall 1985; Hurlet 2002, 171.
127 Scheid 1999, 390–93.
128 Bendlin 1997; Rüpke 2001; 2020.
129 Beltrán 2002.
130 See Campo in this volume.
131 Corbier 1995.
132 Tac., *Ann.* IV.37.1–3 and V.1.1, respectively.
133 Cid 2019, 343–44.
134 *CIL* II 2018.
135 *CIL* II 194; *AE* 1915, 95; Cid 2019, 344.
136 *CIL* II 2156 from Montoro; 4603 from Badalona; 5063 from Antequera.
137 Dardenay 2010, 95.
138 *CIL* II²/7, 93(I).
139 Marco 2015.
140 Beltrán Fortes 2017, 804–05.

## Conclusions

Étienne alluded to the important role that the army played in the diffusion of the imperial cult.[141] That said, the same scholar underlined the well-known connection between the indigenous *devotio* (i.e. the consecration of the warrior to his leader) and the establishment of the imperial cult in Hispania. Subsequent scholars, such as Curchin,[142] Fishwick,[143] Abascal, Almagro-Gorbea, Noguera, and Cebrián,[144] have followed this analysis, maintaining the role of the indigenous leader cult in facilitating the attested worship of the Roman emperor.

Nevertheless, Salinas de Frías[145] was correct to point out that if the relationship that Étienne, basing his work on that of Ramos Loscertales,[146] posited were correct, we would expect to find a greater flourishing of the imperial cult in the very places where the indigenous institutions of the *devotio* and *clientela* were especially pronounced, something for which there is no solid evidence. In fact, manifestations of the imperial cult are rather scarce in Celtiberia. On the contrary, it is in the more urbanized parts of Hispania, such as Tarraconensis and Baetica,[147] where we find evidence for the rapid spread of the imperial cult. The origins of the imperial cult in Hispania, then, ought to be understood not as a relic of an indigenous practice, but rather as the influence of Hellenistic king worship, which was already on display in the honours devoted to late republican *principes*. The series of divine honours paid to Octavian in Rome, some of which had also been conferred on Caesar, are well known:[148] one only needs to think of the celebration of his birthday, victories, and *adventus* in Rome, offerings to his *genius* in public and private banquets beginning in 30 BCE, the honorific title of *Augustus* in 27, or even the placing of his image between the *Lares Compitales* of the crossroads[149] in 7 BCE, a variation of what would later become the *Lares Augusti*.

In contrast to the great spontaneity with which the imperial cult appeared in the East, the beginnings of this worship in Hispania are more in line with the general tendencies of the western provinces. The initiative on the part of the central Roman administration, especially in relation to individuals with a high military rank, such as Paulus Fabius Maximus in Bracara and Lucus or L. Sestius Quirinalis, who set up the altars that bear his name, is analogous to the actions of Drusus in Gaul and Germany.[150] As Lozano Gómez and Alvar Ezquerra have convincingly proposed,[151] it is the direct action of the central authority that explains the early adoption of the imperial cult instead of a longstanding indigenous *devotio*, which is furthermore difficult to differentiate from other types of interpersonal dependence in the ancient Mediterranean.[152] That said, already in the Augustan period, local elites were also taking the initiative to worship the *princeps*: the first landmark in this respect is seen in the altar in Tarraco, after which both public and private examples carried out by local priests and members of the college of *Seviri Augustales* would continue to proliferate. This much is attested in the epigraphic and numismatic records. The establishment of a standardized provincial cult devoted to the *divi* would have to wait until the Flavian period, even though an inscription like that of the *flamen* Cornelius Bocchus from Salacia opens up the possibility that the *concilium provinciae* met before that time. Be that as it may, through the consensus rituals mentioned above, Hispanic elites partook in the system of symbolic capital, not only in a bid to demonstrate their high social position, but also as a means of manifesting their adhesion to the new order embodied by the emperor.

---

141 Étienne 1974, 380–86.
142 Curchin 1996.
143 Fishwick 1996.
144 Abascal and others 2007, 690–91.
145 Salinas de Frías 1986, 186–87.
146 Ramos Loscertales 1942.
147 González 2007.
148 Galinski 2007.
149 Ov., *Fast.* v.145–46.
150 Marco 2017.
151 Lozano Gómez and Alvar 2009, 431.
152 Alvar 2004, 29.

# 13. Localizing 'Oriental Cults' in Roman Iberia

*Relationality, Power, and Place*

MATTHEW M. McCARTY and KIMBERLY EDHER

From the moment Franz Cumont yoked together a group of cults spread widely across the Mediterranean as 'Oriental cults', evidence for such cults has played an outsize role in narratives of the cultural and religious history of the Roman Empire and specific regions within it.[1] The Iberian Peninsula is no exception. Although Cumont could quip that Spain was 'the country of the Occident which is poorest in Mithraic monuments',[2] and Antonio García y Bellido could emphasize that he was unwilling to write a history of Oriental Cults in Roman Spain on the basis of scant documentation,[3] a dizzying quantity of new finds related to these deities in the last three decades has augmented and transformed the evidentiary basis for looking at these cults (Fig. 13.1). Yet these discoveries have done little to alter the types of questions posed of them, and older metanarratives continue to govern interpretation of these finds, particularly as they are problematically grouped together as 'Oriental' cults, or even as discrete cults like Mithraism or worship of Egyptian gods.[4]

These traditional questions often focus on where and how the cults of Isis/Serapis and Mithras spread into the Hispanic provinces, and what their appearance and popularity (or lack thereof) might reveal about the cultural backgrounds and identities of people living in the region. The particular answers to these questions have changed thanks to new data. As one example, García y Bellido, following Cumont, saw the spread of Mithras-cult as closely linked to soldiers who had adopted the cult elsewhere returning to Spain.[5] While these views have generally been accepted,[6] others have challenged the precise dynamics at play; Alvar, for example, rightly recognizes the importance of the social milieux of worshippers, arguing for a much smaller role played by the military and a greater role played by imperial administrators based largely on the recent discovery of a Mithraeum at Els Munts.[7] New arguments about the worship of Egyptian gods offer a second example of how recent discoveries are offering new answers to these types of questions: instead of accepting earlier arguments about continuity of a cult brought by an earlier wave of Phoenician colonization, or trickle-down diffusion of such cults from provincial capitals to *conventus* capitals, Alvar uses recent finds to argue for the cult of Isis penetrating the peninsula in multiple waves to a range of individual sites.[8] Even when careful attention is paid to the precise social dynamics of cult transfer, the predominant model in all cases is one of diffusion, where a relatively stable cult is transferred and spread as a bounded, reified entity.

The other core tenet underlying such accounts — which stretches well beyond studies of Isis-, Serapis-, and Mithras-worship to most narratives of the history

---

\* We are grateful to Jaime Alvar for his generosity in sharing material and his broad perspective on Mithras-worship in Spain; to the anonymous reviewers for their very thoughtful suggestions which will also serve as the basis for future work; and to the editors for their invitation to step outside our areas of focus and create new dialogues around religion in the Roman Empire.

1 Cumont 1906.
2 Cumont 1956 [1903], 59.
3 García y Bellido 1967, ix.
4 For example, in the context of a volume offering critiques of the notion of 'Oriental' cults, Alvar 2009 argues for the continued value of this category, although he has more recently shifted focus to seeing these as 'initiatory cults', see Alvar 2016. Alvar 2013, following the precedents set by García y Bellido 1967, likewise groups together anything related to Egyptian deities as evidence for their cult.

5 García y Bellido 1948, 22–23.
6 e.g. de Francisco Casado 1989; Adán and Cid 1998, 129; Barrientos 2001, 379; Bricault 2009, 153.
7 Alvar 2016; 2018. Cappai 2010 suggests a broad social catchment for worshippers.
8 Alvar 1999, 41.

---

**Matthew McCarty**, Assistant Professor of Roman Archaeology (University of British Columbia)

**Kimberly Edher**, Instructor (Langara College)

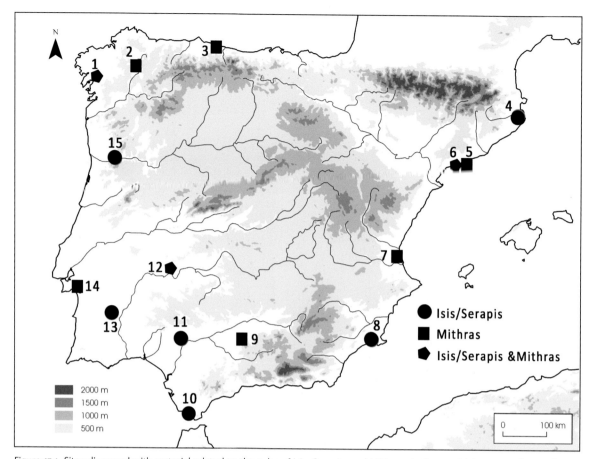

Figure 13.1. Sites discussed with material related to the cults of Isis, Serapis, and Mithras. Authors, with basemap data under license from esri, USGS, NOAA. 1. Caldas de Reyes/Aquae Calidae. 2. Lugo/Lucus Augusti. 3. San Juan de la Isla. 4. Empúries/Emporion. 5. Els Munts. 6. Tarragona/Tarraco. 7. Benifaió. 8. Cartagena/Carthago Nova. 9. Cabra/Igabrum. 10. Belo/Baelo Claudia. 11. Santiponce/Italica. 12. Mérida/Augusta Emerita. 13. Beja/Pax Iulia. 14. Setúbal/Caetobriga. 15. Panóias.

and religion of Roman Hispania — is that an individual's prior membership in a group dictates which gods that person worships.[9] Indigenous peoples are assumed to worship indigenous deities, Romans or 'Romanized' peoples worship 'Roman' gods like Jupiter, and peoples from the East or connected to specific groups predisposed to accept such gods (merchants, soldiers) worship 'Oriental' gods like Isis or Mithras.[10] Given the assumption that worship of a given god is the product of belonging to a specific ethnic (or occupational) group, cults have served as a means of mapping the socio-cultural geography of the Hispanic provinces and their transformations (or stasis) through time in different ways: that is, they are evidence of Romanness or Romanization, Indigeneity, or Resistance.

Building on these ideas about religion and cultural background, both old and new discoveries continue to be fitted into much wider narratives about the place of Iberia and 'Oriental cults' within the Roman Empire. Alvar has argued that these imported cults are markers or products of 'Romanization': the appearance of a cult like that of Mithras was evidence of cultural change, part of a process of becoming integrated into the Roman Empire.[11] Similarly, the spread and popularity of Isis-worship in Spain has regularly been directly connected to rhythms of imperial patronage (or rejection) of the cult at Rome, tied to a core–periphery model where emperors in the capital dictate the cultural trends of the provinces.[12] Laurent Bricault has even gone so far as partially to reject the archaeological ceramic chronology of the Iseum at Baelo Claudio in favour of one predicated on patronage of Isis in Italy; the narrative from the centre is imposed on local material even in

---

9 Examples include: Blázquez Martínez 1991; Curchin 2003, 169–92.
10 The view owes much to Toutain 1905–1911; cf. McCarty 2016 for the model and its problems in Roman Africa.

11 Alvar 1981, 60; cf. also Adán and Cid 1998, 258; Pla and Revilla 2002, 212.
12 Alvar and Muñiz 2004 directly calque the waxing and waning popularity of the cult of Isis in Spain with that at Rome.

those rare cases where there are external, well-dated chronological pegs to understand the development of a site.[13] Assumed narratives strongly shape interpretation of primary data. 'Oriental cults' have been marshalled to demonstrate either Iberia's full participation in a Romanized koine or its status as 'provincial', dependent on external imperial impetus to shape its religious life.

In essence, interpretation of finds related to Isis, Serapis, and Mithras in Roman Spain depend — implicitly or explicitly — on models of reified religions, cultural practice, and national identity that privilege perceived origins. These sorts of models have repeatedly been problematized and rejected in other parts of the Empire, particularly within the search for alternatives to teleological cultural narratives like 'Romanization'. Practices — including those that involve choosing to worship a particular god in a particular manner and with a particular group — are not evolutionarily fixed, or done *because* one automatically belongs to a group or lives in a particular place. As a host of postcolonial literature has emphasized, fixed identities based on a person's origin do not dictate practice; rather, practices work discursively to claim and negotiate multiple, situational associations (and dissociations).[14] Groups and claims of belonging did not exist independent of the practices and experiences that actively created groupings-together.[15] Nor do origins — real or imagined — or diffusion offer explanations for why a practice might be taken up by groups or individuals at a given moment, appropriated and freighted with new significances; such models simply allow for the latent possibilities that this could happen.[16] Rather, cult and its material correlates were the products of discrete choices by agents that created discursive networks of connections, in society, in time, in space, and in meaning.

Recognizing that worship practices and their archaeological remains were not tightly defined entities or the product of fixed cultural backgrounds opens the possibility for analysing the creative agency of religious actors in society. Mithras-cult and Isis-cult were not reified religions that could be diffused, but rather composed of sets of cultural building-blocks that could be recombined, mobilized, and deployed by individual practitioners and (often self-proclaimed) experts to create novel relationships.[17] These bricolages of practice and material were deployed to create the social power of individuals; making a sanctuary place, establishing or maintaining cult, was contiguous with creating a particular form of authority.[18] The types of implicit associations that were activated in these cults in Iberia were not broad claims of being or becoming 'Oriental' or 'Roman', but rather targeted much closer to home, at creating localized senses of physical and social place.

Three case studies suggest the ways that viewing these cults in relational and creative perspectives can offer new understandings. The first is an unusual sanctuary to Isis and Serapis (among others) at Panóias, which shows how traditional frames of interpretation fail to capture the dynamics of individual agency at play on a site-specific level: gods and ritual practices were building blocks that could be mobilized for the creation of social authority. The second, a Mithraic sculpture assemblage from Augusta Emerita, points to the ways a charismatic cult founder might deploy similar strategies in a rather different cult context, creating a place and practice that set himself at its centre. If both Isis/Serapis-cult and Mithras-cult might create similar types of social authority, a broader look at the emplacement of sanctuaries to Isis/Serapis and to Mithras in their localized contexts demonstrates the different types of wider social relationships created — the cults cannot be grouped as homogenously 'Oriental' — as well as the ways that even sanctuaries that seem more 'canonical' create highly localized relationships of association.

## Creativity, Place, and Power at Panóias

In the middle of inland Lusitania, on the edges of the Conventus Bracarum, a sanctuary constructed around and atop a series of rocky outcrops demonstrates the problems with interpretative models that privilege the origins of dedicants or practices as explanations for a worshipper's actions or choice of deities, or that cast imported cults as part of teleological narratives. Instead, the sanctuary at Panóias points to the ways that individual agents could, in the course of establishing their own social authority, create cultic places that were wholly localized.

---

13 Bricault 2010 for the ceramic chronology; Dardaine and others 2008, 48–53, although also privileging imperial pressures and Neronian interest in the cult and not without problems raised by Bricault.
14 e.g. Mattingly 2011, 203–45; Revell 2015.
15 Lichtermann and others 2017.
16 For diffusionism in anthropology, its problems, and alternatives, Hahn 2008; Mills and Peeples 2019.
17 For Mithras-cult, see similar points made by Adrych and others 2017, on the deity as relational rather than fixed, and McCarty and Egri 2020 on the practices.
18 Smith 1987.

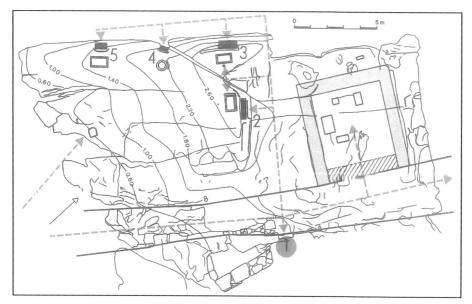

Figure 13.2. The sanctuary at Panóias, with locations of the inscriptions recorded (numbered) and associated features cut in the rock; the dashed line represents Alföldy's proposed path progressing through the sanctuary. Plan: after Alföldy (1997), fig. 7, with kind permission of the German Archaeological Institute, Madrid.

The sanctuary at Panóias, already having suffered various depredations post-antiquity, was first documented in the eighteenth century as eleven plugs of limestone, converted into a built sanctuary space through the carving of ascending staircases, various pools and channels, postholes, and a series of at least five Latin (including one bilingual Greek-Latin) inscriptions (Fig. 13.2).[19] Weathering and intentional destruction has made the readings of these texts uncertain, but the application of digital imaging technologies has recently clarified many of the proposed texts, and demonstrated that the sanctuary was, in various inscriptions, dedicated to 'Isis, Serapis, and all the gods and goddesses', 'the gods and goddesses and all the spirits, [including those] of the Lapitae', 'Hypsistos Serapis', and 'the gods'.[20] That is, the site represents an expansive sanctuary dedicated to a range of deities, but Isis and Serapis loom large in that list.

Strikingly, all five inscriptions also include the name of the dedicant: Gaius C(?) Calpurnius Rufinus, *vir clarissimus*. This figure of senatorial status must be seen as the agent responsible for creating and organizing the sanctuary; two of the inscriptions flag that, if nothing else, he is responsible for building an *aedes* (temple building) and *lacus* (water-pool), probably in the early third century CE.[21]

Calpurnius Rufinus also demonstrates the ways that modern scholarship has yoked worship habits to ethnicity. The inscriptions reveal nothing about the man's origin, and his common name offers little purchase for onomastic analysis. Still, most recent discussions suggest that he or his family come from Asia Minor, and try to locate Rufinus's homeplace close to known sanctuaries of Serapis.[22] The problematic process of reasoning thus runs: Rufinus worships 'Oriental' deities and therefore must himself be 'Oriental' (never mind that Asia Minor is quite geographically, socially, culturally, and religiously distinct from Egypt!). His own origin created a link with Serapis worship. The deeply ingrained linkage between the origins and ethnicities of gods and their worshippers continues to mould and shape interpretation; moving beyond this impulse is central to creating new understandings of cult in the Roman Empire.

At the same time, the sanctuary defies neat cultural categorization. Rocky sanctuaries like this — preserved mostly as undatable cuts in bedrock — have long been recognized as a particular regional phenomenon in this part of Iberia.[23] Because distinctively regional practices often get explained as continuities of pre-Roman traditions, such sites — including Panóias — are almost always cast as part of an indigenous religiosity.[24] These attributions are problematic on both conceptual and evidentiary grounds. On the one hand, the social structures of

---

19 Alföldy 1997 provides the most thorough account, joined now by Rodríguez Colmenero 1999; cf. also Tranoy 2004. Gasparini 2020 appeared after submission of this manuscript.
20 *CIL* II 2395a–e. Alföldy 1997 also provides canonical readings of the texts, updated using digital modelling by Correia Santos and others 2014.
21 The formula he uses, *diis deabus omnibus*, in *CIL* II 2395a, may suggest a third-century date based on the general popularity of this invocation in the Western Empire: Raepsaet-Charlier 1993, 41–42. The theonym 'Serapidi', recently uncovered in a new reading of *CIL* II 2395a by Corriea Santos and others 2014, is also more standardized in the third century CE when Serapis was increasingly assimilated with Jupiter and Sol Invictus.
22 Alföldy 1997, 239–41, suggesting the possibility that Rufinus came from a family of Calpurnii Rufi in Asia Minor, noting the presence of a Serapeum at nearby Perge; Alföldy's hesitations about this attribution are ignored — and the Pergene origin of Rufinus accepted as fact — in later publications, including Alvar 2013, 239. Note that Alföldy 1969, 110, earlier suggested an African origin for the family. The shift in proposed origin is not based on new evidence, but the assumption of 'Orientalness' of cult and worshipper.
23 Correia Santos 2010.
24 e.g. Alvar 2013, 239.

the Roman Empire worked to create new patterns of regionalized practices; 'local' does not stand opposed to 'imperial', nor does 'imperial' automatically mean homogenous or universal.²⁵ On the other hand, at one of the few rock-cut 'sanctuaries' where stratigraphic excavations have taken place, Mogueira, the cuttings have proven to be medieval, drawing into question the entire notion that these rock-cut sites are pre-Roman or cultic.²⁶ At Panóias, the close physical association between the Latin inscriptions and cuttings probably indicates that at least some of the rock-cut features were ritual in nature, but there is no positive evidence for religious activity here prior to Calpurnius Rufinus's interventions. That is, the sanctuary is a product of Rufinus's interventions in the third century, but one that harnesses the rocky landscape in a way that localizes the cult and connects it to regional traditions.

Similarly, the sanctuary is hardly an affair of the Roman state or of urban cults in general, despite the emphasis often placed on the Roman Empire and its personnel as the agents who drove the spread of 'Oriental deity'-worship. Panóias sits far from any known urban agglomeration. Even if Calpurnius Rufinus was a Roman senator, his dedications here are of a personal character. Attempts at divining the reasons Rufinus may have invested in this rural sanctuary have generated a host of proposals; most suggest that he was a judicial legate passing through the area.²⁷ As such, Rufinus's interventions have sometimes been read as an act of official Romanization: an imperial administrator promoting a pan-Mediterranean cult, grafting it upon a pre-existing tradition.²⁸ There is, of course, no evidence for Rufinus playing this official role besides his status as a *vir clarissimus*; he is simply a senator, otherwise unattested epigraphically. The inscriptions are silent on any other individuals and groups who might have been involved; there is no comment about the land being provided by a landholding group like the *conventus* or the dedications being approved by pre-existing sanctuary authorities. While there is little direct evidence for land-tenure patterns in the region around Panóias, it seems most likely that the construction of such a sanctuary took place on private land owned by the dedicant: senators like Rufinus were, after all, large landholders in the provinces. The sanctuary and the cult were, then, wholly 'private' affairs. Even if conquest and incorporation into the empire shaped the patterns of land ownership in the region, Rufinus's dedication should not be seen as the work of a provincial, acculturating administrator, but rather as an individual.

If not 'native' or 'state', the sanctuary is also not 'Oriental'. Serapis is named twice (thanks to Correia Santos's rereading of *Dis Severis* in *CIL* II 2395a as *Diis Serapidi Isidi*), but set alongside an entire pantheon of gods, goddesses, and *numina* within the same sanctuary space.²⁹ The practice of worshipping Egyptian gods was not isolated from the worship of other deities in any meaningful way, despite the predilection of modern scholarship to isolate 'Oriental cults' from their wider religious ecosystems. Still, the inscriptions emphasize Serapis's foreignness as a key aspect of his cult here; one of the rock-cut inscriptions couches its invocation in Greek: 'To Highest (*Hypsistos*) Serapis, together with Kore and the Mysteries'.³⁰ The dedicatory information, including Rufinus's name, is in Latin below; as the only surviving Greek script in the sanctuary, the invocation immediately stands out for its otherness. This odd set of deities is both part of a wider sanctuary pantheon, but also distinct from it, constructing and instrumentalizing the foreignness of these gods in the text.

In short, Rufinus's sanctuary at Panóias defies interpretation according to the standard lines that privilege the origins of gods and worshippers, or seek out indigenous continuities or state-led efforts of religious acculturation. The challenges posed by the site invite new frames of interpretation: in this case, recognition of the ways that one figure, Rufinus, created and expressed his own power over landscape to make a bricolage of place and practices.

Rufinus's texts also work to establish his status and authority as a ritual expert, prescribing the manner in which rites ought to unfold at specific places within the sanctuary. Rufinus's name is everywhere across the site, emphasizing the role he played in manufacturing a sanctuary out of a rocky landscape. Geza Alföldy has demonstrated how the series of texts and the artificial topography created by cutting into the rock create a processional path through the landscape, providing a sense of the ritual dimensions of this sanctuary.³¹ In so doing, Rufinus is not only omnipresent in the texts, but in the unfolding ritual experience of visitors to the site; his power as producer and director of that experience is acutely felt.

---

25 McCarty 2017.
26 Correia Santos 2012.
27 e.g. Tranoy 2004, 90.
28 Alvar 2016, 402.

29 Correia Santos and others 2014.
30 *CIL* II 2395c; Correia Santos 2014, 213–18. Alternative readings have been proposed: for example, instead of *sun an Kora*, Rodríguez Colmenero 1999, 88–90, reads *kanoorō*; García y Bellido 1967 reads *moira*. All agree, however, on reading Serapis.
31 Alföldy 1997.

But the inscriptions go further in prescribing ritual action and emphasizing Rufinus's authority; for example, one inscription lays out that Rufinus dedicated an *aeternus lacus* and temple, 'in which victims are burned by vow', offering a model for future rituals to take place on the site.[32] Another inscription — which, admittedly, does not survive but was recorded — offers even more detail: 'the victims which fall are burned here. Their innards are burned in the squares opposite [here]. The blood is poured out in the adjacent little pools'.[33] The passive verbs and present tenses stand opposed to the verbs of Rufinus's dedicatory acts in the inscription, providing an anonymized account of acts that continue from that moment into the future.

The final aspect of the texts and the rites they perpetuate is their emphasis on locativity, on the rituals taking place *here*. The repeated use of demonstrative pronouns that gesture to structures at the site (*hoc templo*,[34] *hanc aedem*[35]), or of adverbs like *hic*,[36] or of prepositions and other relational adjectives (*contra, iuxta*)[37] take the constructed landscape and turn it into a sacred space. As Jonathan Z. Smith has emphasized, it is ritual practice that empowers and imparts significance to a place;[38] here, Rufinus's texts and the practices they normalize and project freight a rocky landscape with sacredness.

The sanctuary at Panóias combines an unusual — indeed, a unique — set of deities and practices to create a place marked by Rufinus's presence, and at the same time, through the billboard inscriptions, making apparent his power over landscape and rite. The gods he chooses to venerate and to place in this landscape have little to do with his own origin; they are convenient building-blocks that he mobilizes to create this place. Whatever Rufinus's role beyond the sanctuary — landowner, judicial legate, something else entirely — cult 'taking place' establishes his social and ritual authority. What emerges at the site is Rufinus's ability, as an individual, to take shared cultural references — particular gods, practices like sacrifice or making vows — and creatively recombine them to sustain his own social place and ritual authority.

Rufinus's sanctuary thus shows how the inability of past models based around perceived cultural divisions, the origins of worshippers, or the teleological direction of practices ('Romanization') fail to capture creative innovation or bricolage; idiosyncratic and unique practices; or the agency of seemingly self-made religious authorities. But Rufinus's strange sanctuary also goes further in presenting an alternative model: one that recognizes how a constructed and furnished sanctuary was recursively implicated in creating and perpetuating the authority of an individual by making a localized place.

## Defining Mithras-Worship: Hedychrus's Mithraeum in Augusta Emerita

The unusual worship of Serapis, Isis, and other deities at a rural site constructed by a single figure may seem the exception, rather than the rule, but a sculpture assemblage from a Mithraeum at Augusta Emerita points to rather similar dynamics at play. There, a Mithraic expert worked to create a sense of place and personal authority by assembling a bricolage of cultural building-blocks in creative ways. Here, too, an individual, his choices, and his practices worked to create a sense of place that privileged his own (continued) centrality to the cult. The origins of this expert or of those who worshipped in the sanctuary were not what mattered. Instead, the rather unique combination of statues, motifs, and inscriptions created a distinctive sense of place: tightly bound to Augusta Emerita itself, and to an expert who was set at the heart of the worship community in physically tangible ways. That expert did not bring an 'Oriental cult' to town; he borrowed from a shared iconographic repertoire to weave together and materialize a community around himself and his own authority.

During work building Merida's Plaza de Toros in 1902, six marble statues came to light on the building site and around the foreman's house, along with a range of sculptural fragments and inscriptions; these attracted the attention and curiosity of scholars who chanced to see them.[39] In 1913, further building works turned up more statuary, prompting an excavation of the area and leading to the discovery of seven more statues.[40] The subjects depicted range widely and include everything from a head of a senior male deity (usually identified as Serapis), to a draped female figure sometimes identified as Isis, to two statues of nude Venus, to a nude youth with chlamys, to two male figures encircled by snakes

---

32  *CIL* II 2395b.
33  *CIL* II 2395e: *hostiae quae ca|dunt hic immolantur | exta intra quadrata | contra cremantur | sanguis laciculis iuxta | superfunditur.*
34  *CIL* II 2395b.
35  *CIL* II 2395a, but this reading is uncertain.
36  *CIL* II 2395e.
37  *CIL* II 2395e.
38  Smith 1987.

39  Monsalud 1903; Paris 1904.
40  Mélida 1914; Paris 1914.

Figure 13.3. Sculpture probably displayed in a Mithraeum at Augusta Emerita. Left: lion-headed personification. Centre-left: snake-wrapped youthful personification. Centre-right: youth with seated lion. Right: Venus with Cupid riding a dolphin. Museo Nacional de Arte Romana, Mérida. Photos: M. McCarty.

(Figs 13.3–4). The statuary found in the area is both eclectic and fragmentary.[41]

Given that three of the statues have Mithraic inscriptions, and that at least two (if not three) inscribed altars found in the area are dedicated *Invicto Deo*, the finds assemblage has been taken to reflect the furnishings of a Mithraeum; two of the inscriptions also provide a date of 155 CE for the dedication.[42] Still, caution is necessary, given that the statues seem to have been discovered in secondary context; excavations in 1913 turned up no trace of architectural remains housing the statues — only fragments of painted wall plaster.[43] Mélida suggests that the statues were discarded or awaiting reuse by those who destroyed the temple or temples. Instead of the furnishings of a single sanctuary (or an 'Oriental sanctuary district'), though, we may well be looking at material culled from various places and awaiting its turn in the lime kiln or similar fate, or even a late antique collection of statues taken from various places in the city.[44] That all — with the exception of a headless figure identified as Aesculapius — are carved of local Lusitanian white marble does not imply that they were all displayed together; after all, by the second century CE, most sculpture in Augusta Emerita seems to have been carved from this local stone.[45] That is, this full group need not represent a coherent statuary assemblage from a sanctuary or sanctuaries.

---

41 For discussion of the group Caccioti 2008; Romero Mayorga 2016a; Alvar 2018, 81–113.

42 *CIMRM* 794 = *ERAE* 24 = *CMBad* 765, with discovery described by Monsalud 1903, 244–45 no. 5; *CIMRM* 795 = *CMBad* 766, with discovery described by Monsalud 1904, 445 no. 1. *CIMRM* 796 = *ERAE* 26 = *CMBad* 767 is claimed in *CMBad* to come from the Cerro de San Albín area, but is not recorded by either original publication of the finds.

43 Mélida 1914, 444.

44 It is worth noting that Monsalud 1903 also publishes epitaphs from the Cerro de San Albín alongside the Mithraic material, although it is not clear that they were found at the same point on the hill. 'Oriental' sanctuary zone: Mélida 1914; 1925. Late Antique redisplay: Caccioti 2008, 180–81. Alvar 2013, 47 proposes a statue cache formed to protect the statues from Christians; this seems improbable given the intentional damage visible (general head removal, smashing of lion-headed figure's head and sawing his body in half from transport) and recognition that perceived pagan 'statue caches' were rarely that; he has revised his view in Alvar 2018, 25, and now sees the group as in a generically secondary context.

45 Lapuente and others 2014.

Still, at least five of the sculptures, the altars, and recently published fragments of a bull-stabbing relief[46] do seem certainly to be related to a Mithras-sanctuary, and another two are probably connected. The statues with inscriptions dedicating them to Mithras include one of a figure wearing a knee-length, long-sleeved tunic and a mantle fastened over his right shoulder (one form of 'Eastern' dress), often identified either as Mithras himself or a Mithraic torch-bearer; a reclining, bare-chested figure holding a cornucopia, whose plinth is carved with waves and a sea monster to establish his identity as a water deity (usually identified either as Oceanus or localized as the nearby Anas River); and a youthful Mercury with winged sandals, seated on a rocky outcrop with a lyre at his left. Two other statues show figures with snakes wrapped around their bodies, often identified as allegories of time (Kronos or Aion):[47] one has the head of a lion and is bare-chested, wearing trousers, with wings on his back and his (broken) right arm extending forward; the other has a human head with drilled locks falling down his shoulders, is nude, and has a miniature lion's head at his sternum. Although his arms seem to be held downwards based on the positions of his shoulders, the presence of broken struts at thigh level suggest a more complex tableau. Such figures can be found in Mithraea — either free-standing or carved onto reliefs — but also appear in other contexts.[48] Still, it seems probable that these two statues were displayed in a Mithraeum. The other statues found are less certainly from the Mithraeum, but some details — especially in the struts and supports — suggest that they may have formed part of a coherent group with the certainly Mithraic sculptures. For example, a nude youth with chlamys pinned by a round brooch over his right shoulder has a lion seated in front of the tree trunk that serves as his leg support; the lion draws connections to the two snake-wrapped figures and perhaps to the broader importance of the Mithraic grade of Leo. One of the figures of Venus has a Cupid riding a dolphin in front of the trunk-support at her left side, echoing the dolphin-support on the statue of Mithras, and perhaps suggesting the kind of visual riffs popular in Roman statue groups. These seven statues, then, represent the minimum number of sculptures that could have been part of a Mithraic sanctuary.

Most studies have focused on the iconography and identification of individual figures within this assemblage, connecting them with parallel figures (sometimes loosely, sometimes more closely) from Mithraea across the Empire and deciphering the presumed symbolic content of each one.[49] While identifications are important, recent work on Mithras-cult has challenged the notions that images signify complex concepts in such a straightforward manner, and that there was a shared, core Mithraic doctrine that can be decoded through this process.[50] Given the possibilities of polysemy and the ability for practices and individuals to freight the images with changing or unique meanings, it may only be possible to reconstruct the ways these images related to one another, especially via concrete visual connections, and to the community of Mithras-worshippers. That is, here, too, rather than fixed significances, understanding webs of association may prove more useful.

The collection of material comes from the edge of the Roman city, although it is not entirely clear from the published accounts on which side of the Plaza de Toros they were found; because the city wall seems to have run through the site of the bullring, it is impossible to say whether the material was even discovered intra- or extra-mural.[51] It is also worth noting that an elite Roman house was excavated nearby (just to the south of the Plaza de Toros); the house was paved with a late second- or third-century allegorical mosaic full of cosmological figures which scholars have attempted to read as related to Mithraism (among other interpretations), giving the house the misleading modern name, 'Casa del mitreo'.[52] The house, however, suggests that the statues were found near a residential quarter; it would not be far-fetched to suppose that at least those statues related to Mithras may have stood within a sanctuary connected to an elite house, akin to those at Lugo and Els Munts. Again, the personal and domestic dynamics of the cult community comes to the fore.

The sculptural programme also suggests something about the scale of the space in which these

---

46 For these fragments, Rodríguez Azcárraga 2006–2007.
47 Cumont 1956, 105–10 sees these lion-headed figures as a syncretism of Kronos/Aion and the Iranian Zuvan; Gordon 1996, 59 sees the figure as representing the conjunction of constellations.
48 For iconographic analysis and parallels, albeit privileging origins and trying to label the figures, Romero Mayorga 2016a, 324–95.
49 e.g. Cumont 1905; Bendala 1982; Caccioti 2008; Romero Mayorga 2016a.
50 Beck 2006.
51 For the course of the wall and its relationship to Merida's topography, Barrientos and others 2007.
52 García Sandoval 1969 for the discovery. Blanco 1971 and Blázquez Martínez 1986 argue most strongly for Mithraic associations. Quet 1981 argues for broader philosophical contexts and the glorification of Rome; Alföldy and Rosenbaum 1993 as a copy of a Hellenistic painting.

images were displayed: it must have been substantial. Even the minimum probable assemblage from the Mithraeum would have occupied over 23 m² of floor space: nearly the equivalent of the average space not taken up by benches within the Mithraea of Ostia. The scale of the sculptural assemblages points to a large space, a veritable sculpture gallery that is nearly unique among Mithraic sanctuaries known in the Empire.[53] And given the inscriptions, it seems that one figure in particular was responsible for developing this assemblage.

At least three of the sculptures and one altar were dedicated around the same time, for each records that it was erected by or under the *pater* of the community, Gaius Accius Hedychrus.[54] The fact that a *pater* is named at all suggests that there was an organized, hierarchical community of Mithras-worshippers here. At least three other dedicants set up monuments in the sanctuary: one whose name is unclear due to a break;[55] Gaius Avitus; and Marcus Valerius Secundus, *frumentarius* of the Legio VII Gemina.

The latter has been taken as proof that soldiers were the key vector by which Mithras-worship spread to Spain, but several features of Secundus's dedication give us pause.[56] The altar Secundus dedicates is relatively small in scale (66 × 47 × 25 cm), especially when compared to the over-life-size statuary that would have surrounded it; it seems improbable that this was the main altar or dedication within the sanctuary. The language of the inscription points in a similar direction: it is dedicated to the Genesis of Invictus Mithras (presumably his rock-birth), a moment and type of dedication that seems to have played a secondary role in sanctuaries, and Secundus himself is responsible for its setting-up (*curavit aram ponendam*) as a deserved gift (*dono merito*). In ded-

Figure 13.4. Inscribed sculpture from the Mithraic sculptural assemblage at Augusta Emerita. Arrows indicate location of inscriptions. Museo Nacional de Arte Romana, Mérida. Photos: M. McCarty.

icatory contexts, such constructions are unusual, for they take some agency away from the overseer, and place weight on the expectation of the act to be performed through the gerundive. This sort of phrasing is used when the impetus for erecting a monument comes not from the erector, but from an outside agent: for example, when individuals set up monuments decreed by city councils or stipulated by wills.[57] Secundus may have overseen the dedication of this secondary altar, but he is not cast as a primary agent or the 'founder' of the community.

It is striking, though, that Hedychrus is the central figure here who oversees multiple dedications, including some of the main cult furniture; the Mithraeum and its decor did not depend on a soldier's presence and investment, but rather upon this Mithraic expert.

---

53 The only attested parallel, based either on sculptures themselves or bases within a Mithraeum, comes from Sidon and is dated by inscription to the year '500': if this is by the Seleucid calendar, it would be 188 CE; if the local Sidonian calendar, 398 CE: Will 1950. Questions of the nature of this assemblage (whether it belongs to a Mithraeum or late antique re-display) and its authenticity have also been raised: e.g. Baratte 2001. If re-display, then the Augusta Emerita assemblage would truly be unique. Another assemblage was discovered in Skikda in the nineteenth century: CIMRM 121–28. Fragments from S. Prisca also suggest a rich sculptural ensemble.

54 CIMRM 773, 781, 793.

55 Monsalud 1904, 445 proposes Firmus, followed by Garcia y Bellido 1948, 48; CMBad 766 reads Galiu(s); ERAE 25 prefers Gai(us) Iuli(us).

56 e.g. García y Bellido 1948, 45; Alvar 1981, 60; 2018, 21–25 argues for Secundus being a co-founder alongside Hedychrus, based largely on the assumption that his military background mattered; there is, however, no reason to see Secundus as more important than other attested dedicants.

57 e.g. AE 1972, 298; 1979, 348; 2014, 735.

Seen in this way, the military dimension of the cult is incidental; it just happens that one dedicant of a small altar was a military officer. We should not overstate his apparent role in the cult; we might instead recognize the central place occupied by Hedychrus, and the way his substantial role was reiterated through the inscriptions of the sanctuary.

Unusually, the inscriptions are carved on the figures themselves, rather than upon separate bases (Fig. 13.4). This might suggest either that the sculptures were not placed upon such bases, or that there were specific reasons for wanting the texts to appear directly upon the figures. The inscriptions are cut on the plinth of the figure in Eastern dress; on the lower knee of the reclining water god; and on the seated Mercury's lyre. It is, of course, rare to include dedicatory information on the body of a statue itself, rather than on the base; there are no other parallels from Augusta Emerita. The exception for inscribing directly upon a statue at Mérida seems to be for sculptors' signatures;[58] yet although the figure in Eastern dress from the Mithraeum assemblage does have an artist's signature — that of the Greek Demetrios — this appears on the plinth, a more usual place for such inscriptions. It is as though, on the water god and Mercury, Hedychrus is claiming an even greater degree of authorship for the works, as if he were a sculptor.[59] The inscriptions also render the statues inalienable, or at least less easily reusable; the texts mark the statues as permanently part of Hedychrus's dedication and part of his particular sanctuary. The rich sculptural furnishings of the sanctuary were made inseparable from Hedychrus's authorship: he filled the temple space with statuary, and at the same time those same stone monuments recursively worked to delineate, materialize, and perpetuate Hedychrus's own place at the heart of the community.

The local orientation of the sanctuary also appears in other ways. Although Mélida identified the water god as the River Anas, given its find-spot close to the river, it is more probable that the deity is the same water god (usually identified as Oceanus) that appears in Mithraea across the empire.[60] Yet even if the individual figures like Oceanus can be related to the wider iconographic possibilities used in Mithraea across the Empire, the sculptures here are local-

ized via their inscriptions: dates on Mercury and Secundus's altar are provided according to the calendar of Augusta Emerita itself: the 180th year of the *colonia*. Proclaiming a colonial date in any context was unusual at Mérida; the only other surviving examples are an early second-century dedication for a temple to the Lares in the city's theatre and on water pipes laid in 180 CE.[61] Including such unusual information here serves to locate the dedications within a wholly local framework of time-reckoning, one rarely used otherwise: it makes Hedychrus's cult particular to the flow of time as experienced in this place.

In many ways, Hedychrus's inscribed assertions parallel those of Rufinus at Panóias, claiming (and making) himself central to the cult, in a way that exerts his authorship and control into the future. The entire surviving cult apparatus is about making a localized place for cult and an authoritative place for one individual. It is dangerous, when interpreting material related to cults that seem to stretch across the empire with some measure of homogeneity, to lose sight of the role played by such individuals in creatively adopting shared schemata as a means of placing themselves in localized social milieux.

## Beyond 'Oriental' Cults: Locating Practices and Spaces

It would be easy, of course, to dismiss Rufinus's and Hedychrus's sanctuaries as exceptional, especially when set against sanctuaries to Isis, Serapis, and Mithras in Hispania that are immediately more recognizable from a Mediterranean perspective in their layouts and furnishings. Yet the dynamics at play at these two sanctuaries can also be seen, in different ways, at these other sanctuaries. In particular, all of these sanctuaries demonstrate the ways individual agents, through their patronage of the temples, created highly localized places. The connections these places drew may have been less oriented towards the Orient or towards one another than towards groups and practices experienced on a more local level. And here, we see — from the ways sanctuaries to Isis/Serapis and Mithras were placed within the physical fabric of cities or houses — that each cult defined the social place of its users in rather different ways. In essence, the groups who used Isis-sanctuaries were nested within the physical and social milieu of the wider civic, urban communities in which they sat, whereas Mithras-worship took place under the

---

58 García y Bellido 1955.
59 Romero Mayorga 2016b argues instead that the inscription on the lyre symbolizes the association of musical scales with the doctrines of Mithraism.
60 Mélida 1914, 447–48. Alvar 2018, 93 suggests that the dolphin precludes identifying the figure as the Anas; dolphins, though, can be used as generic markers of watery contexts.

61 *HEp* 4, 1994.167; Trillmich 1989–1990; Saquete 2001.

aegis of various households. Each type of cult took place in a rather different manner.

Every space dedicated to worshipping Egyptian deities in Spain reflects the ways in which the cults of Isis and Serapis were enmeshed physically, socially, and ideologically with the civic communities in which the temples sat. Four other probable sanctuaries dedicated to Isis and/or Serapis have been excavated across Iberia: at Italica; at Baelo Claudia; at Carthago Nova; and probably at Emporion, the earliest sanctuary to the Egyptian deities on the peninsula and one seemingly paid for by a dedicant from Alexandria.[62] At Emporion, the identification of Temple M as a temple to the Egyptian gods is debated, being based on the find-spots of pieces of the Alexandrian Nomous's bilingual inscription and a statue variously identified as Asklepios, *Agathos Daimon* ('Good Spirit'), or Serapis.[63] Still, the structure occupies important real estate on the edge of the city, part of a larger sanctuary complex. At Baelo Claudia, the temple to the Egyptian gods was built in the mid-first century CE in a precinct set alongside the north-east corner of the forum: the centre of the city (Fig. 13.5).[64] At Italica, the temple to Isis was inserted into the portico behind the city's theatre in the mid-second century CE, a generation or two after the portico had been completed.[65] Although the legal status and ownership of such porticos is unclear, its connection to a space for public use is striking; this repurposing for Isis-worship may have involved either the transfer of public land to private (or divine) hands, or it may suggest that the cult was incorporated into the civic religious life of the *colonia*.[66] Similarly, at Carthago Nova, the recently discovered Flavian temple to the Egyptian gods sits in a portico one block west of the forum, occupying an irregular city block perhaps shared with a bath building.[67] The nature of the block and its functional connection to a structure in the neighbouring block that was constructed around the same time (the so-called 'Atrium') is unclear; the excavators suggest that the building may be the *schola* of a *collegium* or similar group linked to the temple

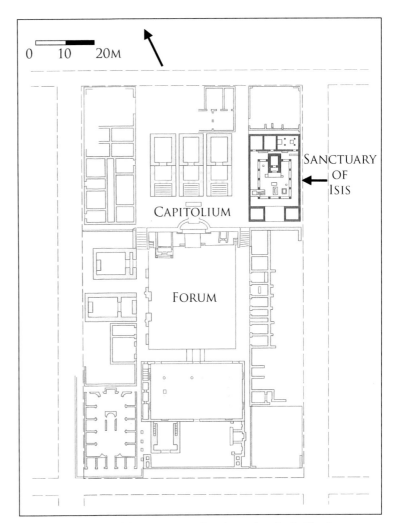

Figure 13.5. Location of the sanctuary to Egyptian gods at Baelo Claudia. Plan adapted from Dardaine and others 2008, fig. 4.

next door (their collegial shrine), on the model of the Serapeum and Domus del Serapeo at Ostia.[68] Still, the Ostian example had a direct physical connection between the spaces; no such connection exists at Carthago Nova; it seems unlikely, based on the plan, that the Iseum was a collegial temple, but whether it served a publicly funded cult, or sat on private land close to the forum, is impossible to say. Still, it is an urban temple in the heart of the city. All of which is to say that these sanctuaries all sat in prime, urban locations, and — even if marked off by high precinct walls — were highly visible and central within the fabric of towns.

Other dedications to Egyptian deities throughout the peninsula also set them in relatively public places. An 'antique' serpentine statue, probably originally carved during the 26th Dynasty, depicting a seated male figure, was discovered in the amphi-

---

62 For the dedication by Noumas, son of Numenios, the Alexandrian and its interpretation, Rodá 1990.
63 Ruiz de Arbulo 1994a, 17–18; Puccio 2010.
64 Dardaine and others 2008.
65 Jiménez and others 2013 revises the plan and layout based on recent excavations.
66 Alvar 2013, 31 assumes the former, but given the latitude that towns and their magistrates had to create their own pantheons, see Rüpke 2006, there is no reason to assume that Isis could not form part of a publicly supported pantheon.
67 Noguera and others 2018.

68 Noguera and others 2018, 70.

theatre of Italica, and may have been displayed in a small shrine there.[69] Even if the deity cannot be identified from the fragmentary piece, its medium and style set it apart and evoke its distant origin, and its find-spot suggests its cultic function. While other inscribed dedications to Isis and Serapis lack precise archaeological contexts — most are stray finds — the texts themselves can include Egyptian gods amid a much broader pantheon, suggesting the contiguity of Isis and Serapis with the publicly worshipped gods of various cities.[70]

Moreover, the specific practices of worshippers in these sanctuaries created a distinctly localized sense of place. The layout of the Italica Iseum has been called 'canonical', given that the sanctuary includes a raised temple to the goddess, a pool and an L-shaped crypt in front, and a nilometer.[71] Yet even with such shared architectural features, and a display that draws an imagined link to distant Egypt, the sanctuary and those who invested in its furnishings create a localized and personalized sense of place. Set just in front of the stairs of the temple, in a walkway marked off from the courtyard of the portico, a series of four marble pavers displayed votive feet.[72] Each invokes a deity in slightly different terms — Isis Domina, Isis Regina, Isis Victrix, Domnula Bubastis — and each was dedicated by an individual, three by women and one by a man. The reasons for dedication are also specific to each person: Marcia Voluptas dedicates out of a vow and a divine command (*ex voto et iussu*); Soter and Iunia Cerasa out of a vow alone; and Privata out of an order from Juno (*imperio Iunonis*). Each is the product of individuals and their distinct circumstances.

The meaning of such monuments is debated; proposals range from memorials of the worshippers themselves, to memorials of their arriving at (and/or leaving) the sanctuary, to indices of the goddess's own presence.[73] But no matter whose feet they indicate, the footprints mark someone's presence in this specific place: locativity matters. At the same time, the footprints serve to mark the focus of a sanctuary-visitor's attention; the feet at Italica face both towards and away from the temple, but with the feet placed side-by-side, they imply a stationary figure standing in a fixed direction. These are not the feet of a moving 'pilgrim',[74] part of a motion narrative where a distant origin is implied; they instead work to define a particular place through a fixed and ritualized act. By creating a model of ritual comportment and attention-direction, these plaques (and by extension, their dedicators) shape the behaviour of future worshippers, much like Rufinus's dedications at Panóias — where, it should be added, sets of footprints also dotted the sanctuary.[75]

Italica is not the only Isis-sanctuary where such votive footprints are dedicated, though; if particular places mattered for individual worshippers and their communities, the practice was more widely shared. Votive footprints appear widely across the Mediterranean in a number of cults (even if Isis is the most common deity so honoured), including a set from Alexandria that are explicitly labelled as Isis's footprints.[76]

The seemingly Egyptian origin of such monuments is often taken as the interpretative crux,[77] yet two distinctive features stand out in Iberia that suggest the general practice was freighted with specifically local significance, taken as a redeployable building block in the creative composition of new localized rites. First, the sheer number of dedications at Italica is striking: five from the Iseum, three near it, but not in archaeological context,[78] and another fifteen from in and around the amphitheatre at Italica.[79] No other site has produced nearly this many examples; even if a ritual possibility across the Mediterranean, the popularity of the practice here must be linked to specifically local dynamics. Second, the group from the amphitheatre, contemporary with those at the Iseum, seems to be dedicated primarily to Nemesis and Caelestis. Bounding interpretation of the practice within the realm of Isis-worship fails to recognize the networks of local association and the dialogues between practices at different places. It is also telling that the Iseum at Baelo Claudia is the only other Isis sanctuary known to include such footprints, with two plaques set at

---

69 For identification, Gamer-Wallert 1998. On display context: Beltrán Fortes 2002, 369–71; Beltrán Fortes and Rodríguez Hidalgo 2004, 159–61.
70 *RICIS* 603/1001 (Legio VII) to Aesculapius, Salus, Serapis, and Isis; *RICIS* 603/1101 (Asturica) to Serapis, Isis Myrionyma, Invicta Kore, Apollo Grannus, and Mars Sagato.
71 Alvar 2013, 61.
72 Corzo 1991, 128–37. Several other plaques have been discovered at Italica, including one at the site of the Iseum, but in a secondary context: Alvar 2013, 65 no. 74.
73 Dedicant in action: Takács 2005. Puccio 2010b proposes that outward-facing footprints are those of the deity, while inward-facing ones are worshippers. Dunbabin 1990 recognizes the multiple ways such monuments signify.

74 *Pace* Takács 2005.
75 The footprints do not survive, but were recorded in the eighteenth century; see Alföldy 1999, 215; Castiglione 1970, 100.
76 Manganaro 1964. For such dedications more broadly, Dunbabin 1990.
77 e.g. Puccio 2010b.
78 Corzo 1991, 128–37.
79 Canto 1984.

the base of its staircase, creating a microregional network of ritual associations.

Similarly, the penchant at Italica for dedicating footprints creates a link between the seemingly personal dedications in the Iseum and the wider civic realm; the footprints from the amphitheatre include a public priest and have been connected with the civic elite of the colony.[80] Dedicatory practices in the Iseum evoke those of other public spaces and civic practices in the town. Instead of seeing Isis-worship as a closed entity and context for interpretation, it is necessary to recognize the ways that practices might be framed within much more localized contexts. Relationality, and the interoperability of practices that defined specific places, offer a clearer understanding and framework for cult choices.

These public locations and associations, within designated precincts in the hearts of cities, stand in sharp contrast to the known Mithraea of the peninsula, which create tight associations with individual households. The Mithraeum at Els Munts, recognizable from its layout with a centre aisle flanked by two benches, was inserted into the lower terrace of a substantial villa outside Tarraco in the mid–late second century CE (Fig. 13.6).[81] A seal and a plaque commemorating the construction of a cistern suggest that, by the mid-second century, the villa was owned by Caius Valerius Avitus and his wife Faustina; a lost inscription from Tarraco itself records that Avitus was a duumvir at Tarraco, *translato ab Divo Pio ex municipio August(obrigensi) in col(oniam) Tarrac(onensium)* ('moved by Divus Antoninus Pius from the Municipium of Augustobriga to the Colony of Tarraco'). Avitus was a figure with some imperial connection; why an emperor should relocate him some three hundred kilometres from inland Augustobriga to Tarraco is unclear, but Ruiz de Arbulo plausibly suggests that the power vacuum at Tarraco created by a plot against the emperor hatched by the governor of Hispania Citerior might offer a historical context.[82] In moving to Tarraco, Avitus invested (or was persuaded to invest by a ritual expert like Hedychrus) in converting part of his villa into one of the largest Mithraea in the empire; still, the sanctuary was part of this private estate.

Similarly, at Lucus Augusti, a Mithraeum was inserted into a high-status house on the edge of the city, constructed as a nave flanked by a colonnade.[83] The main cult image seems to have been a free-standing bronze statue of the god, pointing to

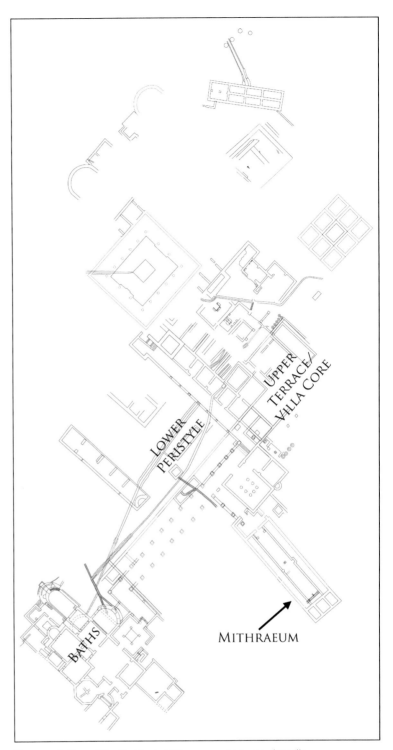

Figure 13.6. Plan of the Els Munts Mithraeum, set into an elite villa. Plan: MNAT Archive, with kind permission of Josep Anton Remolà Vallverdú.

the richness of the sanctuary's furnishings.[84] The inscribed altar found in the sanctuary was dedicated by Gaius Victorius Victorinus of the VII Legio Gemina (assumed to be a centurion, but his rank is

---

80 Canto 1984.
81 Tarrats and others 2006, 219–22; Tarrats and Remolà 2008.
82 Ruiz de Arbulo 2014.
83 Alvar and others 2006; Rodríguez Cao 2014.

84 Fernández Colmenero and Rodríguez Cao 2012, 107.

not recorded).⁸⁵ The placement of the Mithraeum within a house — the excavators assume that it is Victorinus's house, and note that such a luxurious residence was within the means of a centurion — points to the cult's more private, household orientation here. Yet given the centrality of the text itself to understanding the use of this elongated room as a Mithraeum, and to understanding the social dynamics of the cult and its integration within a public or private sphere, it is worth looking at the text in full:

> Invic(to) Mithrae | G(aius) Victorius Vic|torinus |(centurio) leg(ionis) VII G(eminae) | Antoninianae P(iae) F(elicis) | in honorem sta|tionis Lucensis | et Victoriorum | Secundi et Vic|toris lib(ertorum) suor|um aram po|suit libenti | animo.⁸⁶

The fact that the legion receives the title Antoniniana in the inscription offers a date for its dedication: probably under Caracalla (211–218 CE).⁸⁷ The offering *in honorem stationis Lucensis* is highly unusual, but reflects the ways the offering is situated to create a sense of localness. The other part of the dedication is even more unusual, as a high-status individual (Victorinus) dedicates to his freedmen Victorius Secundus and Victorius Victor; in Roman dedicatory practice, social inferiors always dedicate 'up', for the wellbeing of higher-status individuals in a way that maintains structures of social authority.⁸⁸ This problem might be remedied by reading *lib(erorum)* and seeing Secundus and Victor as Victorinus's children, a reading rejected when the inscription was published given that such a designation would more commonly be spelled out *liber(orum)*.⁸⁹ The onomastics of the two honoured figures do not help clarify the situation, as both children and freedmen calqued their names on father/patron. Still, at least one clear example from Africa Proconsularis uses *lib* for *liberorum*, suggesting that this is a possibility; in the context of a small household community, it may have been obvious who Secundus and Victor were.⁹⁰ In either case, the dedication reflects a familial (in the Roman sense) community, practising the cult within a private house.

In the second half of the third century, the house was partially demolished in order to build a street on the inside of the city wall; the Mithraeum, however, seems to have stayed in use until the mid-fourth century based on pottery and coins.⁹¹ This suggests that, even if the sanctuary began as a familial sanctuary, it grew to serve a wider community independent of the house where it originally stood: a community that maintained the Mithraeum for several generations and through important changes in the city more broadly.

In both certain cases, regardless of urban or peri-urban setting, the Mithraeum was set off by a central peristyle, not accessible from outside the house or villa. Even if worshippers came from outside the household, their engagement in the cult required passing through the house (by invitation?), entering the homeowner's domain and catching glimpses of other spaces beyond the peristyle. That is, the location of these Mithraea speaks not only to their patronage by the owners of such elite residences, but also to the way the cult was integrated into the practices and social structures of the household. Every visitor to the sanctuary would experience the authority of the homeowner as if he were a guest; in that sense, cult taking place within such Mithraea worked to establish the power of the homeowner within that space.

At Cabra, a marble statue of Mithras stabbing the bull seems to have been a garden ornament in the peristyle of a luxurious villa.⁹² The statue was set in a niche that framed an ornamental pool in the centre of the court, with a statue of Bacchus in a niche on the other side. The original excavators, expecting — based on the statue that had been discovered there twenty years earlier — to discover a Mithraeum, instead found a villa without any trace of a Mithraic *spelaeum*. They concluded that the statue represented a re-display of the piece which had originally stood in a sanctuary to Mithras, and that the building may have been the seat of a Mithraic *collegium*, assuming (falsely, as subsequent discoveries have shown) that Mithraea were never located in private houses.⁹³ An excavation campaign in 1981 worked to clarify the diachronic development of the

---

85 Alvar and others 2006.
86 *HEp* 9, 1999, 418.
87 Le Roux 2007, 375.
88 Alvar and others 2006, 275–76 also note this oddity, and suggest that these freedmen persuaded Victorinus to dedicate part of the house to Mithras.
89 Le Roux 2007, 376 n. 6, seems to be the only commentator to have considered this possibility, but dismisses it as he sees no need for a centurion to emphasize the freeborn status of his children. Depending on the status of the children's mother (centurions were prohibited from marrying women in the province where they served: *Dig.* XXIII.2.63), it might have been worth emphasizing their legal status and claims. Examples of military officers using *liberi* for children in votives: *AE* 2012, 1262; *CIL* VIII 9023.

90 *CIL* VIII 23022; cf. also *CIL* X 3334.
91 Rodríguez Cao 2014, 26–27.
92 For the statue, discovered in 1952, García y Bellido 1952. For subsequent excavations, Blanco and others 1972; Jiménez Salvador and Martín-Bueno 1992; Alcaide 2011.
93 Blanco and others 1972, 319.

villa, and demonstrated — thanks to a sestertius of Philip the Arab under one of the floors — that the villa underwent substantial renovation in the second half of the third century, and that it was in this period that the statues of Mithras and Dionysus, stylistically dated to the second century, were transformed into garden ornaments.[94] If the Mithras-statue was originally the focus of an as-yet undiscovered sanctuary in the second-century phase of the villa (and there are no guarantees that it had this cultic function, as opposed to being a garden ornament), this would have been a sanctuary linked to the occupants of the villa, rather than a wider public sanctuary.

At what seems to have been a Roman coastal villa at Islas, an inscribed, difficult-to-understand stele records that Fronto placed an altar dedicated to Invictus Deus Au(gu)stus, possibly with figures holding the titles of *pater patratus* and *leo* (or a *pater patratus* named Leo) involved.[95] The piece has been variously dated to the third century on palaeographic grounds,[96] or to the fourth based on an African parallel using Austa for Augusta.[97] While Adán and Cid propose that the sanctuary was set in a grotto along the coast, no evidence supports their conclusion.[98] Despite the problems of interpretation, it seems probable that an organized Mithras-worshipping community was based at a substantial villa here.

A recently discovered structure built into a recess in bedrock in Augusta Emerita (at 22, calle Espronceda, just north-west of the modern Plaza des Toros) has been identified as a Mithraeum.[99] The excavation area was limited by the boundaries of a modern cellar, but revealed a series of walls that seemed to create a nave flanked by plastered benches. Part of a plastered and painted altar showing a bare-legged standing figure, set alongside a triangular altar which was claimed to resemble a bull's head, was found in the nave. The finds associated with the occupation include two lamps and fineware beakers, mostly datable to the first and early second centuries CE. While the proposed reconstructions of the structure do resemble a Mithraeum, the state plan and published description reflect a far more complex sequence of constructions and associations between features; until full publication of the stratigraphic sequence and the finds assemblage, caution is needed in accepting the preliminary conclusions. Regardless, given the limited scope of the excavation, little can be said of the wider context of the structure — whether in a house or freestanding — besides the fact that one wall continued well beyond the boundaries of the nave/benches and thus belonged to a larger structure.

Less is known about the context of other Mithraic finds from the Iberian Peninsula. The dedication to Cautes at Aquae Calidae was a stray find,[100] as was the altar to Mithras at Benifaió.[101] At Saguntum, a fragmentary inscription found in a secondary context may have been the monumental dedication for a Mithraeum, but the reading is not certain.[102] At Caeteobriga, the find-spot in 1925 of the fragmentary Mithraic relief (within a Roman town) was not scientifically excavated and documented.[103] Can Modolell, whose finds assemblage has circularly been interpreted as Mithraic thanks to votive altars dedicated to a local deity abbreviated variously as *K*, *K D(eus)*, or *D(eus) K( ) M( )*, problematically assumed to be K(autes), is probably not a Mithraeum at all.[104] The assemblage from Augusta Emerita may have come from a substantial domestic Mithraeum. The examples of more 'public' Mithras-worship are problematic and can be discounted. For example, although a four-sided altar found in the amphitheatre of Italica has often been linked to Mithras, nothing about its iconography is specific to the Persianate cult; the walking bull is simply a bull (who appears to be rendered as a steer, which makes the Mithraic association even less probable), and the grapes, wheat sheaves, and tree on the other three sides point generally to agro-pastoral fertility.[105]

The close link between household — whether within a city (Lucus Augusti, maybe Augusta Emerita) or in a villa (Els Munts, Cabra) — and Mithraeum in Spain is striking and stands in contrast with the

---

94 Jiménez Salvador and Martín-Bueno 1992, 73–76.
95 *CIL* II 2705 = *ERAsturias* 7. The fragmentary Roman remains have been variously interpreted, but are most probably those of a villa: Adánn and Cid 1998.
96 García y Bellido 1948, 301.
97 Adán and Cid 1998, 133.
98 Adán and Cid 1998, 135.
99 Barrientos 2001.
100 *CIL* II 5635; García y Bellido 1967, 39.
101 *CIL* II 96; García y Bellido 1967, 37.
102 Corell and Seguí 2008, 74–76.
103 *CIMRM* 798. Romero Mayorga 2016a, 242 n. 976, suggests the possibility that the relief was found in a secondary context.
104 Pla and Revilla 2002, 212 as Mithraic 'con total seguridad'. Inscriptions: *IRC* I, 85–86; the reading as Mithras was first put forward by Mariner 1976, and accepted since. On the site and attribution, Sinner and Revilla 2017. Alvar 2016, 398; 2018, 30 accepts the site as a Mithraic cave.
105 García y Bellido 1950, 355 perhaps overstates the case for a 'clara alusión a conceptos puramente mitraicos', but has been followed by (*inter alii*) Alvar 1981, 56; Cappai 2010, 308; Romero Mayorga 2016a, 196–206. Beltrán Fortes and Rodríguez Hidalgo 2004, 167–73 see the altar as belonging to a syncretistic sanctuary, rather than having direct Mithraic connection. Campos Mendez 2015 rightly offers scepticism on the Mithraic nature of the altar.

seemingly more public, urban or peri-urban Mithraea that were the norm in most of the Western Empire. Villa- and house-based Mithraea were not, of course, absent in these areas.[106] But in the Iberian Peninsula, the worship of Mithras seems to have had an especially close link with household communities. In some cases, Mithraic communities seem to have expanded beyond the immediate circle of an elite homeowner (Lucus Augusti), allowing for the longevity of the cult and its sanctuary space; in other cases, as at Cabra, the seemingly short life of the cult statue as a cult object may point to the failure of the community to move beyond its initial group of adherents. This matters because this particular type of social context and ties to individual households speaks to the ways Mithras-worship might be taken in different directions by the heads of such households than in either Mithraic communities across the Empire or even in those within Iberia.

The cults of Isis/Serapis and Mithras thus seem to have occupied rather different social spaces, physically and conceptually, on the Iberian Peninsula. The ways that each related worshippers to one another and to other groups within society were markedly different and suggest that the conflation of the two sets of worship practices along the spectrum of Oriental or initiatory cults may paper over key distinctions. Again, greater focus on the ways these cults created place — for themselves and for individuals — within distinctly localized societies requires greater attention.

## Place-Making and Imported Cults in Roman Iberia

That the Roman Empire provided the structural frameworks in which the worship of deities like Isis and Mithras could be taken up, could attract interest and investment, and could spread across vast geographic spaces is an obvious point. None of these sanctuaries, their furnishings, their users, or their dedicators would have existed in the ways they did without that framework. But the social, political, cultural, and economic structures of the Roman Empire did not create provincial religion. Individuals — often, like Rufinus or Hedychrus, working to generate their own localized social power in religious terms — were the agents who creatively generated gods, places, and practices.

What has been less obvious are the ways that Isis-worship or Mithras-worship were largely building blocks that could be marshalled, deployed, and contextualized by creative agents in very different manners. Instead of fitting into (or mapping onto) bounded and reified cultural groups, the worship of these deities provided opportunities for individuals like Rufinus and Hedychrus to create localized social authority.

Making 'provincial religion' or religion under the Roman Empire was, far more than has been recognized in Roman Spain, about making localized religion: about making discrete places for gods, sanctuaries, and individuals in space and in society.

---

106 In the Gauls and Germaniae, for example, villa Mithraea are known at Orbe-Boscéaz and Bornheim-Sechtem and Bordeaux. In Italy, several of the Ostian Mithraea are linked to houses, and the find of a statue of Mithras stabbing the bull in an elite house in Tarquinia may closely parallel the situation at Cabra.

# Bibliography

Abad Casal, L., S. Keay, and S. Ramallo (eds). 2006. *Early Roman Towns in Hispania Tarraconensis*, *JRA* Supplementary Series, 62 (Portsmouth, RI: Journal of Roman Archaeology)

Abad Lara, R. 2008. 'La divinidad celeste/solar en el panteón céltico peninsular', *Espacio, Tiempo y Forma*, 2nd ser., *Historia Antigua*, 21: 79–103

Abad Varela, M. 1992. 'La moneda como ofrenda en los manantiales', *Espacio, Tiempo y Forma*, 2nd ser., *Historia Antigua*, 5: 133–92

Abascal, J. M. 1995. 'Las inscripciones latinas de Santa Lucía del Trampal (Alcuéscar, Cáceres) y el culto de Ataecina en Hispania', *AEA*, 68: 31–105

——. 1996. 'De nuevo sobre Ataecina y Turobriga. Exploraciones del año 1900 en *Las Torrecillas* (Alcuéscar, Cáceres)', *AEA*, 69: 275–80

——. 2002. 'Ataecina', in J. C. Ribeiro (ed.), *Religiões da Lusitânia: Loquuntur saxa* (Lisbon: Museu Nacional de Arqueologia), pp. 53–60

——. 2006. 'Los tres viajes de Augusto a Hispania y su relación con la promoción jurídica de las ciudades', *Iberia*, 9: 63–78

——. 2017. 'Augusto y el eco epigráfico de *Munda* en *Carthago Nova, Saguntum y Tarraco*', *Gerión*, 35: 571–81

Abascal, J. M., and G. Alföldy. 1998. 'Zeus Theos Megistos en Segobriga', *AEA*, 71: 157–68

Abascal, J. M., M. Almagro-Gorbea, J. M. Noguera, and R. Cebrián. 2007. 'Segobriga. Culto imperial en una ciudad romana de la Celtiberia', in T. Nogales and J. González Fernández (eds), *Culto Imperial: política y poder; Aactas del Congreso Internacional Culto Imperial; política y poder; Mérida, Museo Nacional de Arte Romano, 18–20 de mayo, 2006* (Rome: L'Erma di Bretschneider), pp. 685–704

Abascal, J. M., and R. Cebrián. 2004. 'Grandes familias y riqueza en la sociedad saguntina', in P. P. Ripollès and M. del M. Llorens (eds), *Arse-Saguntum: Historia monetaria de la ciudad y su territorio* (Sagunto: Fundación Bancaja), pp. 123–32

Abásolo, J. A. 1998. 'Indígenas e hispanorromanos en la Meseta Norte. Recientes descubrimientos de inscripciones hipogeas', in S. Rascón (ed.), *Complutum: Roma en el interior de la Península Ibérica. Catálogo de la Exposición* (Alcalá de Henares: Fundación Caja Madrid), pp. 29–38

Abásolo, J. A., and M. Mayer. 1997. 'Inscripciones latinas', in M. S. Corchón (ed.), *La Cueva de la Griega de Pedraza (Segovia)* (Zamora: Junta de Castilla y León), pp. 183–259

Abásolo, J. A., and M. Mayer. 1999 [published 2000]. 'Transcripción de las inscripciones romanas de la Cueva del Puente (Junta de Villalba de Losa, Burgos)', in Grupo Espeleológico Edelweiss, 'El Karst de Monte Santiago, Sierra Salvada y Sierra de la Carbonilla', *Kaite: Estudios de Espeleología Burgalesa*, 7: 283

Abásolo, J. A., and D. Ríos. 2009. 'Escribir en las paredes: graffiti de Astudillo y Pallantia', *PITTM*, 80: 454–64

Aberson, M., and R. Wachter. 2010. 'Les "lois sacrées" en Italie du VI$^e$ au I$^{er}$ siècle av. J.-C.: auteurs, formulations, applications', in L. Lamoine, C. Berrendonner, and M. Cebeillac-Gervasoni (eds), *La praxis municipale dans l'Occident romain* (Clermont-Ferrand: Presses Universitaires Blaise Pascal), pp. 401–19

Adams, J. N. 2005. *Bilingualism and the Latin Language* (Cambridge: Cambridge University Press) (reprint of the first edition 2003)

Adán, G. E., and R. M. Cid. 1998. 'Testimonios de un culto oriental entre los astures transmontanos. La lápida y el santuario mitraicos de San Juan de La Isla (Asturias)', *Boletín de la Real Instituto de Estudios Asturianos*, 152: 125–46

Adroher, A. M. 2005. 'Santuarios y necrópolis fuera de las murallas. El espacio periurbano de los oppida bastetanos', in M. C. Belarte and R. Plana (eds), *El paisatge periurbà a la Mediterrània occidental durant la protòhistoria i l'antiguitat: actes del Col·loqui internacional, Institut Català d'Arqueologia Clàssica, Tarragona, 6–8 maig 2009 / Le paysage périurbain en Méditerranée occidentale pendant la Protohistoire et l'Antiquité: actes du colloque international, Institut Catalan d'Archéologie Classique, Tarragone, 6–8 mai 2009*, ICAC Documenta, 26 (Tarragona: Institut Català d'Arqueologia Clàssica), pp. 231–44

Adrych, P., R. Bracey, D. Dalglish, S. Lenk, and R. Wood. 2017. *Images of Mithra* (Oxford: Oxford University Press)

Alarcão, J. de. 1988. *Roman Portugal*, 2 vols (Warminster: Aris & Phillips)

Alarcão, J. de, and A. Tavares. 1988. 'A Roman Marble Quarry in Portugal', in R. I. Curtis (ed.), *Studia Pompeiana et classica in Honor of Wilhelmina F. Jashemski*, II (New Rochelle: Caratzas), pp. 1–12

Albiach, R., and J. L. de Madaria (eds). 2006. *La villa de Cornelius (L'Ènova, Valencia)* (Valencia: Ministerio de Fomento)

Alcaide, M. M. 2011. 'La Villa del Mitra (Cabra). Puesta al día de las investigaciones', *Antiquitas*, 23: 177–87

Alcock, S. E., and R. Osborne (eds). 1994. *Placing the Gods: Sanctuaries and Sacred Space in Ancient Greece* (Oxford: Clarendon)

Alfaro, C. 1993. 'Uso no monetal de algunas monedas púnicas de la península ibérica', *Rivista Italiana di Numismatica e Scienze Affini*, 95: 261–76

——. 2003. 'Isis en las monedas de Baria y Tagilit', *Numisma*, 247: 7–18

Alfayé, S. 2005. 'Santuarios celtibéricos', in *Celtíberos: tras la estela de Numancia* (Soria: Diputación de Soria), pp. 229–34

——. 2007. 'Contexts of Cult in *Hispania Celtica*', in D. A. Barrowclough and C. Malone (eds), *Cult in Context: Reconsidering Ritual in Archaeology* (Oxford: Oxbow), pp. 311–20

——. 2009. *Santuarios y rituales en la Hispania Céltica*, BAR, International Series, 1963 (Oxford: Archaeopress)

——. 2010. 'Hacia el lugar de los dioses: una aproximación a la peregrinación religiosa en la Hispania indoeuropea', in F. Marco, F. Pina, and J. Remesal (eds), *Viajeros, peregrinos y aventureros en el mundo antiguo*, Col·lecció Instrumenta, 36 (Publicacions i edicions de la Universitat de Barcelona), pp. 177–218

——. 2014. 'Relecturas de algunas inscripciones latinas de la cueva-santuario de "La Griega", Pedraza (Segovia)', *Veleia*, 31: 279–87

——. 2016. 'Expresiones religiosas en las ciudades del poder de la Hispania Céltica: el caso de Clunia', in M. D. Dopico (ed.), *Ciudades del poder en Hispania*, Revista de Historiografía, 25 (Madrid: Universidad Carlos III de Madrid), pp. 355–83

Alfayé, S., and F. Marco. 2008. 'Religion, Language and Identity in Hispania: Celtiberian and Lusitanian Rock Inscriptions', in R. Häussler (ed.), *Romanisation et épigraphie: études interdisciplinaires sur l'acculturation et l'identité dans l'Empire romain* (Montagnac: Monique Mergoil), pp. 281–305

Alfayé, S., and F. Marco. 2014. 'Las formas de memoria en Celtiberia y el ámbito vacceo', in T. Tortosa (ed.), *Diálogo de identidades: Bajo el prisma de las manifestaciones religiosas en el ámbito mediterráneo (s. III a.C.– s. I d.C.)*, Anejos de *Archivo Español de Arqueología*, 72 (Mérida: Consejo Superior de Investigaciones Científicas), pp. 169–82

Alföldy, G. 1969. *Fasti Hispanienses: Senatorische Reichsbeamte und Offiziere in den spanischen Provinzen des römischen Reiches von Augustus bis Diokletian* (Wiesbaden: Steiner)

——. 1977. *Los Baebii de Saguntum* (Valencia: Diputación de Valencia)

——. 1981. 'Die älteste römische Inschrift der Iberischen Halbinsel', *ZPE*, 43: 1–12

——. 1984. 'Drei städtische Eliten im römischen Hispanien', *Gerión*, 2: 193–238

——. 1985. 'Epigraphica Hispanica VI. Das Dian-Heiligtum von Segobriga', *ZPE*, 58: 139–59

——. 1991. 'Augustus und die Inschiften: Tradition und Innovation. Die Geburt der imperialen Epigraphik', *Gymnasium*, 98: 289–324

——. 1997. 'Die Mysterien von Panóias (Vila Real, Portugal)', *Madrider Mitteilungen*, 38: 176–246

——. 1999. *Städte, Eliten und Gesellschaften in der Gallia Cisalpina; Epigraphisch-historische Untersuchungen* (Stuttgart: Steiner)

——. 2000. 'Zur Lage und zu den Inschriften des Diana–Heiligtums von Saguntum', *ZPE*, 129: 275–80

——. 2002. 'Desde el nacimiento hasta el apogeo de la cultura epigráfica de Tarraco', in L. Hernández, L. Sagredo, and J. M. Solana (eds), *Actas del I Congreso Internacional de Historia Antigua: La península Ibérica hace 2000 años* (Valladolid: Universidad de Valladolid), pp. 61–74

Alföldy, G., and E. Rosenbaum. 1993. 'Mérida Revisited: The Cosmological Mosaic in Light of Discussions since 1979', *Madrider Mitteilungen*, 34: 254–74

Almagro Basch, M. 1953. *Las necrópolis de Ampurias*, I: *Introducción y necrópolis griegas*, Monografías Ampuritanas, 3 (Barcelona: Seix y Barral)

——. 1976. 'El "delubro" o Sacellum de Diana en Segóbriga', *Revista de Archivos, Bibliotecas y Museos*, 79: 187–214

Almagro-Gorbea, M. 1988. 'El área superficial de las poblaciones ibéricas', in *Los asentamientos ibéricos ante la romanización* (Madrid: Casa de Velázquez), pp. 21–34

——. 1995a. 'La moneda hispánica con jinete y cabeza varonil: ¿tradición indígena o creación romana?', *Zephyrus*, 48: 235–66

——. 1995b. 'El *lucus Dianae* con inscripciones rupestres de Segóbriga', in A. Rodríguez Colmenero and L. Gasperini (eds), *'Saxa scripta' (inscripciones en roca): Actas del Simposio Internacional Ibero-Itálico sobre epigrafía rupestre*, Anejos de *Larouco*, 2 (A Coruña: Ediciós do Castro), pp. 61–97

Almagro-Gorbea, M., A. Domínguez de la Concha, and F. López Ambite. 1990. 'Cancho Roano. Un palacio orientalizante en la Península Ibérica', *Madrider Mitteilungen*, 31: 251–308

Alvar, J. 1981. 'El culto de Mitra en Hispania', *Memorias de Historia Antigua*, 5: 51–72

——. 1993a. 'Los cultos mistéricos en la Tarraconense', in M. Mayer and J. Gómez Pallarès (eds), *'Religio Deorum': Actas del coloquio internacional Culto y Sociedad en Occidente, Tarragona, 1988* (Sabadell: Ausa), pp. 27–46

——. 1993b. 'Los cultos mistéricos en la Bética', in J. F. Rodríguez (ed.), *Actas del I Coloquio de Historia Antigua de Andalucía, Córdoba, 1988* (Córdoba: Monte de Piedad y Caja de Ahorros de Córdoba), pp. 225–36

——. 1993c. 'Cinco lustros de investigaciones sobre cultos orientales en la Península Ibérica', *Gerión*, 11: 313–26

——. 1999. 'Las religiones mistéricas en Hispania', in J. M. Blázquez and R. Ramos (eds), *Religión y mágia en la antigüedad* (Valencia: Generalidad de Valencia), pp. 35–48

——. 2004. 'Discusión sobre las instituciones ibéricas', in M. Garrido-Hory and A. Gonzáles (eds), *Histoire, espaces et marges de l'Antiquité*, III: *Hommages à Monique Clavel-Lévêque* (Besançon: Institut des Sciences et Techniques de l'Antiquité), pp. 11–31

——. 2009. 'Promenade por un campo de ruinas. Religiones orientales y cultos mistéricos: el poder de los conceptos y el valor de la taxonomía', in C. Bonnet, V. Pirenne-Delforge, and D. Praet (eds), *Les religions orientales dans le monde grec et romain: cent ans après Cumont (1906–2006); Bilan historique et historiographique; Academia Belgica – Institut Suisse de Rome – Accademia dei Lincei. Roma, 16–18 noviembre 2006* (Turnhout: Brepols), pp. 119–34

——. 2013. *Los cultos egipcios en Hispania* (Besançon: Presses Universitaires de Franche-Comté)

——. 2016. 'Las ciudades del poder en la innovación religiosa: Introducción y difusión de los cultos iniciáticos en hispania', *Revista de Historiografía*, 25: 385–403

——. 2018. *El culto de Mitra en Hispania* (Madrid: Editorial Dykinson)

Alvar, J., and E. Muñiz. 2004. 'Les cultes égyptiens dans les provinces romaines d'Hispanie', in B. Bricault (ed.), *Isis en Occident: actes du III<sup>ème</sup> colloque international sur les études isiaques, Lyon III, 16–17 mai 2002*, Religions in the Graeco-Roman World (Leiden: Brill), pp. 69–94

Alvar, J., R. L. Gordon, and C. Rodríguez. 2006. 'The Mithraeum at Luco (Lucus Augusti) and its Connection with Legio VII Gemina', *JRA*, 19: 266–77

Álvarez, J., and G. Ruiz Zapatero. 2001. 'Cementerios y asentamientos: bases para una demografía arqueológica de la Meseta en la Edad del Hierro', in L. Berrocal Rangel and P. Gardes (eds), *Entre Celtas e Iberos: las poblaciones protohistóricas de las Galias e Hispanias* (Madrid: Real Academia de la Historia), pp. 61–76

Álvarez Arza, R., M. Duran i Caixal, I. Mestres, M. D. Molas, and J. Principal. 2000. 'El jaciment del Camp de les Lloses (Tona, Osona), i el seu taller de metalls', in C. Mata and G. Pérez (eds), *Ibers: agricultors, artesans i comerciants; III Reunió sobre economía en el Món Ibèric (Valencia, 24–27 November 1999)* (Valencia: Universitat de València), pp. 271–81

Álvarez Martínez, J. M. 1982. 'El foro de Augusta Emerita', in *Homenaje a Saenz de Buruaga* (Badajoz: Institución Cultural 'Pedro de Valencia'), pp. 53–68

Álvarez Martínez, J. M., and P. Mateos Cruz (eds). 2011. *1910–2010: El yacimiento emeritense; Actas del congreso internacional* (Merida: Ayuntamiento de Mérida)

Álvarez Martínez, J. M., and T. Nogales. 2003. *Forum Coloniae Augustae Emerita: 'Templo de Diana'* (Mérida: Asamblea de Extremadura)

Álvarez Martínez, J. M., and T. Nogales. 2015. 'La ideología del Principado en la fundación de Augusta Emerita', in J. García Sánchez, I. Mañas Romero, and F. Salcedo Garcés (eds), *Navigare necesse est. Estudios en homenaje a José María Luzón Nogué* (Madrid: Universidad Complutense), pp. 54–67

Álvarez Martínez, J. M., and T. Nogales. 2019. 'La fundación de la *Colonia Augusta Emerita*, una consecuencia significativa de las guerras cántabras', in J. J. San Vicente, C. Cortés, and E. González González (eds), *Hispania et Roma: Estudio en homenaje al profesor Narciso Santos Yanguas* (Oviedo: Universidad de Oviedo), pp. 327–36

Amela, L. 2009. *Hispania y el segundo triunvirato (44–30 a.C.)* (Madrid: Signifer Libros)

——. 2011. 'Sagunto, Colonia', *Arse*, 45: 153–61

——. 2012. 'Una moneda con letrero griego de Sagunto (RPC 485)', *Arse*, 46: 171–80

Anderson, B. R. O'G. 1991. *Imagined Communities: Reflections on the Origin and Spread of Nationalism* (London: Verso)

Ando, C. 2000. *Imperial Ideology and Provincial Loyalty in the Roman Empire* (Berkeley: University of California Press)

——. 2003. 'A Religion for the Empire', in A. J. Boyle and W. J. Dominik (eds), *Flavian Rome: Culture, Image, Text* (Leiden: Brill), pp. 321–44

——. 2007. 'Exporting Roman Religion', in J. Rüpke (ed.), *A Companion to Roman Religion* (Malden, MA: Blackwell), pp. 429–45

——. 2008. *The Matter of the Gods: Religion and the Roman Empire* (Berkeley: University of California Press)

——. 2020. 'Public Law in North Africa', in K. Czajkowski, B. Eckhardt, and M. Strothman (eds), *Law in the Roman Provinces* (Oxford: Oxford University Press), pp. 332–45

Andreu, J. 2017a. 'Conimbriga. Condeixa-a-velha (Conimbriga)', in M. J. Peréx and C. Miró (eds), *Vbi aquae ibi Salus: Aguas mineromedicinales, termas curativas y culto a las aguas en la península Ibérica (desde la Protohistoria a la Tardoantigüedad)* (Madrid: Universidad Nacional de Educación a Distancia), pp. 211–12

——. 2017b. 'Lantarón (Álava)', in M. J. Peréx and C. Miró (eds), *Vbi aquae ibi Salus: Aguas mineromedicinales, termas curativas y culto a las aguas en la península Ibérica (desde la Protohistoria a la Tardoantigüedad)* (Madrid: Universidad Nacional de Educación a Distancia), p. 179

——. 2017c. 'Valladolid, Casa Santa (Valladolid)', in M. J. Peréx and C. Miró (eds), *Vbi aquae ibi Salus: Aguas mineromedicinales, termas curativas y culto a las aguas en la península Ibérica (desde la Protohistoria a la Tardoantigüedad)* (Madrid: Universidad Nacional de Educación a Distancia), p. 296

——. 2017d. 'Talavera de la Reina (Toledo)', in M. J. Peréx and C. Miró (eds), *Vbi aquae ibi Salus: Aguas mineromedicinales, termas curativas y culto a las aguas en la península Ibérica (desde la Protohistoria a la Tardoantigüedad)* (Madrid: Universidad Nacional de Educación a Distancia), pp. 292–93

——. 2017e. 'Duratón (Segovia)', in M. J. Peréx and C. Miró (eds), *Vbi aquae ibi Salus: Aguas mineromedicinales, termas curativas y culto a las aguas en la península Ibérica (desde la Protohistoria a la Tardoantigüedad)* (Madrid: Universidad Nacional de Educación a Distancia), p. 333

Andringa, W. van. 2002. *La religion en Gaule romaine: Piété et politique (I<sup>er</sup>–III<sup>e</sup> siècle apr. J.-C.)* (Paris: Errance)

Antunes, M., and A. Cunha. 1986. 'O crânio de Garvão (século III a. C.). Causa mortis, tentativa de interpretação', *Trabalhos de Arqueología do Sul*, 1: 9–85

Aquilué, X., and P. Cabrera (eds). 2012. *Iberia Graeca: el legado arqueológico griego en la península Ibérica* (Girona: Centro Iberia Graeca)

Aranegui, C. 1992. 'Evolucion del area civica saguntina', *JRA*, 5: 56–68

——. 1994. 'De la ciudad ibérica a la ciudad romana: Sagunto', in X. Dupré (ed.), *La ciudad en el mundo romano: actas del XIV Congreso Internacional de Arqueología Clásica. Tarragona* (Madrid: Consejo Superior de Investigaciones Científicas), pp. 69–78

——. 1997. 'La favissa del santuario urbano de Edeta–Liria (Valencia)', *Cuadernos de Prehistoria y Arqueología Castellonenses*, 18: 103–13

——. 2002. 'Ob restitutam Saguntum bello punico secundo', in A. Ribera and J. L. Jiménez Salvador (eds), *Valencia y las primeras ciudades romanas de Hispania* (Valencia: Ajuntament de Valencia), pp. 245–54

——. 2004a. *Saguntum: oppidum, emporio y municipio romano* (Barcelona: Bellaterra)

——. 2004b. 'El fòrum i els edificis d'espectacles', in P. P. Ripollès and M. del M. Llorens (eds), *Arse-Saguntum: historia monetaria de la ciudad y su territorio* (Sagunto: Fundación Bancaja), pp. 99–111

——. 2005. 'Nuevos datos sobre el templo republicano de Sagunto', in *Théorie et pratique de l'architecture romaine: mélanges Pierre Gros* (Aix-en-Provence: Publications de l'Université de Provence), pp. 133–50

——. 2006. 'From Arse to Saguntum', in L. Abad Casal, S. Keay, and S. Ramallo (eds), *Early Roman Towns in Hispania Tarraconensis*, JRA Supplementary Series, 62 (Portsmouth, RI: Journal of Roman Archaeology), pp. 63–75

——. 2011. 'The Most Important Roman Cities in Valencia until the 3rd Century', *Catalan Historical Review*, 4: 9–26

Aranegui, C., P. Izquierdo, E. Hernández Hervás, and R. Graells. 2018. 'La romanización de los bronces ibéricos: el conjunto de Muntanya Frontera de Sagunto (Valencia)', in L. Prados, C. Rueda, and A. Ruiz Rodríguez (eds), *Bronces ibéricos: una historia por contar; Homenaje al prof. Gérard Nicolini (Madrid 2018)* (Madrid: Ediciones de la Universidad Autónoma de Madrid), pp. 455–90

Aranegui, C., and J. L. Jiménez. 2013. 'La curia de *Saguntum*', in B. Soler, P. Mateos, J. M. Noguera, and J. Ruiz de Arbulo (eds), *Las sedes de los 'ordines decurionum' en Hispania: Análisis arquitectónico y modelo tipológico* (Instituto de Arqueología de Mérida: Consejo Superior de Investigaciones Científicas), pp. 43–53

Arasa, F. 1998. 'Escultures romanes de Castelló', *Quaderns de Prehistòria i Arqueologia de Castelló*, 19: 311–47

Arce, J. 1988. *Funus Imperatorum: Los funerales de los emperadores romanos* (Madrid: Alianza)

Arévalo, A. 2002–2003. 'Las imágenes monetales hispánicas como emblemas de estado', *Cuadernos de Prehistoria y Arqueología de la Universidad Autónoma de Madrid*, 28–29: 241–58

——. 2006. 'El valor simbólico y el uso cultual de la moneda en la costa gaditana', in *Moneda, cultes i ritus* (Barcelona: Museu nacional d'art de Catalunya), pp. 75–98

Arévalo, A., and C. Marcos Alonso. 2000. 'Sobre la presencia de moneda en los santuarios hispánicos', in *XII Internationaler Numismatischer Kongress Berlin 1997* (Berlin: Staatliche Museen zu Berlin), pp. 28–37

Arévalo, A., and E. Moreno. 2016. 'La moneda en las necrópolis de Gadir/Gades', in A. Arévalo (ed.), *Monedas para el más allá: uso y significado de la moneda en las necrópolis tardopúnicas y romanas de Ebusus, Gades y Malaca* (Cádiz: Universida de Cádiz), pp. 75–193

Ariño, E., and J. M. Gurt. 1992–1993. 'Catastros romanos en el entorno de Augusta Emerita. Fuentes literarias y documentación arqueológica', *Studia Historica*, 2nd ser., *Historia Antigua*, 10–11: 45–66

Arruda, A. M., and S. Celestino. 2009. 'Arquitectura religiosa en Tartessos', in P. Mateos, S. Celestino, A. Pizzo, and T. Tortosa (eds), *Santuarios, 'oppida' y ciudades: arquitectura sacra en el origen y desarrollo urbano del Mediterráneo Occidental* (Merida: CSIC-Instituto de Arqueología de Mérida), pp. 29–77

Asensio, J. A. 2003. 'El *sacellum in antis* del Círculo Católico de Huesca (*Osca*, Hispania Citerior), un ejemplo precoz de arquitectura templaria romana en el Valle del Ebro', *Salduie*, 3: 93–127

Aubet, M. E. 2001. *The Phoenicians and the West: Politics, Colonies and Trade*, 2nd edn (Cambridge: Cambridge University Press)

Ayerbe Vélez, R., T. Barrientos, and F. Palma (eds). 2009. *El foro de Augusta Emerita: Génesis y evolución de sus recintos monumentales*, Anejos de *Archivo Español de Arqueología*, 53 (Mérida: Consejo Superior de Investigaciones Científicas)

Bakker, J. T. 1994. *Living and Working with the Gods: Studies of Evidence for Private Religion and its Material Environment in the City of Ostia (100–500 A.D.)* (Leiden: Brill)

Baños, J. M. 2003. 'Los *sodales Heliconi* de la Cueva Negra de Fortuna (Murcia): una propuesta de interpretación', in A. González Blanco and G. Matilla (eds), *La cultura latina en la Cueva Negra: en agradecimiento y homenaje a los Profs. A. Stylow, M. Mayer e I. Velázquez*, Antigüedad y Cristianismo, 20 (Murcia: Universidad de Murcia), pp. 355–72

Baratta, G. 2001. *Il culto di Mercurio nella Penisola Iberica* (Barcelona: Universitat de Barcelona)

Baratte, F. 2001. 'Le mithreum de Sidon: certitudes et questions', *Topoi: Orient-Occident*, 11.1: 205–27

Barberarena Nuñez, M. L., and J. L. Ramírez Sádaba. 2010. 'El sincretismo entre divinidades romanas y divinidades indígenas en el Conventus Emeritensis', in J. Arenas-Esteban (ed.), *Celtic Religion across Space and Time* (Toledo: Junta de Comunidades de Castilla-La Mancha), pp. 115–29

Barrientos, T. 2001. 'Nuevos datos para el estudio de las religiones orientales en Occidente: un espacio de culto mitraico en la zona sur de Merida', *Mérida: Excavaciones arqueológicas 1999; Memoria*, 5: 357–81

Barrientos, T., I. Arroyo, and B. Marín. 2007. 'Proyecto de renovación del sistema de gestión de datos arqueológicos en el Consorcio: el SIG de patrimonio emeritense (1a fase: 2004–2007). Diseño y configuración', *Mérida: Excavaciones arqueológicas; Memoria*, 10: 551–75

Barzanò, A. 1992. 'La questione dell'identità zacintio–ardeate dei Saguntini: invenzione erudita, falso diplomatico o realtà storica?', in M. Sordi (ed.), *Autocoscienza e rappresentazione dei popoli nell'antichità* (Milan: Vita e Pensiero), pp. 135–43

Bassani, M. 2003. 'Gli spazi di culto', in S. Bullo and F. Ghedini (eds), *'Amplissimae atque ornatissimae domus' (Aug. civ., II, 20, 26). L'edilizia residenziale nelle città della Tunisia romana* (Rome: Quasar), pp. 153–87

——. 2007. 'Culti domestici nelle province occidentali: alcuni casi di ambienti e di edifici nella Gallia en nella Britannia romane', *Antenor*, 6: 105–23

——. 2008. *Sacraria: ambienti e piccoli edifici per il culto domestico in área vesubiana* (Rome: Quasar)

Bats, M. 2013. *D'un monde à l'autre: contacts et acculturation en Gaule Méditerranéenne*, XLII: *Collections Centre Jean Bérard* (Naples: Centre Jean Bérard)

——. 2014. 'L'Artémis de Marseille et la Diane de l'Aventin: de l'amitié à la rupture entre Marseille et Rome', in S. Bouffier and D. Garcia (eds), *Les territoires de Marseille antique* (Arles: Errance), pp. 133–42

Beard, M. 1987. 'A Complex of Times: No More Sheep on Romulus' Birthday', *Proceedings of the Cambridge Philological Society*, 33: 1–15

Beck, R. 2006. *The Religion of the Mithras Cult in the Roman Empire: Mysteries of the Unconquered Sun* (Oxford: Oxford University Press)

Bedon, R. 2001. 'Mise en scène de la puissance, du pouvoir, et de l'adhésion des élites gauloises à l'idéologie du régime impérial dans les villages indigènes des Trois Gaules', in M. Molin (ed.), *Images et représentations du pouvoir et de l'ordre social dans l'Antiquité: actes du Colloque d'Angers, 28–29 mai 1999* (Paris: De Boccard), pp. 238–48

Beirão, C. de, C. Tavares da Silva, J. Soares, M. Varela Gomes, and R. Varela Gomes. 1985. 'O depósito votivo da II Idade do Ferro de Garvão. Notícia da primeira campanha de escavações', *O Arqueólogo português*, 4th ser., 3: 45–136

Belarte, M. C. (ed.). 2009. *L'espai dòmestic i l'organització de la societat a la Protohistòria de la Mediterrània occidental (I$^{er}$ millenni aC): actes de la IV Reunió Internacional d'Arqueologia de Calafell (Calafell-Tarragona, 8–9 març 2007)* (Barcelona: Universitat de Barcelona)

Belarte, M. C., and S. Valenzuela-Lamas. 2013. 'Zooarchaeological Evidence for Domestic Rituals in the Iron Age Communities of North-Eastern Iberia (Present-Day Catalonia) (Sixth-Second Century BC)', *Oxford Journal of Archaeology*, 32.2: 163–86

Belén Deamos, M. 2011–2012. 'Notas sobre la religiosidad turdetana. Los depósitos sagrados del oppidum de Alhonoz (Herrera, Sevilla)', *Cuadernos de Prehistoria y Arqueología*, 37/38: 333–48

Beltrán, F. 1980. *Epigrafía latina de Saguntum y su territorium (Cronología. Territorium. Notas prosopográficas. Cuestiones municipales)* (Valencia: Servicio de Investigación Prehistórica)

—— (ed.). 1995. *Roma y el nacimiento de la cultura epigráfica en occidente: actas del Coloquio Roma y las Primeras Culturas Epigráficas del Occidente Mediterráneo siglos II a.E.–I d.E., Zaragoza, 4 a 6 de noviembre de 1992*, Publicación de la Institución Fernando el Católico 1684 (Zaragoza: Institución Fernando el Católico)

——. 1999. 'Writing, Language and Society. Iberians, Celts and Romans in Northeastern Spain in the 2nd and 1st Centuries BC', *Bulletin of the Institute of Classical Studies*, 43: 131–51

——. 2002. 'Identidad cívica y adhesión al príncipe en las monedas municipales hispanas', in F. Marco, F. Pina, and J. Remesal (eds), *Religión y propaganda política en el mundo romano* (Barcelona: Publicacions Universitat de Barcelona), pp. 159–87

——. 2003. 'La romanización temprana en el valle medio del Ebro (siglos II–I a. E.): una perspectiva epigráfica', *AEA*, 76: 179–91

——. 2011. 'Lengua e identidad en la Hispania romana', *Palaeohispanica*, 11: 19–59

——. 2012. 'Roma y la epigrafía ibérica sobre piedra del nordeste peninsular', *Palaeohispanica*, 12: 9–30

——. 2013. 'Almost an Oxymoron: Celtic Gods and Palaeohispanic Epigraphy. Inscriptions, Sanctuaries and Monumentalisation in Celtic Hispania', in W. Spickermann (ed.), *Keltische Götternamen als individuelle Option? Celtic Theonyms as an Individual Option? XI. Workshop F.E.R.C.AN.*, Osnabrücker Forschungen zu Altertum und Antik-Rezeption, 19 (Rahden: Leidorf), pp. 165–84

——. 2017. 'Acerca del concepto de romanización', in T. Tortosa and S. Ramallo (eds), *El tiempo final de los santuarios ibéricos en los procesos de impacto y consolidación del mundo romano*, Anejos de *Archivo Español de Arqueología*, 79 (Madrid: Consejo Superior de Investigaciones Científicas), pp. 17–26

Beltrán, F., and B. Díaz Ariño. 2007. 'Altares con teónimos hispano–célticos de la Meseta norte (Museos de Palencia, Burgos y Valladolid)', in M. Hainzmann (ed.), *Auf den Spuren keltischer Götterverehrung: Akten des 5. F.E.R.C.A.N.–Workshop (Graz, 9.–12. Oktober 2003)* (Vienna: Österreichischen Akademie der Wissenschaften), pp. 29–56

—— (eds). 2018. *El nacimiento de las culturas epigráficas en el occidente mediterráneo: modelos romanos y desarrollos locales (III–I a. E.)*, Anejos de *Archivo Español de Arqueología*, 85 (Madrid: Consejo Superior de Investigaciones Científicas)

Beltrán, F., C. Jordán, and F. Marco. 2005. 'Novedades epigráficas en Peñalba de Villastar (Teruel)', *Palaeohispanica*, 5: 911–56

Beltrán Fortes, J. 2002. 'Descubrimentos arqueológicos en el anfiteatro de Itálica en 1914', *SPAL*, 11: 365–75

——. 2012. 'L'origen del culte imperial a Hispània i el seu reflex en les emissions romanoprovincials', in M. Campo (ed.), *Déus i mites de l'antiguitat: l'evidència de la moneda d'Hispània* (Barcelona: Museu Nacional d'Art de Catalunya), pp. 78–83

——. 2017. 'El mundo funerario augusteo en la Hispania meridional. Una aproximción arqueológica', in J. Mangas and A. Mayorgas (eds), *La Hispania de Augusto, Gerión*, 35 (Madrid: Editorial Complutense), pp. 791–808

Beltrán Fortes, J., and J. M. Rodríguez Hidalgo. 2004. *Espacios de culto en el anfiteatro de Itálica* (Seville: Universidad de Sevilla)

Beltrán Fortes, J., and A. U. Stylow. 2007. 'Un aspecto del culto imperial en el sureste bético: el puteal de Trigueros (Huelva), un altar dedicado a Augusto', in T. Nogales and J. González Fernández (eds), *Culto Imperial: política y poder; actas del Congreso Internacional Culto Imperial; política y poder; Mérida, Museo Nacional de Arte Romano, 18–20 de mayo, 2006* (Rome: L'Erma di Bretschneider), pp. 239–49

Belloni, G. 1987. *Le res gestae Diui Augusti. Augusto: il nuovo regime e la nuova urbe* (Milan: Vita e Pensiero)

Bendala, M. 1982. 'Reflexiones sobre la iconografía mitraica de Mérida', in *Homenaje a Sáenz de Buruaga* (Badajoz: Institución Cultural Pedro de Valencia), pp. 99–108

——. 1986. 'Die orientalischen Religionen Hispaniens in vorrömischer und römischer Zeit', *ANRW*, 2.18.1: 345–408

Bendlin, A. 1997. 'Peripheral Centres – Central Peripheries: Religious Communication in the Roman Empire', in H. Cancik and J. Rüpke (eds), *Römische Reichsreligion und Provinzialreligion* (Tübingen: Mohr Siebeck), pp. 35–68

Benedito, J. J. 2015. 'Las infraestructuras viarias de *Saguntum* en época imperial: propaganda, prestigio social y poder municipal', *Potestas*, 8: 9–35

Benoist, S. 2018. 'Des empereurs et des dieux: peut-on parler d'une "théocratie" impériale romaine?', in M. F. Baslez and C. G. Schwentzel (eds), *Les dieux et le pouvoir: aux origines de la théocratie* (Rennes: Presses universitaires de Rennes), pp. 83–99

Bérard, G. 1997. *Carte archéologique de la Gaule: 04. Les Alpes-de-Haute-Provence* (Paris: Éditions de la Maison des sciences de l'homme)

Bérenguer, A. 2010. 'Ambassades et ambassadeurs a Rome aux deux derniers siècles de la République', in *État et société aux deux derniers siècles de la République romaine: hommage à François Hinard* (Paris: De Boccard), pp. 65–76

Bermejo, J. 1994. *Mitología y mitos de la Hispania Prerromana*, I, 2nd edn (Madrid: Tres Cantos)

Berrocal-Rangel, L. 1994. *El altar prerromano del Castrejón de Capote: ensayo etno-arqueológico de un ritual céltico en el Suroeste peninsular*, Excavaciones Arqueológicas en Capote (Beturia Céltica), 2 (Madrid: Universidad Autónoma de Madrid)

——. 2004. 'Banquetes y rituales colectivos en el suroeste peninsular', *Cuadernos de Prehistoria y Arqueología*, 30: 105–19

——. 2018. 'La segunda Edad del hierro', in *150 Años del Museo Arqueológico Provincial de Badajoz 1867–2017* (Badajoz: Junta de Extremadura), pp. 159–67

Berrocal-Rangel, L., and C. Ruiz-Triviño. 2003. *El depósito alto-imperial del Castrejón de Capote o La historia de una ciudad sin historia*, Memorias de arqueología extremeña, 5 (Mérida: Consejería de Cultura)

Berrocal-Rangel, L., M. Blech, A. Morillo, G. Rodríguez Martín, A. Salguero, and M. Zarzalejos. 2009. 'Das frühkaiserzeitliche Votivdepot von San Pedro (Valencia del Ventoso, prov. Badajoz). Augusta Emerita in der Baeturia und der Kult der Ataecina-Bandue', *Madrider Mitteilungen*, 50: 196–295

Bianchi, E. 2010. *Il rex sacrorum a Roma e nell'Italia antica* (Milan: Vita e Pensiero)

Bickerman, E. 1952. 'Origines gentium', *Classical Philology*, 47.2: 65–81

Blanco, A. 1971. 'El mosaico de Merida con la alegoria del saeculum aureum', *Estudios sobre el mundo helenistico: anales de la Universidad Hispalense*, 8: 151–78

Blanco, A., J. García, and M. Bendala. 1972. 'Excavaciones en Cabra (Córdoba): la casa del Mitra (Primera campaña, 1972)', *Habis*, 3: 297–320

Blázquez Martínez, J. M. 1974. 'Propaganda dinástica y culto imperial en las acuñaciones de Hispania', *Numisma*, 120–31: 311–29

——. 1975. *Diccionario de las religiones prerromanas de Hispania* (Madrid: Ediciones Istmo)

——. 1986. 'Cosmología mitraica en un mosaico de Augusta Emerita', *AEA*, 59: 89–100

——. 1991. *Religiones en la España antigua* (Madrid: Cátedra)

Blázquez Martínez, J. M., and J. Alvar (eds). 1996. *La romanización en Occidente* (Madrid: Actas Editorial)

Blech, M. 2009. 'Die figürlichen Terrakotten', in L. Berrocal Rangel, M. Blech, Á. Morillo Cerdán, G. Rodríguez Martín, A. S., and M. Z. Marin Prieto, 'Das frühkaiserzeitliche Votivdepot von San Pedro (Valencia del Ventoso, Prov. Badajoz). Augusta Emerita in der Baeturia und der Kult der Ataccina-Bandue', *Madrider Mitteilungen*, 50: 197–294 (204–24)

Boatwright, M. T. 1989. *Hadrian and the City of Rome* (Princeton: Princeton University Press)

——. 2000. *Hadrian and the Cities of the Roman Empire* (Princeton: Princeton University Press)

Bodel, J. 1997. 'Monumental Villas and Villa Monuments', *JRA*, 10: 5–35

Bonet, H. 2010. 'Ritos y lugares de culto de ámbito doméstico', in T. Tortosa, S. Celestino, and R. Cazorla (eds), *Debate en torno a la religiosidad protohistórica* (Mérida: CSIC-Instituto de Arqueología de Mérida), pp. 177–201

Bonet, H., I. Grau, and J. Vives-Ferrándiz. 2015. 'Estructura social y poder en las comunidades ibéricas de la franja central mediterránea', *Arqueomediterrània*, 14: 251–72

Bonet, H., and C. Mata. 1997. 'Lugares de culto edetanos: propuesta de definición', in A. O. Foix *Espacios y lugares cultuales en el mundo ibérico*, Quaderns de prehistòria i arqueologia de Castelló, 18 (Castelló de la Plana: Servei d'Investigacions Arqueològiques i Prehistòriques), pp. 115–46

Bonnet, C. 1988. *Melqart: cultes et mythes de l'Héraclès Tyrien en Méditerranée*, Studia Phoenicia (Leuven: Presses Universitaires de Namur)

Bonnet, C., and C. Jourdain-Annequin (eds). 1992. *Héraclès: d'une rive à l'autre de la Méditerranée* (Rome: Institut Historique Belge de Rome)

Bonnet, C., and L. Bricault. 2016. *Quand les dieux voyagent: cultes et mythes en mouvement dans l'espace méditerranéen antique* (Geneva: Labor et Fides)

Bonneville, J. N. 1987. 'La epigrafía romana', in C. Aranegui (ed.), *Guía de los monumentos romanos de Castillo y Sagunto* (Valencia: Conselleria de Cultura, Educació i Ciència), pp. 133–41

Bookidis, N. 2003. 'The Sanctuaries of Corinth', in C. K. Williams II and N. Bookidis (eds), *Corinth: The Centenary, 1896–1996* (Princeton: American School of Classical Studies at Athens), pp. 247–59

Bouma, J. W. 1996. *Religio votiva: The Archaeology of Latial Votive Religion; The 5th – 3rd Centuries BC Votive Deposit South West of the Main Temple at Satricum–Borgo Le Ferriere* (Groningen: University of Groningen)

Bourdieu, P. 1998. *Praktische Vernunft: Zur Theorie des Handelns* (Frankfurt: Suhrkamp)

Bowes, K. 2006. 'Building Sacred Landscapes: Villas and Cult', in A. Chavarria, J. Arce, and G. P. Brogiolo (eds), *Villas tardoantiguas en el Mediterráneo occidental*, Anejos de *Archivo Español de Arqueología*, 39 (Madrid: Consejo Superior de Investigaciones Científicas), pp. 73–95

Boyce, G. K. 1937. *Corpus of the Lararia of Pompeii* (Rome: American Academy in Rome)

Bradbury, S. 1995. 'Julian's Pagan Revival and the Decline of Blood Sacrifice', *Phoenix*, 49: 331–56

Bradley, K. R. 1991. '*Tatae* and *mammae* in the Roman Family', in *Discovering the Roman Family: Studies in Roman Social History* (Oxford: Oxford University Press), pp. 76–102

Brandt, J. R. 2014. 'Blood, Boundaries, and Purification. On the Creation of Identities between Memory and Oblivion in Ancient Rome', in B. Alroth and C. Scheffer (eds), *Attitudes towards the Past in Antiquity: Creating Identities; Proceedings of an International Conference Held at Stockholm University, 15–17 May 2009* (Stockholm: Stockholms universitet), pp. 101–16

Braudel, F. 1986. *L'identité de la France*, 3 vols (Paris: Flammarion)

Bremmer, J. N. 1987. 'Romulus, Remus and the Foundation of Rome', in J. N. Bremmer and N. M. Horsfall (eds), *Roman Myth and Mythography* (London: Institute of Classical Studies), pp. 76–88

Bricault, L. (ed.). 2000. *De Memphis à Rome: Actes du I$^{er}$ colloque international sur les études Isiaques, Poitiers-Futuroscope, 8–10 avril 1999*, Religions in the Graeco-Roman World (Leiden: Brill)

——(ed.). 2004a. *Isis en Occident: Actes du III$^{ème}$ colloque international sur les études isiaques, Lyon III, 16–17 mai 2002*, Religions in the Graeco-Roman World (Leiden: Brill)

——. 2004b. 'La diffusion isiaque. Une esquisse', in P. C. Bol, G. Kaminski, and C. Maderna (eds), *Fremdheit–Eigenheit: Ägypten, Griechenland und Rom; Austausch und Verständnis* (Stuttgart: Scheufele), pp. 548–56

——. 2009. 'Les "religions orientales" dans les provinces occidentales sous le Principat', in Y. Le Bohec (ed.), *Rome et les provinces de l'Occident de 197 av. J.C. à 192 ap. J.C.* (Pornic: Éditions du Temps), pp. 129–53

——. 2010. 'Le sanctuaire d'Isis au Municipium Claudium Baelo', *JRA*, 23: 681–88

Bricault, L., M. J. Versluys, and P. G. P. Meyboom (eds). 2007. *Nile into Tiber: Egypt in the Roman World; Proceedings of the IIIrd International Conference of Isis Studies, Leiden, May 11–14 2005*, Religions in the Graeco-Roman World (Leiden: Brill)

Briquel, D. 1996. 'Remarques sur le dieu Quirinus', *Revue Belgique de Philologie et d'Histoire*, 74.1: 99–120

Broodbank, C. 2013. *The Making of the Middle Sea: A History of the Mediterranean from the Beginning to the Emergence of the Classical World* (Oxford: Oxford University Press)

Brotons, F., and S. Ramallo. 2010. 'Ornamento y símbolo: las ofrendas de oro y plata en el santuario ibérico del Cerro de la Ermita de la Encarnación de Caravaca', in T. Tortosa, S. Celestino, and R. Cazorla (eds), *Debate en torno a la religiosidad protohistórica* (Mérida: CSIC-Instituto de Arqueología de Mérida), pp. 123–68

Brunt, P. A. 1971. *Italian Manpower, 225 B.C.–A.D. 14* (Oxford: Oxford University Press)

Burton, P. 2011. *Friendship and Empire: Roman Diplomacy and Imperialism in the Middle Republic (353–146 B.C.)* (Cambridge: Cambridge University Press)

Caballero Zoreda, L., A. Almagro Gorbea, and J. Madroñero de la Cal. 1991. 'Iglesia de época visigoda de Santa Lucía del Trampal, Alcuéscar (Cáceres)', *Extremadura Arqueológica*, 2: 497–525

Caballero Zoreda, L., and F. Sáez Lara. 1999. *La iglesia mozárabe de Santa Lucía del Trampal, Alcuéscar (Cáceres): Arqueología y arquitectura* (Mérida: Junta de Extremadura)

Caballos, A. 2010. 'Hitos de la historia de Itálica', in A. Caballos Rufino (ed.), *Itálica-Santiponce: Municipium y Colonia Aelia Augusta Italicensium*, Ciudades romanas de Hispania, 7 (Rome: L'Erma di Bretschneider), pp. 1–16

—— 1990. *Los senadores hispanorromanos y la romanización de Hispania (siglos I al III p. C.)*, I: *Prosopografía* (Écija: X Gráficas Sol)

Caballos, A., W. Eck, and F. Fernández. 1996. *Das Senatus Consultum de Cn. Pisone patre* (Munich: Beck)

Cabrera, P., and C. Sánchez Fernández (eds). 2000. *Los griegos en España: tras las huellas de Heracles* (Madrid: Caja de Ahorros del Mediterráneo)

Caccioti, B. 2008. 'Culti orientali in Spagna: alcune osservazioni iconografiche', in J. M. Noguera and M. E. Conde (eds), *Escultura Romana en Hispania*, V: *Reunión sobre Escultura Romana en Hispania (5. 2005. Murcia)* (Murcia: Tabularium), pp. 163–86

Cadiou, F. 2008. *Hibera in terra miles: Les armées romaines et la conquête de l'Hispanie sous la République (218–45 av. J.-C.)* (Madrid: Casa de Velázquez)

Calado, M. 1993. *Carta arqueológica do Alandroal* (Alandroal: Câmara Municipal)

——. 2012. *O Santuário de Santa Bárbara de Padrões: uma Perspectiva Religiosa e Artística na Lusitânia dos Séculos I a III d. C.* (Lisbon: Faculdade de Ciências Sociais e Humanas, Universidade Nova de Lisboa)

Calado, M., and C. Roque. 2013. *O tempo dos deuses: nova carta arqueológica do Alandroal* (Lisbon: Câmara Municipal and Faculdade de Belas-Artes, Universidade de Lisboa)

Calza, G. 1916. 'Ostia–Scavi sul Piazzale del Corporazioni, nell'isola tra il Decumano e la via della Casa di Diana', *Notizie degli Scavi di Antichità*, 13: 138–48

Campbell, J. B. 2000. *The Writings of the Roman Land Surveyors: Introduction, Text, Translation and Commentary*, Journal of Roman Studies, Monographs, 9 (London: Society for the Promotion of Roman Studies)

Campo, M. 1993. 'Objetos paramonetales y monedas objeto en *Emporion/Emporiae*', *Rivista Italiana di Numismatica e Scienze Affini*, 95: 193–205

——. 2003. 'Les primeres imatges gregues: l'inici de les fraccionàries d'*Emporion*', in *Les imatges monetàries: llenguatge i significat; VII Curs d'Història monetària d'Hispània* (Barcelona: Museu Nacional d'Art de Catalunya), pp. 25–45

——. 2006. 'Usos rituals i valor religiós de la moneda a l'illa d'Ebusus (s. III aC–inici I dC)', in *Moneda, cultes i ritus* (Barcelona: Museu nacional d'art de Catalunya), pp. 47–74

—— (ed.). 2012. *Déus i mites de l'antiguitat. L'evidència de la moneda d'Hispània* (Barcelona: Museu Nacional d'Art de Catalunya)

——. 2012. 'Usos cultuals de la moneda: ofrenes i amulets', in M. Campo (ed.), *Déus i mites de l'antiguitat: l'evidència de la moneda d'Hispània* (Barcelona: Museu Nacional d'Art de Catalunya), pp. 58–63

Campo, M., P. Castanyer, M. Santos, and J. Tremoleda. 2016a. 'Tesoro de denarios romanos hallado en la Ínsula 30 de Empúries (74–73 a.C.)', *Numisma*, 260: 7–37

Campo, M., B. Costa, J.-H. Fernández, and A. Mezquida. 2016b. 'La moneda en la necrópolis de Ebusus', in A. Arévalo (ed.), *Monedas para el más allá: uso y significado de la moneda en las necrópolis tardopúnicas y romanas de Ebusus, Gades y Malaca* (Cádiz: Universida de Cádiz), pp. 27–73

Campo, M., M. Santos, P. Castanyer, E. Hernández, and J. y Tremoleda. 2022. 'Uso y circulación de la moneda en una ciudad griega: Emporion', in X. Aquilué and P. P. Ripollès (eds), *La moneda griega en Iberia: cecas y circulación monetaria (in memoriam Paloma Cabrera)* (Barcelona: Centro Iberia Graeca), pp. 55–70

Campos Mendez, I. 2015. 'Revisión del culto mitraico en la Colonia *Aelia Augusta Italica*', *Habis*, 46: 175–86

Cancik, H., and C. Hitzl (eds). 2003. *Die Praxis der Herrscherverehrung in Rom und seinen Provinzen* (Tübingen: Mohr Siebeck)

Cancik, H., and J. Rüpke (eds). 1997. *Römische Reichsreligion und Provinzialreligion* (Tübingen: Mohr Siebeck)

Cancik, H., and J. Rüpke (eds). 2009. *Die Religion des Imperium Romanum* (Tübingen: Mohr Siebeck)

Canto, A. M. 1984. 'Les plaques votives avec *plantae pedum* d'Italica: un essai d'interprétation', *ZPE*, 54: 183–94

——. 1999. 'La *vetus urbs* de Italica, quince años después. La planta hipodámica y de D. Demetrio de los Ríos, y otras novedades', *Cuadernos de Prehistoria y Arqueología de la Universidad Autónoma de Madrid*, 25.2: 145–91

Cappai, L. 2010. 'Testimonianze archeologiche della diffusione del culto mitraico nella Penisola Iberica', *Ricerca e confronti*, 2010: 305–16

Carneiro, A. 2019. 'A exploração romana do mármore no anticlinal de Estremoz: extração, consumo e organização', in V. Serrão, C. M. Soares, and A. Carneiro (eds), *Mármore: 2000 anos de História*, I: *Da Antiguidade à Idade Moderna* (Lisbon: Theya Editores), pp. 57–122

Casas, J., and J. Ruiz de Arbulo. 1997. 'Ritos domésticos y cultos funerarios. Ofrendas de huevos y gallináceas en villas romanas del territorio emporitano (s. III d.C.)', *Pyrenae*, 28: 211–27

Castanyer, P., and J. Tremoleda. 1999. *La villa romana de Vilauba: un exemple de l'ocupació i explotació del territorio a la comarca del Pla de l'Estany* (Girona: Ajuntament de Banyoles)

Castiello, A. 2021. *Augusto il fondatore: la rinascita di Roma e il mito romuleo* (Wiesbaden: Harrassowitz)

Castillo, M. J. 2000. 'Las propiedades de los dioses: los *loca sacra*', *Iberia: Revista de la Antigüedad*, 3: 83–109

Celestino, S., and C. López-Ruiz. 2016. *Tartessos and the Phoenicians in Iberia* (Oxford: Oxford University Press)

Cenerini, F. 1992. 'Scritture di santuari extraurbani tra le Alpi e gli Appenini', *Mélanges de l'École française de Rome*, 104.1: 91–107

Chaves, F. 2008a. '*Lupa Romana. Municipium Italicense*: una mirada al pasado', in E. La Rocca, P. León, and C. Parisi (eds), *Le due Patrie adquisite: studi di Archeologia dedicati a Walter Trillmich* (Rome: L'Erma di Bretschneider), pp. 117–27

——. 2008b. 'Monedas en la Hispania republicana ¿integración o autoafirmación?', in J. Uroz, J. M. Noguera, and F. Coarelli (eds), *Iberia e Italia: modelos romanos de integración territorial* (Murcia: Tabularium), pp. 353–77

——. 2012a. 'Les religions indígenes davant la presència romana: cultes i iconografies', in M. Campo (ed.), *Déus i mites de l'antiguitat: l'evidència de la moneda d'Hispània* (Barcelona: Museu Nacional d'Art de Catalunya), pp. 40–45

——. 2012b. 'Il riflesso dell'iconografia ellenistica nelle coniazioni della Hispania Ulterior', in R. Pera (ed.), *Il significato delle immagini: numismatica, arte, filologia, storia; atti del secondo incontro internazionale di studio del 'Lexicon iconographicum numismaticae'* (Rome: Giorgio Bretschneider), pp. 171–92

——. 2017. 'La evolución de la identidad cívica a través de los documentos monetales: el sur de Hispania siglos III a.C. – I d.C.', in J. J. Ferrer Maestro, C. Kunst, D. Hernández de la Fuente, and E. Faber (eds), *Entre los mundos: homenaje a Pedro Barceló* (Besançon: Presses universitaires de Franche-Comté), pp. 285–305

Chaves, F., and M. C. Marín Ceballos. 1992. 'L'influence phénico-punique sur l'iconographie des frappes locales de la Péninsule Ibérique', in T. Hackens and G. Moucharte (eds), *Numismatique et histoire économique phéniciennes et puniques*, Studia Phoenicia, 9 (Louvain-la-Neuve: Seminaire de Numismatique Marcel Hoc), pp. 167–94

Chaves, F., and M. C. Marín Ceballos. 2004. 'Las cabezas galeadas en la amonedación hispánica', in M. Caccamo Caltabiano, D. Castrizio, and M. Puglisi (eds), *La tradizione iconica come fonte storica: il ruolo della numismatica negli studi di iconografia; atti del I Incontro di Studio del Lexicon Iconographicum Numismaticae (Messina. 6–8 Marzo 2003)* (Reggio Calabria: Falzea), pp. 351–84

Chaniotis, A. 2005. 'Ritual Dynamics in the Eastern Mediterranean: Case Studies in Ancient Greece and Asia Minor', in W. V. Harris (ed.), *Rethinking the Mediterranean* (Oxford: Oxford University Press), pp. 141–66

Cid, R. M. 2019. 'Livia y los homenajes a las mujeres de la *Domus Augusta*. Algunos testimonios de Hispania', in J. I. San Vicente González de Aspuru, C. Cortés-Bárcena, and E. González González (eds), *Hispania et Roma: Estudios en homenaje al profesor Narciso Santos Yanguas* (Oviedo: Universidad de Oviedo), pp. 337–48

Cifani, G., and S. Stoddard (eds). 2012. *Landscape, Ethnicity and Identity in the Archaic Mediterranean Area* (Oxford: Oxbow)

Civera, M. 2014–2015. 'El santuari de la Muntanya Frontera de Sagunt (de Tu a Liber Pater)', *Arse*, 48–49: 151–72

Clauss, M. 1999. *Kaiser und Gott: Herrscheskult im römischen Reich* (Stuttgart: Teubner)

Coarelli, F. 2001. '*Origo Sagunti*: l'origine mitica di Sagunto e l'alleanza con Roma', in V. Fromentin and S. Gottleland (eds), *Origines gentium* (Bordeaux: Ausonius), pp. 321–26

——. 2012. *Palatium: il Palatino dalle Origini all'Impero* (Rome: Quasar)

Coarelli, F., M. Torelli, and J. Uroz (eds). 1992. *Conquista romana y modos de intervención en la organización urbana y territorial*, Dialoghi di Archaeologia Tersa Serie. Anno 10 (Rome: Quasar), pp. 1–2

Colominas, L. 2008. 'Els animals en el conjunt de les práctiques socials desenvolupades a l'establiment rural de Mas Castellar (Pontós, Girona)', *Cypsela*, 17: 219–32

Collar, A. 2007. 'Network Theory and Religious Innovation', *Mediterranean Historical Review*, 22.2: 149–62

Comino, A. 2015. 'El santuario de la Luz (Santo Ángel, Murcia) como elemento de identidad territorial (s. IV/III a.C.– I d.C)' (unpublished doctoral thesis, Universidad de Murcia)

Cooley, A. E. (ed.). 2002. *Becoming Roman, Writing Latin: Literacy and Epigraphy in the Roman West*, *JRA* Supplementary Series, 48 (Portsmouth, RI: Journal of Roman Archaeology)

Corbier, M. 1995. 'Male Power and Legitimacy through Women: The *Domus Augusta* under the Julio-Claudians', in R. Hawley and B. Levick (eds), *Women in Antiquity: New Assessments* (London: Routledge), pp. 178–93

Cordero, T. 2010. 'Una nueva propuesta sobre los límites del "ager emeritensis" durante el Imperio Romano y la Antigüedad Tardía', *Zephyrus*, 65: 149–65

Corell, J. 1994. 'La "Muntanyeta de Santa Bàrbara" (La Vilavella, Castellón): ¿Un santuario de Apolo?', *Sylloge Epigraphica Barcinonensis*, 1: 155–87

——. 1996. 'Tres santuaris de l'antic territori de Sagunt', *Fonaments*, 9: 125

——. 2002. *Inscripcions romanes del País Valencià: Saguntum i el seu territori*, Fonts històriques valencianes, 12, 2 vols (Valencia: Publicacions de la Universitat de València)

Corell, J., and J. J. Seguí. 2008. 'Fragmentos de inscripciones monumentales romanas de Sagunto', *Sylloge epigraphica Barcinonensis*, 6: 73–80

Cornell, T. J. 1975. 'Aeneas and the Twins: The Development of the Roman Foundation Legend', *Proceedings of the Cambridge Philological Society*, 21: 1–32

——. 1977. 'Aeneas' Arrival in Italy', *Liverpool Classical Monthly*, 2.4: 77–85

Corrales, Á. 2016. *La arquitectura doméstica de Augusta Emerita*, Anejos de *Archivo Español de Arqueología*, 76 (Madrid: Consejo Superior de Investigaciones Científicas)

Corrales, Á., J. Bermejo, and J. M. Campos. 2016. 'El lararium de la Casa Norte de Arucci: un nuevo testimonio de culto doméstico en la Provincia Baetica', *Antiquitas*, 28: 65–74

Correia Santos, M. J. 2007. 'El sacrificio en el occidente de la Hispania romana. Para un nuevo análisis de los ritos de tradición indoeuropea', *Palaeohispanica*, 7: 175–217

——. 2010. 'Santuarios rupestres no Ocidente da Hispania Indo-europeia: ensaio de tipologia e classificação', *Paleohispanica*, 10: 147–72

——. 2012. 'La arqueología, lo imaginario y lo real. El santuario rupestre de Mogueira (São Martinho de Mouros, Portugal)', *Madrider Mitteilungen*, 53: 455–96

——. 2015. 'Santuarios rupestres de la Hispania indoeuropea' (unpublished doctoral thesis, Universidad de Zaragoza)

Cortés, A. 2014. *L'arquitectura domèstica d'època tardorrepublicana i altimperial a les ciutats romanes de Catalunya* (Barcelona: Institut d'Estudis Catalans)

Cortes Bárcena, C. 2013. *Epigrafía de los confines de las ciudades romanas: Los 'termini publici' en Hispania, Mauretania y Numidia*, Hispania Antigua. Serie histórica, 7 (Rome: L'Erma di Bretschneider)

Corzo Sánchez, R. 1991. 'Isis en el teatro de Itálica', *Boletín de Bellas Artes*, 19: 125–48

Crawford, M. H. 1985. *Coinage and Money under the Roman Republic: Italy and the Mediterranean Economy* (London: Methuen)

——. 2008. 'States Waiting in the Wings. Population Distribution and the End of the Roman Republic', in L. de Ligt and S. Northwood, *People, Land and Politics: Demographic Developments and the Transformation of Roman Italy 300 BC – AD 14* (Leiden: Brill), pp. 631–43

Crawley Quinn, J., and N. C. Vella (eds). 2014. *The Punic Mediterranean: Identities and Identification from Phoenician Settlement to Roman Rule* (Cambridge: Cambridge University Press)

Crawley Quinn, J. 2017. *In Search of the Phoenicians* (Princeton: Princeton University Press)

Crespo, S., and A. Alonso. 2000a. *Corpus de inscripciones romanas de la provincia de Burgos: fuentes epigráficas para la historia social de Hispania romana* (Valladolid)

——. 2000b. *Auctarium a los corpora de epigrafía romana en el territorio de Castilla y León: novedades y revisiones; Fuentes epigráficas para la historia social de la Hispania romana* (Valladolid)

Cristóbal, V. 2003. 'Fuego en la fuente: sobre dos epígrafes de la Cueva Negra de Fortuna y su conexión con Virgilio y otros poetas latinos', in A. González Blanco and G. Matilla (eds), *La cultura latina en la Cueva Negra: en agradecimiento y homenaje a los Profs. A. Stylow, M. Mayer e I. Velázquez*, Antigüedad y Cristianismo, 20 (Murcia: Universidad de Murcia), pp. 345–53

Cruz Andreotti, G. (ed.). 1999. *Estrabón e 'Iberia': nuevas perspectivas de estudio* (Málaga: Servicio de Publicaciones de la Universidad de Málaga)

——. 2007. 'Acerca de Estrabón y la Turdetania ibérica', in G. Cruz Andreotti, P. Le Roux, and P. Moret (eds), *La invención de una geografía de la Península Ibérica*, II: *La época imperial* (Málaga: Centro de Ediciones de la Diputación de Málaga and Casa de Velázquez), pp. 251–70

——. 2009. 'Acerca de las identidades meridionales en época prerromana: algunos planteamientos geográficos', in F. Wulff Alonso and M. Álvarez Martí-Aguilar (eds), *Identidades, culturas y territorios en la Andalucia prerromana* (Málaga: Universidades de Málaga), pp. 297–316

——. 2011. 'Identidad e identidades en el sur de la Península Ibérica en época romana: un problema histórico y geográfico', in A. Sartori and A. Valvo (eds), *Identità e autonomie nel mondo romano occidentale, Iberia-Italia Italia-Iberia*, III, Epigrafia e Antichità, 29 (Faenza: Fratelli Lega), pp. 151–71

——. 2015. 'Rome and Iberia: The Making of a Cultural Geography', in M. Cataudella and H.-J. Gehrke (eds), *Brill's Companion to Ancient Geography: The Inhabited World in Greek and Roman Tradition* (Leiden: Brill), pp. 274–97

—— (ed.). 2018. *Roman Turdetania: Romanization, Identity and Socio-Cultural Interaction in the South of the Iberian Peninsula between the 4th and 1st Centuries BCE*, Cultural Interactions in the Mediterranean, 3 (Leiden: Brill)

Cruz Andreotti, G., P. Le Roux, and P. Moret (eds). 2006. *La invención de una geografía de la Península Ibérica*, I: *La época republicana* (Málaga: Centro de Ediciones de la Diputación de Málaga and Casa de Velázquez)

—— (eds). 2007. *La invención de una geografía de la Península Ibérica*, II: *La época imperial* (Málaga: Centro de Ediciones de la Diputación de Málaga and Casa de Velázquez)

Cuesta, R. 2011. 'Cueva de Román: fuente de abastecimiento, lugar de culto de la colonia Clunia Sulpicia', in A. Costa, L. Palahí, and D. Vivó (eds), *Aquae sacrae: Agua y sacralidad en época romana* (Girona: Universitat de Girona: Institut de la Recerca Histórica), pp. 167–80

Cugusi, P. 2003. 'Doppioni e ritornelli epigrafici', *Bolletino di Studi Latini*, 33: 449–66 (= Cugusi and Sblendorio Cugusi 2016, 266–85)

———. 2007. 'Culto e letteratura nei testi della Cueva Negra di Fortuna (Murcia)', *Invigilata Lucernis*, 20: 61–81 (= Cugusi and Sblendorio Cugusi 2016, 1415–38)

———. 2011. 'Gusto "pompeiano" nei graffiti ispanici', *Maia*, n.s., 63: 96–106 (= Cugusi and Sblendorio Cugusi 2016, 1439–55)

Cugusi, P. and M. T. Sblendorio Cugusi. 2012. *Carmina Latina Epigraphica Hispanica post Buechelerianam collectionem editam reperta cognita (CLEHisp)* (Faenza: Fratelli Lega)

———. 2016. *Versi su pietra: studi sui Carmina Latina Epigraphica; metodologia, problema, tematiche, rapporti con gli auctores, aspetti filologici e linguistici, edizione di testi; Quaranta anni di ricerche*, III, Epigrafia e Antichità, 38 (Faenza: Fratelli Lega)

Cumont, F. 1905. 'Note sur une statue provenant du mithraeum d'Emerita', *Comptes rendus des séances de l'Académie des Inscriptions et Belles-Lettres*, 49.2: 148–51

———. 1906. 'Les cultes d'Asie Mineure dans le paganisme romain', *Revue de l'Histoire des Religions*, 53: 1–24

———. 1956. *The Mysteries of Mithra* (New York: Dover)

Cunliffe, B. 1995. 'Diversity in the Landscape. The Geographical Background to Urbanism in Iberia', in B. Cunliffe and S. Keay (eds), *Social Complexity and the Development of Towns in Iberia: From the Copper Age to the Second Century AD* (Oxford: Oxford University Press), pp. 5–28

Cunliffe, B., and J. T. Koch (eds). 2010. *Celtic from the West: Alternative Perspectives from Archaeology, Genetics, Language and Literature* (Oxford: Oxbow)

Curchin, L. 1991. *Roman Spain: Conquest and Assimilation* (New York: Routledge)

———. 1996. 'Cult and Celt: Indigenous Participation in Emperor Worship in Central Spain', in A. Small (ed.), *Subject and Ruler: The Cult of the Ruling Power in Classical Antiquity; Papers Presented at a Conference Held in the University of Alberta on April 13–15, 1994 to Celebrate the 65th Anniversary of Duncan Fishwick*, JRA Supplementary Series, 17 (Ann Arbor, MI: Journal of Roman Archaeology), pp. 143–52

———. 2003. *The Romanization of Central Spain: Complexity, Diversity, and Change in a Provincial Hinterland* (New York: Routledge)

Czajkowski, K., B. Eckhardt, and M. Strothmann (eds). 2020. *Law in the Roman Provinces*, Oxford Studies in Roman Society and Law (Oxford: Oxford University Press)

Dardenay, A. 2007. 'Le rôle de l'image des *primordia Vrbis* dans l'expression du culte imperial', in T. Nogales Basarrate and J. González Fernández (eds), *Culto imperial: política y poder; actas del Congreso Internacional Culto Imperial; política y poder* (Rome: L'Erma di Bretschneider), pp. 153–68

———. 2010. *Les mythes fondateurs de Rome: images et politique dans l'Occident romain* (Paris: Picard)

———. 2011. 'La diffusion iconographique des mythes fondateurs de Roma dans l'Occident romain: spécificités hispaniques', in A. Caballos Rufino and S. Lefebvre (eds), *Roma generadora de identidades: la experiencia hispana* (Madrid: Collection de la Casa de Velázquez), pp. 79–96

———. 2012. *Images des fondateurs: d'Énée à Romulus* (Bordeaux: Ausonius)

Dardaine, S., M. Fincker, J. Lancha, and P. Sillières. 2008. *Belo*, VIII: *Le sanctuaire d'Isis* (Madrid: Collection de la Casa de Velázquez)

De la Barrera Antón, J. L. 1996. 'Apéndice. Nuevas aportaciones al estudio y configuración del programa iconográfico del "Pórtico del Foro" de *Augusta Emerita*', in J. Massó and P. Sada (eds), *Actas de la II Reunión sobre escultura romana en Hispania* (Tarragona: Museu Nacional Arqueòlogic de Tarragona), pp. 109–13

De Ruggiero, E. 1910. *Dizionario epigrafico di antichità romane*, II.2 (Spoleto: Premiata Tipografia dell'Umbria)

Delgado, J. A. 1998. *Élites y organización de la religión en las provincias romanas de la Bética y las Mauritanias: sacerdotes y sacerdocios* (Oxford: Archaeopress)

———. 1999. 'Flamines Provinciae Lusitaniae', *Gerión*, 17: 433–61

———. 2000. 'Los sacerdotes de rango local de la provincia romana de Lusitania', *Conimbriga*, 39: 107–52

———. 2005. 'Priests of Italy and the Latin Provinces of the Roman Empire', in V. Lambrinoudakis and J. Ch. Balty (eds), *Thesaurus cultus et rituum antiquorum*, V (Los Angeles: The J. Paul Getty Museum), pp. 116–39

———. 2014. 'El sacerdocio salio de Sagunto. La recepción del programa religioso de Augusto en un municipio de Hispania Citerior', *Veleia*, 31: 143–62

———. 2016. 'Religión y culto en el *ara Pacis Augustae*', *AEA*, 89: 71–94

Demarrais, E., L. J. Castillo, and T. Earle. 1996. 'Ideology, Materialization and Power Strategies', *Current Anthropology*, 37.1: 15–31

Deonna, W. 1927. 'L'ornementation des lampes romaines', *Revue archéologique*, 26: 233–63

Derks, T. 1998. *Gods, Temples and Ritual Practices: The Transformation of Religious Ideas and Values in Roman Gaul* (Amsterdam: Amsterdam University Press)

Dias, M. M. A., and L. Coelho. 1995–1997. 'Endovélico: caracterização social da romanidade dos cultuantes e do seu santuário (S. Miguel da Mota, Terena, Alandroal)', *O Arqueólogo Português*, 4th ser., 13–15: 233–65

Díaz y Pérez, N. 1887. *Extremadura: Badajoz y Cáceres* (Barcelona: Establecimiento tipográfico-editorial de Daniel Cortezo)

Dietler, M. 1989. 'Greeks, Etruscans and Thirsty Barbarians. Early Iron Age Interaction in the Rhône Basin of France', in T. Champion (ed.), *Centre and Periphery: Comparative Studies in Archaeology* (London: Unwin Hyman), pp. 127–41

——. 2005. *Consumption and Colonial Encounters in the Rhône Basin of France: A Study of Early Iron Age Political Economy*, Monographes d'Archéologie Méditerranéene, 21 (Lattes: Association pour le Développement de l'Archéologie en Languedoc-Roussillon)

——. 2009. 'Colonial Encounters in Iberia and the Western Mediterranean. An Exploratory Framework', in M. Dietler and C. López-Ruiz (eds), *Colonial Encounters in Ancient Iberia: Phoenician, Greek and Indigenous Relations* (Chicago: Chicago University Press), pp. 3–48

Dietler, M., and C. López-Ruiz (eds). 2009. *Colonial Encounters in Ancient Iberia: Phoenician, Greek and Indigenous Relations* (Chicago: Chicago University Press)

Díez de Velasco, F. 1992. 'Divinités des eaux thermales dans les Nord-Ouest de la provincia Tarraconensis et dans le Nord de la provincia Lusitania: une approche au phénomène du thermalisme romain dans l'occident des provinces ibériques', in R. Chevalier (ed.), *Les eaux thermales et les cultes des eaux en Gaule et dans les provinces voisines: actes du colloque*, Caesarodunum, 26 (Tours: Centre de recherches A. Piganiol), pp. 133–49

——. 1998. *Termalismo y religión: la sacralización del agua termal en la Península Ibérica y el norte de África en el mundo antiguo*, 'Ilu: Revista de Ciencias de las Religiones, 3 (Madrid: Universidad Complutense. Instituto Universitario de Ciencias de las Religiones)

——. 1999. 'Religión provincial romana en la Península Ibérica: reflexiones teóricas y metodológicas', in J. M. Blázquez Martínez and R. Ramos (eds), *Religión y Magia en la antigüedad* (Valencia: Generalidad de Valencia), pp. 89–102

——. 2012. *Religiones en España: pasado y presente* (Madrid: Akal)

——. 2017. 'Balnearios y divinidades indígenas testificadas en la epigrafía de época romana en la Península Ibérica: reflexiones en torno a Bormanico', in J. C. Bermejo and M. García Sánchez (eds), *Desmoì philías = Bonds of Friendship: Studies in Ancient History in Honour of Francisco Javier Fernández Nieto* (Barcelona: Universitat de Barcelona), pp. 123–36

Domínguez Arranz, A. 2004. 'La expresión del sacerdocio en las monedas cívicas de Hispania: el poder de las imágenes', *Anejos de Archivo Espanol de Arqueologia*, 33: 163–83.

Domínguez Arranz, A., and A. Aguilera. 2012. 'Ritus sagrats i sacerdots', in M. Campo (ed.), *Déus i mites de l'antiguitat: l'evidència de la moneda d'Hispània* (Barcelona: Museu Nacional d'Art de Catalunya), pp. 72–77

Domínguez Monedero, A. 1997. 'Los lugares de culto en el mundo ibérico: espacio religioso y sociedad', *Quaderns de Prehistòria y Arqueologia de Castelló*, 18: 391–404

——. 2009–2011. 'Los foceos y sus ciudades, entre Jonia, la Magna Grecia y el occidente. Diversidad material e identidad étnica', *Empúries*, 56: 9–24

——. 2011–2012. 'Sagunto, el *emporion* de Arse, punto de fricción entre las políticas de Roma y Cartago en la península Ibérica', *Cuadernos de Prehistoria y Arqueología de la Universidad Autónoma de Madrid*, 37–38: 395–417

Dopico, Mª D. 1988. *La tabula Lougeiorum: estudios sobre la implantación romana en Hispania*, Anejos de *Veleia*, 5 (Vitoria: Universidad de Santiago de Compostela)

Downs, M. 1998. 'Turdetani and Bastetani. Cultural Identity in Iberian and Early Roman Baetica', in S. Keay (ed.), *The Archaeology of Early Roman Baetica*, JRA Supplementary Series, 29 (Portsmouth, RI: Journal of Roman Archaeology), pp. 39–53

Dubourdieu, A. 1989. *Les origines et le développement du culte des pénates à Rome*, Collection de l'école française de Rome, 118 (Paris: De Boccard)

Dueck, D. (ed.). 2017. *The Routledge Companion to Strabo* (London: Routledge)

Duliére, C. 1979. *Lupa romana: recherches d'iconographie et essai d'interpretation*, 1 (Rome: Institut historique belge de Rome)

Dumézil, G. 1974. *La religion romaine archaïque: avec un appendice sur la religion des Étrusques* (Paris: Payot)

Duplouy, A. 2019. *Construire la cité Essai de sociologie historique sur les communautés de l'archaïsme grec* (Paris: Les Belles Lettres)

Duran, M., I. Mestres, and J. Principal. 2004. 'El jaciment del Camp de les Lloses (Tona, Osona)', in M. Genera Monells (ed.), *Actes de les Jornades d'Arqueologia i Paleontologia, comarques de Barcelona, 1996–2001 (La Garriga, 29 i 30 de novembre, 1 de desembre de 2001)* (Barcelona: Generalitat de Catalunya), pp. 423–42

Duran, M., I. Mestres, and M. D. Molas. 2015. 'Maternidad e inhumaciones perinatales en el vicus romanorrepublicano de el Camp de les Lloses (Tona, Barcelona)', in M. Sánchez, E. Alarcón, and G. Aranda (eds), *Children, Spaces and Identity* (Oxford: Oxbow), pp. 294–309

Duran, M., I. Mestres, C. Padrós, and J. Principal. 2017. 'El Camp de les Lloses (Tona, Barcelona): evolución y significado del vicus romanorrepublicano', in J. Principal, T. Ñaco, M. Duran, and I. Mestres (eds), *Roma en la Península Ibérica presertoriana: escenarios de implantación militar provincial* (Barcelona: Universitat de Barcelona), pp. 153–89

Dury-Moyaers, G. 1981. *Énée et Lavinium: à propos des découvertes archéologiques récentes* (Brussels: Latomus)

Edmondson, J. 1987. *Two Industries in Roman Lusitania: Mining and Garum Production*, British Archaeological Reports, International Series, 362 (Oxford: BAR)

———. 1992–1993 [1994]. 'Creating a Provincial Landscape. Roman Imperialism and Rural Change in Lusitania', *Studia Historica*, 2nd ser., *Historia Antigua*, 10–11: 13–30

———. 1997. 'Two Dedications to Divus Augustus and Diva Augusta from Augusta Emerita and the Early Development of the Imperial Cult in Lusitania Re-examined', *Madrider Mitteilungen*, 38: 89–105

———. 2006a. *Granite Funerary Stelae from Augusta Emerita*, Monografías Emeritenses, 9 (Mérida: Ministerio de Cultura)

———. 2006b. 'Cities and Urban Life in the Western Province of the Roman Empire 30 BCE – 250 CE', in D.S. Potter (ed.), *A Companion to the Roman Empire* (Oxford: Blackwell), pp. 250–80.

———. 2007. 'The Cult of Mars Augustus and Roman Imperial Power at Augusta Emerita (Lusitania) in the Third Century A.D.: A New Votive Dedication', in T. Nogales and J. González Fernández (eds), *Culto imperial: política y poder; actas del Congreso Internacional Culto Imperial; política y poder; Mérida, Museo Nacional de Arte Romano, 18–20 de mayo, 2006* (Rome: L'Erma di Bretschneider), pp. 543–75

———. 2011. 'A Tale of Two Colonies: Augusta Emerita (Mérida) and Metellinum (Medellín), 25 B.C. – A.D. 100', in R. J. Sweetman (ed.), *Roman Colonies in the First Century of their Foundation* (Oxford: Oxbow), pp. 32–54

———. 2016. 'Monuments of Empire in Roman Spain and Beyond: Augusta Emerita (Mérida), the "Spanish Rome"', in J. M. D. Pohl and C. L. Lyons (eds), *Altera Roma: Art and Empire from the Aztecs to New Spain* (Los Angeles: The Cotsen Institute of Archaeology), pp. 69–107

———. 2018. 'La formación de una sociedad colonial en Augusta Emerita', in T. Nogales, and N. Barrero (eds), *La fundación de Augusta Emerita y los orígenes de Lusitania*, Monografías Emeritenses, 11 (Mérida: Fundación de Estudios Romanos), pp. 53–84

———. 2020. 'La administración de la provincia de Lusitania en el siglo III d.C.: nuevas aportaciones', in D. Moreau and R. González Salinero (eds), *Academica Libertas: Essais en l'honneur du Professeur Javier Arce; Ensayos en honor del Profesor Javier Arce*, Bibliothèque de l'Antiquité Tardive, 39 (Turnhout: Brepols), pp. 167–81

———. forthcoming. 'Onomástica y sociedad de una *colonia ciuium Romanorum* y *caput prouinciae*: la colonia *Augusta Emerita*', in J. Edmondson and M. Navarro Caballero (eds), *Onomástica, sociedad e identidad cultural en Lusitania romana*, ADOPIA, 1 (Bordeaux: Institut Ausonius)

Edmondson, J. and L. Á. Hidalgo Martín. 2008. 'Hallazgo de dos epitafios de *veterani* en Mérida: vidas paralelas de dos soldados *Augustani* (emeritenses) a finales del siglo I d.C.', *Mérida: excavaciones arqueológicas. 2004*, Memoria, 10: 479–507

Ekroth, G. 2007. 'Heroes and Hero-Cults', in D. Ogden (ed.), *A Companion to Greek Religion* (Malden, MA: Blackwell), pp. 100–14

Encarnação, J. d' 1975. *Divindades indígenas sob o domínio romano em Portugal* (Lisbon: Imprensa Nacional)

———. 1984. *Inscrições romanas do Conventus Pacensis [IRCP]* (Coimbra: Universidade de Coimbra)

———. 1995. 'Panorâmica e problemática geral da epigrafia rupestre em Portugal', in A. Rodríguez Colmenero and L. Gasperini (eds), *'Saxa scripta' (inscripciones en roca): actas del Simposio Internacional Ibero-Itálico sobre epigrafía rupestre*, Anejos de Larouco, 2 (A Coruña: Ediciós do Castro), pp. 261–77

———. 2015. 'Era aqui que Febo adormecia', *Estudos arqueológicos de Oeiras*, 22: 315–28

Ennabli, L. and J. Scheid. 2007–2008. 'Une *lex sacra* de Carthage relative au culte des Cereres? Nouvelles observations sur les fragments découverts dans la basilique de Carthagenna', *Atti della Pontificia Accademia Romana di Archeologia, Rendiconti*, 80: 37–76

Erskine, A. 2005. 'Unity and Identity: Shaping the Past in the Greek Mediterranean', in E. Gruen (ed.), *Cultural Borrowings and Ethnic Appropriations in Antiquity* (Stuttgart: Steiner), pp. 121–36

Escrivá, V. and A. Ribera. 1993. 'Els primers vestigis monumentals del període tardorepublicà a Valentia', in J. Padró i Parcerisa (ed.), *Homenatge a Miquel Tarradell* (Barcelona: Curial), pp. 577–84

España-Chamorro, S. 2021. 'Los esquivos *oppida* de Brutobriga y Turobriga: una propuesta sobre su ubicación y su relación con las deportaciones célticas', *Revue des Études Anciennes*, 123.1: 139–72

Espigares, A. 2003. '¿Ecos del Pro Archia en la Cueva Negra?', in A. González Blanco and G. Matilla (eds), *La cultura latina en la Cueva Negra: en agradecimiento y homenaje a los Profs. A. Stylow, M. Mayer e I. Velázquez*, Antigüedad y Cristianismo, 20 (Murcia: Universidad de Murcia), pp. 313–16

Espinosa, A. 2006. 'Sobre el nombre de la ciudad ibérica y romana de Villajoyosa y la ubicación del topónimo *Alonís/ Alonai/ Allon*', *Lucentum*, 25: 223–48

Estarán, M. J. 2016. *Epigrafía bilingüe del Occidente romano: el latín y las lenguas locales en las inscripciones bilingües y mixtas* (Zaragoza: Universidad de Zaragoza)

———. 2022. 'The Epigraphy and Civic Identity of Saguntum: A Historical and Sociolinguistic Study of a Bilingual City in the Roman West (2nd Century BC to Early 1st Century AD)', *Pyrenae*, 53.1: 135–58

Esteban Ortega, J. 2012–2013 [2015]. 'Epigrafía romana de Moraleja. Una nueva inscripción de *Iuppiter Solutorius* y algunas consideraciones sobre su culto', *Anas*, 25–26: 173–87

Étienne, R. 1958. *Le culte impérial dans la péninsule ibérique d'Auguste à Dioclétien*, BÉFAR, 191 (Paris: De Boccard)

——. 1974. *Le culte impérial dans la péninsule ibérique d'Auguste à Dioclétien* (Paris: De Boccard).

——. 1982. 'Sénateurs originaires de la province de Lusitanie', in *Epigrafia e ordine senatorio: atti del Colloquio internazionale AIEGL, Roma, 14–20 maggio 1981*, Tituli, 4–5 (Rome: Edizioni di storia e letteratura), pp. 521–29 (repr. in F. Mayet (ed.), *Itineraria hispanica: Recueil d'articles de Robert Étienne*, Scripta Antiqua, 15 (Bordeaux: Institut Ausonius, 2006), pp. 215–23)

——. 1990. 'Le culte impérial, vecteur de la hiérarchisation urbaine', in J.-G. Gorges (ed.), *Les villes de Lusitanie romaine: hiérarchies et territoires* (Paris: Centre national de la recherche scientifique), pp. 215–13 (repr. in F. Mayet (ed.), *Itineraria hispanica: Recueil d'articles de Robert Étienne*, Scripta Antiqua, 15 (Bordeaux: Institut Ausonius, 2006), pp. 79–92)

——. 1995. 'À propos du territoire d'Emerita Augusta (Mérida)', in M. Clavel-Lévêque and R. Plana-Mallart (eds), *Cité et territoire*, I: *Colloque européen, Béziers, 14–16 oct. 1994* (Paris: Presses universitaires de Franche-Comté), pp. 27–32 (repr. in F. Mayet (ed.), *Itineraria hispanica: Recueil d'articles de Robert Étienne*, Scripta Antiqua, 15 (Bordeaux: Institut Ausonius, 2006), pp. 269–76)

Étienne, R. and F. Mayet. 1984. 'La dénomination antique de Mérida', in *Lucerna: Homenagem a D. Domingos de Pinho Brandão* (Porto: Ministério da Cultura, Delegação Regional do Norte, Centro de Estudos Humanísticos), pp. 159–72

Evans, J. D. 1992. *The Art of Persuasion: Political Propaganda from Aeneas to Brutus* (Ann Arbor: University of Michigan Press)

Fabião, C. 1996. 'O povoado fortificado da Cabeça de Vaiamonte (Monforte), A Cidade', *Revista Cultural de Portoalegre*, 11: 35–84

Fabre, G. 1993. 'Les divinites "indigènes" en Aquitaine meridionale sous l'empire romain', in M. Mayer and J. Gómez Pallarès (eds), *'Religio Deorum': Actas del coloquio internacional Culto y Sociedad en Occidente, Tarragona, 1988* (Sabadell: Ausa), pp. 177–92

Fayer, C. 1976. *Il culto della dea Roma: origine e diffusione nell'Impero* (Pescara: Editrice Trimestre)

Fear, A. T. 1996. *Rome and Baetica: Urbanization in Southern Spain, c. 50 BC–AD 150* (Oxford: Oxford University Press)

Fernandes, L. da S. 2002. '*Genii, Lares* e *Tutela* na província da Lusitânia', in J. Cardim Ribeiro (ed.), *Religiões da Lusitânia, Loquuntur saxa* (Lisbon: Museu Nacional de Arqueologia), pp. 179–88

Fernandes, T. M. 1986. 'O crânio de Garvão (século III a. C.). Análise antropológica', *Trabalhos de Arqueología do Sul*, 1: 75–78

Fernández Ardanaz, S. 2003. 'Símbolos y rituales en las inscripciones de la "Cueva Negra de Fortuna" (Murcia): correlaciones entre etnolingüística y etnohistoria', in A. González Blanco and G. Matilla (eds), *La cultura latina en la Cueva Negra: en agradecimiento y homenaje a los Profs. A. Stylow, M. Mayer e I. Velázquez*, Antigüedad y Cristianismo, 20 (Murcia: Universidad de Murcia), pp. 405–22

Fernández Colmenero, A., and C. Rodríguez Cao. 2012. 'Anastilosis virtual de "A domus do mitreo de Lucus Augusti"', *Virtual Archaeology Review*, 3: 104–08

Fernández López, M. C. 2003. 'Tierra, cielo e inspiración: una lectura de tres pasajes de la Cueva Negra', in A. González Blanco and G. Matilla (eds), *La cultura latina en la Cueva Negra: en agradecimiento y homenaje a los Profs. A. Stylow, M. Mayer e I. Velázquez*, Antigüedad y Cristianismo, 20 (Murcia: Universidad de Murcia), pp. 335–44

Fernández Nieto, F. J. 2003. 'La función de la Cueva de Fortuna: el antro báquico-sabazio y sus antecedentes', in A. González Blanco and G. Matilla (eds), *La cultura latina en la Cueva Negra: en agradecimiento y homenaje a los Profs. A. Stylow, M. Mayer e I. Velázquez*, Antigüedad y Cristianismo, 20 (Murcia: Universidad de Murcia), pp. 437–64

Fernández Ochoa, C., Á. Morillo, and Á. Villa. 2005. 'La torre de Augusto en la Campa Torres (Gijón, Asturias). Las antiguas excavaciones y el epígrafe de Calpurnio Pisón', *AEA*, 78: 129–46

Ferrer Albelda, E. 2012. 'El sustrato púnico en las urbes meridionales: persistencias culturales e identidades cívicas', in J. Santos Yanguas and G. Cruz Andreotti (eds), *Romanización, fronteras y etnias en la Roma Antigua: el caso Hispano* (Vitoria: Universidad del País Vasco), pp. 665–89

Ferrer i Jané, J., J. Velaza, and O. Olesti. 2018. 'Nuevas inscripciones rupestres latinas de Oceja y los *IIIviri* ibéricos de *Iulia Lybica*', *Dialogues d'histoire ancienne*, 44.1: 169–95

Ferrer Maestro, J. J., J. Benedito, J. M. Melchor-Montserrat. 2018. 'A New Impression of the Roman City of Saguntum (Spain) Based on Recent Findings', *Archeologia classica*, 69: 357–78

——. 2019. 'Saguntum: The Remains of an Honorary Arch and Urban Planning outside the City Walls', *European Journal of Archaeology*, 23.1: 43–63

Ferri, G. 2017. 'Brelich e Quirino', *Anabases: Traditions et Réceptions de l'Antiquité*, 25: 179–90

Ferriès M.-C. 2008. 'Les Lupercales, rite urbain et fête populaire. Les avatars d'une célébration séculaire', in G. Bertrand and I. Taddei (eds), *Les destin de rituels: faire corps dans l'espace urbaine; Italie-France-Allemagne* (Rome: École française de Rome), pp. 21–40

——. 2009 'Luperci et Lupercalia de César à Auguste', *Latomus*, 68.2: 373–92

Fincker, M., and F. Tassaux. 1992. 'Les grands sanctuaires "ruraux" d'Aquitaine et le culte impérial', *Mélanges de l'École française de Rome – Antiquité MEFRA*, 104.2: 41–76

Fishwick, D. 1996. 'On the Origins of Africa Proconsularis III: The Era of the Cereres again', *Antiquités africaines*, 32: 13–36

——. 2002. *The Imperial Cult in the Latin West: Studies in the Ruler Cult of the Western Provinces of the Roman Empire*, III.1: *Provincial Cult: Institution and Evolution* (Leiden: Brill)

——. 2004. *The Imperial Cult in the Latin West: Studies in the Ruler Cult of the Western Provinces of the Roman Empire*, III.3: *Provincial Cult: Provincial Centre. Provincial Cult* (Leiden: Brill)

——. 2014. 'Augustus and the Cult of the Emperor', *Studia Historica*, 2nd ser., *Historia Antigua*, 32: 47–60

——. 2017. *Precinct, Temple and Altar in Roman Spain: Studies on the Imperial Monuments at Mérida and Tarragona* (Farnham: Ashgate)

Fita, F., and the Marqués de Hinojares. 1918. 'Informe inédito del R. P. Fita S. J., Director de la Academia [Epigrafía romana y visigótica de Montemolín]', *Boletín de la Real Academia de la Historia*, 72: 152–55

Fitas, A. P. (ed.). 2013. *Cadernos do Endovélico*, I: *Caminhos da identidade* (Lisbon: Edições Colibri)

Flaig, E. 1992. *Den Kaiser herausfordern: Die Usurpationen im römischen Reich* (Frankfurt: Campus)

Fox, E. W. 1971. *History in Geographic Perspective: The Other France* (New York: Norton)

Franco, G. L., and T. J. Gamito. 1997. *Ossonoba: Noventa séculos entre a Terra e o Mar* (Lisbon: Ministério da Cultura), pp. 343–66

Francisco, M. A. de. 1989. *El culto de Mithra en Hispania* (Granada: Editorial Universidad de Granada)

Francisco Casado, A. 1989. *El culto de Mithra en Hispania* (Granada: Universidad de Granada)

Fridh, A. 1990. 'Sacellum, sacrarium, fanum, and Related Terms', in C. Delannoy and S. Teodorsson, *Greek and Latin Studies in Memory of Cajus Fabricius*, Studia Graeca et Latina Gothoburgensia, 54 (Göteborg: Acta Universitatis Gothoburgensis), pp. 173–87

Frija, G. 2019. 'Cultes impériaux et pouvoir impérial: diffusion et circulation des cultes des empereurs dans le monde romain', in F. Cadiou and S. Pittia (eds), *Religion et pouvoir dans le monde romain de 218 avant notre ère à 235 de notre ère: Actes du colloque de la SoPHAU (Bordeaux, 13–15 juin 2019)*, Pallas, 111 (Toulouse: Presses universitaires du Midi), pp. 77–94

Fröhlich, T. 1991. *Lararien- und Fassadenbilder in den Vesuvstädten: Untersuchungen zur 'volkstümlichen' pompejanischen Malerei*, Römische Mitteilungen, Supplement, 32 (Mainz: Von Zabern)

Gabba, E. 1973. *Esercito e società nella tarda repubblica romana* (Florence: La Nuova Italia)

——. 1976. 'Sulla valorizzazione politica della leggenda delle origini troiane di Roma fra III e II sec. a.C.', in M. Sordi (ed.), *I canali della propaganda nel mondo antico* (Milan: Vita e Pensiero), pp. 84–101

Galinsky, K. 1969. *Aeneas, Sicily, and Rome* (Princeton: Princeton University Press)

——. 2007. 'Continuity and Change: Religion in the Augustan Semi-Century', in J. Rüpke (ed.), *A Companion to Roman Religion* (Oxford: Blackwell), pp. 71–82

Gamer, G. 1989. *Formen römischer Altäre auf der Hispanischen Halbinsel*, Madrider Beiträge, 12 (Mainz: Von Zabern)

Gamert-Wallert, I. 1998. 'Una deidad del antiguo Egipto en Itálica', *Revista de Arqueológica*, 206: 6–9

Gamo, E., and J. M. Murciano Calles. 2016–2017 [2020]. 'Una nueva dedicatoria emeritense a Augusto', *Anas*, 29–30: 161–68

Garcia, J. M. 1991. *Religiões antigas de Portugal: aditamentos e observações às 'Religiões da Lusitânia' de J. Leite de Vasconcelos; fontes epigráficas* (Lisbon: Imprensa Nacional)

García, O. 1990. 'Baco en Hispania. Economía y religión a través de las fuentes epigráficas, arqueológicas y literarias' (unpublished doctoral thesis, Universidad Complutense de Madrid)

García Bueno, C. 2015. 'Aspectos constructivos y decorativos de la villa romana de Puente de la Olmilla (Albaladejo, Ciudad Real)', *Lucentum*, 34: 207–30

García Iglesias, L. 1984. 'Notas de epigrafía emeritense. II', *Revista de Estudios Extremeños*, 40: 145–59

García Jurado, F., and I. Velázquez Soriano. 2003. 'Interpretación semántica de *venis infestus et docilis et mobilis* (inscripción nº 31) en el contexto de la Cueva Negra (Fortuna, Murcia)', in A. González Blanco and G. Matilla (eds), *La cultura latina en la Cueva Negra: en agradecimiento y homenaje a los Profs. A. Stylow, M. Mayer e I. Velázquez*, Antigüedad y Cristianismo, 20 (Murcia: Universidad de Murcia), pp. 325–34

García Riaza, E., and M. L. Sánchez León. 2000. *Roma y la municipalización de las Baleares* (Palma: Universitat de les Illes Balears)

García i Roselló, J., A. Martín, and X. Cela. 2000. 'Nuevas aportaciones sobre la romanización en el territorio de *Iluro* (*Hispania Tarraconensis*)', *Empúries*, 52: 137–72

García y Bellido, A. 1943. 'Algunos problemas de arte y cronología ibéricos', *AEA*, 16.50: 78–108

——. 1948. 'El culto a Mithras en la Península Ibérica', *Boletín de la Real Academia de la Historia*, 122: 283–349

——. 1949. *Esculturas romanas de España y Portugal* (Madrid: Consejo Superior de Investigaciones Científicas)

——. 1950. 'Cuatro esculturas romanas inéditas del Museo Arqueológico de Sevilla', *AEA*, 23: 361–70

——. 1952. 'El Mithras Tauroktonos de Cabra (Córdoba)', *AEA*, 25: 289–92

——. 1955. 'Nombres de artistas en la España romana', *AEA*, 28: 3–19

——. 1963. 'Das Artemision von Sagunt', *Madrider Mitteilungen*, 4: 87–98

——. 1967. *Les religions orientales dans l'Espagne romaine*, Études préliminaires aux religions orientales dans l'Empire romain, 5 (Leiden: Brill)

García-Bellido, M. P. 1991. 'Las religiones orientales en la Península Ibérica: documentos numismáticos, I', *AEA*, 64: 37–81

——. 1993. 'Las cecas libio–fenicias', in *Numismática hispano-púnica: estado actual de la investigación. VII Jornadas de Arqueologia fenicio-punica (Eivissa, 1992)* (Ibiza: Govern Balear. Conselleria de Cultura Educació i Esports), pp. 67–146

——. 2001. '*Lucus Feroniae emeritensis*', *AEA*, 74: 53–71

García-Bellido, M. P., and C. Blázquez. 2001. *Diccionario de cecas y de pueblos hispánicos* (Madrid: Consejo Superior de Investigaciones Científicas)

García-Cardiel, J. 2015a. 'El Cerro de los Santos: paisaje, negociación social y ritualidad entre el mundo ibérico y el hispano', *AEA*, 88: 85–104

——. 2015b. 'Pebeteros en la costa. Santuarios, peregrinaciones y rituales en la Contestania ibérica (ss. III–II a.C.)', *Zephyrus*, 76: 77–98

García-Dils de la Vega, S., S. Ordóñez, and O. Rodríguez. 2007. 'Nuevo templo augusteo en la Colonia Augusta Firma Astigi (Écija, Sevilla)', *Romula*, 6: 75–114

García-Sandoval, E. 1969. 'El mosaico comogónico de Mérida', *Boletin del Seminario de Estudios de Arte y de Arqueologia*, 34–35: 9–29

Garrido, A., R. Mar, and M. Martins. 2008. *A fonte do Ídolo: análise, interpretação e reconstituição do santuario*, Bracara Augusta, – Excavaciones arqueológicas, 4 (Braga: Unidade de Arqueología da Universidade do Minho)

Garriguet, J. A. 2007. 'La decoración escultórica del templo romano de las calles Claudio–Marcelo–Capitulares y su entorno (Córdoba). Revisión y novedades', in T. Nogales and J. González Fernández (eds), *Culto imperial: política y poder; actas del Congreso Internacional Culto Imperial; política y poder; Mérida, Museo Nacional de Arte Romano, 18–20 de mayo, 2006* (Rome: L'Erma di Bretschneider), pp. 299–321

Gasca, J., A. Solís, and S. Viana. 2003. 'Preinforme del estado de conservación de las inscripcions de la Cueva Negra', in A. González Blanco and G. Matilla (eds), *La cultura latina en la Cueva Negra: en agradecimiento y homenaje a los Profs. A. Stylow, M. Mayer e I. Velázquez*, Antigüedad y Cristianismo, 20 (Murcia: Universidad de Murcia), pp. 387–402

Gasparini, V. 2020. 'Renewing the Past. Rufinus' Appropriation of the Sacred Site of Panóias (Vila Real, Portugal)', in V. Gasparini, M. Patzelt, R. Raja, A.-K. Rieger, J. Rüpke, and E. Urciuoli (eds), *Lived Religion in the Ancient Mediterranean World* (Berlin: De Gruyter), pp. 319–50

Gasperini, L. 1992a. *RVPES LOQVENTES: Atti del Convegno internazionale di studio sulle iscrizioni rupestri di età romana in Italia; Roma–Bomarzo 13–15. X. 1989*, Studi pubblicati dall'Istituto Italiano per la Storia Antica, 53 (Rome: Istituto Italiano per la Storia Antica)

——. 1992b. 'Sul complesso ipogeico cluniense della Cueva de Román e le sue iscrizioni', *Miscellanea greca e romana*, 17: 283–96

——. 1998. 'Sobre el hipogeo cluniense de la Cueva de Román y sus inscripciones', in J. Mangas and J. Alvar (eds), *Homenaje a J. M.ª Blázquez*, v (Linares: Centro de Estudios Linarenses), pp. 161–82

Geertz, C. 1983. *Local Knowledge: Further Essays in Interpretative Anthropology* (New York: Basic Books)

Giacobello, F. 2008. *Larari pompeiani: Iconografia e culto dei Lari in ambito domestico* (Milan: LED)

Gimeno, H. 1997. 'El "peñasco" de Alange (Badajoz) (CIL II 1024)', *Revista de Estudios Extremeños*, 53: 15–29

——. 2003. 'La sociedad de Munigua a través de sus inscripciones', in S. Armani, B. Hurlet-Martineau, and A. U. Stylow (eds), *Epigrafía y sociedad en Hispania durante el Alto Imperio: estructuras y relaciones sociales; actas de la mesa redonda organizada por la Casa de Velázquez, el Centro CIL II de la Universidad de Alcalá y L'Année épigraphique Madrid–Alcalá de Henares, 10–11 de abril de 2000; Acta Antiqua Complutensia IV (Alcalá 2003)* (Alcalá de Henares: Universidad de Alcalá), pp. 177–92

G.I.P. (Grup d'Investigació Prehistòrica). 2005. 'Dos hogares orientalizantes de la fortaleza de Els Vilars (Arbeca, Lleida)', in S. Celestino and J. Jiménez (eds), *El periodo orientalizante: actas del III Simposio Internacional de Arqueología de Mérida; Protohistoria del Mediterráneo Occidental*, 1, Anejos de AEspA, 35 (Merida: Consejo Superior de Investigaciones Científicas), p. 651

Giral, F. 2006. 'El lobo en las acuñaciones de Iltirta. Imagen monetaria de un mito', *Pyrenae*, 37: 71–82

Glinister, F. 1997. 'What Is a Sanctuary?', *Cahiers du Centre Gustave Glotz*, 8: 61–80

Gnade, M. 2002. *Satricum in the Post-Archaic Period: A Case Study of the Interpretation of Archaeological Remains as Indicators of Ethno-cultural Identity*, Satricum, 6 (Leuven: Peeters)

Goffaux, B. 2004. 'Le culte au Génie de la cité dans la péninsule ibérique romaine', *Pallas*, 66: 157–79

——. 2006. 'Formes d'organisation de culte dans la Colonia Augusta Emerita (Lusitanie)', in M. Dondin-Payre and M.-T. Raepsaet-Charlier (eds), *Sanctuaires, pratiques cultuelles et territoires civiques dans l'Occident romain* (Brussels: Le Livre Timperman), pp. 51–97

Gomes, F. B. 2012. *Aspectos do sagrado na colonização fenícia: contextos de culto de influência oriental na Idade do Ferro do Sul de Portugal (séculos VIII–III a.n.e.)* (Lisbon: Centro de Arqueologia da Universidade de Lisboa)

Gomes, M. V., and C. T. Silva. 1994. 'Garvão. Un sanctuaire protohistorique du sud du Portugal', *Les Dossiers d'Archéologie*, 198: 34–39

Gómez Espelosín, F., A. Pérez Largacha, and M. Vallejo Girvés. 1995. *La imagen de España en la antigüedad clásica* (Madrid: Gredos)

Gómez Moreno, M. 1949. *Misceláneas: historia-arte-arqueología; primera serie; la antigüedad* (Madrid: Consejo Superior de Investigaciones Científicas. Instituto Diego Velazquez)

Gómez Pallarés, J. 1995. 'Initia de los carmina latina Epigraphica Hispania (Conventus Tarraconensis) I', *Faventia*, 17.1: 67–86

González Fernández, J. 1988. 'The First Oath *pro Salute Augusti* Found in Betica', *ZPE*, 72: 113–27

——. 1996. 'Mansio Mons Mariorum (*It. Ant.* 432.4)', *Habis*, 27: 83–95

——. 2007. 'El origen del culto imperial en la Bética según la documentación epigráfica', in T. Nogales and J. González Fernández (eds), *Culto Imperial: política y poder; actas del Congreso Internacional Culto Imperial; política y poder; Mérida, Museo Nacional de Arte Romano, 18–20 de mayo, 2006* (Rome: L'Erma di Bretschneider), pp. 173–89

González Fernández, J., and J. Arce (eds). 1988. *Estudios sobre la Tabula Siarensis*, Anejos de *Archivo Español de Arqueologia*, 9 (Madrid: Consejo Superior de Investigaciones Científicas), pp. 307–15

González Blanco, A. 1996 [1999]. 'Los calcos de los *tituli* en las sucesivas etapas del trabajo e investigación', in A. González Blanco, M. Mayer, A. U. Stylow, and R. González Fernández (eds), *El balneario romano y la Cueva Negra de Fortuna (Murcia): Homenaje al prof. Ph. Rahtz*, Antigüedad y Cristianismo, 13 (Murcia: Universidad de Murcia), pp. 323–60

——. 2003. 'Los calcos de los *tituli* en las sucesivas etapas del trabajo e investigación', in A. González Blanco and G. Matilla (eds), *La cultura latina en la Cueva Negra: en agradecimiento y homenaje a los Profs. A. Stylow, M. Mayer e I. Velázquez*, Antigüedad y Cristianismo, 20 (Murcia: Universidad de Murcia), pp. 275–312

González Blanco, A., M. Mayer, and A. U. Stylow. 1987. *La Cueva Negra de Fortuna (Murcia) y sus tituli picti: un santuario de época romana; homenaje al profesor D. Sebastián Mariner Bigorra*, Antigüedad y Cristianismo, 4 (Murcia: Universidad de Murcia)

——. 1993. 'La Cueva Negra (Fortuna, Murcia). Memoria-informe de los trabajos realizados en la campaña de 1989', *I Jornadas sobre Arqueología de la Región de Murcia, tenida en Murcia en mayo de 1990, Memorias de Arqueología*, 1989: 149–52

González Blanco, A., M. Amante, P. Rahtz, and L. Watts. 1996. 'Primer acercamiento a los restos arqueológicos del balneario romano', in A. González Blanco, M. Mayer, A. U. Stylow, and R. González Fernández (eds), *El balneario romano y la Cueva Negra de Fortuna (Murcia): Homenaje al prof. Ph. Rahtz*, Antigüedad y Cristianismo, 13 (Murcia: Universidad de Murcia), pp. 153–78

González Blanco, A., M. Mayer, A. U. Stylow, and R. González Fernández (eds). 1996 [1999]. *El balneario romano y la Cueva Negra de Fortuna (Murcia): Homenaje al prof. Ph. Rahtz*, Antigüedad y Cristianismo, 13 (Murcia: Universidad de Murcia)

González Blanco, A., R. González Fernández, M. Mayer, and I. Velázquez Soriano. 2002. 'Últimas lecturas en la Cueva Negra (Fortuna, Murcia), mayo de 1995', in *VII Jornadas de arqueología en Murcia, Memorias de Arqueología 10. Séptimas Jornadas de Arqueología Regional 14–17 de mayo 1996* (Murcia: Servicio de Patrimonio Histórico), pp. 241–46

González Blanco, A., and G. Matilla (eds). 2003. *La cultura latina en la Cueva Negra: en agradecimiento y homenaje a los Profs. A. Stylow, M. Mayer e I. Velázquez*, Antigüedad y Cristianismo, 20 (Murcia: Universidad de Murcia)

González Fernández, R. 2003. 'La diosa fortuna. Relaciones con las aguas y los militares. El caso particular del balneario de Fortuna (Murcia)', in A. González Blanco and G. Matilla (eds), *La cultura latina en la Cueva Negra: en agradecimiento y homenaje a los Profs. A. Stylow, M. Mayer e I. Velázquez*, Antigüedad y Cristianismo, 20 (Murcia: Universidad de Murcia), pp. 373–86

González Fernández, R., G. Matilla, and F. Fernández Matallana. 1996. 'La recuperación arqueológica del balneario romano de Fortuna', in A. González Blanco, M. Mayer, A. U. Stylow, and R. González Fernández (eds), *El balneario romano y la Cueva Negra de Fortuna (Murcia): homenaje al prof. Ph. Rahtz*, Antigüedad y Cristianismo, 13 (Murcia: Universidad de Murcia), pp. 179–220

González Herrero, M. 2015. *La implantación del culto imperial de la provincia en Hispania*, Roman Archaeology, 11 (Oxford: Archaeopress)

González Román, C. 2010. 'Romanos e itálicos en la Hispania republicana', in L. Pons Pujol (ed.), *Hispania et Gallia: dos provincias del Occidente romano* (Barcelona: Universitat de Barcelona), pp. 13–32

Gordon, R. 1990. 'The Veil of the Power: Emperors, Sacrificers and Benefactors', in J. North and M. Beard (eds), *Pagan Priests: Religion and Power in the Ancient World* (London: Duckworth), pp. 199–232

——. 1996. *Image and Value in the Graeco-Roman World: Studies in Mithraism and Religious Art* (Aldershot: Variorum)

——. 2011. 'The Roman Imperial Cult and the Question of Power', in J. North and S. Price (eds), *The Religious History of the Roman Empire: Pagans, Jews and Christians* (Oxford: Oxford University Press), pp. 37–70

Gorges, J.-G., and F. G. Rodríguez Martín. 2011. 'Le territoire antique de Mérida: un état de la question du *territorium emeritense*', in J. M. Álvarez Martínez and P. Mateos Cruz (eds), *1910–2010: El yacimiento emeritense; actas del congreso internacional* (Merida: Ayuntamiento de Mérida), pp. 267–90

Gorrochategui, J. 1987. 'En torno a la clasificación del Lusitano', in *Actas del IV Coloquio sobre Lenguas y Culturas Paleohispanicas (Vitoria, 1985)*, Studia Paleohispanica, Veleia, 2–3 (Vitoria-Gasteiz: Instituto de Ciencias de la Antigüedad), pp. 77–91

Gozalbes García, H. 2019. 'El origen de la imagen del toro en la moneda provincial hispana: propaganda religioso-castrense en las emisiones de la *Colonia Iulia Victrix Lepida* (Velilla del Ebro, Zaragoza) (44–36 aC)', *Pyrenae*, 50.2: 29–54

Gozalbes, M. 2006a. 'Jinetes sin escudo. Las representaciones ecuestres en la Citerior', *Numisma*, 250: 295–317

——. 2006b. 'Las emisiones de la Citerior y su vertiente religiosa', in *Moneda, cultes i ritus* (Barcelona: Museu nacional d'art de Catalunya), pp. 111–30

——. 2012. 'Divinitats i herois a les emissions iberes i celtiberes de la Citerior', in M. Campo (ed.), *Déus i mites de l'antiguitat: l'evidència de la moneda d'Hispània* (Barcelona: Museu Nacional d'Art de Catalunya), pp. 46–51

Gradel, I. 2002. *Emperor Worship and Roman Religion* (Oxford: Clarendon)

Grandazzi, A. 2008. *Alba Longa, histoire d'une légende: recherches sur l'archéologie, la religion, les traditions de l'ancien Latium* (Rome: Publications de l'école française de Rome)

Grau, I. 2016. 'Forging Communities: Coalitions, Identity Symbols and Ritual Practices in Iron Age Eastern Iberia', *World Archaeology*, 48.1: 110–24

Grau, I., and I. Amorós. 2017. 'Los santuarios del área central de la Contestania en tiempos de la implantación romana', in T. Tortosa and S. Ramallo (eds), *El tiempo final de los santuarios ibéricos en los procesos de impacto y consolidación del mundo romano*, Anejos de *Archivo Español de Arqueología*, 79 (Madrid: Consejo Superior de Investigaciones Científicas), pp. 75–92

Grau, I., I. Amorós, and J. M. Segura. 2017. *El santuario ibérico y romano de La Serreta: prácticas rituales y paisaje en el área central de la Contestania* (Alcoi: Publicaciones del Museu d'Alcoi)

Grau, I., I. Amorós, M. P. de Miguel, P. Iborra, and J. M. Segura. 2015. 'Fundar la casa: prácticas rituales y espacio doméstico en el *oppidum* ibérico de El Puig d'Alcoi (Alacant)', *Archivo Español de Arqueología*, 88: 67–84

Grau, I., and C. Rueda. 2018. 'La religión en las sociedades iberas: una visión panorámica', *Revista de Historiografía*, 28: 47–72

Gros, P. 1991. 'Les autels des Caesares et leur signification dans l'espace urbain des villes julio-claudiennes', in R. Étienne and M. T. Le Dinahet (eds), *L'Espace sacrificiel dans les civilisations méditerranéennes de l'Antiquité (actes du colloque tenu à la Maison de l'Orient, Lyon, 4–7 juin 1988)* (Paris: De Boccard), pp. 179–86

——. 2006. *L'architecture romaine*, II: *Maisons, palais, villas et tombeaux*, 2nd edn (Paris: Picard)

Gruel, K., V. Bernollin, and V. Brouquier-Reddé. 2008. 'Les sanctuaires, éléments structurels du territoire antique', in R. Compatangelo-Sussignan, J. R. Bertrand, J. Chapman, and P. Y. Laffont (eds), *Marqueurs des paysages et systèmes socio-économiques* (Rennes: Presses Universitaires de Rennes), pp. 35–44

Grüner, A. 2005. 'Die Altäre des L. Sestius Quirinalis bei Kap Finisterre. Zum geopolitischen Konstruktion des Römischen Herrschaftsraums', *Madrider Mitteilungen*, 46: 246–66

Guerra, A. 2008. 'La documentation épigraphique sur Endouellicus et les nouvelles recherches dans son sanctuaire à S. Miguel da Mota', in R. Häussler and A. C. King (eds), *Continuity and Innovation in Religion in the Roman West*, II, JRA Supplementary Series, 67 (Portsmouth, RI: Journal of Roman Archaeology), pp. 159–67

Guerra, A., T. Schattner, C. Fabião, and R. Almeida. 2003. 'Novas investigações no santuário de Endovélico (S. Miguel da Mota, Alandroal): a campanha de 2002', *Revista Portuguesa de Arqueologia*, 6.2: 415–79

——. 2005. 'São Miguel da Motta (Alandroal/Portugal) 2002. Bericht über die Ausgrabungen im Heiligtum des Endovellicus', *Madrider Mitteilungen*, 46: 184–234

Gusi, F., and S. Muriel, 2008. 'Panorama actual de la investigación de las inhumaciones infantiles en la protohistoria del sudoeste mediterráneo europeo', in F. Gusi, S. Muriel, and C. R. Olaria (eds), *Nasciturus: infans, puerulus, vobis mater terra; la muerte en la infancia* (Castellón: Diputació de Castelló. Servei d'Investigacions Arqueològiques i Prehistòriques), pp. 257–329

Gutsfeld A., A. Lichtenberger, T. G. Schattner, H. Schnorbusch, and D. Wigg-Wolf. 2019. 'Prozesse der Romanisierung', in T. G. Schattner, D. Vieweger, and D. Wigg-Wolf (eds), *Kontinuität und Diskontinuität, Prozesse der Romanisierung: Fallstudien zwischen Iberischer Halbinsel und Vorderem Orient; Ergebnisse der gemeinsamen Treffen der Arbeitsgruppen 'Kontinuität und Diskontinuität: Lokale Traditionen und römische Herrschaft im Wandel' und 'Geld eint, Geld trennt'* (Rahden: Leidorf), pp. 193–99

Hahn, H. P. 2008. 'Diffusionism, Appropriation, and Globalization. Some Remarks on Current Debates in Anthropology', *Anthropos*, 103: 191–202

Halbwachs, M. 1971. *La topographie légendaire des évangiles en Terre Sainte* (Paris: Presses Universitaires de France)

Haley, E. W. 1991. *Migration and Economy in Roman Imperial Spain*, Aurea Saecula (Barcelona: Publicacions Universitat de Barcelona)

Hard, G. 2003. 'Eine "Raum"-Klärung für aufgeweckte Studenten. Dimensionen geographischen Denkens, Aufsätze zur Theorie der Geographie 2', *Osnabrücker Studien zur Geographie*, 2003: 15–30

Hartog, F. 2001. *Memories of Odysseus: Frontier Tales from Ancient Greece*, trans. by Janet Lloyd. (Edinburgh: Edinburgh University Press; original edn: Paris: Éditions Gallimard, 1996)

Häussler, R. 1999. 'Architecture, Performance and Ritual: The Role of State Architecture in the Roman Empire', in P. Baker, C. Forcey, S. Jundi, and R. Witcher (eds), *TRAC 98: Proceedings of the Eighth Annual Theoretical Roman Archaeology Conference, Leicester 1998* (Oxford: Oxbow), pp. 1–13

—— (ed.). 2008a. *Romanisation et épigraphie: études interdisciplinaires sur l'acculturation et l'identité dans l'Empire romain* (Montagnac: Monique Mergoil)

——. 2008b. 'Signes de la "romanisation" à travers l'épigraphie: possibilités d'interprétations et problèmes méthodologiques', in R. Häussler (ed.), *Romanisation et épigraphie: études interdisciplinaires sur l'acculturation et l'identité dans l'Empire romain* (Montagnac: Monique Mergoil), pp. 9–30

——. 2012. '*Interpretatio indigena*. Re-inventing Local Cults in a Global World', *Mediterraneo Antico*, 15.1–2: 143–74

Häussler, R., and G. F. Chiai (eds). 2019. *Sacred Landscapes in Antiquity: Creation, Transformation and Manipulation* (Oxford: Oxbow)

Heras, F. J. 2018. 'El territorio de *Augusta Emerita* un siglo antes de su fundación', in J. C. López Díaz, J. Jiménez Ávila, and F. Palma García (eds), *Historia de Mérida*, I: *De los antecedentes de Augusta Emerita al fin del medievo* (Mérida: Consorcio de la Ciudad Monumental, Histórico-Artística y Arqueológica de Mérida), pp. 269–310

Heras, F. J., M. Bustamente, and J. A. Aranda. 2012. 'Figurillas femeninas en hueso. Función y contexto de un tipo particular de amuleto romano en Lusitania', *Habis*, 43: 177–212

Hermanns, M. H. 2004. *Licht und Lampen im westgriechischen Alltag: Beleuchtungsgerät des 6.–3. Jhs. v. Chr. in Selinunt*, Internationale Archäologie, 87 (Rahden: Leidorf)

Hernández Pérez, R. 2007. 'Los tituli picti de la Cueva Negra de Fortuna (Murcia)', *Epigraphica*, 69: 287–320

Hernández Pérez, R., and X. Gómez Font. 2006. *Carmina Latina epigraphica Carthaginis Novae* (València: Universitat de València)

Hernández-Hervás, E. 2004. 'Evolución del urbanismo antiguo en la ciudad de Sagunto', in P. P. Ripollès and M. del M. Llorens (eds), *Arse-Saguntum: Historia monetaria de la ciudad y su territorio* (Sagunto: Fundación Bancaja), pp. 113–22

Hernández-Hervás, E., M. López Piñol, and I. Pascual Buyé. 1996. 'La implantación del circo en el área suburbana de Saguntum', *Saguntum*, 29: 221–30

Herzig, H. E. 2006. 'Novum genus hominum: Phänomene der Migratione im römischen Heer', in E. Olshausen and H. Sonnabend (eds), *Troianer sind wir gewesen Migrationen in der antiken Welt: Stuttgarter Kolloquium zur Historischen Geographie des Altertums*, 8 2002 (Stuttgart: Steiner), pp. 325–28

Hidalgo Martín, L. Á., and J. J. Chamizo. 2012–2013 [2018]. 'Una posible *mensa* sacra circular dedicada por un soldado (o varios) de la *Legio VII Gemina* en *Augusta Emerita*', *Anas*, 25–26: 247–60

Hild, J. A. 1896. 'Fortuna', in C. V. Daremberg and E. Saglio (eds), *Dictionnaire des Antiquités Grecques et Romains d'après les textes et les monuments*, II.2 (Paris: Hachette), pp. 1264–77

Hingley, R. 2005. *Globalizing Roman Culture: Unity, Diversity and Empire* (London: Psychology Press)

——. 2011. 'Globalization and the Roman Empire: The Genealogy of "Empire" Sémata', *Ciencias Sociais e Humanidades*, 23: 99–113

Hitchner, R. B. 2008. 'Globalization avant la lettre: Globalization and the History of the Roman Empire', *New Global Studies*, 2.2: article 2

Hobsbawm, E. 1983. 'Introduction: Inventing Traditions', in E. Hobsbawm and T. Ranger (eds), *The Invention of Tradition* (Cambridge: Cambridge University Press), pp. 1–14

Hobsbawm, E., and T. Ranger (eds). 1983. *The Invention of Tradition* (Cambridge: Cambridge University Press)

Hölkeskamp, K.-J. 2017. *Libera res publica: Die politische Kultur des antiken Rom; Positionen und Perspektiven* (Stuttgart: Steiner)

——. 2018. '*Memoria* by Multiplication: The *Cornelii Scipiones* in Monumental Multiplication', in K. Sandberg and C. Smith (eds), '*Omnium annalium monumenta*': *Historical Writing and Historical Evidence in Republican Rome* (Leiden: Brill), pp. 422–76

Hopkins, K. 1978. *Conquerors and Slaves* (Cambridge: Cambridge University Press)

Horden, P., and N. Purcell. 2000. *The Corrupting Sea: A Study of Mediterranean History* (Oxford: Blackwell)

Horsfall, N. M. 1987. 'The Aeneas-Legend from Homer to Virgil', in J. N. Bremmer and N. M. Horsfall (eds), *Roman Myth and Mythography* (London: Institute of Classical Studies), pp. 12–24

Houten, P. H. A. 2021. *Urbanisation in Roman Spain and Portugal: 'Civitates Hispaniae' in the Early Empire* (Abingdon: Routledge)

Howgego, C., V. Heuchert, and A. Burnett (eds). 2005. *Coinage and Identity in the Roman Provinces* (Oxford: Oxford University Press)

Hoz, J. de. 1995. 'Panorama provisional de la epigrafía rupestre paleohispánica', in A. Rodríguez Colmenero and L. Gasperini (eds), '*Saxa scripta*' (*inscripciones en roca*): *actas del Simposio Internacional Ibero-Itálico sobre epigrafía rupestre*, Anejos de Larouco, 2 (A Coruña: Ediciós do Castro), pp. 9–33

Hoz, M. P. de. 2014. 'Santuário do Alto da Vigia (Colares, Sintra)', in M. P. de Hoz, *Inscripciones griegas de España y Portugal*, Bibliotheca Archaelogica Hispana, 40 (Madrid: Real Academia de la Historia), pp. 360–61

Hurlet, F. 2002. 'Le consensus et la concordie en Occident (I$^{er}$.-III$^{e}$. siècles apr. J.-C.). Réflexions sur la diffusion de l'idéologie impériale', in H. Inglebert (ed.), *Idéologies et valeurs civiques dans le monde romain. Hommage à Claude Lepelley* (Paris: Picard), pp. 163–78

Hurtado, T. 2013. 'Las emisiones monetarias de la Colonia Victrix Iulia Lepida-Celsa' (unpublished doctoral thesis, Universidad de Valencia)

Iglesias Gil, J. M. 1986. '*Genius Turgalensis*', in C. Chaparro Gómez (ed.), *Primeras Jornadas sobre Manifestaciones religiosas en la Lusitania* (Cáceres: Universidad de Extremadura), pp. 127–32

——. 2019. 'El protagonismo de Augusto y sus viajes a Hispania: de las guerras cántabras al proceso de fundación y promoción de las ciudades', in J. I. San Vicente González de Aspuru, C. Cortés-Bárcena, and E. González González (eds), *Hispania et Roma: estudios en homenaje al profesor Narciso Santos Yanguas* (Oviedo: Universidad de Oviedo), pp. 315–26

Inês Vaz, J. L. 1995. 'Algumas inscrições rupestres da *civitas* de Viseu', in A. Rodríguez Colmenero and L. Gasperini (eds), '*Saxa scripta*' *(inscripciones en roca): actas del Simposio Internacional Ibero-Itálico sobre epigrafía rupestre*, Anejos de *Larouco*, 2 (A Coruña: Ediciós do Castro), pp. 279–95

Jaczinowska, J. 1989. 'Une religion de la loyauté au débuts de l'Empire romain', *Dialogues d'Historie Ancienne*, 15.2: 159–78

Jaeggi, O. 1996. 'El helenismo en la Península Ibérica y algunas reflexiones sobre el helenismo en las periferias: el ejemplo de los santuarios', in *Actas del XXIII Congreso Nacional de Arqueología (Elche, 1995)* (Elche: Ayuntamiento de Elche), pp. 427–32

Jarrett, M. G. 1971. 'Decurions and Priests', *American Journal of Philology*, 92: 513–38

Jimeno Martínez, A. 2011. 'Las ciudades celtibéricas de la Meseta Oriental', *Complutum*, 22.2: 223–76

Jiménez, A., O. Rodríguez, and R. Izquierdo. 2013. 'Novedades arqueológicas adrianeas en el teatro de Itálica y su entorno', in R. Hidalgo and P. León (eds), *Roma, Tibur, Baetica: Investigaciones Adrianeas* (Seville: Universidad de Sevilla), pp. 271–91

Jiménez Díez, A. 2015. 'The Western Empire and the "People without History". A Case Study from Southern Iberia', in K. Galinsky and K. Lapatin (eds), *Cultural Memories in the Roman Empire* (Los Angeles: Getty Publications), pp. 170–90

Jiménez Salvador, J. L., and M. Martín-Bueno. 1992. *La Casa del Mitra* (Cabra: Delegación de Cultura del Ayuntamiento)

Jodin, A. 1975. *Recherches sur la metrologie du Maroc punique et hellénistique* (Tangier: Editions Marocaines et Internationales)

Johnston, A. 2017. *The Sons of Remus: Identity in Roman Gaul and Spain* (Cambridge, MA: Harvard University Press)

Jones, H. J. (trans.). 1923. *Strabo: Geography*, II: *Books 3–5*, Loeb Classical Library, 50 (Cambridge, MA: Harvard University Press)

Jones, S. 1997. *The Archaeology of Ethnicity: Constructing Identities in the Past and Present* (London: Routledge)

Jordan, H. 1879. 'Über die Ausdrücke, aedes, templum, fanum, delubrum', *Hermes*, 14: 567–83

Jordán Montés, P. F. 1992. 'Prospección arqueológica en la comarca de Hellín-Tobarra', *Al-Basit: Revista de Estudios Albacetenses*, 31: 183–227

Juan Castelló, J. 2005. 'La celebración del *Natalis Vrbis* en Cales Coves (Menorca): ritual y oficiantes', paper presented at: *Congrés Internacional d'Història de les Religions Homo Religiosus. Mediadores con lo divino en el mundo mediterráneo antiguo. Palma de Mallorca, Centre de Cultura Fundació 'Sa Nostra'. 13–15 octubre 2005*, pp. 747–70 <http://diposit.ub.edu/dspace/handle/2445/112045> [accessed 8 August 2020]

Kantirea, M. 2007. *Les dieux et les dieux Augustes: le culte impérial en Grèce sous les Julio-claudiens et les Flaviens: études épigraphiques et archéologiques* (Athens: Centre de Recherche de l'Antiquité grecque et romaine)

——. 2011. 'Étude comparative de l'introduction du culte impérial à Pergame, à Athènes et à Éphèse', in P. I. Panagiotis, A. Chankowski, and C. C. Lorber (eds), *More than Men, Less than Gods: Studies on Royal Cult and Imperial Worship; Proceedings of the International Colloquium Organized by the Belgian School at Athens* (Leuven: Peeters), pp. 521–51

Keay, S. 1988. *Roman Spain* (Berkeley: University of California Press)

——. 1990. 'Processes in the Development of the Coastal Communities of Hispania Citerior in the Republican Period', in T. Blagg and M. Millett (eds), *The Early Roman Empire in the West* (Oxford: Oxbow), pp. 120–50

—— (ed.). 1998. *The Archaeology of Early Roman Baetica*, JRA Supplementary Series, 29 (Portsmouth, RI: Journal of Roman Archaeology)

——. 2001. 'Romanization and the Hispaniae', in S. Keay and N. Terrenato (eds), *Italy and the West: Comparative Issues in Romanization* (Oxford: Oxbow), pp. 117–44

——. 2003. 'Recent Archaeological Work in Roman Iberia (1990–2002)', *JRS*, 93: 146–211

Knust, J. W., and Z. Várhelyi (eds). 2011. *Ancient Mediterranean Sacrifice* (Oxford: Oxford University Press)

Koch, J. T., and B. Cunliffe (eds). 2013. *Celtic from the West*, II: *Rethinking the Bronze Age and the Arrival of Indo-European in Atlantic Europe* (Oxford: Oxbow)

—— (eds). 2016. *Celtic from the West*, III: *Atlantic Europe in the Metal Ages: Questions of Shared Language* (Oxford: Oxbow)

Koch, M. 2019. *Die epigraphische Hinterlassenschaft des römisch-keltischen Heiligtums auf dem Monte do Facho (O Hío/Cangas, Galicien) – El legado epigráfico del santuario céltico–romano en el Monte do Facho (O Hío/Cangas, Galicia)*, Madrider Beiträge, 38.2 (Wiesbaden: Reichert)

Koppel, E.-M. 1990. 'Relieves arquitectónicos de Tarragona', in W. Trillmich and P. Zanker (eds), *Stadtbild und Ideologie: Die Monumentalisierung hispanischer Städte zwischen Republik und Kaiserzeit* (Munich: Verlag der Bayerischen Akademie der Wissenschaften), pp. 327–39

Koortbojian, M. 2013. *The Divinization of Caesar and Augustus: Precedents, Consequences, Implications* (Cambridge: Cambridge University Press)

Kuckenburg, M. 2004. *Die Kelten in Mitteleuropa* (Stuttgart: Konrad Theiss)

La Rocca, E. 2011. 'Il Foro di Augusto e le provincie dell'Impero', in T. Nogales Basarrate and I. Rodá (eds), *Roma y las provincias: modelo y difusión* (Rome: L'Erma di Bretschneider), pp. 991–1010

Lambrino, S. 1951. 'Le dieu lusitanien Endovellicus', *Bulletin des Études Portugaises*, n.s., 15: 93–147

Lancel, S. 1973. 'Lachau. Informations Archéologiques circonscription Rhône-Alpes', *Gallia*, 31.2: 534–35

Lapuente, P., T. Nogales, H. Royo, and M. Brilli. 2014. 'White Marble Sculptures from the National Museum of Roman Art (Mérida, Spain): Sources of Local and Imported Marbles', *European Journal of Mineralogy*, 26: 333–54

León Alonso, M. P. 1995. *Esculturas de Itálica* (Seville: Consejería de Cultura de Andalucía)

Le Gall, J. 1985. 'Le serment à l'empereur: une base méconnue de la tyrannie impériale sous le Haut-Empire', *Latomus*, 44: 767–83

Le Roux, P. 1995. 'L'émigration italique en Citérieure et Lusitanie jusqu'à la mort de Néron', in F. Beltrán (ed.), *Roma y el nacimiento de la cultura epigráfica en occidente: actas del Coloquio Roma y las Primeras Culturas Epigráficas del Occidente Mediterráneo siglos II a.E.–I d.E., Zaragoza, 4 a 6 de noviembre de 1992*, Publicación de la Institución Fernando el Católico 1684 (Zaragoza: Institución Fernando el Católico), pp. 85–95

———. 2006. 'Les dévotions des gouverneurs de province dans la Péninsule Ibérique au Haut-Empire romain', in A. Vigourt, X. Loriot, A. Bérenger-Badel, and B. Klein (eds), *Pouvoir et religion dans le monde romain, en hommage à Jean-Pierre Martin* (Paris: Presses de l'Université de Paris-Sorbonne), pp. 367–85

———. 2007. 'Statio Lucensis', in J. Dalaison (ed.), *Espaces et pouvoirs dans l'antiquité de l'Anatolie à la Gaule: hommages à Bernard Rémy* (Grenoble: CRHIPA), pp. 371–82

———. 2019. 'L. A. S. sur une *arula* de Mérida de Lusitanie: le *votum* d'un *miles leg. VII G. F.*', *Epigraphica*, 81: 676–83

Letzner, W. 1992. *Römische Brunnen und Nymphaea in der westlichen Reichshälfte*, Charybdis, 2 (Münster: Lit)

Leveau, P. 1983. 'La ville antique et l'organisation de l'espace rural: villa, ville, village', *Annales: Histoire, Sciences Sociales*, 38.4: 920–42

Lichtermann, P., R. Raja, A.-K. Rieger, and J. Rüpke. 2017. 'Grouping Together in Lived Ancient Religion: Individual Interacting and the Formation of Groups', *Religion in the Roman Empire*, 3.1: 3–10

Ligt, L. de. 1993. *Fairs and Markets in the Roman Empire* (Amsterdam: Gieben)

Ligt, L. de, and L. E. Tacoma (eds). 2016. *Migration and Mobility in the Early Roman Empire* (Leiden: Brill)

Lillo, P. A. 1991–1992. 'Los exvotos de bronce del Santuario de La Luz y su contexto arqueológico', *Anales de Prehistoria y Arqueología*, 7–8: 107–42

———. 1995–1996. 'El Peribolos del templo del Santuario de La Luz y el contexto de la cabeza marmórea de la diosa', *Anales de Prehistoria y Arqueología*, 11–12: 95–128

Llobregat, E., E. Cortell, J. Juan, and J. M. Segura. 1992. 'El urbanismo ibérico en La Serreta', *Recerques del Museu d'Alcoi*, 1: 37–70

Llorens, M. del M. 2002. 'Las imágenes', in P. P. Ripollès and M. del M. Llorens (eds), *Arse-Saguntum: historia monetaria de la ciudad y su territorio* (Sagunto: Fundación Bancaja), pp. 63–120

Loidi, J. 2017. 'Introduction to the Iberian Peninsula, General Features: Geography, Geology, Name, Brief History, Land Use and Conservation', in J. Loidi (ed.), *The Vegetation of the Iberian Peninsula* (Cham: Springer), pp. 3–27

López, E., and A. M. Niveau de Villedary. 2014. 'Acerca de un pebetero indígena del Cortijo de La Negra (El Puerto de Santa María, Cádiz)', in Mª C. Marín and A. M. Jiménez (eds), *Imagen y culto en la Iberia prerromana, II: Nuevas lecturas sobre los pebeteros en forma de cabeza femenina* (Seville: Universidad de Sevilla), pp. 173–96

López Castro, J. L. 1995. *Hispania poena: los fenicios en la Hispania Romana (206 a.C.–96 d.C.)* (Barcelona: Crítica)

López Díaz, J. C., J. Jiménez Ávila, and F. Palma García (eds). 2018. *Historia de Mérida, I: De los antecedentes de Augusta Emerita al fin del medievo* (Mérida: Consorcio de la Ciudad Monumental, Histórico-Artística y Arqueológica de Mérida)

López-Mondéjar, L. 2016. 'Placing Sanctuaries in their Socio-Political Landscapes: A Diachronic Approach to the Late Iron Age Communities in South-East Iberia (Fourth–Second Centuries BC)', *Oxford Journal of Archaeology*, 35.1: 101–21

———. 2019. *De íberos a romanos: poblamiento y territorio en el Sureste de la Península Ibérica (siglos IV a.C.–III d.C.)*, BAR, International Series, 2930 (Oxford: BAR)

López Monteagudo, G. 1973. 'El toro en la numismática ibérica e ibero–romana', *Numisma*, 120–21: 233–47

———. 1982. 'Las esculturas zoomorfas célticas de la Península Ibérica y sus paralelos polacos', *AEA*, 55: 3–25

López-Ruiz, C., and B. R. Doak (eds). 2019. *The Oxford Handbook of the Phoenician and Punic Mediterranean* (Oxford: Oxford University Press)

Lorencio, C., F. Puig, and M. Julia. 1998. 'Enterraments infantils a l'edifici imperial de la Magdalena (Lleida)', in M. Mayer, J. M. Nolla, and J. Pardo (eds), *De les estructures indígenes a l'organització provincial romana de la Hispània Citerior; homenatge a Josep Estrada i Garriga* (Barcelona: Institut d'Estudis Catalans, Societat Catalana d'Estudis Clàssics), pp. 209–315

Löw, M. 2001. *Raumsoziologie* (Frankfurt: Suhrkamp)

Lozano Gómez, F. 2011. *Un dios entre los hombres: la adoración a los emperadores romanos en Grecia* (Barcelona: Universidad de Barcelona)

Lozano Gómez, F., and J. Alvar. 2009. 'El culto imperial y su proyección en Hispania', in J. Andreu Pintado, C. Cabrero Piquero, and I. Rodà de Llanza (eds), *Hispaniae: las provincias hispanas en el mundo romano* (Tarragona: Institut Català d'Arqueologia Clàssica), pp. 425–37

Luján, E. R. 2019. 'Language and Writing among the Lusitanians', in A. G. Sinner and J. Velaza (eds), *Palaeohispanic Languages and Epigraphies* (Oxford: Oxford University Press), pp. 304–34

Machuca, F. 2019. *Una forma fenicia de ser romano: identidad e integración de las comunidades fenicias de la Península Ibérica bajo el poder de Roma*, SPAL Monografías Arqueología, 29 (Seville: Universidad de Sevilla)

Mackie, N. K. 1983. *Local Administration in Roman Spain AD 14–212*, BAR, International Series, 172 (Oxford: British Archaeological Reports)

MacMullen, R. 2000. *Romanization in the Time of Augustus* (Yale: New Haven)

Malkin, I. 1998. *The Returns of Odysseus: Colonization and Ethnicity* (Berkeley: University of California Press)

——. 2002. 'A Colonial Middle Ground: Greek, Etruscan and Local Elites in the Bay of Naples', in C. Lyons and J. K. Papadopoulos (eds), *The Archaeology of Colonialism* (Los Angeles: Getty Research Institute), pp. 151–81

Manganaro, G. 1964. 'Nuove dediche con impronte di piedi alle divinità egizie', *Archeologia Classica*, 16: 291–95

Mangas, J. 1982. 'La religión romana en Hispania', in J. Mª Jover (ed.), *Historia de España, España romana (218 a. de J.C.–414 de J.C.), la sociedad, el derecho, la cultura*, II.2 (Madrid: Espasa Calpe), pp. 323–69

Mangas, J., and M. A. Novillo (eds). 2014. *Santuarios suburbanos y del territorio de las ciudades romanas (Madrid 28–29 de mayo de 2009)* (Madrid: Universidad Autónoma de Madrid), pp. 87–112

Marco, F. 1986. 'El dios céltico Lug y el santuario de Peñalba de Villastar', in *Estudios en homenaje al Dr Antonio Beltrán Martínez* (Zaragoza: Universidad de Zaragoza: Facultad de Filosofía y Letras), pp. 731–59

——. 1990. 'Iconografía y propaganda ideológica. Júpiter Amón y Medusa en los foros imperiales', in J. M. Croisille (ed.), *Neronia, IV: Alejandro Magno, modelo de los emperadores romanos; actes du IVᵉ. Colloque International de la S.I.E.N.*, Coll. Latomus, 209 (Brussels: Peeters), pp. 143–62

——. 1993. '*Nemedus Augustus*', in I. J. Adiego, J. Siles, and J. Velaza (eds), *Studia palaeohispanica et indogermanica J. Untermann ab amicis Hispanicis oblata*, Aurea Saecula, 10 (Universitat de Barcelona), pp. 165–78

——. 1994. 'La religión indígena en la Hispania indoeuropea', in *Historia de las religiones de la Europa Antigua* (Madrid: Cátedra), pp. 313–400

——. 1996a. 'Integración, interpretatio y resistencia religiosa en el occidente del Imperio', in J. Alvar and J. M. Blázquez (eds), *La romanización en Occidente* (Madrid: Editorial Actas), pp. 217–38

——. 1996b. 'Romanización y aculturación religiosa: los santuarios rurales', in S. Reboreda Morillo and P. López Barja (eds), *A cidade e o mundo: romanización e cambio social* (Xinzo de Limia: Concello de Xinzo de Limia), pp. 83–100

——. 2002. 'Mito y bipartición simbólica del espacio en el *Ara Pacis* y el *Forum Augustum*', in F. Marco, F. Pina, and J. Remesal (eds), *Religión y propaganda política en el mundo romano* (Barcelona: Publicacions Universitat de Barcelona), pp. 105–18

——. 2004. 'Lex Narbonensis y agon capitolinus: el sacerdote de Júpiter en la política religiosa de los Flavios', in L. Hernández Guerra and J. Alvar (eds), *Jerarquías religiosas y control social en el mundo antiguo: actas del XXVII Congreso internacional GIREA-ARYS IX* (Valladolid: Universidad de Valladolid), pp. 417–22

——. 2009. 'Las inscripciones religiosas hispanas del ámbito rural como expresión del hábito epigráfico', in *Espacios, usos y formas de la epigrafía hispana en épocas antigua y tardoantigua: homenaje al Dr A. Stylow*, Anejos de *Archivo Español de Arqueología*, 48 (Mérida: Consejo Superior de Investigaciones Científicas), pp. 197–210

——. 2011. 'Roman Policy regarding Native and Provincial Cults in the West (2nd c. BC – 2nd c. AD)', in G. A. Cecconi, and C. Gabrielli (eds), *Politiche religiose nel mondo antico e tardoantico: poteri e indirizzi, forme di controllo, idee e prassi di tolleranza; atti del Convegno internazionale di studi (Firenze, 24–26 settembre 2009)* (Bari: Edipuglia), pp. 135–46

——. 2012. 'Patterns of *interpretatio* in the Hispanic Provinces', in G. F. Chiai, R. Häussler, and C. Kunst (eds), *Interpretatio: Religiöse Kommunikation zwischen Globalisierung und Partikularisierung; Proceedings of the Conference at Osnabrück University, 9th–11th September 2010, Mediterraneo Antico*, 15.1: 217–32

——. 2013a. 'Ritual y espacios de memoria en la Hispania Antigua', *Palaeohispanica*, 13: 137–65

——. 2013b. 'Local Cult in Global Context: *Interpretatio* and the Emergence of New Divine Identities in the *provincia Tarraconensis*', in A. Hofeneder and P. de Bernardo Stempel (eds), *Théonymie celtique, cultes, 'interpretatio' / Keltische Theonymie, Kulte, 'interpretatio': X. Workshop F.E.R.C.AN., Paris, 24.–26. Mai 2010* (Vienna: Verlag der Österreichischen Akademie der Wissenschaften), pp. 221–32

——. 2015. 'Priests of the Groves. (Re)creating Ancient Cults in the Augustan Culture', *Symposium Veronense: The Age of Augustus, Gazzo Veronese, Acta Antiqua Academiae Scientiarum Hungaricae*, 55: 79–90

———. 2017a. 'Santuarios en la Celtiberia: ejemplos de monumentalización y de romanización religiosa', in T. Tortosa and S. Ramallo (eds), *El tiempo final de los santuarios ibéricos en los procesos de impacto y consolidación del mundo romano*, Anejos de *Archivo Español de Arqueología*, 79 (Madrid: Consejo Superior de Investigaciones Científicas), pp. 201–12

———. 2017b. 'Los inicios del culto imperial en la Hispania augustea', in J. Mangas and A. Mayorgas (eds), *La Hispania de Augusto*, Gerión, 35 (Madrid: Editorial Complutense), pp. 773–89

———. 2019. 'Un *pontifex nemoris* en la Bética', in V. Revilla, A. Aguilera, L. Pons, and M. García Sánchez (eds), *'Ex Baetica Romam': Homenaje a José Remesal Rodríguez* (Barcelona: Universitat de Barcelona), pp. 353–68

Marco, F., and S. Alfayé. 2008. 'El santuario de Peñalba de Villastar (Teruel) y la romanización religiosa en la Hispania indoeuropea', in X. Dupré, S. Ribichini, and S. Verger (eds), *Saturnia Tellus: definizioni dello spazio consacrato in ambiente etrusco, italico, fenicio-punico, iberico e celtico; atti del convegno internazionale svoltosi a Roma dal 10 al 12 novembre 2004* (Rome: Consiglio Nazionale delle Ricerche), pp. 507–26

Marcos Celestino, M. 2002. *El aniversario de la fundación de Roma y la fiesta de Pales* (Madrid: Signifer Libros)

Marín Ceballos, M. C. 2001. 'Les contacts entre Phéniciens et Grecs dans le territoire de Gadir et leur formulation religieuse; histoire et mythe', in S. Ribicini, M. Rocchi, and P. Xella (ed.), *La questione delle influenze vicino-orientali sulla religione greca (Stato degli studi e prospettive della ricerca. Atti del Colloquio Internazionale, Roma 1999)* (Rome: Consiglio Nazionale delle Ricerche), pp. 315–31

———. 2012. 'Les encunyacions de la Hispània Ulterior des de la perspectiva de la religió feniciopúnica', in M. Campo (ed.), *Déus i mites de l'antiguitat: l'evidència de la moneda d'Hispània* (Barcelona: Museu Nacional d'Art de Catalunya), pp. 32–37

Marín Ceballos, M. C., and F. Horn (eds). 2007. *Imagen y culto en la Iberia prerromana los pebeteros en forma de cabeza femenina* (Seville: Universidad de Sevilla, Secretariado de Publicaciones)

Marín Díaz, M. A. 1986. 'La emigración itálica a Hispania en el siglo II a.C.', *Studia Historica*, 2nd ser., *Historia Antigua*, 4–5: 53–63

———. 1988. *Emigración, colonización y municipalización en la Hispania Republicana* (Granada: Universidad de Granada)

Márquez, C. 2004. 'La decoración arquitectónica en la colonia patricia en el período julio-claudio', in S. Ramallo Asensio (ed.), *La decoración arquitectónica en las ciudades romanas de Occidente* (Murcia: Universidad de Murcia), pp. 337–53

Martín Bueno, M. 2007. 'El culto imperial en el Valle del Ebro', in T. Nogales and J. González Fernández (eds), *Culto Imperial: política y poder; actas del Congreso Internacional Culto Imperial; política y poder; Mérida, Museo Nacional de Arte Romano, 18–20 de mayo, 2006* (Rome: L'Erma di Bretschneider), pp. 721–38

Martín Menéndez, A. 2004. 'Intervencions arqueològiques a Ca l'Arnau–Can Mateu (Cabrera de Mar, Maresme), 1997–1998', in M. Genera Monells (ed.), *Actes de les Jornades d'Arqueologia i Paleontologia, comarques de Barcelona, 1996–2001 (La Garriga, 29 i 30 de novembre, 1 de desembre de 2001)* (Barcelona: Generalitat de Catalunya), pp. 376–408

Martínez Pinna, J. 2008. 'Las tradiciones fundacionales en la Península Ibérica', in P. Annello and J. Martínez Pinna (eds), *Relaciones interculturales en el mediterráneo antiguo: Sicilia e Iberia* (Málaga: Diputación de Málaga), pp. 245–59

Mateos, P. (ed.). 2006. *El 'Foro Provincial' de Augusta Emerita: un conjunto monumental de culto imperial*, Anejos de *Archivo Español de Arqueología*, 42 (Madrid: Consejo Superior de Investigaciones Científicas)

Mateos, P., S. Celestino, A. Pizzo, and T. Tortosa (eds). 2009. *Santuarios, oppida y ciudades: arquitectura sacra en el origen y desarrollo urbano del Mediterráneo occidental*, Anejos de *Archivo Español de Arqueología*, 45 (Mérida: Consejo Superior de Investigaciones Científicas)

Matilla, G., J. Gallardo, and A. Egea. 2002. 'El santuario romano de las aguas de Fortuna (el balneario de Carthago Nova)', *Mastia*, 1: 179–90

———. 2003. 'El balneario romano de Fortuna. Estado de la cuestión y perspectivas de futuro', in A. González Blanco, M. Mayer, A. U. Stylow, and R. González Fernández (eds), *El balneario romano y la Cueva Negra de Fortuna (Murcia): Homenaje al prof. Ph. Rahtz*, Antigüedad y Cristianismo, 13 (Murcia: Universidad de Murcia), pp. 79–182

Mattingly, D. J. 1997. *Dialogues in Roman Imperialism: Power, Discourse and Discrepant Experience in the Roman Empire*, Journal of Roman Archaeology, Supplement 23 (Portsmouth, RI: Journal of Roman Archaeology)

———. 2002. 'Vulgar and Weak "Romanization" or Time for a Paradigm Shift', *Journal of Roman Archaeology*, 15: 536–40

———. 2011. *Imperialism, Power, and Identity: Experiencing the Roman Empire* (Princeton: Princeton University Press)

Mayer, M. 1990. 'La pervivencia de cultos púnicos: el documento de la Cueva Negra (Fortuna, Murcia)', *VII Convegno Internazionale sull'Africa Romana, Sassari 1989, L'Africa romana VII* (Sassari: Gallizzi), pp. 695–702

———. 1992. '¿Rito o literatura en la Cueva Negra?', in M. Mayer and J. Gómez Pallarès (eds), *'Religio Deorum': actas del coloquio internacional Culto y Sociedad en Occidente, Tarragona, 1988* (Sabadell: Ausa), pp. 347–57

———. 1993. 'La presència de Virgili en la epigrafia d'Hispania. Notes per a un corpus de citacions directes', in J. Padró (ed.), *Homenatge a Miquel Tarradell* (Barcelona: Curial), pp. 859–64

———. 1995a. 'Aproximación sumaria a la epigrafía rupestre e hipogea de la *Hispania citerior*', in A. Rodríguez Colmenero and L. Gasperini (eds), *'Saxa scripta' (inscripciones en roca): actas del Simposio Internacional Ibero-Itálico sobre epigrafía rupestre*, Anejos de *Larouco*, 2 (A Coruña: Ediciós do Castro), pp. 35–46

———. 1995b. 'Las inscripciones pintadas en Hispania. Estado de la cuestión', in H. Solin, O. Salomies, and U.-M. Liertz (eds), *Acta colloquii epigraphici Latini Helsingiae 3.-6. sept. 1991 habiti*, Commentationes Humanarum Litterarum, 104 (Helsinki: Societas Scientiarum Fennica), pp. 79–92

———. 1996 [1999]. 'La Cueva Negra de Fortuna (Murcia). *Tituli picti*', in A. González Blanco, M. Mayer, A. U. Stylow, and R. González Fernández (eds), *El balneario romano y la Cueva Negra de Fortuna (Murcia): homenaje al prof. Ph. Rahtz*, Antigüedad y Cristianismo, 13 (Murcia: Universidad de Murcia), pp. 407–22

———. 2008. 'A propósito de las canteras de Vila Viçosa – Estremoz y de *CIL* II 133', *O Arqueólogo Português*, 4th ser., 26: 545–52

———. 2012. 'Tabulae ansatae votivas en santuarios. Algunas reflexiones a propósito de las halladas en el posible mitreo de Can Modolell en Cabrera de Mar (Barcelona)', in G. Baratta and S. M. Marengo (eds), *Inscriptiones inscriptae*, III: *Manufatti iscritti evita dei santuari in età romana* (Macerata: Edizioni Università di Macerata), pp. 113–43

———. 2016. 'Santuario en época romana de la Cova dels Jurats o Església: estudio epigráfico de los paneles en el exterior de la gruta', in M. Orfila, G. Baratta, M. Mayer, E. Sánchez, M. Gutiérrez, and P. Marín, *Los santuarios de Cales Coves (Alaior, Menorca)* (Alaior: Ajuntament d'Alaior), pp. 77–88

———. 2019a. '¿Espeleología romana? Las inscripcions de la Cueva del Puente (Junta de Villalba de Losa, Burgos)', in A. Sartori (ed.), *L'iscrizione nascosta: atti del Convegno Borghesi 2017*, Epigrafia e antichità, 42 (Faenza: Fratelli Lega), pp. 153–67

———. 2019b. 'Escribir para qué y para quién. Algunas consideraciones sobre el valor y el uso de la escritura a propósito de su presencia epigràfica', in G. Baratta (ed.), *L'ABC di un impero: iniziare a scrivere a Roma*, Armariolum, 1 (Rome: Scienze e Lettere), pp. 3–28

———. 2019–2020. 'Algunas observaciones sobre la epigrafia rupestre e hypogea de Hispania', *Rendicontti della Pontificia Accademica Romana di Archaeologia*, 92: 193–223

Mayer, M. and J. A. Abásolo. 1997. 'Inscripciones latinas', in M. S. Corchón (ed.), *La cueva de la Griega de Pedraza (Segovia)* (Zamora: Junta de Castilla y León), pp. 83–259

Mayer, M. and J. Gómez Pallarès (eds). 1993. '*Religio Deorum*': Actas del coloquio internacional Culto y Sociedad en Occidente, Tarragona, 1988 (Sabadell: Ausa)

Mayer, M. and A. González Blanco. 1995. 'Novedades en la Cueva Negra (Fortuna, Murcia)', in A. Rodríguez Colmenero and L. Gasperini (eds), *'Saxa scripta' (inscripciones en roca): actas del Simposio Internacional Ibero-Itálico sobre epigrafía rupestre*, Anejos de *Larouco*, 2 (A Coruña: Ediciós do Castro), pp. 109–15

Mayorgas, A. 2007. *La memoria de Roma: oralidad, escritura e historia en la República romana*, BAR International Series, 1641 (Oxford: John and Erica Hedges)

———. 2010. 'Romulus, Aeneas, and the Cultural Memory of the Roman Republic', *Athenaeum*, 98.1: 89–109

———. 2017. 'Reimagining Hispania. History to Epic in Silius Italicus' *Punica*', *Quaderni Urbinati di Cultura Classica*, 117.3: 129–49

McCarty, M. M. 2016. 'Gods, Masks, and Monstra. Situational Syncretisms in Roman Africa', in S. Alcock, M. Egri, and J. Frakes (eds), *Beyond Boundaries: Connecting Visual Cultures in the Provinces of Ancient Rome* (Los Angeles: Getty Publications), pp. 266–80

———. 2017. 'Africa Punica? Child Sacrifice and Other Invented Traditions in Early Roman Africa', *Religion in the Roman Empire*, 3.3: 393–428

McCarty, M. M. and M. Egri (eds). 2020. *The Archaeology of Mithraism* (Leuven: Peeters)

McLynn, N. 2008. 'Crying Wolf. The Pope and the Lupercalia', *The Journal of Roman Studies*, 98: 161–75

Melchor Gil, E. 2006. '*Solo publico – solo suo*. Sobre la ubicación de los homenajes estatuarios en las ciudades de la Bética', *Cahiers du Centre Gustave-Glotz*, 17: 201–11

———. 2017. 'El patrocinio de Augusto y de los herederos del *Princeps* sobre las comunidades cívicas Hispanas', in J. Mangas and A. Mayorgas (eds), *La Hispania de Augusto*, Gerión, 35 (Madrid: Editorial Complutense), pp. 327–47

Melchor-Monserrat, J. M., J. Benedito, J. J. Ferrer-Maestro, F. García, and F. Buchón. 2017. 'Nuevas aportaciones al conocimiento del circo romano de Sagunto y su entorno monumental', in J. López Vilar (ed.), *Actes 3er Congrés Internacional d'Arqueologia i Món Antic: la glòria del circ: curses de carros i competicions circenses* (Tarragona: Institut Català d'Arqueologia Clàssica), pp. 155–60

Mellor, R. 1981. 'The Goddess Roma', *ANRW*, 17.2: 950–1030

Mélida, J. R. 1914. 'Cultos emeritenses de Serapis y de Mithras', *Boletín de la Real Academia de Historia*, 64: 439–57

———. 1925. *Catálogo Monumental de España: provincia de Badajoz* (Madrid: Ministerio de Instrucción Pública y Bellas Artes)

Méndez Grande, G. 2015. 'Hallazgo de dos nuevas piezas de mármol con dedicaciones a Ataecina/Proserpina en *Augusta Emerita*', *Mérida: Excavaciones arqueológicas. 2005*, Memoria, 11: 447–63

Metzler, J., M. Millet, N. Roymans, and J. Slofstra (eds). 1997. *Integration in the Early Imperial West: The Role of Culture and Ideology*, Dossiers d'archéologie du Musée national d'histoire et d'art, 4 (Luxembourg: Musée national d'histoire et d'art)

Mielke, D. P. 2012. 'Zu den Anfängen der entwickelten figürlichen Kunst bei den Iberern: Die Großskulptur', in C. Pare (ed.), *Kunst und Kommunikation: Zentralisierungsprozesse in Gesellschaften des europäischen Barbarikums im 1. Jahrtausends v. Chr.; Teilkolloquium im Rahmen des Schwerpunktprogrammes 1171 der Deutschen Forschungsgemeinschaft 'Frühe Zentralisi-*

erungs- und Urbanisierungsprozesse. Zur Genese und Entwicklung frühkeltischer Fürstensitze und ihres territorialen Umlandes' Mainz 4.–6. April 2008* (Mainz: Verlag des Römisch-Germanischen Zentralmuseums), pp. 17–58

Miggelbrink, J. 2002. *Der gezähmte Blick: Zum Wandel des Diskurses über 'Raum' und 'Region' in humangeographischen Forschungsansätzen des ausgehenden 20. Jahrhunderts*, Beiträge zur regionalen Geographie, 55 (Leipzig: Institut für Länderkunde)

Millar, F. 1977. *The Emperor and the Roman World (31 BC – AD 337)* (London: Cornell University Press)

Mills, B., and M. Peeples. 2019. 'Reframing Diffusion through Social Network Theory', in K. Harry and B. Roth (eds), *Interaction and Connectivity in the Greater Southwest* (Boulder: University Press of Colorado), pp. 40–62

Minar, E. L., F. H. Sandbach, and W. C. Hembold (eds). 1969. *Plutarch's Moralia*, IX: *697C–711E* (Cambridge, MA: Harvard University Press)

Mínguez, J. A. 1989–1990. 'Enterramientos infantiles domésticos en la Colonia Lepida/Celsa (Velilla de Ebro, Zaragoza)', *Caesaraugusta*, 66–67: 105–22

Moatti, C. 2015. *The Birth of Critical Thinking in Republican Rome* (Cambridge: Cambridge University Press)

Molina, J. A. 2003. 'La inspiración poética en los textos del santuario romano de la Cueva Negra (Fortuna). Ensayo de interpretación', in A. González Blanco and G. Matilla (eds), *La cultura latina en la Cueva Negra: en agradecimiento y homenaje a los Profs. A. Stylow, M. Mayer e I. Velázquez*, Antigüedad y Cristianismo, 20 (Murcia: Universidad de Murcia), pp. 213–24

Mols, S. T. A. M. 2003. 'The Cult of *Roma Aeterna* in Hadrian's Politics', in L. de Blois, P. Erdkamp, O. Hekster, and G. de Kleijn (eds), *The Representation and Perception of Roman Imperial Power* (Leiden: Brill), pp. 458–65

Monsalud, M. C. 1903. 'Nuevas inscripciones romanas y visigóticas de Extremadura', *Boletín de la Real Academia de Historia*, 43: 242–45

——. 1904. 'Epigrafía romana y visigótica de Extremadura', *Boletín de la Real Academia de Historia*, 44: 445–48

Montero Herrero, S. 2017a. 'Octaviano y el prodigio de *Munda*', in J. Mangas and A. Mayorgas (eds), *La Hispania de Augusto*, Gerión, 35 (Madrid: Editorial Complutense), pp. 747–61

——. 2017b. 'Augusto y los altares del culto imperial', in M. D. Dopico Caínzos and M. Villanueva Acuña (eds), *Clausus est Ianus: Augusto e a trasformacion do noroeste hispano*, Philtáte, 1 (Lugo: Deputación), pp. 135–61

——. 2017c. 'Octaviano y el prodigio de Munda', *Gerión*, 35: 741–61

Montero Herrero, S., and S. Perea Yébenes. 1996. 'Augusto y el Bidental de Bracara (ad VIL II 2421)', in J. M. Blázquez Martínez and J. Alvar (eds), *La romanización en Occidente* (Madrid: Editorial Actas), pp. 299–316

Montón, F. J. 1996. *Las arulas de Tárraco* (Tarragona: Museu Nacional Arqueològic de Tarragona)

Mora, B. 2003. 'La iconografía de la moneda hispano-púnica', in *Les imatges monetàries: llenguatge i significat; VII Curs d'Història monetària d'Hispània* (Barcelona: Museu Nacional d'Art de Catalunya), pp. 47–66

——. 2012. 'Divinitats poliades a les emissions de tradició feniciopúnica del sud de la península Ibèrica', in M. Campo (ed.), *Déus i mites de l'antiguitat: l'evidència de la moneda d'Hispània* (Barcelona: Museu Nacional d'Art de Catalunya), pp. 26–31

——. 2014–2015. 'Altares y monedas: topografía religiosa y continuidad de cultos fenicios en Malaka (Málaga)', *Byrsa*, 25–26/2014, 27–28/2015: 131–47

——. 2019. 'Across the Looking Glass: Ethno-Cultural Identities in Southern Hispania through Coinage', in G. Cruz Andreotti (ed.), *Roman Turdetania: Romanization, Identity and Socio-Cultural Interaction in the South of the Iberian Peninsula between the 4th and 1st Centuries BCE* (Leiden: Brill), pp. 148–63

Morais, R., M. Mandeira, and E. Manuel Pinho. 2010. *Itineraria sacra: Bracara Augusta Fidelis et Antica* (Coimbra: Imprensa da Universidade de Coimbra)

Moret, P. 2006. 'La formation d'une toponymie et d'une ethnonymie grecques de l'Ibérie. Étapes et acteurs', in G. Cruz Andreotti, P. Le Roux, and P. Moret (eds), *La invención de una geografía de la Península Ibérica*, I: *La época republicana* (Málaga: Centro de Ediciones de la Diputación de Málaga and Casa de Velázquez), I, pp. 39–76

Morillo Cerdán, Á., and G. Rodríguez Martín. 2009. 'Lampen', in L. Berrocal Rangel, M. Blech, Á. Morillo Cerdán, G. Rodríguez Martín, A. S., and M. Z. Marin Prieto, 'Das frühkaiserzeitliche Votivdepot von San Pedro (Valencia del Ventoso, Prov. Badajoz). Augusta Emerita in der Baeturia und der Kult der Ataecina-Bandue', *Madrider Mitteilungen*, 50: 197–294 (224–34)

Muñoz Tomás, B. 1995. 'Poblamiento rural en el Sureste. El altiplano, Jumilla', in J. M. Noguera (ed.), *Poblamiento rural romano en el sureste de Hispania: actas de las Jornadas celebradas en Jumilla del 8 al 11 de noviembre de 1993* (Murcia: Universidad de Murcia, Servicio de Publicaciones), pp. 107–32

Museo de Arqueología de Sagunto. 2009. *Arse-Saguntum y el Castillo de Murviedro: guía oficial* (Sagunto: Pentagraf)

Navarro Caballero, M. 2000. 'Notas sobre algunos gentilicios romanos de Lusitania: una propuesta metodológica acerca de la emigración itálica', in J.-G. Gorges and T. Nogales (eds), *Sociedad y cultura en la Lusitania romana: IV Mesa Redonda Internacional* (Mérida: Junta de Extremadura), pp. 281–98

——. 2006. 'L'émigration italique dans la Lusitanie côtière: une approche onomastique', in A. Caballos and S. Demougin (eds), *Migrare: la formation des élites dans l'Hispanie romaine*, Ausonius Études, 11 (Bordeaux: Institut Ausonius), pp. 69–100

———. 2017. '*Perfectissima femina*': *femmes de l'élite dans l'Hispanie romaine*, Scripta Antiqua, 101 (Bordeaux: Institut Ausonius)
Nicolai, C. von. 2011. 'Viereckschanzen tra sacro e profano', in G. Cantino Wataghin and C. Colombara (eds), *Finem dare: il confine tra sacro, profano e immaginario, a margine della stele bilingue del Museo Leone di Vercelli; atti del convegno internazionale, Vercelli, cripta di S. Andrea, 22–24 maggio 2008*, Studi umanistici, 22 (Vercelli: Mercurio), pp. 217–41
Nicolau, M. R. 1998a. 'La Montaña Frontera: Historia de la investigación, Braçal', *Revista del Centre d'Estudis del Camp de Morvedre*, 17/18: 147–55
———. 1998b. 'Un santuario iberorromano saguntino situado en la Montaña Frontera (Sagunto, Valencia)', *Anales de Arqueología Cordobesa*, 9: 25–49
Nicolini, G. 1973. *Les Ibères: art et civilisation* (Paris: Fayard)
Nieto, F. J. 1982. 'El pecio del Cap del Vol. Nuevas aportaciones', *Cypsela*, 4: 165–68
Nock, A. D. 1972. 'Synnaoi theoi', in A. D. Nock, *Essays on Religion and the Ancient World* (Oxford: Clarendon), pp. 202–51
Nogales, T. 2000a. *Espectáculos en Augusta Emerita: espacios, imágenes y protagonistas del ocio y espectáculo en la sociedad romana emeritense*, Monografías Emeritenses, 5 (Mérida: Fundación de Estudios Romanos)
———. 2000b. 'El relieve histórico de M. Agrippa, los relieves de Pan Caliente y el Altar del Foro emeritense', *Espacio, Tiempo y Forma*, 2nd ser., *Historia Antigua*, 13: 391–423
Nogales, T., and J. M. Álvarez Martínez. 2014. '*Colonia Augusta Emerita*. Creación de una ciudad en tiempos de Augusto', *Studia Historica*, 2nd ser., *Historia Antigua*, 32: 209–47
Nogales, T., and J. González Fernández (eds). 2007. *Culto Imperial: política y poder; actas del Congreso Internacional Culto Imperial; política y poder; Mérida, Museo Nacional de Arte Romano, 18–20 de mayo, 2006* (Rome: L'Erma di Bretschneider)
Noguera, J. M. 1994. *La escultura romana de la provincia de Albacete (Hispania Citerior – Conventus Carthaginensis)*, Instituto de Estudios Albacetenses. Serie 1: Estudios 76 (Albacete: Diputación de Albacete)
Noguera, J. M., and M. J. Madrid. 2013. 'Pebetero', in M. Bendala, M. Pérez Ruiz, and I. Escobar (eds), '*Fragor Hannibalis*': *Aníbal en Hispania* (Madrid: Comunidad de Madrid y Museo Arqueológico Regional), p. 508
———. 2014. 'Carthago Nova: fases e hitos de monumentalización urbana y arquitectónica (siglos III a.C.–III d.C.)', *Espacio, Tiempo y Forma*, 1st ser., *Prehistoria y Arqueología*, 7: 13–60
Noguera, J. M., J. M. Abascal, and M. J. Madrid. 2018. 'Nuevas inscripciones romanas del Molinete (Cartagena) (campañas 2008–2017)', *Mastia: Revista del Museo Arqueológico Municipal de Cartagena*, 14: 63–101
Noreña, C. 2019. 'Romanization in the Middle of Nowhere: The Case of Segobriga', *Fragments*, 8: 1–32
North, J. 1995. 'Religion and Rusticity', in T. J. Cornell and K. Lomas (eds), *Urban Society in Roman Italy* (London: Psychology Press), pp. 135–50
Obrador, B., J. C. de Nicolás, and C. Múrcia. 2020. 'L'epigrafia antiga dels hipogeus de Menorca', *Pyrenae*, 51: 31–67
Ojeda, D. 2018. 'La decoración escultórica del frente escénico', in P. Mateos Cruz (ed.), *La 'scaenae frons' del teatro romano de Mérida*, Anejos del *AEspA*, 86 (Mérida: Consejo Superior de Investigaciones Científicas), pp. 193–205
Olesti, O. 2014. *Paisajes de la Hispania romana: la explotación de los territorios del Imperio* (Sabadell: Dstoria)
Olivares, J. C. 2002. *Los dioses de la Hispania Céltica*, Bibliotheca Archaeologica Hispana, 15; Anejos de *Lucentum*, 8 (Madrid: Real Academia de la Historia)
Olmos, R. 1988–1989. 'Originalidad y estímulos mediterráneos en la cerámica ibérica: el ejemplo de Elche', *Lucentum*, 7–8: 79–102
Orfila, M., G. Baratta, and M. Mayer. 2010. 'Los santuarios de Cales Coves (Alaior, Menorca): Coberxo Blanc y Cova del Jurats o de l'Eglesia. Informe preliminar', *Cuadernos de Prehistoria y Arqueología de Granada*, 20: 395–433
———. 2013. 'El Santuario de Calescoves (Alaior, Menorca: la Cova dels Jurats o Església', in T. Riera, and J. Cardell (eds), *V Jornades d'Arqueologia de les Illes Balears* (Palma: Edicions Documenta Balear), pp. 109–17
Orfila, M., G. Baratta, M. Mayer, E. Sánchez, M. Gutiérrez, and P. Marín. 2015. *Los santuarios de Cales Coves (Alaior, Menorca)* (Alaior: Ayuntamiento de Alaior)
Orlin, E. (ed.). 2016. *Routledge Encyclopaedia of Ancient Mediterranean Religions* (London: Routledge)
Orr, G. K. 1972. 'Roman Domestic Religion: A Study of the Roman Household Deities and their Shrines at Pompeii and Herculaneum' (unpublished doctoral dissertation, University of Maryland)
Ortega, A. I. 1999. 'Arqueología y paleontología del Karst de Monte Santiago, Sierra Salvada y Sierra de la Carbonilla', in Grupo Espeleológico Edelweiss, 'El Karst de Monte Santiago, Sierra Salvada y Sierra de la Carbonilla', *Kaite Estudios de Espeleología Burgalesa*, 7: 243–81
———. 2004. 'Inscripciones romanas de la Cueva del Puente de Villalba de Losa (Sierra Salvada burgalesa)', *Aunia*, 4: 50–58
Otto, B.-C., S. Rau, and J. Rüpke (eds). 2015. *History and Religion: Narrating a Religious Past*, Religionsgeschichtliche Versuche und Vorarbeiten, 68 (Berlin: De Gruyter)
Padilla Monge, A. 2017. 'Escipión e *Italica*: algunas notas', *Polis: Revista de Ideas y Formas Políticas de la Antigüedad*, 29: 69–100
Paganismo y Cristianismo. 1981. *Paganismo y cristianismo en el occidente del imperio romano* (Oviedo: Universidad de Oviedo: Instituto de Historia Antigua)

Palol, P. de, and J. Vilella. 1986. '¿Un santuario priápico en Clunia?', *Koiné*, 2: 15–25

——. 1987. *Clunia*, II: *La epigrafía de Clunia*, Excavaciones Arqueológicas en España, 150 (Madrid: Ministerio de Educación, Cultura y Deporte)

Panciera, S. 2003. 'Umano, sovrumano o divino? Le divinirà auguste e l'imperatore a Roma', in P. Erdkamp, O. Hekster, G. de Kleijn, S. T. A. M. Mols, and L. De Blois (eds), *The Representation and Perception of Roman Imperial Power* (Amsterdam: Gieben), pp. 215–39

Paniego, P., J. L. Ramírez Sádaba, and N. Guillén Vázquez. 2020. 'Nuevo *terminus augustalis* de Valencia del Ventoso (Badajoz, España), que confirma la prefectura emeritense meridional', *Cuadernos de Prehistoria y Arqueología de la Universidad Autónoma de Madrid*, 46: 239–47

Panzram, S. 2003. 'Los *flamines provinciae* de la *Baetica*; autorrepresentación y culto imperial', *AEA*, 76: 121–30

Paris, P. 1904. 'Un sanctuaire de Mithra à Merida (Espagne)', *Comptes rendus des séances de l'Académie des Inscriptions et Belles-Lettres*, 48.6: 573–75

——. 1914. 'Restes du culte de Mithra en Espagne. Le mithraeum de Mérida', *Revue Archéologique*, 24: 1–31

Parker, R. 2017. *Greek Gods Abroad: Names, Natures, and Transformations* (Oakland: University of California Press)

Pascual Buyé, I. 2002. 'El circo romano de Sagunto', in T. Nogales and F. J. Sánchez Palencia (eds), *El circo en la Hispania Romana: Museo Nacional de Arte Romano, Mérida, 22, 23 y 24 de marzo de 2001* (Madrid: Ministerio de Educación y Cultura), pp. 155–74

Pascual, G. and P. Jardón. 2014. 'Un espacio de culto rural romano en Montesa, comarca de La Costera, Valencia', *Saguntum: Papeles del Laboratorio de Arqueología de Valencia*, 46: 129–45

Patterson, J. 1992. 'The Romanization of Samnium and Lycia', in J. Rich and A. Wallace-Hadrill (eds), *City and Country in the Ancient World* (London: Routledge), pp. 149–64

Peeters, F. 1938. 'Le culte de Jupiter en Espagne', *Revue belge de Philologie et d'Histoire*, 17: 157–93

Pena, M. J. 2000. 'Les cultes d'*Emporion*', in A. Hermary and H. Tréziny, *Les cultes des cités phocéennes: actes du colloque international Aix-en-Provence/Marseille 4–5 juin 1999*, Études Massaliètes, 6 (Aix-en-Provence: Edisud), pp. 59–68

——. 2007. 'Reflexiones sobre los pebeteros en forma de cabeza femenina', in M. C. Marín and F. Horn (eds), *Imagen y culto en la Iberia prerromana: los pebeteros en forma de cabeza femenina* (Seville: Universidad de Sevilla), pp. 17–40

——. 2012. 'Imatges gregues a emissions d'Ibèria', in M. Campo (ed.), *Déus i mites de l'antiguitat: l'evidència de la moneda d'Hispània* (Barcelona: Museu Nacional d'Art de Catalunya), pp. 20–25

——. 2016. 'El culto a Artemis Efesia en *Massalia* y las costas de *Iberia*. ¿Una leyenda tardía con trasfondo político? Análisis crítico de las fuentes literarias', *Latomus*, 75: 960–84

——. 2022. 'Notas saguntinas', *Saguntum: Papeles del Laboratorio de Arqueología de Valencia*, 54

Peña Jurado, A. 2005. 'Imitaciones del *Forum Augustum* en Hispania. El ejemplo de *Italica*', *Romula*, 4: 137–62

Pera, J. 2001. 'Aproximació a la circulació monetària de la ciutat romana de Iesso (Guissona, Lleida)', in *Moneda i vida urbana: V Curs d'Història monetària d'Hispània* (Barcelona: Museu Nacional d'Art de Catalunya), pp. 53–63

Perea Yébenes, S. 2017. 'Julio César y el joven Octavio en Hispania en el año 45 a.C. La cuestión del itinerario cesariano y las apelaciones de los saguntinos en *Carthago Nova* según Nicolás de Damasco, *Bíos Καίσαρος*, 23–27', *Hispania Antiqua*, 41: 68–106

Pereira, M., and M. Maia. 1997. *Lucernas de Santa Bárbara* (Castro Verde: Cortiçol Cooperativa)

Pérez Almoguera, A. 1998. 'Tres casos de rituales fundacionales o propiciatorios en construcciones domésticas en el Alto Imperio Romano. ¿Latinidad o indigenismo?', *ARYS (Antigüedad: Religiones y Sociedades)*, 1: 195–206

Pérez Ruiz, M. 2007–2008. 'El culto en la casa romana', *Anales de Prehistoria y Arqueología de la Universidad de Murcia*, 23–24: 195–225

——. 2008. 'Un caso singular de estatua romana de culto doméstico', *AEA Arqueología*, 81: 273–87

——. 2011. 'Aproximación a la cultura material asociada al culto doméstico en el mundo romano', *Espacio, Tiempo y Forma*, 1st ser., *Nueva época: Prehistoria y Arqueología*, 4: 285–308

——. 2013. 'Topografía del culto en las casas romanas de la Baetica y la Tarraconensis', *Madrider Mitteilungen*, 54: 399–441

——. 2014. *Al amparo de los Lares: el culto doméstico en las provincias romanas Bética y Tarraconense*, Anejos de *Archivo Español de Arqueología*, 68 (Madrid: Consejo Superior de Investigaciones Científicas–Universidad Autónoma de Madrid)

——. 2015. 'Un emperador en el larario. Reformas religiosas en época de Augusto y su repercusión en la ritualidad doméstica', in J. López Vilar (ed.), *Actes del 2on Congrés Internacional d'Arqueologia i Món Antic: August i les províncies occidentals; 2000 Aniversari de la mort d'August (Tarragona, 26–29 novembre 2014)* (Tarragona: Fundació Privada Mútua Catalana), pp. 93–98

Pérez Villatela, L. 1990. 'El origen de Sagunto en Silio Itálico', *Arse*, 25: 23–39

Pina Polo, F. 2018. 'How Much History Did the Romans Know? Historical References in Cicero's Speeches to the People', in K. Sandberg and C. Smith (eds), *'Omnium Annalium Monumenta': Historical Writing and Historical Evidence in Republican Rome* (Leiden: Brill), pp. 205–33

Pitts, M., and M. J. Versluys. 2015. *Globalisation and the Roman World: World History, Connectivity and Material Culture* (Cambridge: Cambridge University Press)

Pla, C., and V. Revilla. 2002. 'El santuario romano de Can Modolell (Cabrera de Mar, Barcelona). Nuevas aportaciones para su interpretación', *Empúries*, 53: 211–39

Plácido, D. 2002. 'La *pietas* romana, el culto imperial y las religiones de salvación', in S. Crespo and A. Alonso (eds), *Scripta antiqua: in honorem Ángel Montenegro Duque et José María Blázquez Martínez* (Valladolid), pp. 475–84

Pons Pujol, L. 2003. 'Les ofrenes de fundació', in V. Revilla (ed.), *Economia i poblament romà al curs inferior de l'Ebre: la villa de Casa Blanca (Tortosa)* (Tarragona: Diputació de Tarragona), pp. 263–74

Pons i Brun, E. 1997. 'Estructures, objectes i fets culturals en el jaciment protohistòric de Mas Castellar (Pontós, Girona)', *Quaderns de Prehistòria y Arqueologia de Castelló*, 18: Espacios y lugares cultuales en el mundo ibérico, 71–89

—— (ed.) 2002. *Mas Castellar de Pontós (Alt Empordà): un complex arqueològic d'època ibèrica (excavacions 1990-1998)*, Museu d'Arqueologia de Catalunya: Sèrie Monogràfica, 21 (Girona: Museu d'Arqueologia de Catalunya)

Pons i Brun, E., J. Ruiz de Arbulo, and D. Vivó. 1998. 'El yacimiento ibérico de Mas Castellar de Pontós (Girona). Análisis de algunas piezas significativas', in C. Aranegui (ed.), *Los Iberos: príncipes de Occidente; estructuras de poder en la sociedad Ibérica* (Barcelona: Fundación 'la Caixa'), pp. 55–64

Poveda, A. M. 1999. 'Reinterpretación del relieve histórico emeritense de M. Agrippa a partir de un nuevo fragmento', *Espacio, Tiempo y Forma*, 2nd ser., 12: 389–405

Porte, D. 1981. 'Romulus-Quirinus, prince et dieu, dieu des princes. Études sur le personnage de Quirinus et sur son évolution, des origines à Auguste', *ANRW*, 2.71.1: 300–45

Prag, J. R. W. 2013. 'Epigraphy in the Western Mediterranean: A Hellenistic Phenomenon?', in J. R. W. Prag and J. C. Crawley Quinn (eds), *The Hellenistic West: Rethinking the Ancient Mediterranean* (Cambridge: Cambridge University Press), pp. 320–47

Price, S. 1984. *Rituals and Power: The Roman Imperial Cult in Roman Asia Minor* (Cambridge: Cambridge University Press)

Prontera, F. 1984. *Strabone: contributi allo studio della personalità e dell'opera*, I (Perugia: Università degli studi)

——. 1999. 'Notas sobre Iberia en la Geografía de Estrabón', in G. Cruz Andreotti (ed.), *Estrabón e 'Iberia': nuevas perspectivas de estudio* (Málaga: Servicio de Publicaciones de la Universidad de Málaga), pp. 17–30

Puccio, L. 2010a. 'Les cultes isiaques à *Emporion*', *Pallas*, 84: 207–27

——. 2010b. 'Pieds et empreintes de pieds dans les cultes isiaques: Pour une meilleure compréhension des documents hispaniques', *Mélanges de la Casa de Velázquez*, 40: 137–55

Purcell, N. 1987. 'Tomb and Suburb', in H. von Hesberg and P. Zanker (eds), *Römische Gräberstrassen: Selbstdarstellung – Status – Standard* (Munich: Bayerische Akademie der Wissenschaften), pp. 25–41

——. 1995. 'The Roman Villa and the Landscape of Production', in T. J. Cornell and K. Lomas (eds), *Urban Society in Roman Italy* (London: Psychology Press), pp. 151–79

Quaglia, A. 2019. '*Fera sodalitas*. Los *Lupercalia*, de Evandro a Augusto' (unpublished doctoral dissertation, Complutense University of Madrid)

Quet, M. H. 1981. *La mosaïque cosmologique de Mérida* (Paris: De Boccard)

Raddatz, K. 1969. *Die Schatzfunde der Iberischen Halbinsel vom Ende des dritten bis zur Mitte des ersten Jahrhunderts vor Chr.*, Madrider Forschungen, 5 (Berlin: De Gruyter)

Raepsaet-Charlier, M.-T. 1993. '*Diis deabusque sacrum*': Formulaire votif et datation dans les trois Gaules et les deux Germanies (Paris: De Boccard)

Ramage, E. S. 1987. *The Nature and Purpose of Augustus' 'Res gestae'* (Stuttgart: Steiner)

Ramallo, S. 1991. 'Un santuario de época tardo-republicana en La Encarnación, Caravaca, Murcia', in *Templos romanos de Hispania*, Cuadernos de arquitectura romana, 1 (Murcia: Universidad de Murcia), pp. 39–65

——. 1993. 'La monumentalización de los santuarios ibéricos en época tardorrepublicana', *Ostraka*, 2: 117–44

——. 1999. *El programa ornamental del teatro romano de Cartagena* (Murcia: Fundación Caja Murcia)

Ramallo, S. 2006. 'Carthago Nova: urbs opulentissima omnium in Hispania', in L. Abad Casal, S. Keay, and S. Ramallo (eds), *Early Roman Towns in Hispania Tarraconensis*, JRA Supplementary Series, 62 (Portsmouth, RI: Journal of Roman Archaeology), pp. 91–104

Ramallo, S. and F. Brotons. 1997. 'El santuario ibérico de la Encarnación (Caravaca de la Cruz, Murcia)', *Quaderns de Prehistòria i Arqueologia de Castelló*, 18: 257–68

——. 2014. 'Depósitos votivos y ritos en los santuarios ibéricos e íbero-romanos. Continuidades y rupturas a través de las evidencias de culto en el santuario del Cerro de la Ermita de la Encarnación (Caravaca de la Cruz, Murcia)', in T. Tortosa (ed.), *Diálogo de identidades: Bajo el prisma de las manifestaciones religiosas en el ámbito mediterráneo (s. III a.C.– s. I d.C.)*, Anejos de *Archivo Español de Arqueología*, 72 (Mérida: Consejo Superior de Investigaciones Científicas), pp. 17–44

Ramallo, S., J. M. Noguera, and F. Brotons. 1998. 'El Cerro de los Santos y la monumentalización de los santuarios ibéricos tardíos', *Revista de Estudios Ibéricos*, 3: 11–69

Ramírez Sádaba, J. L. 1993. 'Panorámica religiosa de *Augusta Emerita*', in M. Mayer and J. Gómez Pallarès (eds), *'Religio Deorum': Actas del coloquio internacional Culto y Sociedad en Occidente, Tarragona, 1988* (Sabadell: Ausa), pp. 389–98

——. 2000. 'Lo sagrado en el proceso de municipalización del Occidente latino. Fuentes', *Iberia: Revista de la Antigüedad*, 3: 11–24

——. 2003a. *Catálogo de las inscripciones imperiales de Augusta Emerita*, Cuadernos emeritenses, 21 (Mérida: Museo Nacional de Arte Romano)

——. 2003b. 'El culto a Baco en la religión romana y los textos de Fortuna (Murcia)', in A. González Blanco and G. Matilla (eds), *La cultura latina en la Cueva Negra: en agradecimiento y homenaje a los Profs. A. Stylow, M. Mayer e I. Velázquez*, Antigüedad y Cristianismo, 20 (Murcia: Universidad de Murcia), pp. 317–24

——. 2013. *Badajoz antes de la ciudad: el territorio y su población durante la Edad Antigua* (Badajoz: Diputación Provincial de Badajoz)

——. 2019. 'Las creencias en *Augusta Emerita*', in A. Alvar (ed.), *Siste, viator: La epigrafía en la antigua Roma* (Alcalá de Henares: Universidad de Alcalá), pp. 161–72

——. 2019 [2021]. *Catálogo de las inscripciones votivas de Augusta Emerita*, Cuadernos emeritenses, 48 (Mérida: Museo Nacional de Arte Romano)

Ramírez Sádaba, J. L., and M. Jiménez Losa. 2011. 'Panorámica religiosa de *Augusta Emerita* II: territorium y centro urbano', in J. C. Ribeiro (ed.), *Diis Deabusque: Actas do II Coloquio Internacional de Epigrafia 'Culto e Sociedade' [Sintria 3–4, 1995–2007]* (São Miguel de Odrinhas: Museu Arqueológico de São Miguel de Odrinhas), pp. 429–56

Ramos, A., and R. Ramos. 1976. *Excavaciones en La Alcudia de Elche durante los años (1968 a 1973)*, Excavaciones arqueológicas en España, 91 (Madrid: Ministerio de Educación y Ciencia)

Ramos Loscertales, J. M. 1942. 'Hospicio y Clientela en la España céltica', *Emerita*, 10: 308–37

Ramos Martínez, F. 2018. *Poblamiento ibérico ss V–III a.n.e. en el sureste de la península ibérica: nuevos datos para el estudio a través de la arqueología del paisaje*, BAR, International Series, 2903 (Oxford: British Archaeological Reports)

Religión romana 1981. *La Religión romana en Hispania: symposio organizado por el Instituto de Arqueología 'Rodrigo Caro' del C.S.I.C. del 17 al 19 de diciembre de 1979* (Madrid: Ministerio de Cultura, Subdirección General de Arqueología y Etnología)

Renberg, G. 2006. 'Was Incubation Practiced in the Latin West?', *Archiv für Religionsgeschichte*, 8: 105–47

Renfrew, C. 1985. *The Archaeology of Cult: The Sanctuary at Philakopi* (Athens: British School at Athens)

Renfrew, C., and J. F. Cherry (eds). 1986. *Peer Polity Interaction and Socio-political Change*, New Directions in Archaeology (Cambridge: Cambridge University Press)

Revell, L. 2009. *Roman Imperialism and Local Identities* (Cambridge: Cambridge University Press)

——. 2015. *Ways of Being Roman: Discourses of Identity in the Roman West* (Oxford: Oxbow Archaeological Monographs)

Revilla, V. 2002. 'Santuarios, élites y comunidades cívicas: consideraciones sobre la religión rural en el conventus Tarraconensis', in F. Marco, F. Pina, and J. Remesal (eds), *Religión y propaganda política en el mundo romano* (Barcelona: Publicacions Universitat de Barcelona), pp. 189–226

Ribeiro, A. 2002a. 'Árula consagrada aos Lares Aquites, por Gaius Caecilius (?) Rufus', in J. C. Ribeiro (ed.), *Religiões da Lusitânia: Loquuntur saxa* (Lisbon: Museu Nacional de Arqueologia), p. 472

——. 2002b. 'Manifestações particulares de devoção. As árulas de Conimbriga', in J. C. Ribeiro (ed.), *Religiões da Lusitânia: Loquuntur saxa* (Lisbon: Museu Nacional de Arqueologia), pp. 193–99

Ribeiro, J. C. (ed.). 2002a. *Religiões da Lusitânia: Loquuntur saxa* (Lisbon: Museu Nacional de Arqueologia)

——. 2002b. 'Endovellicus', in J. C. Ribeiro (ed.), *Religiões da Lusitânia: Loquuntur saxa* (Lisbon: Museu Nacional de Arqueologia), pp. 79–90

Ribeiro, J. 2007. 'Soli Aeterno Lvnae. Cultos astrais em época pré-romana e romana na área de influência da Serra de Sintra: um caso complexo de sincretismo?', *Sintria*, 3–4: 595–624

——. 2013. 'Damos-te esta ovelha, ó Trebopala! A invocatio lusitana de Cabeço das Fráguas (Portugal)', *Palaeohispanica*, 11: 237–56

——. 2016. 'Ad Antiquitates Vestigandas. Destinos e itinerários antiquaristas nos campos olisiponenses ocidentais desde inícios a meados do século XVI', in G. González Germain (ed.), *Peregrinationes ad inscriptiones colligendas: Estudios sobre epigrafía de tradición manuscrita* (Barcelona: Universitat Autònoma de Barcelona), pp. 135–249

Ribera, A. 2008. '*Valentia* (*Hispania Citerior*), una fundación itálica de mediados del siglo II a. C. Novedades y complementos', in J. Uroz, J. M. Noguera, and F. Coarelli (eds), *Ibéria e Italia: modelos romanis de integración territorial* (Murcia: Tabularium), pp. 169–97

Ribera, A., and J. L. Jiménez. 2012. '*Valentia*, ciudad romana: su evidencia arqueológica', in J. Beltrán Fortés and O. Rodríguez Gutiérrez (eds), *'Hispaniae Vrbes': Investigaciones arqueológicas en ciudades históricas* (Seville: Universidad de Sevilla), pp. 77–120

Richardson, J. S. 1976. 'The Spanish Mines and the Development of Provincial Taxation in the Second Century B.C.', *JRS*, 66: 139–52

——. 1983. 'The Tabula Contrebiensis. Roman Law in Spain in the Early First Century B.C.', *JRS*, 73: 33–41

——. 1986. *Hispaniae: Spain and the Development of Roman Imperialism, 218–82 BC* (Cambridge: Cambridge University Press)

——. 2000. 'Tarraco in the Age of Trajan: The Testimony of Florus the Poet', in J. González Fernández (ed.), *Trajano emperador de Roma: actas del congreso internacional (Sevilla, 14–17 septiembre 1998)* (Rome: L'Erma di Bretschneider), pp. 427–46

Richert, E. A. 2005. *Native Religion under Roman Domination: Deities, Springs and Mountains in the North-West of the Iberian Peninsula*, BAR, International Series, 1382 (Oxford: British Archaeological Reports)

Rioseras, M. A., M. A. Martín, and I. A. Ortega. 2011. 'El Karst de Monte Santiago, Sierra Salvada y Sierra de la Carbonilla', *Cubía*, 15: 54–69

Ripollès, P. P. 1988. *La ceca de Valentia* (Valencia: Generalitat Valenciana)

——. 1998. 'Las acuñaciones cívicas romanas de la Península Ibérica (44 a.C.–54 d.C.)', in C. Alfaro Asins (ed.), *Historia monetaria de Hispania Antigua* (Madrid: Jesús Vico), pp. 335–95

——. 2002a. 'La ordenación y la cronología de las emisiones', in P. P. Ripollès and M. del M. Llorens (eds), *Arse-Saguntum: Historia monetaria de la ciudad y su territorio* (Sagunto: Fundación Bancaja), pp. 273–302

——. 2002b. 'El panorama monetario', in P. P. Ripollès and M. del M. Llorens (eds), *Arse-Saguntum: Historia monetaria de la ciudad y su territorio* (Sagunto: Fundación Bancaja), pp. 319–46

——. 2010. *Las acuñaciones provinciales romanas de Hispania*, Bibliotheca Numismatica Hispana, 8 (Madrid: Real Academia de la Historia)

——. 2012a. 'El reflejo de la iconografía helenística en las emisiones de Iberia oriental: el siglo III a.C.', in R. Pera (ed.), *Il significato delle immagini: numismatica, arte, filologia e storia; atti del secondo incontro internazionale di studio del Lexicon Iconographicum Numismaticae (Genova, 10–12 novembre 2005)* (Rome: Giorgio Bretschneider), pp. 193–218

——. 2012b. 'The Ancient Coinages of the Iberian Peninsula', in W. E. Metcalf (ed.), *The Oxford Handbook of Greek and Roman Coinages* (Oxford: Oxford University Press), pp. 356–73

Ripollès, P. P., and J.-A. Chevillon. 2013. 'The Archaic Coinage of Emporion', *The Numismatic Chronicle*, 173: 1–21

Ripollès, P. P., and M. del M. Llorens (eds). 2002. *Arse-Saguntum: Historia monetaria de la ciudad y su territorio* (Sagunto: Fundación Bancaja)

Ripollès, P. P., and J. Velaza. 2002. 'Saguntum colonia Latina', *Zeitschrift für Papyrologie und Epigraphik*, 141: 285–94

Ripollès, P. P., and A. G. Sinner. 2019. 'Coin Evidence for Ancient Hispanic Languages', in A. G. Sinner and J. Velaza (eds), *Palaeohispanic Languages and Epigraphies* (Oxford: Oxford University Press), pp. 365–95

Rives, J. B. 1995. *Religion and Authority in Roman Carthage from Augustus to Augustine* (Oxford: Clarendon)

——. 2001. 'Civic and Religious Life', in J. Bodel (ed.), *Epigraphic Evidence: Ancient History from Inscriptions* (London: Psychology Press), pp. 118–36

——. 2007. *Religion in the Roman Empire*, Blackwell Ancient Religions, 2 (Oxford: Blackwell)

——. 2010. 'Graeco-Roman Religion in the Roman Empire', *Currents in Biblical Research*, 8.2: 240–99

——. 2015. 'Religion in the Roman Provinces', in C. Brun and J. Edmondson (eds), *The Oxford Handbook of Roman Epigraphy* (Oxford: Oxford University Press), pp. 420–44

Rodá, I. 1990. 'La integración de una inscripción bilingüe ampuritana', *Boletín del Museo Arqueológico Nacional*, 8: 79–80

——. 2004. 'El culto a Augusto y su reflejo en la colonia de *Barcino*', in E. Marin and I. Rodà (eds), *Divo Augusto: El descubrimiento de un templo romano en Croacia* (Split: Arheološki muzej), pp. 418–23

——. 2007. 'Documentos e imágenes de culto imperial en la Tarraconense septentrional', in T. Nogales and J. González (eds), *Culto Imperial: política y poder* (Rome: L'Erma di Bretschneider), pp. 739–61

Roddaz, J.-M. 2014. 'Augusto y el Imperio Romano', *Studia Historica: Historia Antigua*, 32: 21–46

Rodríguez Azcárraga, A. M. 2006–2007. 'Fragmentos relivarios del santuario de los dioses orientales de Augusta Emerita', *Anas*, 19–20: 267–78

Rodríguez Bordallo, R., and A. Ríos Graña. 1985. 'El simbolismo, la localización y el número de las Aras Sestianas', in *Actas del II Coloquio Galaico-Minhoto*, 1 (Santiago de Compostela: Instituto Cultural Galaico-Minhoto), pp. 255–70

Rodríguez Cao, C. 2014. *A domus do Mitreo* (Santiago de Compostela: Universidade, Servizo de Publicacións e Intercambio Científico)

Rodríguez Colmenero, A. 1993. *Corpus-Catálogo de inscripciones rupestres de época romana del cuadrante noroccidental de la Península Ibérica*, Anejos de *Larouco*, 1 (A Coruña: Ediciós do Castro)

——. 1995. 'Corpus de inscripciones rupestres de época romana del cuadrante NW de la Península Ibérica', in A. Rodríguez Colmenero and L. Gasperini (eds), *'Saxa scripta' (inscripciones en roca): actas del Simposio Internacional Ibero-Itálico sobre epigrafía rupestre*, Anejos de *Larouco*, 2 (A Coruña: Ediciós do Castro), pp. 117–259

—— (ed.). 1996. *Lucus Augusti*, 1: *El amanecer de una ciudad* (Coruña: Fundación Pedro Barrié de la Maza)

——. 1999. *O santuário rupestre galaico-romano de Panóias (Vila Real, Portugal): novas achegas para a sua reinterpretação global* (Lisbon: Ministério da Cultura)

——. 2003. 'La Cueva Negra de Fortuna (Murcia), un posible *témenos* indígena posteriormente sincretizado', in A. González Blanco and G. Matilla (eds), *La cultura latina en la Cueva Negra: en agradecimiento y homenaje a los Profs. A. Stylow, M. Mayer e I. Velázquez*, Antigüedad y Cristianismo, 20 (Murcia: Universidad de Murcia), pp. 423–36

Rodríguez Colmenero, A., and L. Gasperini (eds). 1995. *'Saxa scripta' (inscripciones en roca): actas del Simposio Internacional Ibero-Itálico sobre epigrafía rupestre*, Anejos de *Larouco*, 2 (A Coruña: Ediciós do Castro)

Rodríguez, F. J., and E. Melchor. 2001. 'Evergetismo y *cursus honorum* de los magistrados municipales en las provincias de Bética y Lusitania', in C. Castillo, J. F. Navarro, and R. Martínez (eds), *De Augusto a Trajano: un siglo de la Historia de España* (Pamplona: Ediciones Universidad de Navarra), pp. 139–238

Röring, N., and W. Trillmich. 2010. 'Agrippina y la Concordia Augusti. Elementos para la interpretación del "foro provincial" de la Colonia Augusta Emerita', in T. Nogales (ed.), *Ciudad y foro en Lusitania romana*, Studia Lusitana, 4 (Mérida: Museo Nacional de Arte Romano), pp. 273–83

Rojas, M. R. 2016. '*Ataecina*, un análisis de la continuidad de los cultos locales o indígenas en la Hispana romana', *Ligustinus: Revista digital de Arqueología de Andalucía occidental*, 5: 8–25

Romero Mayorga, C. 2016a. 'Iconografía Mitraica en Hispania' (unpublished doctoral thesis, Universidad Complutense de Madrid)

——. 2016b. 'Mercury with Lyre: A New Interpretation of a Mithraic Sculpture Found in Hispania', in A. C. Luigi Bravi, L. Lomiento, A. Meriani, and G. Pace, *Tra Lyra e Aulos Tradizioni Musicali e Generi Poetici*, Quaderni della '*Rivista di cultura classica e medioevale*', 14 (Pisa: Fabrizio Serra editore), pp. 199–206

Ronda, A. M., and M. Tendero. 2014. 'Producciones locales de época augustea de *Ilici*: las imitaciones de paredes finas y de la vajilla metálica romana', in R. Morais, A. Fernández, and M. J. Suosa (eds), *As produções cerâmicas de imitação na Hispania* (Porto: Faculdade de Letras da Universidade do Porto), pp. 191–213

——. 2015. 'La reinterpretación de un depósito augusteo: el *cantharus* de *Ilici*', in J. López Vilar (ed.), *August i les províncies occidentals: 2000 aniversari de la mort d'August; actes del 2on Congrés Internacional d'Arqueologia i Mon Antic: Tarraco Biennal*, 1 (Tarragona: Institut Català d'Arqueologia Clàssica), pp. 263–68

Ros, A. 2005. 'Ideologia i ritual: aportació a l'estudi sobre la religiositat de la Cessetània', *Revista de la Fundació Privada Catalana per a l'Arqueologia Ibèrica*, 1: 147–82

Rothaus, R. M. 2000. *Corinth: The First City of Greece; An Urban History of Late Antique Cult and Religion*, Religions in the Graeco-Roman World, 139 (Leiden: Brill)

Rothenhöfer, P. 2009. 'Te rogo, oro, obsecro … Bemerkungen zu indigenen Kulten in Mérida', in *Espacios, usos y formas de la epigrafía hispana en épocas antigua y tardoantigua: homenaje al Dr Armin U. Stylow*, Anejos de *Archivo Español de Arqueología*, 48 (Madrid: Consejo Superior de Investigaciones Científicas), pp. 307–17

Rouillard, P., A. Espinosa, and J. Moratalla. 2014. *Villajoyosa Antique (Alicante, Espagne): territoire et topographie; Le sanctuaire de la Malladeta*, Collection de la Casa de Velázquez, 141 (Madrid: Casa de Velázquez)

Roymans, N. 1997. 'Romanization, Cultural Identity and the Ethnic Discussion: The Integration of Lower Rhine Populations in the Roman Empire', in J. Metzler, M. Millet, N. Roymans, and J. Slofstra (eds), *Integration in the Early Imperial West: The Role of Culture and Ideology*, Dossiers d'archéologie du Musée national d'histoire et d'art, 4 (Luxembourg: Musée national d'histoire et d'art), pp. 47–64

Royo, M. M. 2016. 'La identidad de las ciudades hispanas a través de sus emisiones provinciales romanas', in A. L. Morelli and E. Filippini (eds), *Moneta e indentità territoriale: dalla polis antica alla civitas medievale; atti del III Incontro internazionale di studio del Lexicon Iconographicum Numismaticae (Bologna, 12–13 settembre 2013)* (Reggio Calabria: Falzea), pp. 213–32

Ruano, E. 1987. 'La escultura humana de piedra en el mundo ibérico' (doctoral thesis, published by the author, Universidad Autónoma de Madrid)

Rueda, C. 2011. *Territorio, culto e iconografía en los santuarios iberos del Alto Guadalquivir (ss. IV a.n.e.–I d.n.e.)*, Textos CAAI no. 3 (Jaén: Universidad de Jaén)

Rueda-Galán, C., A. García-Luque, C. Ortega-Cabezudo, and C. Rísquez-Cuenca. 2008. 'El ámbito infantil en los espacios de culto de Cástulo (Jaén, España)', in F. Gusi i Jener, S. Muriel, and C. R. Olaria (eds), *Nasciturus: infans, puerulus; Vobis mater terra; La muerte en la infancia* (Castelló: Diputació de Castelló), pp. 473–96

Ruiz, A. 1998. 'Los príncipes íberos: procesos económicos y sociales', in C. Aranegui (ed.), *Los Iberos: príncipes de Occidente; estructuras de poder en la sociedad Ibérica* (Barcelona: Fundación 'la Caixa'), pp. 289–300

Ruiz Bueno, M. D. 2018. *Dinámicas topográficas urbanas en Hispania: el espacio intramuros entre los siglos II y VII d.C.* (Bari: Edipuglia)

Ruiz de Arbulo, J. 1994a. 'El Gimnasio de Emporion (S.II–I a.C.)', *Butlletí Arqueòlogic*, 5th ser., 16 (Tarragona): 11–44

——. 1994b. 'Los cernos figurados con cabeza de Core. Nuevas propuestas en torno a su denominación, función y origen', *Saguntum*, 27: 155–71

——. 2002–2003. 'Santuarios y fortalezas. Cuestiones de indigenismo, helenización y romanización en torno a *Emporion* y *Rhode* (s. VI–I a.C.)', *Cuadernos de Prehistoria y Arqueología de la Universidad Autónoma de Madrid*, 28–29: 161–202

——. 2009. 'El altar y el templo de Augusto en la *Colonia Tarraco*. Estado de la cuestión', in J. M. Noguera (ed.), *'Fora Hispaniae': Paisaje urbano, arquitectura, programas decorativos y culto imperial en los foros de las ciudades hispanorromanas* (Murcia: Museo Arqueológico de Murcia), pp. 155–89

——. 2014. 'El signaculum de Caius Valerius Avitus, duoviro de Tarraco y propietario de la villa de Els Munts (Altafulla)', *Pyrenae*, 45: 125–51

Ruiz Bremón, M. 1986. 'Esculturas romanas en el Cerro de las Santos', *AEA*, 59: 67–88

——. 1989. *Los exvotos del santuario ibérico del Cerro de los Santos*, Instituto de Estudios Albacetenses. Serie 1. Ensayos históricos y científicos, 40 (Albacete: Instituto de Estudios Albacetenses)

Rüpke, J. 2001. 'Religiöse Kommunikation in provinzialen Raum', in W. Spickermann, H. Cancik, and J. Rüpke (eds), *Religiöse Kommunikation in provinzialen Raum* (Tübingen: Mohr Siebeck), pp. 71–88

——. 2006a. 'Religion in the Lex Ursonensis', in C. Ando, and J. Rüpke (eds), *Religion and Law in Classical and Christian Rome* (Stuttgart: Steiner), pp. 34–46

——. 2006b. 'Urban Religion and Imperial Expansion: Priesthoods in the *Lex Ursonensis*', in L. de Blois, P. Funke, and J. Hahn (eds), *The Impact of Imperial Rome on Religions, Ritual and Religious Life in the Roman Empire* (Leiden: Brill), pp. 11–23

—— (ed.). 2013a. *The Individual in the Religions of the Ancient Mediterranean* (Oxford: Oxford University Press)

——. 2013b. 'Individualization and Individuation as Concepts', in J. Rüpke (ed.), *The Individual in the Religions of the Ancient Mediterranean* (Oxford: Oxford University Press), pp. 3–38

——. 2015. 'Religious Agency, Identity, and Communication: Reflecting on History and Theory of Religion', *Religion*, 45: 344–66

——. 2016. *On Roman Religion: Lived Religion and the Individual in Ancient Rome* (Ithaca: Cornell University Press)

——. 2017. 'Una prospettiva individualizzata sulla religione antica', *Mythos* [online]: <https://journals.openedition.org/mythos/659> [accessed 28 September 2019]

——. 2018 [2016]. *Pantheon: A New History of Roman Religion* (Princeton: Princeton University Press)

——. 2020. 'Establishing Self-World Relations in Socio-Religious Practices. Looking at Roman Religious Communication', in A. Begemann, A.-K. Rieger, J. Rüpke, W. Spickermann, and K. Waldner (eds), *Rituals and Habitus in the Ancient World*, ARYS (Antigüedad: Religiones y Sociedades), 18 (Madrid: Biblioteca de la facultad de Humanidades, Universidad Carlos III de Madrid), pp. 19–50

Sagona, C. (ed.). 2008. *Beyond the Homeland: Markers in Phoenician Chronology* (Leuven: Peeters)

Salas, J., J. A. Redondo, and J. L. Sánchez Abal. 1983. 'Un sincretismo religioso en la Península ibérica: Jupiter Solutorio-Eaeco', *Norba*, 4: 243–61

Salinas de Frías, M. 1986. *Conquista y romanización de Celtiberia*, Acta Salmanticensia: Estudios históricos & geográficos, 50 (Salamanca: Ediciones Universidad de Salamanca)

——. 1995. 'Los inicios de la epigrafía en Lusitania oriental', in F. Beltrán Lloris (ed.), *Roma y el Nacimiento de la cultura epigráfica en Occidente: actas del Coloquio Roma y las primeras culturas epigráficas del occidente mediterráneo (siglos II a. E.-I d.E.)* (Zaragoza: Institución 'Fernando el Católico'), pp. 281–92

Salinas de Frías, M., and J. Rodríguez. 2007. 'El culto imperial en el contexto político y religioso del *conventus emeritensis*', in T. Nogales and J. González Fernández (eds), *Culto Imperial: política y poder; actas del Congreso Internacional Culto Imperial; política y poder; Mérida, Museo Nacional de Arte Romano, 18–20 de mayo, 2006* (Rome: L'Erma di Bretschneider), pp. 579–90

Sallnow, M. J. 1981. 'Communitas Reconsidered: The Sociology of Andean Pilgrimage', *Royal Anthropological Institute of Great Britain and Ireland*, 16.2: 163–82

Sánchez González, L., and J. J. Seguí. 2005. *La romanización en tierras valencianas: una historia documental* (Valencia: Universitat de València)

Sánchez Palencia, J., and J. Mangas (eds). 2000. *El edicto del Bierzo: Augusto y el Noroeste de Hispania* (Ponferrada: Fundación Las Médulas)

Sandberg, K., and C. Smith (eds). 2018. *'Omnium Annalium Monumenta': Historical Writing and Historical Evidence in Republican Rome* (Leiden: Brill)

Sanmartí, E., P. Castanyer, and J. Tremoleda. 1990. 'Emporion: un ejemplo de monumentalización precoz en la Hispania republicana (los santuarios helenísticos de su sector meridional)', in W. Trillmich and P. Zanker, *Stadtbild und Ideologie: Die Monumentalisierung hispanischer Städte zwischen Republik und Kaiserzeit; Kolloquium in Madrid vom 19. bis 23. Oktober 1987* (Munich: Verlag der Bayerischen Akademie der Wissenschaften), pp. 117–44

Sanmartí, E., and R. A. Santiago. 1987. 'Une lettre grecque sur plomb trouvée a Emporion', *ZPE*, 68: 119–27

Sanmartí, J. 1984. 'Edificis sepulcrals romans dels Països Catalans, Aragó i Múrcia', *Fonaments*, 4: 87–160

Santiago, R. A. 1990. 'En torno a los nombres antiguos de Sagunto', *Saguntum*, 23: 123–40

——. 1994. 'Enigmas en torno a Saguntum y Rhoda', *Faventia*, 16.2: 51–64

Santos, J., A. L. Hoces, and J. del Hoyo. 2005. *Epigrafía romana de Segovia y su provincia* (Caja Segovia: Diputación Provincial de Segovia)

Santos, M., and J. C. Sourisseau. 2011. 'Cultes et pratiques rituelles dans les communautés grecques de Gaule méditerranéenne et de Catalogne', in R. Roure and L. Pernet (eds), *Des rites et des hommes: les pratiques symboliques des Celtes, des Ibères et des grecs en Provence, en Languedoc et en Catalogne* (Paris: Errance), pp. 19–34

Santos, M. J., H. Pires, and O. Sousa. 2014. 'Nuevas lecturas de las inscripciones del santuario de Panóias (Vila Real, Portugal)', *Sylloge Epigraphica Barcinonensis*, 12: 197–224

Saquete, J. C. 2001. 'Fistulae aquariae con sello halladas en Augusta Emerita', *Anas*, 14: 119–69

——. 2005. 'Materiales epigráficos procedentes del área del gran templo de culto imperial de Augusta Emerita: una revisión necesaria', *Habis*, 36: 72–98

——. 2016–2017 [2020]. 'Vettilla, Paculus y sus relaciones familiares', *Anas*, 29–30: 355–62

Sartori, A. 1992. 'L'alto Milanese, terra di culti', *Mélanges de l'École française de Rome*, 104: 77–90

——. 1993. 'Epigrafia sacra e appariscenza sociale', in M. Mayer and J. Gómez Pallarès (eds), *'Religio deorum': Actas del coloquio internacional Culto y Sociedad en Occidente, Tarragona, 1988* (Sabadell: Ausa), pp. 423–34

'Saxa scripta' 2001. *'Saxa scripta': Actas do III Simpósio Ibero-Itálico de Epigrafia Rupestre*, Colecção Ser e Estar, 6 (Viseu: Governo civil do distrito de Viseu)

Sayas, J. J. 1982. 'Religiones mistéricas', in J. Mª. Jover (ed.), *Historia de España*, II.2 (Madrid: Espasa Calpe), pp. 371–97

Scardigli, B. 1991. *I trattati romano-cartaginesi* (Pisa: Scuola normale superiore)

Schattner, T. G. 2012. 'Kurze Bemerkung zu den Figurenfriesen und Prozessionsdarstellungen auf westhispanischen Denkmälern', *Madrider Mitteilungen*, 53: 403–28

——. 2013. 'Die Romanisierung einheimischer Heiligtümer im Westen der Iberischen Halbinsel unter besonderer Berücksichtigung von Votiv und Ritual', in I. Gerlach and D. Raue (eds), *Sanktuar und Ritual: Heilige Plätze im archäologischen Befund*, Menschen — Kulturen — Traditionen, 10 (Rahden: Leidorf), pp. 393–415

——. 2015. 'Pre-Roman and Roman Sanctuaries of the Hispanic West and their Rituals, an Archaeological Contribution to the Linguistic Division of the Country', in C. Zinko and M. Zinko (eds), *Der antike Mensch im Spannungsfeld zwischen Ritual und Magie*, I: *Grazer Symposium zur indogermanischen Altertumskunde. Graz, 14./15. November 2013; Grazer Vergleichende Arbeiten am Zentrum Antike der Karl–Franzens–Universität Graz 28 (Vormals: Arbeiten aus der Abteilung, Vergleichende Sprachwissenschaft Graz)* (Graz: Leykam), pp. 341–75

——. 2017. 'Projet d'étude des cultes et des sanctuaires de l'ouest de la péninsule ibérique à l'époque romaine, réflexions sur les nouvelles fondations', in S. Agusta-Boularot, S. Huber, and W. van Andringa (eds), *Quand naissent les dieux: fondation des sanctuaires antiques; motivations, agents, lieux, Kolloquium Rom, les 18–20 juin 2015*, Collection de l'école française de Rome, 534 (Rome: École française de Rome), pp. 351–81

——. 2019a. 'Vielfalt in der Distanz. Römische Götterdarstellungen im hispanischen Westen', in T. G. Schattner and A. Guerra (eds), *Das Antlitz der Götter – O rosto das divindades: Götterbilder im Westen des Römischen Reiches – Imagens de divindades no ocidente do Império romano, Internationales Kolloquium in Boticas/Colóquio internacional em Boticas (Portugal). 24 a 27 de maio de 2012*, Iberia Archaeologica, 20 (Wiesbaden: Reichert)

——. 2019b. 'Vorarbeiten für eine archäologische Typologie der Heiligtümer und Votivdepots des vorrömischen und römischen hispanischen Westens', *Madrider Mitteilungen*, 60: 133–81

——. 2022. 'Men, Women, Children, Animals: The Votive Statuary from the Sanctuary of Endovellicus at São Miguel da Mota/Alandroal (Portugal)', in T. D. Stek and A. Carneiro (eds), *The Archaeology of Roman Portugal in its Western Mediterranean Context* (Oxford: Oxbow), pp. 257–73

Schattner, T. G., A. Guerra, and C. Fabião. 2005. 'La investigación del Santuario de Endovelico en São Miguel da Mota (Portugal)', in *Actas del IX Coloquio sobre Lenguas y Culturas Paleohispanicas, 20–24 de octubre de 2004*, Palaeohispanica, 5 (Zaragoza: Institución 'Fernando el Católico'), pp. 893–908

——. 2008. 'La cariátide de São Miguel da Mota y su relación con las cariátides de Mérida', in J. M. Noguera and E. Conde Guerri (eds), *Escultura Romana en Hispania V: actas de la reunión internacional, Murcia 2005* (Murcia: Tabularium), pp. 697–729

——. 2013. 'A investigação em torno do Santuário de S. Miguel da Mota: o ponto de situação', *Cadernos de Endovélico*, 1: 65–98

Schattner, T. G., J. Suárez Otero, and M. Koch. 2005. 'Monte do Facho, Donón (O Hío/Prov. Pontevedra) 2003. Bericht über die Ausgrabungen im Heiligtum des Berobreus', *Madrider Mitteilungen*, 46: 135–83

Schattner, T. G., J. Suárez Otero, and M. Koch. 2014. 'Weihaltäre im Heiligtum des deus lar Berobreus auf dem Monte do Facho (O Hío, Galicien)', in A. W. Busch and A. Schäfer (eds), *Römische Weiheealtäre im Kontext: Internationale Tagung in Köln vom 3. bis 5. Dezember 2009* (Friedberg: Likias), pp. 249–68

Scheid, J. 1981. *Commentarium fratrum Aravlium qui supersunt: Les copies épigraphiques des protocoles annuels de la confrérie arvale (21 av. – 304 ap. J.-C.)* (Rome: École française de Rome)

——. 1992. 'Épigraphie et sanctuaires guérisseurs en Gaule', *Mélanges de l'École française de Rome Antiquité*, 104.1: 25–40

——. 1996. 'Pline le Jeune et les sanctuaires d'Italie. Observations sur les Lettres IV, 1, VIII, 8 et IX, 39', in A. Chastagnol, S. Demougin, and C. Lepelley, *Splendidissima civitas: Études d'histoire romaine en hommage à François Jacques* (Paris: Éditions de la Sorbonne), pp. 241–58

——. 1997. 'Comment identifier un lieu de culte?', *Cahiers du Centre Gustave Glotz*, 8: 51–59

——. 1999. 'Aspects religieux de la municipalisation. Quelques réflexions générales', in M. Dondin-Payre and M.-T. Raepsaet-Charlier (eds), *Cités, municipes, colonies: les processus de municipalisation en Gaule et en Germanie sous le Haut Empire romain* (Paris: Éditions de la Sorbonne), pp. 381–423

——. 2005. 'Augustus and Roman Religion: Continuity, Conservatism, and Innovation', in K. Galinsky (ed.), *The Cambridge Companion to the Age of Augustus* (Cambridge: Cambridge University Press), pp. 175–96

——. 2012. 'Epigraphy and Roman Religion', in J. K. Davies and J. Wilkes (eds), *Epigraphy and the Historical Sciences* (Oxford: Oxford University Press), pp. 31–44

Scheid, J., and M.-T. Granino. 1999. 'Les sacerdoces publics équestre', in S. Demougin, H. Devijver, and M. T. Raepsaet-Chalier (eds), *L'ordre équestre: histoire d'une aristocratie (II$^e$ siècle av. J.-C. – III$^e$ siècle ap. J.-C.)* (Rome: Ecole française de Rome), pp. 79–189

Schettino, M. T. 2006. 'Sagunto e lo scoppio della guerra in Silio Italico', *Aevum Antiquum*, 6: 53–63

Seco, I. 2010. *Piedras con alma: el betilismo en el mundo antiguo y sus manifestaciones en la Península Ibérica* (Seville: Universidad de Sevilla)

Shaw, B. D. 1981. 'The Elder Pliny's African Geography', *Historia: Zeitschrift für Alte Geschichte*, 30.4: 421–71

——. 2004. 'A Peculiar Island. Maghrib and Mediterranean', *Mediterranean Historical Review*, 18.2: 93–125

Silva, A. da and M. C. Lopes. 2007. *La contribution de la prospection géomagnétique pour la compréhension de la paléoforme de Matabodes (Beja, Portugal)*, 1.º Colloque d'Archéogéographie (6 à 8 Septembre 2007 à Paris) <http://ia.regiaocentro.net/paginas/index.php?nIDPagina=64> [accessed on 7 January 2020]

Simón Cornago 2012: I. Simón Cornago, *La epigrafía ibérica de Montaña Frontera (Sagunto)*, *Madrider Mitteilungen*, 53, 2012: 239–61

Sinner, A. G. 2015. 'Cultural Contacts and Identity Construction: A Colonial Context in NE Spain (2nd–Early 1st c. B.C.)', *JRA*, 28: 7–38

——. forthcoming. 'Human Mobility between Italy and NE Hispania during the Late Republican Period', in L. Gosner and J. Hayne (eds), *Local Experiences of Connectivity and Mobility in the Ancient West-Central Mediterranean*, Monographs in Mediterranean Archaeology (Sheffield: Equinox)

Sinner, A. G. and J. Ferrer i Jané. 2022. 'Rock Sanctuaries, Sacred Landscapes, and the Making of the Iberian Pantheon', *Religions*, 13: 722.

——. 2020. 'Baitolo, a Native Shipowner's Vessel, and the Participation of Northern Iberians in the Laietanian Wine-Trade under the Late Republic', *JRA*, 33: 365–82

Sinner, A. G., and V. Revilla. 2017. 'Rural Religion, Religious Places and Local Identities in *Hispania*: The Sanctuary at Can Modolell (Cabrera de Mar, Barcelona)', *JRA*, 30: 267–82

Sinner, A. G., and J. Velaza. 2018. 'Epigraphy: The Palaeohispanic Languages', in C. Smith (ed.), *Encyclopedia of Global Archaeology* (Cham: Springer), pp. 1–13

—— (eds). 2019. *Palaeohispanic Languages and Epigraphies* (Oxford: Oxford University Press)

Small, A. (ed.). 1996. *Subject and Ruler: The Cult of the Ruling Power in Classical Antiquity; Papers Presented at a Conference Held in the University of Alberta on April 13–15, 1994 to Celebrate the 65th Anniversary of Duncan Fishwick*, JRA Supplementary Series, 17 (Ann Arbor, MI: Journal of Roman Archaeology)

Smith, J. Z. 1987. *To Take Place: Toward Theory in Ritual* (Chicago: University of Chicago Press)

Solana, J. M., and L. Hernández. 2000. *Religión y sociedad en época romana en la Meseta septentrional* (Valladolid: Universidad de Valladolid)

Solin, H. 1996. *Die Stadtrömischen Sklavennamen: Ein Namenbuch*, II: *Griechische Namen*, Forschungen zur Antiken Sklaverei Beihefte, 2 (Stuttgart: Steiner)

Sopeña, G. 1995. *Ética y ritual: aproximación al estudio de la religiosidad de los pueblos celtibéricos* (Zaragoza: Institución 'Fernando el Católico')

Spaeth, B. S. (ed.). 2013. *The Cambridge Companion to Ancient Mediterranean Religions* (Cambridge: Cambridge University Press)

Spannagel, M. 1999. *Exemplaria Principis: Untersuchungen zu Entstehung und Ausstattung des Augustusforums*, Archäologie und Geschichte, 9 (Heidelberg: Verlag Archäologie und Geschichte)

Spawforth, A. J. S., and S. Walker. 1985. 'The World of the Panhellenion. I. Athens and Eleusis', *JRS*, 75: 78–104

——. 1986. 'The World of the Panhellenion. II. Three Dorian Cities', *JRS*, 76: 88–105

Stek, T. D. 2009. *Cult Places and Cultural Change in Republican Italy: A Contextual Approach to Religious Aspects of Rural Society after Roman Conquest* (Amsterdam: Amsterdam University Press)

——. 2014. 'Roman Imperialism, Globalization, and Romanization in Early Roman Italy. Research Questions in Archaeology and Ancient History', *Archaeological Dialogues*, 21: 30–40

——. 2015. 'The Importance of Rural Sanctuaries in Structuring Non-Urban Society in Ancient Samnium: Approaches from Architecture and Landscape', *Oxford Journal of Archaeology*, 34.4: 397–406

——. 2016. 'Romanizzazione religiosa' tra modello poliadico e processi culturali. Dalla destrutturazione postcoloniale a nuove prospettive sull'impatto della conquista romana', in M. Aberson, M. C. Biella, M. Di Fazio, P. Sanchez, and M. Wullschleger, *L'Italia centrale e la creazione di una 'koiné' culturale? I percorsi della 'romanizzazione'* (Bern: Lang), pp. 291–306

Stek, T., and G.-T. Burgers. 2015. *The Impact of Rome on Cult Places and Religious Practices in Ancient Italy*, BICS Supplement 132 (London: Institute of Classical Studies, School of Advanced Study, University of London)

Stephens, J. 2016. *Ancient Mediterranean Religions: Myth, Ritual and Religious Experience* (Newcastle: Cambridge Scholars)

Strothmann, M. 2000. *Augustus – Vater der Res publica: Zur Funktion der drei Begriffe restitutio – saeculum – pater patriae im augusteischen Prinzipat* (Stuttgart: Steiner)

——. 2020. 'Roman City-Laws of Spain and their Modelling of the Religious Landscape', in K. Czajkowski, B. Eckhardt, and M. Strothmann, *Law in the Roman Provinces* (Oxford: Oxford University Press), pp. 332–45

Stylow, A. U. 1987. 'Beiträge zur lateinischen Epigraphik im Norden der Provinz Córdoba', *Madrider Mitteilungen*, 28: 57–126

——. 1992. 'La Cueva Negra de Fortuna (Murcia): ¿un santuario púnico?', in M. Mayer and J. Gómez Pallarès (eds), *'Religio deorum': Actas del coloquio internacional Culto y Sociedad en Occidente, Tarragona, 1988* (Sabadell: Ausa), pp. 449–60

——. 1995. 'Von Emil Hübner zur Neuauflage von CIL II. Anhang: Zu einer neuen Pales-Inschrift aus Mirobriga', *Madrider Mitteilungen*, 36: 17–29

——. 1997. 'Nuevo testimonio emeritense de Ataecina', *Revista de Estudios Extremeños*, 53: 11–14

Stylow, A. U., and M. Mayer. 1987. 'Los *tituli* de la Cueva Negra. Lectura y comentarios literario y paleográfico', in *La Cueva Negra de Fortuna (Murcia) y sus tituli picti: un santuario de época romana; homenaje al profesor D. Sebastián Mariner Bigorra*, Antigüedad y Cristianismo, 4 (Murcia: Universidad de Murcia), pp. 191–236

——. 1996 [1999]. 'Los tituli de la Cueva Negra. Lectura y comentarios literario y paleográfico', in A. González Blanco, M. Mayer, A. U. Stylow, and R. González Fernández (eds), *El balneario romano y la Cueva Negra de Fortuna (Murcia): homenaje al prof. Ph. Rahtz*, Antigüedad y Cristianismo, 13 (Murcia: Universidad de Murcia), pp. 367–406

——. 2003. 'Los *tituli* de la Cueva Negra. Lectura y comentarios literario y paleográfico', in A. González Blanco and G. Matilla (eds), *La cultura latina en la Cueva Negra: en agradecimiento y homenaje a los Profs. A. Stylow, M. Mayer e I. Velázquez*, Antigüedad y Cristianismo, 20 (Murcia: Universidad de Murcia), pp. 225–64

Stylow, A. U., and Á. Ventura Villanueva. 2018. 'Inscripciones asociadas a la *scaena* del teatro', in P. Mateos Cruz (ed.), *La 'scaenae frons' del teatro romano de Mérida*, Anejos del *Archivo Español de Arqueología*, 86 (Mérida: Consejo Superior de Investigaciones Científicas), pp. 157–95

Swain, S. 1996. *Hellenism and Empire: Language, Classicism and Power in the Greek World, AD 50–250* (Oxford: Clarendon)

Syme, R. 1981. 'Rival Cities. Notably Tarraco and Barcino', *Ktema*, 6: 271–85

Tacoma, L. E. 2016. *Moving Romans: Migration to Rome in the Principate* (Oxford: Oxford University Press)

Takács, S. A. 2005. 'Divine and Human Feet: Record of Pilgrims Honouring Isis', in J. Elsner and I. Rutherford (eds), *Pilgrimage in Graeco-Roman and Early Christian Antiquity: Seeing the Gods* (Oxford: Oxford University Press), pp. 353–69

Tarradell, M. 1973. 'Cuevas sagradas o cuevas santuario: un aspecto poco valorado de la religión ibérica', *Memoria del Instituto de Arqueología y Prehistoria de la Universidad de Barcelona*, 1973: 25–40

——. 1979. 'Santuaris ibèrics i ibero-romans a llocs alts', *Memòria de l'Institut d'Arqueologia i Prehistòria de la Universitat de Barcelona*, 1979: 35–45

Tarrats, F. B., and J. A. Remolà. 2008. 'Vil·la romana dels Munts', in J. A. Remolà (ed.), *El Territori de Tarraco: villes romanes del Camp de Tarragona* (Tarragona: Museu Nacional Arqueològic de Tarragona and Institut Català d'Arqueologia Clàssica), pp. 95–117

Tarrats, F. B., J. A. Remolà, and J. Sánchez. 2006. 'La villa romana dels Munts (Altafulla, Tarragonès) i Tarraco', *Tribuna d'Arqueologia*, 2006: 213–28

Terrenato, N. 1998. 'The Romanization of Italy: Global Acculturation of Cultural Bricolage', in C. Forcey, J. Hawthorne, and R. Witcher (eds), *TRAC 97: Proceedings of the Seventh Annual Theoretical Roman Archaeology Conference* (Oxford: Oxbow), pp. 20–27

——. 2007. 'The Essential Countryside: Farms, Villages, Sanctuaries, Tombs', in S. Alcock and R. Osborne (eds), *Classical Archaeology* (Oxford: Blackwell), pp. 139–61

——. 2008. 'The Cultural Implications of the Roman Conquest', in E. Bispham (ed.), *Roman Europe (Short Oxford History of Europe)* (Oxford: Oxford University Press), pp. 234–64

——. 2013. 'Patterns of Cultural Change in Roman Italy. Non-Elite Religion and the Defense of Cultural Self-Consistency', in M. Jehne, B. Linke, and J. Rüpke (eds), *Religiöse Vielfalt und soziale Integration: Die Bedeutung der Religion für die kulturelle Identität und politische Stabilität im republikanischen Italien* (Heidelberg: Verlag Antike), pp. 43–60

Thonemann, P. 2011. *The Maeander Valley: A Historical Geography from Antiquity to Byzantium*, Greek Culture in the Roman World (Cambridge: Cambridge University Press)

Torelli, M. 1985. 'Introduzione', in S. Stopponi (ed.), *Case e palazzi d'Etruria* (Florence: Regione Toscana), pp. 21–32

Torregaray, E. 1998. *La elaboración de la tradición sobre los 'Cornelii Scipiones': pasado histórico y conformación simbólica* (Zaragoza: Institución Fernando el Católico)

——. 2002. 'Contribución al estudio de la memoria como instrumento en Historia Antigua: la transmisión de la memoria de los Cornelii Scipiones', *Latomus*, 61: 295–311

——. 2006. 'Los espacios de la diplomacia en la Roma republicana', *Caesarodunum*, 40: 254–58

——. 2018. 'Marsella en el imaginario político-diplomático romano', in V. Bonet and G. Viard (eds), *Marseille en Méditerranée: échanges économiques et culturels de la ville grecque à la ville médiévale: actes du XLVI$^e$ congrès de l'APLAES (2013)*, Les Annales de l'APLAES, 5: 1–11

Tortosa, T. 2004. 'Tipología e iconografía de la cerámica ibérica figurada en el enclave de La Alcudia (Elche, Alicante)', in T. Tortosa (ed.), *El yacimiento de La Alcudia: pasado y presente de un enclave ibérico*, Anejos de *Archivo Español de Arqueología*, 30 (Madrid: Consejo Superior de Investigaciones Científicas), pp. 71–222

——. 2006. *Los estilos y grupos pictóricos de la cerámica ibérica figurada de la Contestania*, Anejos de *Archivo Español de Arqueología*, 38 (Mérida: Consejo Superior de Investigaciones Científicas)

—— (ed.). 2014. *Diálogo de identidades: Bajo el prisma de las manifestaciones religiosas en el ámbito mediterráneo (s. III a.C.– s. I d.C.)*, Anejos de *Archivo Español de Arqueología*, 72 (Mérida: Consejo Superior de Investigaciones Científicas)

Tortosa, T., and A. Comino. 2013. 'Observaciones sobre una nueva mirada en el contexto de los espacios sacros murcianos: el Santuario de la Luz (Verdolay, Murcia)', in C. Rísquez and C. Rueda (eds), *Santuarios Iberos: territorio, ritualidad y memoria; actas del Congreso: el Santuario de la Cueva de la Lobera, Castellar* (Jaén: Asociación para el Desarrollo Rural de la Comarca de El Condado), pp. 115–44

Tortosa, T., and S. Ramallo (eds). 2017. *El tiempo final de los santuarios ibéricos en los procesos de impacto y consolidación del mundo romano*, Anejos de *Archivo Español de Arqueología*, 79 (Madrid: Consejo Superior de Investigaciones Científicas)

Toutain, J. 1905–1911. *Les cultes païens dans l'Empire romain*, 3 vols (Paris: Leroux)

Tovar, A. 1985. 'La inscripción del Cabeço das Fráguas y la lengua de los Lusitanos', in *Actas del III Coloquio sobre Lenguas y Culturas Paleohispanicas (Salamanca 1985)* (Salamanca: Universidad de Salamanca), pp. 227–54

Tranoy, A. 1981. *La Galice romain* (Paris: De Boccard)

——. 2004. 'Panóias ou les rochers des dieux', *Conimbriga*, 43: 85–97

Trillmich, W. 1989–1990. 'Un *sacrarium* del culto imperial en el teatro de Mérida', *Anas*, 2–3: 87–102

——. 1996. 'Reflejos de un programa estatuario del *forum Augustum* en Mérida', in J. Massó and P. Sada (eds), *Actas de la II Reunión sobre escultura romana en Hispania* (Tarragona: Museu Nacional Arqueologic), pp. 95–168

——. 2007. 'Espacios públicos de culto imperial en *Augusta Emerita*: entre hipótesis y dudas', in T. Nogales and J. González Fernández (eds), *Culto Imperial: política y poder; actas del Congreso Internacional Culto Imperial; política y poder; Mérida, Museo Nacional de Arte Romano, 18–20 de mayo, 2006* (Rome: L'Erma di Bretschneider), pp. 415–46

——. 2016–2017 [2020]. 'Una promesa de fidelidad al Genio de los emeritenses', *Anas*, 29–30: 385–94

Trillmich, W., and P. Zanker. 1990. *Stadtbild und Ideologie: Die Monumentalisierung hispanischer Städte zwischen Republik und Kaiserzeit; Kolloquium in Madrid vom 19. bis 23. Oktober 1987* (Munich: Verlag der Bayerischen Akademie der Wissenschaften)

Truszkowski, E. 2006. *Étude stylistique de la sculpture du sanctuaire ibérique du Cerro de los Santos, Albacete (Espagne)*, Monographies instrumentum, 33 (Drémil-Lafage: Éditions Mergoil)

Tuchelt, K. 1970. *Die archaischen Skulpturen von Didyma: Beiträge zur frühgriechischen Plastik in Kleinasien*, Istanbuler Forschungen, 27 (Berlin: Mann)

Ubiña, J. F. 1996. 'Magna Mater, Cybele and Attis in Roman Spain', in *Cybele, Attis and Related Cults: Essays in Memory of M. J. Vermaseren*, Religions in the Graeco-Roman World, 131 (Leiden: Brill), pp. 405–33

Untermann, J. 1983. 'Die Althispanischen Sprachen', *ANRW*, 29.2: 791–818

Urciuoli, E. R., and J. Rüpke. 2018. 'Urban Religion in Mediterranean Antiquity: Relocating Religious Change', *Mythos*, 12: 117–35 <https://doi.org/10.4000/mythos.341>

Uribe, P., L. Íñiguez, and M. Pérez Ruiz. 2014. 'Arquitectura y repertorios decorativos domésticos de la Osca romana', *Bolskan*, 25: 11–25

Vallejo Ruiz, J. M. 2005. *Antroponimia indígena de la Lusitania romana*, Anejos de *Veleia*, Serie minor, 23 (Vitoria-Gasteiz: Universidad del País Vasco)

Van Andringa, W. 2002. *La religion en Gaule romaine: Piété et politique ($I^{er}$–$III^e$ siècle apr. J.-C.)* (Paris: Errance)

Van Dommelen, P., and N. Terrenato (eds). 2007. *Articulating Local Cultures: Power and Identity under the Expanding Roman Republic*, JRA Supplementary Series, 63 (Portsmouth, RI: Journal of Roman Archaeology)

Vasconcellos, J. 1905. *Religiões da Lusitania*, II (Lisbon: Imprensa Nacional)

——. 1913. *Religiões da Lusitania*, III (Lisbon: Imprensa Nacional)
Vázquez Hoys, A. 1977. 'La religión romana en Hispania I: análisis estadístico', *Hispania Antiqua*, 7: 7–45
——. 1982. *La religión romana en Hispania: fuentes epigráficas, arqueológicas y numismáticas* (Madrid: Universidad Complutense)
——. 1987. 'La religiosidad de la España romana', in *Historia general de España y América*, II (Madrid: Rialp), pp. 405–45
——. 1995. *Diana en la religiosidad hispanorromana*, I: *Las fuentes. Las diferentes diosas* (Madrid: UNED)
Vé, K.K. 2018. 'La cité et la sauvagerie : les rites des Lupercales', *Dialogues d'Historie Ancienne*, 44.2: 139–90
Velaza, J. 2002. 'Las inscripciones monetales', in P. P. Ripollès and M. del M. Llorens (eds), *Arse-Saguntum: Historia monetaria de la ciudad y su territorio* (Sagunto: Fundación Bancaja), pp. 121–48
——. 2003. 'Los textos de la Cueva Negra y sus modelos literarios', in A. González Blanco and G. Matilla (eds), *La cultura latina en la Cueva Negra: en agradecimiento y homenaje a los Profs. A. Stylow, M. Mayer e I. Velázquez*, Antigüedad y Cristianismo, 20 (Murcia: Universidad de Murcia), pp. 265–74
——. 2018. 'Epigrafía ibérica sobre soporte pétreo: origen y evolución', in F. Beltrán and B. Díaz Ariño (eds), *El nacimiento de las culturas epigráficas en el occidente mediterráneo*, Anejos de *Archivo Español de Arqueología*, 85 (Madrid: Consejo Superior de Investigaciones Científicas), pp. 169–83
——. 2018–2019. 'Escritura y ritualidad en los santuarios rupestres de la Cerdanya', *Bandue*, 11: 83–93
Ventura, Á. 2007. 'Reflexiones sobre la arquitectura y la advocación del templo de la calle Morería e el *fórum adiectum* de la *Colonia Patricia Corduba*', in T. Nogales and J. González Fernández (eds), *Culto Imperial: política y poder; actas del Congreso Internacional Culto Imperial; política y poder; Mérida, Museo Nacional de Arte Romano, 18–20 de mayo, 2006* (Rome: L'Erma di Bretschneider), pp. 215–37
Veny, C. 1965. *Corpus de las inscripciones baleáricas hasta la dominación árabe* (Madrid: Consejo Superior de Investigaciones Científicas)
Ver Eecke, M. 2008. *La République et le roi: le mythe de Romulus à la fin de la République romaine* (Paris: De Boccard)
Versluys, M. J. 2004. '*Isis Capitolina* and the Egyptian Cults in Late Republican Rome', in B. Bricault (ed.), *Isis en Occident: actes du III<sup>ème</sup> colloque international sur les études isiaques, Lyon III, 16–17 mai 2002*, Religions in the Graeco-Roman World (Leiden: Brill), pp. 421–48
Vessey, D. 1974. 'Silius Italicus on the Fall of Saguntum', *Classical Philology*, 69.1: 28–36
Veyne, P. 1983. '*Titulus praelatus*: offrande, solennisation et publicité dans le ex-voto gréco-romain', *Revue Archéologique*, 2: 281–300
Viana, A. 1954. 'Notas históricas, arqueológicas e etnográficas do Baixo Alentejo', *Arquivo de Beja*, 11: 3–31
——. 1957. 'Lucernas de Peroguarda', *Arquivo de Beja*, 13: 123–38
Vicent, J. A. 1979. 'Excavacions al santuari hispano-romà de Santa Bárbara', *Cuadernos de Prehistoria y Arqueología Castellonenses*, 6: 181–221
Vilaça, R. 2007. 'A Cachouça (Idanha-a-Nova, Castelo Branco). Construção e organização de um caso singular de inícios do I milénio AC', in S. Oliveira Jorge, A. M. S. Bettencourt, and I. Figueiral (eds), *Actas do IV Congresso de Arqueologia Peninsular Faro: a concepção das paisagens e dos espaços na Arqueologia da Península Ibérica, Faro 14 a 19 de Setembro de 2004*, Promontoria monográfica, 8 (Faro: Centro de Estudos de Património), pp. 67–75
——. 2008. *Através das Beiras: pré-história e proto-história* (Coimbra: Palimage Editora)
Villaronga, L. 1978. *Las monedas ibéricas de Ilerda* (Barcelona: CSIC)
Visedo, C. 1922a. *Excavaciones en el monte La Serreta, próximo a Alcoy*, Memoria de la Junta Superior de Excavaciones y Antigüedades, 41 (Madrid: Tip. de la Revista de Archivos)
Vukovic, K. 2017. 'The Topography of the Lupercalia', *Papers of the British School at Rome*, 86: 37–60
Weber, E. 1976. *Peasants into Frenchmen: The Modernization of Rural France, 1870–1914* (Stanford: Stanford University Press)
Webster, J. 1996. 'Roman Imperialism and the "Post-Imperial Age"', in J. Webster and N. J. Cooper (eds), *Roman Imperialism: Post-Colonial Perspectives*, Leicester Archaeology Monograph, 3 (Leicester: Leicester University, School of Archaeological Studies), pp. 1–17
——. 1997. 'Necessary Comparisons: A Post-Colonial Approach to Religious Syncretism in the Roman Provinces', *World Archaeology*, 28.3: 324–38
——. 2001. 'Creolizing the Roman Provinces', *AJA*, 105.2: 209–25
Webster, J., and N. J. Cooper (eds). 1997. *Roman Imperialism: Post-Colonial Perspectives*, Leicester Archaeology Monograph, 3 (Leicester University: School of Archaeological Studies)
Weinstock, S. 1971. *Divus Julius* (Oxford: Clarendon)
Whitmarsh, T. (ed.). 2010. *Local Knowledge and Microidentities in the Imperial Greek World: Greek Culture in the Roman World* (Cambridge: Cambridge University Press)
Whittaker, C. R. 1999. 'Imperialism and Culture: The Roman Initiative', in D. J. Mattingly (ed.), *Dialogues in Roman Imperialism: Power, Discourse, and Discrepant Experience in the Roman Empire*, JRA Supplementary Series, 23 (Portsmouth, RI: Journal of Roman Archaeology), pp. 143–63

Wicha, S. 2002–2003. 'Urbs fide atque aerumnis incluta. Zum Saguntmythos in augustischer Zeit', *Lucentum*, 22–23: 179–90

Will, E. 1950. 'Le date du Mithréum de Sidon', *Syria*, 27: 261–69

Williamson, C. 2012. 'Sanctuaries as Turning Points in Territorial Formation. Lagina, Panamara and the Development of Stratonikeia', *Byzas*, 13: 113–50

Wilson, A. J. N. 1966. *Emigration from Italy in the Republican Age of Rome* (New York: Barnes & Noble)

Wiseman, T. P. 1974. 'Legendary Genealogies in Late-Republican Rome', *Greece & Rome*, 21.1: 153–64

Wissowa G. 1912. *Religion und Kultus der Römer* (Munich: Beck)

Witcher, R. 2000. 'Globalization and Roman Identity: Perspectives on Identities in Roman Italy', in E. Herring and K. Lomas (eds), *The Emergence of State Identities in Italy in the First Millennium BC* (London: Accordia Research Institute, University of London), pp. 213–25

——. 2017. 'The Global Roman Countryside: Connectivity and Community', in T. C. A. de Hass and G. Tol (eds), *The Economic Integration of Roman Italy: Rural Communities in a Globalising World*, Mnemosyne Supplement, 404 (Leiden: Brill), pp. 28–50

Woolf, G. D. 1992. 'The Unity and Diversity of Romanisation', *JRA*, 5: 349–52

——. 1994. 'Becoming Roman, Staying Greek: Culture, Identity and the Civilizing Process in the Roman East', *Proceedings of the Cambridge Philological Society*, 40: 116–43

——. 1995. 'The Formation of Roman Provincial Cultures', in J. Metzler, M. Millet, N. Roymans, and J. Slofstra (eds), *Integration in the Early Imperial West: The Role of Culture and Ideology*, Dossiers d'archéologie du Musée national d'histoire et d'art, 4 (Luxembourg: Musée national d'histoire et d'art), pp. 9–18

——. 1997a. 'Beyond Romans and Natives', *World Archaeology*, 28.3: 339–50

——. 1997b. 'Polis-Religion and its Alternatives in the Roman Provinces', in H. Cancik and J. Rüpke (eds), *Römische Reichsreligion und Provinzialreligion* (Tübingen: Mohr Siebeck), pp. 71–84

——. 1998. *Becoming Roman: The Origins of Provincial Civilization in Gaul* (Cambridge: Cambridge University Press)

——. 2004. 'A Sea of Faith?', *Mediterranean Historical Review*, 18.2: 126–43

——. 2008. 'Divinity and Power in Ancient Rome', in N. Brisch (ed.), *Religion and Power: Divine Kingship in the Ancient World and Beyond* (Chicago: Oriental Institute of the University of Chicago), pp. 243–59

——. 2009a. 'World Religion and World Empire in the Ancient Mediterranean', in H. Cancik and J. Rüpke (eds), *Die Religion des Imperium Romanum: Koine und Konfrontationen* (Tübingen: Mohr Siebeck), pp. 19–35

——. 2009b. 'Found in Translation. The Religion of the Roman Diaspora', in O. Hekster, S. Schmidt-Hofner, and C. Witschel (eds), *Ritual Dynamics and Religious Change in the Roman Empire: Proceedings of the Eighth Workshop of the International Network Impact of Empire* (Leiden: Brill), pp. 239–52

——. 2011. *Tales of the Barbarians: Ethnography and Empire in the Roman West* (Oxford: Blackwell)

——. 2016. 'Movers and Stayers', in L. de Ligt and L. E. Tacoma (eds), *Migration and Mobility in the Early Roman Empire* (Leiden: Brill), pp. 438–61

Zanker, P. 1989. *Augusto e il potere delle immagini* (Turin: Einaudi) (Italian translation of *Augustus und die Macht der Bilder* (Munich: Beck, 1987))

——. 1990. *The Power of Images in the Age of Augustus* (Ann Arbor: University of Michigan Press)

Zucca, R. 1998. *Insulae Baliares: Le isole Baleari sotto il dominio romano* (Rome: Carocci)

# Index of Sources

## Literary Sources

AGEN.
*De controv. agrim.*
    37: 86
    44: 79

AMM. MARC.
    XV.10.10: 156

APP.
*Hann.*
    29: 156
*Hisp.*
    7: 154, 157, 158
    10: 158
    11: 158
    19: 162
    23: 162
    26: 162
    95–98: 156

ATH.
    VIII.63: 141
    XII.36: 156

CATUL.
    61: 62

CIC.
*Rep.*
    XI.11: 162
*Att.*
    XII.18: 76
    XII.19: 76
*Phil.*
    V.27: 159
    VI.6: 159
*Balb.*
    23: 153
    50–51: 157

CASS. DIO
    XLIII.41: 168
    LIII.26.1: 171
    LIV.32.1: 171

*DIG.*
    XXIII.2.63: 190

DION. HAL.
*Ant. Rom.*
    I.56: 148

FABIUS PICTOR
    F3 (Cornell): 148
    *Fest. P.* 329: 160

FLOR.
*Epit.*
    I.34.18.11–17: 156

FRONTIN.
*De controv.* 9: 86
*De limit.* 9: 79
*Str.*
    IV.5.18: 156

GELL.
    II.10: 49
    VI.1: 162
    XVI.13.1–9: 122
    XVI.13.8–9: 91

HYGIN. GROM.
*De limit constit.*
    135–36: 79

IUST.
    XXXI.8.1–4: 162
    XLIII.3: 159
    XLIII.5: 159

JUV.
    XII.80: 58

LIV.
*Praef.* 7–8: 139
    I.2.6: 140
    I.16.3: 140
    I.40.3: 140
    III.20: 153
    XVI.216: 154
    VXIII.39: 158
    XXI.6: 157
    XXI.7.2–3: 153, 156
    XXI.10.13: 157
    XXI.12.6: 158
    XXI.12.7–8: 157
    XXI.13.2: 158
    XXI.14.1: 157
    XXI.19.6–11: 156
    XXI.21.9: 155
    XXI.41.7: 155
    XXIII.20.4–10: 156
    XXIII.30.1–5: 156
    XXVI.19.1–7: 162
    XXVIII.38: 161
    XXVIII.39: 157, 161–62
    XXXVII.33.7: 162
    XXXVII.37.1–3: 162
    LXIII.3: 133
*Per.*
    XXI.2: 156
    XXVI.7: 162
    139: 171

MART.
    XII preface: 123

MELA
    II.92: 156
    III.1.11: 171
    III.13: 170

NIC. DAM.
*Vit.Caes.*
    11: 153

Oros.
    VI.21.9: 168

Ov.
*Pont.*
    XII.3.3: 170
    XII.4.6: 170
*Fast.*
    IV.793–806: 141
    V.145–46: 176

Petr.
    60: 109

Plin. (Pliny the Elder)
*Nat.*
    III.1.6: 121
    III.1.8: 123
    III.3.7–17: 121, 174
    III.3.30: 121
    III.4: 156
    III.20: 153, 171
    IV.4.18–30: 121
    IV.14.110: 171
    IV.20.110–20: 121, 170
    IV.35.113–18: 121
    XVI.216: 154
*Is.*
    IV.117: 87

Plin. (Pliny the Younger)
*Ep.*
    3.4: 123
    3.9: 123
    5.14.8: 75
    7.30.3: 75
    8.2: 75
    9.15.1: 75
    9.36.6: 75
    9.37: 75
    9.39: 75
    10.35–36: 173

Plut.
*Moralia*
    L.1: **62**
*Num.*
    XIII: 160

Polyb.
    III.15.5–8: 156
    III.17.7: 156
    III.30.1: 156
    III.97.6–8: 155
    VII.1: 156

Ptol.
*Geog.*
    II.6.3: 170

Quint.
*Inst.*
    VI.3.77: 135, 168

Sal.
*Hist.*
    II.70: 109

Sen.
*Apocol.*
    III: 123

Sil.
    I.271–75: 155
    I.291–93: 155
    I.332: 155
    I.377–79: 155
    I.378–425: 155
    I.572: 155
    I.654–61: 155
    I.665–69: 155
    II.541: 155
    II.567: 155
    II.604–05: 155
    III.178: 155
    IV.4–5: 155
    IV.62: 155

Solin.
    I.18: 141

Str.
    II.4.6: 154
    III.2.15: 13, 80
    III.4.8: 126
    III.4.13: 121
    III.5.5: 128
    IV.1.4: 126
    IV.1.4–5: 159

Suet.
*Aug.*
    VII.2: 140
    XXVI.3: 168
    XCII.1: 168
*Jul.*
    XCIV.11: 168
*Nero*
    VII: 155

Tac.
*Ann.*
    I.5: 170
    I.39.2: 171
    I.73: 169
    I.78.1: 135, 169
    IV.37.1–3: 175
    IV.45.2: 54
    V.1.1: 175
    XII.58: 155
    XVI.22: 173

Var.
*R.*
    II.4.18: 148

Verg.
*A.*
    I.159: 63
    IV.298: 160
    VIII.285: 160

Val. Max.
    I.8.7: 144
    VI.6. *ext*.1: 156, 159
    VI.6 *ext*. 2: 156

# Epigraphic Sources

*AE*
  1905, 24: 95
  1905, 25: 95
  1905, 26: 95
  1907, 249: 90
  1908, 151: 82
  1915, 67; 1919, 87: 95
  1915, 68; 1919, 86: 95
  1915, 95: 175
  1946, 199: 84
  1955, 151: 82
  1955, 234: 94
  1961, 48: 95
  1962, 67; 1984, 487: 95
  1971, 147: 90
  1971, 159: 84
  1972, 298: 185
  1976, 269; 1983, 486: 93
  1979, 348: 185
  1983, 630: 70
  1984, 485: 82
  1984, 486: 95
  1984, 505: 82
  1987, 655: 62
  1987, 729: 70
  1990, 515: 81
  1992, 1078: 62
  1992, 938: 98
  1992, 957: 94
  1993, 892: 80
  1993, 917a: 80
  1993, 917b: 80
  1994, 877: 83
  1995, 734: 96
  1995, 735: 96
  1995, 736: 96
  1995, 737: 96
  1995, 738: 96
  1995, 739: 96
  1995, 740: 96
  1995, 741: 96
  1995, 742: 96
  1995, 743: 96
  1995, 744: 96
  1995, 745: 96
  1995, 746: 96
  1995, 747: 96
  1995, 748: 96
  1995, 749: 97
  1995, 751: 97
  1995, 752: 97
  1995, 753: 97
  1996, 864a: 146
  1997, 785: 80
  1997, 804a: 85
  1997, 883–907: 56
  1999, 1835–41: 91
  2000, 698: 90
  2000, 1179: 90
  2002, 849: 62
  2003, 87: 931
  2003, 868: 93
  2003, 869: 93
  2003, 870: 93
  2003, 872: 93
  2003, 1012: 70
  2004, 703: 98
  2004, 704: 88, 98
  2004, 705: 99
  2004, 758: 170
  2005, 760; 2006, 582: 93
  2006, 587: 93
  2006, 597: 80
  2006, 615–16: 86
  2007, 721: 81, 94
  2007, 1721–37: 91
  2009, 527–28: 93
  2009, 529: 93
  2009, 530: 95
  2012, 1262: 190
  2014, 735: 185
  2015, 541: 95
  2015, 542: 93
  2015, 544: 94
  2015, 698–702.: 59
  2016, 686: 93
  2017, 646: 84
  2018, 832: 81

CIBal., nos 135–56: 59

*CIIAE*
  20: 93
  26: 81
  27: 93
  28: 93
  29: 93
  30: 93
  31: 93
  32: 93
  33: 94
  52, Röring and Trillmich 2010: 93

*CIL*
  I² 756: 74

  II 96: 191
  II 127: 98
  II 128: 98
  II 129: 98
  II 130: 98
  II 131: 98
  II 132: 98
  II 132: 98
  II 133: 89, 98
  IL II 134: 88, 99
  II 135: 99
  II 136: 98–99
  II 137: 99
  II 138: 99
  II 139: 98
  II 140 = 5201: 98–99
  II 141: 98
  II 142: 98–99
  II 143 = IRCP 570: 97
  II 144 = IRCP 571: 97
  II 145 = IRCP 572: 97
  II 172: 174
  II 194: 175
  II 461: 93
  II 462: 84, 96
  II 464: 93
  II 465: 93
  II 466: 94
  II 467: 94
  II 468: 81, 94
  II 469: 95
  II 470: 95
  II 471: 93
  II 473, rev. Edmondson 1997, 91–103 no. 2 (AE 1997, 777b; HEp 7, 1997, 111): 93
  II 618: 84
  II 656: 79
  II 657: 84
  II 661: 84
  II 728: 84
  II 756: 90
  II 944: 84
  II 980: 96
  II 981: 96
  II 1015: 97
  II 1024, rev. AE 1997, 805: 97
  II 1044: 85
  II 1223: 90

II 2017: 172
II 2018: 175
II 2126: 148
II 2156: 148, 163, 175
II 2395a: 180–82
II 2395b: 180, 182
II 2395c: 180, 181
II 2395d: 180
II 2395e: 180, 182
II 2411: 170
II 2411: 170
II 2479: 172
II 2581: 170
II 2705: 191
II 3093b: 76
II 3093d: 76
II 3718–24: 73, 144
II 4255: 170
II 4528: 73
II 4603: 148, 163
II 5031–32: 84
II 5063: 147, 163
II 5182: 172
II 5202: 90, 98
II 5203: 99
II 5204: 98–99
II 5205: 98
II 5206: 98
II 5207: 88, 99
II 5208: 99
II 5260: 94
II 5261, rev. Stylow 1987,
   116–17 no. A3 (AE 1987,
   484; HEp 2, 1990, 36): 94
II 5262: 94
II 5276: 84
II 5290: 84
II 5635: 191
II 5874b: 76
II 5874d: 76
II 5937: 94
II 5992: 144
II 6265: 98–99
II 6265a: 98
II 6266: 98
II 6267: 98
II 6267a: 98–99
II 6267b: 99
II 6268: 99
II 6269: 99
II 6269a: 99

II 6269b: 99
II 6330: 98
II 6331: 99
II 6333: 91

II²/13, 207–11: 58
II²/14, 291: 164
II²/14, 292: 166
II²/14, 293: 166
II²/14, 296: 164
II²/14, 297: 164
II²/14, 298: 164
II²/14, 305: 164
II²/14, 305: 153
II²/14, 306: 164
II²/14, 307: 164
II²/14, 308: 164
II²/14, 309: 164
II²/14, 310: 164
II²/14, 327: 161
II²/14, 328: 162
II²/14, 329: 164
II²/14, 329: 164
II²/14 349: 142
II²/14 351: 142
II²/14 352: 142
II²/14 359: 142
II²/14 364: 142
II²/14 365: 142
II²/14 390: 142
II²/14, 579: 164
II²/14, 597–598: 70, 164
II²/14, 656: 71, 73–74, 164
II²/14, 731: 164
II²/70: 172

III 1090: 174
III 3491: 110
III 4581: 85

V 6657: 83

VI 4,2 31267: 174
VI 646: 110
VI 35067: 90

VIII 6353: 88
VIII 9023: 190
VIII 12220: 148
VIII 22699: 148
VIII 23022: 190

X 3334: 190

XI, 406: 142
XI 1421: 174

XII 6038: 173

XIII 1668: 173
XIII 3570: 171
XIII 5207: 169
XIII 6978: 169
XIII 7011: 169

XIV 5032: 90

CILA
II, 15*: 82
II.1, 64: 90
II.1, 336: 85

CILAE
1501: 95
1502: 95
1503: 95
1504: 95
1505: 95
1506: 95
1507: 94
1508: 94
1509: 93
1510: 95
1511: 94
1512: 93
1513: 95
1514: 93
1516: 94
1517: 96
1519: 95
1520: 94
1521: 94
1522: 95
1523: 93
1525: 95
1526: 93
1528: 95
1529: 95
1530: 94
1532: 94
1533: 94
1538: 95
1540: 93
1541: 94

1543: 93
1545: 95
1546: 94
1547: 93
1548: 94
1549: 94
1550: 95
1551: 94
1552: 93
1553: 94
1555: 94
1556: 94
1557: 94
1558: 95
1559: 93
1560: 95
1561: 93
1562: 95
1564: 94
1565: 94
1566: 94
1567: 93
1577: 93
1586: 93
1603: 93
1604: 93
1605: 93
1606: 93
1612: 93
1613: 93
1622: 93
1674: 93
2001: 96
2002: 96
2003: 96
2004: 96
2005: 96
2006: 96
2007: 96
2008: 96
2009: 96
2010: 96
2011: 96
2012: 96
2013: 96
2014: 96
2015: 97
2016: 96
2017: 97
2018: 97
2019: 97
2020: 97

2032: 97
2047: 97
2055: 97
2075: 97
2087: 97
2090: 97
2115: 97
2117: 96
2133: 97
2138: 97
2139: 96
2143: 97
2147: 97
2153: 96
2170: 96

*CILCC*
 I 2: 83
 I 24: 90
 I 32: 96
 I 33: 96
 I 34: 96
 I 35: 96
 I 36: 96
 I 37: 96
 I 38: 96
 I 39: 96
 I 40: 96
 I 41: 96
 I 42: 96
 I 43: 96
 I 44: 96
 I 45: 96
 I 46: 97
 I 47: 96
 I 48: 97
 I 49: 97
 I 50: 97
 I 51: 97
 I 63: 97
 I 353: 83
 I 383, 342: 84

 II 485: 83, 84
 II 637: 84
 II 718: 84
 II 726: 84
 II 728: 84
 II 842: 84

 IV 1268–69: 84
 IV 1313: 90

*CIMRM*
 121–28: 185
 773: 185
 781: 185
 793: 185
 794: 183
 795: 183
 796: 183
 798: 191

 I, 773: 95
 I, 779: 95
 I, 781: 95
 I, 792: 95
 I, 793: 95
 I, 794: 95
 I, 795: 95
 I, 796: 95

*CIVAE*
 1: 96
 2: 93
 3: 93
 4: 93
 5: 93
 6: 93
 7: 93
 8: 93
 9: 93
 10: 96
 11: 96
 12: 96
 13: 96
 14: 96
 15: 96
 16: 96
 17: 96
 18: 96
 19: 96
 20: 96
 21: 96
 22: 96
 23: 96
 24: 96
 25: 94
 26: 94
 27, rev. JE: 94
 28: 93
 29: 96
 30: 94
 31: 94
 32: 94

33: 94
34: 94
35: 94
36: 94
37: 97
38: 97
39: 94
40: 94
41: 83, 94
42: 96
44: 97
45: 97
46: 97
47: 97
48: 97
49; cf. Le Roux 2019: 94
50: 94
51: 94
52: 94
53: 94
54: 97
55: 95
56: 95
57: 95
58: 97
59: 97
60: 95
61: 93
62: 93
63: 81
64: 93
65: 93
66: 93
67: 93
68: 93
69: 93
70: 94
72: 93
73: 94
74: 96
75: 95
76: 95
77: 95
78: 95
79: 95
80: 95
81: 95
82: 93
83: 95
84: 95
85: 95
86: 95
88: 95
90: 95
92: 95
94: 93
95: 95
96: 95
97: 97
98: 97
99: 97
100: 97
102: 97
103: 94
110: 96
Apéndice no. 2: 93

*CMBad*
757: 94
758: 93
759: 93
761: 94
762: 94
763: 95
764: 95
765: 183
765: 95
766: 183, 185
767: 95, 183
768: 94
769: 93
776: 95
1083: 95
1088: 95
1089: 95

*CNH*
102.18: 128
124.5: 128
125.1–3: 128
126.1: 129
160.16: 132
160–61.17–19: 132
264.19: 132
315–16.8–10: 132
324.1–2: 132
357.1–5: 131
365.1: 131
383.9–12: 129
394.1: 131
394.3: 131
401–02.1–6: 133

Díaz y Pérez 1887, 354: 95

Edmondson 1997, 89–91 no. 1 (AE 1997, 777a; HEp 7, 1997, 110): 93
Edmondson 2007, 547–48 no. 3, fig. 6: 94
Edmondson 2007, 548 no. 4, fig. 7a–b: 95
Edmondson 2007: 94

*EE*
VIII 9 = IRCP 573: 97
VIII 10 = IRCP 574: 97
VIII 16: 95
VIII 23: 94
VIII, 280: 170

IX 42: 93
IX 43: 93
IX 44: 94
IX 72: 94
IX 156: 97
IX 160: 97
IX 161a: 97
IX 162: ERBC 98; Ramírez Sádaba 2013, 152 no. 69: 96
IX 169: 97
IX 181: 97
IX, p. 108: 170

*ERAE*
6: 94
8: 95
24: 183
25: 185
26: 183
30: 94
33: 95

*ERAsturias*
7: 191

*ERItalica*
11: 82

*FE*
188: 98

Gamer 1989, BA 57, fig. 85d: 94

Gamo and Murciano 2016–2017 [2020] (AE 2018, 825): 93

*HAE*
  409: 94
  557, rev. AE 1984, 485; cf. Étienne and Mayet 1984, 168: 94
  666: 95
  667, 1637: 95
  HAE (cont.)
  668, 2694: 95
  669: 95
  686, 2693: 95
  815, 2691: 95
  1483: 80
  1840: 95
  2681: 93
  2692: 95

*HEp*
  1, 1989, 99: 95
  1, 1989, 105: 95
  1, 1989, 108: 94
  2, 1990, 34; 6, 1996, 135: 93
  2. 1990, 74: 70
  3, 1993, 477: 98
  4, 1994, 167: 81, 186
  4, 1994, 754: 82
  5, 1995, 52: 80
  5, 1995, 76: 96
  5, 1995, 81: 94
  5, 1995, 109: 80
  5, 1995, 112; 7, 1997, 155: 97
  5, 1995, 115: 80
  5. 1995, 135: 70
  6, 1996, 127, rev. EAOR VII 58, reading Fhilo rather than Felic(i)o: 95
  6, 1996, 148: 144
  6, 1996, 187: 83
  6, 1996, 194: 96
  6, 1996, 196: 97
  6, 1996, 204: 97
  6, 1996, 205: 97
  6, 1996, 208: 97
  6, 1996, 226: 83
  6, 1996, 249: 83
  7, 1997, 22: 84
  7, 1997, 33: 97
  7, 1997, 109a: 146
  7, 1997, 124; rev. Edmondson 2006, 57 and n. 115, fig. 1.50: 94
  7. 1997, 659–763: 56
  9, 1999, 95: 80
  9, 1999, 237: 142
  9, 1999, 418: 190
  9, 1999, 511: 82
  11, 2001, 58: 90
  13, 2003–2004, 980: 98
  13, 2003–2004, 981: 88, 98
  13, 2003–2004, 982: 99
  15, 2006, 53: 93
  15, 2007, 12: 94
  16, 2010, 12: 81
  16. 2010, 65–76: 59
  18, 2009, 42: 94
  19, 2010, 71: 144
  20, 2011, 19: 93
  20, 2011, 21: 93
  21, 2012, 179: 84
  2013, 18: 97
  2013, 43: 97

Hidalgo Martín and Chamizo 2012–2013 [2018] (AE 2017, 626): 95

*ILAlg.*
  II.3: 88
  II. 10123–24: 88

*ILER*
  278: 95
  280: 95
  284: 95
  367: 94
  527: 93
  541: 94
  732: 93
  733: 93
  859: 94
  1028: 170
  6004: 94

*ILS*
  103: 174
  140: 174
  190: 174
  6741a: 83
  6964: 173
  9297: 95

*IMAPB*
  10: 97
  56: 97

*IRC*
  I, 85–86: 191
  I, 88: 70, 73, 74
  I, 89: 70
  I, 126: 73
  I, 207: 70

  II, 17: 70

*IRCP*
  195: 90
  408: 90
  482c: 91
  483: 98
  484: 88, 98–99
  485: 98
  486: 98
  487: 90, 98
  488: 88, 98
  489 (Fig. 6.5a): 98
  490: 98
  491: 98
  492: 98
  493: 98
  494: 98
  495: 88, 98
  496: 98
  497: 89, 98
  498: 98
  499: 98
  501: 98
  502: 98
  503: 98
  504: 88, 98–99
  505: 99
  506: 99
  507: 99
  508: 88, 99
  509: 99
  510: 99
  511: 88, 99
  512: 99
  513: 88, 99
  514: 98–99
  515: 98–99
  516: 88, 99
  517: 99

518: 99
519: 98–99
520: 88, 99
521: 99
522: 99
523: 99
524: 99
525: 99
526: 98
527: 98–99
528: 99
529: 98
530: 88, 99
531: 99
532: 99
533: 99
534: 99
535: 99
536: 98
540: 99
543: 98
548: 99
566: 85, 96
575: 97

*IRPToledo*
19: 84
81: 84

*OPEL*
3.112: 90
4.161: 90

Ramírez Sádaba 2013,
51–52 no. 1: 97

*RGDA*
34: 172

*RICIS*
603/1001: 188
603/1101: 188

*RPC*
48: 135
73: 135
120–23: 133
167a: 136
192: 135
225: 135
261–62: 136
262–64: 136
264: 133
322: 136
346: 135
371: 135
429: 136

*RS*
25: 81

*Senatus Consultum de Cn. Pisone patre*
150-60: 174

*Tabula Siarensis*
151-60: 174

TIR K–29:1991: 170

Trillmich 2016–2017 [2020]
(AE 2018, 827): 94

# Index of Names

## Names of Persons

Personal names have been organized, when possible, according to Latin onomastics;
in other cases, it has been decided to use those that are most recognizable to the reader

Aemilius Aemilianus, v.p.,
   p(raeses) p(rov.) U(lterioris)
   L(usitaniae): 94
Accius Hedychrus, Gaius: 95,
   185–86, 189, 192
Aemilius Rectus, Lucius: 34
Agennius Urbicus: 86
Agrippa: 163, 172, 174
Albia Ianuaria: 98
Albinus, Albui f., flamen d[ivi
   Augusti et] divae Aug(ustae)
   provinciae Lusitan[iae]: 93
Allius, C. Tangini f.: 80
Alexander the Great: 126, 170
Amoena Antubeli f.: 90
Anchises: 146, 172
Ann(ia) Q. f. Mariana: 98
Annius Aper, T.: 98
Annius Severus: 86, 96
Antiochus III the Great: 162
Antistius C. lib. Iucundus, C.: 94
Antistius Marcellianus, M.: 95
Antonia L. [f.?] Manliola: 98
Antony, Mark: 159
Antoninus Pius (emperor): 144
Antubellicus Priscus: 90, 98
Appian: 154, 157–58
Arcontius: 56
Arrius Badiolus: 90, 98
Arrius Laurus, M.: 94
Arrius Reburrus, Marcus: 82, 94
Artema, slave of Claudius
   Martilinus: 84, 93
Articuleius Rufus, Quintus: 172
Asinius Gallus, C.: 170
Augustus: 28, 32, 37, 51, 73, 79, 87,
   106, 118, 133–36, 139, 142, 143
   (Divus), 145–49, 153, 160–65,
   170 (as Caesar), 168–76
   *see also* Octavian

Aulus Gellius: 49, 91
Aurelia Vibia Sabina: 89
Aurelius Fhilo, M.: 82, 95
Aur(elius) [---], M.: 93
Aurelius, Marcus (emperor): 89, 91
Autobulus: 62
Avitus, Caius: 185

Bergius Seranus: 59
Blandus, slave of Caelia Rufina: 89, 98
Boutius Antibue(i) f.: 90

Caecilius Metellus, Quintus: 144
C(aecilius?) Severus, C.: 86, 96
Caelia Rufina: 89
Caelius Philinus, Lucius: 84, 93
Caesar, Caius: 164
Caesius Crescens: 86, 96
Caligula (emperor): 125, 133–34, 138,
   174–75
Calpurnius Andronicus, L.: 98
Calpurnius Dobetianus: 90, 98
Calpurnius Piso, Gn.: 171
Calpurnius Rufinus, Gaius C.:
   180–82, 186, 188, 192
Camilius Superat(us), C.: 95
Caracalla (emperor): 89, 123, 190
Catullus: 62
Cav(---) S(exti) (f.?) [B]alanus, L.:
   83
Chares of Teichiussa: 45
Claudius (emperor): 143 (Divus),
   145–47, 172–73, 175
Claudius II (emperor): 48
Claudius Aurelius Quintianus,
   Lucius Tiberius: 57
Claudius Daphnus: 94
Claudiu[s] Donatus, L.: 95
Claudius Martilinus: 84
Claudius Severus, Gnaeus: 57

Cocceius Craterus Honorinus,
   Sextus: 89, 98
Cocceius Vi[---], L.: 94
Conicodius: 90, 98
Constantius II (emperor): 48
Cordius Symphorus, L., medicus: 95
Cornelius Bocchus: 176
Cornelius Caeso, Caius: 175
Cornelius Herculanus, Lucius: 84, 93
Cornelius Primigenius, Marcus: 147
Cornelius Scipio, Gnaeus: 37
Cornelius Scipio Africanus, Publius:
   146, 157, 160–62
Cornelius Scipio Asiaticus, Lucius:
   162
Cor(nelius) Baria, Gn(eus): 144
Cornelius, Quintus: 84, 93
*Critonia C. f. [---]: 98
Critonia Maxuma: 98
Critonius: 90
Curius Avitus, C.: 95

De Gaulle, Charles: 119
Dionisius: 95
Domitia Vettilla: 82, 94 (Paculi uxor)
Domitian (emperor): 79, 143, 169, 173
Drusus Caesar: 164, 171, 176
Drusus minor: 164

Euainetos: 126
Eustatius: 56
Eutichius: 98

Fabius Felix: 71, 164
Fabius Fabianus: 71, 164
Fabius Maximus, Paulus: 170, 176
Fabius Maximus, Quintus: 133
Fannius Augurinus, M.: 98
Faustina Minor: 169
Festianus, Valerius: 83

Flavi Baetici, Quintio: 95
Flavia Patricia: 86, 96
Flavianus: 62
Florus: 23
Frontinus: 86
Fulcininus Trio, Lucius: 171
Furnia G. F(urnii) l. Turran(ia): 97

Galba (emperor): 173
Germanicus: 163–64, 171, 174
Gracchus, Tiberius: 121

Hadrian (emperor): 43, 59, 122, 141, 144–48
Hannibal: 153, 155–57, 161, 165
Hector Cornelior(um), slave: 95
Helanicus of Lesbos: 140
Helvia Avita: 98
(H)elvia Ybas: 98
Helvius Silvanus, Quintus: 85, 97
Hermes [...]P.[l]ib: 89, 98
Hermes, slave of Aurelia Vibia Sabina (daughter of Marcus Aurelius): 89, 91, 98
Herodes Atticus: 43
Hiero II of Syracuse: 131
Horatius Bodonilur, Marcus: 175
Hymenaeus: 62

Iulia Anus: 98
*Iul(ia) Marcella: 98
Iulia Maxuma: 98
Iulia [Pro]cula: 98
Iulia Severa: 86, 96
Iuli, G.: 95
Iulius Amminus, T.: 83
?Iul. Ascani[u]s: 94
[I]ulius [---], C(aius): 83
Iulius Caesar, Caius: 51, 121, 133, 142–43, 146–47, 149, 153, 159, 163, 168–69, 172–73, 176
Iulius Capito, G.: 99
Iulius Caturonis, Caius: 90, 99
[Iu]lius Clemens: 97
I(ulius) Em(eritus?), Q.: 96
Iul. Lupu[s]: 94
Iulius Iulianus, L.: 97, 99

Iulius Mandi f. Sangenus, C.: 80
Iul. Maximinu[s], v.p., proc(urator) Aug(usti) n(ostri), a(gens) v(ice) p(raesidis) p(rov.) L(usitaniae)]: 94
[Iul]ius Nicero[s]: 97
Iuliu[s ?P]aesicus, L.: 99
Iulius Panthenopaeus, Gnaeus: 85, 97
I(ulius) Pelecus, G.: 83
Iulius Proculus, Marcus: 99
Iulius Pultarius, Q.: 99
I(ul.) Saturninus: 95
Iu[lius Se]ptumi[nus?], Caius: 99
Iullius Pollio, Sextus: 136
Iulus: 139
*Iunia (A)Eliana: 99
Iunia Cerasa: 188
Iunius Paetus, Lucius: 169
Iunius Silvanus Melanius, Caius: 75, 77
Iuventius Iulianus, Lucius: 84, 93

Juba II: 163
Juvenal: 58

L(icinia?) Marciana: 88, 99
Licinius, Lucius: 45
L(icinius?) Catullus, Q.: 89, 99
L(icinius?) Nigellius, M.: 88, 99
Licinius Rusticus: 86, 97
Licinius Serenianus: 84, 97
Livia: 135, 169, 172 and 175 (Diva)
Livius Severus, M.: 99
Livy: 139–40, 153–54, 156–57, 160–62
Lucretia Sergieton: 175

Magolius C[ar?]us, M.: 89, 99
Manilia: 88
Marcia Voluptas: 188
Maroanus: 97
Maximus, Valerius: 143, 156, 164–65
Meduttus Caturonis f.: 90
Metellus, Marcus: 121
Metellus Pius: 109
Michael the Archangel, S: 88
Musa[---] (Mus[aeus]?): 84, 93

Nero (emperor): 155
Nicolaus of Damascus: 163
Nicolavus: 57
Nonius Prim(us), Q., miles leg. VII Gemin(a)e F(elicis): 94
Norbanus Severus, Lucius: 86, 96
Numa Pompilius: 160

Oclatius Severus, Tiberius: 56
Octavian: 176
Olius: 89
Otho (emperor): 173
Ovid: 141

Paccia Flaccilla, 94
Paccius Agathopus, D.: 95
Pertinax (emperor): 59
Petronia Albilla: 99
Philip the Arab (emperor): 190
Placidus: 57
Pliny the Elder: 121–23, 153–55, 170–71
Pliny the Younger: 72–75, 123
Plutarch: 62
Polybius: 13, 121, 155–56, 164
*Pompeia Prisca: 99
Pompeius Trogus: 158
Pompey: 121, 153, 159, 163
Pompeius Saturninus, M.: 99
Pomponia Marcella: 99
Pomponius Mela: 170–71
Pontius Severinus, Lucius: 86, 96
Posidonius: 121
Proculus, Valerius: 83
Ptolemy (author): 170

Qu[inctius?] V[---], C.: 99
Quintilian: 135, 168
Quintio: 82

Roscius Paculus, Lucius: 83
Rubenus: 57
Rufus: 93

Scandiliae C. f. Campanae: 96
Sallust: 109
Secun[d]u[s]: 86, 96

Secundytius Victori[nus]: 97
Sempronius Celer, P.: 99
Sempronius Fronto: 82
Sentius Marsus: 84, 93
Seranus: 94
Servius: 63
Sestio: 98
Sestius Quirinalis, Lucius: 170, 176
Severus, Caius: 86
Severianus Aug(ustalis): 96
Severus Macer, Quintus: 148
Sevius Firmanus, Quintus: 89
Silius Italicus: 155
Silius Nerva, Publius: 163
Sitonia Victorina: 88, 98
Sitonius Equestris, (*)Q.: 89, 99
Statorius Taurus, *Quintus: 99
Strabo: 13–14, 121, 126, 128, 138, 154, 158
Suetonius: 140, 168
S(ulpicius?) C(---), C.: 99
S(ulpicia?) Romula: 99

Tacitus: 54, 118, 169, 175
Tarquin the Elder: 158
Terentia G. f.: 98
Terentius Varro, Marcus: 123, 148
Teusca Petrei f.: 97
Theodosius: 141
Tiberius (emperor): 133–35, 138, 163–64, 171–75
Titus (emperor): 143 (Divus)
Toncius / Tongius: 85, 97
Trajan (emperor): 81, 147
Trophimus: 83, 94
Tullia C.f. Modesta: 98
Tullius Cicero, Marcus: 76, 153, 158–59, 162
Turrecia I[---]: 99
Turrecius: 89
Tusca Olia Tauri f.: 98

Val(eria) Avita: 94
Valerius Avitus, Caius: 189
Valerius CIICA ... ?: 99
Val(erius) Festianus: 83, 94

Valerius Phoebus, Marcus: 147–48
Valerius Proculus: 83, 94
Valerius Secundus, Marcus: 95, 185–86
Valerius Telesphorus, Caius: 86, 96
Valerius Vitulus: 83, 94
Va(lerius?) V(---), Q.: 97
Varinia Flaccina: 84, 97
Varinia Serena: 84, 97
Varius Rufus, Caius: 136
Veranus Caturonis f.: 90
Vernacla, slave of Treb(ia?) Musa or Treb(icia) Musa: 89, 98
[-][Ve?]sidiu[s ---], father of Vesidius Fuscus, G.: 99
Vesidius: 89–90
Vesidius Fuscus, *G.: 99
Vespasian (emperor): 30, 80, 121, 143 (Divus), 172
Vettius Silvinus, Caius: 85, 97
Vibius Avitus, M.: 99
Vibius Bassus, M.: 99
Victorius Secundus: 190
Victorius Victor: 190
Victorius Victorinus, Gaius: 189–90
Virgil: 60, 63
Visellius Tertius, Lucius: 148
Vitalis, slave of Messius Sympaeron: 89, 98
Vitia[---], P.: 84, 93
Vitellius (emperor): 173
Vitulus, Valerius: 83
Vivennia Badia: 90
*Vivennia Venusta: 88, 99
Vivennius: 89

Incerti
[-] [Calp?]urni[us] [---]: 98
[---]atius [D]emetrius: 94
[I]uli[us ---], C.: 94
Iu[l. ---?]: 99
[-][---]ius [N]arcissus: 99
[---] Rustri? (f.): 97
[---]s Saturninus: 99

## Names of Deities and Mythological Characters

Abbadir: 91
Aeneas: 21, 139–40 (Indiges), 141, 143–44, 146–50, 155, 160, 163, 172, 175
Aesculapius: 62 and 77 (Ibizan), 82, 183, 187 (Asklepios), 188
see also Asclepius
Aeternitas Augusta: 135
Agathos Daimon: 187
Aion: 184 (Kronos/Aion)
Alcmena: 140
Ammon: 172 (Jupiter/Ammon)
Anchises: 146, 172
Antoninus Pius, Divus: 189
Aphrodite: 155, 164
Apollo: 45, 66, 71, 126, 131, 138, 140, 168, 188 (Apollo Granus)
Artemis: 58, 74, 126, 138, 154, 155, 158, 166
see also Diana
Ascanius: 139, 146
see also Iulus
Asclepius: 140, 164 (Asclepius Augustus)
Astarte: 49 (Astarte/Demeter), 128 (Astarte marine Venus; Astarte–Isis), 138 (Astarté–Isis)
Ataecina: 19, 39 (Bandue), 69, 82, 84 (Ataecina Sancta, Dea Ataecina Turobrigensis Sancta, Dea Sancta Turibrigensis, Dea Turibrigensis, Dea Sancta, Ataecina Turibrigae Proserpina, Dea Sancta Proserpina, Dea Sancta Ataecina Turibrigensis), 85 (Dea Ataecina Turibrigensis Proserpina, Dea Sancta Ataecina), 86–88, 92, 93, 96, 111
see also Proserpina
Athena: 126, 137
Attis: 62, 109, 110
Augusta, Diva (Livia): 93, 175
Augustus, Divus: 93, 135, 138, 143, 168 (Numen)–175

Baal: 117 (of Tyr), 128 (Hammon)
Bacchus: 109–10, 110
Bandue: 39 (Ataecina)
Berus breus: 39, 47
Betatun: 37
Bes: 128, 137–38

Bokon: 37
Bona Dea: 91

Caelestis: 188
Castor: 131
Cautes: 93, 191
Ceres: 82, 91 (Cereres), 124
Chares: 45
Christ: 140
Chronos: 82
Chusôr: 128, 138 (Ptah)
Claudius, Divus: 143
Concord: 81, 93 (Concordia Augusta)
Cornutus Cordonus: 145
Coronis: 140
Cupid: 132–33, 183–84
Cybele: 62, 109, 110

Dea Caelestis: 106
Dea Sancta Burrulobrigensis: 85
Dagda: 102
    see also Dis Pater
Demeter: 102, 103
Deva: 71
Diana: 58 (Frugifera, Nemorensis), 74, 76 (Frugifera), 81, 84–85, 96, 154, 158, 166, 171, 173
Dis Pater: 102
Diis omnibus: 82, 93, 180 (diis deabus omnibus)
Diis Severis: 75
Dionisus: 82, 191
Divus Iulius: 81, 171

Edigenius Domnicus: 83, 94
Endovellicus: 19, 39, 41–45, 51, 87–92, 98
Eros: 62
Europa: 131, 138
Eulalia, Santa: 81

Feronia: 85, 86
Fides: 165
Fontanus: 82, 84 (and Fontana, fontibus?)
Fortuna: 66, 82, 94, 109–11, 137; Balnearis: 62, 111; Fortis: 62; Redux: 168; Romanorum: 62; Mulieribus: 62

Genius: 82 (Colonia Iulia Augusta Emerita), 84 (Turgalensium), 94 (Colonia Iulia Augusta Emerita), 94 (Augusti), 106 (domèstic), 109, 143 (Domitiani), 146 (Populi Romani), 148 (of the Municipium), 163 (Populi Romaní), 168 (or Numen Augusti), 170 (Caesaris, Augusti), 175 (Municipalis), 176 (Caesaris)

Helios: 128
    see also Sol
Hephaestus: 128
Heracles: 68, 123, 128, 132, 140, 155
    see also Hercules; Melqart
Hercules: 45, 109, 117, 123–24, 126, 139–40, 155, 160

Iccona Loiminna: 48
Indiges: 140 (Jupiter, Aeneas), 146, 149 (Pater)
Invictus Deus: 183, 191
Isis: 39, 47, 75, 84, 91, 96 (domina), 109, 117–18, 128, 138, 177–79, 181–82, 187–88, 192
Iulus: 139

Janus: 136
Juno: 82, 84 (Regina), 94, 97 (Regina), 124, 135, 188
Jupiter: 70 (Augustus), 83 (Solutorius), 84 (Optimus Maximus), 94 (Deus, Augustus, Solutorius), 97, 109–10 (Optimus Maximus), 117–18, 124 (Optimus Maximus), 133, 135, 140 (Indiges), 143–44, 149, 158, 162, 172, 174 (Optimus Maximus), 178

Kore: 102–03, 181
Kronos: 184

Lacipaea: 83, 94
Laebo: 39, 48
Lares: 81, 82 (Augusti), 84–85 (Viales), 94 (Augusti), 97 (Viales), 106, 109–11 (Aquites), 164 (Augusti), 168 (Augusti), 172, 176 (Compitales, Augusti), 186

Liber/Liber Pater: 22, 39, 45, 55, 66, 70–71, 74, 82, 94 (Augustus, Pater), 123, 164–65
Livia, Diva: 172, 175 (as Iulia Augusta)
Lug: 63
Lugus: 132
Luna: 135
Lupa: 147, 148 (Romana, Augusta), 163

Magna Mater: 62, 82, 111
Mars: 81, 82–83, 94 (Deus Mars Augustus), 109–10, 133, 139–40, 142, 146 (temple of Mars Ultor), 147–48, 164 (Augustus), 188 (Sagato)
Mater Deorum: 82
Melqart: 62, 117, 123, 128–29, 132, 137–38
    see also Heracles
Mercury: 46, 82, 84, 97 (Deus Dominus Sanctus Mercurius), 109–11, 129, 132, 138, 184, 186
Mithras: 82, 95 (Deus Invictus, Invictus Deus, Invictus), 118, 124, 177–79, 182, 184–86, 190–92
Minerva: 18 (Men(e)rva), 46, 109
Muses: 62

Nemedus: 56, 71
    see also Nemeton
Nemesis: 81, 82, 95 (Dea Invicta Caelestis, Domina curatrix anima), 188
Nemeton: 56, 169
Neptune: 82, 95
Neton: 37
Nike: 126
Numen Augusti: 168
    see also Augustus
Nymphs: 63–64 (and Venus), 66, 82, 95 (Nympha), 111

Oceanus: 95 (statue), 184, 186
Odysseus: 123, 140

Pales: 37, 39, 44, 141, 145
Pan: 123
Penates: 109, 111, 143 (Populi Romaní)–144, 149, 155

Pietas Augusta: 169
Pluto: 82
Pollux: 131
Proserpina (sincreticed with Ataecina): 82, 83–84 (Dea Sancta Proserpina), 85 (Sancta, Dea, Servatrix), 86, 93, 95–97
Ptah: 128, 138 (Chusor)
Pyrene: 123

Quirinus: 140–41 (Romulus), 146, 149, 168

Remus: 141
Romulus: 139–41, 144, 146–47, 149–50
Reve: 39, 48
Roma: 64, 141 (Aeterna), 142 and 145 (flamen Romae et Augusti), 168, 170 (sacerdos Romae et Augusti)

Salaeco: 37
Salus: 83, 188
Saturn: 88, 123, 133
Serapis: 39, 47, 75, 82, 95 (Sarapis), 177, 179–82, 187–88, 192
Sertundo: 37
Shamash: 128
Sigerius Stillifer, Divus: 83, 94
Silvanus: 66, 84, 97, 109–11
Spes: 91
Sol: 128 (Helios–Sol)

Tanit: 102–03, 129, 137
Titus, Divus: 143
Trebaruna: 39, 48
Trebopala: 48
Tutela: 109

Venus: 49, 63–64 (and Nymphs), 74, 82 (Victrix), 95 (Victrix), 128 (Astare-Marine), 133, 135 (Venus-Luna), 139–41 (Felix), 143, 145 (temple of Venus and Rome), 149, 164 (Augusta), 182–84
Vespasianus, Divus: 143
Vesta: 144
Victoria: 174 (Augusta)
Victory: 136, 169
Volcanus: 91
Vulcan: 124, 128 (Hephaistos)

Zeus: 75 (Theos Megistos), 131, 140
Zuvan: 184

Incerti
??Dea [---] Genius [---]??: 93

## Names of Places

Abdera: 127–29
Acinipo: 105
Actium: 86, 133, 136, 171
Adriatic, (sea): 118
Aegean (sea): 118, 123
Africa Proconsularis: 91, 117, 120, 123–24, 148, 190
Agri Decumates: 170
Alameda Alta: 39–40
Alange: 80, 84, 97
Alba Longa: 140, 143, 148, 150
Alcoi: 14–15, 31, 36, 68
Alexandria (Egypt): 187–88
Algaida, La: 137
Alicante: 30–31, 103, 109
Allone: 30
Alon: 30
Alps (range): 119, 121
Altava: 142
Altos de Solaparza, Los: 79
Ammaia: 79, 83–84
Anatolia: 118, Anatolian plateau: 119
Anas (river; modern Guadiana): 79, 184, 186
Andalusia: 124
Ankara: 119
Anticaria: 175
Apulum: 174
Aquae Calidae (modern Caldas de Reyes): 178, 191
Ara Augusta: 170
Arabia: 118
Ardea: 34, 154–55
Aritium: 174
Armenia: 118
Arsa: 79
Arse: 79, 126–27, 132, 152–53, 155
Artigi: 79, 172
Arucci: 108
Asia (continent): 170
Asia Minor: 45, 175, 180

Asido: 127–29
Astigi: 173
Astorga see Asturica Augusta
Asturias: 121
Asturica Augusta: 86, 168, 170
Atlantic (ocean): 19, 119
Atlas (range): 118
Augusta Emerita: 13, 18, 43, 69, 79–87, 89–91, 107, 111, 124, 134–35, 146–47, 150, 163, 171–73, 175, 178–79, 182–83, 185–86, 191
Augustobriga: 85, 189
Axati: 172
Azuaga: 79

Badajoz: 79, 80, 85, 90, 97
Baelo Claudia: 136, 178, 187–88
Baetis (river; modern Guadalquivir): 13, 15
Baetulo: 148, 175
Bagacum: 89
Bailo: 129, 131, 136
Barcelona: 119, 169
Barcino (modern Barcelona): 165
Baria: 126, 128, 138
Bastetania: 41
Bavacum: 171
Benifaió: 178, 191
Beuvray, Mont: 121
Bilbilis: 112
Bolskan: 137
Bordeaux: 119
Bracara Augusta: 38, 90, 168, 170
Bracarum, Conventus: 178
Britain: 121
Burrulobriga: 85

Ca l'Arnau: 112
Cabeço das Fráguas: 39, 4
Cabo de Peñas: 171
Cabra: 190–92
Cabriana: 111
Cachouça: 39, 40
Cádiz see Gadir
Caesaraugusta: 13, 83, 134–36, 169, 175 see also Zaragoza
Caesarea (Mauretania Caesariensis): 142
Caesarobriga: 83–84
Caetobriga: 178, 191
Cales Coves: 15, 18, 21, 59, 64, 70, 73–74, 144–45, 149

Camp de les Lloses: 101, 104–05, 112
Campa Torres: 171
*Campus Martius* (Rome): 171
Can Mateu: 112
Can Modolell: 70–71, 73–74, 76–77, 191
Canari, El: 32
Cañuelo, El: 79
Cap de Creus: 137
Cap de Vol: 137
Capitoline Hill (Rome): 158, 162
Caravaca: 34
Carmo: 129–31
Carteia: 122, 133–34, 136, 138
Carthage: 91, 128
Carthago Nova: 28, 62, 103, 105, 108, 134, 136, 163, 169, 178, 187
Casa Blanca (Spain): 112
Casa Santa: 111
Casablanca (Morocco): 119
Castellet de Bernabé: 109
Castellum Elefantum: 88
Castrejón, El: 39
Castro Capote: 39, 41, 49
Castulo: 129–31
Catalonia: 112
Caurium: 83
Cayster (river): 119
Celsa: 105, 112, 134
Celtiberia: 13, 121, 132, 176
Central Iberian Mountain System: 48
Central, Massif: 118
Cerro de los Santos: 18, 32–34, 36, 38–39, 42–45, 51
Cerro de San Albín: 183
Chemtou: 73
Cilicia Pedias: 119
Città Castellana: 34
Civitas Igaeditanorum: 83
Clunia: 18, 55, 58–59, 63, 73–74, 108, 111
Clusium: 142
Cocentania: 31
Cocosa, La: 80, 85, 96–97
Cogull, El: 70
Colonia: 168, 171
Conimbriga: 82, 111
Conobaria/Colobana: 174
Contributa Iulia Ugultunia: 79
Corbins: 112
Corduba: 106, 133, 138, 147, 150, 163, 172–73

Corsica: 118
Cosa: 34
Cova de l'Església: 144
Cova dels Jurats *see also* Cales Coves: 144
Crete: 118
Cueva de La Griega: 55–57, 63
Cueva de la Losa: 64
Cueva de Román: 55, 58, 63
Cueva del Puente: 56–57,
Cueva Negra: 15, 18, 60–64, 70, 71, 77
Cyprus: 118

Dalmatia: 90, 142
Danube: 117, 118
Didyma: 45
Douro (river): 48, 119, 120, 122
Duratón: 111

Ebora: 79, 87, 90–91, 173
Ebro (river): 14, 32, 119, 121, 122, 136
Ebusus: 77, 126–28, 137–38, 152
Edeta: 77
Egypt: 180
Elvas (Portugal): 80, 85, 96–97
Emporiae: 105–06, 111, 133, 172
Emporion: 32, 37, 68, 102–03, 125–27, 136–38, 152, 178, 187
Encarnación, La: 33–35
Enova, L': 104
Ensérune: 121
Epora: 147–48
Estremoz: 87, 89
Etruria: 117
Europe: 117, 118

Feria (dehesa de Los Rapados): 80, 96
Ferreira do Alentejo: 39, 47
Finisterre: 170
Fonte do Ídolo: 38
Forum Augustum: 147, 172, 174
Fráguas: 39
France: 119, 121
*see also* Gallia

Gabarda: 32
Gadir: 68, 117, 126–29, 137–38, 152
Garvão: 39–41, 49
Galicia: 121

Gallia: 39, 47, 90, 109, 110, 118, 120–21, 124 (Tres Galliae), 148, 169, 171, 176, 192; Aquitania: 123; Belgica: 89; Comata: 173; Narbonensis: 123, 142, 173; Transpadana: 83, 90
Garrovilla, La: 96
Gaul *see* Gallia
Germania: 110, 176, 192
Gracchuris: 122, 134, 136
Greece: 45, 47, 49, 117
Griega, La: 14, 71, 74, 77
Guadalquivir (river): 68, 80, 119–22, 137, 174
*see also* Baetis
Guadiana (river): 79, 85, 119, 120
*see also* Anas

Hasta Regia: 174
Helicon (Mount): 62
Henchir-El-Meden: 148
Herculaneum: 107
Herdade da Fonte Branca, Caia e Sao Pedro: 80, 97
Hermus, river: 119
Hispalis: 90
Hispania: 14, 16–24, 34, 37, 39–41, 47, 49, 51, 53–54, 58, 63, 65–68, 73, 75, 101, 104–05, 107, 109–13, 124–25, 131, 135, 137–39, 142–52, 158–59, 161–66, 170–73, 175–78, 185, 187
  Citerior/Tarraconensis: 54, 65, 69, 79, 83, 107, 121, 129, 131, 133, 136, 138, 145, 148, 165, 168–71, 175–76, 189
  Lusitania: 13, 38, 47, 79, 81, 86, 88–92, 111, 121, 171–73, 175
  Transduriana: 170
  Ulterior/Baetica: 22, 41, 79, 80, 84, 90, 107, 121–24, 126, 129, 131, 133, 138, 147, 172–76
Hispellum: 73
Hornachos: 80, 97
Horta das Faias: 39, 46
Horta do Pinto: 47

Iamo: 144–45
Iberia: 13–14, 16, 27–30, 32, 90, 117, 119, 121–24, 139, 146, 177–79
    Iberian Peninsula: 13–14, 16–19, 21–22, 27, 36–39, 41, 43, 48, 53–54, 64–67, 75, 79, 90, 101–04, 106, 110–12, 118, 123, 125–26, 128, 131, 136–38, 155, 171, 177, 191–92
Ibiza *see* Ebusus
Ida (Mount): 62
Iesso: 136
Igabrum: 178
Ikalesken: 132
Ilerda: 110, 112, 145–46
Ilici: 103–04, 106–07, 134, 172
Ilipa: 129
Ilium: 155, 162
Iltirkesken: 136
Iltirta: 130, 145–46
Ilturir: 131
Iluro: 70
India: 118, 168, 170
Iponuba: 175
Ipora: 131
Iptuci: 128
Iran: 118
Ireland: 118
Irni: 143
Islas: 191
Israel: 47, 49
Italian Peninsula: 14, 16, 18, 41, 49, 54, 72, 74, 90, 91, 104, 109, 112, 118, 123, 139, 142, 149, 178, 192
Italica: 21, 122, 146–47, 149, 163, 172–73, 178, 187–89
Italy *see* Italian Peninsula
Iulia Lybica: 59, 60
Iulipa: 79

Kese: 130, 132, 136

Lacinimurga: 79
Lambaesis: 142
Languedoc: 119
Lanuvium: 142
Lascuta: 127–29
Latium: 22, 139–41, 148–49, 155, 160, 175
Laurentum: 146
Lavinium: 34, 140, 143, 149, 175
León: 123
Lepida: 133–34, 136

Llívia *see* Iulia Lybica
Loire (river): 119
Lucus Augusti (Lugo): 169–70, 178, 184, 189, 191–92
Lucus Augusti (Luc-en-Diois): 169
Lugdunum: 119, 124, 168, 171–73
Lugdunum Convenarum: 171
Luz de Verdolay, La: 33–34
Lyon *see* Lugdunum

Macedonia: 122
Madrid: 119
Maeander (river): 119
Maghreb: 118
Mago: 144–45
Malaca: 126–29, 138
Malladeta, La: 30
Malpica de Bergantiños: 170
Manching: 121
Marrakesh: 119
Marseille: 119
Mas Castellar de Pontós: 102, 103, 105
Mas Gusó: 112
Massalia (modern Marseille): 126, 158–59
Matabodes: 39, 40
Mauretania: 124; Caesariensis: 90, 142
Mérid *see* Augusta Emerita
Mediterranean (sea): 14, 16–19, 23, 36–37, 47, 66, 91, 117, 119, 149, 176–77, 188
Menorca: 145
Meseta (central Spanish plateau): 40, 118, 119
Metellinum: 79
Middle Sea *see* Mediterranean
Molón, El: 104
Monte do Facho: 39, 47
Monte Louro: 170
Montealegre del Castillo: 32
Montoro: 163, 175
Morera, La: 80, 97
Munigua: 51, 173
Muntanya Frontera: 14–15, 18, 38–39, 44–45, 51, 70–71, 73, 76–77, 164
Munts, Els: 177–78, 184, 189, 191
Muziris: 118
Mytilene: 168

Nabrissa Veneria: 174
Nemausus: 142, 169, 173
Nemetobriga: 169

Nepet: 142
Nogales (cortijo de Maricara; Endrines Altos): 80, 97
Norba Caesarina: 79, 83, 86
North Africa: 117, 123, 128, 142, 148, 178
Numantia: 51, 121
Numicus (river): 140
Numidia: 88, 142

Obulco: 129–31, 148–49, 175
Oceja: 59, 60
Olisipo: 85
Olivenza: 80, 97
Olontigi: 128
Opitergium: 142
Orippo: 131
Orose: 127
Osca: 32, 105
Ostia: 90, 109–10, 185, 187
Otricoli: 142

Palatine Hill (Rome): 141
Palestine: 140
Palma: 142–43, 145
Palmillas, Las: 174
Pamphylia: 119
Pan Caliente: 172
Panóias: 14, 18, 54, 72, 75–76, 178–82, 186
Paris: 119
Patavium: 142
Pax Augusta: 13
Pax Iulia: 178
Penàguila: 31
Peñalba de Villastar: 14, 60, 63, 70–71, 145
Perge: 180
Petelia: 156
Pisa: 174
Po (river): 142
Pompeii: 107, 108
Pontus (kingdom): 122
Porcuna: 163
Portugal: 90
Portus Victoriae Iuliobrigensium: 171
Praeneste: 141
Praia das Mãças: 39
Proserpina roman reservoir, 7.5 km N. of Mérida: 80, 85, 96
Puente de la Olmilla: 108
Puig des Molins: 137
Pyrenees: 37, 70, 119
Pyrgi: 34

Rambla de la Boltada: 106
Regina: 79
Rhine (river): 119
Rhineland: 117, 124
Rhode: 102, 126–27, 138
Rhône: 119, 121
Ribeira de Lucefecit: 88
Rihuete, El: 105, 108
Rome (city): 22, 43, 59, 83, 90, 139–41, 143–46, 149, 162–63, 168, 171
Romula: 134–35, 175
Rottweil: 170
Rabat: 119

Saguntum: 21–22, 68, 70, 77, 132, 142, 149, 151–56, 158–66, 191
Sahara: 118
Salacia: 172, 176
Salvacañete: 136
San Juan de la Isla: 178
San Miguel de Liria-Edeta: 46
San Pedro: 39, 46
　see also Valencia del Ventoso
Santa Bárbara de Padrões: 39, 46
Santa Bàrbara: 69, 71, 164
Santa Lucía del Trampal: 14, 69, 85–86, 96–97
Santo Angel: 35
São Miguel da Motta: 39, 41–45, 50–51, 87–88, 91
Sar (river): 171
Sardinia: 49, 90, 118
Satricum: 41
Saucedo: 111
Scallabis: 174
Scythia: 168
Segida Restituta Iulia: 79
Segobriga: 58, 71, 75–76, 169
Seine (river): 119

Sekaisa: 136
Semelhe: 169
Seria Fama Iulia: 79
Serreta, La: 14, 31–33, 36, 69
Seville: 119
Sexs: 127–29
Sicily: 39, 47, 49, 118
Sidon: 131, 185
Sierra de Monesterio: 85
Singilia Barba: 147
Skikda: 185
Somorrostro (Hill): 171
Spain see Hispania
Stradonice: 121
Strasbourg: 119
Syracuse: 126
Syria: 118, 124

Tagus (river): 48, 119–20, 122, 174
Tangier: 119
Tarquinia: 192
Tarraco: 23, 77, 81, 123–24, 134–35, 146–47, 150, 165, 168–69, 171–72, 178, 189
*Tarraconensis, conventus*: 105, 152
Tarragona see Tarraco
Tartessos: 120
Teichiussa: 45
Termes: 54, 83
Tibus: 142
Ticinum: 142
Tiermes see Termes
Tolegassos: 112
Torre de Miguel Sesmero: 80, 96–97
Torrecillas, Las: 85
Torremejía: 80, 97
Torreparedones: 103
Trebula Suffenas: 142
Trigueros: 172

Troy: 146, 175
Trull dels Moros: 70
Tunisia: 109
Turbie, La: 171
Turdetania: 13
Turgalium: 79, 83–84, 86
Turiazu: 132
Turibriga/Turobriga: 85
Turkey: 119
Turris Augusti: 171
Tyr: 117

Ucubi: 79
Ulia: 129
Ullastret: 120–21
Untikesken: 130, 132
Urgabo Alba: 172
Urgavo: 175
Urso: 73, 122, 143, 144, 149
Utrera: 174
Uxama Argaela: 112

Valencia (modern Valentia): 119
Valentia: 28, 32, 77, 130, 133, 138, 154, 159, 163
Valencia del Ventoso: 46, 79, 80
Vercellae: 83
Vila Joiosa, La: 30
Vila Viçosa: 87, 89
Vilauba: 104, 110–13
Villar del Rey: 80, 97
Vispesa: 32
Volubilis: 51

Zacynthus: 154–55
Zaragoza: 38
Zarza (river): 80

# ARCHAEOLOGY OF THE MEDITERRANEAN WORLD

All volumes in this series are evaluated by an Editorial Board, strictly on academic grounds, based on reports prepared by referees who have been commissioned by virtue of their specialism in the appropriate field. The Board ensures that the screening is done independently and without conflicts of interest. The definitive texts supplied by authors are also subject to review by the Board before being approved for publication. Further, the volumes are copyedited to conform to the publisher's stylebook and to the best international academic standards in the field.

## In Preparation

*Perspectives on Byzantine Archaeology: From Justinian to the Abbasid Age (6th–9th Centuries AD)*, ed. by Angelo Castrorao Barba and Gabriele Castiglia

*Adoption, Adaption, and Innovation in Pre-Roman Italy: Paradigms for Cultural Change*, ed. by Jeremy Armstrong and Aaron Rhodes-Schroder